The Crisis of the American Republic

The St. Martin's Series in
U.S. History

The Crisis
of the
American Republic

A History of
the Civil War
and Reconstruction Era

Allen C. Guelzo
Eastern College

The St. Martin's Series in
U.S. History

ST. MARTIN'S PRESS, New York

For Debra, a true "Civil War Lady,"
on our twelfth anniversary

Acquisitions editor: Louise H. Waller
Manager, publishing services: Emily Berleth
Publishing services associate: Kalea Chapman
Project management: Richard Steins
Production supervisor: Alan Fischer
Art director: Sheree Goodman
Text design: Gene Crofts
Cover design: Rod Hernandez
Cover photo: Massachusetts Commandery, Military Order of the Loyal Legion and the US
Army Military History Institute

Manufactured in the United States of America.
98765
fedcba

For information, write:
St. Martin's Press, Inc.
175 Fifth Avenue
New York, NY 10010

ISBN: 0–312–09515–5

Preface

The Crisis of the American Republic was written to provide college-level history classes on the Civil War and Reconstruction era with a mid-sized narrative of the war's major events, personalities, and issues. Although I have included an overview of Reconstruction, the major focus is on the war itself. I deliberately have paired the word crisis with republic, for I regard the Civil War as fundamentally a challenge to the viability of a 19th-century liberal republic, or at least to a republic constructed from such potentially divisive materials and beliefs as the American republic. Although the rhetoric of the "republican" ideology is often associated with American political thinking in the late 18th or the early 19th century, the Americans who advanced to political leadership in the Civil War years had been shaped by the contours of that rhetoric in the 1820s and 1830s. They continued to employ it as a way of explaining what they thought was most at stake in the Civil War. Accordingly, it will become quickly apparent that I have moved political ideology to the front of the stage when discussing the causes of the war, and that the heart of that ideology is to be found in the various interpretations and attenuations of the "republicanism" that exercised such fascination for the revolutionaries of the 18th century and that the 19th-century Whigs and Democrats clearly believed they were still fighting to define. I have given particular attention to the Whigs as a political party, if only to counterbalance in some measure the excessive attention usually bestowed upon the Democrats (who, after all, won most of the presidential contests in the six decades prior to the war). Whatever else they accomplished in the Civil War, both Lincoln (who consistently described himself as "an old Whig" even while president) and his Congress managed to bring to life so much of the old Whig political agenda that the years of Lincoln's administration are fully as much an ideological watershed in American history as Jefferson's.

But I might also have used the plural crises to describe this book. The central struggle of the 1860s over the political organization of the American republic quickly spawned a series of secondary questions and struggles during the Civil War years over religion, race, and gender—how they were to be defined and what role they were to play in whatever republic emerged from "our fiery trial." Thus, I have granted race and slavery a central place in the coming of the war, the course of the war, and the uncertain results of the war in Reconstruction. And though the book makes no pretense of telling the whole story of the Civil War and Reconstruction era, I have chosen to tell some stories about republican crisis that have not usually made it into earlier Civil War surveys—stories about religion, race, and gender that historians have vigorously pushed to the forefront over the last twenty years.

Chapter 1 begins with the state of the Union in the post-Revolutionary period and the threat to the stability of the Union posed by slavery from 1820 onward. Chapters 2 and 3 describe how American leaders used the techniques of compromise to head off confrontation, and how the compromises eventually failed to work as the stakes of the debate rose ever higher. Chapters 4 and 5 provide a narrative of the first years of the Civil War and lay out the steady progress by which Lincoln managed to turn a war about preservation of the Union into a war for the abolition of slavery. Chapter 6 focuses on the world of the Civil War soldier, while Chapter 7 analyzes how North and South tried to supply and organize their war efforts and attempted to invite or prevent foreign intervention. Chapter 8 discusses a variety of climaxes, including Lincoln's search for a general who would back up the new political agenda of emancipation, the great battles of 1863, and the challenge of the Confederate regime to states' rights in the South. Chapter 9 raises the question of racial and gender conflicts in the Civil War, while chapters 10 and 11 bring the war to its end and weigh the ambiguous accomplishments of postwar Reconstruction of the South.

It is one measure of the abiding intensity of Civil War issues that racial terminology remains a matter of great sensitivity to readers of all races in all parts of the country. In describing both slave and free persons of color in the era of the Civil War and Reconstruction, I have chosen to use *black* and *African American* without any intention to suggest a meaning wider than that which I would imply by the similar use of *white* or *Irish American*. Both of these terms are common and easily recognizable for modern readers, which is the primary reason for their usage. However, the reader should bear in mind that neither *black* nor *African American* were the terms of choice in the 1860s. For African Americans like Frederick Douglass, *black* was actually a term of abuse in the 1860s, and the preferred terminology in the writings of Douglass and his contemporaries leans toward the use of *Negro* or *colored.* I have preserved these terms wherever they occur in quotations from African-American writers. The racial epithet *nigger* was a frequent and unpleasant characteristic of white, and sometimes even African-American, discourse in the 1860s. I have preserved its use as parts of quoted speech, comments, or writing only because some quotations make it impossible to avoid.

Acknowledgments

No survey of this subject can be written without accumulating vast debts to a number of specialists in the Civil War's many subfields of interest. I want to single

out, in particular, Gabor Boritt of Gettysburg College for his original encourage-
ment of this work; Tom Legg of the College of William and Mary, Stephen Fratt of
Trinity College, Steven E. Woodworth of Toccoa Falls College, Thomas Askew of
Gordon College, and James Geary of Kent State University for their careful reading
of the manuscript. I also thank Steven J. Wright, the Curator of the Civil War
Library and Museum in Philadelphia, for cheerfully providing access to rare Civil
War materials in the CWLM collections and for reading chapters 5 and 6; William
Marvel of South Conway, New Hampshire, for his gracious cooperation in tracking
down information on Civil War veterans; Roland Bauman, the Archivist of the
Oberlin College Archives, for access to the papers of Charles Grandison Finney;
and Monica Mealy, who forced me to think about Frederick Douglass in a fresh way.
Dorothy Bruton of Dallas, Texas, knows what the rebel yell really sounded like, and
generously granted me the use of the letters of her grandfather, George Asbury
Bruton of the 19th Louisiana.

Special care has been taken in selecting the photographs in this book to
present, as much as possible, previously unpublished images of the Civil War, or at
least relatively little-used ones. In this effort, I have been greatly assisted by the
cooperation of two major private collectors, Henry Deeks of Acton, Massachusetts,
and David Charles of Havertown, Pennsylvania, and by the staffs of the Union
League of Philadelphia and the Library Company of Philadelphia. I also wish to
acknowledge Richard S. Dunn and the Philadelphia Center for Early American
Studies, who made office space available for the academic year 1992–93.

The academic building blocks for any history of the Civil War are found in
libraries, and in my case I want to acknowledge with thanks the librarians and staff
of the C. P. Van Pelt Library at the University of Pennsylvania, the W. W. Hagerty
Library at Drexel University, the Warner Library at Eastern College, the Magill
Library at Haverford College, the Oberlin College Archives, and the McCabe
Library at Swarthmore College. In these places I have been able to work not only
with the monographs cited in the footnotes of this book but also the major Civil
War reference works, which I shall list here rather than repeating them at length in
the text itself.

1. *The Official Records of the Union and Confederate Armies* (Washington, D.C.,
1887–1900), 128 volumes, noted in the text simply as *Official Records* with the
appropriate series, volume (and part), and page; the *Official Records of the Union and
Confederate Navies in the War of the Rebellion* (Washington, D.C., 1894–1922), 30
volumes noted in the same fashion, except as *Official Records/Navies*.

2. *The Collected Works of Abraham Lincoln*, edited by Roy P. Basler and published in nine volumes (and two later supplements) by Rutgers University Press; a
full citation to this series is made only on its first occurence in chapter 1; thereafter
throughout the book it is noted simply as *Collected Works*, with the volume and page
number following. My one departure from the text of the Basler Lincoln edition is
the new text of the Lincoln-Douglas debates edited by Harold Holzer as *The
Lincoln-Douglas Debates: The First Complete, Unexpurgated Text* (New York, 199?`

3. *The Encyclopedia of the Confederacy,* edited by Richard N. Current and published by Simon and Schuster (New York, 1993).

4. *Historical Times Illustrated Encyclopedia of the Civil War,* edited by Patricia Faust and published by Harper & Row (New York, 1986), to which I was a contributor.

5. *The Civil War Dictionary,* edited by Colonel Mark M. Boatner and published by David McKay (New York, 1959). The Boatner *Dictionary* is shorter and more compact than the Faust *Encyclopedia,* but also more confined to strictly military matters.

6. *The Civil War Day by Day: An Almanac, 1861–1865,* by E. B. Long (New York, 1971), who may have known more about the Civil War than any other person.

7. *The West Point Atlas of American Wars,* volume 1 (1689–1900), which contains some of the best tactical maps of Civil War battles ever drawn.

Several great Civil War surveys of past years deserve to be counted as reference works in their own right. These include J. G. Randall and David Donald, *The Civil War and Reconstruction* (originally published, 1937; second revised edition, Boston, 1961), Peter Parish, *The American Civil War* (New York, 1975), James M. Mc-Pherson, *Ordeal By Fire: The Civil War and Reconstruction* (New York, 1982), and James M. McPherson, *Battle Cry of Freedom: The Civil War Era* (New York, 1988). Much as I admire these works, and have used some of them in teaching the Civil War and Reconstruction course, I have not consciously attempted to model myself on any of them. For surveys of the current state of Civil War historiography since these works were published, several excellent bibliographical essays have recently appeared, including Gary W. Gallagher, "Home Front and Battlefield: Some Recent Literature Relating to Virginia and the Confederacy," in *Virginia Magazine of History and Biography* 98 (June 1990); James Geary, "Blacks in Northern Blue: A Select Annotated Bibliography of Afro-Americans in the Union Army and Navy during the Civil War," in *Bulletin of Bibliography* 45 (September 1988); and Joseph T. Glatthaar, "The 'New' Civil War History: An Overview," in *Pennsylvania Magazine of History and Biography* 115 (July 1991).

I owe a particular debt of gratitude to Louise Waller of St. Martin's Press, who I hope will still be amused when I tell people how this book began. My wife, Debra, has been a loving and faithful reader and exhorter all through the writing of this book, and I have at times had the peculiar pleasure of being outrun by her in a mutual enthusiasm for this history. She has hallowed it far above my poor power to add or detract.

Allen C. Guelzo

Contents

Photographs

Prologue

They are all gone now.

They have all vanished, the young men and the old men who left their April orchards and their rain-washed city brownstones and marched off between 1861 and 1865 to enter what became known among Americans as simply "the Civil War." Terrible numbers of them never returned, and those who did faded quietly off the scene even while the story of their battles grew more crimson and epochal with the passing years. Some of them were still around in 1910, when they came to visit my grandmother's elementary-school classroom in north Philadelphia. In their blue jackets and their little blue hats, the veterans shuffled to the front of her class before each Decoration Day to prod the guttering flame of remembrance to life again, so that a new generation of children would know what these men had suffered and what they had fought for. A few were still alive when I was born in 1953. The last survivor of the Civil War, a New York–born Minnesotan named Albert Henry Woolson, died at the age of 109. A few others claimed to have been survivors of the Civil War, including a Texan named Walter Washington Williams, who died in 1959 at what he claimed was the age of 117. But Williams had faked his age and his Civil War service in order to coax a pension out of the Texas state government. Sylvester Mack Magee died in 1971 at the astounding age of 130, insisting that he had been born a slave in Mississippi and dug soldiers' graves at Vicksburg in the summer of 1863. But there were no papers to substantiate anything Magee described. Without those records, Albert Woolson was really the last certifiable veteran of the Civil War.[1] Once he was gone, the remembrance of the shining bayonets and the dry bite of powder smoke in the harsh afternoon sun disappeared forever.

Yet this American Civil War continues to exert a mysterious and powerful hold on our imaginations. In the late 1980s, during observances of the 125th anniversary

---

[1]Jay S. Hoar, "Our Last Civil War Veterans," in *Blue and Gray Magazine* (April/May 1985), 33–42; on the debunking of Walter Williams, see William Marvel, "The Great Imposters," in *Blue and Gray Magazine* (February 1991), 12–15.

of the Civil War, over 40,000 Americans donned re-creations of the uniforms of the armies, shouldered replicas of rifles, and marched off to reenact the battles. A developer who wanted to open a 1.2 million-square-foot shopping mall adjoining the first battlefield of the Civil War incurred the wrath of a million-and-a-half people, who plunked down money for a lawsuit to stop the mall. A little-known film director named Ken Burns vaulted into overnight national fame in 1990 for his television documentary on the Civil War. And Georgia state legislators are still arguing over the propriety of maintaining their Civil War–era flag motif as part of the modern state flag.[2]

The families and communities, the statesmen, and the soldiers are all gone now. Once more, and not for the last time, this is their story.

[2]Lew Lord, "In the Grip of the Civil War" in *U.S. News and World Report* (August 15, 1988), pp. 48–59; Peter Applebome, "Enduring Symbols of the Confederacy Divide the South Anew," in *New York Times* (January 27, 1993), p. A16.

The Crisis of the American Republic

The St. Martin's Series in
U.S. History

CHAPTER 1

A Nation
Announcing Itself

Inauguration Day, the fourth of March, 1865, dawned over the city
of Washington with a blustery, overcast chill. There, in the Capitol,
the principal actor in this inauguration pageant, Abraham Lincoln,
the president of the United States, was already at work, signing the
last pieces of legislation passed by the outgoing Congress and witness-
ing a new Senate being sworn into office. The ceremonies held few surprises for
Lincoln, since this day would mark his second presidential inauguration. He had
come to this Capitol four years before, on the fourth of March in 1861, as a newly
elected president, untried and unprepared, and now four years later, the country
had chosen him a second time as its chief executive. When the congressional
ceremonies within the Capitol were over, a great file of legislators, cabinet secretaries, diplomats, and judges streamed out onto the Capitol steps, where a broad
platform had been constructed for the president to take his oath of office in public
view. Last of all onto the platform came Lincoln, holding in his hand a single large
sheet of paper.

Four years before, when Lincoln had taken his first presidential oath, the
weather was still thick with early-spring chilliness and damp, but the sun shone
with a hard and resolute cheerfulness. And the sunshine, in 1861, was almost the
only thing smiling then upon Abraham Lincoln. Even as he swore to "preserve,
protect and defend the Constitution of the United States," seven of those supposedly united states had renounced their attachment to the Constitution. They had
already organized a rival government, and elected a rival president, and they had
demanded that all property of the United States government sitting within their
boundaries be turned over to them at once. Lincoln had refused, and within six
weeks, war had broken out. The rebel states insisted that they were now an
independent country with a right to determine their own future, but Lincoln
maintained that they were only insurgents who had to be suppressed like any
other treasonous coup d'état. And it became a war such as few Americans had
ever dreamt: four years of it, with horrendous costs in life and property, and the

ghoulish echo of homespun place-names made hideous in blood—Gettysburg, Chancellorsville, Shiloh.

Now the spring of 1865 was coming, and Lincoln's armies had finally turned the tide, and the war was stumbling haltingly toward what looked like the end. As he arose to deliver his inaugural address, the exhausted president was ready to begin asking why the great horror of civil war had spread itself across his country. At that moment, the clouds parted and the long-hidden sun shone a golden aura down on Lincoln, the Capitol, and the hushed citizens below him. There were, Lincoln said, three fundamental causes that had pushed the United States into war. One of them was political, the fact that the United States had been organized, since its birth as a republic, as a *union* of thirteen former English colonies that had declared themselves independent states in 1776. And ever since, there had been voices within those states pointing out that their union with each other was a bad bargain that ought to be terminated. Those voices had come to a crescendo in the southern states of the Union in 1861, and Lincoln had found himself as president "devoted altogether to *saving* the Union without war" while at the same time having to deal with people who thought it right and proper "to *destroy* it without war—seeking to dissolve the Union, and divide effects, by negotiation."

But simply because the southern states thought the Union *could* be legally dissolved did not necessarily mean that it *had* to be—and that led Lincoln to the next fundamental reason for civil war. "One eighth of the whole population were colored slaves, not distributed generally over the Union, but localized in the Southern part of it." And this slavery, Lincoln declared, had become the irritant that provoked the southernmost states to reach for the solution of disunion. "These slaves constituted a peculiar and powerful interest," Lincoln insisted, and "all knew that this interest was, somehow, the cause of the war." Waving aside all the other supposed reasons for secession and war, Lincoln insisted that "to strengthen, perpetuate, and extend this interest was the object for which the insurgents would rend the Union, even by war."

But even that much did not explain matters entirely. Lincoln had come into office in 1861, swearing to uphold a Constitution that gave explicit guarantees to slave holding in the fifteen southern states where it was legal. But across the Mississippi River, out over the broad prairies of the western half of the North American continent, were the immense miles of United States—owned territory that had not yet been peopled and organized by white Americans, and that would one day want to be recognized and admitted to the Union as states equal to all the other states. Should slavery be permitted to plant itself in those territories? There, Lincoln and his party had drawn the line: They would not crush slavery where it was, but they would not allow it to spread, either. The southern states were outraged at this denial, fearful that a slavery that could not grow and extend itself was doomed to slow death. "The government claimed no right to do more than to restrict the territorial enlargement of it," but that was more than sufficient to make the slaveholding South begin thinking of canceling its membership in the Union.

"Both parties deprecated war," Lincoln said, "but one of them would *make* war rather than let the nation survive; and the other would *accept* war rather than let it perish." Lincoln paused for a long moment, looking out over the upturned faces crowding the Capitol steps. "And the war came."[1]

Since Lincoln uttered those words—and they amount to no more than two paragraphs in an inaugural address only four paragraphs long—something close to 50,000 books and articles on the American Civil War have been published. But if we want to understand what plunged the American republic into its greatest crisis, and map out the paths and highways that led Americans to four years of unplanned-for and unlooked-for carnage, we can hardly do better than to take our bearings from the three signposts that Abraham Lincoln left us.

1. The American Union

Underlying everything else that pushed or pulled 19th-century Americans toward the abyss of civil war was one very plain fact about the United States of America. Its political structure—that of a federation of states—was a standing invitation to chaos.

The origins of this situation extend far into the American past, all the way to the founding of the first English-speaking colonies in North America. Beginning with the Jamestown colony of 1607 in Virginia, these settlements had been individually laid out, individually funded, individually settled, and organized individually, with next to nothing in the way of supervision from the English government. In 1776, after a dozen years of spectacular political bungling by the British government, thirteen of those colonies declared themselves independent of British rule. But even in the face of British armies sent to suppress their revolt, the American colonies were unwilling to cooperate with one another on more than a hit-or-miss basis. The Continental Congress that they formed to act as their parliament looked more like a steering committee than a government, and even then its deliberations were racked by dissension and bickering. Frequently on the run from the British, the Continental Congress had no power to levy taxes and only the slimmest public credibility.

It took five years after the Declaration of Independence before the Continental Congress persuaded the new states to adopt some form of unified national government, and the states agreed only because they could not obtain an alliance with France (which they needed for survival) without forming themselves into something that the French could recognize as a government. What they finally created in 1781 was based on a flimsy document known as the Articles of Confederation. Under the Articles, each of the thirteen new states would receive equal representation in a new

[1]Lincoln, "Second Inaugural Address," in *The Collected Works of Abraham Lincoln*, Roy F. Basler, ed. (New Brunswick, NJ, 1953), vol. 8, pp. 332–333.

Confederation Congress, regardless of each state's size or population—a formula that amounted to allowing the states to come to the Confederation Congress as separate but equal powers, rather than participants in a national assembly.[2]

The outcome was inevitable. Soon enough, individual states found themselves quarreling with one another, while the Confederation Congress stood on the sidelines, wringing its hands. And then the quarrels would explode into civil war; and the war would so weaken the United States that some powerful European monarchy (perhaps the British again) would intervene and reduce the Americans to European control all over again. For almost all the rest of the world was still governed in the 1780s by kings who looked upon the king-less American republic as a bad example to their own restless subjects, and those kings had armies and navies which were too close to the American borders for comfort. Britain still occupied Canada to the north, and Spain still ruled the western half of North America and all of Central and South America, and neither of them liked what they saw in the new republic. Let the American states divide, and the European powers might take the opportunity to conquer.

So it was fear more than unity of purpose that finally drove the Americans to scrap the Articles of Confederation and write a new Constitution in 1787. This Constitution equipped the national government with the power to raise its own income by imposing taxes on the states, and created an executive president who had the authority and the means to enforce the decisions of Congress. But even so, there were still ambiguities and compromises in the Constitution that allowed the individual states to retain a large measure of their jealously guarded autonomy. The most obvious example of compromise concerned the Congress. The Constitution divided the old Confederation Congress into two "houses," the Senate and the House of Representatives. Members of the House were elected directly by the voters of each state, with the population of each state determining how many representatives each state could elect; but the members of the Senate were elected by the state legislatures (two from each state) giving each state equal voice in the Senate, just like the Confederation Congress.

There were other telltale problems, too. The Constitution created a confusing and cumbersome system for electing the national president. As it was, the Constitution did not precisely clarify who was permitted to vote for the president (the eligibility of voters was a question left to the individual states). For those who could vote, the Constitution specified that they would cast their ballots, not for a particular presidential candidate, but for a handful of state *electors*, who would then assemble in an electoral college and vote as state delegations for the next president. Even more ominous, the states made no pledge in the text of the Constitution to treat it as a perpetual arrangement and some declared the right to retrieve their autonomy at will. In 1798, the second president, John Adams, attempted to quell

---

[2]Kenneth Stampp, "Unam Aut Plures? The Concept of a Perpetual Union," in *The Imperiled Union: Essays on the Background of the Civil War* (New York, 1980), pp. 21–29.

political opposition to his administration through the so-called Alien and Sedition Acts. In reply, two of the foremost American political thinkers, Thomas Jefferson (the author of the Declaration of Independence) and James Madison (the architect of the Constitution) drafted the Virginia and Kentucky Resolutions, which announced to President Adams that the individual states still reserved the privilege of declaring acts of the national Congress unconstitutional and nonoperative.

As late as the 1830s, the United States of America looked more like a league or a compact of states than a single country, and its Constitution was still regarded as something of an experiment embraced mostly for its practical usefulness. "Asking a State to surrender a part of her sovereignty is like asking a lady to surrender part of her chastity," declared the eccentric Virginia politician, John Randolph of Roanoke; and Randolph, even on the floor of Congress, made his loyalties clear by insisting that, "When I speak of my country, I mean the Commonwealth of Virginia." The framers of the Constitution, fearing the possibility that state antagonisms, economic competition, and political corruption would easily derail the national system, appealed to the spirit of political compromise to defuse the threat of divisive issues, and not to national unity or some elusive national spirit. The ultimate sense in which that was expressed was in the name Americans used to describe their political order. For Americans spoke, not of their *nation* (which might have implied a uniform cultural and political system) but of their *Union* or their *Federal Union* (as though they were speaking of an alliance).[3]

This is not to say, though, that Americans were not becoming a nation in other ways. No matter how jealously the states regarded and defended their individual political privileges and identities, it would have been hard for a people who spoke the same English language, read the same books and heard the same music, and voted in the same elections, not to develop some sort of fellow-feeling, irrespective of state boundaries. This was especially true for those Americans who had actually borne the brunt of the fighting in the revolutionary war, and who carried out of the Revolution a highly different perspective on the unity of the American republic. One of these soldiers, John Marshall, began the Revolution as a Virginia militiaman, then enlisted in the Continental army, and endured the horrors of Valley Forge. He remembered later, "I was confirmed in the habit of considering America as my country and Congress as my government." And Marshall would later rise, as chief justice of the United States, to shape a system of national jurisprudence that transcended state boundaries and loyalties. A South Carolinian (turned Tennessean) named Andrew Jackson lost two brothers and his mother to the Revolution. Captured by the British, he refused a British officer's order to clean the officer's boots, and was rewarded with a blow across the face from the officer's sword. It left a scar Jackson carried with him for the rest of his life, and it also left a burning hatred

[3]Robert Dawidoff, *The Education of John Randolph* (New York, 1979), pp. 34, 154; Peter B. Knupfer, *The Union As It Is: Constitutional Unionism and Sectional Compromise, 1787–1861* (Chapel Hill, NC, 1991), pp. 115–117.

of all enemies of his country, whether they were British invaders or (as it turned out later) his fellow Southerners, trying to nullify congressional legislation.

By the end of the 1830s, an entire political generation had come to maturity under the Constitution and the Union. And for many members of this generation, the Union, crisscrossed by "mystic chords of memory," had ascended to the level of a political faith. The Union, for Abraham Lincoln, "rose to the sublimity of a religious mysticism," and even a perfectly straightforward politician like William H. Bissell of Illinois felt no embarrassment in claiming that whenever anyone carelessly broached the idea of "destroying this Union" to his neighbors in the West, there would not be "a man throughout that vast region who will not raise his hand and swear by the Eternal God, as I do now, that it shall never be done, if our arms can save it." When, as it turned out, other members of the American Union did just that, and asked the Lincolns and Bissells to choose between state or local interests and the Union, the answer would more and more be, the Union.[4]

The experience of the Revolution and political maturity were only the first steps away from disunity and suspicion. The new political generation of Americans in the 1830s found two other important ways to rise above their divisions. One of these was the experience of a common religion. Although the federal Constitution forbade Congress from singling out any particular religion or religious denomination as a national "established" church, it was nevertheless clear that Protestant, evangelical Christianity was the overwhelming favorite among Americans in all parts of the country. Evangelical Protestant churches claimed approximately 15 percent of the American population as full members, and as much as 40 percent of all Americans as "attenders" or "hearers."[5] The evangelicalism espoused by these churches was a blend of Protestant religious individualism, a rigorous moralism, and the need for spiritual renewal, aided and encouraged by the powerful preaching of evangelical ministers and a vast network of evangelical newspapers, tracts, and books. There were, of course, many differences between various groups of evangelical Protestants, and they organized themselves into more separate and subdivided denominations—Presbyterians, Baptists, Methodists, Congregationalists, and so on—than there were states. But many of these differences were not often apparent to the unaided eye, since they all shared a common commitment to the basic outlines of evangelical piety. Even more important, the differences separating these Protestant denominations were not tied to geography, like state boundaries. American Methodists from Michigan and South Carolina could meet and enjoy fellowship in national conventions. Presbyterians and Congregationalists could swap pulpits and cooperate in church planting in frontier districts.

[4]William G. Brownlow, *Sketches of the Rise, Progress, and Decline of Secession* (Philadelphia, 1862), p. 227; Eric Foner, *Free Soil, Free Labor, Free Men: The Ideology of the Republican Party before the Civil War* (New York, 1970), p. 179.

[5]Richard J. Carwardine, *Evangelicals and Politics in Antebellum America* (New Haven, CT, 1993), pp. 3–18.

The influence of this common evangelicalism was heightened by the control these denominations exercised over American higher education. Almost all of the seventy-eight American colleges founded by 1840 were church-related, with clergymen serving on the boards and the faculties. In this way, not only American religion, but the development of American ethics and philosophy were shaped by a common Protestant evangelicalism. Evangelical educational influence was accompanied on the popular level by the promotion of evangelical Protestant revivalism. Revivals of religion were seasons of heightened religious excitement and piety involving energetic and emotional preaching of the Christian message before great audiences by famous and skillful preachers who invited and demanded conversion to "the new birth" and a sanctified Christian life. Although revivals could sometimes be crude and manipulative affairs, they could also be moments of commitment to renewal and reform. Revivals could also be great levelers of distinctions. Although the leadership of America's Protestant churches remained almost exclusively in the hands of white males, the Protestant ministry did concede some limited room for African-American leadership, and white women could find in the revivals one of the rare opportunities for their joys and their anxieties to obtain a hearing equal to those of men.

Blacks/ women

Supporting and instructing these revivals was a substantial and impressive body of analysis and theory, chiefly from the pen of the Massachusetts Congregationalist, Jonathan Edwards (1703–1758). Edwards's writings continued to provide models and examples for thoughtful movers of revivals of religion well into the 19th century, especially since Edwards had set his own personal example for leading revivals as one of the most famous preachers of the colonial revival of the 1740s known as the "Great Awakening." Through his oft-republished books and his own accomplishments as a preacher, Edwards was probably the most influential American thinker before the Civil War.

Just as powerful a common bond as evangelical Christianity was the common political ideology that Americans embraced in the Revolution. However much the structure of American politics was compromised and frustrated by state demands and state loyalties, Americans in all the states agreed that the states and the federal government alike were to be a republic, and follow a republican form of government. This all-pervading republican ideology had its sources in 18th-century British political thinking (much of it dangerously radical in its criticism of kingly government). But much of it can also be traced back to the civic humanism of the Italian Renaissance, and even to the political writings of the ancient Greeks and Romans. The primary lesson these older examples taught Americans was the priority of *liberty*, or independence. Republicanism insisted that no individual—or at least, in the 1700s, no white, English-speaking male—should be subject to the arbitrary rule of another. People should be free from having to cringe before aristocrats, or beg their bread from wealthy landowners. For not only was this debasing and humiliating, but it meant that dependent people could always be manipulated by the powerful into subjugating others, or forced into silence when the great and powerful did wrong. The opposite of liberty was *power*, and republicans feared concentrations of power, political or economic, as inevitable threats to liberty.

The lessons of political history also taught that republican liberty had to be securely based on *virtue*. Liberty, left merely to its own devices, could easily decay into anarchy, and the resulting loss of self-control could only lead to control by others—the very opposite of liberty—or to corruption—putting your own profit first or manipulating public trust to your own ends. To keep liberty unspoiled, republican writers yoked it to the necessity of civic, or public, virtue, by which they meant the willingness to lay aside one's private interests, personal desires, luxuries, and family, and labor for the sake of a higher good. And yet republicanism, while it lauded public virtue as a kind of civil holiness, was also pulled in a somewhat opposite direction by its respect for individual rights to an acceptance of a large measure of private self-interested behavior from its citizens. Civic virtue demanded that citizens in a republic actively participate in a search for a nonpartisan public good that benefitted all citizens equally. But as James Madison wrote in the celebrated *Federalist Papers,* one of the best ways of arriving at a genuinely nonpartisan public order was to permit every faction and every interest to compete against each other openly in the public square. And by the same token, one of the best ways to ensure a common economic benefit to the republic was to place as few barriers as possible in the way of individual economic self-interest. American civic virtue would be based not on regulations, sumptuary laws (statutes prescribing modes of dress), or state-sponsored religion, as in the classical republics, but on a new liberal republicanism that rested civic virtue on what Alexander Hamilton called "rational liberty" and "the equality of political rights, exclusive of all hereditary distinction."

Ultimately, the security of both liberty and virtue rested on *property*. Liberty and virtue could never survive so long as an individual was trapped in the nets of dependence and patronage, where obligation and power could easily corrupt and compel. Consequently, it was vitally important that a republican government guarantee the economic independence of its citizens by securing rights to the ownership of property. Indentured servants, tenants, and all other propertyless persons either had to have the way to property ownership opened up for them, or else they must be excluded from the political process. Otherwise, their masters and landlords could corrupt and coerce them into political actions that served only private interests and power. So, while kings and aristocrats sneered at dirtying their hands in commerce or farming, the republicans praised it as the best means of acquiring the property that would guarantee independence and liberty.

Of course, it was also important that property not turn into another ugly species of power. Too much property concentrated in too few hands resulted in too much power, and power was the enemy of liberty. So, the republican ideal of property became the small, independent farmer who grew what he needed for his own needs, or the small-scale manufacturer, the shipbuilder, the tailor, the shoemaker and other self-developed enterprises based, by-and-large, in the large urban seaports of New York, Boston, Philadelphia, Baltimore, and Charleston. It occurred to relatively few Americans before the 1830s that there was something remarkably inconsistent about praising liberty, virtue, and property, when one out of every eight people in America was an African American who was either a slave or could not vote, or when many American women could neither vote nor hold property legally in their names. Even for an enlightened republican like Thomas Jefferson, republicanism was a creed for white men, and even then, only some white men.

The roles played by religion, revivalism, and republicanism were all tools that pushed Americans away from narrow state loyalties and dissolved the stresses that might upset the delicate scaffolding of the federal Union. But all the same, there were also problems on the American horizon that were just as likely to operate in the other direction and encourage more and more division and conflict. The most serious and divisive set of problems in the new republic were economic. The Americans chose to create a republic just at the moment when Europe, and especially Great Britain, was moving into a new and unprecedented age of economic development. Ever since the end of the 1600s, Great Britain had dominated the Atlantic ocean's trade routes, and that dominance had created an immense reserve of commercial capital in the British economy. Much of that reserve was drained away by Britain's wars in Europe in the 1700s, and by the wars against Napoleon's France. But those wars had the advantage of eliminating what was left of Britain's international competitors on the world trading markets and on the high seas, and allowed the British to stake out the richest trading markets of Asia and Africa as commercial or political colonies. At the same time, after 1780, British inventors devised new sources of cheap power and production through the development of the steam engine, which sharply reduced the amounts of start-up capital required for the production of goods that could be sold to those colonies. That technology, in turn, allowed British capitalists to create a new form of cheap labor organization, the factory. With the forces of industrial capitalism and technology thus joined, Britain emerged by 1850 as the world's first genuinely international economic empire.

As the British economy moved its laborers out of the traditional agricultural economy and into industrial production, it needed new sources for feeding and clothing that new work force, and it found them in American agriculture. Before 1800 in the United States, only farmers in the hinterlands of the major ports, like Philadelphia, Charleston, and the Chesapeake Bay, were seriously committed to raising crops to sell for cash on foreign markets. Most American farmers were organized around a household economy that sold little except small surpluses off the farm, and that relied on barter and extended loans for the few manufactured goods it needed. But the allurement of selling agricultural produce to British and foreign markets slowly moved American farmers away from independent subsistence farming and into capitalist market relationships that saw farmers turning to single-crop agriculture, selling produce for cash, and using the cash to buy manufactured clothing or tools made in other peoples' factories. No agricultural commodity sold better than American cotton, for the production of cheap cotton textiles was the cornerstone of British capitalism. The close connections that arose between the cotton-growing states of the American republic and British cotton consumers gave many of those states a stronger link to Liverpool than to Washington.[6]

This hit republicanism at a sensitive spot. Republicanism was based upon liberty, and liberty was based upon independence. But how could American farmers really be considered independent if their well-being now hung on the price that wheat or cotton might get on a faraway exchange market? And how independent could a shoemaker be when he was forced to close up his shop because cheaply manufactured British shoes cost less than his handmade ones? On the other hand, how independent would America remain if it stuck its economic head in the sands, persisted in the old patterns of household agriculture, and became a relative weakling among the ravenous capitalist economies of Europe?

These questions were posed by republicans who now found themselves differing seriously from one another. Beginning with Alexander Hamilton and the old Federalist party, some republicans argued that American independence depended on the strength and competitiveness of its economy on the world capitalist markets. Hamilton, in particular, favored direct federal government intervention in the American economy to encourage manufacturing development, trade (through publicly funded roads, bridges, and canals), and finance (by chartering a national bank to lend money to entrepreneurs). But other republicans, championed by Thomas Jefferson and the Democratic party, argued that encouraging Americans to join the system of world capitalist markets would only mortgage the American republic to foreign interests and encourage Americans to thirst for money and power over their fellow citizens. The Jeffersonian Democrats especially opposed calls for government-financed public works, or "internal improvements," since it was obvious that the new roads, bridges, and canals could serve only one purpose—to make it easier for farmers to reach distant markets, and for the markets to tempt American farmers into their grasp. It also went without saying that "internal improvements" could only be financed through federal taxation; and farmers who grew or manufactured only for their own households would never be able to find the money to pay those taxes without surrendering their cherished independence and growing what the market would pay them in cash. "The market is a canker," warned a contributor to *The New England Farmer* in 1829, "that will, by degrees, eat you out, while you are eating upon it."[7]

The Democrats reserved their greatest venom for the two newest instruments of capitalist finance, the bank and the chartered corporation. America had known no banks until the very end of the American Revolution, and had only eighty banks by

[6]Charles G. Sellers, *The Market Revolution: Jacksonian America, 1815–1846* (New York, 1991), pp. 8–23, 27–28.

[7]Christopher Clark, *The Roots of Rural Capitalism: Western Massachusetts, 1780–1860* (Ithaca, NY, 1990), p. 154.

1810. But by 1840, there were nearly a thousand of them, including a congression-ally chartered "monster" Bank of the United States in Philadelphia, organized in 1816 with an initial capitalization of $35 million. Democrats hated the banks because the banks were the chief processing agents of the markets: They extended credit for investment (which Democrats attacked as "phoney" wealth) and either made windfall profits from manufacturers and farmers when those investments succeeded or else seized the property of those whose enterprises failed. Either way, the banks looked like precisely the enormous concentrations of power that republi-cans feared as the source of corruption, and those fears of corruption were not eased when large-scale banks like the Bank of the United States began paying handsome retainers to members of Congress to sit on its board of directors. Democrats were equally fearful of chartered corporations, since large-scale corporations could just as easily acquire the same enormous wealth as banks, and with it, the same power for corrupting state and local legislatures.

For the first three decades of the American republic, it was clearly the fears of the Democrats that had the upper hand. Although the first two presidents, Wash-ington and Adams, favored development and competition on the world markets as the best method for toughening the independence of the American economy, the costs of that encouragement were federal taxes, and a country that had formed as a revolt against British taxes was in no mood to pay them to the federal government. Thomas Jefferson was swept into the presidency in 1800 in a tremendous landslide that secured Democratic control of the federal government for the next quarter-century. Accordingly, the Democrats allowed banks and corporate charters to wither, and in 1807, Jefferson briefly imposed an absolute embargo on all foreign trade, as if to seal America off by edict from the world markets.

What Jefferson had not entirely counted upon was the degree to which isola-tion really did translate into weakness. Britain, then at the height of its titanic grapple with Napoleon, discovered that a government without a bank for borrowing or taxes for spending had no way to fund a navy for protection, and so British warships shamelessly stopped and boarded American ships and hijacked (or "im-pressed") American sailors to fill up depleted British crews. In 1812, Jefferson's hand-picked successor as president, James Madison, led the country into war against the British. It was a catastrophe. "Our commerce [had been] put in fetters by non-importation acts and embargoes; and the crisis that succeeded found us without the most ordinary resources of an independent people," complained John Pendleton Kennedy of Kentucky. "Our armies went to the frontier clothed in the fabrics of the enemy; our munitions of war was gathered as chance supplied them from the four quarters of the earth; and the whole struggle was marked by the prodigality, waste and privation of a thriftless nation, taken at unawares and challenged to a contest without the necessary armor of a combatant."[8] The unprepared American armies

[8] John Pendleton Kennedy, "Address of the Friends of Domestic Industry" [October 26, 1831], in *Political and Official Papers* (New York, 1872), pp. 119–120, 122–123.

were routed by a British empire already fighting with one arm tied behind its back by Napoleon, and the household-based American economy fell apart. Only British exhaustion from its European wars kept Britain from turning the American republic back into British colonies.

The disaster of the War of 1812 frightened many republicans away from Jefferson's fond dream of an agricultural republicanism. "These disasters opened our eyes to some important facts," Kennedy recalled in 1831, "They demonstrated to us the necessity of extending more efficient protection, at least, to those manufactures which were essential to the defence of the nation" as well as the establishment of "the value of a national currency, and the duty of protecting it from the influence of foreign disturbance" through the protection of a national banking system. Led by Henry Clay of Kentucky, a new party of "National Republicans," or Whigs (as Clay renamed them in the 1830s) resurrected the old program of government support for internal improvements, government-sponsored banking, and a new program of protective tariffs to keep out cheap imported British manufactured goods and stimulate manufacturing at home. Although the presidency remained firmly in the hands of the Democrats (except for a brief interlude under John Quincy Adams from 1825 until 1829), Clay's influence in Congress pushed large elements of this "American System" into being, anyway. It was not until the election of Andrew Jackson, an unreconstructed Jeffersonian radical, as president in 1828 that the Democrats struck back. Jackson vetoed congressional appropriations for public roads, effectively destroyed the Bank of the United States by refusing to deposit federal money in it, and paid off the national debt so that there would no need for federal taxes and (above all) no need for federal tariffs.

Jackson's war against market-based power was, in the long run, far from successful. His nemesis, Henry Clay, remained a powerful figure in American politics, and many banks protected themselves from Jackson's republican wrath by obtaining charters from cooperative state legislatures. But that lack of success cannot obscure the anger and violence with which Whigs and Democrats—both supposedly dedicated to republicanism—had come to regard each other. By the 1840s the Whigs had defined themselves as the party of an upwardly mobile middle class, willing to embrace the fluidity of the market, happy to leave "yeoman" republicanism behind, and eager to promote national unity and government support for railroads, canals, and even steamship lines. Perhaps most important, the Whigs had enlisted the support of a vast majority of the evangelicals, and they wedded their economic gospel of hard work and thrift to the evangelical gospel of moral self-control.[9] The Democrats remained the party of localism and diversity, dedicated to resisting "consolidated" national government with its tariffs and "improvements." It appealed most strongly to the old elite families of the republic, who feared and resented the ambitious rise of Whig entrepreneurs, and to the poorest farmers and

[9]Carwardine, Evangelicals and Politics in Antebellum America, pp. 103–110; Daniel Walker Howe, The Political Culture of the American Whigs (Chicago, 1979), pp. 152–178.

urban workers who suspected that the Whigs were merely the agents of a "money power" out to rob them, through taxes or through financial chicanery, of the little they had. Both parties spoke the language of liberal republicanism, although both were also convinced that their brand of republicanism was the best guarantee of civic virtue. As one historian has summed up, the Whigs were the party of America's hopes, the Democrats the party of its fears.[10]

Sometimes, division and conflict could thrive on simple local self-interest, without any extra help from political ideology. During the War of 1812, New Englanders were hard hit by the naval blockade that British warships imposed on them, and the more they suffered from this blockade, the more the suffering seemed to be the fault of people from other sections of the country, like President Madison (a Virginian) or Henry Clay (a Kentuckian), whose sections presumably had something to gain (or less to lose) from the war that New England did not. In December, 1814, delegates from Massachusetts, Connecticut, and Rhode Island met at Hartford, Connecticut, to express their opposition to the war and make ugly suggestions about seceding from the Union and making a separate peace with Great Britain. It all blew over because the war ended a month later, but it was a dangerous indication that states or sections of the country who suspected that they were losing in some way might take advantage of the autonomy left them by the federal Union, and leave the Union for good.

A more dramatic example of the dangerous power of local self-interest occurred in 1832, over a federal tariff. For more than a decade, South Carolina and the southern states had been vigorously protesting the use of tariffs to protect American industry. Tariffs like the one imposed in 1816 boosted the price of imported manufactured goods by 25 percent over their original valuation, and forced consumers to buy American-made goods that were considerably more costly than the imports had originally been. South Carolinians like John Caldwell Calhoun observed that this was fine for New England, which was home to many of America's infant industries, but it was very hard on South Carolina, which specialized in cotton-growing and needed to buy manufactured goods from elsewhere. But Congress was not inclined to give the South Carolinians relief, and in 1828, it passed a tariff so stiff (imposing import costs up to 50 percent on the value of some imports) that South Carolina dubbed it "the Tariff of Abominations."

Calhoun saw the tariff not just as an economic issue but as a challenge by the federal government to South Carolina's integrity as a state. For two years, while he was serving as Andrew Jackson's vice-president, Calhoun fought the tariff through his political lieutenants in Congress, insisting that South Carolina had the authority to nullify any federal law it deemed unsatisfactory (including tariffs) unless three-quarters of the other states had the opportunity to review the law and approve

[10]Marvin Meyers, *The Jacksonian Persuasion: Politics and Belief* (Stanford, CA, 1957), p. 13; Marc W. Kruman, "The Second American Party System and the Transformation of Revolutionary Republicanism," in *Journal of the Early Republic* 12 (Winter 1992), pp. 509–537.

it. Early in 1830, Robert Hayne of South Carolina, acting as Calhoun's mouth-piece, delivered a long and powerful polemic on the floor of the Senate, defending the state sovereignty of South Carolina against a "consolidated" Union. But Hayne was argued down by Massachusetts Senator Daniel Webster, who proclaimed (in a speech that subsequent generations of American schoolchildren were required to memorize) that the federal government was "the peoples' constitution; the peoples' government" and could not be splintered by one state under the plea of liberty. "Liberty and Union," Webster concluded, "now and forever, one and inseparable." Undeterred by Webster's eloquence, Calhoun hoped to play on the antitariff sympathies of President Jackson, calculating that Jackson would not use force to impose a tariff he did not welcome, and in the state in which he had been born. In one of the most dramatic moments in the history of the American presidency, Jackson was invited by Calhoun and his friends to a Jefferson's birthday dinner on April 13, 1830, in the hope that Calhoun might prod an antitariff statement out of Jackson. After dinner, the toasts went round the table, beginning with Calhoun and building one-by-one to a carefully orchestrated anthem of praise for state sovereignty. But when Jackson rose to present his toast, he stared point blank at Calhoun and proposed, "Our Union: it must be preserved!" And he held his glass aloft as a sign that the toast was to be drunk by all standing. Calhoun and the others struggled weakly to their feet, Calhoun spilling a trickle of wine as he trembled in shock. "The Union," Calhoun gasped in response, "next to our liberties most dear."

Calhoun had greatly misjudged Jackson's loyalty to the Union, and realizing that he had lost all hope of influencing Jackson, he resigned his vice-presidency and returned to South Carolina. On November 24, 1832, the Calhounites led a specially called convention in South Carolina in formally nullifying the collection of the tariff within South Carolina, and threatening secession from the Union if the federal government interfered. But on December 10, 1832, Jackson replied that nullification was "incompatible with the existence of the Union. . . . The Constitution forms a government, not a league." Jackson went on to take a further swipe at secession by adding, "To say that any state may at pleasure secede from the Union is to say that the United States is not a nation." The president obtained from Congress a Force Bill, which authorized him to use the army and navy to suppress South Carolina resistance. But before force became necessary, the more conciliatory Henry Clay produced a compromise measure that provided for the graduated reduction of the tariff, and on March 15, 1833, Calhoun and the South Carolinians rescinded their nullification ordinance.

They did not, however, renounce the principle of secession. And that meant that whatever else Americans might hold in common, their political structure—a Union of sometimes grudging and suspicious states—remained vulnerable in a crisis where any state with a grievance might try to end its cooperation with the others and stalk out of the Union. Jackson might have prevented disunion over the tariff, and Clay might have demonstrated how compromise was the best method for disarming confrontation, but as far as Calhoun was concerned, that did not mean the remedy of secession would not be available for future use if a more demanding set of circumstances called for it. And as many Americans could already see, such a set of circumstances was very likely to appear in the form of the issue of slavery, as it was practiced in the southern states. And no one less than Andrew Jackson had already glumly predicted, after the nullification crisis had passed, that "The nullifiers in the South intend to blow up a storm on the slave question. . . ." Nullification might be defeated, he told his aide, John Coffee, but "they will try to arouse the Southern people on this false tale. This ought to be met, for be assured these men will do any act to destroy the union, & form a southern Confederacy, bounded north, by the Potomac river."[11]

2. Sociology for the South

Cadet Jefferson Davis did not like Yankees.

Born in Kentucky, and raised in Mississippi, Davis found it something of a novelty to meet Northerners when he arrived at the United States Military Academy at West Point as a cadet in 1824. But it was not a novelty he enjoyed. He found Yankees tight-fisted, chilly, and unsociable. "The Yankee part of the corps [of cadets] . . . are not . . . such associates as I would at present select." Northerners were dedicated to money-making, penny-pinching, and building factories; they were all "vulgar parvenus . . . vulgar landlords, capitalists, and employers." Southerners were another quantity altogether. Southerners preferred the relaxed pace of agricultural life, close to the rhythms of nature, aristocratic, noble-minded, generous, traditional. In fact, Southerners even *looked* different than Northerners. "Foreigners have all remarked on the care-worn, thoughtful, unhappy countenances of our people," George Fitzhugh, a Virginian, wrote in 1854, but that description "only applies to the North, for travellers see little of us at the South, who live far from highways and cities, in contentment on our farms."[12]

Fitzhugh was at least partly right. After the Revolution, European tourists and journalists flocked to America to gawk at the operation of the new republic, and they *did* agree that the southern states of the American republic seemed like a country unto themselves.

The first appearance to shape the initial impressions of onlookers was the dominance of cotton agriculture in the South. Single-crop agriculture was actually a habit with a long history in the southern states, stretching back into colonial times, when the South's prosperity had relied almost entirely on tobacco growing

---

[11]Richard E. Ellis, *The Union at Risk: Jacksonian Democracy, States Rights, and the Nullification Crisis* (New York, 1989), p. 191; Robert V. Remini, *Andrew Jackson and the Course of American Democracy, 1833–1845* (New York, 1984), p. 42.

[12]Davis to Joseph Davis [January 12, 1825], in *The Papers of Jefferson Davis*, H. M. Monroe and J. T. McIntosh, eds. (Baton Rouge, LA, 1971), vol. 1, p. 18; George M. Fitzhugh, *Sociology for the South, or the Failure of Free Society* (Richmond, VA, 1854), p. 258.

around the Chesapeake Bay, and rice or indigo in the South Carolina lowlands. By the time of the Revolution, however, tobacco and indigo had gone into decline, and the South faced an agricultural crisis of alarming proportions. But in 1793, a New England–born inventor, Eli Whitney, constructed a simple device known as the cotton gin, which was able to take raw cotton, separate the fiber of the cotton from the seeds, and produce a usable textile product with no more than the effort needed to turn a handle. At one stroke, cotton production became mechanically simple and economically viable.

Whitney's gin shaped the future of southern agriculture, for cotton grew well in the soil of the American South—in fact, the soils of the lower tier of the South were the finest agricultural soils in the world—and the gin made cotton production on that soil a profitable venture. Then, at virtually the same moment that Whitney's gin simplified the production process, Great Britain's factory-based textile industry began its clamor for new, cheap sources of cotton. Demand met supply, and between the 1790s and 1850, British cotton imports from the South leapt from 12 million pounds a year to 588 million pounds; in the same period, British exports of the finished cotton products rocketed from 40 million square yards to 2 billion square yards, while the costs of cotton goods fell by 1850 to 1 percent of what they had been in the 1780s. Cotton brought Britain power and prosperity, employing a million-and-a-half workers in the cotton factories alone, and a world empire. Cotton, in return, brought the South economic and political power in the American republic. By 1860, southern cotton constituted 57 percent of all American exports; compared to northern grain agriculture, which exported only 5 percent of its total crop, southern cotton plantations shipped 75 percent of their cotton abroad.[13]

But cotton also brought the South bane as well as blessing. The rage for cotton profits drove the development of manufacturing out of southern minds, and that, in turn, meant that the South was forever having to import manufactured goods, either from the new and expensive factories of the North or else from abroad over the intolerable hurdle of federal tariffs. To buy these goods, southern planters were compelled to mortgage their next crop to northern manufacturers and bankers in order to buy the cotton gins and other tools they needed to plant and harvest the crop in the first place. And the money that flowed from English cotton buyers back to the South generally came in the form of bills and drafts that were then forwarded to New York banks to pay southerners' bills to northern merchants. This created cycles of debt for cotton growers, especially in the oldest parts of the South, and most of the debt was owed to northern bankers. "We have been good milk cows," South Carolinian Mary Boykin Chesnut complained, "Milked by the tariff, or skimmed. . . . Cotton pays everyone who handles it, sells it, manufactures it, &c &c—rarely pays the men who make it."[14] The faster planters in the old cotton

[13]Allan Nevins, *Ordeal of the Union: Fruits of Manifest Destiny, 1847–1852* (New York, 1947), p. 466; Eric Hobsbawm, *The Age of Revolution, 1789–1848* (New York, 1962), pp. 51–55.

[14]Chesnut, in *Mary Chesnut's Civil War*, C. Vann Woodward, ed. (New Haven, CT, 1981), p. 410.

states ran to produce more cotton, the faster they piled up debts for the costs of production. By 1850, some of them were surviving on profit margins as low as two or three percent.

In the effort to understand why Southerners would set aside the opportunity to diversify their economy, the journalists and travelers could only guess that southerners were in some peculiar way willing to exchange solid modern profits for the social values that came attached to traditional agriculture. They were helped to this conclusion by those unceasing southern voices that proclaimed they preferred a way of living which (whether it was profitable or not) provided more graciousness of style, more leisure, and more sense of the past than the frantic, money-grubbing lives of modern northern manufacturers and their armies of faceless wage-paid factory hands. Edward Pollard, the editor of the Richmond *Examiner*, liked to think of the southern cotton planters as a sort of American aristocracy, the last survival of a noble and knightly virtue, holding its own against the onslaught of Yankee capitalism. "The South had an element in its society—a landed gentry—which the North envied, and for which its substitute was a coarse ostentatious aristocracy which smelt of the trade," Pollard explained. He acknowledged that "the South was a vast agricultural country," and its "waste lands, forest and swamps" featured "no thick and intricate nets of internal improvements to astonish and bewilder the traveller." But all the same, "However it might decline in the scale of gross prosperity, its people were trained in the highest civilization."[15] And so a social virtue was made out of an economic necessity, and the appearance of backwardness and decline crept over the South.

But it was not only the South's mysterious preoccupation with cotton agriculture that seemed to foreign observers to have shaped a culture of romantic conservatism. It was the particular *form* of labor that the South used in cotton agriculture—slaves—which seemed to set it off, not only from the North, but from the rest of the 19th century. Western Europeans had kept slaves ever since the end of the Roman Empire, and even in the heyday of classical Greece and Rome, slavery had been an everyday feature of urban and rural life. The reason for this was simple: In ages that knew only the most basic forms of labor-saving machinery, slaves provided a docile work force that did not require an equal share of one's wealth or success. And yet slavery was not always successful and slaves were not always docile, and throughout the Middle Ages, the institution of slavery was gradually narrowed to serfdom, and serfdom slowly yielded to simple renter, or tenant, status. Still, slavery did not disappear entirely. Western Christianity, although it gave little reason to encourage slavery, did not forbid it either, and Christian Europeans found no explicit condemnation of slavery on the pages of the New Testament. And the rediscovery of ancient Greek and Roman literature in the Renaissance further reminded western Europeans that slavery had once been an important part of great societies admired by European humanists. Above all, the decimation of European society resulting

[15]Pollard, *The Lost Cause: A New Southern History of the War of the Confederates* (New York, 1867), p. 51.

from the waves of lethal epidemics and national warfare in the 14th century created a revived need for cheap labor, and slave labor was the easiest way to fill that bill. By the end of the 1400s, one-tenth of the population in the Portuguese seafaring capital of Lisbon was in some form of slavery.[16]

Slavery in the American South appeared, at first glance, to be simply a continuation of the slavery people knew from the Bible or from Caesar, Livy, or Suetonius. But in many respects, southern slavery, like the other forms of New World slavery from Columbus onward, was a very different affair from the kind Europeans had known in ancient times. Like ancient slavery, southern slavery had been called into being by economic circumstances—in colonial Virginia, by the need for a cheap labor force to harvest tobacco, a crop that became profitable only when harvested in greater volume than one tobacco farmer could undertake. But in this case, there was a significant difference from all the other forms of slavery that western civilization had known. This time, it was based on race.

Although colonial Southerners searched for cheap sources of labor in white indentured servants, redemptioners, and prisoners-of-war, almost all of these forms of forced labor had time limits and legal obligations attached to them, and European attitudes were already starting to question the legitimacy of extracting forced labor from other Europeans. But before the end of the 1600s, southern white colonists had found a permanent solution to their labor problems by opening their ports and plantations to the thriving transatlantic African slave trade. African slave labor turned out to be easily transferrable to Chesapeake tobacco-growing. And using captured Africans as slaves paid an additional social dividend to colonial slaveholders, for just as their color marked them off as "outsiders" to European eyes, so their labor could be bounded with an entirely different set of assumptions than would prevail for white labor. This lent the twist of racism to southern slavery, making what had ordinarily been a matter of economic exploitation into a system of racial exploitation as well.[17]

Colonial slavery was also a far more brutal and ruthless system of labor organization than the slaveries found in the dim past. American slavery involved from the start the kidnapping of other human beings from their homes, subjecting them to the horrors of transportation across the Atlantic Ocean in fetid and disease-ridden slave ships, where as many as half died en route, and then selling them like cattle without any real hope of ever obtaining their freedom again. This kind of brutality toward other human beings, which departed dramatically from anything Protestant Americans could read concerning slavery in their Bibles, could not be justified in an avowedly Christian society—unless, of course, it could be shown that the slaves were not really human beings at all. It was here that racism served its purpose, for to

---

[16]J. J. Sharp, *Discovery in the North Atlantic, from the 6th to the 17th century* (Halifax, NS, 1991), pp. viii–ix.

[17]David Eltis, "Europeans and the Rise and Fall of African Slavery in the Americas: An Interpretation," in *American Historical Review* 98 (December 1993) pp. 1399–1423.

varying degrees, slaveowners protected themselves from the charge of kidnapping and murder by claiming that the black African was really subhuman. It was also at this point that slavery revealed its most vicious and dehumanizing face. For a slave, by simple definition, has no legal or social existence: The slave could have no right to hold property, could enjoy no recognition of marriage or family, and could not give testimony (even in self-defense) before the law.[18] There was nothing, therefore, that protected the slave from dehumanization and dishonor, since law exists in human societies to protect what a society deems to be human or the possessions of humans. Therefore, slaves could be beaten and whipped: Josiah Henson, born a slave in 1789 in Charles County, Maryland, remembered that his father had "received a hundred lashes on his back" and had "his right ear . . . cut off close to his head" for stopping a white overseer from beating Josiah's mother. Slaves could be bullied and brutalized: Frederick Bailey, also born a slave in Maryland in 1818, was turned over by a fearful owner to a professional "slave-breaker," Edward Covey, who whipped and beat Bailey without mercy for six months to bring him into "submission." Slaves could be raped: In 1855, Celia, the slave of Robert Newsom, killed Newsom in self-defense when Newsom attempted to rape her. The Missouri court she appealed to in *State of Missouri v. Celia* would not admit her testimony. But it did execute her.[19] Above all, slaves could be bought and sold, and slave families broken up for auction, without any regard for ties of kinship or marriage.

And yet, slaveholders could not have had everything their own way, no matter what the law said. A black slave was a human being, and any master who aspired to civilized refinement had to recognize that fact just to get any work out of the slave at all. What was more, no master could easily deny that slaves spoke the same language, worshiped the same God, and obstinately behaved like people. It also went without saying that a beaten or dead slave was one less production unit, and in a system where the labor force *was* the capital investment of the owner, it did not do to live too much by the whip alone. Nor did African-American slaves wait upon the indulgence of whites to work out their own stubborn degrees of independence. They formed their own black Christian congregations, which became (and have remained) the center of African-American community life; they sang their own songs; and to a degree that would ordinarily seem unimaginable, kept their fragile families together. For their part, white masters frequently had little choice but to accept these manifestations of extremely human behavior and quietly tolerate them. As Eugene Genovese had suggested in his numerous studies of the slave South, the practical realization that real human beings were providing free goods and services induced a sense of guilt and obligation among the whites that cushioned the slaves from the excesses of white behavior that the law otherwise permitted.[20]

And as whites made the grudging concession that their slaves were human

[18]James Oakes, *Slavery and Freedom: An Interpretation of the Old South* (New York, 1990), p. 3–14.

[19]Melton A. McLaurin, *Celia: A Slave* (New York, 1991), pp. 134–135.

[20]Eugene D. Genovese, *Roll, Jordan, Roll: The World the Slaves Made* (New York, 1972), pp. 89–91.

beings after all, this produced a clamorous urge on the part of white Southerners to justify the continuation of slavery on the grounds that slavery was actually a benefit of sorts to African Americans. The captain of the steamboat that carried William Howard Russell down the Alabama River insisted on arranging a "dance of Negroes . . . on the lower deck" to demonstrate "how 'happy they were.' " " 'Yes sir,' " Russell's host intoned," 'they're the happiest people on the face of the earth.' " At almost the same moment, in Georgia, Susan Cornwall Shewmake was writing, "It is certain there is not so much want among then. They are the happiest laboring people on the globe." In the same state, Georgia Senator T. R. R. Cobb assuringly repeated, "Our slaves are the most happy and contented, best fed and best clothed and best paid laboring population in the world, and I would add, also, the *most faithful* and least feared." And at the same moment in Virginia, Governor Henry Wise was claiming that "the descendants of Africa in bondage" find themselves in "bodily comfort, morality, enlightenment, Christianity. . . . universally fed and clothed well, and they are happy and contented."[21] This "universal hymn of the South" was a peculiar claim that would have otherwise been unnecessary to make about subhumans. At the same time, though, the same guilt that provoked whites to justify slavery on the grounds of its good works also provoked revealing displays of disgust and helplessness over slaveholding. Senator James Chesnut of South Carolina told his wife, Mary Boykin Chesnut, that his slaves owed him $50,000 for the food and clothing he had given them; when asked if his slaves had ever attempted to run away, he exclaimed, "Never. It's pretty hard work to keep me from running away from them."

> Take this estate [Chesnut suggested]. John C. says he could rent it from his grandfather and give him fifty thousand a year—then make twice as much more for himself. What does it do, actually? It all goes back in some shape to what are called slaves here—operatives, tenants, &c elsewhere. . . . This old man's [money] goes to support a horde of idle dirty Africans—while he is abused and vilefed as a cruel slave owner. . . . I hate slavery.

Richard Taylor, a Louisianian and the son of a president, commented bitterly long after slavery had disappeared that "Extinction of slavery was expected by all and regretted by none." Even in the throes of slavery, enslaved African Americans imposed a strong psychological tension on their masters that robbed the whites of whatever joys there are to be had in owning another human being.[22]

And so, once again, the question emerged: *Why,* if slavery held so much woe,

[21]Russell, *My Diary North and South,* Fletcher Pratt, ed. (New York, 1954), p. 106; Randall Jimerson, *The Private Civil War: Popular Thought During the Sectional Conflict* (Baton Rouge, LA, 1988), p. 54; Cobb, "T. R. R. Cobb's Secessionist Speech," in *Secession Debated: Georgia's Showdown in 1860,* William H. Freehling and Craig M. Simpson, eds. (New York, 1992), p. 11; Craig M. Simpson, *A Good Southerner: The Life of Henry A. Wise of Virginia* (Chapel Hill, NC, 1985), p. 103.

[22]Chesnut, in *Mary Chesnut's Civil War,* p. 246; T. Michael Parrish, *Richard Taylor: Soldier Prince of Dixie* (Chapel Hill, NC, 1992), p. 446.

not only for black slaves but for white masters as well, did Southerners cling to slavery with the same hold they clung to cotton agriculture? The answer was similar: Because slavery promoted a peculiar culture, certain way of living that white Southerners were willing to pay the price for. "It was a medieval civilization, out of accord with the modern tenor of our time," Fanny Andrews, a Georgian, recalled, "It stood for gentle courtesy, for knightly honor, for generous hospitality; it stood for fair and honest dealing of man with man in the common business of life, for lofty scorn of cunning greed and ill-gotten gain through fraud and deception of our fellowmen. . . ."[23] This was an ingenious rationalization, and it has enjoyed a certain following among modern historians as well. The problem is that it is too simple. The slave-based cotton agriculture of the southern states was an intricate and complicated system of political economy in which cultural appearances were not always the safest guide. Alongside the irrational display of carelessness and waste in cotton agriculture lay a relentless economic rationality; alongside the facade of racial reciprocity lay resistance and revolt; and alongside the image of stability and elegance lurked an aggressiveness that was willing to bring down the federal Union in order to protect its future.

The dominance of cotton agriculture in the South distracted observers then, and distracts historians now, from the real meaning of that agriculture. Whatever else cotton agriculture was in the South before the Civil War, it was based on two critical economic facts: Cotton-growing dealt in the most highly prized commodity in the capitalist world, and it dealt at great distances on an international market. Cotton, unlike the agricultural commodities produced in the household-based agriculture of the North, was a cash crop, not a self-sufficiency crop. It could not be eaten and it could not be worn without being manufactured into garments, and the money that was to be made from it resulted in long-range, high-volume exchanges of cash and financial instruments that followed a highly sophisticated network of transatlantic trade. Instead of cotton-growing being a sign of an aristocratic Southerner's withdrawal from the "vulgar" world of the market economy, cotton was actually the American commodity most likely to bring a grower into the closest possible engagement with it.

Not only planter profits, but planter behavior reveals an economic logic in the South much more sophisticated and much more closely tied to the international markets than the planters wanted to admit. Much as it was true that slave-based cotton agriculture was generating more prestige than profits for planters in the oldest parts of the South, there were other, newer parts of the South where the situation was radically different; and this was because there was a third, and not so obvious variable, in the equation of successful cotton-growing, and that was *land*. Land as much as slavery dictated the rise or fall of a cotton plantation, largely because intensive cotton-growing wore out even the best soil. For that reason, as

[23]Randall Jimerson, *The Private Civil War: Popular Thought During the Sectional Conflict* (Baton Rouge, 1988), p. 249

William H. Freehling has shown in his survey of the slave economy, cotton-growing in the southern states turned out to be a highly mobile occupation, with a constant slide of transient masters, slaves, and cotton out of the original cotton-growing regions of the 1790s and toward the new southwest territories of the United States. In 1800, almost the whole North American cotton crop came from the Carolinas and Virginia. Then, with the suden boom in cotton, slaves and masters began shifting south and west, first to Georgia, and then after 1810 into the new territories of Alabama and Mississippi, finally lapping up the Mississippi River into Tennessee and across the Mississippi into Arkansas and Missouri. By 1860, Virginia and Maryland had only 18 percent of all southern slaves within their borders, and only a quarter of the South's cotton output, while the alluvial bottomlands of Mississippi produced more than all the old cotton states combined.[24] And, provided the land was right, there were immense profits to be made. While the worn-out plantations of the Upper South were declining to marginal profitability, Harriet Martineau toured cotton plantations in Alabama in the mid-1830s where the profit margin was 35 percent. "One planter whom I knew had bought fifteen thousand dollars' worth of land within two years. . . . He expected to make, that season, fifty or sixty thousand dollars of his growing crop." J. H. Ingraham in 1835 had met raw new cotton planters in southwestern Mississippi with net annual incomes between $20,000 and $40,000. Making the adroit move to the most advantageous location could generate immense and quick wealth in cotton. It was ambitious Alabama planters, and not avaricious Northern factory owners, that Martineau described as being, "from whatever motive, money-getters; and few but money-getting qualifications are to be looked for in them."

And of course, the great and singular advantage for cotton capitalists of using a labor force consisting of slaves was that it could, by simple order, be *moved.* Much as defenders of slavery argued the rights and benefits of slavery from biblical or classical examples, the slavery that was first introduced into North America in the 1600s was the direct offspring, not of a traditional or feudal social system, but of the needs of commercial capitalism. North American slavery was only part of that larger cycle of slavery reinvented in the 16th century when Europeans first realized what awesome wealth the American continents contained and what few hands they had to extract it. The purpose of slavery, then, was not to create an antique social system where a fox-hunting aristocracy would rule a balanced and organic society of helots in the spirit of reciprocity and mutual obligation. It was a labor system fueled by violent and sometimes lethal coercion, designed for the maximum production of commodities and wealth at the cheapest imaginable labor cost.

The slaves harbored the fewest illusions of all about the South's social economy. Slaves rebelled when they could, as Denmark Vesey and his conspirators tried to do in Charleston in 1822, and as Nat Turner and his band of slaves actually did in

[24]William W. Freehling, *The Road to Disunion: Secessionists at Bay, 1776–1854* (New York, 1990), pp. 18, 24, 35, 201–207.

Virginia in 1831. When outright rebellion was impossible, slaves found other ways to isolate and terrify their tormentors, including work slowdowns, breakage of tools, and abusing work animals. And they ran away. Sometimes for short periods of time to evade punishments, sometimes to escape from slavery entirely, the slaves ran whenever the threats or the opportunities became too great to resist. When Josiah Henson's master moved him from Maryland to a new plantation down the Ohio River in 1830, and then began toying with the idea of selling Henson away from his wife and children, Henson "determined to make my escape to Canada, about which I had heard something, as beyond the limits of the United States." In mid-September, 1830, he arranged to collect his wife and children, persuaded a fellow slave to ferry them over the Ohio River by night, and trudged all the way to Canada on foot. Frederick Bailey returned to his master, scheming all the while how to buy his freedom with the money he earned on odd jobs performed for other whites. But when his master suspended his outside work privileges, Bailey decided that he had paid his master all he deserved, and in 1838, he boarded a train headed for Philadelphia, dressed as a sailor and carrying false identification papers. He found his way to New Bedford, Massachusetts, where he changed his name to Frederick Douglass. In 1841, Douglass was recruited as an agent for the Massachusetts Anti-Slavery Society; four years later he published his *Narrative of the Life of Frederick Douglass, an American Slave*. Within a decade he had become the most famous African American on the continent, and one of slavery's deadliest enemies.

But nothing questions the complacent, relaxed, and sentimental image of the planter aristocracy more than the plain fact that this aristocracy spent so much of its time wheedling, persuading, and soliciting the good will of the rest of the white South. Much as it is easy to speak of the South as though it was a single homogenized region, there were really several different Souths. For instance: although many Northerners thought of the South as "the land ob Cotton," by the 1850s, large-scale cotton plantations and large-scale slave labor was concentrated mainly along the lower Mississippi River valley (where slaves could constitute up to 70 percent of the population of the fertile cotton-growing districts) and the Carolina and Georgia coastlines; a lesser concentration of slavery and cotton-growing stretched in a broad belt from southern Arkansas, through central Mississippi and Alabama and up through the Carolinas to the shores of the Chesapeake Bay. That left large stretches of the South—especially in the thinly settled districts of lower Florida, the wiregrass and piney woods counties of Alabama, and the mountain districts of east Tennessee, Kentucky, and western North Carolina— with only a relatively thin sprinkling of cotton-growing and slaveholding. In eastern Tennessee, only 10 percent of the population were slaves, and in central Tennessee, only four out of ten. And it was not cotton that most of Tennessee grew, but wheat.[25]

---

[25]Thomas V. Ash, *Middle Tennessee Society Transformed, 1860–1870: War and Peace in the Upper South* (Baton Rouge, LA, 1988), pp. 10, 18.

Large-scale slavery was confined, not only by geography, but by class. Although slaves were held by a remarkably broad section of southern society—overall, one out of every four white families in the South in 1860 owned slaves, an extraordinary figure considering that by 1860 the cost of a strong, healthy field hand had reached $1,500—the distribution of that ownership varied considerably. Less than one percent of southern white families (comprising less than 12,000 people across the South) owned more than 100 slaves; the largest group of slaveowning families held between one and four slaves, and those families accounted for almost half the slaveholding in the entire South. This meant that southern slavery was, in most cases, an affair of small-scale farming, in which white farmers enlisted the help of a slave or two to plow up and harvest holdings of less than a hundred acres. It also meant that, beyond the actual slaveholders themselves, there existed a large population of nonslaveholding whites, and they created almost as great a problem for the great planters as rebellious slaves.

What frightened the planters was the possibility, however remote, that an economically and politically alienated population of white yeoman farmers with a curiosity about such subjects might, at some point, decide that its mutual interests lay in other directions than those of the great planters, and become an engine for abolition or (in the most hideous scenario) a refuge for slave runaways and rebellion. Southern planters fantasized about northern plots "to array one class of our citizens against the other, limit the defense of slavery to those pecuniarily interested, and thereby eradicate it." It thus became vital to the peace of the planters' minds that the frustrations of the "crackers," or "sandhillers," or simply "poor white trash" be diminished or placated at all costs. This involved, first and foremost, keeping the bogeyman of racism ever before the nonslaveholders' eyes, for whatever hatreds the poor whites nursed against the planters, they nursed still greater ones against African Americans. "Now suppose they was free," an Alabama dirt farmer asked Frederick Law Olmstead, "How'd you like to hev a nigger feelin' just as good as a white man? How'd you like to hev a nigger steppin' up to your darter?" Even if slavery was wrong, its wrongs were canceled out for nonslaveholders by the more monstrous spectre of racial equality. Abolish slavery, and white farmers would find that blacks were now their legal equals and economic and social competitors. "You very soon make them all tenants and reduce their wages for daily labor to the smallest pittance that will sustain life," warned Georgia Governor Joseph E. Brown, and that will eventually force poor whites and blacks "to go to church as equals; enter the Courts of Justice as equals, sue and be sued as equals, sit on juries together as equals, have the right to give evidence in court as equals, stand side by side in our military corps as equals, enter each others houses in social intercourse as equals; and very soon their children must marry together as equals. . . ." Southern elites like Brown felt certain that when nonslaveholding whites realized the full racial consequences of abolition, they would become slavery's strongest supporters. "The strongest pro-slavery men in these States are those who do not own one dollar of slave property," insisted a Louisville newspaper, "They are sturdy yeomen who cultivate the soil, tend their own crops; but if need be, would stand to their section till the last one of them fell."[26]

Ensuring the loyalty of nonslaveholding whites also involved a measure of social humiliation on the part of the planters, who found themselves forced at every election to advocate as a social ideal, not aristocracy, but *herrenvolk* democracy—a kind of equality in which all the members of a superior race are more equal, socially and politically, to each other than to any members of an inferior race. "In all social systems there must be a class to do the menial duties, to perform the drudgery of life," explained James Henry Hammond in 1858, there must be a class which "constitutes the very mud-sill of society and political government." And white Southerners had found that "menial" class, that "mud-sill," in the black slave. Built on top of that "mud-sill," and performing the "duties" no white man would stoop to, all southern whites could feel that they were members of a ruling class. Of course, arguing thusly forced slavery's apologists to sing a different tune than the one that assured the world that slavery existed to bestow the benefits of civilization and Christianity on the African. Instead, alongside the happiest-people-on-the-earth argument, planters had to offer a parallel argument for slavery, based on the vilest form of racism and calculated to enlist the racist sympathies and fears of the nonslaveholders. "The privilege of belonging to the superior race and of being free was a bond that tied all Southern whites together," wrote the Alabama lawyer Hilery Abner Herbert, "and it was infinitely strengthened by a crusade that seemed from a Southern stand-point, to have for its purpose the leveling of all distinctions between the white man and the slave hard by."[27]

The appeal to white racial solidarity disguised the fact that southern yeomen may have had a great deal more to fear from slavery, so far as their economic futures were concerned, than they suspected. Slavery has become so fixed in the historical memory as a form of agricultural labor that it has been easy to miss how steadily, in the 1850s, African-American slaves were being slipped into the South's small industrial work force. More than half of the workers in the new iron furnaces along the Cumberland River in Tennessee were slaves, and after 1845, most of the ironworkers in the Richmond iron furnaces in Virginia were slaves as well. The hemp factories of Kentucky, which had actually begun using slave labor as early as the 1820s, defended the decision to use slave operatives on the grounds that they were so much easier to exploit than free white workers: "they are more *docile*, more constant, and cheaper than freemen, who are often refractory and dissipated; who waste much time by frequenting public places, attending musters, elections, etc.,

[26]"An Appeal to Non-Slaveholders" [Louisville, KY, *Statesman*, October 5, 1860] in *Southern Editorials on Secession*, ed. Dwight Lowell Dumond (New York, 1931), pp. 174–175; Olmstead, *The Cotton Kingdom, A Selection*, D. F. Hawke, ed. (Indianapolis, 1971), p. 106; Brown, in *Secession Debated*, eds. Freehling and Simpson, p. 153.

[27]Hammond, "Mud-Sill Speech," in *Slavery Defended: The Views of the Old South*, Eric L. McKitrick, ed. (Englewood Cliffs, NJ, 1963), p. 122–123; Hugh B. Hammett, *Hilery Abner Herbert: A Southerner Returns to the Union* (Philadelphia, 1976), p. 37.

which the operative slave is not permitted to frequent." And, added Tennessee iron producer Samuel Morgan in 1852, they did not strike. Furthermore, when the great California gold rush of the late 1840s opened up for Americans the prospect of large-scale mining in the West, it was not forgotten by Southerners how successful slave-based gold mining had been in South America.[28] The South thus presented the spectacle, peculiar to a number of subcultures in the Euro-American 19th century, that wedded nonmarket social ideals to a market economy. With only the right circumstances and sufficient amount of time, slave labor could have easily become the industrial "mud-sill," a new proletariat made permanent by its identification through race.

For slavery was neither a backwards nor a dying system in the 1850s. It was aggressive, dynamic, mobile, and by pandering to the racial prejudices of a white republic starved for labor, it was perfectly capable of expansion. In 1810, the southern states had a slave population of just over one million; by 1860, in defiance of every expectation for what a system of organized violence could do to the survival of a people, the slave population stood at just under four million. No matter that, to outside observers, the South looked like anything but a market *society;* cotton, and the economic rationalization needed to sustain it, had made the South as much a part of the market *economy* as the North. No matter that slavery was based on the absurd and irrational prejudice of race; its greatest attraction was its cheapness, its capacity for violent exploitation, and its mobility. If California had been turned over to Southerners, speculated Virginia Governor Henry Wise, "every cornfield in Virginia and North Carolina, in Maryland, Missouri, Tennessee and Kentucky, would have been emptied of black laborers, and I doubt whether many slaves would have been left to work the cotton and sugar estates of the other Southern plantations." But to expand, slavery would need protection and reassurance. Southerners would tolerate the annoyance of tariffs and the like, but they would not permit interference with or restriction upon slavery or its growth. And the federal Union in which the southern states participated was a sufficiently rickety structure that any serious attack on slavery would be an excuse for Southerners to tear the whole structure of the Union down.

3. The Rise of Abolitionism

The economic aggressiveness of the slave system and the political weakness of the Union were an unhappy combination within the American republic, but there was nothing in either of them that necessarily threw one into war with the other. South

[28]Robert S. Starobin, *Industrial Slavery in the Old South* (New York, 1970), pp. 214–222; Eugene D. Genovese, *The Political Economy of Slavery* (New York, 1965), pp. 222–223; T. Stephen Whitman, "Industrial Slavery at the Margin: The Maryland Chemical Works," in *Journal of Southern History* 51 (February 1993), pp. 31–62.

and North still shared large areas of cultural continuity, and northern merchants happily made fortunes feeding slavery's economic drives. In fact, there might never have been a civil war at all in 1861 had it not been for two facts of geography that forced the sections onto a collision course. The first of these facts was that by 1860 there were virtually no slaves at all in the northern states; and the second was that there was an enormous amount of land in the American West that no one quite knew what to do with.

Under British rule, nearly all white American colonists who owned their own farm or merchandise had servants of various sorts, although *servant* was a term that included everything from wage laborers to outright bondage. Slavery was part of this overall use of servant labor, and it persisted in all parts of the American colonies until the American Revolution and beyond. Rhode Island and Connecticut still possessed a smattering of slaves as late as 1810; Pennsylvania still had some slaves living within its borders in 1830; in New Jersey, there were still eighteen lifetime black "apprentices" when the Civil War broke out.[29] Had slavery remained a legal and economic force in every northern state and survived in any significant numbers, then slavery would still have posed a moral problem to the republic. But it would have been a problem that every state shared and one that would never have developed into a sectional issue, fanning animosities between states where slavery was legal and those where it was not.

But slavery did not remain a national institution. Apart from the small pockets of slaves surviving in the North in the early 19th century, slavery gradually became a dead letter north of the famous Mason-Dixon line (which separated Pennsylvania and Maryland) and the Ohio River. This disappearance has often been explained as a result of climate and soil: The agriculture practiced in the northern states was small-scale and required little or no slave assistance. Especially, the northern climate was too cold to grow cotton, and Northerners felt none of the enthusiasm Southerners felt for the explosive growth of cotton agriculture in the 19th century. Therefore, they had no need for slaves. Instead, the North welcomed factory-based manufacturing, which could afford to dispense with a large permanent labor force and get along with a smaller, wage-paid labor supply. Beginning in 1813, when Francis Cabot Lowell built the first cotton textile factory (on plans stolen from British textile manufacturers), the old Northeast sprouted textile mills and manufacturing operations, some 140,000 of them by 1860, employing 1.3 million workers. As early as 1826, Pennsylvania's Chester County already had fourteen woolen factories and thirteen cotton mills, and by 1860, there were forty-nine mills and workshops along just one five-mile stretch of the Connecticut River in western Massachusetts. The coming of the mills to the cold and stony northern states left only the cotton fields of the South as a viable home for slavery. By the time slavery

---

[29]C. Duncan Rice, *The Rise and Fall of Black Slavery* (New York, 1975), pp. 210–211; Freehling, *The Road to Disunion*, pp. 132–135.

began to be seen as a moral problem in the United States, it had become a southern problem as well.

And yet, the climate-and-soil argument cannot carry all the weight of explaining why the North lost its slaves while the South multiplied them. After all, neither the climate nor the soil of much of the northern states differed all that much from a good deal of the slaveholding South. Even if cotton could not be easily grown in Connecticut, wheat could; and wheat was being harvested by slave labor in both Kentucky and Tennessee. Wheat, in fact, had been planted and harvested by slave labor in Pennsylvania as early as the 1680s, and 20 percent of all the manual labor in Quaker Philadelphia in the 1750s was being performed by black slaves. And as Southerners themselves had begun to realize, there was no reason why slave labor could not run the mills as easily as hired white labor.

The reasons for slavery's disappearance in the North also have to be looked for in a number of more-or-less intangible sources. One of the least intangible of these causes was the American Revolution. In an effort to weaken American resistance, British occupation forces frequently lured slaves to desert their masters and enter British lines, where freedom was promised as a reward. That promise was, more often than not, honored in the breach. Slaves who ran away in Pennsylvania to join Sir William Howe's occupation of Philadelphia or who ran away in Virginia to join Lord Dunmore's "Ethiopian regiment" found themselves dumped by their erstwhile allies in Nova Scotia or sold back into slavery in the Bahamas. But the effect on the structures of slavery was significant: over 5,000 Georgia slaves fled to the protection of the King George when the British invaded Georgia in 1779, and another 20,000 South Carolina slaves found refuge under British guns in Charleston. In New York City, which the British had occupied for most of the Revolution, runaway slaves swelled the free black population, while in Philadelphia, by the close of the Revolution, the slave population had fallen from 1,400 to 400.[30]

The political idealism of the Revolution also encouraged, and sometimes forced, white slaveowners to liberate their slaves. The political ideology of republicanism owed an immense debt to the political ideals of the Enlightenment, with its glorification of individual liberty and freedom of conscience, and opposition to slavery was only a logical extension of republican liberty. There were, as Samuel Johnson remarked, few things more incongruous than listening to yelps for liberty from the mouths of slave drivers. A number of Americans felt the pain of that comparison enough to manumit their slaves or pass laws that provided an end to the slave trade in their states. As early as 1774, the Massachusetts Provincial Convention turned to "consider the propriety that while we are attempting to free ourselves from our present embarrassments, and preserve ourselves from slavery, that we also take into consideration the state and circumstances of the negro slaves in this province." By the time the Constitution was written, laws prohibiting the slave

[30]Gary B. Nash, Forging Freedom: The Formation of Philadelphia's Black Community, 1720–1840 (Cambridge, MA, 1988), p. 65.

trade had been passed in Pennsylvania, Rhode Island, and Connecticut. But free African Americans also took their future into their own hands. "Freedom suits" were filed by black Americans in northern courts, and litigious slaves in Massachusetts like Quok Walker in *Jennison v. Caldwell* (1781) claimed freedom on the grounds that the new Massachusetts constitution had declared that all individuals were "born free and equal." Others organized manumission societies to assist in purchasing the freedom of other blacks still in bondage, or prosecute slaveowners guilty of abuse.[31]

But more than secular political ideas, it was religious commitment that formed the backbone of much of the North's hostility to slavery. The Protestant evangelicalism that grew out of the Great Awakening was fully as devoted to the importance of individual spiritual freedom as republicanism was devoted to political freedom, and the two ideologies found a common cause in opposing slavery. Fueling evangelical opposition to slavery was the relentless urge toward "disinterested benevolence" that evangelicals found in the writings of Jonathan Edwards and his disciples, Joseph Bellamy and Samuel Hopkins. Edwards's great *Freedom of the Will* taught that no action of the human will could be considered morally responsible unless it was free from physical compulsion and restraint, or "natural necessity." His last and posthumously published treatise on *The Nature of True Virtue* (1758) insisted that the only truly moral actions were those performed with an utter disregard to self-interest and in a spirit of perfect charity toward "being in general." Both Hopkins and Bellamy saw at once that Edwards's doctrines were incompatible with slavery, since by Edwards's logic slavery served no other purpose than the self-interest of the slaveowner and imposed "natural necessity" on the actions of the slave at every point. Bellamy voluntarily emancipated his only slave; from then onward, Hopkins emptied his Second Congregational Church in Newport, Rhode Island, by preaching against slavery. And the most famous heir of the Edwardsean tradition, Charles Grandison Finney, openly denied communion in 1833 to slaveholders "and all concerned in the traffic." The Edwardseans were joined by other streams of religious dissent. The Quakers, awakened by the writing and preaching of Anthony Benezet and John Woolman, moved to admonish and then discipline slaveholders in the 1750s, and by the time of the Revolution, slavery had disappeared almost entirely from American Quakerism.

Not all of the rising agitation against slavery was limited to the North. Prior to the 1830s, many Southerners expressed a sense of shame over slavery for both political and religious reasons. Thomas Jefferson offers one of the best-known and most ambivalent cases of southern antislavery feeling, for Jefferson fully understood that slavery was a vicious and unjust system that mocked the liberty and equality he had made his political gospel. "Nothing is more certainly written in the book of fate

---

[31]Arthur Zilversmit, "Slavery and Its Abolition in the Northern States" (unpublished Ph.D. dissertation, University of California—Berkeley, 1962), pp. 147, 152–153; Duncan J. McLeod, *Slavery, Race, and the American Revolution* (Cambridge, 1974), pp. 121–122; Benjamin Quarles, "The Revolutionary War as a Black Declaration of Independence," in *Slavery and Freedom: The Age of the American Revolution*, Ira Berlin and Ronald Hoffman, eds. (Urbana, IL, 1986), pp. 283–301.

than that these people are to be free," Jefferson declared; without any effort to free the slaves, he could only "tremble for my country," for in that case he knew "that God is just; that his justice cannot sleep forever; that considering numbers, nature and natural means only," a slave uprising "is among possible events." In that case, "the Almighty has no attribute which can takes sides with us in such a contest." And so Jefferson wrote the Northwest Ordinance of 1787, which organized the new territories of Ohio, Indiana, Illinois, Michigan, and Wisconsin, so that slavery would be permanently illegal there. And the new federal Constitution was written to ban the importation of further slaves from Africa after 1808. Abolition societies like the North Carolina Manumission Society were, for a time, more numerous in the South than the North.

But antislavery opinion in the South remained weak, and was palsied by racism. For all of Jefferson's guilt over slaveholding, the right time and the right conditions for emancipation never quite seemed to come. As president, he deliberately turned a deaf ear to cooperation with a new black revolutionary republic in Haiti, which was at that moment struggling to throw back an invasion by the soldiers of a man Jeffersonn had declared to be a tyrant, Napoleon Bonaparte. The Virginians in the state constitutional convention who called for an end to slavery also wanted an end to African Americans in Virginia, and wanted them bundled out of the sight of white people entirely. Further south, as cotton grew more and more profitable, republican enthusiasm for abolition waned past the vanishing point. More and more whites who once had no reason to own slaves were now drawn into the cotton culture, and the desire for cotton profits lured numbers of Southerners into defending those profits by defending slavery.

The symbolic deathblow to any southern abolition movement came in August of 1831, when a religious visionary named Nat Turner led seventy of his fellow slaves in a short-lived but bloody insurrection in southeastern Virginia. The revolt was quickly and brutally put down, with Turner and his followers captured or butchered, but not before fifty-seven whites had also died. At Turner's trial, it became apparent that he had methodically ordered the execution of every white man, woman, and child he had encountered, whether they were slaveowners or not, and had hoped to spread his revolt throughout Virginia. Turner's confessions served notice on southern whites that it mattered nothing what their personal opinions on slavery were—Nat Turner would have massacred them all if given the chance. This realization served to drive nonslaveholding yeomen straight into the arms of planters, simply in the interest of self-protection. And when the Virginia House of Delegates resumed its debate over the future of slavery in 1832, the question was put purely in terms of white survival: Either expel the blacks completely from Virginia or institute more repressive measures and end all discussion of abolition as dangerous incitement. By a narrow margin, the decision came down, in effect, on the side of repression. After 1832, Virginian calls for abolition and transportation faded, and elsewhere in the South any further attempts by whites to advocate freeing the slaves were denounced as felonies and punished accordingly.

This steady swing back in favor of the continuation of slavery produced, in the North, an equal but opposite reaction. With all the energies of religious and secular idealism flowing, free African Americans raised their voices in a chorus of eloquent protest. "I speak, Americans, for your good," wrote David Walker, a free black shopowner in Boston in 1829, "We must and shall be free, I say, in spite of you . . . God will deliver us from under you. And wo, wo, will be to you if we have to obtain our freedom by fighting." Northern antislavery societies denounced the slide backward with new militancy, and on January 1, 1831, William Lloyd Garrison published the first issue of the antislavery newspaper, *The Liberator*. With one sweep of defiant rhetoric, Garrison demanded an unconditional and immediate end to slavery. "I *will be* as harsh as truth, and as uncompromising as justice," Garrison promised on the first page of *The Liberator*, "I will not equivocate—I will not excuse—I will not retreat a single inch—AND I WILL BE HEARD." Garrison gave up any hope of converting the South to antislavery opinions. He was bent upon radicalizing the North, and his weapons were provocation and shock: "Be not afraid to look the monster SLAVERY boldly in the face," Garrison cried in 1832, "He is your implacable foe—the vampyre who is sucking your life-blood—the ravager of a large portion of your country, and the enemy of God and man." If necessary, Garrison was willing to have the free states secede from the Union rather than continue in an unholy federation with slave states. "It is said if you agitate this question, you will divide the Union," Garrison editorialized, "but should disunion follow, the fault will not be yours. . . . Let the pillars thereof fall—let the superstructure crumble into dust—if it must be upheld by robbery and oppression." In 1833, Garrison joined with the wealthy evangelical brothers, Arthur and Lewis Tappan (who were also bankrolling Charles Grandison Finney), and founded the American Anti-Slavery Society in Philadelphia, and demanded the "immediate abandonment" and "entire abolition of slavery in the United States."[32]

These demands were infinitely more than Southerners could take. But they were also more than many Northerners could take, either. Just as the South's cotton agriculture bound southern whites to the defense of slavery, it also bound the northern bankers and merchants who lent the planters money to the toleration of slavery. Immediate abolition meant the disappearance of the immense fortunes that had been invested in the purchase of slaves, which would not only bankrupt the planters, but every Northerner who had invested in southern cotton. Even the ordinary northern millowner, who depended on shipments of southern cotton for the manufacture of finished textile products, stood to lose by Garrison's frank willingness to break up the Union over slavery. There was, as it turned out, a very significant gap between being antislavery and being abolitionist. A Northerner

[32]Garrison, "Introduction" and "The Great Crisis" [December 29, 1832], in *Documents of Upheaval: Selections from William Lloyd Garrison's The Liberator, 1831–1865*, Truman Nelson, ed. (New York, 1966), pp. xiii–xiv, 57; Russel B. Nye, *William Lloyd Garrison and the Humanitarian Reformers* (Boston, 1955), p. 72.

could oppose, criticize, and even denounce slavery without being at all inclined to take the risks of abolition.

It was for just this reason that northern factory workers could be thoroughly hostile to slavery and yet also be suspicious of the abolitionists. The northern labor movement was, like the antislavery movement, making its first attempts at large-scale organization in the late 1820s, and northern workers were hostile to an abolitionism that concerned itself only with the plight of slave laborers and not northern "wage slaves." Garrison did not help matters when he discounted any comparisons between slavery and the working conditions in many northern mills: "it is an abuse of language to talk of the slavery of wages. . . . We cannot see that it is wrong to give or receive wages." The close identification of evangelical Protestant-ism with the American Anti-Slavery Society did not improve the workers' opinion of the abolitionists. Many northern workers were new immigrants from Roman Catholic Ireland or southern Germany, and they spurned the antislavery zealots as part of a strategem of evangelical Protestants to Americanize the immigrant. And it could not have been far from the mind of northern workers that a sudden flood of free black labor onto the country's labor market would depress white wages and jeopardize white jobs.[33]

Farmers in the free states also pulled shy of the abolitionists in the 1830s. Although Illinois was technically a free state (under the original mandate of the Northwest Ordinance), large parts of the state had been settled by Southerners moving northward up the Mississippi valley and by immigrants moving westward over the Great Lakes. These Illinoisans banned slavery, but they also discouraged settlement by free African Americans, too, and they all looked upon the abolition-ists as an unholy alliance of religious bigots and tight-fisted Yankee meddlers. So, when the militant evangelical abolitionist, Elijah Lovejoy, was murdered by a mob in Alton, Illinois, in November, 1837, there was more at work than the making of an abolition martyr. Lovejoy was a rabid anti-Catholic who described Roman Catholicism as "an unmixed evil" in the pages of his newspaper, the St. Louis *Observer,* and his murderers were immigrants and Southerner migrants who looked on him as a threat to their community identities. So long as the abolition move-ment chose men like Lovejoy as its martyrs and examples, large segments of north-ern society would balk at abolition.[34]

As it was, Garrison could scarcely hold his own followers together. The Ameri-can Anti-Slavery Society was supposed to draw its support from a network of local and state auxiliary societies, but few of those auxiliary societies kept their donations up to the necessary level. Although the antislavery societies claimed as many as 250,000 members, *The Liberator* had only 1,400 subscribers, and the Tappan broth-ers had continually to bail Garrison's newspaper out. Garrison himself only made matters more difficult. When evangelical ministers questioned Garrison's "harsh,

[33]Eric Foner, *Politics and Ideology in the Age of the Civil War* (New York, 1980), pp. 64–76.
[34]Merton L. Dillon, *Elijah P. Lovejoy, Abolitionist Editor* (Urbana, IL, 1961), pp. 38–43.

unchristian vocabulary," Garrison lashed out at them as "a cage of unclean birds and a synagogue of Satan." When the Tappan brothers and other evangelical supporters of the American Anti-Slavery Society began to balk at Garrison's criticism of the ministers, Garrison immediately accused them of wanting "to see me cashiered, or voluntarily leave the ranks."[35]

Instead, Garrison cashiered the evangelicals. Garrison had been deeply impressed in the 1830s with the fervency and eloquence of two former South Carolina cotton heiresses, Sarah and Angelina Grimké, who had been converted to abolition. Garrison promoted them as lecturers on the circuit of the local antislavery societies, and they brought Garrison into close contact with the new womens' rights movement and its leaders, Elizabeth Cady Stanton, Abby Kelley, and Lydia Maria Child. These early feminists argued that a campaign to emancipate slaves could not avert its eyes from the need to emancipate American women from social conventions and legal restraints that prevented them, like the slave, from owning property and voting, and kept them altogether subservient to the interests of white males. "Woman," declared Stanton, is "more fully identified with the slave than man can possibly be . . . for while the man is born to do whatever he can, for the woman and the negro there is no such privilege." And even if womens' rights did not fall precisely within the goals of an antislavery society, at least that Society could admit women to its membership and leadership and allow them to bear their "subjective" testimony against slavery. But when Garrison attempted to place Abby Kelley on the business committee of the American Anti-Slavery Society at its annual meeting in 1840, the Tappan brothers and fully half of the Society's delegates rose and withdrew.

Garrison was left with a rump Society, and although he now had a free hand to place three feminists—Lucretia Mott, Lydia Child, and Maria Chapman—on the Society's executive committee, the American Anti-Slavery Society was never more than a shadow of what it had been in the 1830s. The Tappans, meanwhile, organized a rival antislavery society, the American and Foreign Anti-Slavery Society, whose constitution expressly barred women from voting in its deliberations. Many of the other leaders and followers of the abolitionists wandered off to support various schemes of "gradual emancipation" or colonization for freed blacks in Africa or the Caribbean. Colonization turned out to be a particularly popular solution to the slavery problem, since it treated slavery more as a problem for whites than blacks, and promised to eliminate the problem for whites by removing both slavery and blacks from white view. So long as slavery was eliminated, the colonizationists did not much worry about the injustice of colonizing African Americans back to a continent from which many of them were six to eight generations removed.

But the South increasingly failed to see these evidences of fragmentation, poverty, and outright resistance to abolition in the North, and ignored how easily Northerners might oppose slavery on a variety of grounds without necessarily wishing

[35]Bertram Wyatt-Brown, *Lewis Tappan and the Evangelical War Against Slavery* (New York, 1971), p. 190.

for its abolition in the South. Instead, South Carolina Governor James Hamilton thrust copies of *The Liberator* under the noses of state legislators, claiming that Nat Turner's revolt had been "excited by incendiary newspapers and other publications, put forth in the nonslaveholding states," and the legislatures of South Carolina, Virginia, Georgia, and Alabama formally appealed to legislatures of ten northern states in 1836 with requests that the publication and distribution of "newspapers, tracts, and pictorial representations, calculated and having an obvious tendency to excite the slaves of the slave states to insurrection and revolt" be made a criminal offense.[36] Never mind that no connection between Turner and Garrison was ever demonstrated—southern pressure forced Postmaster General Amos Kendall to turn a blind eye when southern postmasters began censoring suspicious mail and newspapers from the North.

And because northern state and local governments did not likewise act at once to silence the abolitionists, Southerners concluded that Northerners were actually in quiet collusion with the abolitionists to produce more Nat Turners. Throughout the 1840s and early 1850s, Southerners turned away from the Whig party to the Democrats, convinced that the Whig programs for federal intervention in the economy were only laying the groundwork for federal tampering with slavery. The tide of southern suspicion and southern temper rose higher and higher, and Southerners forgot that they had ever discussed emancipating their slaves. The happiest-people-on-the-face-of-the-earth argument silenced Jefferson's warning that the South had a wolf by the ears that it could neither master nor release. Southerners who extolled independence and liberty also found themselves extolling *herrenvolk* democracy and passing solemn resolutions warning that "Freedom of speech and press do not imply a moral right to freely discuss the subject of slavery. . . ." And eventually, by the mid-1850s, they came to the point of claiming that the political liberties enjoyed by northern workers were useless frauds compared to the cradle-to-the-grave care given by the slaveholder to the slave. "The negro slaves of the South are the happiest, and, in some sense, the freest people in the world," George Fitzhugh intoned yet again in 1856. "We do not know whether free laborers ever sleep," Fitzhugh snickered, "the free laborer must work or starve" while the slaves "enjoy liberty, because they are oppressed neither by care nor labor." The northern worker is actually "more of a slave than the negro, because he works longer and harder for less allowance than the slave, and has no holiday, because the cares of life with him begin when its labors end. He has no liberty, and not a single right."

But it was not enough for Southerners merely to justify the "positive good" of slavery in books and learned treatises and sermons. Nat Turner had been no respecter of arguments, and so the proslavery defenses began to sprout demands that the federal government and the northern state issue assurances that the abolitionists would never be allowed to tamper with what John Calhoun delicately described as the South's "peculiar domestic institution." Still, southern slaveholders need not

[36]Nye, *William Lloyd Garrison*, pp. 54, 98–100.

have worried overmuch, since the Constitution had sanctioned the existence of slavery by allowing the slave states to count three-fifths of their slave populations toward the creation of federal congressional districts. (This arrangement, to the disgruntlement of the free states, effectively granted the South something like two dozen extra members of Congress whose constituents could not vote.) "Slavery existed in the South when the constitution was framed," declared Calhoun on the floor of the Senate in 1848, and "It is the only property recognized by it; the only one that entered into its formation as a political element, both in the adjustment of the relative weight of the States in the Government, and the apportionment of direct taxes; and the only one that is put under the express guaranty of the constitution." William Lloyd Garrison found himself powerless to disagree: "It is absurd, it is false, it is an insult to the common sense of mankind, to pretend that the Constitution . . . or that the parties to it were actuated by a sense of justice and the spirit of impartial liberty. . . ."[37] And when it came to choosing between abolition and the Constitution, Garrison knew that most Northerners would choose the Constitution.

But then there came into being all that territory in the West.

At the end of the Revolution, the outward fringe of the thirteen newly independent United States stopped pretty much at the foothills of the Appalachians. But the British surrendered to the American republic complete title to all their remaining colonial lands below Canada, stretching west beyond the Appalachians to the Mississippi River. Then, in 1803, President Jefferson bought up 830,000 square miles of old Spanish land beyond the Mississippi River for the United States for $15 million in spot cash. Both the midwestern land won from the British and the western lands bought by Jefferson originally had next to nothing in the way of American settlers in them, but there was no reason why any of it could not soon fill up with settlers, who could organize themselves as federal territories and then petition Congress for admission to the Union as states on an equal footing with the original states. Because the Northwest Ordinance had already barred slaery from the upper midwestern land, the territories of Ohio, Indiana, Illinois, and Michigan all entered the Union as free states; and slaveholders, skirting southward below the Ohio River, were content to organize Alabama, Mississippi, Tennessee, Kentucky, and Louisiana as states where slavery would remain legal. The trouble began when people began looking westward, beyond the Mississippi, where no Northwest Ordinance mandated the slave or free status of the land. Southerners anxious to keep the way to new cotton land open reasoned fearfully that if nonslaveholding Northerners squatted in the Purchase lands and settled them as free states, the South could easily find itself barricaded in behind the Mississippi and Ohio Rivers. Surrounded by free states on the Mississippi and Ohio lines, and by Louisiana's border

[37]Calhoun, "Speech on the Oregon Bill" [June 27, 1848], in *Union and Liberty: The Political Philosophy of John C. Calhoun*, Ross M. Lence, ed. (Indianapolis, IN, 1992), p. 543; Garrison, "Massachusetts Resolutions" [May 3, 1844], in *Documents of Upheaval*, p. 201.

with Spanish-held Mexico, cotton and slavery would suffocate, no matter what the Constitution said.

And so came the first of the great southern demands for assurance, and the first in a series of threats that the slave states would leave the Union if assurances were not forthcoming. In 1820, and then again in 1850, slaveholders would turn the Garrisonian gospel on its head and ask the rest of the United States to choose between slavery and the Constitution.[38] And both times, desperate politicians would find a way to avert the choice. Until finally, in 1861, the choice would have to be made.

And the war came.

Further Reading

On the fragility of the American Union, there are few better guides than the essays in Kenneth Stampp's *The Imperiled Union: Essays on the Background of the Civil War* (New York, 1980) and the work of Gordon Wood, *The Creation of the American Republic* (Chapel Hill, NC, 1969). The importance of Protestant Evangelicalism in the formation of the new republic has been skillfully treated in a wide variety of sources, including Nathan O. Hatch, *The Democratization of American Christianity* (New Haven, CT, 1989), Richard J. Carwardine, *Evangelicals and Antebellum Politics* (New Haven, CT, 1993), and Bruce Kuklick, *Churchmen and Philosophers: From Jonathan Edwards to John Dewey* (New Haven, CT, 1985). The republican ideology has been the focus of Gordon Wood's *The Radicalism of the American Revolution* (1991), J. G. A. Pocock's *The Machiavellian Moment* (1975), Lance Banning's *The Jeffersonian Persuasion* (1978), Isaac Kramnick's *Republicanism and Bourgeois Radicalism* (1990), and Joyce Appleby's *Economic Thought and Ideology in Seventeenth-century England* (1978). My understanding of the world context of the early republic's economy has been shaped by my reading of Eric Hobsbawm's *The Age of Revolution, 1789–1848* (1962) and *The Age of Capital, 1848–1875* (1975), Charles G. Sellers' *The Market Revolution: Jacksonian America, 1815–1846* (New York, 1991), and Christopher Clark's *The Roots of Rural Capitalism: Western Massachusetts, 1780–1860* (Ithaca, NY, 1991). The politics of the Jacksonian era have been richly covered in Robert V. Remini's three-volume biography of Andrew Jackson, *Andrew Jackson and the Course of American Empire* (New York, 1973), *Andrew Jackson and the Course of American Freedom* (New York, 1981), and *Andrew Jackson and the Course of American Democracy* (New York, 1984). Remini has also produced a biography of Jackson's nemesis, Henry Clay, in *Henry Clay: Statesman for the Union* (New York, 1991). Whig political thinking has been superbly dissected by Daniel Walker Howe in *The Political Culture of the American Whigs* (Chicago, 1979) and Thomas Brown in *Politics and Statesmanship: Essays on the American Whig Party* (New York, 1985), while the Democrats have their remembrancers in Jean Baker, *Affairs of Party: The Political Culture of Northern Democrats in the Mid-Nineteenth Century* (Ithaca, NY, 1983) and Marvin Meyer, *The Jacksonian Persuasion* (1957).

Simply listing the literature available on American slavery could easily consume a book

---

[38]David Potter, *The Impending Crisis, 1848–1861* (New York, 1976), pp. 44–50.

on its own. The best single-volume compilation of first-person accounts by African Americans of the slave experience is *Slave Testimony: Two Centuries of Letters, Speeches, Interviews and Autobiographies*, edited by John W. Blassingame (Baton Rouge, LA, 1977). Among the many interpretations and scholarly analyses of slave life, the most concise and readable are Leslie Howard Owen's *This Species of Property: Slave Life and Culture in the Old South* (New York, 1976), Albert Raboteau's *Slave Religion: The 'Invisible Institution' in the Antebellum South* (New York, 1978), John W. Blassingame's *The Slave Community: Plantation Life in the Antebellum South* (New York, 1972), Herbert Gutman, *The Black Family in Slavery and Freedom* (New York, 1976), and Ann Patton Malone, *Sweet Chariot: Slave Family and Household Structure in Nineteenth-Century Louisiana* (Chapel Hill, NC, 1992). For this chapter, I have relied extensively on the insights into southern slavery offered by Eugene Genovese and James Oakes, especially Genovese's *The Political Economy of Slavery* (1965) and Oakes's *Slavery and Freedom: An Interpretation of the Old South* (New York, 1990), despite the fact that Genovese and Oakes represent two very different ways of interpreting slavery. The arguments of southern slaveholders in defense of slavery have been collected and analyzed by Drew Faust, especially in *A Sacred Circle: The Dilemma of the Intellectual in the Old South, 1840–1860* (Baltimore, MD, 1977). On the struggles of free blacks and slaves in the new republic, I have turned to Gary B. Nash, *Forging Freedom: The Formation of Philadelphia's Black Community, 1720–1840* (1988), William McFeely, *Frederick Douglass* (1991), Leon Litwack, *North of Slavery: The Negro in the Free States, 1790–1860* (1961), and Sylvia R. Frey, *Water from the Rock: Black Resistance in a Revolutionary Age* (1991). For the bird's-eye view of the slave South and for a number of specific illustrations, I have used William W. Freehling's *The Road to Disunion: Secessionists at Bay, 1776–1854* (New York, 1990), and I have drawn statistics on slave numbers from Louis M. Hacker, *The Triumph of American Capitalism* (1940).

CHAPTER 2

The Disillusion of Compromise

The fatal sequence of public events in the United States that stretches from the year 1820 until 1861 and the outbreak of the American Civil War can be visualized as a game of balances, with the federal Union as the balance point along the beam. Of all the issues that divided Americans and provoked them to threaten that balance—tariffs, trade, banks, reform—nothing proved so heavy or so liable to plunge the balance off the table entirely as slavery. Slavery pitted cultures (or at least perceptions of culture), economic interests, and moral antagonisms against one another; and worse, it pitted states against other states; and worst of all, it pitted whole associations of states (in this case, the South) against other whole associations of states (namely, the free North of the old colonies and the free West of the Northwest Ordinance). It was bad enough that in 1832 one single state had been willing to defy and disrupt the Union over the tariff question. It was almost unimaginable what might happen if several states, sharing common borders in a common region, with a common culture and common economy, came to believe that their very way of life was at stake, and would decide that self-preservation required disunion.

But so long as Americans still believed that the federal Union was only a union—only a league or federation of quasi-independent states that could be terminated at will—and so long as Southerners continued to believe that northern antislavery attacks on slavery constituted a real and present danger to southern life and property, then disunion could not be ruled out. And if the northern states, and the federal government in Washington, failed to place on their balance pan a weight of assurances equal to southern demands for reassurance about slavery, then the South would drop onto its pan the immense and destructive weight of disunion and the balance would be wrecked, perhaps forever.

And that made the threat of secession useful.

The key word in understanding the South's behavior throughout the four critical decades before the Civil War is *threat*. The life of the Constitution rested on the assumption that compromise could settle disputes, and in any compromise situation, threats are the weightiest chips to bargain with. So, Southerners would begin talking a great deal about seceding from the Union from the 1820s onward, but frequently, it was little more than loud talk, meant to squeeze concession during the compromise process rather than to announce action. There were few Southerners in 1820 who seriously wanted to leave the Union, and most of them lived only in South Carolina. But Southerners were willing to *talk* secession because of the leverage such talk easily acquired within a federal Union as shaky as the one that held together the American republic. If it was believed that disunion was a possible political outcome to the balancing game, then using secession as a threat could be highly useful in cajoling favorable responses out of the rest of the Union. It mattered little enough whether secession was likely or even desirable, or whether in fact the balance itself was far more indestructible than any of the players realized. So long as the threat of secession and disunion continued to pry assurances out of the rest of the country that slavery would never be imperilled, then the South would stay in the Union.

And so the threats were issued.

1. You Have Kindled a Fire

The first round of threats and assurances was played out in February of 1819, when Missouri applied for admission to the Union with a state constitution legally recognizing slavery. Missouri's application was a moment for celebration, since it was the first state that lay entirely west of the Mississippi, in the Louisiana Purchase lands, to apply to Congress for statehood. What was less obvious was that Missouri's petition also represented a challenge to the free states, since the Union in 1819 was perfectly balanced between eleven free states (where slavery was being phased out through nonimportation laws or had been barred by outright prohibition) and eleven slave states, where slavery remained legal. Allow Missouri to enter the Union as a slave state, and it would add two "slave" senators to the Senate and an indeterminate number of representatives to the House (artificially swollen, as Northerners saw it, by the three-fifths rule). That, in turn, might give the South enough of an edge in Congress to disrupt the northern campaign to protect American manufacturing and weaken the demands of Henry Clay and the National Republicans for an "American System" of federally tax-supported roads, turnpikes, canals and other "internal improvements." And so, on February 13, 1819, Representative James Tallmadge of New York rose in the House to add an amendment to the Missouri statehood bill barring the further importation of slaves into Missouri and emancipating any slave living in the state who reached the age of twenty-five.

Southern congressional delegations erupted in rage and panic. Missouri was not only the first of the Louisiana Purchase territories to be added to the Union, but it also represented the only highway the South possessed to further western land in the Purchase. President Jefferson's Purchase ran within a long, rough triangle, with the long side running from a point on the north Pacific coast in Oregon to Louisiana's border with the old Spanish empire and the great bulk of the Purchase lying along the United States' northern boundary with British Canada. Northern settlers could expand straight westward, across the Mississippi River, without being cramped together; but southern settlers moving west were forced into the narrow lower corner of the triangle, against the border of Spanish Texas. Unless Southerners and slavery were allowed to expand equally into the Purchase territories with Northerners, then the South could hope to develop only one or two future slave states. In short order, their alarm turned into threats of disunion and demands for assurance. "If you persist," roared Thomas W. Cobb of Georgia across the aisle in the House at Tallmadge, "the Union will be dissolved. You have kindled a fire which all the waters of the ocean cannot put out, which seas of blood can only extinguish."[1] But the Tallmadge restrictions passed through the House, with representatives voting along virtually exclusive North-South lines; only the balance of southern senators in the Senate (and five free-state allies) killed the amended Missouri bill there. The House sent the amendments back to the Senate again, and at that point, in March, 1819, Congress adjourned and left matters hanging.

The brief pause the intersession of Congress brought did nothing to allay the fears of onlookers. For the first time, slavery and sectionalism had reared their heads in Congress as a matter of national debate, and almost immediately, Congress had divided along sectional lines in the debate. "This momentous question, like a firebell in the night, awakened and filled me with terror," wrote an aging Thomas Jefferson, "I considered it at once the knell of the Union." To Jefferson's relief, a solution quickly appeared in the form of Maine and Henry Clay. By the time Congress had settled back into Washington, another petition for admission to the Union had been received from Maine, which had been governed since colonial times as a province of Massachusetts. Henry Clay, then the Speaker of the House of Representatives, proposed to damp down the anxieties about upsetting the sectional balance in Congress by simultaneously admitting Missouri (as a slave state) and Maine (as a free state) to the Union. For the future, Clay called for the division of the Louisiana Purchase into two zones along a line of 36°30' (the southern boundary line of Missouri), with the northern zone forever reserved for free settlement and the southern zone left open to the extension of slavery. Adroitly sidestepping the partisans of both sections, Clay maneuvered the legislation through the House and greased its way through a joint House-Senate reconciliation committee to the desk of President James Monroe, who signed it on March 6, 1820.

The Missouri Compromise made the reputation of Henry Clay as a national reconciler and champion of the Union, and the 36°30' line became the mutually agreed-upon line of settlement that was supposed to squelch the need for any further

[1]Robert V. Remini, Henry Clay: Statesman for the Union (New York, 1991), p. 178.

antagonistic debates over the extention of slavery. It is difficult, looking back on the Missouri Compromise, to see just what advantages slaveholders believed they had won, since the available Purchase territory lying south of the 36°30′ line was actually fairly minimal (only one other slave state, Arkansas, would ever be organized from it). Most of the Purchase territory lay north of the 36°30′, and even then, it was by no means certain in the 1820s that the Canadian border was so permanently fixed that the United States could not expand further north. Great Britain and the United States had agreed to govern mutually the Oregon territory after 1812, and the Oregon boundaries then ran as far north as Russian Alaska. With the right use of bluster and bluff on the British, the opportunities for free settlement above 36°30′ could be made almost unlimited. The South's acquiescence in the 36°30′ agreement makes sense only if, by 1820, it had become fairly widely assumed that the United States would also apply some bluff, bluster, and expansion to the Spanish territory that lay south of the Purchase boundary, in Texas.

That some Americans were prepared to act on that assumption was clear from what was already beginning to happen in Texas. As late as 1820, Spain still clung tenaciously to large parts of the New World empire it had won under the conquistadors of the 1500s. But Spain's political strength had been ebbing for 200 years, and by 1800 it had proven more and more difficult for the Spaniards to control an American dominion that still stretched from the southern cone of South America up to the Missouri and Mississippi Rivers. One by one, pieces of that dominion in South America had thrown off Spanish rule and established republics based on the liberties and slogans of the American Revolution of 1776. Then, in 1820, the Spanish king, Ferdinand VII, was challenged by an uprising among his own officers, demanding reform and a republic. While Spanish attention was preoccupied with its own revolution, the Spanish vice-royalty of Mexico took its future in its own hands and established a revolutionary monarchy under Augustín de Iturbide in 1821. Iturbide's monarchy proved only marginally more popular that Spain's. In 1823, Iturbide was overthrown and the following year a republic was established.

The Mexican republic had a rocky history, especially since the individual Mexican states had notions of independence and autonomy that were not unlike some of those held by their North American neighbors. At length, in 1834, an ambitious general, Antonio López de Santa Anna, solved the republic's problems by overthrowing it and setting up a personal dictatorship. In the meanwhile, the Mexican states dealt with their internal problems pretty much by their own lights. For the state of Coahuila, which included the province of Texas, the principal problem was the sparsity of the population. From the 1820s onward, Coahuila proposed to cure that barrenness by franchising out large, vacant stretches of eastern Texas prairie to land-hungry North Americans. Guided by *empresarios* and land brokers like Moses and Stephen Austin, who acted as middlemen between Coahuila and potential American settlers, large colonies of Americans migrated to Texas, some 20,000 of them by the end of the decade and 30,000 by 1835. They found under the Mexican flag a land perfectly suited to livestock and farming—

especially cotton. And cotton meant slaves. By 1830, the Americans in Texas already had 1,000 African-American slaves working in the rich, new cotton fields of east Texas.

What had at first seemed like the ideal solution to the emptiness of their land soon turned sour for the Mexicans. For not only did the American colonists blithely disregard agreements that bound the colonists to convert to Roman Catholicism and adopt Spanish as the civil language, but their numbers eventually dwarfed the tiny Mexican population of Texas. Anxious that the Americans would soon attempt to set up an independent Texan government, Santa Anna attempted to seal off the Texas border with Louisiana to control further immigration. But the Mexican troops, under the clumsy command of Santa Anna's brother-in-law, instead provoked an uprising in Texas and in December, 1835, the enraged Texans drove Santa Anna's men back across the Rio Grande into Coahuila.

The resulting Texan war of independence was short but spectacular. Many of the Mexican grandees of Texas had no more love for Santa Anna's dictatorship than the American colonists, and the *tejanos* and their Anglo neighbors declared Texas an independent republic in March, 1836. The odds for the Texan republic's survival were, at first, not very good. Santa Anna gathered an army of 4,000 and staged a midwinter march into Texas that threw the Texans into a panic. The small Anglo-*tejano* garrison in San Antonio barricaded itself into a crumbling Catholic mission known as the Alamo, and held up Santa Anna's advance for thirteen days until a pre-dawn Mexican attack overwhelmed the Alamo's 183 defenders. The Alamo was not particularly significant from a military point of view (the Alamo garrison had originally been instructed to blow the place up and retreat), although Santa Anna did waste the lives of a few hundred of his men in the effort to capture it. What turned the Alamo from a military annoyance into a catastrophic misjudgment was Santa Anna's temperamental decision to put every survivor of the Alamo garrison to death. Across east Texas, the American colonists were both terrified and outraged, and "Remember the Alamo," became an electrifying war cry. A ragtag Texan army, under an old protégé of Andrew Jackson named Sam Houston, fell back before Santa Anna's advance, lulling the Mexicans into a sense of assured conquest. And then, on April 21, 1836, Houston and the Texan army turned and struck the Mexicans at San Jacinto, routing the Mexican army and capturing Santa Anna himself. As a condition of his release, Santa Anna signed an agreement recognizing Texan independence (an agreement that was, of course, promptly repudiated when Santa Anna reached Mexico City again).

The aim of the Texans, however, was not to remain independent, but to join the United States as a new state as soon as possible. And here the trouble began anew. President Martin Van Buren was Andrew Jackson's anointed successor in the presidency, and as a Democrat, he owed a great deal to the Democratic constituencies of the southern states. But Van Buren was also a New Yorker who was less than eager to promote the expansion of slavery, or involve the United States in a dispute over a province that was still, technically, the property of Mexico. It did not help that Van Buren found himself embroiled at that moment in a major economic depression, and he was not willing to annex Texas and assume responsibility for the debts the Texans had run up in financing their revolution. In fact, the depression cost Van Buren the White House in the election of 1840, and brought a Whig to the presidency for the first time in the person of William Henry Harrison. The Whigs preferred to pour the nation's resources into developing the internal American economy rather than picking up the bills for expansionist adventures, and so Texas remained an unwilling but independent republic.

But poor William Henry Harrison died in 1841, only one month after his inauguration as president, and the Whig party suddenly found itself saddled with John Tyler, Harrison's vice-president, as the country's chief executive. Although Tyler was nominally a Whig, he soon found himself at odds with Henry Clay and Daniel Webster, the real chiefs of the Whig party, and two men who were sure that they deserved the presidency more than the man people sneered at "His Accidency." Every bill that Clay and a Whig Congress wrote for the pet projects of the Whigs—internal improvements, protectionist tariffs, a new Bank of the United States—was vetoed by Tyler, and eventually all the Whigs in the Cabinet resigned. Shunned by the Whigs, Tyler tried to assemble his own independent political power base, and as a Virginian and a slaveholder, he was not shy of bidding for southern support. As bait to his fellow Southerners, Tyler and his new secretary of state, Abel Upshur, negotiated an annexation treaty for Texas and tried to turn Texas annexation into a campaign issue that Tyler could ride back into the White House in 1844.[2]

Tyler succeeded in making Texas an issue, but not himself president. The Democrats snubbed the unhappy Tyler and ran one of Andrew Jackson's old lieutenants, James Knox Polk of Tennessee, for the presidency in 1844. The Whigs had no time at all for Tyler, and ran Henry Clay instead, hoping to feed on fears that an annexation of Texas would provoke war with Mexico. But Clay undercut his own candidacy by conceding to southern Whigs that he might be willing to accept the annexation of Texas if could be done "without dishonor, without war, with the common consent of the Union." What Clay gained among the southern Whigs he promptly lost among the northern ones, and Polk squeezed into the White House after winning Pennsylvania and New York with majorities of only 7,000 votes.

There was no question about James Knox Polk's plans for Texas—Polk was an outright annexationist, and even hoped to edge the British out of Oregon—and even before his inauguration, the disheartened Whigs gave up the fight and allowed a joint congressional resolution to adopt the Texas annexation treaty in December, 1844. The Mexican government was not bluffed by Polk's determination to have Texas, and Mexico withdrew its diplomats from Washington in protest. Sensing trouble (and not finding trouble with Mexico all that unwelcome), President Polk sent Brigadier General Zachary Taylor to the Texas border with 1,500 United States soldiers in July

[2]Charles G. Sellers, *The Market Revolution: Jacksonian America, 1815–1846* (New York, 1991), p. 413.

of 1845. Ten months later, there was a bloody clash between Mexican and American troops over a disputed border area, and Polk used the clash as an excuse for rallying Congress to declare war on Mexico on May 13, 1846.

The Mexican-American War was, compared to the Alamo and San Jacinto, a relatively unglamorous affair. The American forces were divided into four field forces under John Ellis Wool, Zachary Taylor, Stephen Kearny, and Alexander Doniphan for the invasion of Mexican territory. Taylor (alongside Wool) won a major victory over Santa Anna at Buena Vista and occupied most of northern Mexico. Kearny plunged into New Mexico and chased Mexican forces from Santa Fe, and then moved on into southern California, where scattered colonies of American settlers helped him overthrow the Mexican provincial government. But the greatest laurels were won by Major General Winfield Scott, who led a daring invasion column from Mexico's Gulf coast inland to Mexico City, which fell to Scott on September 13, 1847. The following February, the Treaty of Guadalupe-Hidalgo was signed, with Mexico grudgingly surrendering New Mexico, California, and parts of what are now Arizona, Colorado, Utah, and Nevada to the United States. And as if to illustrate that fortune favors the bold, no sooner was California an American possession than one James Marshall discovered gold in a streambed near Sacramento, thus setting off the mighty California gold rush and stampeding thousands of American settlers into the newly acquired territories.

It was at this point that the old balancing game of threats and assurances began again.

The Missouri Compromise had settled what to do with that half of the far West that the United States had owned in 1820, and the South had been anxious to settle the question then because in 1820, most of the old Louisiana Purchase looked like it was going to fall into the hands of free-state settlers. Now, in 1848, the Mexican-American War had brought the United States the other half of the far West—the southern half, running in a clear straight line from Louisiana to the southern California coast—and this time, it appeared that these new territories would surely develop into slave states. In fact, there was no reason to assume that the United States might not want to keep pecking away at Mexico, or at the Spanish-held island of Cuba, or even Central America, and obtain still more territory that would obviously come under the wing of the old slave states. And this, announced Southerners, was a fact that the rest of the country had better respect. Robert Toombs of Georgia boldly warned Congress "in the presence of the living God, that if by your legislation you seek to drive us from the territories of California and New Mexico, purchased by the common blood and treasure of the whole people . . . thereby attempting to fix a national degradation upon half the states of this Confederacy, *I am for disunion.*"[3]

What Toombs did not reckon with was the feeling of many Americans that the Mexican-American War had been something other than a source of national pride.

[3]David M. Potter, *The Impending Crisis, 1848–1861* (New York, 1976), p. 94.

In Congress, southern Whigs like Alexander Stephens of Georgia repeatedly assailed Polk's war as "dishonorable . . . disgraceful and infamous," and other Whigs questioned the political ethics of one republic making war on another. Even in the army, young lieutenants out of West Point like Ulysses Simpson Grant acknowledged that "the Mexican War was a political war," and nearly 7,000 American soldiers (of the 115,000 mustered into service) actually deserted. But the most unpopular aspect of the war was the realization that slavery stood to gain a political windfall from it. To the disappointment of Northerners, Polk had negotiated a fairly timid treaty with Great Britain that surrendered most of the bolder American claims to northern territory and put what amounted to a geographical cap on northern expansion; but Polk had grabbed nearly 1.5 million square miles of Mexican territory to the south, and with no certainty that slaveholders might not go on from there to destabilize other Latin American republics, transplant slavery there, and claim them for admission to the Union. As it was, the size of just the newly acquired western lands offered enough material to create so many new states below the 36°30′ line that slaveholders might at last acquire a decisive numerical advantage in the Senate, if not the House as well. With that prospect before him, Frederick Douglass denounced the war as "this slaveholding crusade" from which "no one expects any thing honorable or decent . . . touching human rights." Lieutenant Grant could hardly avoid the conclusion that everything from the Texas annexation onward had been "a conspiracy to acquire territory out of which slave states might be formed for the American Union."[4]

As early, then, as August of 1846, four basic political agendas took shape for dealing with the "Mexican cession" (the territory in the far West surrendered by Mexico). The first of these was proposed on August 8, 1846, when President Polk, admitting publicly for the first time that "a cession of territory" by Mexico was a possible result of the war, asked the House to approve $2 million in negotiating funds. A first-term Democratic representative from Pennsylvania named David Wilmot rose to move an amendment to the appropriations bill that added a deadly proviso: "that, as an express and fundamental condition to the acquisition of any territory from the Republic of Mexico . . . neither slavery nor involuntary servitude shall ever exist in any part of said territory, except for crime. . . ." The Wilmot Proviso was essentially a paraphrase of the Northwest Ordinance of 1787, whose sweeping ban against slavery Wilmot now wanted applied to the southwestern territories of the Mexican cession. And more than its frank declaration against slavery, it was an even more frank assertion that Congress (based on Article 3, Section 3 of the Constitution) had the authority to make judgments about the future of the territories. Just as in 1820 with the Tallmadge amendment, Congress immediately broke up along sectional rather than party lines. The northern Whigs

[4]Douglass, "The War with Mexico" [January 21, 1848], in *The Life and Writings of Frederick Douglass*, Philip S. Foner, ed. (New York, 1950), vol. 1, p. 293; Grant, "Personal Memoirs," in *Memoirs and Selected Letters*, M. D. McFeely and W. S. McFeely, eds. (New York, 1990), pp. 41, 83.

and all but four northern Democrats in the House overrode southern votes in the House and sent the appropriations bill with its lethal proviso to the Senate, where Polk and the southern Democrats killed it.

Polk was particularly mortified at the Wilmot Proviso, since the blow had come from a member of his own party. But the administration had its own plan ready to launch: extend the Missouri Compromise line all the way through the Mexican cession. This does not seem like a particularly imaginative proposition. But the idea had behind it the indisputable fact that the Missouri Compromise had worked for twenty-six years in keeping the slavery issue from polarizing Congress, and it offered what looked like a solution that everyone had already agreed to earlier, and what was most important of all, President Polk was prepared to swing all the weight of his office behind it. The trouble with this, however, was that a good deal of dark water had flowed under the bridge since 1820, and most of it was really a flood of ink from the tireless and reckless presses of the northern abolitionists. Antislavery Northerners were beginning to wonder if the Missouri Compromise might not have been wrong in the first place, and the proposal to give it further lease on life looked like a covert plan for handing the slave states everything they wanted in the Mexican cession.

But the southern leadership in Congress was not interested in securing their rights to slavery by covert means only. On February 19, 1847, the white-haired and hollow-cheeked John Calhoun rose to offer a set of resolutions arguing that "the territories of the United States belong to the several States composing this Union, and are held by them as their joint and common property." This meant (and Calhoun explained his meaning with frightening lucidity) that "Congress, as the joint agent and representative of the States of this Union, has no right to make any law . . . that shall . . . deprive the citizens of any of the States of this Union from emigrating, with their property, into any of the territories of the United States. . . ."[5] By Calhoun's logic, the territories were the common property of all the United States, not the federal government. Congress, in organizing and readying federal territories for statehood, was merely acting as a trustee on behalf of the entire people of the United States. Citizens of any one of the United States had equal title to the territories, and therefore ought to be able to take any of their property into any of the territories, including slaves. Hence, not only did Congress have no authority to enact a Wilmot Proviso, which banned the transportation of slave "property" to *any* of the territories, but it had no authority in 1820 to enact the Missouri Compromise, which banned the transportation of slaves to *some* of the territories. With this one gesture, Calhoun swung the door of every federal territory open to slavery, and swung delighted southern Whigs and Democrats behind him as the South's great political figurehead.

The northern Democrats, however, were less than enthralled with Calhoun's logic. In December, 1847, one of Polk's chief rivals within the Democratic party,

[5]Calhoun, "Speech on the Introduction of his Resolutions on the Slave Question," in *Union and Liberty: The Political Philosophy of John C. Calhoun*, Ross M. Lence, ed. (Indianapolis, IN, 1992), pp. 513–521.

Michigan Senator Lewis Cass, brought forward yet another solution to the problem of the Mexican cession territories. In a letter published in the Washington *Union,* Cass gingerly agreed with Calhoun that Congress had no authority to impose a settlement of the slavery issue on any of the territories. But surely, observed Cass, the people who were actually living in each of the territories had the right to adopt a "slave" or "free" settlement for themselves. Let the popular will be sovereign in the territories—and let popular sovereignty defuse the confrontations in Washington over slavery and free Congress from the responsibility of solving the problem. Cass's proposal appealed to that fundamental American ideological instinct that an independent and republican people have the right to make their own political decisions, and Cass's letter might have taken Cass further along the road to the presidency if he had not already managed to make a host of enemies within the Democratic party. As it was, an unpersuaded President Polk attempted to ram the Missouri Compromise solution through Congress during the summer of 1848, and came out at the end of the session with nothing more to show for his efforts than a single bill authorizing the organization of the Oregon territory without slavery. Chronically ill and disappointed at the defections from Democratic unity by Calhoun, Wilmot, and Cass, Polk announced that he would not seek a second term as president in 1848.

The worst for the Democrats was yet to come. The party convention, as might have been expected, nominated Lewis Cass for the presidency. But agitated northern Democrats wanted the Wilmot Proviso or nothing, and they suspected that if Cass and popular sovereignty were allowed to rule the future of the territories, the popular will could just as easily announce itself in favor of slavery as not. "I am jealous of the *power* of the South," wrote David Wilmot, "The South holds no prerogative under the Constitution, which entitles her to wield forever the Scepter of Power in this Republic," and if Wilmot could "strike an effectual & decisive blow against its dominion at this time, I would do so even at the temporary loss of other principles."[6] Wilmot got his chance in June of 1848, when a group of antislavery Northern Democrats met in Utica, New York, to organize a splinter movement based on the principle that Congress had full authority to ban slavery from the territories. Two months later, in Buffalo, a national "Free-Soil" convention assembled under a great tent, with luminaries as varied as Wilmot and Frederick Douglass among the delegates. In a decisive repudiation of the Democratic party's leadership, they nominated Martin Van Buren as the presidential candidate for the "Free-Soil" party under the banner, "free soil, free speech, free labor, and free men."

The Whigs might have suffered the same splintering had it not been clear that the divisions among the Democratic party were the Whigs' golden opportunity. Rather than risk North-South bickerings within the party, the Whigs nominated Zachary Taylor for the presidency, a Louisiana slaveholder who was, nevertheless, a

[6]Michael F. Holt, *Political Parties and American Political Development from the Age of Jackson to the Age of Lincoln* (Baton Rouge, LA, 1992), p. 69.

highly popular war hero with no known stand on the territorial question. And after reflecting upon the wisdom of nominating a candidate with no inconvenient political views to disturb the voters, the Whig party decided as a whole to do likewise and adopted no party platform. By the end of the summer, it was plain that Taylor was going to beat Cass handily.

But Zachary Taylor, to nearly everyone's surprise, turned out to have a plan of his own for the territories. By the time he was inaugurated in March, 1849, the California gold rush was in full swing, and Sacramento, the site of the original gold strike, had exploded from a village of four houses into a boom city of 10,000.[7] In order to provide California and the New Mexico territory with some sense of public order, a bill for territorial organization had to be offered at once, and Taylor dispatched his own personal emissaries to prod the California and New Mexico settlers into organizing new governments. But Taylor was responding to more than just the practical demands of the California situation. A political novice, Taylor had fallen under the sway of some of the most radical antislavery Whigs, especially William H. Seward of New York, and under their influence Taylor was determined to secure California and New Mexico as "free and Whig," even at the risk of more southern threats of disunion. By December of 1849, Taylor had pushed the Californians to the point where they were ready to make an application to Congress for immediate statehood, bypassing the whole question of Congress's authority over the territorial stage completely. And the application would be as a free state.

Southerners read President Taylor's proposal as nothing less than the Wilmot Proviso in disguise, and in the early spring of 1850, fearful Southerners like Robert Barnwell Rhett and James Henry Hammond were calling for a convention of the slaveholding states to discuss what their future could be in the Union. At the same time, Taylor faced a challenge from within his own party in the person of Henry Clay, who still believed, even at age seventy-three and after three unsuccessful nominations, that he would have made a better Whig president than Taylor, the "Military Chieftain." On January 29, 1850, Clay laid before the Senate a "comprehensive scheme" of eight resolutions offering to settle the territorial dispute in practical little pieces rather than by sweeping formulas like "common property" or "popular sovereignty." Basically, Clay proposed to admit California as a free state (the California constitutional convention had already adopted free-state provisions and there was nothing gained by trying to force them to change their minds), but, in order to show that this established no principle for the other territories, New Mexico and a separate Mexico cession territory of Deseret (or Utah) would be allowed to organize themselves as territories on the basis of popular sovereignty (which left open the possibility that these territories *might* become slave states). To sweeten the loss of the "common property" principle for Southerners, Clay added a provision for a new Fugitive Slave Law, which would give slaveholders new powers to stop the flow of runaway slaves

[7]Allan Nevins, *Ordeal of the Union: Fruits of Manifest Destiny, 1847–1852* (New York, 1947), p. 237.

northward to the free states, and he offered a final resolution denying that Congress had any authority to regulate the interstate slave trade.

Clay's two-day presentation of his compromise was a rhetorical masterpiece, but he fell considerably short of winning the votes he needed for it. The partisans of slavery in the Senate regarded the concession of California as tantamount to accepting the principle, if not the fact, of the Wilmot Proviso, while northern Free-Soilers regarded the popular sovereignty allowance for New Mexico and Deseret as little more than surrendering the territories outright to slavery. Clay also committed a major tactical error by insisting that all the resolutions be voted upon together as one "omnibus," without recognizing that while all of the senators would like some of the resolutions, only some of the senators would like all of the resolutions, and some was not enough to carry the day. In particular, Clay's "comprehensive scheme" did not satisfy the mortally ailing John Calhoun. On March 4, 1850, Calhoun had another senator, James Mason of Virginia, read a lengthy and shrewd attack on Clay's plan, calling again for "an equal right in the acquired territory . . . to cease the agitation of the slave question, and to provide for the insertion of a provision in the constitution, by an amendment, which will restore to the South, in substance, the power she possessed of protecting herself, before the equilibrium between the sections was destroyed by the action of this government." Otherwise, threatened Calhoun, "the Southern States . . . cannot remain, as things now are, consistently with safety and honor, in the Union."[8]

Three days later, Daniel Webster of Massachusetts took the floor of the Senate to deliver what many anticipated would be an equally scathing critique of Clay's omnibus, this time from an antislavery position. But to the amazement of the packed Senate galleries (and the howls of indignation from antislavery Northerners), Webster rose "to speak today not as a Massachusetts man, nor as a Northern man, but an American. . . . I speak today for the preservation of the Union. Hear me for my cause." And from there, Webster's great oratory rolled on for three hours, denouncing disunion and calling for the adoption of Clay's omnibus. Webster paid dearly in Massachusetts for befriending Clay, with muttered hints of treason and derangement. But Clay and Webster were acting to save a Union that they could easily see was headed for the breakers, and a Union that Calhoun was only too ready to see hit them. Day after exhausting day, Clay dragged himself to the Senate floor to defend his resolutions on the wings of words that soared far above his own personal political ambitions for the presidency. Americans North and South must stop and "by all their love of liberty—by all their veneration for their ancestors—by all their regard for posterity . . . pause—solemnly to pause—at the edge of the precipice, before the fearful and disastrous leap is taken into the yawning abyss below." And if the grappling sections did hurl themselves over the cliff into civil

[8]Calhoun, "Speech on the Admission of California—And the general State of the Union" [March 4, 1850], in *Union and Liberty*, pp. 591, 600.

war, Clay's prayer was that "I may not survive to behold the sad and heart-rending spectacle."[9]

One person, at least, who was moved by none of this rhetorical display in the Senate was President Taylor, and between the upper and nether millstones of Taylor and the Calhounites, the omnibus was ground to dust. When the Senate Committee on Territories finally reported out Clay's resolutions as a single bill, its component pieces were crushed down by amendments and counterproposals, and on July 31, 1850, all but the provisions for the territorial organization of Utah were turned back. An enfeebled Henry Clay left the Senate, his political career effectively over and sick with the tuberculosis that would kill him in less than two years; Webster returned to Massachusetts to be vilified by the antislavery press as a "fallen angel" and followed Clay to the grave by four months. But at this last point before the "abyss," the enemies of compromise obligingly removed themselves from the scene. John Calhoun was dead on March 31, 1850, less than three weeks after his last defiant speech in the Senate. The death of Calhoun was followed by the unexpected death of President Taylor in July, and his successor, a self-made and surprisingly capable antislavery New Yorker named Millard Fillmore, quickly proclaimed his support for Clay's compromise. Clay himself withdrew from the Senate after the July 31st debacle, but into his shoes stepped the junior senator from Illinois, a short, scrappy Democrat named Stephen A. Douglas.

Committed from the beginning of the debates to the principle of popular sovereignty, Douglas had sided with Clay for the sake of the popular sovereignty provisions in the "comprehensive scheme." But since he had never favored the omnibus approach, Douglas craftily split the defeated omnibus bill into five separate new bills, and built separate Congressional coalitions around each of them, with his own fellow Democrats cajoled and caressed into supporting them. With President Taylor out of the way, Fillmore (in an unusual display of bipartisanship) linked forces with Douglas and pressured Congressional Whigs to back the Douglas bills. By mid-September, all five of them had been passed, and the substance of Clay's compromise—if not the form—became law. "The difference between Mr. Clay's Compromise Bill & my . . . Bills was a wafer," wrote Douglas before the final votes, "and when they are all passed, you see, they will be collectively Mr. Clay's Compromise."[10]

What, exactly, did this great Compromise of 1850 do? In general, it averted a showdown over who would control the new western territories, and that was the chief reason people around the country celebrated the passage of the bills with bell ringing, and in Congress with a falling-down drunken spree. In specific terms, the Compromise of 1850 allowed the Missouri Compromise to stand for the old Louisiana Purchase territories, but it established the principle of popular sovereignty as the rule for organizing the Mexican cession. California, of course, was allowed to dodge both compromises completely and enter the Union directly as a free state

[9]Irving Bartlett, *Daniel Webster* (New York, 1978), pp. 116–121; Remini, *Henry Clay*, p. 737.
[10]*The Letters of Stephen A. Douglas*, Robert W. Johannsen, ed. (Urbana, IL, 1961), p. 192.

without passing through the debated stage of territorial government. But the territory of Utah, which lay above the 36°30′ line, and New Mexico, which lay below it, would be allowed to make their own determinations about slavery or nonslavery as they saw fit. The Compromise of 1850 also added a new Fugitive Slave Law to the federal code, and promised noninterference by Congress in the interstate slave trade. And it made Stephen A. Douglas into "the Little Giant." Douglas would emerge, after the deaths of Calhoun, Clay, and Webster, as one of the most powerful men in the Senate.

The "abyss" of disunion had thus been averted, but only for the time being.

2. The Destruction of Compromise

The Compromise of 1850 had been created by a Whig (Henry Clay) and pushed through at last by the influence of a Whig president (Fillmore). But the laurels for this victory went to Stephen A. Douglas and the Democrats, and the Democrats used the political capital that the Compromise gave them to regain their political wind and win the presidential election of 1852. Both parties ran Mexican-American war heroes—the Whigs nominated Winfield Scott and the Democrats nominated Franklin Pierce of New Hampshire—but Scott proved dull and aristocratic, while the handsome, likable Pierce stood on a pro-Compromise platform and won election easily.

But there was a fly in the ointment of the Compromise of 1850. With all the attention in the debates of 1850 focused on the Mexican cession territories, few people paid attention to the contents of the new Fugitive Slave Law. There had actually been such a law on the federal books since 1793 (based on Article 4, Section 2 of the Constitution) allowing southern slaveholders to pursue and retrieve runaway slaves even in the free states. For that reason, until 1842, runaway slaves like Josiah Henson had found it safer to run until they had made it to Canada and the safety of British law (where slavery was illegal and where the presumption of the law had always been in favor of freedom). But as northern opinion turned colder toward slavery, the free states offered pursuing slaveholders less and less cooperation. Then, in 1842, the Supreme Court (in *Prigg v. Pennsylvania*) ruled that the 1793 federal law did not necessarily require the cooperation of state magistrates and justices of the peace, especially where slave recaptures encroached on state due-process laws. The result, of course, was that numerous northern state officials then refused to cooperate at all in capturing runaways.

The new Fugitive Slave Law was an attempt to plug the holes that *Prigg v. Pennsylvania* had put in the 1793 law. A federal enforcement apparatus was created, consisting of United States commissioners with powers to issue federal warrants for fugitive slaves and to make judgments in fugitive cases on the basis of as little as a simple affidavit of ownership from a slaveowner (the commissioner was to receive a $10 fee for each fugitive returned to slavery and only $5 otherwise, so that it was clear from the start what the preferred judgement would be). Ominously, the new law established no statute of limitations for runaways, which meant that runaways from as long as twenty years before (and more) could be captured and re-enslaved. And it threatened both local marshals and citizens with fines of up to $1,000 and liability for civil suits if they harbored fugitives or refused to cooperate in capture proceedings. This last provision was the most potentially explosive, for it virtually made every Northerner who had enjoyed little or no contact with slavery, or who thought of slavery as merely an unpleasant moral abstraction, now were forced to consider how they would act if a slaveowner or federal marshal in hot pursuit of a runaway should summon them to join a federal slave-catching posse.

Neither Clay nor Douglas had expected the Fugitive Slave Law to attract much controversy, if only because the actual number of runaways was fairly small compared to the entire slave population of the South. They at once learned how badly they had underestimated northern reaction. Northerners who had never entertained a serious antislavery thought were now treated to a series of public captures and extraditions of runaway slaves that only showed slavery off at its most revolting. Overeager slaveowners and hired slave catchers tracked down long-time runaways like Euphemia Williams, who had run away from Maryland twenty-two years before, and tried to drag her and the six children she had raised in Philadelphia back into slavery. In September, 1851, a Maryland slaveowner named Edward Gorsuch crossed into Pennsylvania in pursuit of four runaways. Gorsuch enlisted the aid of a federal marshal and a posse, and tracked the runaways to the home of William Parker, a free black, in Christiana, Pennsylvania. There, the runaways and their allies shot it out with the posse, killing Gorsuch; Parker and the runaways immediately fled for Canada. Frederick Douglass, then living and editing an antislavery newspaper in Rochester, New York, sheltered them and got the fugitives on board a Great Lakes steamer. At parting, one of them gave Douglass a momento that he treasured all his life: Edward Gorsuch's revolver.[11] All over the North, prisons were broken into, posses disrupted, and juries refused to convict.

Much more dramatic, and adding more fuel to the fire of opposition to the Act, were the cases of fugitives who could not be helped. On May 24, 1854, an escaped Virginia slave named Anthony Burns was seized by three federal deputies as he walked home from the Boston clothing store where he worked. White and black Bostonians at once assembled, and on the evening of May 26th, Boston abolitionists led an assault on the prison where Burns was held, only to fail in their attempts to retrieve him. President Pierce was determined to demonstrate his support for the Compromise laws, and sent in federal troops and marines to ensure that Burns was put on a ship to carry him back to Virginia. Two Bostonians actually offered to pay Burns's market price, and more if necessary, to Burns's owner, an Alexandria merchant named Charles Suttle. But the Pierce administration was determined to

---

[11]Thomas Slaughter, *Bloody Dawn: The Christiana Riot and Racial Violence in the Antebellum North* (New York, 1991), p. 78.

return Burns to Suttle for the symbolic importance of the gesture. So, on June 2, 1854, while thousands of silent, pale Bostonians looked on, Burns was marched to a waiting ship between files of soldiers. The Burns affair was a massive, public disgrace, and it drove many Northerners to conclude that slavery itself was a disgrace that deserved extermination rather than assurances. Amos Lawrence, a pro-Compromise Whig, remembered that after the Burns affair, "We went to bed one night old-fashioned, conservative, Compromise Union Whigs & waked up stark mad abolitionists."[12]

But even the anger stirred up by the Fugitive Slave Law was limited to the relatively small number of fugitive slave warrants that were actually issued and the even smaller number of fugitives who were actually returned to slavery (probably around eighty, in all). What brought the plight of the runaway under the Fugitive Slave Law into every northern parlor was a novel, *Uncle Tom's Cabin or, Life Among the Lowly,* written by Harriet Beecher Stowe, the wife of a theology professor at Bowdoin College in Maine. Stowe was the daughter of Lyman Beecher, one of the best-known northern evangelicals and a distant admirer of the ever-present Jonathan Edwards. Stowe shared her father's ambivalent interest in Edwards but she also shared with her sister Catharine an unwillingness to accept the polite, self-effacing model of "republican womanhood" that taught that a woman's proper sphere was that of "a wife, a sister, a mother." In a revealing parallel with Frederick Douglass, who found his way to freedom through literacy and publishing, Stowe and numerous other American women found release (not to mention added income for struggling families) through writing popular fiction.

Uncle Tom's Cabin was Stowe's first novel, but it drew on a wealth of observation she had acquired when living in Cincinnati in the 1840s while her husband was a professor at Lane Theological Seminary, and a wealth of reading she had done in slave narratives (including Josiah Henson, who turns up in *Uncle Tom's Cabin* as one of the models for Uncle Tom). In 1851, her sister-in-law urged her to "use a pen if you can" to denounce the Fugitive Slave Law and "make this whole nation feel what an accursed thing slavery is." "I will if I live," she announced, and one Sunday shortly thereafter in church, the plot and characters of the novel broke upon her "almost as a tangible vision." The story poured out of her pen in a matter of weeks, sentimental and mushy and short on story line, but faultless in its character construction and perfect in its appeal to a sentimental and mushy age.[13] The plot can be stated briefly: Tom, the faithful slave of the Shelby family, is sold away from his Kentucky home to pay the debts of his guilt-ridden master. He is purchased by a Louisiana planter, the disillusioned Augustine St. Clare, who believes that slavery is wrong but who cannot imagine a way of life without slaves. Tom wins the hearts

[12]Richard H. Abbott, *Cotton and Capital: Boston Businessmen and Antislavery Reform, 1854–1868* (Amherst, MA, 1991), p. 26.

[13]Edmund Wilson, *Patriotic Gore: Studies in the Literature of the American Civil War* (New York, 1962), pp. 31–32.

of the St. Clare household, especially St. Clare's frail daughter, Little Eva. In what may be the most saccharine-laden chapter in American literature, Little Eva dies and the remorseful St. Clare resolves to free his slaves. But before that can happen, St. Clare is stabbed in a brawl; and when he dies, Tom is not freed. Instead, he is sold to Simon Legree, whose unalloyed villainy drives him to murder the hymn-singing Tom just before George Shelby, the son of Tom's old master, arrives to purchase to his freedom. As if this were not enough, Stowe throws in some hair-raising adventure to offset the tackiness of the plot: the escape of the runaway Eliza Harris, who eludes the fugitive-slave-catchers by dashing across the wintry Ohio River, her infant son in her arms, bobbing precariously from ice floe to ice floe; and a shootout between Eliza's husband, George Harris, and the fugitive-slave posse.

The real genius of the book, however, lies in the care with which Stowe made her chief attack on slavery itself rather than merely taking quick shots at slavehold-ers. Slavery, for Stowe, was an evil that held well-intentioned Southerners like the Shelbys and St. Clare as much in its grip as any slave. Stowe made her readers hate slavery, and she made them hate the Fugitive Slave Law, too, for her immediate objective was to awaken Northerners to the hideous realities that the new law was bringing to their own doorsteps. "His idea of a fugitive," wrote Stowe of one stunned northern character, John Bird, who finds a half-frozen Eliza Harris in his kitchen,

> was only an idea of the letters that spell the word. . . . The magic of the real presence of distress,—the imploring human eye, the frail trembling hand, the despairing appeal of helpless agony,—these he had never tried. He had never thought that a fugitive might be a hapless mother, a defenseless child,—like that one which was now wearing his lost boy's little well-known cap. . . .

Uncle Tom's Cabin began as a serial in the antislavery newspaper National Era on June 1, 1851, and ran until April 1, 1852. When it was issued in book form, 3,000 of the first 5,000 copies flew from the booksellers' stalls on the first day of publica-tion; within two weeks it had exhausted two more editions, and within a year it had sold 300,000 copies.

The controversial captures of runaways and the sensational impact of Uncle Tom's Cabin soured peoples' confidence in the Compromise of 1850. The sourness then proceeded to turn into outright bitterness as it became apparent that the Compromise's key doctrine, popular sovereignty, was not going to work. The Com-promise of 1850 allowed the popular vote of the people of the New Mexico and Utah territories to decide the future status of those territories as free or slave states. This not only seemed to be the responsible and republican way of doing things, but it made the problem of the future of the territories seem to disappear in a peaceful application of true republicanism.

And it was the apparent ease with which popular sovereignty seemed to charm away all difficulties that led Stephen A. Douglas to carry it one step too far. Eager to open up the trans-Mississippi lands to further settlement (and, incidentally, position Douglas's Illinois as a pathway for a new transcontinental railroad), Douglas and the Senate Committee on Territories, which had saved the Compromise of 1850 from defeat, reported out a new bill to the Senate on January 4, 1854, that would organize a new territory of Nebraska and provide for eventual statehood on the basis of popular sovereignty (after some brief reflection, Douglas agreed to split the proposed Nebraska territory into two separate territories, with the southernmost section to be known as the Kansas territory). This proposal shocked northern congressional leaders, not only because they remained uneasy about popular sovereignty, but because Douglas was now proposing to unleash it in a region where it was not supposed to operate. The proposed Kansas and Nebraska territories both lay within the old Louisiana Purchase lands and above the old 36°30′ line of the Missouri Compromise; and although the compromisers of 1850 had agreed not to apply the Missouri Compromise rule to the Mexican cession territories, nothing had been said with any clarity about changing that rule for the territories that still lay within the old Louisiana Purchase. The state of Iowa, for example, had been organized as a free territory and admitted as a free state in 1846 precisely because it *did* lie within the Missouri Compromise lands and above 36°30′, and there were many in Congress who assumed that Kansas and Nebraska ought to be organized under the same rule.

But by 1854, Douglas knew well that the South would balk at the organization of the new Kansas territory on an antislavery basis, since in that event, the slave state of Missouri would be surrounded on three sides by "free" land. Of course, Douglas knew equally well that Northerners would howl at the prospect of scuttling the Missouri Compromise and opening Kansas and Nebraska to so much as the bare possibility, through popular sovereignty, of slavery. Salmon P. Chase, the antislavery Democratic giant of Ohio, tore into Douglas's Kansas-Nebraska bill with "The Appeal of the Independent Democrats" in the *National Era* on January 24, 1854, savagely attacking Douglas and accusing him of subverting the Missouri Compromise in the interest of opening Kansas and Nebraska to slavery. But Douglas was nothing if not a skillful political manager. He had the ear of the Pierce administration and the whip-handle of the Democratic party in Congress, and on March 3, 1854, he successfully bullied the Kansas-Nebraska bill through the Senate. It was a closer call in the House, where Kansas-Nebraska slipped through by a thirteen-vote margin, but it gave Douglas what he wanted.

And it was at this point that the entire doctrine of popular sovereignty began to come unraveled.

When Stephen Douglas spoke of popular sovereignty, it was clear that he imagined a peaceful territory, filling up gradually with contented white settlers (and evicting, if necessary, any contented Indian inhabitants) and eventually arriving at the place where enough white settlers were on hand to justify an application for statehood and the writing of a state constitution. It seems never to have occurred to Douglas before Kansas-Nebraska that popular sovereignty might also mean that if a majority of antislavery settlers could camp in New Mexico, Utah, Kansas, or

Nebraska before any equal numbers of slaveholding settlers (or vice versa), that simple majority would constitute the slave or free majority of the territory and determine its future status as a state. Douglas simply ignored the possibility that there might be other ways of achieving majorities than gradual and painless ones. But majorities do not just occur; they can also be manufactured, and in the case of Kansas, they could be manufactured simply by cramming a territory full of proslavery or antislavery white males, and then clamoring for statehood before the other side could rush in to make up a new majority. In that case, it might be possible to engineer Kansas or any other territory into the Union on the side of whichever faction could first fill up the territory to the required numbers for statehood.

And this, of course, is precisely what happened in the new Kansas territory. Antislavery New Englanders organized a New England Emigrant Aid Society in the summer of 1854 to send trains of armed antislavery Northerners to Kansas; in Missouri, bands of armed proslavery whites crossed over the border into Kansas to claim it for slavery. In the process, both sides learned yet another way of creating majorities, namely, by killing off one's opponents, and so a fiery sparkle of violent clashes and raids between proslavery and antislavery emigrants danced along the creeks and rivers of the new territory. And by the time a territorial governor, Andrew Reeder, had been dispatched by Congress to supervise a preliminary territorial election, the Missourians had developed yet another variation on popular sovereignty—sending "border ruffians" over into Kansas on voting days to cast illegal ballots.

The situation only grew worse in the spring of 1855, when Governor Reeder called for elections to create a territorial legislature for Kansas. The "border ruffians" crossed over in droves to vote for proslavery candidates for the legislature, and when the balloting was over, and some 6,000 votes had materialized from the 3,000 eligible white male voters of the Kansas territory, it was clear that the election had been stolen. The beleaguered Governor Reeder was too intimidated by the "border ruffian" gangs to invalidate it, and the new legislature ignored Reeder's vetoes and enacted a territorial slave code so severe that even verbal disagreement with slavery was classified as a felony. President Pierce, still staked (like Douglas) to popular sovereignty, refused to take any action. The angered free-soil settlers at once feared for the worst from their new legislature, and so they armed and fortified the free-soil town of Lawrence. They also organized a rival antislavery legislature and wrote a free-state constitution. But in May of 1856, the proslavery legislature responded by equipping a small proslavery army that sacked and burned Lawrence. Two hundred people were killed in subsequent clashes between proslavery and antislavery factions in Kansas before President Pierce finally sent in John White Geary, an ex-army officer, as territorial governor. A more skillful arbitrator than Reeder, Geary was at last able to bring a measure of peace to what had become known to the rest of the country as "Bleeding Kansas."

What happened in Kansas was disturbing evidence that Douglas's popular sovereignty cure-all was no help whatsoever in sorting out the complex problem of the expansion of slavery into the territories. Far from bringing peace, popular sovereignty in Kansas had only brought Americans two of the most spectacular scenes of violence they had ever witnessed outside of outright war. One of them occurred in Kansas itself. A Connecticut-born abolitionist named John Brown, a man with the selfless benevolence of the Edwardseans wrought into a fiery determination to crush slavery, became convinced from the reports he had heard that five antislavery men had died in the sack of Lawrence. Seeking an eye for an eye, Brown and four of his sons went on a murderous rampage along Pottawatomie Creek on May 24, 1856. They dragged five proslavery farmers from their beds and from the arms of their wives and deliberately hacked them to death with old surplus artillery broadswords that Brown had thoughtfully bought up and brought from Ohio.

The second event happened almost at the same time as Brown's raid, but it took place on the floor of the United States Senate. On May 19, 1856, the antislavery senator from Massachusetts, Charles Sumner, rose and delivered what turned out to be a two-day diatribe on "The Crime Against Kansas." In the body of his speech, he took time to unleash some particularly nasty personal insults at a number of southern senators, including Andrew Butler of South Carolina. Butler, Sumner declared, "has chosen a mistress to whom he has made his vows, and who, though ugly to others, is always lovely to him; though polluted in the sight of the world, is chaste in his sight . . . the harlot, Slavery."[14] Two days after Sumner finished his speech, South Carolina Representative Preston Brooks, a relative of Butler's, entered the almost empty Senate chamber and found Sumner alone at his desk, writing. Brooks addressed Sumner, accused Sumner of slandering Butler, and then began beating Sumner over the head with his cane. Sumner, pinned into place by his desk, sank under the rain of blows until Brooks's cane broke and Brooks could only hit him with the butt end of it. Sumner tore himself free and was rescued by several colleagues, but his injuries would keep him out of political life for three years. This act of almost wanton violence on the floor of Congress appalled the northern states, fully as much as Brown's raid appalled the South with its equally wanton barbarism.

Both incidents were testimony to the fact that popular sovereignty, the great guarantee of the Compromise of 1850, would breed only violence and not peace. And assuming that the passage of six years had made neither the Wilmot Proviso nor Calhoun's "common property" doctrine any more appealing than they had been in 1850 as a way of dealing with the extension of slavery in the territories, the last possible option in Congress might be a return to some form of the Missouri Compromise.

But Congress was not to have any further say in the matter.

[14]David Donald, *Charles Sumner and the Coming of the Civil War* (New York, 1960), pp. 285–286.

3. Dred Scott and the Collapse of National Spirit

Kansas was a double misfortune for Stephen Douglas. The Little Giant believed with all his heart that popular sovereignty was the golden key that unlocked the peaceful settlement of the territories, and he had made promises to both North and South about that settlement, which Kansas had shown he could not keep. Now, Northerners distrusted him as the man who had carelessly torn down the old safeguard of the Missouri Compromise and allowed slavery into Kansas, and Southerners mistrusted him because the uncertainty over Kansas's future was preventing Kansas from entering the ranks of the slave states.

But Douglas's reputation suffered less in the wake of Bleeding Kansas than the reputations of the two national political parties. The Whigs had gone into the election of 1852 in poor shape to begin with. Both of their most recent presidents, Harrison and Taylor, had died in office, and in 1852, their two greatest standard-bearers, Clay and Webster, died as well. For some of the southern Whigs, of course, their deaths could not have come sooner. Southern Whigs were especially bitter over Taylor, a slaveowner and Southerner who had betrayed both slaveowners and Southerners by advocating the free-state admission of California and New Mexico. So, even though the Whigs still had a sitting president in 1852 in the person of the New York Whig, Millard Fillmore, the southern Whigs refused to allow a northern Whig's nomination and held the Whig presidential convention hostage over 52 ballots until the Virginian, Winfield Scott, was nominated. But Scott balked at wholeheartedly endorsing the Compromise, and the southern Whigs promptly deserted. Scott carried only two of the slave states in the 1852 election.

The controversy over Kansas-Nebraska finished off what little fellow-feeling remained between northern and southern Whigs, and most of the northern Whigs wandered off to experiment with a series of short-lived anti-Nebraska "fusion" coalitions or bitter-end antiimmigrant hate groups like the American party (or "Know-Nothings," a name they earned from their pledge to respond, when questioned about their political loyalties, "I know nothing"). Although some of the most prominent Whigs, like William Henry Seward of New York, openly spurned the Know-Nothings and curried the political favor of the immigrant population, other Whigs found the Know-Nothing hatred for foreigners and immigrants a perfectly congenial match to their own brand of nationalism. But the Know-Nothings were poorly organized to function as a national political party, and their opinions were fatally divided over the slavery issue. Eventually, both nativist Whigs and antislavery Know-Nothings would be compelled to find their way to a new free-soil party where Know-Nothing nativism could be blended into the more moderate strains of Whig nationalism, and both absorbed into the more volatile issue of slavery. It did not take long for such a new party to emerge. In May of 1854, a group of thirty northern ex-Whig and anti-Nebraska Democratic congressmen met in Washington to issue a call for a new party that would unite all the "fusion" and anti-Nebraska groups into a "Republican" party, and in July, a state convention in

Jackson, Michigan, nominated the first slate of candidates to run under the name *Republican.* [15]

The core of the new Republican party were the remnants of what had once been the mainstream northern Whigs—Seward of New York, Charles Sumner and Henry Wilson of Massachusetts, Zachariah Chandler of Michigan. And like the old Whigs, the new Republicans saw themselves as the party of an enterprising white middle-class. They glorified the manufacturer and the independent farmer, "freeholders, educated men, independent men." On the other hand, they were suspicious of planters who grew too great and of manufacturers whose mills grew to gargantuan sizes. They had seen the uncontrolled growth of northern manufacturing generate immense wealth for owners and investors, and great poverty for the faceless gangs of workers who ran the great machines, and they feared for the spread of an urban underclass of wage laborers who owned no property of their own and who had no real hope of rising out of mass poverty. What became important, then, for the Republicans was to ensure that economic independence could be made open to all, so that "even the poorest and humblest in the land, may, by industry and application, attain a position which will entitle him to the respect and confidence of his fellow-men." Independence, however, required opportunity, and so the Republicans rallied around the old Whig program of tariffs to encourage new manufacturing. But they also proposed to head off the problem of working-class poverty by selling off public lands in the territories as "homesteads" at cheap prices, so that even the poorest urban worker could hope to find new life and new economic opportunity beyond the Mississippi. [16]

And this, of course, is what frightened the Republicans about Kansas-Nebraska. Mobility, development, and "the chance to rise" seemed stagnant in a slave system, and now Douglas and the Democrats wanted to fasten that very system onto the very territories that the Republicans hoped to make into the safety valve of opportunity for northern industry. For the Republicans, slavery was not an economic system, but a deadly conspiracy, a conscious "Slave Power" that had possessed the soul of the Democratic party and that was determined to seize the territories and turn them into nurseries for slavery. The Republicans were not the first to accuse the South of hatching a "Slave Power" conspiracy. Salmon Chase claimed in 1854 that the entire Kansas-Nebraska bill was "part and parcel of an atrocious plot" to create "a dreary region of despotism, inhabited by masters and slaves" in the territories. But no one made better use of the accusation than the Republicans, and in short order, the Republicans attracted Chase and the most antislavery of the northern Democrats to their banner. The great danger in this was that, by the mid-1850s, an antislavery party was most likely to be an almost entirely

[15]William E. Gienapp, *The Origins of the Republican Party, 1852–1856* (New York, 1987), pp. 194, 265–271.

[16]Eric Foner, *Free Soil, Free Labor, Free Men: The Ideology of the Republican Party before the Civil War* (New York, 1971), pp. 15–19.

northern party, devoted to expressing northern opinions and representing northern interests. The Whigs had been a national party laboring to reduce sectional strife by inducing its northern and southern members to cooperate and compromise in the service of larger, national goals. But the time for compromises between Northerners and Southerners was fast slipping away, and the Republicans had as their goal the abolition of an institution that Southerners regarded as nonnegotiable.

With the death of the Whigs, one of the principal agencies for binding the sections of the fragile American Union disappeared. The same fate nearly overtook the Democrats. President Pierce, who had supported Kansas-Nebraska, was denounced with Douglas as a traitor by the northern Democrats and as a halfheart by the southern Democrats, and Democratic candidates who were pledged to support their party's president were mowed down in the Congressional by-elections in 1854. When the Democratic presidential convention met in Cincinnati in 1856, the fearful Democrats jettisoned Pierce and rejected Douglas as their presidential candidate, and on the 18th ballot, nominated a Pennsylvania Democrat, James Buchanan.

Buchanan was a veteran Democratic politician who had long coveted a presidential nomination. But in 1856 his chief political merit lay in the fact that he had been out of the country as American minister to Great Britain during the Kansas-Nebraska debates and so had avoided taking any side publicly. Buchanan was also a Northerner (to reassure the northern Democrats), but one with many friends in the South (to reassure the southern Democrats). And so, by nominating a party machine man who had no well-known opinions on the crying issues of the moment, the Democrats managed to avoid a North-South split. With the old Whig party in shambles and the Republican party still only two years old, Buchanan's victory in the 1856 election was a foregone conclusion. But even under those circumstances, the Republicans pulled off what struck proslavery people as an alarmingly good show at the polls. Nominating the famous explorer, John Charles Frémont, for president, the Republicans scooped up a third of the nation's votes, and virtually all of them from the North, where voters turned out in record numbers.[17] As many Southerners quickly realized, had the antislavery northern Democrats not been mollified by Buchanan's nomination, they might have bolted to the Republicans and handed them the election on the first try, just on the strength of northern votes alone. The next time around, the Democrats might not be so fortunate.

The political parties were not the only national institutions cracking under the strain of sectional controversy. The Protestant churches, which had for many years been yet another agency of union within the Union, were also splitting under the stress of southern threats and demands for assurance. Part of the strain was caused by the South's unceasing search for moral arguments in defense of slavery. Once slavery was being defended in the 1830s as a "positive good," it was only a matter of time before Southerners appealed to the Bible to show that the "positive good" also

[17]Gienapp, *Origins of the Republican Party*, p. 414.

had divine approval. "We assert that *the Bible teaches that the relation of master and slave is perfectly lawful and right,*" declared the old-school Presbyterian, Robert Lewis Dabney, and from a litany of Old Testament and New Testament examples, from Abraham to St. Paul, Dabney concluded that slavery "was appointed by God as the punishment of, and remedy for . . . the peculiar moral degradation of a part of the [human] race."[18]

When southern divines offered these arguments, northern evangelicals were quick to correct them, at first patiently and then angrily, as Southerners responded with accusations of apostasy and unbelief. By 1850, the year of the Compromise, one southern Presbyterian's temper had frayed to the point where he denounced his northern counterparts in terms fit for the Devil: "The parties in this conflict are not merely Abolitionists and Slaveholders; they are Atheists, Socialists, Communists, Red Republicans, Jacobins on the one side, and the friends of order and regulated freedom on the other." But the greatest of the American Presbyterian theologians, Charles Hodge of Princeton, who at first condemned the abolitionists as trouble-makers in the 1830s, turned to accuse the South of the troublemaking in 1856 and voted for Frémont.[19] With antagonisms of this order dividing the theologians, it was no little time before they divided the churches as well. The Methodists split into northern and southern branches in 1844; in 1845, the Baptists also split; and in 1857, the southern presbyteries of the Presbyterian church simply walked out of the Presbyterian General Assembly, taking with them some 15,000 southern members. These church splits were significant, not only because they helped destroy vital national institutions and turn them into sectional ones, but because (as John Calhoun happily pointed out in his last speech) they were successful. The southern Methodists, Baptists, and Presbyterians all seceded peacefully from the larger fellow-ships and successfully set up operations that, in the case of the Baptists, have endured to the present day. The churches were a living refutation of Webster's argument to Hayne, that Liberty and Union were inseparable, for here were South-erners who had terminated unions with Northerners without any hurt to their religious liberty. In fact, secession had brought peace to the quarrels in their churches. Thus, the church separations provided an illusory guarantee to Southern-ers that, if matters warranted, secession from the Union was an easy, profitable, and moral way of putting an end to the strife over slavery.[20]

Stephen A. Douglas, however, was unconvinced. Douglas had managed to survive much of the wreckage that his policies had caused, and although he once remarked that he could have traveled from Massachusetts to Illinois by the light of

[18]Dabney, *A Defense of Virginia, and Through Her, of the South* (1867; rept. Harrisonburg, VA, 1977), p. 103.

[19]Thornwell, "The Christian Doctrine of Slavery," in *The Collected Writings of James Henley Thornwell* (1875; rept. Edinburgh, 1974), vol. 4, pp. 405–406; Archibald Alexander Hodge, *The Life of Charles Hodge* (New York, 1880), p. 463.

[20]Clarence C. Goen, *Broken Churches, Broken Nation: Denominational Schisms and the Coming of the Civil War* (Macon, GA, 1985), pp. 113–127.

fires kindled to burn him in effigy, once he was back in Illinois, he was able to rebuild his strength and his credibility. Swinging back at his critics, Douglas claimed that popular sovereignty would fail only where the ill-will of abolitionists and radicals in both North and South made it fail.

And in Illinois, Douglas was speaking to an audience strongly inclined to agree with him. Illinois was part of the old Northwest, filled with German immigrants who hated the South for trying to bring black slaves into territories that they desired, and southern migrants who hated the abolitionists because they feared that emancipation of the slaves would loose free blacks into the territories, with the same result. Douglas played to the fears of the small farmers and the immigrants, held up popular sovereignty as the only safe method for keeping slavery (and African Americans in general) out of the territories, and blamed the uproar over the Kansas-Nebraska bill on the agitators. By October of 1854, Douglas had won back the home-state loyalty he had nearly forfeited in ramming Kansas-Nebraska through Congress, and on October 3rd, he used the state fair at Springfield, Illinois, as a stage for preaching the gospel of popular sovereignty and Kansas-Nebraska.

One voice was raised in dissent. A Springfield lawyer, a former member of Congress and longtime Whig named Abraham Lincoln, took over Douglas's platform in the Springfield statehouse the day after Douglas's defense of Kansas-Nebraska at the state fair. In the course of a three-hour speech, Lincoln proceeded to tear Kansas-Nebraska and popular sovereignty to shreds. Was popular sovereignty really the most peaceful and effective method for settling the territories? Then why hadn't the Founding Fathers in 1787 thought of that when they organized the Northwest territories? Instead, the Northwest had been declared free territory, and the states of the Northwest did not appear to have suffered for it.

Lincoln then pinned Douglas on the question of whether popular sovereignty was really going to keep the territories free. "It is vain," argued Lincoln, to claim that popular sovereignty "gives no sanction or encouragement to slavery." If I have a field, Lincoln shrewdly remarked, "around which the cattle or the hogs linger and crave to pass the fence, and I go and tear down the fence, will it be supposed that I do not by that act encourage them to enter?" Just so with Kansas-Nebraska: The Missouri Compromise had been the fence that kept slavery out of most of the old Louisiana Purchase, but now came Douglas, tearing down the fence in the name of popular sovereignty, and expecting people to believe that slavery would not make every possible effort, climate or not, to camp there. "*Even the hogs would know better*," Lincoln sneered.

But most of all, Lincoln condemned popular sovereignty because it tried to dodge the moral issue of slavery. Douglas hoped to pacify southern anxieties by showing how popular sovereignty gave slavery at least the appearance of a "fair chance" in the territories. Lincoln did not believe that slavery ever deserved to have a "fair chance," and even if all the voters of a territory unanimously demanded it, their demanding it did not make it right. It was, Lincoln declared, "a descending from the high republican faith of our ancestors" to have the United States government adopt as its territorial policy "that we have no longer a choice between freedom and slavery—that both are equal with us—that we yield our territories as readily to one as the other!"[21] This was not the last time Stephen A. Douglas would hear from the tall Springfield lawyer, and those three themes—the authority of Congress over the territories, the incapacity of popular sovereignty to keep slavery from any territory, and the moral injustice of slavery itself—would be Lincoln's constant hammers at Douglas's position in Illinois for the next four years.

For the moment, however, Douglas and popular sovereignty faced a more serious challenge than Lincoln, and it came in the form of the United States Supreme Court. In 1834, a United States Army surgeon named John Emerson was transferred from the Jefferson Barracks in St. Louis, Missouri, to Fort Armstrong, in Illinois, and with him he brought his slave, Dred Scott. Two years later, Emerson was transferred again to Fort Snelling, a frontier army post in what was then still the Wisconsin territory, and once again he brought Scott with him. Technically, Emerson had violated both the free-state statutes of Illinois and the Missouri Compromise (since Fort Snelling was located in a federal district that had been part of the Louisiana Purchase), but since he was a transient rather than a settler, no charges were levied. In 1840, Emerson was transfered again to Florida, and in 1842, he left the army and returned to St. Louis. The next year, Emerson died, and in his will Dred Scott and his wife and children passed into the hands of Emerson's wife, Eliza Sanford Emerson.

It was at this point that Dred Scott and his family made a bid for freedom, not by running away, but by filing suit against Eliza Emerson in April, 1846, for wrongful imprisonment, on the grounds that their residence in a state and a territory that forbade slavery had made them free. This was not an unusual suit, and the St. Louis county circuit court hearing the case in 1850 ordered Dred Scott and his family freed. But Eliza Emerson then appealed to the Missouri Supreme Court, and the Missouri high court truculently reversed the circuit ruling on the grounds that Scott was now a resident of Missouri, and Missouri was not necessarily bound to recognize the antislavery statutes of other states or territories. In the meantime, Eliza Emerson remarried and moved to New York, transferring effective ownership of the Scotts to her brother, John Sanford, of St. Louis. Scott now filed a new suit in the federal district court, arguing that his federal civil rights had been violated: Once on free territory, Scott claimed, he was a free man, and if free, then a citizen and entitled to all the "immunities and privileges" of citizenship specified in the Fifth Amendment to the federal Constitution. The federal district court eventually ruled against Scott in a jury trial in May, 1854, but Scott and his attorneys now

---

[21]Lincoln, "Speech at Springfield, Illinois" [October 4, 1854], in *Collected Works*, vol. 2, pp. 240–247.

appealed on a bill of exceptions to the Supreme Court of the United States, which began hearing *Scott v. Sanford* in February of 1856.[22]

The decision was handed down on March 6, 1857, two days after James Buchanan was inaugurated as the 15th president, and it rocked the country. First, Chief Justice Roger Brooke Taney (writing for a seven-to-two majority) denied that Scott had the privilege of appealing to the Supreme Court, on the grounds that Scott was not only a slave but also an African American, and on both counts, Scott could not be legally considered a citizen of the United States. "The class of persons described in the plea . . . are not included, and were not intended to be included under the word 'citizens' in the Constitution," Taney announced, "They were at that time considered as a subordinate and inferior class of beings, who. . . had no rights which the white man was bound to respect." Even if Scott's master had violated free state laws by taking Scott into free territory, Scott had no legal standing as a citizen before the federal courts, and the federal courts had no reason to listen to his suit, justified or not.

But Taney's argument from race only caused one part of the sensation, since, after all, Taney's notions about Scott's "inferior" race were not much different from what most white Americans and even many abolitionists believed. The political blockbuster of the Dred Scott decision came when Taney actually turned to consider Scott's plea, that residence in a free state or territory could terminate his slave status. Taney proceeded to deny this plea in the clearest and most chilling terms. No territorial government in any federally administered territory had the authority to alter the status of a citizen's property, much less to take that property out of a citizen's hands, unless as a punishment for some crime. And this, of course, meant any property of any citizen in any territory. In effect, Taney had resurrected John Calhoun's "common property" doctrine and overturned any federal or territorial law that in any way interfered with a citizen's "enjoyment" or use of his property—which in the case of Surgeon Emerson had been his slaves, Dred and Harriet Scott. Taney then attacked the Missouri Compromise as unconstitutional on the grounds that it deprived slaveholders of the use of their slave property north of the 36°30' line. In the process, he also destroyed popular sovereignty, the Compromise of 1850, and the Kansas-Nebraska bill as well, for if it was unconstitutional for Congress to ban slavery from the territories, it was equally unconstitutional for the federal territories to do it for themselves, no matter what the majority vote of a territory on the question might be.

The two sections of the Taney opinion, running over 250 tightly printed pages in the Court *Reports*, fit together as integral parts. The first reduced Dred Scott to noncitizenship and a condition fit only to become some real citizen's "property," and the second denied the federal government any authority to restrain in any way the spread of slavery in any place where the federal government—as opposed to the

---

[22]A court clerk misspelled John Sanford's name as *Sandford*, and so the case appears as *Scott v. Sandford* in the court reports.

individual state governments—had jurisdiction. In fact, only the states themselves were left by Taney with any constitutional authority to deal with slavery within their own borders, and even that might be the next safeguard to be questioned by a federal court.[23]

In terms of what the Dred Scott appeal actually required before the law, Taney need not have done more than declare that Scott simply had no standing before the Court, and left matters at that. The explanation for the Taney decision to reach beyond Dred Scott himself and strike down the great Compromises lies largely in Taney and his Court. Five of the seven justices who voted in the majority were Southerners: John A. Campbell, an Alabamian, would later serve as an assistant secretary of war in the Confederacy, and Robert Wayne Grier, John Catron, and Peter Daniel were all proslavery partisans. Taney was a Marylander and an old Jacksonian Democrat who had served as Jackson's attorney general in destroying the Bank of the United States. His opinions as a Supreme Court chief justice consistently tried to brake the social mobility and market-oriented economy so beloved of the Whigs (and later the Republicans). And his opinion in *Scott v. Sanford* became Taney's effort to settle the slavery question where both Congress and the presidents had failed, where Clay and Webster and Taylor and Wilmot had failed, and to settle it in favor of the South.

But far from settling the slavery question, *Scott v. Sanford* only aggravated it. The new Republican party replied that a decision so repugnant to popular opinion could never be binding as law, and Abraham Lincoln denounced Taney's attack on the right of blacks to citizenship as a turning of the Declaration of Independence upside down. "Our Declaration of Independence was held sacred by all, and thought to include all," Lincoln declared, "but now, to aid in making the bondage of the Negro universal and eternal, it is assailed, and sneered at, and construed, and hawked at, and torn, till, if its framers could rise from their graves, they could not recognize it at all."[24] Meanwhile, Stephen A. Douglas was coming up for re-election to the Senate in 1858, and it was clear that the Illinois Republicans would be quick to challenge Douglas on how he could reconcile popular sovereignty—and the right of territories to vote slavery in or out according to their popular majorities—with Taney's declaration that neither Congress nor a federal territory had the authority to ban the transportation of slaves to those territories.

And President James Buchanan, relieved at not having to deliver an opinion on the slavery controversy himself, would happily announce his full intention of

---

[23]At the time the Dred Scott decision was handed down, there was already a case working its way through the New York state courts, involving eight Virginia slaves who claimed that a temporary stopover in New York City had made them free men. This case, *New York v. Lemmon*, might have given Taney the opportunity to overturn every antislavery statute in the free states, as well, and paved the way for the reintroduction of slavery into the free states. The case, however, did not reach the Supreme Court before the outbreak of the Civil War, and Taney never had the chance to hand down a companion ruling to *Scott v. Sanford*.

[24]Lincoln, "Speech at Springfield, Illinois" [June 26, 1857], in *Collected Works*, vol. 2, p. 404.

applying the Dred Scott decision to the trouble in Kansas, and welcoming the application of the proslavery legislature for the admission of the Kansas territory to the Union as a slave state.

Further Reading

The political history of the United States for the dozen years before the outbreak of the Civil War has enjoyed a remarkably rich crop of histories and biographies. For an overall narrative of the movement of North and South toward confrontation over slavery and its extension into the territories, Allan Nevins's "Ordeal of the Union" volumes, *Ordeal of the Union: The Fruits of Manifest Destiny, 1847–1852* and *Ordeal of the Union: A House Dividing, 1852–1857* (New York, 1947) are still without peer in terms of their scope and excitement. David Potter's *The Impending Crisis: 1848–1861* (New York, 1976) offers a superb overview of these same events in a much shorter scope. The significance of the idea of compromise as an operative political principle in holding together the Union is explained in Peter B. Knupfer, *The Union As It Was: Constitutional Unionism and Sectional Compromise, 1787–1861* (Chapel Hill, NC, 1991).

The politics of the Mexican-American War obviously deserve their own nod, and from this angle, I have found Charles G. Sellers's two-volume *James K. Polk* (Princeton, NJ, 1957, 1966) and Paul Bergeron's *The Presidency of James K. Polk* (Lawrence, KS, 1987) quite helpful. But the other aspects of the war have also been well-covered in a number of newer books on this almost-forgotten conflict by K. Jack Bauer, *The Mexican-American War, 1846–1848* (New York, 1974), by Robert W. Johannsen, *To The Halls of the Montezumas: The War with Mexico in the American Imagination* (New York, 1985), and by John S. D. Eisenhower, *So Far From God: The War with Mexico* (New York, 1989).

The Compromise of 1850 was the offspring of the Mexican-American War, and the connection of the two events is magisterially handled by Nevins, Potter, and Holman Hamilton's brief but illuminating *Prologue to Conflict: The Crisis and Compromise of 1850* (New York, 1966). The opposition to the Compromise can be understood through K. Jack Bauer's biography of *Zachary Taylor: Soldier, Planter, Statesman of the Old Southwest* (Baton Rouge, LA, 1986), Charles Wiltse's three-volume *John C. Calhoun* (Indianapolis and New York, 1944–1951), and John Niven, *John C. Calhoun and the Price of Union* (Baton Rouge, LA, 1988). Calhoun's political papers, and the two great Compromise speeches he gave in 1847 and 1850, have recently been collected and published by Ross E. Lence, *Union and Liberty: The Political Philosophy of John C. Calhoun* (Indianapolis, IN, 1992). In addition to Calhoun, the southern point of view on Compromise is available through Thomas A. Scott, *Alexander H. Stephens of Georgia: A Biography* (Baton Rouge, LA, 1988) and William Y. Thompson, *Robert Toombs of Georgia* (Baton Rouge, LA, 1966). On the other side of the Compromise, Daniel Webster's great Seventh of March speech is presented in detail in Irving Bartlett's *Daniel Webster* (New York, 1978), while Stephen A. Douglas, the rescuer of the Compromise, has been capably analyzed in Robert W. Johannsen's *Stephen A. Douglas* (New York, 1973). Douglas was also the father of the Kansas-Nebraska bill, which has been treated in both James C. Malin, *The Nebraska Question, 1852–1854* (Lawrence, KS, 1953) and Gerald M. Wolf, *The Kansas-Nebraska Bill: Party, Section, and the Coming of the Civil War* (New York, 1977). Lincoln's early criticisms of Douglas and Kansas-Nebraska are discussed in

Don E. Fehrenbacher, *Prelude to Greatness: Lincoln in the 1850s* (Stanford, CA, 1962). Kansas itself has almost been eclipsed by the notorious partisans who sought to pull it toward slavery or freedom. Stephen B. Oates's, *To Purge This Land With Blood: A Biography of John Brown* (New York, 1970) presents a sympathetic interpretation of "Old Brown," stressing Brown's intellectual and emotional debt to the Edwardsean theology. I have found David Donald's *Charles Sumner and the Coming of the Civil War* (New York, 1961) to be as useful as it is legendary. On the religious roots of northern opposition to slavery, one should not miss John R. McKivigan's excellent *The War Against Pro-Slavery Religion: Abolitionism and the Northern Churches, 1830–1865* (Ithaca, NY, 1984).

Without wanting to dwell too much on political history, it is still true that political history and the behavior of the political parties has become one of the most fruitful species of historical writing on the 1850s. On the Whigs, I have turned to Thomas Brown, *Politics and Statesmanship: Essays on the American Whig Party* (New York, 1985) and Michael Holt's essay on the vanishing Whigs in *Political Parties and American Political Development from the Age of Jackson to the Age of Lincoln* (Baton Rouge, LA, 1992). The most impressive study of the Republicans remains Eric Foner's *Free Soil, Free Labor, Free Men: The Ideology of the Republican Party before the Civil War* (New York, 1970), although William E. Gienapp, in *The Origins of the Republican Party, 1852–1856* (New York, 1987), has argued that Foner underestimated the importance of nativism and other isssues in the creation of the Republicans. Local politics have also had their due, especially in the form of Michael F. Holt's *Forging a Majority: The Formation of the Republican Party in Pittsburgh, 1848–1860* (New Haven, CT, 1969) and Stephen E. Maizlish's *The Triumph of Sectionalism: The Transformation of Ohio Politics, 1844–1856* (Kent, OH, 1983). Among the many political biographies available, one of the most thorough is Frederick J. Blue, *Salmon Chase: A Life in Politics* (Kent, OH, 1986).

The Fugitive Slave Law and the Dred Scott decision were clearly the two greatest political hot potatoes of the 1850s, and I have been able to turn to important books on each: Don E. Fehrenbacher, *The Dred Scott Case: Its Significance in American Law and Politics* (New York, 1978) and Stanley W. Campbell, *The Slave Catchers: Enforcement of the Fugitive Slave Law, 1850–1860* (Chapel Hill, NC, 1968). I have borrowed from Paul Finkelman's article on "Prigg v. Pennsylvania and Northern State Courts" in *Civil War History* 25 (March 1979), pp. 5–35, and his article on *Prigg V. Pennsylvania* in the *Oxford Companion to the Supreme Court*, Kermit L. Hall, ed. (New York, 1992) in explaining the bearing of that case on the creation of the Fugitive Slave Law; Finkelman has also discussed the overall context of comity between the states and its bearing on the fugitive slave cases in *An Imperfect Union: Slavery, Federalism, and Comity* (Chapel Hill, 1980). I have also borrowed examples of resistance to the Fugitive Slave Law from Thomas P. Slaughter's *Bloody Dawn: The Christiana Riot and Racial Violence in the Antebellum North* (New York, 1992) and from Nat Brandt, *The Town That Started the Civil War* (New York, 1991).

CHAPTER 3

From Debate
to Civil War

 The behavior of northern and southern politicians in the ten years before the Civil War is often described as *irrational* by many historians, as though the Civil War was a product of an undiagnosed madness, or a paralysis of communications so great as to make the Tower of Babel the only worthwhile comparison. The great Allan Nevins described Southerners "in the final paroxysm of 1860–61" as being "filled with frenzy," while Northerners turned "grimly implacable" over slavery. "The thinking" of North and South alike, concluded Nevins, "was largely irrational, governed by subconscious memories, frustrated desires, and the distortions of politicians and editors." Dominated by "stereotypes" of each other, Northerners and Southerners were possessed by "fear," and "fear was largely the product of ignorance, and ignorance—or misinformation—largely the product of propaganda."[1] Over the generation since Nevins wrote those words, the struggle to understand the causes of the Civil War has gone on unabated, but many of these interpretations continue to hover around the theme of *irrationality*. Sometimes, the irrationality takes the form (as it did for Frank Lawrence Owsley) of an "egocentric sectionalism" or (as in James G. Randall) a kind of political dementia that caused a systematic failure in the American political system.

The difficulty with the plea of irrationality arises from the ease with which it permits our attention to slide away from the political crisis of the 1850s, and the political ideologies that were then at work. As much as Nevins was correct to point to the exaggerated rhetoric of proslavery and antislavery forces in the 1850s as a point of serious abrasion between North and South, both the South's fears of territorial and economic strangulation, and the North's fears of a "slave power" conspiracy, are anything but irrational—implausible, maybe, and only with the benefit of hindsight, but not irrational given what was at stake. "Is it nothing to *yell*

---

[1]Nevins, *The Emergence of Lincoln: Douglas, Buchanan, and Party Chaos, 1857–1859* (New York, 1950), pp. 15–16, 19.

about," asked South Carolinian William Gimball in a letter to Elizabeth Gimball in 1861, "that we are prevented from carrying our property into the common territory of the United States? Is it nothing to yell for that the government is to be in the hands of men pledged to carry on the 'irrepressible conflict' against us? Is it nothing that they send incendiaries to stir up the slaves to poison & murder us? Is it nothing that our brothers at the North rob us of our property and beat us when we reclaim it?"[2] On the northern side, Abraham Lincoln is not usually considered a candidate for irrationality, but he was convinced of the existence of a "slave power" conspiracy, and he did not hesitate to suggest the entire train of events from Kansas-Nebraska to Dred Scott had been cunningly devised by two presidents, the chief justice of the Supreme Court, and the junior senator from Illinois.

Until the firing of the very first gun, Northerners and Southerners were driven, not by irrationality, but by the clearest political logic on offer. "As long as slavery is looked upon by the North with abhorrence; as long as the South is regarded as a mere slave-breeding and slave-driving community; as long as false and pernicious theories are cherished respecting the inherent equality and rights of every human being, there can be no satisfactory political union between the two sections," declared the New Orleans *Bee* in December of 1860. And while the premises of that proposition may be questionable, the logic that flowed from them was not. "If one-half the people believe the other half to be deeply dyed in inquity; to be daily and hourly in the perpetration of the most atrocious moral offense," continued the editor of the *Bee*, "how can two such antagonistic nationalities dwell together in fraternal concord under the same government?"[3] On those terms, secession and disunion were dismayingly coherent and logical political choices within a political system that had all along confirmed that secession and disunion were viable options. The political system did not break down—as James McPherson has written, the southern states simply decided that it had fallen into the wrong hands, and that they would no longer choose to use it.[4] And so far from losing confidence in that system, Northerners and Southerners struggled for workable compromises right down to last minutes, even while the room for creating those compromises narrowed beyond all hope of maneuver, and they continued to agitate for them almost all the way through the war in the form of northern and southern peace movements. If there is anything genuinely appalling in the political context of the Civil War, it is the dominance of the most glittering and hard-edged political rationality, and it was the hard edge of that rationality which, in the end, made a final compromise impossible.

[2]Randall C. Jimerson, *The Private Civil War: Popular Thought During the Sectional Conflict* (Baton Rouge, LA, 1988), pp. 8–9.

[3]"Vain Hopes," in the New Orleans *Bee* [December 14, 1860], in *Southern Editorials on Secession*, Dwight Lowell Dumond, ed. (New York, 1931), p. 336.

[4]McPherson, "Antebellum Southern Exceptionalism: A New Look at an Old Question," in *Civil War History* 29 (September 1983), p. 243.

1. The "Little Engine" of Abraham Lincoln

The Dred Scott decision was a deep embarrassment for Stephen A. Douglas. The doctrine of popular sovereignty, on which Douglas had pegged his hopes for achieving sectional peace (and achieving his own nomination to the presidency), initially assumed that the inhabitants of any given territory could, if they wished, exclude slavery simply by passing the active legislation necessary to ban it from their midst. The Dred Scott decision, however, made it clear that no one—not Congress, not the inhabitants of a territory, not even a territorial legislature—had any power to keep any United States citizen from taking property (which had now become a euphemism for *slaves*) anywhere a citizen wanted and erecting the slave system in any territory of the Union. And if it was pressed far enough, it might also open the way to claiming that no state, either, could ban slavery. But Douglas was nothing if not resourceful, and after the initial shock of the decision wore off, he announced that the Dred Scott decision would not contradict the operation of popular sovereignty after all. True, a territory could not pass legislation *actively* banning slavery; but the people of a territory could *passively* make it impossible for slavery to exist in their territory by refusing to enact the usual array of slave codes and police measures that all the other slave states needed in order to keep slavery intact. The right to take slaves into the territories, claimed Douglas in a speech in Springfield in the summer of 1857, was "practically a dead letter" without "appropriate police regulations and local legislation." Withhold those, and slavery had no chance of surviving within a territory's boundaries. By Douglas's logic, *Scott v. Sanford* not only left popular sovereignty intact, but left it as the only weapon remaining by which slavery could be legally kept out of the territories.[5]

This line of reasoning did nothing to stanch the hemorrhaging of Douglas's reputation among southern Democrats. Southerners, who were overjoyed at the Dred Scott decision, were furious at Douglas's refusal to submit tamely to the Supreme Court's dictum. What was more, the new president, James Buchanan, had welcomed the Dred Scott decision as a convenient way of declaring the Kansas problem settled. Buchanan, surrounded by a mostly southern cabinet, was irritated that Douglas was threatening to spoil that settlement by suggesting that antislavery Kansans might yet have the means to obstruct a proslavery settlement and prolong the Kansas turmoil still longer. And as Douglas approached senatorial re-election in Illinois in 1858, it was becoming a real question as to whether Buchanan might manipulate party patronage against Douglas to prevent the troublesome Illinois Democrat from returning to the Senate.

The Republicans had been thrown into similar disarray by the Dred Scott decision. They had assumed that their task was the creation of a congressional coalition large enough to block any attempt to organize Kansas or any other new territory with slavery. Now, Dred Scott had pulled the rug out from under them by

[5]Robert A. Johannsen, *Stephen A. Douglas* (New York, 1973), pp. 570–572.

declaring that neither Congress nor anyone else had the authority to create such an obstacle. For that reason, desperate Republicans—especially in the East—began to hearken to the song of Stephen A. Douglas. Douglas's argument that popular sovereignty (at least in its passive form) was now the only workable means of keeping slavery from the territories convinced many Illinois Republicans that, especially for the 1858 senatorial race, it was time to stymie Taney and Buchanan and throw their support behind Douglas.

There was, however, one Illinois Republican who dissented from this view of Douglas, and that was Abraham Lincoln. In 1858, Lincoln was forty-nine years old, one of the most outstanding lawyers in Illinois and equally one of the most prominent state Republicans. Lincoln had come by his successes the hard way. Born in a crude log cabin in 1809 in Kentucky, Lincoln had known little before his twenty-fifth birthday but the poverty and hardships that were the substance of backcountry life. He had, as he wrote of himself in 1860, "had an axe put into his hands at once; and from that time till within his twenty-third year, he was almost constantly handling that most useful instrument—less, of course, in plowing and harvesting seasons." Lincoln had also imbibed antislavery opinions almost with his mother's milk, since his parents, Thomas and Nancy Lincoln, were both members of an ultra-Calvinistic Baptist sect that banned slaveholding members from their fellowship. In fact, the spread of slavery across Kentucky was one of the motivations for Thomas Lincoln to uproot his family and move, first to Indiana, and then finally to Illinois.

Their views on slavery may have been almost the only things that Thomas and Abraham Lincoln shared in common. Thomas Lincoln was content to be a farmer, only marginally literate—Lincoln recalled that his father "never did more in the way of writing than to bunglingly sign his own name"—but at least moderately successful in his calling. Abraham, however, grew up with a passion for self-education and social betterment, fed at the beginning by his stepmother, Sarah Bush Johnston, whom Thomas married after the death of Nancy Lincoln in 1818. "Abe was a good boy: he didn't like physical labor—was diligent for knowledge," Sarah Lincoln recalled in 1865.

> He read all the books he could lay his hands on. . . . When he came across a passage that struck him he would write it down on boards if he had no paper. . . . He cyphered on boards when he had no paper . . . and when the board would get too black he would shave it off with a drawing knife and go on again. . . . As a usual thing Mr. Lincoln never made Abe quit reading to do anything if he could avoid it. He would do it himself first. Mr. Lincoln could read a little & could scarcely write his name: hence he wanted . . . his boy Abraham to learn. . . .[6]

In 1831, Abraham Lincoln struck out on his own, trying his hand at anything that offered him a way up the ladder. He tried clerking and postmastering in a store in

---

[6]David Donald, *Lincoln's Herndon: A Biography* (New York, 1948), p. 182.

the village of New Salem, Illinois, but succeeded at neither, and in 1832, took his first turn at politics.

Politically, Lincoln found himself almost instinctively drawn to the Whigs rather than the Democrats. The Whig ideology celebrated nationalism and deplored the loud demands of the states for first loyalties; and it called for a strong central government and a prominent role for the federal government in the economy, in railroads and internal improvements, and in protective tariffs. The Whigs were the party of up-and-coming men, the western men, the frontier men like Lincoln, who did not want to be bound by the old loyalties of the past. And so Lincoln became a Whig, and took the great Whig statesman Henry Clay (a fellow Kentuckian) as his political idol. Lincoln's first electoral platform—he ran for the state legislature but came in only eighth in a field of thirteen candidates—advocated tax-funded internal improvements, attacked the repudiation of debts (this was a covert Democratic tactic for undermining the hated banking system), and promoed "the principles of true republicanism."

In 1834, Lincoln won his first seat in the Illinois state legislature as a Whig, and served four successive terms there. In the process, he helped lead the Illinois legislature into the sponsorship of transportation projects, and, in 1837, the passage of a $10 million appropriation for railroad construction. His first major speech in the Illinois legislature praised the operation of the Illinois State Bank for having "doubled the prices of the products" of Illinois farms, and filled farmers' pockets "with a sound circulating medium, and they are all well-pleased with its operations." The Democratic attacks on banks and bank charters, Lincoln explained, would never hurt "men of wealth" who are "beyond the power of fortune," but they would "depreciate the value of its paper [currency] in the hands of the honest and unsuspecting farmer and mechanic."[7] But once having helped to put much of this program in place, it promptly turned to ashes. A national economic depression, caused in large measure by the Democratic assault on the banks, crushed the American economy in 1837. Illinois had financed its railroad appropriation on bank borrowing, and the collapse of the banks saddled the state legislature (and the unforgiving taxpayers) with an indebtedness that it took years to pay off. Lincoln, defending the Illinois State Bank to the bitter end, left the legislature in defeat in 1841.[8]

Meanwhile, Lincoln's urges for social betterment and education persisted. While still a state legislator, Lincoln began teaching himself law out of an assortment of borrowed law books, and in 1836 he was licensed to practice in the state circuit courts. The choice of law as a profession was part and parcel of his Whiggish economic aspirations, since lawyers were (in the phrase of Charles G. Sellers) the "shock troops" of market capitalism, and from John Marshall's Supreme Court on down, American lawyers were becoming the guardians of commercial contracts and

[7]"Speech in the Illinois Legislature Concerning the State Bank," in Collected Works, vol. 1, p. 69.

[8]Gabor Boritt, Lincoln and the Economics of the American Dream (Memphis, TN, 1978), pp. 15–22, 30–31, 47, 59.

property.[9] It was in pursuit of the market—and of the financial and social respect-ability that came with it—that Lincoln moved to the Illinois state capital, Spring-field, and entered a law firm there with another young lawyer, John Todd Stuart. "His ambition," wrote another law partner, William Herndon, "was a little engine that knew no rest." Eventually, that "little engine" succeeded. In 1842, Lincoln married Mary Todd, the daughter of a prominent Lexington, Kentucky, family, who brought him a lifelong schooling in social graces. But even more important, Lincoln labored with ferocious intensity at becoming a successful lawyer and Whig politi-cian. Herndon noticed that Lincoln seemed to think "that there were no limita-tions to the force and endurance of his mental and vital powers," and he watched Lincoln wear himself to the point of breakdown in "continuous, severe, persistent, and exhaustive thought" on a problem.[10]

His thoroughness, his feel for the practical in legal issues, and his remarkably retentive memory made Lincoln an outstanding courtroom performer. He was not "a learned lawyer," recalled Herndon, but he was a first-rate "case lawyer" who ignored grand legal theory in favor of settling cases by practical precedent and considerations. Much as Lincoln cared for the rightness of a case, he was just as concerned about whether it could be won on reasonable terms; and if it could not, he did not hesitate to change the terms. "Discourage litigation," was Lincoln's own advice to aspiring lawyers, "Persuade your neighbors to compromise whenever you can. Point out to them how the nominal winner is often a real loser—in fees, expenses, and waste of time." This was a pattern which, in later years, would also characterize his political solutions, for the practice of law developed a strong ele-ment of the pragmatic in Lincoln, and his bent for what Herndon called "case law" tempted Lincoln to reach for the quickest and not always the most exalted means for getting a favorable solution. "Secret, silent, and a very reticent-minded man," Lincoln was "a riddle and a puzzle to his friends and neighbors," and in political combat he could be indirect, evasive, and easy to underestimate.[11]

The plainest example of this evasiveness was his awkward embarrassment over his crude origins. "Lincoln's ambition," remarked Herndon, was "to be distinctly understood by the common people." Yet, no man wanted less to be one of those "common people." Once Lincoln moved to Springfield, he rarely cast a backward glance at his humble origins: Neither Thomas nor Sarah Lincoln were invited to their son's wedding, and Lincoln was too embarrassed and alienated by his father's crudeness even to attend the old man's funeral in 1851. His stepbrother's pleas that Lincoln come down to the Coles County farmhouse where Thomas Lincoln lay

---

[9]Charles G. Sellers, Jr., *The Market Revolution: Jacksonian America, 1815–1848* (New York, 1991), p. 47.

[10]Herndon to Jesse Weik [December 9, 1886], and to C. O. Poole [January 5, 1886] in *The Hidden Lincoln, from the Letters and Papers of William H. Herndon*, Emanuel Hertz, ed. (New York, 1938), pp. 124, 148.

[11]Lincoln, "Fragment: Notes for a Law Lecture" [July 1, 1850], in *Collected Works*, vol. 2, p. 81; Herndon to C. O. Poole, in *The Hidden Lincoln*, pp. 119–120, 124.

dying were met with a frosty refusal: "Say to him that if we could meet now, it is doubtful whether it would not be more painful than pleasant." Lincoln lost no love on Thomas Jefferson's dream of a republic of yeoman farmers. What he wanted for the Union was what he wanted for himself: an upwardly mobile society of successful, small-scale producers and professionals, whose participation in the world markets held out for them the promise of republican independence. "I hold the value of life is to improve one's condition," Lincoln said in 1861, and he lived by the "promise that in due time the weights should be lifted from the shoulders of all men, and that *all* should have an equal chance."[12]

The practice of law gave Lincoln his first "equal chance." Although much of his reputation as a trial lawyer was made out on the state circuit courts, riding from one plank-and-shingle little courthouse to another over the Illinois prairies, he made his fortune pleading before the Illinois Supreme Court, where he handled appeals in 402 cases, and in the federal circuit court, where he handled over 300 cases for bankruptcy and debt. In addition to a demanding legal practice that may have amounted to more than 5,000 cases and as many as 100,000 separate legal documents, Lincoln managed to sit as a judge in over one hundred cases on the state circuit courts when a regular judge was sick or unavailable. He was involved in two cases before the United States Supreme Court, dabbled in a variety of Patent Office cases, and developed a long-term association as counsel for the Illinois Central Railroad (confident in the benefits of pushing the boundaries of markets deeper and deeper into the west, Lincoln managed to persuade the state court to have the Illinois Central declared tax-exempt as a "public work"). By the 1850s, Lincoln was commanding an annual income of more than $5,000 per annum—approximately twenty times that figure if we reckon in today's currency—owned a large frame house in Springfield, had his oldest son in a private school in Springfield, and had investments in real estate, mortgages, notes, bank accounts, and insurance policies amounting to over $20,000.[13]

And yet, despite his successes, Abraham Lincoln arrived at his mid-forties dissatisfied and restless. Rigidly self-controlled, Lincoln refused even the relaxation of liquor, and Robert Lincoln, his oldest son, afterward recollected that he had "seen him take a sip of a glass of ale and also of a glass of champagne . . . on two or three occasions in my life, not more. . . ." When self-control or his control of his circumstances escaped him, Lincoln became possessed by a strain of moody introspection, and he easily lapsed into periods of sustained and almost suicidal depression. Whatever religion he may have been taught by his parents he had exchanged for an emotionless rationalistic deism, and he proclaimed his faith, not in a per-

[12]Lincoln, "To John D. Johnston" [January 12, 1851], and "Speech in Independence Hall" [February 22, 1861], in *Collected Works*, vol. 2, pp. 96–97, and vol. 4, p. 240; Stephen B. Oates, *With Malice Toward None: The Life of Abraham Lincoln* (New York, 1977), p. 95.

[13]Harry E. Pratt, *The Personal Finances of Abraham Lincoln* (Springfield, IL, 1943), pp. 52–53, 82; Herbert Mitgang, "Document Search Shows Lincoln the Railsplitter was Polished Lawyer," in *New York Times*, February 14, 1993.

sonal God, but in "Reason, cold, calculating, unimpassioned reason" as "all the materials for our future support and defence." Yet he retained a streak of the superstitious—in the form of dreams and omens—all his life, and he transmuted the Calvinist predestination of his evangelical parents into "the Doctrine of Necessity—that is, that the human mind is impelled to action, or held in rest by some power, over which the mind itself has no control. . . ."[14]

His one remedy for the manic depression he called "the hypo" lay in his peculiarly clownish sense of humor and the almost bottomless fund of jokes and funny stories he had collected from the folk humor of the Illinois frontier. His reputation as a storyteller was almost as legendary as his eloquence as a lawyer, reeking of the cornfield, and occasionally of the barnyard. Some measure of Lincoln's humor was consciously cultivated to appeal to popular audiences, and Lincoln used laughter to deadly effectiveness as a stump speaker (Douglas would later claim that he never feared Lincoln's arguments, but "every one of his stories seems like a whack upon my back"). And woe to the courtroom rival who mistook Lincoln's folksiness for brainlessness: "Any man who took Lincoln for a simple-minded man," remembered Leonard Swett, "would very soon wake up with his back in a ditch." But in a larger sense, Lincoln craved the escape from melancholy offered him by the jokes he could tell to a crowd of howling friends and admirers. "Some of the stories are not so nice as they might be," Lincoln admitted, "but I tell you the truth when I say that a funny story, if it has the element of genuine wit, has the same effect on me that I suppose a good square drink of whiskey has on an old toper; it puts new life into me. The fact is I have always believed that a good laugh was good for both the mental and the physical digestion."[15] It also reflected the divisions of Lincoln's character, one half all seriousness and ambition and republican honesty, the other bawdy, cunning, homespun, and secretive.

Part of Lincoln's brooding was rooted in his complex and sometimes unhappy marriage to Mary Todd. Painfully aware of his own social awkwardness, Lincoln's relationships with women were tentative and uncertain. His early passion for Ann Rutledge, the daughter of a New Salem tavern keeper, has often been dismissed as a fairytale shaped by William Herndon to discomfit Mary Lincoln, but the evidence Herndon accumulated for the Rutledge story has more substance to it than the dismissals imply. Rutledge's premature death, if we can rely on Herndon's interviews with New Salemites years afterward, devastated Lincoln. A subsequent engagement to Mary Owens in 1836 fell through due to Lincoln's hasty and not entirely becoming retreat from matrimony. For the most part, he avoided intimate contact with women, fearing rejection, and even his marriage to Mary Todd almost

---

[14]Robert Todd Lincoln to Isaac Markens [February 13, 1918], in *A Portrait of Abraham Lincoln in Letters by His Oldest Son*, Paul Angle, ed. (Chicago, 1968), p. 55; Lincoln, "Address before the Young Men's Lyceum of Springfield, Illinois," and "Handbill Replying to Charges of Infidelity," in *Collected Works*, vol. 1, pp. 115, 382.

[15]J. F. Farnsworth, in Carl Sandburg, *Abraham Lincoln: The War Years* (New York, 1939), vol. 3, p. 305.

fell through due to his anxieties about his sexual adequacy. In the end, only the determined intervention of friends and the equally determined strategy of Mary herself managed to tie the knot for Lincoln. As it was, Mary Todd was both a burden and a blessing to Lincoln. Criticized by her wealthy, slaveholding family for having married beneath herself, Mary constantly fed Lincoln's "little engine" and provided him with the kind of reassurance and devotion he needed to keep himself going. She was, said Herndon, "like a toothache, keeping her husband awake to politics day and night." On the other hand, she could goad her husband into rage as easily as politics. Mary was high-strung and irritable, and Herndon thought her a "terror . . . imperious, proud, aristocratic, insolent, witty, and bitter," and he (and almost everyone else who knew the Lincolns personally) characterized the Lincolns' marriage as a "domestic *hell.*" By the mid-1850s, much of the intimacy of the first decade of the Lincoln-Todd union had begun to fade, and Lincoln began to spend increasing amounts of time away from Springfield on the circuit or on railroad cases.[16]

Further aggravating Lincoln's melancholy was his persistent failure at politics. In 1840, he had campaigned as a loyal Whig for William Henry Harrison, and in 1843 the Whig state committee recruited him to write a state party platform. He campaigned for Whig nominees in 1844, including his "beau ideal of a statesman," Henry Clay, and in 1846, the Illinois Whigs successfully ran him for Congress as the representative for the 7th congressional district. But Lincoln's performance in Washington fell far short of impressive. Although he struggled hard to make a name for himself as a Whig, little in Lincoln's freshman term as a congressman was noticed, not even his opposition to President Polk and the Mexican-American War. In 1848, he stepped aside in accordance with party wishes to allow another Whig, Stephen Logan, to win the 7th District seat, and instead Lincoln was sent out on the stump to promote the election of Zachary Taylor, the Whig candidate for president. Despite falling on his spear so loyally, Lincoln was offered as a political reward only the governorship of the Oregon territory, a lusterless post so far removed from real political life that Lincoln turned it down.

Thus, Abraham Lincoln in the mid-1850s was a man who had accomplished much, but not nearly as much as he craved. And then, conveniently, his vision shifted from the unsatisfied and ambiguous conflicts of his private world to the equally unsatisfied and ambiguous conflicts of national politics.

Lincoln had long harbored antislavery instincts. But his dislike of slavery was generated less by a concern over racial injustice, and more by the economic experience of dependency he had suffered as a young man working first for his father and then for others but hardly ever for himself. Through the 1830s and 1840s, his rankling at slavery never actually took the route of abolitionism, and he paid scant attention to the moral question of human bondage based on race. The debate over

---

[16]Jean Baker, *Mary Todd Lincoln: A Biography* (New York, 1987), pp. 135, 152; Herndon to Jesse Weik [January 9, 1886], in *The Hidden Lincoln,* p. 131.

Kansas-Nebraska and then Dred Scott, however, convinced Lincoln that the threatened expansion of slavery represented a personal challenge to the pattern of his own life. Slavery now came to mean more than just an insufferable form of economic dependence; it now meant the establishment and spread of a planter aristocracy who meant to use the slave system to fasten a permanent system of economic dependence onto the American republic, with no more opportunity for a "poor man's son" (which was as much concession as Lincoln would make to his father or his past) to acquire a homestead of his own and begin the same ascent to bourgeois respectability that Lincoln had achieved. And so he threw himself into the anti-Nebraska fight, hoping to rebuild the shattered unity of the Whig party on a platform that offered northern Whigs a resurrection of the Missouri Compromise, and southern Whigs new reassurances for the safety of slavery in the southern states. That platform came near to winning him one of Illinois' U.S. senate seats in 1855, when Lincoln outpolled a pro-Nebraska Democratic candidate, James Shields. But the Whigs in Illinois no longer had the strength to push Lincoln over the finish line, and Lincoln was forced to throw his support to a free-soil Democrat, Lyman Trumbull, in order to keep another Douglasite out of the Senate.

Lincoln clung to the Whigs long after the party had, for all practical political purposes, asphyxiated. He had no sympathy with the Know-Nothings, and until he was convinced that another Whiggish alternative would survive as a platform for his ambitions, he was reluctant to abandon the party of Clay and the one party that had got him elected to Congress. But by the end of 1855, the slavery issue and Kansas-Nebraska had put the Whigs past any hope of resuscitation as far as Lincoln was concerned, and the mounting demands of the mysterious "Slave Power" for the free extension of slavery everywhere in the territories tipped Lincoln over to the new Republican party. In May, 1856, Lincoln helped lead a coalition of antislavery Whigs (like his partner, William Herndon) and free-soil Democrats (like Lyman Trumbull) into the Republican camp. And at length, in 1858, Lincoln got what he wanted most, the chance to bring down one of the chief perpetrators of the Kansas-Nebraska betrayal, Stephen A. Douglas, as Douglas ran for reelection in Illinois to the Senate. Not surprisingly, he was dumbfounded when he began to hear suggestions of eastern Republicans that Illinois Republicans stand aside and let Douglas be reelected without opposition. "What does the New-York Tribune mean by it's constant eulogising, and admiring, and magnifying [of] Douglas?" Lincoln demanded of Lyman Trumbull during the last week of 1857, "Have they concluded that the republican cause, generally, can be best promoted by sacrificing us here in Illinois? If so we would like to know it soon; it will save us a great deal of labor to surrender at once."[17]

But Lincoln need not have feared: His standing among the Illinois Republicans was too high to be jeopardized by the editorials of the New York *Tribune*. On June 16, 1858, Lincoln was nominated by a Republican state convention in Springfield

[17]Lincoln, "To Lyman Trumbull" [December 28, 1857], in *Collected Works*, vol. 2, p. 430.

for the Senate, and that evening Lincoln addressed the convention in one of his greatest speeches, the "House Divided" speech. At the very beginning, Lincoln hammered at the folly of expecting that popular sovereignty could resolve the sectional crisis.

> We are now far into the *fifth* year, since a policy was initiated, with the avowed object, and confident promise, of putting an end to slavery agitation. Under the operation of that policy, that agitation has not only *not ceased,* but has *constantly augmented.* In *my* opinion, it *will* not cease, until a *crisis* shall have been reached, and passed. "A House divided against itself cannot stand." I believe this government cannot endure, permanently half *slave* and half *free.*

He then attacked the notion that Douglas, the author of this failed policy, was now to be hailed as the adopted son of the Republicans. "*They* do *not* tell us, nor has *he* told us, that he *wishes* any such object to be effected," Lincoln observed. Just because Douglas has a quarrel with Buchanan and Taney does not mean that he has become a Republican, or, more to the point, that Douglas has now become an opponent of slavery. "How can he oppose the advances of slavery?" Lincoln asked, "He don't *care* anything about it." To the contrary, Lincoln argued, the entire progress of events from Kansas-Nebraska up through Dred Scott showed that everything in it had been prearranged deliberately to advance slavery, and that Douglas was as much as part of that conspiracy as Buchanan, Pierce, or Taney. "Let any one who doubts, carefully contemplate that now almost complete legal combination— piece of *machinery* so to speak—compounded of the Nebraska doctrine, and the Dred Scott decision," Lincoln declared darkly:

> When we see a lot of framed timbers, different portions of which we know have been gotten out at different times and places and by different workmen—Stephen, Franklin, Roger, and James, for instance—and when we see these timbers joined together, and see they exactly make the frame of a house or a mill, all the tenons and mortices exactly fitting . . . we find it impossible to not *believe* that Stephen and Franklin and Roger and James all understood one another from the beginning, and all worked upon a common *plan* or *draft.* . . .[18]

With that, Lincoln called upon Illinois Republicans to rally to his standard, and display a united front against Douglas.

Douglas cast a wary eye on Lincoln, recognizing him as "the strong man of the [Republican] party—full of wit, facts, dates—and he is the best stump speaker, with his droll ways and dry jokes, in the West."[19] His best policy would have been to stay away from Lincoln and rely on his own prestige in Illinois to carry him back to the Senate. But Douglas could never resist a fight when offered, and when Lincoln challenged Douglas to a series of fifty debates across the state, Douglas accepted— with the stipulation that the number of debates be reduced to seven and that

---

[18] "'A House Divided': Speech at Springfield, Illinois" in *Collected Works,* vol. 2, pp. 461–462, 465–466.
[19] Johannsen, *Stephen A. Douglas,* pp. 640–641.

Douglas be given the upper hand in rebuttals. The debates began on August 21st in Ottawa, Illinois, and ranged across the state to Freeport on August 27th, at Jonesboro on September 15th, at Charleston on September 18th, at Galesburg on October 7th, at Quincy on October 13th, and at Alton (where Elijah Lovejoy had been murdered twenty-one years before) on October 15th.

Douglas's original plan for dealing with Lincoln was to paint himself as the champion of law and order, and Lincoln as an abolitionist fanatic whose opposition to popular sovereignty would let down Illinois' barriers to black immigration. The "House Divided" speech, in Douglas's hands, was the principal evidence that Lincoln was a reckless "Black Republican" partisan who wanted equal rights for blacks more than he wanted a stable and peaceful Union. "He tells you this Republic cannot endure permanently divided into slave and free states," Douglas roared. *Why not?* "Why can't it last, if we will execute the government in the spirit and on the same principles upon which it was made?" Douglas asked during the third debate at Jonesboro. It would, Douglas insisted, last just fine if Lincoln and the Republicans would simply leave off trying to impose abolition on the South or upon the territories. "It can thus exist if each state will carry out the principles upon which our institutions were founded . . . the right of each State to do as it pleases, and then let its neighbours alone." Giving each state active popular sovereignty over its affairs (and each territory passive popular sovereignty over its organization) was the only way to guarantee peace among the states. "There is but one path of peace in this Republic," Douglas declared, "and that is to administer the Government as our Fathers made it, divided into free States and slave States," and the best signpost to that path was popular sovereignty, "allowing each State to decide for itself whether it wants slavery or not." It mattered nothing to Douglas whether slavery itself was right or wrong or whether there was a moral imperative that justified its restriction no matter what damage that requirement did to individual state rights. "If Kentucky and every other Southern State will settle the question to suit themselves, and mind their own business and let others alone, there will be peace between the North and South, and the whole Union."

And lest this seem too much a triumph of political expediency over a question of morality, Douglas was quick to remind his white Illinois listeners of who their moral discomforts were being lavished upon—blacks, whose presence they loathed anyway. Suppose slavery was wrong, and so wrong that restriction and abolition was the only cure: What would the result be for Illinois? "Do you desire to turn this beautiful State into a free negro colony, in order that when Missouri abolishes slavery she can send one hundred thousand emancipated slaves into Illinois, to become citizens and voters, on an equality with yourselves?" Douglas asked. Thus racism came to the rescue of expediency, and calmed the queasy consciences of those who were wondering if peace by popular sovereignty might come at too high a price. Douglas, in fact, played the race-hatred card repeatedly and shamelessly throughout the debates. "All I have to say on that subject is this," Douglas announced in Freeport, "those of you who believe that the nigger is your equal and ought to be on an equality with you socially, politically, and legally, have a right to entertain those opinions, and of course will vote for Mr. Lincoln." *Down with the negro,* growled the vast throng of listeners.[20]

But Lincoln was not willing to be thrown on the defensive so easily. Principally, Lincoln attacked the popular sovereignty scheme as having no meaning after Dred Scott. Not only did popular sovereignty offer no practical way of excluding slaves from the territories, but the very suggestion that it might flew in the face of the Dred Scott dictum, which threw the territories open to slaveholder and nonslaveholder alike. In the debate at Freeport, Lincoln forced the spotlight onto the incompatibility of popular sovereignty with Dred Scott by posing a question to Douglas: 'Can the people of the United States territories in any lawful way against the wishes of any citizen of the United States, exclude slavery from their limits prior to the formation of a state constitution?" Douglas had no choice, at Freeport and elsewhere, but to answer *yes* in order to preserve his own political integrity and win a northern election. "The people of a territory have the lawful means to admit it or exclude it as they please," Douglas irritably responded, "for the reason that slavery cannot exist a day or an hour anywhere unless supported by local police regulations."[21] But that then meant, as Lincoln later pointed out, that what is lawful (slavery in the territories) can somehow be rendered unlawful without the rendering being in any way contradictory.

Moreover, urged Lincoln, even if popular sovereignty could somehow ensure that the Union could peacefully endure half-slave and half-free, that divided arrangement flew in the face of the real intentions of the framers of the American republic. "When our government was first established," Lincoln said, "it was the policy of the government to prohibit the spread or extension of slavery into the territories of the United States where it did not then exist." All that Lincoln asked "is that it should be put back on the basis that our fathers originally placed it on, and I have no sort of Doubt that it would there be extinguished in God's own time. . . ."[22] Douglas's popular sovereignty dogma was not perpetuating the American republic, it was perverting it.

But Lincoln had a larger point to make than merely the theoretical inconsistencies of popular sovereignty. Douglas's error lay not only in failing to see that popular sovereignty was an impractical instrument for containing slavery, but that Douglas had failed to see that slavery itself was a moral wrong that did not deserve, and should not claim, the protection of state sovereignty. In the spirit of "true

---

[20]Douglas, "The Third Joint Debate at Jonesboro" [September 15, 1858], "The Second Joint Debate at Freeport" [August 27, 1858] and "The Fifth Joint Debate at Galesburg" [October 7, 1858], in *The Lincoln-Douglas Debates,* Harold Holzer, ed. (New York, 1993), pp. 111, 149, 153, 250–251.

[21]Lincoln, "The Second Joint Debate at Freeport" with "Mr. Douglas' Reply" [August 27, 1858] and "Seventh Joint Debate at Alton" [October 15, 1858], in *Lincoln-Douglas Debates,* Holzer, ed., pp. 96, 106, 356.

[22]Lincoln, "The Third Joint Debate at Jonesboro" [September 1, 1858], in *Lincoln-Douglas Debates,* Holzer, ed., pp. 156–157, 160.

republicanism"—and not Douglas's brand of majoritarian democracy—popular sovereignty must be not simply the vote of the majority, but the choice by the majority of what is morally right, and the position of the Republicans was that slavery was so much a moral wrong that no amount of popular sovereignty could ever make slavery right for an American territory. In the last debate of the series at Alton, Lincoln insisted that "The real issue in this controversy, I think, springs from a sentiment in the mind, and that sentiment is this: on the one part it looks upon the institution of slavery as being wrong, and on the other part of another class, it does not look upon it as wrong."

> It is the eternal struggle between these two principles—right and wrong—throughout the world. . . . It is the same principle in whatever shape it develops itself. It is the same spirit that says, "You work and toil and earn bread, and I'll eat it." [Loud applause.] No matter in what shape it comes, whether from the mouth of a king who seeks to bestride the people of his own nation and live by the fruit of their labor, or from one race of men as an apology for enslaving another race, it is the same tyrannical principle.[23]

In truth, Douglas did not believe that slavery was actually right, nor did Lincoln in 1858 believe that it was wrong enough to justify direct intervention in the affairs of states where it was already domesticated. Nor did Lincoln really believe more than Douglas that African Americans were entirely the social equals of whites, the difference on this point between them being more one of degree than substance. But differences of degree can be critical, too. For Lincoln in 1858, African Americans were certainly the equals of whites in enough senses to make enslaving them wrong, and a wrong that should be contained wherever there was power and opportunity to contain it. For Douglas, African Americans were so far from being the equals of whites that the misfortune of their enslavement was simply not worth antagonizing half the Union, especially when half the continent was at stake. For Douglas, the question about slavery was not morality but politics—*shall we let this quarrel over inferior beings wreck the Union?* And for the time being, that was the basic outlook of most Illinoisans. Douglas Democrats won the majority of the Illinois legislative seats on election day, November 7th, and since the Illinois legislature was still the legal forum for electing the state's U.S. senators, it was the legislature and not the popular vote of the people of Illinois that determined the result between Lincoln and Douglas, and sent Douglas back to Washington.

"I am too big to cry and too badly hurt to laugh," Lincoln remarked. And yet, his loss was a significant one. By forcing out into the open the inconsistencies of the popular sovereignty dogma, Lincoln had made it impossible for antislavery Republicans to see Douglas as an ally and create an amalgamation movement with northern Democrats, and it was worth remembering that in each county where Lincoln and

[23]Lincoln, "Seventh Joint Debate at Alton" [October 15, 1858], in *Lincoln-Douglas Debates*, Holzer, ed., pp. 356–357; Lincoln, "Seventh and Last Debate with Stephen A. Douglas at Alton, Illinois," in *Collected Works*, vol. 3, pp. 312–313, 315.

Douglas had actually debated, the county voters elected Republican representatives to the state legislature. Lincoln had also kept public attention forced on Douglas's disagreement with Buchanan and the southern Democrats, and helped set the stage for the self-destruction of the Democrats in 1860. And incidentally, he had also made himself a national figure, with results that people were already beginning to speculate upon.

2. Election, Compromise, Secession

When James Buchanan became president, it was fervently hoped that he would have the political tools necessary to put the slavery agitation to rest. Buchanan had to his credit almost forty years of experience in Congress, the cabinet, and most recently, in diplomatic service. Although he was a Pennsylvanian by birth and a northern Democrat by conviction, he nevertheless sympathized with the South's ever-mounting demands for reassurance, and the hope that he would be able to please everyone was the single most important factor in his victory in the 1856 election. But Buchanan's skills as a diplomat served, in this instance, to hobble him rather than help him. Anxious to obtain peace in Kansas, Buchanan allowed himself to be intimidated by the violence of southern threats of disunion; and once intimidated by the Southerners in his cabinet and in Congress, he grew spiteful and resentful when northern Democrats balked at his proposals to concede virtually every demand made by the South.

Settling the bloody mess in Kansas was Buchanan's first chore. He was assisted—or so he thought—in dictating a settlement by the Dred Scott decision, since *Scott v. Sanford* apparently relieved him of any responsibility to see that Kansas would choose slavery or freedom. However, Kansas insisted on making trouble for him anyway. The old territorial governor under President Pierce, John W. Geary, had brought a measure of peace to Kansas by the end of 1856; but the rest of the territorial government was still split between two rival legislatures, each claiming to be the legal voice of the people of Kansas. One of these was the official legislature, a proslavery body elected by fraud in 1855 and sitting in the town of Lecompton; the other was a free-soil assembly, sitting in Topeka. In February, 1857, a month before Buchanan's inauguration, the Lecompton legislature, anticipating that the new president would probably appoint a new territorial governor, decided to get the jump on the appointment process. The Lecompton legislature authorized the election of a constitutional convention that would draw up a state constitution for Kansas, a constitution that would then be submitted to Congress for its approval and for the admission of Kansas to the Union. Geary vetoed the convention bill, rightly accusing the proslavery legislature of attempting to stampede a rush to statehood. But the Lecompton legislature overrode his veto, and Geary threw up his post as governor and resigned on March 4, 1857.

Buchanan replaced Geary with a Mississippian, Robert J. Walker, which delighted the proslavery elements in Kansas. But Walker was no proslavery fire-eater. A friend of Stephen A. Douglas, Walker was convinced that slavery had no practical future in Kansas, and that the territory ought to be admitted as a free, but Democratic, state. But that only fed the determination of the Lecompton legislature to nail together a proslavery state constitution as quickly as possible, and in November, 1857, the constitutional convention approved a document that had something in it to offend nearly everyone. In addition to protecting the 200 slaves then in Kansas, the Lecompton Constitution placed restrictions on the chartering of banks, banned free blacks from the state, and prohibited any amendments to the constitution for seven years. As a sop to "popular sovereignty," the new constitution allowed for the calling of a public referendum, but only on the question of whether new slaves could be brought into Kansas, which effectively guaranteed Kansas' admission as a slave state no matter what. And even more amazing was President Buchanan's response to the Lecompton Constitution. Browbeaten by southern congressional delegations and the southern members of his cabinet, Buchanan decided to endorse the Lecompton Constitution and recommended it favorably to Congress in a message on December 8, 1857.

In the light of the repeated electoral frauds in the Lecompton legislature and the refusal of the constitutional convention to submit the entire constitution for popular approval in Kansas, any congressional acceptance of the Lecompton Constitution was tantamount to repudiating popular sovereignty, as well as virtually admitting Kansas as a slave state. Stephen Douglas, righteous in his wrath against Buchanan, took his political life into his own hands and assailed the Lecompton Constitution on the floor of the Senate as a mockery of the popular sovereignty principle. Furthermore, free-soil Kansans boycotted the initial referendum on Lecompton on December 21st, then joined in a second referendum on January 4th where they defeated it by a clear majority. But Buchanan had committed himself to the Lecompton Constitution: He accepted the resignation of the disgusted Governor Walker and proceeded to jam the Lecompton Constitution down the throats of Congress. Pulling every political string a president can conceivably pull, Buchanan twisted approval of Lecompton out of the Senate on March 23, 1858, and then out of the House on April 1st.

Unhappily for Buchanan, the House bill contained an amendment that the Senate version lacked, and the whole question was now thrown into a House-Senate conference committee for resolution. At the urging of William H. English of Indiana, one of the three House conferees, a compromise bill was devised that accepted Lecompton and the statehood of Kansas—provided that the Lecompton Constitution was resubmitted to the people of Kansas for a federally supervised election. Douglas, however, mistrusted Lecompton no matter who supervised an election; and his enemies in congress foolishly persuaded Buchanan that anything Douglas opposed was the perfect thing for the president to support. The English bill passed both House and Senate on April 30, 1858. Accordingly, Lecompton went back to the voters of Kansas for a third time, and to the hideous embarrassment of

Buchanan, the voters of Kansas turned out on August 2nd and rejected Lecompton by a vote of 11,300 to 1,788. Buchanan had lost one of the most vicious political struggles in the history of Congress, southern Democrats had seriously damaged the patience of their northern counterparts, and Buchanan loyalists in the North were unseated wholesale by upstart Republicans in the 1858 Congressional elections. In the state elections a year later, Republicans seized control of the legislatures and governorships of the New England states, Ohio, Pennsylvania, Minnesota, and Iowa. And to add insult to injury, Douglas successfully won reelection to the Senate in November after a grueling campaign against the new rising Republican star of Illinois, Lincoln. In fact, almost the only northern Democrats who survived northern anger over Lecompton were antiadministration Douglasites.

But Buchanan's troubles had only begun, and they were now about to be worsened by one of the weirdest episodes in the history of American politics. Few people outside of Kansas knew anything about John Brown, and those within Kansas knew him only as an antislavery fanatic who taken his own private revenge on the proslavery cause in the murders at Pottawatomie in May of 1856. Unfortunately for Brown, the temporary peace that Governor Geary brought to Kansas after the Pottawatomie massacre dried up most of the excitement Brown had derived from butchering hapless slaveholders. He took little interest in the debate over the Lecompton Constitution, and instead he began to cast around for more substantial opportunities to wreak havoc on what he perceived as the satanic minions of the slave aristocracy. In December of 1858, he led another raid on Fort Scott, where he liberated a free-state prisoner and killed a shopkeeper (Brown had wanted to burn the entire town) and then raided into Missouri, liberating eleven Missouri slaves whom he then transported to Canada. But Brown got no thanks among the free-staters in Kansas, since his raids only drew the wrath of proslavery thugs down on their heads. "I consider it my duty to draw the scene of excitement to some other part of the country," Brown announced, and once he deposited his fugitives in Canada in March, 1859, he gave no more thought to Kansas. Instead, his eye fell upon Virginia.[24] Between January 1857 and June 1859, Brown began recruiting volunteers and money for a guerilla raid into the Old Dominion. Brown's plan was to liberate as many slaves as he could find or who would flock to him, establish himself in a stronghold in the western Virginia mountains, and from there engulf all of the upper South in a massive slave insurrection. The initial object of the raid would be the federal arsenal at Harpers Ferry, on the upper Potomac River, where Brown would be able to seize the arms he would need to defend himself in the Virginia mountains.

Listened to dispassionately, Brown's scheme was bizarre to say the least, and Frederick Douglass, who had known Brown since 1847, tried to talk him out of it down to almost the last minute. "My discretion or my cowardice made me proof

[24]Oswald Garrison Villard, John Brown, 1800–1859: A Biography Fifty Years After (Boston, 1910), pp. 373–375.

against the dear old man's eloquence," and Douglass attempted to convince Brown in his last meeting with him that Harpers Ferry was "a perfect steel trap and that once in he would never get out alive."[25] But Brown had made up his mind, and by mid-October he had managed to recruit and train twenty-one fighters, some of them free blacks like Dangerfield Newby who hoped to liberate their families still in slavery. More significantly, Brown had traded in on his reputation as a hero of antislavery militancy to approach prominent eastern abolitionists like Thomas W. Higginson, Theodore Parker, George L. Stearns, Franklin B. Sanborn, Gerrit Smith, and Samuel Gridley Howe, and easily hypnotized them with his fire-and-brimstone eloquence into giving him the money he needed to finance the attack on Harpers Ferry.

Early in the morning of October 17, 1859, Brown and his followers descended upon the Harpers Ferry arsenal, disposed of its two guards, and captured the Baltimore & Ohio railroad bridge over the Potomac. And then, for some unaccountable reason, instead of carrying off a store of looted weapons toward the safety of the mountains, Brown dallied in Harpers Ferry. By midafternoon, several Virginia militia companies had surrounded the town and recaptured the bridge, and the next morning, a detachment of United States Marines under a lieutenant colonel of cavalry named Robert E. Lee assaulted the engine house of the arsenal, where Brown had holed up, and captured or killed sixteen of Brown's men.

It might have been best for the emotional well-being of the entire country had Brown himself died in the assault. But Brown was only wounded and captured, and he was instead put on trial for treason against the Commonwealth of Virginia. The trial gave Brown what he always really wanted, a public pulpit, and what he revealed about the nature of his plot, the identities of the people who had backed it, and the cold fury with which he was prepared to execute it sent a shiver of horror down the back of the South. It could only have conjured up nightmares of Nat Turner, of slave rebellion, of wholesale race war, to listen to Brown's description of his planned insurrection, especially since it was evident that he had absolutely no regrets about what he had done or what he had planned to do. "I see a book kissed which I suppose to be the Bible," Brown said at his sentencing, "which teaches me that all things whatsoever I would that men should do to me, I should do to them. . . . I believe that to have interfered as I have done in behalf of His despised poor, is no wrong, but right." And if the court found that sufficient grounds for his execution, then he embraced the verdict with the fervor of a Christian martyr. "Now, if it is deemed necessary that I should forfeit my life for the furtherance of the ends of justice, and mingle my blood with the blood of millions in this slave country whose rights are disregarded by wicked, cruel, and unjust enactments, I say let it be done." Brown was declared guilty of treason on November 7, 1859, and hanged on December 2nd in Charlestown. His last words, found written on a slip of paper in his cell, hung like dark thunderclouds over the American horizon:

[25]Douglass, *Life and Times of Frederick Douglass, written by Himself* (New York, 1941), pp. 352–353.

I John Brown am now quite *certain* that the crimes of this *guilty land will* never be purged *away*, but with Blood. I had *as I now think, vainly* flattered myself that without *very much* bloodshed, it might be done.[26]

Brown's raid caused an eruption of anger and panic in the South. Although southern leaders publicly congratulated their slaves on their reluctance to rally to Brown's banner, their behavior showed something entirely different from confidence. "Never has the country been so excited before," wrote one Georgian in December, 1859, "There was great feeling in 1820, but not like the present. The South is deeply stirred." Slave codes were toughened, slave patrols were reinstated, and violence against blacks multiplied. But nonslaveholding white Southerners were also the target of suspicion. It had not escaped the notice of the planters and their friends in the southern state capitals that Brown had chosen western Virginia for his raid, a region of comparatively few slaves but full of resentful white yeomen, and it was even more disturbing to learn that the Harpers Ferry townspeople and the local militia had been less than enthusiastic in attacking Brown (the Virginia militia had, in fact, declined Lieutenant Colonel Lee's invitation to make the final assault on Brown in the arsenal engine house). "Watch Harper's Ferry people," Virginia governor Henry Wise warned his agents in mid-November, and at Brown's hanging, Wise ordered the local commander to "Let no crowd be near enough to the prisoner to hear any speech he may attempt."[27]

But the ultimate message of John Brown for Southerners was the lesson of distrust for the North, for Brown's raid was seized upon as argument-clinching proof that the North was only awaiting its opportunity to destroy the South by force, and the discovery of Brown's private correspondence in his temporary headquarters in Maryland underscored how much support Brown had enjoyed from prominent northern abolitionists. "This mad attempt of a handful of vulgar cut-throats," wrote Robert Lewis Dabney, "would have been a very trivial affair to the Southern people, but for the manner in which it was regarded by the people of the North."[28] Although Lincoln and other Republicans hastened to wash their hands of any association with Brown, across the North Brown's steadfast and unrelenting courage at his trial dimmed the idiocy of his raid and allowed him to emerge as a hero. In Chicago, church bells were tolled at the hour of Brown's execution, and in Boston, William Lloyd Garrison praised Brown as a model fit for repeated imitation. "Was John Brown justified in his attempt?" Garrison asked enthusiastically, "Yes, if Washington was in his . . . If men are justified in striking a blow for freedom, when the

[26]Stephen B. Oates, *To Purge This Land With Blood: A Biography of John Brown* (New York, 1970), pp. 327, 351.

[27]Clarence L. Mohr, *On the Threshold of Freedom: Masters and Slaves in Civil War Georgia* (Athens, GA, 1986), p. 7; Malcolm C. McMillan, *The Disintegration of a Confederate State: Three Governors and Alabama's Wartime Home Front, 1861–1865* (Macon, GA, 1986), p. 11; Craig Simpson, *A Good Southerner: The Life of Henry A. Wise of Virginia* (Chapel Hill, 1985), pp. 211–212.

[28]Dabney, *Life and Campaigns of Lieut.-Gen. Thomas J. Jackson* (Boston, 1866), p. 144.

question is one of a threepenny tax on tea, then, I say, they are a thousand times more justified, when it is to save fathers, mothers, wives and children from the slave-coffle and the auction-block, and to restore to them their God-given rights." Garrison was a pacifist by conviction, "yet, as a peace man—an 'ultra' peace man— I am prepared to say 'Success to every slave insurrection at the South, and in every slave country.' "[29] No wonder the South saw Brown's raid as sinister proof that the Union was turning into an embrace with destruction.

The primary casualty of Harpers Ferry was, ironically, the Democratic party. Persuaded that no Northerners were to be trusted after Harpers Ferry, southern Democrats now began to demand that their voice have the preponderant weight in determining Democratic policy. Addressing the Virginia legislature in January, 1860, Christopher Memminger announced that the South must secure four guarantees in the next election for its continued safety—an equal share for the South of all the western territories, the disbanding of all antislavery societies, the repeal of any laws that obstructed the capture of fugitive slaves, and a ban against any amendment of the Constitution respecting slavery—while others like Jefferson Davis of Mississippi added to that demands for a national slave code and the reopening of the African slave trade. They fully expected the next Democratic national convention in Charleston, South Carolina, to make these demands part of its national platform.

But Douglas and the northern Democrats were unwilling to acquiesce in a legislative program for the destruction of popular sovereignty in the territories, and certainly not for the purpose of pandering to southern anxieties about John Brown and slavery. The stakes were made all the higher since Buchanan, bowing to Democratic tradition and weary of the burdens of the presidency, had announced his intention not to seek reelection as president. This left Douglas as the single most obvious candidate for the Democrats to run for the presidency in 1860. Douglas's defense of popular sovereignty and his defiance of Lecompton in the teeth of Buchanan's rage had made Douglas the champion of the northern Democracy, and the only acceptable presidential candidate to the northern half of the party. Moreover, northern Democrats were convinced that only Douglas, and not the southern fire-eaters, had the national stature to carry both northern and southern states in the presidential election of 1860. Consequently, they regarded Douglas as the only Democrat capable of retaining Democratic control of the presidency, and with that, of the entire apparatus of the federal bureaucracy.

The northern Democracy's unwillingness to follow the demands of the southern ultras, and their determination to see Douglas nominated by the Charleston convention, together with the southern demands for renewal of the slave trade and slave protection in the territories, made the destruction of the Democrats logically

[29]Garrison, "Speech of William Lloyd Garrison" [December 16, 1859], in *Documents of Upheaval: Selections from William Lloyd Garrison's The Liberator, 1831–1865*, Truman Nelson, ed. (New York, 1966), pp. 265–266.

inevitable. When the Charleston convention assembled in April, 1860, southern radicals led by William Lowndes Yancey of Alabama stood for seven days agitating for a proslavery platform, and when it became clear that they would not get it from the Douglas men, all of the lower South delegations except that of Georgia walked out of the convention. The southern withdrawal made it statistically impossible for Douglas to obtain the necessary two-thirds vote for the nomination, and the shattered convention adjourned itself to reconvene in Baltimore on June 18th. But when the Democrats met again, the convention split once more, with still more southern withdrawals. Douglas, still short of the two-thirds majority of delegates, had to be nominated by the convention as part of a resolution. The day after the Baltimore convention closed, the southern ultras nominated their own candidate, John Breckinridge of Kentucky, for president, thus making the party split a political reality. And then, as if things were not already bad enough for the Democrats, a compromise movement, composed largely of old-time southern Whigs and calling down a pox on both Douglas and Breckinridge, met in Baltimore and nominated yet another presidential candidate, the colorless Tennessean, John Bell. The end result was that Douglas captured the Democratic nomination for the presidency, but both southern support and the Democratic party collapsed from under him. "It is an utterly futile and hopeless task to re-organize, re-unite and harmonize the disintegrated Democratic party, unless this is to be done by a total abandonment of principle," editorialized the Augusta *Daily Chronicle and Sentinel*, "No, sensible people might as well make up their minds to the fact that the Democratic party is dissolved forever, that new organizations must take its place. . . ."[30]

The Republicans viewed the splintering of the Democrats with glee, for the collapse of Democratic unity between Douglas and Breckinridge, and the unwillingness of Bell's supporters to vote for either as an acceptable southern candidate, opened the way to a Republican victory in November. But precisely because victory was now within their grasp, the Republicans instantly began to hesitate about nominating their most ultra antislavery standardbearers, like William H. Seward of New York. Seward was a longtime Whig who had once stiffened Zachary Taylor's back against slave expansion, and who was regarded by northern Democrats as a reckless radical. Nominating Seward might be perceived as too violent an antislavery gesture by the Republicans and cost them the votes of the moderates within the party; and even more serious, his championship of the Whig economic agenda in the Senate and as governor of New York might drive northern and southern Democrats back into each other's arms, and cost the Republicans as much as a quarter of the votes they had won from Democrats in the 1856 presidential campaign. The Republicans who assembled in Chicago in May, 1860, for their national nominating convention would be looking for an antislavery man and a Whig economist who had managed to avoid making himself nationally notorious on either of those points, the kind of man Horace Greeley described in a letter to a friend: "I know the

---

[30]"The Washington Abortion," in *Southern Editorials on Secession*, Dumond, ed., p. 111.

country is not Anti-Slavery. It will only swallow a little Anti-Slavery in a great deal of sweetening. An Anti-Slavery man *per se* cannot be elected; but a Tariff, River-and-Harbor, Pacific Railroad, Free Homestead man *may* succeed *although* he is Anti-Slavery." And the man who best fit Greeley's description was already at hand in Illinois in the person of Abraham Lincoln.

Lincoln's run against Douglas for the Illinois Senate seat in 1858 had boosted him to the top of the Illinois Republicans, and in October, 1859, he was invited by prominent New York Republicans to speak in New York City so that they might take his measure. Lincoln was not at all averse to being measured. As early as February, 1860, he admitted to his friends that "I am not in a position where it would hurt much for me to be nominated on the national ticket," and on February 16th, he was pleased to find that the influential Chicago *Tribune* had openly endorsed him for the Republican presidential nomination, claiming that only Lincoln could carry the western states for the Republicans. But the crucial test for Lincoln was the New York invitation, and on February 27th, in the midst of a blinding snowstorm, fifteen hundred New York Republicans turned out to hear Lincoln speak at the Cooper Institute.

His Cooper Institute address started poorly. Tall, gaunt, his wrists dangling out of his sleeves, Lincoln nervously addressed the assembly in a shrill Kentucky drawl that made sophisticated New Yorkers wonder whether a terrible mistake had been made about this man. But after a few moments, Lincoln warmed to his task and in a short while the silent crowd turned increasingly more enthusiastic. He addressed himself first to Douglas, underscoring once again that the intention of the framers of the Constitution was to see slavery contained and gradually extinguished, and not given the tacit approval of the popular sovereignty doctrine. "Those fathers marked it," Lincoln insisted, "as an evil not to be extended, but to be tolerated and protected only because of and so far as its actual presence among us make that toleration and protection a necessity." Lincoln then turned to the southern disunionists and warned them that the Republicans were not going to be frightened out of their principles simply because the South held the pistol of political disruption of the Union to their heads. Republican opposition to slavery was a matter of moral judgment, and not just political expediency. "All they ask, we could readily grant, if we thought slavery right; all we ask, they could as readily grant, if they thought it wrong," Lincoln explained, "Their thinking it right, and our thinking it wrong, is the precise fact upon which depends the whole controversy." And yet, Lincoln tempered his utterances with a large dash of caution: he insisted that he only wanted to contain slavery where it was, not to abolish it outright. "Wrong as we think slavery is, we can yet afford to let it alone where it is, because that much is due to the necessity arising from its actual presence in the nation." And he distanced himself from John Brown by referring to the Harpers Ferry raid as "peculiar" and "absurd."[31] In short, Lincoln said everything he needed to say to make his

[31]"Address at Cooper Institute, New York City," in *Collected Works*, vol. 3, pp. 534, 549–550.

moral opposition to slavery extension clear, while at the same time professing no personal animosity toward the South. Gone was the provocative rhetoric of the "House Divided" speech and the talk of conspiracy between Buchanan, Pierce, Douglas, and Taney; Lincoln as much as conceded that the house could remain divided, so long as one of the divisions could not spread, and in so doing he positioned himself as a firm but not radical antislavery man, the perfect Republican. The Cooper Institute roared its approval, and so did the major Republican newspapers.

But the greatest impact of the Cooper Institute triumph was felt in Illinois. On May 9, 1860, the Illinois Republican state convention riotously pledged its national convention delegates to Lincoln for the presidential nomination, and at the height of a tremendous outburst of enthusiasm, Lincoln's cousin, John Hanks, paraded into the convention, bearing two weather-beaten fence rails bedecked with a banner reading: "Abraham Lincoln. The Rail Candidate for President in 1860. Two Rails From a Lot of 3,000 Made in 1830 by Thos. Hanks and Abe Lincoln." Lincoln had struggled all his adult life to put his past out of sight, and deeply resented anyone's attempt to address him as informally as "Abe". But Lincoln saw at once the value now of identifying himself as a man of the people, and especially of the pioneering West, and so he became, not Mr. Lincoln the railroad lawyer or the Honorable Abraham Lincoln, Esq., of Springfield, but Abe Lincoln the rail-splitter.

When the Republican national convention convened one week later in Chicago, most of the delegates arrived at the convention hall assuming that either Seward or some other party stalwart would be handed the presidential nomination. But Seward's reputation as a radical, unelectable in the West and anathema to antislavery Democrats, crippled him, and he stalled on the first ballot, only sixty delegates shy of the nomination. From that point on, the Illinois contingent (which had been agitating and bargaining for their favorite son for weeks before) now began wheeling and dealing in earnest while Lincoln remained in Springfield so as to be able to turn a blind eye to the politicking the Illinois Republicans were waging on his behalf. On the third ballot Lincoln landslided into the nomination, and the convention exploded into a pandemonium of jubilation. As a running-mate, the Republicans cast a careful eye on northern Democrats and drafted a former Maine Democrat, Hannibal Hamlin.

The southern Democrats were not nearly so jubilant. "The subsequent nomination of LINCOLN was a master-stroke of political craft," the New Orleans *Bee* conceded.[32] With the Democratic party shivered into three splinters, there was little practical hope of defeating Lincoln and the Republicans, and after a glum and lackluster campaign by most of the candidates, Lincoln successfully captured the presidential election on November 6, 1860. Ironically, he had polled almost a million votes less than the combined popular votes of his three opponents, Douglas, Breckinridge, and Bell—which meant that the southern Democrats, by refusing to

---

[32]"The Chicago Nomination," in *Southern Editorials on Secession*, Dumond, ed., pp. 104–105.

unite behind Douglas, had actually helped bring about the very thing they had screamed against, the election of a Republican president. But even with less than a majority of popular votes, Lincoln still commanded the 180 electoral votes of the North, and that would have given him the election even if the South had united both its popular and electoral votes entirely behind Douglas. At last, the game of balances had tipped irrevocably against the South.

One day after the election, interest rates on the New York money markets began to soar nervously toward 12 percent. Three days after the election, the legislature of South Carolina passed a bill calling for the assembling of a state convention that would withdraw South Carolina from the Federal Union.

3. The Sumter Crisis

It will be difficult for us to appreciate the degree of desperation that Lincoln's election to the presidency produced in the South unless we remember what the presidency meant on the local level in the 1860s. The creation of a professional civil service was still another thirty years in the future, and before then, every federal appointive office—from the Cabinet down to the lowliest postmaster—was filled at presidential discretion and usually according to party or philosophical loyalties. Much as Lincoln might protest that he was no John Brown, his identity as a Republican was enough to convince most Southerners that he would appoint only Republicans to postmasterships (where they could ensure the free flow of abolitionist literature into every southern hamlet), only Republicans as federal marshals (who would then turn a deliberately blind eye to fugitive slaves en route to Canada), only Republicans to army commands (and thus turn the federal army into an antislavery militia, and federal forts and arsenals in the South into abolitionist havens), and so forth. And that was entirely aside from the possibility that Lincoln himself harbored hostile designs on the South.

Lincoln, as the president-elect, tried to offer as much in the way of reassurance as he could to the South without violating his own principles or the platform of the Republican party. Late in November, Lincoln wrote that, as president, he would regard himself as bound to obey the Consitution and the laws, including the fugitive slave laws and the security of slavery in the slave states. "I have labored in, and for, the Republican organization with entire confidence that whenever it shall be in power, each and all of the States will be left in as complete control of their own affairs respectively . . . as they have ever been under any administration," Lincoln wrote reassuringly from Springfield two weeks after the election. "I regard it as extremely fortunate for the peace of the whole country, that this point . . . is now to be brought to a practical test, and placed beyond the possibility of Doubt." To his old Whig comrade-in-politics, Alexander H. Stephens of Georgia, Lincoln wrote on December 22nd to reiterate that he had no intention of meddling with slavery in the States, where the Constitution gave him no authority to meddle with it. "Do the people of the South really entertain fears that a Republican administration would, *directly*, or *indirectly* interfere with their slaves, or with them, about their slaves?" Lincoln asked soothingly. "If they do, I wish to assure you, as once a friend, and still, I hope, not an enemy, that there is no cause for such fears."[33]

But at the same time, Lincoln made it plain that he would never countenance the *extension* of slavery into the territories. Territorial governments that entertained notions of applying for admission to the Union as slave states were hereby served notice that the president-elect would send no signals and no appointees who would oil slavery's wheels. "Let there be no compromise on the question of *extending* slavery," Lincoln wrote on December 10th, "If there be, all our labor is lost, and ere long, must be done again." And he was certainly not about to retreat to some form of the popular sovereignty doctrine in the territories in order to pacify southern threats of disunion. "I am sorry any Republican inclines to dally with Pop. Sov. of any sort," Lincoln wrote to an Indiana Republican on December 18th. "It acknowledges that slavery has equal rights with liberty, and surrenders all we have contended for."[34] Beyond his promise to leave slavery alone in the slave states, Lincoln would make no further concessions.

This could have been read as Lincoln's admission that direct intervention in the slave states was out of the question, a hint he hoped Alexander Stephens and other Southerners would take to their comfort. But such an admission, however significant in Republican eyes and disappointing to the abolitionists, fell considerably short of the reassurances about a slave code and reopened slave trade that the South was now demanding in what amounted to the final round in the forty-year-long game of balances. Exclusion of slavery from the territories meant that slave-based agriculture had no future; and since the states that would one day be formed in the territories would now be free states, then no matter what Lincoln's assurances for the present about slavery and the Constitution, the mounting number of free states in the Union would eventually permit the Republicans to create and adopt amendments to the Constitution for abolishing slavery outright, and get them ratified by an ever-increasing free-state majority. This, at least, was the logic of the calmest slaveholders; other Southerners, convinced that the spirit of John Brown was now about to take up residence in the White House, reached for the weapon they had so often threatened to use—immediate secession from the Union. Within twenty-three days of Lincoln's election, five southern states—South Carolina, Alabama, Mississippi, Georgia, and Florida—had authorized the calling of state conventions to debate withdrawal from the Union, and Louisiana's legislature was in special session in order to call such a convention. In Texas, only the stubborn opposition of Governor Sam Houston kept the legislature from calling for a seces-

[33]Lincoln, "Passage Written for Lyman Trumbull's Speech at Springfield, Illinois" [November 20, 1860] and "To Alexander H. Stephens" [December 22, 1860], in *Collected Works*, vol. 4, pp. 142–143, 160.

[34]Lincoln, "To William Kellogg" [December 11, 1860] and "To John D. Defrees" [December 18, 1860], in *Collected Works*, vol. 4, pp. 150, 155.

sion convention, and not even Houston would be able to stave off that demand forever. Even before his state convention met, Alabama's Governor Moore mobilized the state militia and pressured Alabama banks into suspending payments of hard cash (mostly owed to northern banks) and made them guarantee at least $1 million in their vaults for the use of the state. Georgia Governor Joseph Brown asked the Georgia legislature for $1 million to purchase weapons for the state and ordered the Georgia militia to occupy Fort Pulaski, a federal fort at the entrance to the port of Savannah.[35]

Leading all of the Southern states in secession fervor was South Carolina, whose grievances with the federal Union ran all the way back to the nullification crisis of 1832. Moreover, South Carolina was home to some of the most radical and eloquent voices for disunion, and they made themselves heard when the South Carolina secession convention assembled on December 17, 1860, in Columbia. After deliberating for two days, the entire convention shifted to Charleston and there, at 1:15 PM on December 20th, it unanimously passed a secession ordinance and declared that South Carolina had resumed its status as an independent republic. As for the possibility that the federal government might do as Andrew Jackson had done in 1832, and treat the secession as an armed insurrection, South Carolinians sniffed in contempt. J. D. B. DeBow assured a friend that Northerners would turn out to fight each other before they would fight the South over secession. South Carolina Senator James Chesnut even offered to drink all the blood that would be shed in any war over the Union.[36]

South Carolina's boldness carried the other states of the lower South before it. Mississippi passed its own ordinance of secession on January 9, 1861, with Florida adopting a secession ordinance the next day, Alabama the day after that, and Georgia on January 19th. On January 26th, Louisiana followed suit, and Texas joined them on February 1st. In less than the short space between Lincoln's election and his inauguration, seven states had declared their Union with the United States dissolved, convinced that the political situation of the South required disunion, and that the legal and cultural situation of the Union itself permitted it. The Augusta Constitutionalist explained that "The difference between North and South" had been "growing more marked for years, and the mutual repulsion more radical, until not a single sympathy is left between the dominant influences in each section." Now that the national government has fallen into the control of the Republicans, "all the powers of a Government which has so long sheltered" the South "will be turned to its destruction. The only hope for its preservation, therefore, is out of the Union."[37]

And yet the secessionists were not nearly as sure of themselves as their pronouncements implied. "A new confederacy, if the present Union be dissolved, it

[35]McMillan, Disintegration of a Confederate State, pp. 14–15.
[36]Allan Nevins, The Emergence of Lincoln: Prologue to Civil War, 1859–1861 (New York, 1950), p. 335.
[37]"What Should Georgia Do?" in Southern Editorials on Secession (New York, 1931), p. 242.

must be conceded, is a necessity," advised the New Orleans *Daily Picayune* even before South Carolina had seceded, "The history of the world proves the failure of governments embracing very small communities."[38] The brave talk about the irreconcilable differences of North and South and the painlessness of secession notwithstanding, the South Carolinians immediately began casting around for support from their fellow Southerners. It was impossible to be sure how the federal government would actually respond; and what was more, the elections of delegates to the various state secession conventions had given an uncertain sound about the enthusiasm of the southern people for the secession movement. The Mississippi secession convention had voted strongly for secession, but had also passed a resolution against reopening the African slave trade; the Alabama convention voted for secession by a bare majority of eight; in Georgia, it took ballot rigging by the secessionist governor, Joseph Brown, to ensure that enough prosecession delegates would be elected to the secession convention. And, most significant of all, the upper South and the border states were sitting tight. Virginia, Arkansas, and Missouri each called secession conventions, only to have secession resolutions go down to defeat (in Virginia by a two-to-one margin), while North Carolina and Tennessee voted to call no secession convention at all.

So on December 31, 1860, in an effort to provide security for the future of the secession movement, the South Carolina secession convention elected commissioners to meet with the governments of the other seceding states with a view towards organizing a cooperative mutual government. On January 3rd, the commissioners discussed their situation, and concluded their deliberations with a call for a general convention of all the seceding states to meet at Montgomery, Alabama, in one month's time to form a provisional southern government. The Montgomery convention, assembling on February 4, 1861, took just four days to create a new joint government for the southern states. They adopted a new constitution, more or less based on the federal Constitution, but adding to the preamble the cautious reminder that "each State" was "acting in its sovereign and independent character." They chose as the new government's title (again, to underscore that it was a federation of independent powers and not a national union), the Confederate States of America. Two days later, the convention elected a president for the new Confederacy, the former West Point cadet, secretary of war, and senator from Mississippi, Jefferson Davis. Thus, in short order was born a southern slave republic—but not without an ill-concealed case of nerves.

The worries of the Confederates, however, were nothing compared to the woes of President James Buchanan, who became, in the lame-duck months of his unhappy presidency, the closest thing to an American Job. "Probably the unhappiest man, this day, within the whole limits of the Union, is James Buchanan, the President of these nearly disunited States," jeered the New Orleans *Daily Crescent*, "In common with nine-tenths of the people of the North, he has been accustomed

---

[38]"New Lines of Sectionalism," in *ibid.*, p. 312.

to regard the threats of the South as mere idle talk, which really amounted to nothing. He finds out, now, how much mistaken he is."[39] Wearied to death of the incessant din in Congress and in his own Cabinet, Buchanan gradually lost whatever capacity he had to lay out a consistent plan of action and then follow it to the finish. He detested the southern disunionists and utterly repudiated any legal right to secession from the Union. In a major message to Congress on December 3, 1860, Buchanan warned the South that the Union was more than a "mere voluntary association of states" and could not be "annulled at the pleasure of any one of the contracting parties." Secession, he added, "is neither more nor less than revolution." But at the same time, he was inclined to excuse the secessionists on the grounds of abolitionist provocation; and anyway, he was certain that the Constitution gave him no authority as president to "coerce" seceding states back into the Union. As the weeks of his afflicted administration ran out, Buchanan sank further and further into political paralysis, desperately hoping that a crisis could be delayed long enough for him to retire gracefully and turn the government and its problems over to Lincoln.

Unfortunately for Buchanan, neither the newly triumphant Republicans in the North nor the secessionist fire-eaters in the South were willing to grant him a quiet exit. The Republicans, and especially Lincoln, refused to believe that southern secession meant anything more than all the other temper tantrums the South had thrown since the Missouri Compromise. Senator Henry Wilson of Massachusetts, in a speech to the Senate on January 25, 1861, heaped contempt on the secession threats as the "DISUNION FARCE," which was intended only to "startle and appall the timid, make the servility of the servile still more abject, [and] rouse the selfish instincts of nerveless conservatism." Lincoln himself was confidently predicting "that things have reached their worst point in the South, and they are likely to mend in the future." Part of Lincoln's peculiar confidence was due to his own overweening certainty that, as a born Kentuckian, he possessed a special insight and empathy with Southerners. Possessed with this insight, he was sure that Unionism was a far more powerful force in the long run than the apparently illogical rush to secession.[40] But Lincoln was not the only Republican floating on a bubble of confidence. "We shall keep the border states," predicted William H. Seward in February, "and in three months or thereabouts, if we hold off, the Unionists and Disunionists will have their hands on each other's throats in the cotton states." William S. Thayer, the assistant editor of the New York *Evening Post* was heartily assured that "the leading Republicans" were all convinced that "the seceders had no purpose of *remaining* out of the Union."[41] It was also clear to the Republicans that the southern threat of secession

[39]"Meeting of Congress," in *ibid.*, p. 293.

[40]Robert W. Johannsen, *Lincoln, the South, and Slavery: The Political Dimension* (Baton Rouge, 1991), pp. 58ff.

[41]Martin Crawford, "Politicians in Crisis: The Washington Letters of William S. Thayer, December 1860–March 1861," in *Civil War History* 27 (September 1981), p. 232.

gave them an important issue on which to rally northern public opinion, even while the threats of disunion divided hesitant Southerners.

Consequently, neither Lincoln nor the Republicans were going to be at all receptive when Buchanan pleaded for compromises to placate the secessionists and keep the Union together. In his December 3rd message to Congress, Buchanan had called upon Congress to work out a series of compromises that would take the wind out of the secession mongers' sails, including a constitutional convention to consider an amendment to protect slavery in the territories and the purchase of the Spanish colony of Cuba in order to admit it to the Union as a slave state. These proposals were hardly the sort to please either northern Democrats or Republicans, but they might have forced the secessionists to back down long enough to let the storm over Lincoln's election die down. Similarly, a constitutional convention might have been just the instrument to reawaken national interest and loyalty in the South. Congress grudgingly formed two committees, one each for the House and Senate, to discuss Buchanan's proposals for compromise, and by the end of December, the Senate committee was ready to put forth a compromise proposal that had been drafted by John J. Crittenden of Kentucky.

The Crittenden compromise actually called for not one but a series of constitutional amendments: 1) The old Missouri Compromise line of 36°30′ would be revived with slavery forbidden in any state or territory north of the line, and protected anywhere to the south; 2) slavery in the District of Columbia was to be protected from congressional regulation; 3) Congress would be prohibited from interfering in the interstate slave trade; and 4) Congress would compensate any slaveowner whose runaways were sheltered by local northern courts or antislavery measures. Crittenden seriously believed that his compromise could win popular support, and he even urged Congress to submit it to a national referendum. But Lincoln, who refused to believe that the secession threats were finally serious, would have none of it. "Entertain no proposition for a compromise in regard to the *extension* of slavery," Lincoln wrote to a Republican member of the compromise committee, "The instant you do, they have us under again. . . . The tug has to come & better now than later."[42] At Lincoln's cue, the Republicans in Congress gagged on Crittenden's guarantees for the extension of slavery into the territories, and on January 16th, they successfully killed it on the floor of the Senate in a narrow 25–23 vote. In all fairness to Buchanan, the compromise plan had not been a necessarily bad idea, in political terms; and in February, a mostly Democratic "peace convention," with delegates from twenty-one states and chaired by no one less than ex-president John Tyler, attempted to revive the Crittenden proposals. But Buchanan had lost the will and the political force that had enabled him to carry the Lecompton Constitution through an unwilling Congress in 1858, and so his efforts at compromise, sincere but half-hearted, died wordlessly on his own goal line.

But Republican intransigence was hardly Buchanan's only problem. Buchanan

[42]Lincoln, "To William Kellogg," in *Collected Works*, volume four, p. 150.

might have found secession a little more tolerable, or at least a little more ignorable, if the secessionists had not themselves kept pushing on what was, for Buchanan, a particularly touchy question of honor, and that was the disposition of federal property in the seceding states. The United States government owned and operated a mint in New Orleans, a network of post offices throughout the South, arsenals full of weapons, and nine forts. The secessionists solved the question of the mint, the post offices, and the arsenals themselves—since the employees of these federal outposts were all southern civilians the seceding states simply seized them and appropriated them for their own use before Buchanan or anyone else could have anything to say in the matter. But the forts were garrisoned and commanded by the United States Army. And unless the seceders were exceptionally bold (as at Fort Pulaski) or the federal officers exceptionally unreliable, the seceders would hesitate to risk an armed confrontation with the federal government, and so the forts were left alone. But in leaving them alone, the seceders only created trouble for themselves, since the continued presence of the federal government's authority in the forts only irritated and festered in the minds of the secessionists. And none of those forts produced more irritation than the three forts that sat quietly brooding over the harbor of Charleston, South Carolina.

Actually, only one of the Charleston forts, Fort Moultrie, was seriously occupied by the two artillery companies that comprised Charleston's federal garrison. Of the other two, Castle Pinckney was an obsolete relic of the 18th century, and Fort Sumter was an incomplete brick pentagon sitting on a man-made island of granite rubble beside the main ship channel. Under pressure from the southern members of his Cabinet, Buchanan would probably have been willing to negotiate with South Carolina over the future of the forts; and presumably to pave the way for those negotiations, the secretary of war, a prosecession Virginian named John B. Floyd, sent the Charleston garrison a slaveholding Kentucky major, Robert Anderson, as its new commander in November, 1860. Anderson's orders were to avoid provocations, carry out military business as usual, and make no changes in his dispositions unless he felt his garrison was actually threatened in some way. That, and a little time, would ensure that the Charleston forts could be turned over, either to Lincoln so that Buchanan could retire in peace, or to the South Carolinians without a messy confrontation.

But Anderson, even though he was a Southerner, was a regular army man whose first loyalty was to the honor of the United States. Anderson first surveyed the decaying ramparts of Fort Moultrie, sized up the growing numbers of armed South Carolina militia men keeping watch over Fort Moultrie, and then, six days after South Carolina uproariously adopted its secession ordinance, exercised the discretion granted him by his orders and changed his dispositions. Under cover of night, he evacuated his two companies from Moultrie and paddled them over to Sumter, where no one in Charleston had a hope of laying hands on him. "Outrageous breach of faith" was how South Carolina's governor, Francis Pickens, characterized Anderson's move. But the North hailed Anderson as a hero, a patriot who at last had the courage to defy the secession bluster. President Buchanan was angered by Anderson's move and was tempted to order Anderson back to Moultrie. But when it appeared that northern public opinion was solidly behind Anderson, Buchanan changed his mind and attempted to persuade the South Carolinians to accept Anderson's occupation of Fort Sumter as a legitimate exercise of federal authority. The South Carolina government, however, stopped its ears. Nothing would now satisfy their injured pride but the unconditional surrender of Sumter, and on January 9, 1861, when the steamer *Star of the West* entered Charleston habor with provisions for Sumter, South Carolina militia opened fire on it with several cannon and forced the ship to withdraw. Only Anderson's restraint in refusing to open fire himself on the South Carolinians kept civil war from breaking out at that moment. But from that time onward, Anderson took nothing further for granted. His eighty-five man force mounted a total of sixty powerful cannon inside the fort, and he brought the uncompleted fort as close to war readiness as possible.

Anderson's refusal to take the firing on the *Star of the West* as a signal to start firing himself on Charleston also made it possible for Buchanan to escape from the presidency without further incident. Lincoln formally assumed office from Buchanan on March 4, 1861, and in his inaugural address, he made it as clear as he could that he had no intention of backing down from Major Anderson. But, as Anderson himself informed Lincoln in a dispatch received on the evening of the inaugural, the real question was not whether the government would support Anderson, but whether Anderson could support himself. The new Confederate government had taken over control of the Charleston harbor defenses on March 1st, and had immediately cut Sumter off from local food supplies and begun erecting ominous batteries of cannon around the harbor perimeter. In his dispatch, Anderson warned the new president that he had only enough food for six weeks more in the fort, and at the end of that time, he would be compelled to surrender. What did Lincoln propose to do?

For three weeks, Lincoln weighed the alternatives before him. On the one hand, he could attempt to resupply Sumter; but with the example of the *Star of the West* before him, he knew that any such attempt would provoke a shooting match. That, in turn, could easily cause not only a full-fledged civil war but also a fresh round of secessions, this time in the upper South. On the other hand, Lincoln knew that he could order Sumter evacuated; but in that event, he knew that the credibility of his presidency and the Republican administration would be in pieces before either had scarcely begun. On March 29th, Lincoln decided—after polling his Cabinet for the second time on the question—to order a supply flotilla prepared and sent to Charleston, and sat back to await the unpleasant outcome. If the flotilla succeeded in resupplying Sumter, then federal authority in South Carolina had been preserved, and Charleston could do little short of war to change it; if it failed, the failure would be due to Charleston's decision to open fire, and the onus of beginning a civil war would lie on their heads. Clearly, Lincoln was not trying to provoke war; but it was also true that either way, Charleston lost, and Lincoln won, and years afterward people would become convinced that Lincoln had rigged it all deliberately to have a civil war begin that way.[43]

As it turned out the Confederates did not wait for the flotilla to arrive. Jefferson Davis and the Confederate cabinet in Montgomery learned of the Lincoln resupply mission on April 9th, and the next day, they ordered the Confederate commander in Charleston—a dashing French Louisianan named Pierre Gustave Toutant Beauregard—to demand Anderson's surrender, or else proceed to level the fort. Anderson rejected Beauregard's demand, and at 4:30 AM on April 12, 1861, the Confederate batteries ringing Charleston harbor opened fire on Anderson's pitiful little garrison. For thirty-four hours, Anderson's two companies fought back until their ammunition was exhausted and the interior of the fort was hopelessly ablaze. On April 14th, Anderson lowered his flag and marched out of the battered fort, remarkably without having lost a single man of his garrison during the shelling.

It would prove to be the last such bloodless fight for the next four years.

Further Reading

No other single figure in American history has generated so much biography and analysis as Abraham Lincoln. The most famous and durable single-volume biography of Abraham Lincoln is Benjamin P. Thomas's classic *Abraham Lincoln* (New York, 1952), although Stephen B. Oates's controversial *With Malice Toward None: The Life of Abraham Lincoln* (New York, 1977), Oscar and Lillian Handlin's brief *Abraham Lincoln and the Union* (Boston, 1980) and Mark E. Neely, Jr.'s *The Last Best Hope of Earth: Abraham Lincoln and the Promise of America* (Cambridge, MA, 1993) make for delightful and unexpectedly insightful reading. But for those who thirst after every detail, only Mark E. Neely, Jr.'s, fascinating *The Abraham Lincoln Encyclopedia* (New York, 1982) and Earl Schenck Miers's *Lincoln Day-by-Day: A Chronology* (three volumes, Washington, 1960) will suffice.

Among the most useful specific studies of Lincoln in the 1840s and 1850s, Gabor Boritt's *Lincoln and the Economics of the American Dream* (Memphis, TN, 1978) creates an indispensable context for understanding Lincoln's ceaseless drive for "the chance to rise." Don W. Fehrenbacher, the author of a study of Lincoln in the 1850s I have noted elsewhere, offers some finely crafted analyses of Lincoln in *Lincoln in Text and Context: Collected Essays* (New York, 1987). Donald W. Riddle's *Congressman Abraham Lincoln* (Urbana, IL, 1957), examines Lincoln's single term as a member of Congress, while P. M. Zall's collection of humor by and about Lincoln, *Abe Lincoln Laughing: Humorous Anecdotes from Original Sources by and about Abraham Lincoln* (Berkeley, CA, 1982), presents the Lincoln which, perhaps unfortunately, may be the most familiar to most Americans. The finest study of the Lincoln-Douglas debates remains Harry V. Jaffa's *Crisis of the House Divided: An Interpretation of the Issues in the Lincoln-Douglas Debates* (New York, 1959), a book which, for all its brilliant insight, has remained strangely neglected. Lincoln's well-known melancholia has invited a

---

[43]David M. Potter, *Lincoln and His Party in the Secession Crisis* (New Haven, CT, 1942), pp. 373–375.

number of attempts at "psychobiography," and although I have serious reservations about putting Lincoln on Freud's couch (one has only to look up what Freud himself did to Woodrow Wilson to understand why), there is still much to be stimulated by—and provoked by—in Dwight Anderson, *Abraham Lincoln: The Quest for Immortality* (New York, 1982), Charles B. Strozier, *Lincoln's Quest for Union: Public and Private Meanings* (New York, 1982), and most radical of them all, George B. Forgie, *Patricide in the House Divided: A Psychological Interpretation of Lincoln and His Age* (New York, 1979).

Mary Todd Lincoln suffered as much as any other woman in the 19th century in the loss of her husband and three of her four sons, but she suffered even more at the hands of Lincoln biographers and memoirists who remembered her only as a shrew who weighed Lincoln down with needless care and grief. Her biographers have rallied loyally to her cause, however, and Jean Baker's *Mary Todd Lincoln: A Biography* (New York, 1987) offers a sympathetic reading of Mary Lincoln's life, edged with insights into 19th-century women's history. On the other hand, Mark Neely, Jr., and Gerald McMurtry have returned a serious consideration of Mary Lincoln's mental stability to front stage with *The Insanity File: The Case of Mary Todd Lincoln* (Urbana, IL, 1986). And Lincoln's male associates offer an overwhelmingly negative view of Mary Todd Lincoln in their memoirs, some of which can be sampled in Ward Hill Lamon's *Recollections of Abraham Lincoln, 1847–1865* (Chicago, 1865), in John Hay's diaries, as condensed to a single-volume anthology in *Lincoln and the Civil War in the Diaries and Letters of John Hay*, Tyler Bennet, ed. (1939; rept. Westport, CT, 1972), and the rich treasure-trove of Lincoln personalia in William Herndon's papers and letters to his collaborator, Jesse Weik, in *The Hidden Lincoln, From the Letters and Papers of William H. Herndon*, Emanuel Hertz, ed. (New York, 1938). Although aspects of Herndon's recollections have been questioned over the years, several recent publications, including Douglas L. Wilson on "Abraham Lincoln, Ann Rutledge, and the Evidence of Herndon's Informants," in *Civil War History* 36 (December 1990), "Abraham Lincoln and 'that fatal first of January' " in *Civil War History* 38 (June 1992), and John E. Walsh, *The Shadows Rise: Abraham Lincoln and the Ann Rutledge Legend* (Urbana, IL, 1993), help to reposition Herndon as a reliable source on Lincoln's personal life.

In 1984, the Gettysburg College Civil War Institute sponsored a 175th-birthday conference on Lincoln that brought together a broad cross-section of Lincoln scholars to sum up the frontiers of Lincoln interpretation at that time; their essays were collected and published, with commentaries, by Gabor Boritt, the Institute's director, as *The Historian's Lincoln: Pseudohistory, Psychohistory, and History* (Urbana, IL, 1988). Boritt's collection, when taken together with John L. Thomas's collection of essays by major scholars of Lincoln's politics, *Abraham Lincoln and the American Political Tradition* (New York, 1986), offers an excellent summation of modern Lincoln research.

The preeminent survey of the national agony that stretched from Lecompton to Sumter remains Allan Nevins's two volumes, *The Emergence of Lincoln: Douglas, Buchanan, and Party Chaos, 1857–1859* (New York, 1950) and *The Emergence of Lincoln: Prologue to Civil War, 1859–1861* (New York, 1950), which should be read alongside David Potter's elegant and eloquent *The Impending Crisis*. Potter's earlier work on *The South and the Sectional Conflict* (Baton Rouge, 1968) and a still earlier book on *Lincoln and His Party in the Secession Crisis* (New Haven, 1942) are rich in detail and emotional engagement with the four years immediately preceding Fort Sumter, as is Kenneth M. Stampp's *And the War Came: The North and the Sectional Crisis, 1860–1861* (Baton Rouge, 1970). William and Bruce Catton, *Two Roads to*

Sumter (New York, 1963) use the lives of Lincoln and Jefferson Davis to produce a supple and fascinating narrative of the sectional collision.

For specific studies of individuals and institutions, Roy F. Nichols's *The Disruption of the American Democracy* (New York, 1948) is elderly but still useful. The secession crisis itself is best treated in William L. Barney, *The Secessionist Impulse: Alabama and Mississippi in 1860* (Princeton, 1974), Steven A. Channing, *The Crisis of Fear: Secession in South Carolina* (New York, 1970), and Michael P. Johnson, *Toward a Patriarchal Republic: The Secession of Georgia* (Baton Rouge, 1977). The events surrounding the attack on Fort Sumter are thrillingly recounted in William A. Swanberg's *First Blood: The Story of Fort Sumter* (New York, 1957). Richard N. Current's *Lincoln and the First Shot* (Philadelphia, 1963) and Roy Meredith, *Storm Over Sumter: The Opening Engagement of the Civil War* (New York, 1957) also offer evenly balanced accounts of the "opening shot."

CHAPTER 4

Sullen Hymns
of Defeat

The East: 1861–1862

On the "most exquisite morning" of April 15, 1861, Sarah Butler Wister rose early to take a bundle of letters to the post office near her home in the Philadelphia suburb of Germantown. To her annoyance, she found that the newspaper had been stolen from her front door. But then, she and her husband, Dr. Owen Jones Wister, soon found that they needed no newspapers to learn what was happening in the world. "All the world was awake & alive with the news that Ft. Sumter has surrendered," she confided to her diary.

The news of the fall of Fort Sumter set off a string of contradictory emotions in Sarah Butler Wister. Her father was Pierce Butler, a Georgia planter and Democratic politician, and the mail that morning contained a letter from her father describing a guided tour he had received of the Charleston harbor batteries by "Gen. Beauregard & other officers." Her mother, however, was the celebrated English Shakespearean actress Fanny Kemble, who had married Pierce Butler in 1834 and lived to regret it. The life she led on the Butler plantation was miserable beyond description, and the lot of the Butler family slaves even more miserable. Divorcing Butler, Kemble left for Lenox, Massachusetts, in 1845, and would later publish a *Journal of a Residence on a Georgia Plantation*, which painted slavery in its vilest colors. Sarah Butler had been born in 1835 in Philadelphia (Pierce Butler had inherited land in both Philadelphia and Georgia from two different sides of his family) and married Owen Jones Wister there in 1859. Her opinions on slavery flowed all in her mother's direction.

Both the weather and the news turned darker through the day. "The latter part of the day was gloomy and forbidding," and she heard rumors of "thousands . . . furious at the news of the surrender," marching in the streets of Philadelphia "& swearing revenge on all disunionists or disaffected." Robert Tyler, the son of former president John Tyler, "literally fled before them" and the crowd "visited the houses,

102

stores & offices of" Southerners who had made themselves "especially odious in the last few days." The mob was in the streets again the next day ("oh how thankful I am for Father's absence") and had to be pacified by speeches and threats from Mayor Alexander Henry. Not that Sarah Wister really minded them: "they were the most moderate, mannerly mob ever heard of." At the same time, though, she saw in their faces (when she went out to buy "radishes in the market") that "they were in the utmost state of excitement & the least thing would have fired them, & then riots must have followed." Mixed snow and rain fell the next day, but "flags large & small flaunt from every building, the dry-goods shops have red, white & blue materials draped together in their windows, in the ribbon stores the national colors hang in long streamers, and even the book sellers place the red, white, and blue bindings together."

On the day following, "our newspaper" was "stolen from the door step again. . . ."[1]

Fifteen miles away, in rural Chester County, the news of the fall of Fort Sumter came over the telegraph wire to West Chester, the county seat, on Sunday evening, April 14th. The next morning, the national flag was flying everywhere through the town. Across Chester County, in Upper Uwchlan township, an immense Stars and Stripes was hoisted up an 80-foot pole in front of the local tavern, and in the evening the county courthouse was thrown open for a mass Union rally.[2] Far to the north, at Maine's Bowdoin College, a professor and former pupil of Calvin Stowe who had once sat in the Stowe parlor listening to Harriet Beecher Stowe read drafts of *Uncle Tom's Cabin* was seized with anger that "the flag of the Nation had been insulted." His name was Joshua Lawrence Chamberlain, and an "irresistible impulse" came over him to abandon the teaching of rhetoric at Bowdoin and join the army to become God's minister "in a higher sense than the word."[3]

To the west, the news of the first shot fell on the Ohio legislature when "a senator came in from the lobby in an excited way" and cried out, " 'The telegraph announces that the secessionists are bombarding Fort Sumter!' " There was a sick moment of silence, and then "a woman's shrill voice" called out from the gallery, " 'Glory to God!' " It was the voice of Abby Kelly, the veteran abolitionist for whose sake William Lloyd Garrison had broken up the American Anti-Slavery Society two decades before. Kelley had come to believe, with John Brown, that "only through blood" could the freedom of the slaves be won, and now the redeeming blood of the abolition martyrs could begin to flow. The next day, the news of the Anderson's surrender came over the wires, and "the flag—*The Flag*—flew out to

[1]"Sarah Butler Wister's Civil War Diary," Fanny Kemble Wister, ed., in *Pennsylvania Magazine of History and Biography* 102 (July 1978), pp. 271–277.

[2]Douglas R. Harper, *"If Thee Must Fight"*: A Civil War History of Chester County, Pennsylvania (West Chester, PA, 1990), p. 18.

[3]Alice Rains Trulock, *In The Hands of Providence: Joshua L. Chamberlain and the American Civil War* (Chapel Hill, NC, 1992), pp. 60–61.

the wind from every housetop in our great cities." Ohio Judge Thomas Key stopped state senator Jacob Dolson Cox in the Ohio senate hall: "Mr. Cox, the people have gone stark mad!" Cox, a staunch antislavery Whig-turned-Republican (and the son-in-law of the antislavery evangelist, Charles Grandison Finney) replied, "I knew they would if a blow were struck against the flag."[4]

Six hundred miles to the south, the English newspaperman and war correspondent William Howard Russell had gone to church on Sunday morning, April 14th, in a small Episcopal parish in Norfolk, Virginia. "The clergyman or minister had got to the Psalms" when a man slipped into the back of the church and began whispering excitedly to the first people he could speak to. The whispering rose in volume, while some of the people at the back "were stealing on tiptoe out of the church." The minister doggedly plunged on through the Psalter, and the people gradually began to heave themselves up and walk out, until at length, Russell "followed the example" and left the minister to finish the Psalter on his own. Outside in the street, Russell found a crowd running through the street. "Come along, the telegraph's in at the Day Book. The Yankees are whipped!" Russell was told. "At all the street corners men were discussing the news with every symptom of joy and gratification."[5] Further south, in what was now the Confederate States of America, the Confederate president, Jefferson Davis, received a telegram from Pierre Beauregard at 2:00 P.M. on the afternoon of April 13th, informing Davis, "White flag up. Have sent a boat to receive surrender." Davis wired back his congratulations, and lamely added, "If occasion offers, tender my friendly remembrance to Major Anderson." He went to bed, gloomy with the foreboding that Lincoln and the North would soon retaliate. Davis had never been able to make his fellow-Southerners understand that secession would mean war with the northern states, and a long war at that. "You overrate the risk of war," the governor of Mississippi had assured Davis. "I only wish I did," Davis replied.

Outside, in the streets of Montgomery, Alabama, the crowds cheered and cheered.[6]

1. War of the Thousand-Colored Uniforms

The bombardment and seizure of Fort Sumter was an act of aggression that no one, least of all President Lincoln, could afford to ignore. What the Confederate forces had done in Charleston harbor was, technically speaking, nothing different from John Brown's assault on the Harpers Ferry arsenal. It destroyed at one stroke all real hope for negotiation or compromise, and left it up to Lincoln to demonstrate

[4]Cox, "War Preparations in the North," in *Battles and Leaders of the Civil War*, R. U. Johnson and C. C. Buel, eds. (1887; New York, 1956), vol. 1, pp. 85–86.

[5]Russell, *My Diary North and South*, Fletcher Pratt, ed. (New York, 1954), pp. 49–51.

[6]William C. Davis, *Jefferson Davis: The Man and His Hour* (New York, 1991), p. 325.

whether or not the federal government was prepared to back up its denial of the right to secession with force. Long ago, in 1856, Lincoln had warned the Democrats that a Republican administration would not allow the Union to be dissolved, and "if you attempt it, *we won't let you.*" But at the same time he dismissed all serious talk of secession as "humbug—nothing but folly." Now the talk had turned into iron reality.

But what means did Lincoln have at his disposal to suppress the Confederate rebellion? The United States Army consisted of only ten regiments of infantry, four of artillery, and five of cavalry (including dragoons and mounted riflemen)—in all, that worked out to 1,105 commissioned officers, a number of whom were Southerners from the seceded states, and 15,259 enlisted men. Furthermore, few of the regiments were together in one place, almost all of them having been broken up piecemeal to garrison forts in the West or along the borders. Three-quarters of the army's artillery had been scrapped at the close of the Mexican-American War. No force of such tiny peacetime proportions was likely to bring the secessionists easily to heel. What was worse, Congress was at that moment out of session, and without congressional sanction, Lincoln lacked presidential authority to raise a national army. Unlike the Senate, the representatives in the House were still elected in 1860 on a staggered schedule that varied from state to state, and the new Congress did not usually expect to fully assemble itself after an election year until December of the following year—which, in this case, meant December of 1861. At the very best, even with speeding up some state elections, there was little hope of getting the new Congress together before July.

Lincoln did have one other recourse for recruiting soldiers, and that was an antique 1795 militia bill that had originally given President Washington the authority to call up the militia of the various states in the event of insurrection. So, on April 15th, two days after the fall of Fort Sumter, Lincoln issued a proclamation declaring the Confederate states in rebellion and calling for the states of the Union to provide the federal government with 75,000 volunteers for three months. Although Congress approved the expansion of the regular army by 23,000 men when it finally assembled for an emergency session in July, Lincoln's call for the states to supply volunteers for the war remained the chief mechanism by which the federal government would recruit the armies it needed to fight the Confederates, and when Congress did finally meet in July, it authorized the enlistment of a further 1 million three-year volunteers.

This created a parallel system in the federal army, in which the Union forces would be composed of two kinds of military organizations. First, at the core of the army would be the old regular army regiments, which enlisted men directly into the federal service and which were known simply by their regimental numbers (for example, First United States Infantry, Fifth United States Cavalry). Second, rising into existence at the call of the various state governments would be the volunteer regiments, which were recruited by the states, marched under state-appointed officers carrying their state flag as well as the Stars and Stripes, and were identified by their state regimental number (for example, 83rd Pennsylvania Volunteer Infantry, 1st Minnesota Volunteers, 20th Maine Volunteers, 19th Massachusetts Volunteers). This system might have been more confusing had it not been for the fact that the regular army regiments never numbered more than a handful compared to the vast outpouring of volunteer recruits (Pennsylvania alone raised 215 volunteer infantry regiments during the course of the war), and for the fact that the volunteer regiments were organized and generaled by federal officers. But at the beginning of the war, it caused no end of chaos. State volunteer regiments often chose their own uniforms and weapons, elected their own noncommissioned and company officers, and generally behaved little better than a mob of hunters at a turkey-shoot. Regiments like the 79th New York arrived in Washington garbed in Highland kilts; the 72nd Pennsylvania copied from the daring French-Algerian colonial troops known as "Zouaves" the dashing Zouave uniform, complete with baggy red trousers, a cutaway monkey-jacket, and a red fez and turban; the 3rd Maine reported for duty in uniforms of gray. Regimental drill often had to wait until the newly elected officers could learn, from a variety of popular handbooks or from the presence of a few old Regulars, how to give the necessary orders.

Nevertheless, the volunteers were all that Lincoln at first thought he might need, for he was sure that a show of resolute determination on the part of the federal government in raising an army would be all that was necessary to prick the secession bubble. Still confident that southern Unionism would reassert itself, Lincoln "questioned whether there is, to-day, a majority of the legally qualified voters of any State, except perhaps South Carolina, in favor of disunion." At least, he added weakly, "the contrary has not been demonstrated in any one of them." Only let the federal government show its resolve, and the rebellion would collapse before a rebirth of Union loyalty.[7] In fact, almost the exact opposite happened. Virginia had called a state convention soon after Lincoln's election to consider secession. The convention met on February 13, 1861, but debate on a secession ordinance dragged on for a month and a half before it was finally put to a vote on April 4, when it was lost, 88 to 45. The upper South, and especially Virginia, was not willing to go following the will-o-the-wisp of secession, especially when it was led by the hotheads of South Carolina. But Lincoln's call for volunteers put an entirely different complexion on affairs. Virginia would not fight the Union for South Carolina, but it would not join with the rest of the Union in suppressing its fellow Southerners and denying the principle of secession. Forced by Lincoln's proclamation to choose which master it would serve, the Virginia convention reversed itself and voted to secede on April 17th. Three days later, the commandant of the federal navy yard at Norfolk evacuated the yard and burned nine of the ships laid up there to keep them from falling into rebel hands.

Similar reactions set in across the upper South. In Maryland, a secessionist mob stoned the men of the 6th Massachusetts on April 19th as they changed trains

[7]Lincoln, "Message to Congress in Special Session" [July 4, 1861], in *Collected Works*, vol. 4, p. 437.

in Baltimore, en route to Washington; the panicky volunteers responded by open-ing fire, killing or wounding over two dozen civilians. Maryland secessionists had been haranguing Maryland Governor Thomas Hicks for a special session of the state legislature, but Hicks had so far stubbornly refused to yield to them. The Baltimore shootings momentarily unsettled Hicks: he agreed to call the special session and frantically advised Lincoln to call in the British ambassador as a "mediator between the contending parties of our Country." But Hicks soon recovered his Unionist composure and designated the rural town of Frederick as the meeting place for the legislative session, rather than in the agitated atmosphere of the state capital at Annapolis. In the peace and detachment of Frederick, Hicks was able to keep the legislature from bolting down the secession path; in the fall, a new Unionist governor was successfully elected and Hicks was sent to Washington by the legisla-ture as Maryland's new U.S. senator.[8] However, on May 7th, the Tennessee legisla-ture followed the example of Virginia rather than Maryland and voted to join the Confederacy without even bothering to call a special convention into being; the Arkansas state convention passed a secession ordinance on the same day; and on May 20th, North Carolina also seceded. Eventually, Tennessee, Arkansas, Vir-ginia, and North Carolina each joined the Confederacy, and in order to cement Virginia's loyalty to the new southern republic, the Confederate government chose to move its capital from Montgomery to the Virginia capital of Richmond, only 100 miles south of Washington. Lincoln could now look out of the White House windows and see the new Confederate flag waving naughtily from housetops across the Potomac in Alexandria.

No less cheering were the deliberations Lincoln faced about what to do with his new army of volunteers. Lincoln's choice for secretary of war was a political hack from Pennsylvania, Simon Cameron, who quickly proved utterly inadequate to the task of managing a wartime army. But even if Lincoln had appointed a professional soldier to the post, the results might not have been much better. Among the small cadre of professional American army officers, few possessed any real schooling in advanced strategic thinking beyond the basic military education handed out to all regular army officers at West Point. And while that education was remarkably good in many respects, the dispersion of the regular army all over the frontier meant that virtually none of those officers acquired much practical experience in commanding large military formations. Jacob Dolson Cox was appalled to find that the regular army officers whom he met knew little, read little in military science, and were woefully unprepared for the actual conduct of a war. But when Cox complained to one regular whom he knew, the common-sense reply he got was: "What could you expect of men who have had to spend their lives at a two-company post, where there was nothing to do when off duty but play draw-poker and drink whiskey at the sutler's shop?" The result, as Cox could see, was that the regular army was almost useless for the war that was now breaking out, or at least not much more useful than

[8]William Hesseltine, *Lincoln and the War Governors* (New York, 1948), pp. 154–156.

the host of amateur military and militia units across the country. The regulars' "advantage over equally well-educated civilians is reduced to a practical knowledge of the duties of the company and the petty post," complained Cox, "and in comparison with the officers of well-drilled militia companies, it amounted to little more than a better knowledge of the army regulations and the administrative process."[9]

As it was, the strategic wisdom in the regular army was divided between two conflicting schools of military thought. At the head of one of these schools stood the figure of Napoleon, or at least Napoleon as interpreted by one of the more popular of Napoleon's former officers, Antoine Henry Jomini. French military theory, as a legacy of the Napoleonic wars, was considered the most advanced in the world, and a 100-page excerpt of Jomini's *Treatise on Grand Military Operations* was mandatory reading at West Point until 1832. Jomini believed in the virtue of the military offensive: The general who wanted a truly decisive victory (like those of Napoleon) must take the war to the enemy by cutting the enemy's communications, turning the flanks of his armies, or, if all else failed, making a concentrated frontal assault on the enemy's defenses. Jomini acknowledged that the offensive was more costly in lives in the short run. But since it was more likely to achieve a decisive result more quickly, more lives would be saved in the long run.[10] And in Europe, almost all the tactical experience of the major national armies seemed to bear Jomini out. From the French at Solferino in 1859 to the Franco-Prussian War in 1871, it was the army of the offense that won European battles, and at lightning speed. This was enough to convince many prewar American officers, and as a result, the reigning American tactics handbooks—like Winfield Scott's *Infantry Tactics* (1835) and William J. Hardee's *Rifle and Light Infantry Tactics* (1855)— borrowed heavily from Napoleonic sources and stressed the virtue of quick, aggressive offensive movements on the battlefield. And Scott himself had put the offensive to the practical test in the Mexican-American War by driving an outnumbered American army straight through the gates of Mexico City on the momentum of a Napoleonic-style campaign.[11]

But beside the example of Scott's campaign operations in Mexico was the practical example of Zachary Taylor's field tactics in Buena Vista, where Taylor stood his army on the defensive and allowed Santa Anna to bleed his Mexican army to death in repeated assaults on Taylor's position. In fact, most of the great victories in American military history had been defensive ones, with Andrew Jackson's crushing defeat of the British at New Orleans in 1815 being the most famous and the most politically potent example. The politics of the defensive, whether on the level of grand strategy or of battlefield tactics, may have been more important to Americans than the real military value of the defensive, since the American repub-

[9]Jacob Dolson Cox, *Military Reminiscences of the Civil War* (New York, 1900), vol. 1, pp. 175, 187–188.
[10]Herman Hattaway and Archer Jones, *How the North Won: A Military History of the Civil War* (Urbana, IL, 1983), pp. 12–13.
[11]Paddy Griffith, *Battle Tactics of the Civil War* (New Haven, CT, 1989), pp. 99–111.

lic retained a horror of supporting a large professional army (not only did a professional army remind Americans of British occupation during the Revolution, but a
standing army represented the principle of power, the eternal enemy of republican
liberty, and required heavy taxation to maintain). American armies were more
likely to be made up of civilian volunteers and state militia, and it was easier and
safer to put nonprofessional soldiers of that sort on the defensive, rather than
risking them on the offensive where discipline, coordination, and mobility had to
be of the highest order.

This preference for a strategic defensive posture in American wars was reinforced by the fact that West Point, the American military academy, was organized
and run by the Army Corps of Engineers, so that the education given to officers
there was naturally inclined toward such defensive studies as fortification and
military engineering. Then, in 1832, a young meteor named Denis Hart Mahan was
promoted to the professorship of civil and military engineering at West Point, and
he soon succeeded, through his classroom teaching and his publications, in persuading the new officers of the federal army that the Napoleonic lust for the offensive
had to be qualified by a realistic appreciation for the risks that the offensive might
run. Like Jomini, Mahan encouraged future generals to maneuver—but not, like
Jomini, in order to gain advantage for an attack. Instead, fully aware that American
armies were bound to the use of militia and volunteers, the principal object in
Mahan's teaching was to seize and occupy enemy territory, and eventually force the
enemy to launch an attack on one's own defensive fortifications. That required
intensive training in the construction of major fortifications, and instruction in the
creation of temporary fieldworks on the battlefield, and that was what Mahan and
West Point offered. The result was, as Jacob Dolson Cox remembered, that "the
intellectual education at the Military Academy was essentially the same . . . as that
of any polythechnic school, the peculiarly military part of it being in the line of
engineering." Mahan took an academy that had been designed mostly for the
defensive protection of American territory through the construction and garrison of
fortification, and a military tradition shaped by political mandates from Congress to
favor a defensive mission, and raised the art of defense to an American science.[12]
The American regular army officer in 1861 was thus presented with a series of
contradictions: tactics books that encouraged officers to take the offensive and
make the enemy's army their objective, and a professional military culture that
looked to occupy enemy territory and fight defensive war from behind fortifications.

In addition to these theoretical concepts, the officer of the Civil War era would
also have had to come to terms with two new considerations. The first of these was
supplies. From the Napoleonic wars at the turn of the century until the Crimean
War in the 1850s, the size of modern armies had mushroomed from the 5,000–
6000-man forces that served under George Washington to mammoth field armies of

[12]Cox, *Military Reminiscences*, vol. 1, p. 179; Edward Hagerman, *The American Civil War and The Origins of Modern Warfare: Ideas, Organization, and Field Command* (Bloomington, IN, 1988), pp. 4–13.

between 60,000 and 70,000 men, which in turn required equally mammoth numbers of animals (horses and mules) for transportation and, in the case of mounted infantry and cavalry, for combat operations. Keeping both the human and animal forces fed and equipped was an increasingly difficult task, and probably would have been impossible had it not been for the development of railroad technology. But at the same time, the increasing value of supply lines and railroads meant that more attention had to be paid to protecting those lines. Strategically, that meant that a general ought only to take his army along roads, rivers, or rail lines where his supply cord could not be cut, and ought to use the vulnerability of his enemy's supply lines to force him to surrender territory and advantage.

Linked to the problem of supply was the concept of *lines of operations*. No matter how different in size two armies might be, the only thing that mattered was the size of the force each army could bring to a battlefield at a given moment (that is, even an army numerically inferior to its opponent can still achieve victory if it can manage to pick off small sections of the enemy army and defeat them piece-by-piece). Consequently, Denis Mahan impressed on his West Point pupils the vital importance of operating defensively on "interior lines" and forcing the enemy to operate on "exterior lines." What this means is that in any given strategic situation, an army occupying the interior of a position only has to move the chord of the arc surrounding that position to get from one end of it to the other; a general on the exterior of a position has to occupy as well as move around the circumference of the arc, which forces him to spread his troops more thinly to cover the greater distance and take more time in moving from point to point along the arc. By taking up "interior lines," a numerically inferior army could defend itself more easily, and could move to strike at exposed positions along the enemy's arc faster than the enemy could reinforce them. For an attacking army, the best way to overcome the advantage of interior lines was to outflank the enemy's lines entirely by means of *turning movements*. Hence, Civil War battles often found themselves determined by how successful one army was at getting hold of the other's flank and compelling a withdrawal, rather than by head-to-head attacks.[13] On the other hand, turning movements were frequently stymied by a physical problem that never bothered Napoleon, and that was the thickly wooded terrain of North America. Napoleon could fight Wellington across a series of neatly swept and tended farms, but battle in the American Civil War had to deal with the fact that much of the American landscape was tangled, heavily forested, and poorly mapped. Many a clever turning movement floundered off into nowhere, slowed or lost by the inaccessibility of woods and roads and rivers.

All of these lessons were very much in the mind of the man to whom Lincoln eventually turned for military direction and advice, the senior commanding general of the United States Army, who in this case turned out to be the apostle of the American offensive, Major General Winfield Scott. Unfortunately for Lincoln,

[13]Hattaway and Jones, *How the North Won*, pp. 12–17.

Scott in 1861 was seventy-five years old and too badly crippled by gout to mount a horse, much less to think of taking active command in the field. Scott also had little faith in the military capacities of the volunteers Lincoln was calling for, and when he began organizing the state and federal forces along the Ohio and Potomac Rivers, he generally handed out department commands to former or serving protégés from the regular army: the Department of Missouri went to Major General Henry Wager Halleck, a bookish but extremely competent soldier; the Department of the Cumberland was placed under Major General Don Carlos Buell; and the Department of the Ohio was given to a new brigadier general of Ohio volunteers named George Brinton McClellan, who had resigned his commission in the U.S. Army in 1857 to become chief engineer and vice-president of the Illinois Central Railroad.

Although Scott's campaign in Mexico was the very model of the Jominian offensive, Scott's army in Mexico had enjoyed a much higher ratio of regulars to volunteers than the army Lincoln was calling into being, and Scott did not mind telling people how dubious he was about the quality of the volunteers. "Our militia & volunteers, if a tenth of what is said be true, have committed atrocities—horrors—in Mexico, sufficient to make Heaven weep, & every American, of Christian morals *blush* for his country," Scott wrote to the secretary of war in 1847. "Most atrocities are always committed in the absence of regulars, but sometimes in the presence of acquiescing, trembling volunteer officers."[14] Scott's doubts about the reliability of an army of volunteers had not diminished since Mexico, and without a large stiffening of regulars, Scott wanted to take as few risks with the volunteer soldier as possible. Instead of proposing direct action against the Confederates, Scott suggested to Lincoln what derisively became known as the "Anaconda Plan" (so named for the huge snake that squeezes to death its prey), the first comprehensive strategic military plan in the nation's history. First, Scott proposed to use the federal navy to blockade the entire length of the southern coasts; he would then establish a strong defensive cordon across the northern borders of the Confederacy; and last, he would mount a joint expedition of some 80,000 troops, plus gunboats, to move down the Mississippi and secure the entire length of the river from the southern tip of Illinois to the Gulf of Mexico. In effect, Scott was recognizing that the Confederacy occupied its own set of interior lines that a motley army of federal volunteers would be unwise to attack; consequently, the best way to bring the Confederacy to its knees would be to turn its flank (down the Mississippi) and sever its supply lines to the outside world (with the naval blockade). With the Confederacy encircled and squeezed by land and sea, Scott believed that it would only be a matter of time before secessionist fervor would pale (and Scott was a Virginian who might have been presumed to know), and southern Unionists would be able to seize control of their state governments again.

Scott's cautious approach to waging war, however, was overwhelmed in the

[14]Mark E. Neely, Jr., *The Fate of Liberty: Abraham Lincoln and Civil Liberties* (New York, 1991), p. 40.

outpouring of aggressive chest-thumping from Congress and the northern newspapers, which were already demanding that an immediate offensive on Richmond be mounted. Even Lincoln was anxious that some kind of demonstration be made in western Virginia and eastern Tennessee, where he believed that southern Unionists would happily rally to the old flag. Scott reluctantly authorized the 35,000 volunteers who encamped around Washington to prepare for an offensive into Virginia, and put the operation under the command of one of his old Mexican War staff officers, Irvin McDowell.

Scott made the appointment with tight-lipped foreboding: McDowell had only the barest combat experience, and had been jumped to the rank of brigadier general from a desk job in the adjutant general's office. Across the Potomac, and across the Ohio, the Confederate forces were enduring similar confusions. The Confederacy had as one advantage the fact that its president, Jefferson Davis, was a West Point graduate, had served in the Mexican War, and had put in a term under Franklin Pierce as secretary of war. As such Davis had the immediate advantage of being a military man with substantial military experience. In addition to Davis, 296 southern officers serving in the United States Army (almost a quarter of the federal officer corps) resigned their commissions and returned south to offer their services to their respective state governments. Although a few Southerners remained with the federal army, most of them did not, including the one officer whom Winfield Scott had set his heart upon as a possible successor as commander in chief of the federal army, Robert E. Lee, and the most admired and widely respected soldier in the U.S. Army, Albert Sidney Johnston.

Apart from these advantages, the Confederacy encountered the same organizational problems, and worse, as the federal army. The Confederate constitution permitted the Confederate congress to raise and maintain armies, but the precise provisions of the constitution made it clear that the Confederate government was expected to use the state militia as it existed rather than organizing a regular army of its own. Hence, the Confederacy created its "Provisional Army of the Confederate States" mostly by appeal to the states to supply regiments of state volunteers. Only the general organization of these forces and the commission of general officers was kept in the hands of the Confederate government. Unlike the federal volunteers, who were initially enlisted for only three months, the Confederate volunteers were enlisted for a full year (Jefferson Davis would have preferred to enlist all Confederate volunteers for the duration of the war, but in 1861, there was no hope of talking the Confederate congress into such a measure). Arming and equipping the new provisional army was another matter. In terms of men, money, and resources, the Confederacy was dwarfed by the North. The military-age male population of the southern states was outnumbered 3 to 1 by the North, and the Confederate government was so lacking in the means to uniform and arm its new recruits that Confederate soldiers turned out in even more different varieties, styles, and colors of uniforms than their federal counterparts. Alabama volunteers were issued dark blue frock coats and gray pants on March, 1861; the 5th Georgia wore so many different styles of uniform (including a regulation navy-blue U.S. Army frock coat) that they were mocked as the "Pound-Cake Regiment," while the 3rd Georgia featured a mix of red jackets and blue pants; the Louisiana "Tigers" sported jackets of russet brown, and so many Louisiana volunteers were issued blue uniforms in 1861 that the Louisianans were forced to wear red armbands to avoid being mistaken for federal troops.[15] Feeding the new Confederate army was an even greater problem for the state and Confederate commissaries. Private George Asbury Bruton of the 19th Louisiana found that "the first few days that we were here" at Camp Moore, Louisiana, "they fed us well," but within a few weeks the Confederate supply system broke down, and "now they feed us on old poor beef and Cast Iron pies."[16]

The greatest problem, however, was not a shortage of material, but a shortage of the means for moving it where it was needed. The Confederate states had less than one-third the total railroad mileage of the northern states. Only two complete railroad systems connected Richmond with the Mississippi River. One of these was the Memphis & Charleston, which originated in Memphis, picked up connector lines through Chattanooga and up the Piedmont to the Orange & Alexandria Railroad, and then made its way to Richmond over the Richmond & Danville Railroad. The other major lateral rail line, the Memphis & Ohio, connected Memphis with Bowling Green and Louisville, and then hooked onto two other connector lines to arrive in Chattanooga; but since Kentucky remained undecided about joining the Confederacy, the usefulness of the Memphis & Ohio was in some question. Nor was there much likelihood that new railroad systems could now be built, since the southern states possessed few iron foundries capable of rolling iron for rails.

There was, however, a silver lining to these logistical clouds. The South's shortages of manpower and military material dictated that the Confederacy adopt a basically defensive posture. But taking the strategic defensive would allow the Confederacy to operate along interior lines. The broad heartland of the Confederate states would give the southern armies room enough to draw the federal armies in after them, string out their supply lines, and thus render them vulnerable to counterattack on unfriendly territory. Above all, it would force the real expense of waging war onto the federal army, and if the Confederacy made that expense high enough through delay and resistance, the federal government would be forced to give up simply out of exhaustion. And no matter what other material shortages the Confederacy suffered from, it was still the world's leading supplier of cotton, and Southerners fully expected that the voracious demand of European textile manufacturing for southern cotton would draw Great Britain and France to the southern side, either as suppliers of weapons or perhaps even as open allies.

[15]Philip J. Haythornewaite, *Uniforms of the Civil War, 1861–1865* (New York, 1976), pp. 131–133, 175–176.

[16]Nevins, *The War for the Union: The Improvised War, 1861–1862* (New York, 1959), p. 357.

At first, this Confederate war strategy seemed amply justified. By mid-July, the public outcry in the North for an invasion of Virginia had reached a pitch where Generals Scott and McDowell could afford to wait no longer. So, on July 16, 1861, McDowell's poorly trained, gaudily dressed, and marvelously disorganized army of volunteers marched out of Washington to crush the rebellion. Scott and McDowell had before them two basic choices for an invasion of Virginia. They might do as Scott had done in the Mexican War, and use the federal navy to transport the army down the Chesapeake Bay, deposit it on the James River peninsula on the east side of Richmond, and lay siege to the new Confederate capital without risking a pitched battle. Or, they could march overland, using the Orange & Alexandria Railroad as a supply line, cross the Rappahannock River, and attack Richmond from the north, with the certainty that somewhere along the route, a stand-up, knock-down fight would have to be fought with the Confederates.

The first choice was wiser in strictly military terms, since the army was too poorly organized as yet to fight a large-scale battle, and even if they should win such a battle, the impact (even if it was a victory) would disorganize the army so badly that it might have to withdraw anyway. But the second choice was what the newspapers and Congress were demanding, a sensational confrontation, straight out of a picture-book of battles, that would put an end to the war at one stroke. In addition, the three-month enlistments of many of the volunteer regiments were up by the end of July, and without any absolute assurance that they would all re-enlist for longer periods of service. If McDowell meant to use his army while he still had it together, he would have to move at once. And so the long columns of Union volunteers straggled out of their Washington encampments onto the roads of northern Virginia, headed in a more-or-less straight line south for Richmond.

The result was a disaster for the federal army. To defend Richmond, the Confederate government had concentrated approximately 20,000 of its own volunteers under Brigadier General Pierre Beauregard, the hero of Fort Sumter, near the village of Manassas Junction, squarely across the track of the Orange & Alexandria railroad and behind a meandering little stream called Bull Run. There, on July 21st, the hapless McDowell attempted to clinch Beauregard's army in its front and then swing a clumsy turning movement around the end of Beauregard's defenses. It might have succeeded had not some 12,000 Confederate reinforcements under Joseph E. Johnston been brought in from western Virginia to stagger the oncoming Federals with one blow and send them reeling back to Washington. The effect of the battle of Bull Run on Union morale was crushing: over 500 Union volunteers were dead, another 2,600 wounded or missing. The poet Walt Whitman watched the defeated army drag itself back through the streets of Washington under a sullen and rainy sky. "The defeated troops commenced pouring into Washington over the Long Bridge at daylight on Monday, 22nd," Whitman recalled, "During the forenoon Washington gets all over motley with these defeated soldiers—queer-looking objects, strange eyes and faces, drench'd (the steady rain drizzles on all day) and fearfully worn, hungry, haggard, blister'd in the feet." Whitman found "the magnates and officers and clerks" in Washington calling for surrender and the resigna-tion of Lincoln. "If the secesh officers and forces had immediately follow'd, and by a bold Napoleonic movement had enter'd Washington the first day, (or even the second,) they could have had things their own way, and a powerful northern faction to back them."[17]

But in fact the Confederate army did not follow up its victory at Bull Run with a hot pursuit. Fully as ill-prepared for battle as the federal army had been, the Confeder-ates were badly disorganized by their victory and in no condition to undertake an offensive of their own. Nor did they think it was necessary, since they had achieved in this triumph all that a defensive strategy could promise. Even Abraham Lincoln was temporarily shaken by the defeat. But within a day, the president had recovered his composure, and on July 27th, Lincoln sat down to draft a more aggressive program for conducting the war, calling for a three-pronged invasion of the Confederacy in Virginia and in east and west Tennessee. To accomplish that, he needed to do some house-cleaning: He relieved the unfortunate McDowell of his command and called to Washington as his replacement the commander of the Department of the Ohio, George McClellan. Then, in November, Lincoln rid himself of the lumbering Win-field Scott, and promoted McClellan to general-in-chief of all the Union armies, and in January, 1862, Lincoln deposed Secretary of War Cameron and replaced him with a steely-eyed lawyer named Edwin M. Stanton.

The naive war, the glory-to-God war, the war of the thousand-colored uni-forms, was over. The war in earnest had now begun.

2. The Young Napoleon

The arrival of George Brinton McClellan on the scene in Washington was a second wind to the demoralized federal army. At age thirty-four, McClellan was dashing and dapper, the very storybook image of a general, a "Young Napoleon." To support that image, he brought with him from his years as a railroad executive some substantial and useful experience as an organizer. The three-month regiments were re-enlisted for three-year terms of service; the regiments were reorganized into brigades, the brigades were grouped into divisions, and the divisions into corps, and given new commanders. Uniforms and weapons were given some measure of stan-dardization, discipline and drill were imposed properly, and the bedraggled army encamped around Washington was given a name that would stick to it throughout the war—the Army of the Potomac. The army responded by giving to McClellan its whole-souled devotion. He had made them feel like soldiers, and at review after glorious review in the fall of 1861, the men of the Army of the Potomac shouted themselves hoarse for McClellan. "He had a taking way of returning such saluta-

[17]Whitman, "Specimen Days," in The Portable Walt Whitman, Mark Van Doren, ed. (New York, 1945, 1969), pp. 498–501.

tions," recalled Jacob Dolson Cox, the Ohio senator-turned-officer. "He went beyond the formal military salute, and gave his cap a little twirl, which with his bow and smile seemed to carry a little of personal good fellowship even to the humblest private soldier." McClellan even acquired a portable printing press to haul around on campaign with him so that he could keep his exhortations and advice flowing constantly through the hands of his soldiers. "It was very plain that these little attentions to the troops took well, and had no doubt some influence in establishing a sort of comradeship between him and them."[18]

At first, McClellan received the same response from Lincoln, the Cabinet, and Congress. Dinner invitations poured in upon him faster than the time available to schedule them, compliments from young and old were publicly showered upon him, and in a very short while, McClellan was being hailed as the savior of the Union— a view that McClellan himself began to share after old Winfield Scott was retired in November and McClellan made general-in-chief in his place. "By some strange operation of magic I seem to have become *the* power of the land," McClellan wrote to his wife soon after his appointment. "I almost think that were I to win some small success now I could become Dictator or anything else that might please me. . . ."[19] Dictator or not, McClellan found an appreciative audience in Abraham Lincoln, for at the time of McClellan's appointment, he and Lincoln saw the purpose of the war in very much the same terms. Lincoln still believed that secession was a political frenzy that only required some measure of firm dealing before it popped, and he advocated the application of only enough force to persuade the South that armed resistance was in vain.

Lincoln was especially careful not to drag the issue of slavery into the war, although it was a hesitation he did not relish. Privately, Lincoln regarded southern secession as a blow, not just against the federal Union, but against the most basic principles of republican government, and slavery for Lincoln was the uttermost negation of republicanism. No matter what Southerners might claim for their aims in secession, Lincoln was clear that "this is essentially a People's contest," in which the Union was struggling to assert the old Whiggish virtues of economic liberty, social mobility, and personal independence against bank wars, planter aristocracies, and the hopeless caste system of the southern backwoods and the working-class slum. "On the side of the Union, it is a struggle for maintaining in the world, that form, and substance of government, whose leading object is, to elevate the condition of men—to lift artificial weights from all shoulders—to clear the paths of laudable pursuit for all—to afford all, an unfettered start, and a fair chance, in the race of life."[20] But Lincoln dared not push that conviction, or the war, to the point of making it an outright assault on slavery. For one thing (as he repeatedly acknowl-

[18]Jacob Dolson Cox, *Military Reminiscences of the Civil War* (New York, 1900), vol. 1, p. 243.

[19]McClellan to Mary Ellen McClellan [July 27, 1861], in *The Civil War Papers of George B. McClellan,* Stephen W. Sears, ed. (New York, 1989), p. 70.

[20]Lincoln, "Message to Congress in Special Session" [July 4, 1861], in *Collected Works,* vol. 4, p. 438.

edged), he had no constitutional authority to emancipate anyone's slaves. But even more to the point, Lincoln recognized that if the abolition of slavery became a federal war issue, the white southern nonslaveholders (whom Lincoln still looked upon as closet Unionists) would be backed into an irreversible racial alliance with the planters, and make them both resolve to fight to the finish and make the war long, bloody, and expensive. Lincoln also had to remember that there were still three slave states—Delaware, Kentucky, and Maryland—that had not seceded from the Union. Any attempt on his part to expand the war to include the abolition of slavery would drive these border states straight into the Confederacy and render the war unwinnable under any strategic circumstances.

This, then, was why Lincoln had taken such pains in his inaugural address in March to disassociate the federal government from any suggestion that the preservation of the Union would lead to the abolition of slavery. "Apprehension seems to exist among the people of the Southern States, that by the accession of a Republican Administration, their property, and their peace, and personal security, are to be endangered," Lincoln calmly observed. They need not worry, he assured the country, for "the property, peace and security of no section are to be in anywise endangered by the now incoming Administration." Four months later, addressing the July emergency session of Congress, Lincoln again strained to reassure the South that his aim in going to war was only to restore the Union, not to interfere with slavery in the southern states. "Lest there be some uneasiness in the minds of candid men, as to what is to be the course of the government, towards the Southern States, *after* the rebellion shall have been suppressed, the Executive deems it proper to say . . . that he probably will have no different understanding of the powers, and duties of the Federal government, relatively to the rights of the States, and the people, and duties of the Federal government, relatively to the rights of the States, and the people, under the Constitution, than that expressed in the inaugural address."[21] Southern states who wanted to rethink their secession ordinances would thus find a bridge back into the Union still standing, and border states that still suspected the intentions of the Republican president would have a reassuring incentive not to join the Confederacy.

George McClellan, as both general-in-chief of all the Union armies and as the commander of the Army of the Potomac had no argument with Lincoln's conception of the war's purposes. He was relieved to find that "The president is perfectly honest & is really sound on the nigger question. . . ." Born and raised in comfortable circumstances in Philadelphia, and a Democrat by conviction and habit, McClellan genuinely disliked slavery, but without feeling the slightest desire to free the African American. "When I think of some of the features of slavery I cannot help shuddering," he wrote to his wife in November of 1861, and he vowed that ". . . when the day of adjustment comes I will, if successful, throw my sword into

[21]"First Inaugural Address—Final Text" [March 4, 1861] and "Message to Congress in Special Session" [July 4, 1861], in *Collected Works*, vol. 4, pp. 262–263, 438–439.

the scale to force an improvement in the condition of those poor blacks." But McClellan looked only for a day of adjustment, not a day of judgment, for "improvement" and not freedom. He scorned the secessionists and the abolitionists in equal parts, and promised his wife that "I will not fight for the abolitionists. . . ." He begged his fellow-Democrat Samuel Barlow to "Help me to dodge the nigger—we want nothing to do with him. I am fighting to preserve the integrity of the Union & power of the Govt" and "on no other issue. . . ."[22] On those grounds, McClellan was happy to agree with the president that the purpose of waging war was to nudge the Confederacy back into the Union, not to punish the South, seize its property, or subjugate its people.

To that end, McClellan proposed to incorporate most of the features of Scott's passive "Anaconda Plan" into his own strategic initiative. Although in the end he probably would have preferred to mass all the available federal forces in Virginia for a single major blow at Richmond, he was careful to yield to Lincoln's preoccupation with the border states and provide for invasions all around the northern perimeter of the Confederacy. First, McClellan authorized a combined army-navy operation designed to secure critical locations along the Atlantic seaboard of the Confederacy. On November 7, 1861, Captain Samuel F. Du Pont steamed into the Port Royal Sound, fifty miles south of Charleston, landed a small contingent of federal soldiers, and cleared the Hilton Head, Port Royal, and St. Helena islands of Confederates. Two months later, a federal force of 15,000 men under a Rhode Island inventor, manufacturer, and railroad man named Ambrose E. Burnside landed on Roanoke island in the Hatteras Sound and easily drove off a scattering of Confederate defenders. In April, 1862, another naval expedition bombarded Fort Pulaski, at the mouth of the Savannah River, into submission. In five months' time, federal naval and land forces controlled virtually all of the south Atlantic coastline between Savannah and Norfolk, except for Charleston harbor and Wilmington, on the estuary of North Carolina's Cape Fear River. At the same time, McClellan also authorized Major General Don Carlos Buell, now commanding McClellan's old Department of the Ohio, to march a small federal army of 45,000 men through Kentucky and into eastern Tennessee, where (it was assumed) loyal Tennesseans would rise in support of the Union and overthrow the secessionist state government in Nashville. And then, McClellan himself proposed to lead the Army of the Potomac in a major invasion of Virginia, aimed at the capture of Richmond. The result would be "to advance our centre into South Carolina and Georgia; to push Buell either towards Montgomery, or to unite with the main army in Georgia."[23]

This was not a bad plan, and in fact it conformed rather handsomely to the indirect methods of campaigning that Denis Hart Mahan had championed at West

[22]McClellan to Samuel Barlow [November 8, 1861] and Mary Ellen McClellan [November 14, 1861], in *The Civil War Papers of George B. McClellan*, Stephen W. Sears, ed., pp. 128, 132.

[23]McClellan to Stanton [February 3, 1862], in *McClellan's Own Story: The War for the Union* (New York, 1887), p. 234.

Point (and McClellan was one of Mahan's prize pupils at the academy). It aimed at the acquisition of territory, not the expensive confrontation of armies, and even though the Union forces would be forced to operate on exterior lines in coordinating these movements, the Union's superiority in terms of ships and railroad support would help to overcome that deficit. Politically speaking, McClellan's plan also had the advantage of carrying the war to those areas that had shown the least fervor for secession, and would probably show the least resistance.

But there were two factors working against McClellan that no one in a West Point classroom could easily have anticipated, much less corrected, and both of them would help to undercut McClellan and his plan. One of these was McClellan's simple personal vanity. McClellan had at first been flattered by the attention paid to him by official Washington, but the more he listened and believed the complimentary nonsense heaped upon him by the press, the bureaucrats, and the politicians, the more he began to believe himself superior to all three. "I am becoming daily more disgusted with this administration—perfectly sick of it," he wrote to his wife, "There are some of the greatest geese in the Cabinet I have ever seen. . . ." Even "the President is an idiot. . . ." "I am weary of all this," he sighed, "I have no ambition in the present affairs—only wish to save my country—& find the incapables around me will not permit it!" But his conclusion that the administration was incapable was precisely what fired his ambition, and he began to entertain fantasies about "the Presidency, Dictatorship &c."[24] He grew contemptuous of Lincoln and uncooperative with the Cabinet, especially Secretary of War Stanton, and they in turn began to wonder about the wisdom of having put the direction of the war into the hands of this suspiciously inflated Democrat.

There was also a problem with McClellan's fussiness. The debacle at Bull Run had demonstrated the foolishness of rushing untrained soldiers into combat, and so Congress had been willing to give McClellan what it had not given McDowell, the time to train and equip an army. But as the summer of 1861 faded into the autumn, and the autumn into the winter, McClellan showed no desire to do more than train and equip, and organize elaborate reviews. When he finally formulated a plan for a move into Virginia in late 1861, he dismissed the notion of assaulting the Confederates at Manassas directly, and called for an ambitious joint army-navy landing operation that would unload federal forces at Urbanna, on the Rappahannock River in Virginia, and march from there overland to Richmond, only fifty miles away. But by January, 1862, McClellan had changed his mind: He would need to wait on Buell's advance into Kentucky before doing anything in Virginia, and he even considered moving his army to Kentucky and abandoning all notion of a Virginia invasion. Neither of these plans produced any motion on McClellan's part, and by the end of January, Lincoln was so exasperated with his general-in-chief that he issued a presidential order mandating a general advance southward by all Union

[24]McClellan to Ellen McClellan [August 9, August 16, and October 10, 1861], in *The Civil War Papers of George B. McClellan*, Stephen W. Sears, ed., pp. 82, 86, 106.

forces on February 22nd, with McClellan assigned particular responsibility for attacking the Confederate positions around Manassas. McClellan, incensed at what he termed meddling on Lincoln's part, replied by resurrecting the Urbanna plan and proposing to move down to the Rappahannock instead of Manassas. But by March 8th, McClellan was no closer to moving on Urbanna than he was on the moon, and Lincoln called him onto the White House carpet for an explanation. The prodding finally worked, and on March 10th, McClellan and his grand army marched down to Manassas to attack what McClellan was sure would be massive Confederate entrenchments, filled with abundant Confederate soldiers who would inflict thousands of casualties that his Urbanna plan would have avoided.[25]

To McClellan's unspeakable surprise, the Confederate entrenchments at Manassas turned out to be empty. Confederate General Joseph E. Johnston, who now had sole command of the Confederacy's northern Virginia army, had far fewer men than McClellan thought, and he prudently eased himself out of the Manassas lines before McClellan's hammer fell, and withdrew to the Rappahannock. The next day, McClellan read in the newspapers that Lincoln had relieved him of his post of general-in-chief, ostensibly to allow McClellan to concentrate his energies on the Virginia theater. For McClellan, it was a humiliation. But Lincoln had by now learned that humiliation was a remarkably effective medicine for McClellan's case of "the slows," and it worked the next day when McClellan laid out yet another plan for invading Virginia. He had no interest in an overland campaign from Manassas, and the original Urbanna campaign was now impossible with Joe Johnston sitting behind the Rappahannock. But McClellan insisted that the basic idea of a combined army-navy operation was still feasible, provided one changed the target area to the James River, where the Federal government still retained possession of Fortress Monroe, on the tip of the James River peninsula as it protruded into the Chesapeake Bay. He would load the 100,000 men of the Army of the Potomac onto navy transports, and relying on the superiority of the federal navy in the waters of the Chesapeake Bay and the strategic cover provided by Fortress Monroe, he would land his soldiers on the James River peninsula just below Richmond, and then draw up to the Confederate capital and besiege it before Johnston's Confederate army on the Rappahannock knew what was happening.

In McClellan's mind, this plan had all the proper Mahan-ite advantages to it. By using federal seapower, he would overcome the Confederate advantage of interior lines in Virginia; it would constitute a gigantic turning movement that would force the Confederates to abandon everything north of Richmond without a shot; and it would take the rebel capital as the real object of the campaign rather than a rebel army, thus avoiding unnecessary battles and unnecessary loss of life. Secretary of War Stanton at once objected that this plan merely demonstrated how unaggressive McClellan was. And since piloting the Army of the Potomac down to the

[25]Stephen W. Sears, George B. McClellan: The Young Napoleon (New York, 1988), pp. 131, 148–149, 160–161.

James River would leave Washington almost undefended, it also left a question in Stanton's mind as to whether McClellan was deliberately baring the national capital to a Confederate strike from northern Virginia. But McClellan's plan appealed to Lincoln's still-cautious sense of how the war ought to be fought, and so Lincoln (despite Stanton's reservations) decided to authorize the venture—provided that McClellan left approximately 30,000 men in front of Washington to protect the capital. McClellan protested that he needed every last man of the Army of the Potomac for his offensive, but Lincoln was adamant. On March 17, 1862, Mc-Clellan began the laborious process of transporting nearly 70,000 men of the Army of the Potomac to the exposed end of the James River peninsula at Fortress Monroe, leaving the remainder behind in scattered commands and forts around Washington.

The resulting Peninsula campaign confirmed everyone's worst fears about Mc-Clellan's vanity and slowness, and raised a few others' fears about his loyalty to a Republican administration. True to McClellan's prediction, the Army of the Potomac's landing on the James peninsula caught the Confederate army in Virginia totally by surprise. Only a thin force of 15,000 rebel infantry, under the command of a former West Pointer and amateur actor named John Magruder, held a defensive line across the James peninsula at the old Revolutionary War battlefield of Yorktown. If McClellan had but known the pitiful numbers opposing him, he could have walked over Magruder and into Richmond without blinking. But what Magruder lacked in terms of numbers he more than made up for with theatrical displays of parading troops and menacing-looking artillery emplacements, and he successfully bluffed McClellan into thinking that a major Confederate army stood in his path. By the time McClellan was finally ready to open up a major assault on the Yorktown lines on May 4, 1862, Joe Johnston's Confederate army in Virginia had been regrouped around Richmond and was prepared to give McClellan precisely the kind of defensive battle he had hoped to avoid. And to make matters worse, Johnston enjoyed the reputation of being one of the finest defensive strategists in the old army.

For the next three weeks, McClellan slowly felt his way up the peninsula, growing more and more convinced that Johnston had as many as 200,000 rebels defending Richmond (Johnston actually had about 55,000) and demanding that Lincoln send him more reinforcements. By the last week of May, McClellan was beside the Chickahominy River, six miles from Richmond, and as he finally worked himself up to planning an assault on Richmond, he began feeding his army, corps by corps, across to the south side of the Chickahominy, closer to Richmond. Unfortunately for McClellan, torrential spring rains imperiled the Chickahominy bridges after only two of his five army corps had crossed the river. And on May 31st, hoping to crush these two isolated corps before the river subsided, Johnston wheeled out his entire army and struck the exposed Federals at the battle of Seven Pines.

For two days, Johnston and the Confederates hammered at the vulnerable federal corps. But the federal generals handled their untested men well, and the Confederates drew off with the loss of over 6,000 men, including Joe Johnston, who was severely wounded. But far from this putting spirit back into McClellan, the outcome of Seven Pines only operated against him. Frightened by Johnston's aggressiveness, McClellan cautiously slowed his advance across the Chickahominy. And, far more ominously, the wounded Johnston was replaced by an infinitely more skillful and aggressive Confederate general, Robert Edward Lee.

In Lee, the Confederacy possessed one of the great figures of American military culture. The consummate Virginia gentleman, the son of a revolutionary war general and grandson-in-law of George Washington, Lee had enjoyed a spotless career in the old army in Mexico and on the western plains, and had even served briefly as superintendent of West Point. Significantly, Lee was older than most of the generals who would serve in the Civil War—he was fifty-four at the outbreak of the conflict—which meant that he had graduated from West Point before Mahan and the deification of the defensive had taken hold of the West Point curriculum. Although commissioned as an engineer, Lee was aggressive and combative beneath the armor of Virginia gentlemanliness, and he had become one of Winfield Scott's most trusted subordinates in Mexico. By the spring of 1861, Lee had risen to the command of the 1st U.S. Cavalry, and Scott had wanted to see Lee given the position that eventually went to McClellan.

But Lee, unlike Scott, could not tear himself away from his old family and state loyalties. He could not agree with Lincoln's decision to "pin the States in the Union with the bayonet," and on April 20, 1861, he resigned his commission. No Southerner ever went into rebellion with more reluctance. Lee told Frank Blair, Lincoln's personal emmissary, that if it were up to him, he would free all the slaves in the South if they belonged to him in order to avert civil war, but he could not "draw my sword . . . save in defense of my native State." As he explained to his sister the same day, "With all my devotion to the Union, and the feeling of loyalty and duty of an American citizen, I have not been able to make up my mind to raise my hand against my relatives, my children, my home."[26] He offered his services instead to Virginia, where he was made a brigadier general of volunteers, and for a year he served in a variety of capacities, especially as Jefferson Davis's de facto chief of staff. With the wounding of Johnston, Davis would entrust the defense of Richmond to no one but Lee.

Lee had already made more than enough trouble for McClellan even before taking the field. In April, Lee had prevailed on Davis to allow Thomas Jonathan Jackson, a former military institute professor and minor hero of the Bull Run battle who commanded the small Confederate force in Virginia's Shenandoah Valley, to make a threatening feint against the federal forces that Lincoln and Stanton had kept scattered between McClellan and Washington. Jackson, who had acquired the nickname "Stonewall" for his courage at Bull Run, moved menacingly up the Shenandoah toward the Potomac River, confirming all of official Washington's

---

[26]J. W. Jones, *Life and Letters of Robert Edward Lee: Soldier and Man* (1906; rept. Harrisonburg, VA, 1978), pp. 126–133.

fears that McClellan's peninsula operation was going to lay Washington open to capture. Lincoln threw three separate federal forces of about 40,000 men after Jackson's 16,000 "foot cavalry," but Jackson easily eluded or trounced all three, and left all the federal soldiers in northern Virginia tied securely in knots and unavailable to the increasingly nervous McClellan.[27]

Now, Lee took personal command of the Richmond defenses, and, in complete contrast to McClellan, he at once advanced to the offensive and opened what became known as the Seven Days' battle. On June 26th, finding the federal army still straddling the Chickahominy, Lee decided to strike at an exposed federal corps on the north side of the river at Mechanicsville. Lee's attacks were repulsed with over 1,400 rebel casualties, but the next day Lee attacked the same Federal corps again at Gaines' Mill, and this time the Confederate forces forced the Union troops to withdraw with nearly 6,800 casualties. McClellan, imagining himself to be outnumbered and endangered by untold hosts of rebel fiends, concluded that he had no choice but to "save this army" and fall back to a safe spot on the James River. Lee, scenting blood, harried and snapped at McClellan's retreating army at Allen's Farm and Savage's Station (June 29th) and Frayser's Farm (June 30th), hoping to pick off and crush isolated federal brigades and divisions, until at last he was handed a bloody repulse by the federal rear guard at Malvern Hill (July 1st). All in all, the Seven Days' battle cost Lee's army 3,286 men killed and 15,909 wounded—but he had saved Richmond. McClellan, still believing himself outnumbered and blaming his defeat on Lincoln's unwillingness to send him reinforcements, dug the Army of the Potomac into an impregnable defensive position at Harrison's Landing, on the James River. The great Peninsula campaign was over.

And so, it seemed, was McClellan's career. On July 8th, Lincoln himself came down to Harrison's Landing to speak with McClellan, and by the time he returned to Washington two days later, he had become convinced of two things. First, the savage fighting on the Peninsula had shown Lincoln that the Confederates were not in the least inclined to listen to his sweet pleadings for a painless reunion. To the contrary, it was now clear to Lincoln that the Confederates cared little or nothing for Union or re-union and were fighting simply and plainly for slavery. Unless Lincoln was willing to make the war for the Union into a war against slavery, the Union cause would never be able to muster the moral fervor to subdue the rebels. That message was also being dinned into his ear by voices within his own party in Congress and the northern state capitals, which warned that northern public opinion could not forever support a war with such great costs for such unexciting goals. So, even as McClellan was still struggling back to Harrison's Landing, Lincoln had decided to appoint a new commander for the scattered Union forces that had been blackened and blued by "Stonewall" Jackson in northern Virginia. He chose a hard-fighting, no-compromise, antislavery Westerner named John Pope, and had the

[27]Robert G. Tanner, *Stonewall in the Valley: Thomas J. "Stonewall" Jackson's Shenandoah Valley Campaign, Spring 1862* (New York, 1976), pp. 155–161.

forlorn remnants of Washington's defenders reorganized as a new army, the Army of Virginia, and sent them off to launch an invasion of northern Virginia. Under Pope, there would be no observances of polite niceties by Union troops in rebel territory. In a series of general orders, Pope freely authorized his troops to forage from the population at will, to shoot any civilians guilty of taking potshots at federal soldiers and confiscate their property, and to impress local civilians into military road work.

While Pope was spreading premediated devastation into northern Virginia, McClellan remained motionless at Harrison's Landing, demanding that Lincoln supply him with another 50,000 men for a second drive at Richmond. Even if Lincoln had wanted to give them to McClellan, the time it would have taken to reinforce and re-equip McClellan for another campaign on the peninsula would allow Lee and his victorious Confederates to slip northward and menace Washington in force. Lincoln could not risk another close call like the one "Stonewall" Jackson had given the capital in March. And yet, Lincoln hesitated to cashier McClellan outright. Although Lincoln might have wanted to rid himself of "Little Mac" on the dock at Harrison's Landing, McClellan had become too clearly identified with Democratic political interests in the North. With critical state elections in New York, New Jersey, and Pennsylvania, and a congressional by-election hanging over the horizon in November, Lincoln could not afford to alienate any northern Democratic sympathies. What was even more dangerous, McClellan still possessed the loyalty and admiration of the ordinary soldiers of the Army of the Potomac, and he had had fully a year to fill up the officer corps of the army with his friends and subordinates. Not only might those officers refuse to serve under a McClellan replacement, but Lincoln could not be certain that they might not attempt a political action of their own if McClellan was summarily relieved of command. Hence, Lincoln chose not to dismiss McClellan but to ease the Army of the Potomac out from under him. On August 3rd, McClellan was ordered to begin putting elements of the Army of the Potomac back onto their transports to return to Washington, where McClellan's proud divisions and corps would be fed over to Pope to form a new federal army, perhaps with Halleck as its field commander.

This delicate outmaneuvering might have gone off smoothly if it had not been for the ferocious aggressiveness of Robert E. Lee and the simple inadequacy of John Pope. After the Malvern Hill fight, Lee decided to gamble on the likelihood of McClellan's inactivity and catch Pope's Army of Virginia before it could grow any larger. He and "Stonewall" Jackson bounded back up into northern Virginia, and on August 30, 1862, Jackson and Lee trapped the hapless Pope between them on the old Bull Run battlefield. The second battle of Bull Run was an even greater disaster for the Union than the first one: Pope's army of 60,000 men suffered 16,000 casualties and was left a hopeless wreck. Meanwhile, the triumphant Lee lunged across the Potomac on a raid into Maryland, where Lee expected to parley his victories into a massive prosecession uprising among slaveholding Marylanders, and perhaps reach far enough across the Mason-Dixon line into Pennsylvania to disrupt the North's vital east-west railroad junction on the Susquehanna River at Harrisburg.

With Pope utterly discredited and the now-defunct Army of Virginia in pieces, Lincoln had no choice but to put McClellan and the Army of the Potomac back into the gap and order them to pursue Lee into Maryland. Few generals ever get a second chance to redeem themselves, and McClellan's gratitude to Lincoln spurred him on after Lee with unaccustomed vigor—gratitude, that is, plus the unlooked-for gift of a copy of Lee's private orders for the Maryland campaign, which an Indiana private discovered in the grass near Frederick, Maryland, on September 13, 1862. The lost orders revealed that Lee's army was actually dangerously dispersed along Maryland's roads, and could easily be destroyed piece by piece if McClellan hopped to it. And for once, he did. The federals surprised Confederate screening fores at Crampton's Gap and Turner's Gap on September 14th, and three days later, McClellan had pinned Lee's army in between the Potomac and one of the Potomac's little tributary streams, the Antietam creek, near the quaint little town of Sharpsburg, Maryland.

The subsequent battle of Antietam ought to have been McClellan's win-it-all opportunity to redeem his reputation. But once again, his slowness and his discomfort with the headlong offensive were his undoing. In a terrible, bitter all-day battle on September 17th—a battle that cost a total of 26,000 casualities from both armies—McClellan launched a series of poorly coordinated attacks on Lee's army that not only failed to deliver the sledgehammer blow that might have flattened the Confederates, but even failed to prevent Confederate reinforcements from arriving from Harpers Ferry. At the end of the day, Lee's men were only barely holding onto their positions, but McClellan showed no disposition to send in a final knockout assault, even though he had at least 15,000 fresh troops in reserve. Instead, Lee was allowed to creep back across the Potomac into Virginia, and McClellan went into camp to lick his wounds.

And there he stayed, through September and into October. Lincoln tried in vain to move him, even visiting McClellan personally to urge him to pursue Lee. But McClellan waited until the end of October before putting his columns back onto the roads southward, and by then, Lincoln had already nerved himself to fire his truculent general. The president waited until the day after the New York and New Jersey congressional elections to mute the political damage, and on November 7, 1862, dismissed McClellan. The reactions were bad, especially in the Army of the Potomac, where loyal McClellanite officers whispered plots for a coup into the general's ear. "Nay, there was considerable swearing indulged in, and threats of marching on Washington, should McClellan but take the lead," remembered Captain Amos Judson of the 83rd Pennsylvania.[28] But McClellan was not a traitor, and even if he had once talked foolishly about dictatorships, he silenced

---

[28]Amos M. Judson, *History of the Eighty-Third Regiment, Pennsylvania Volunteers* (1865; rept. Dayton, OH, 1986), p. 98.

the gossip in his headquarters and rode away from the army he had built, never to return.

Even the slaughter at Antietam had not been without its merits. Although in military terms the battle had been something of a draw, Lincoln was prepared to treat Lee's withdrawal afterward as evidence of a Union victory. And on the strength of that victory, just five days after Antietam, Lincoln issued the preliminary announcement of a dramatic shift in war policy: As of January 1, 1863, all slaves in whatever southern states were still in rebellion against the Union would be declared free. Lincoln had at last chosen to embrace emancipation. Events had closed off his search for compromise. As he told Congress a month later in his annual message, he had discovered that "The dogmas of the quiet past are inadequate to the stormy present." It was not only the slaves who must be freed, but Americans who must free themselves of thinking about slavery in the old way. "We must disenthrall ourselves, then we shall save our country."[29]

3. Lincoln and Emancipation

On the 22nd of September, 1862, President Lincoln abruptly shifted the moral center of the Civil War with the issue of a document that has become universally known as the "preliminary" Emancipation Proclamation. For more than a year, Lincoln had been trying to wage a war of national reunification without explicitly bringing the moral question of slavery into the picture, but now Lincoln decided to change the course of the war effort and make the emancipation of black slaves in the South a stated aim of the war. The "preliminary" proclamation was couched in the form of a calculated threat: unless the Confederate states laid down their arms by January 1, 1863, "all persons held as slaves within any State or designated part of a State . . . in rebellion against the United States, shall be then, thenceforward, and forever free," and the United States military forces "will recognize and maintain the freedom of such persons, and will do no act to repress such persons . . . in any efforts that may make for their actual freedom."[30] No other single document, except perhaps the Gettysburg Address, has done so much to fix Lincoln permanently in the constellation of American history. And yet debate has not ceased to rage since the day of the proclamation's publication over what its meaning was to be, or what Lincoln's real intentions in issuing it were.

Much of that debate was, and still is, fueled by Lincoln himself. In August of 1862, four months before the actual proclamation took effect, the abolitionist editor of the New York *Tribune*, Horace Greeley, published a lengthy editorial entitled "The Prayer of Twenty Millions," which sharply chided Lincoln for not making the war for the Union more of a war against slavery. Lincoln was so stung by

---

[29]Lincoln, "Annual Message to Congress" [December 1, 1862], in *Collected Works*, vol. 5, p. 537.
[30]Lincoln, "Emancipation Proclamation," in *Collected Works*, vol. 6, p. 29.

the editorial that he sat down on August 22nd and wrote out a reply to Greeley that has often been taken as the summation of his view on the relationship between slavery and the conduct of the war. In it, Lincoln asserted that his paramount intention was always to save the Union, and not to do anything one way or the other about slavery unless the doing of it would assist the Federal government in restoring the Union:

> I would save the Union. I would do it the shortest way under the Constitution. . . . My paramount object in this struggle is to save the Union, and is not either to save or destroy slavery. If I could save the Union without freeing any slave I would do it; and if I could save it by freeing all the slaves I would do it; and if I could save it by freeing some and leaving others alone I would also do that. What I do about slavery and the colored race, I do because I believe that it helps save the Union. . . .[31]

Those words have often come back to haunt the image of Lincoln as the Great Emancipator. In the 1960s, the letter to Greeley gave black activists who mistrusted the reliability of whites in the civil rights struggle reason to denounce Lincoln as just another hypocritical white liberal, willing to make concessions to blacks only when it suited a political purpose. "Was Lincoln a White Supremacist?" asked Lerone Bennett in an article in *Ebony* magazine in February, 1968; "Was Lincoln Just a Honkie?" asked Herbert Mitgang in the *New York Times Magazine* two weeks later. The most damning evidence behind these questions came from Lincoln's own mouth. Almost everyone from Lincoln's most sympathetic biographers to the White Citizens Council of Louisiana pointed, with varying degrees of enthusiasm, to Lincoln's utterances on race relations in the fourth of his debates with Stephen Douglas at Charleston, Illinois, in 1858, as evidence that Lincoln was really as much a racist at heart as Douglas or any other white American of his time. "I am not nor ever have been in favor of bringing about in any way, the social and political equality of the white and black races," Lincoln declared at the opening of the Charleston debate. "There is a physical difference between the white and black races, which I suppose will forever forbid the two races living together on terms of social and political equality, and inasmuch as they cannot so live, while they do remain together, there must be the position of superior and inferior . . . I as much as any other man am in favor of the superior position being assigned to the white man."[32] How are we to understand the Emancipation Proclamation if the president who wrote it held beliefs on race that fly straight in the face of civic equality?

There are actually two questions involved in the debate over the Emancipation Proclamation, and both of them have to do with what Lincoln intended that

---

[31]Lincoln, "To Horace Greeley" [August 22, 1862], in *Collected Works*, vol. 5, p. 388.

[32]"The Fourth Joint Debate at Charleston" [September 18, 1858], in *The Lincoln-Douglas Debates*, Harold Holzer, ed. (New York, 1993), p. 189.

the Emancipation Proclamation, and the Civil War, should lead to. The first question concerns what Lincoln really thought about black slavery and black freedom; and the second concerns what place Lincoln thought blacks ought to have in American life once slavery was finished. There is no reason to doubt Lincoln's numerous protests that he had always disliked slavery. In 1837, while still only a state representative in the Illinois legislature, Lincoln had been the co-signer of a protest to the legislature that branded slavery as "founded on both injustice and bad policy." And four years later, pleading before the Illinois Supreme Court, Lincoln won the freedom of a slave girl whose owners had illegally tried to sell her on Illinois territory. Still, this did not mean that his dislike of slavery ran very deep. It was one thing to condemn the insitution of slavery in Illinois; it was quite another to propose that one should take some action to free the slaves as a national principle. Prior to 1854, Lincoln's opposition to slavery was generated more by local distaste rather than moral conviction, and his appeal to the Illinois Supreme Court in 1841 really amounted to little more than his unwillingness to permit slavery to operate freely in Illinois. In fact, far from agonizing over slavery, Lincoln actually defended the rights of a Kentucky slave-owner in 1847 who had been arrested for trying to transport his slaves through Illinois, and between 1849 and 1851, he handled the distribution of proceeds of his father-in-law's estate, which included the selling off of his father-in-law's slaves. Lincoln did not balk at taking money from these sales. Even his 1837 protest against slavery actually went on to add that "the promulgation of abolition doctrines tends rather to increase than to abate [slavery's] evils."

Then came Kansas-Nebraska and Dred Scott, and with them the hot breath of the "Slave Power" upon the neck of "true republicanism" in the territories and perhaps even in the free states. It is important to note that Lincoln's first anxiety about Kansas-Nebraska was not over African Americans but over the threat posed to republican liberty by the "Slave Power," since Lincoln believed that the spread of slavery into the territories would severely limit the ability of small-time white freeholders to buy land and compete on the agricultural markets. But as Lincoln rose to fight the slave conspiracy he outlined in the "House Divided" speech, he found it increasingly difficult to keep his opposition to slavery's politics from blurring over into a condemnation of slavery's morality. Herndon recalled vividly that "Mr. Lincoln had an active, breathing, and living consience that rooted itself deep down in his very being," and his "main question" in any consideration was "Is the thing right, is it just?" In this case, as Lincoln's "conscience" wrapped itself around the slavery question, he became more and more persuaded that the root problem with slavery was not what it might do to whites and their "chance to rise" in a Whig republic, but what it had been doing all along to blacks by denying them a corresponding "chance to rise." For Lincoln, it had become a "principle of law" that "every negro" taken into the territories was free, and it was one of Lincoln's particular grievances against Kansas-Nebraska that now the proslavery Kansas legislature "gravely passes a law to hang men who shall venture to inform a negro of his legal rights."[33]

It was a significant step for Lincoln to think of African Americans as possessing *rights*, and not just with reference to Illinois' racially motivated antislavery statutes, but *rights* under the mandate of a federal territory. The question, however, was *what rights*, exactly? The core of Republican antislavery opinion as it developed in the 1850s held that African Americans were clearly entitled to the same *natural* rights as every other American on the basis of a simple common humanity, and the Republicans found an initial enumeration of those natural rights in the Declaration of Independence: *life, liberty,* and *the pursuit of happiness.* The Republican argument that blacks possessed *natural* rights implied that blacks were also entitled to *civil* rights, which are the basic legal actions a government takes to protect the free exercise of natural rights. The really thorny question was whether blacks also were entitled to *political* rights (to coverage by the ordinary enactments of legislatures, the right to vote, and so forth), since it was impossible, in a republican government, to disentangle natural or civil equality from political equality.[34] That implication brought Lincoln and the Republicans dangerously close to collision with the prevailing racism of white Americans, North and South, in the 1850s. Any attempt on Lincoln's part to attack slavery and the "Slave Power" led to the conclusion that the slaves ought to be freed as a matter of natural and civil rights; but that entailed the political question of *freedom for what?*

In the 1858 senatorial debates, Douglas had sensed the trouble these questions were likely to cause Lincoln. And it is a backhanded measure of how advanced Lincoln's reputation on the rights of African Americans had become in the 1850s that Douglas hoped to damage Lincoln by pointing out the logical connection between Lincoln's campaign for the natural and civil rights of African Americans and the promotion of racial political equality. "If you desire negro citizenship—if you desire them to come into the State and stay with white men—if you desire to make them eligible to office—to have them serve on juries and judge you of your rights," cried Douglas, "then go with Mr. Lincoln and the Black Republicans in favor negro citizenship." Lincoln, caught in the open on an issue where he knew the white constituency of Illinois would never support him, became again the evasive and pragmatic case lawyer who skillfully dodged an opponent's advantage behind a shower of distinctions. He attempted to protect himself by asserting that there remained an impassable distinction, which he attempted to draw, between natural and civil rights on the one hand and political and social rights on the other.

---

[33]Herndon to C. O. Poole [January 5, 1886], in *The Hidden Lincoln, From the Letters and Papers of William H. Herndon,* Emanuel Hertz, ed. (New York, 1938), pp. 120–121; Lincoln, "To Joshua F. Speed" [August 24, 1855], in *Collected Works,* vol. 2, p. 320.

[34]Eric Foner, *Free Soil, Free Labor, Free Men: The Ideology of the Republican Party before the Civil War* (New York, 1970), pp. 73–90, 290–294.

"Anything that argues me into his idea of perfect social and political equality with the negro, is but a specious and fantastic arrangement of words, by which a man can prove a horse chestnut to be a chestnut horse," Lincoln claimed. "I have no disposition to introduce political and social equality between the white and black races."[35] It is not at all clear that Lincoln really believed that such a rigid distinction between natural and political rights really existed. However, insisting that natural and civil rights had no necessary connection to political or social rights allowed Lincoln to save his political skin in Illinois, while at the same time permitting him to wedge the basic claim of natural rights into the door.

The failure of the Republicans to go beyond the assertion of natural rights for African Americans, and the careful insistence of the Republicans to oppose only the extension of slavery, and not slavery itself, disappointed and demoralized the free black communities of the North. Despite the rise of antislavery sentiment in the North in the 1850s, the economic and social well-being of the 200,000 free blacks in the North was actually declining. "How long! How long! O Lord God of Sabaoth!" Frederick Douglass exclaimed in the columns of *Frederick Douglass's Paper*, an antislavery newspaper he edited in Rochester. "Reason and morality have emptied their casket of richest jewels into the lap of this cause in vain." John Rock, a black Boston dentist turned lawyer, despairingly concluded that while "there is less prejudice here than there is farther South," that did not mean that the North was paradise for African Americans. Ironically, thought Rock, African Americans struggle to improve themselves against every obstacle that whites can place in their path, only to discover that their improvements (whether in education or in business) merely equip them to appreciate more keenly the depths of white bigotry. "This country is perfectly adapted to negro slavery," Rock sardonically remarked, "it is the free blacks that the air is not good for!" When another black Boston lawyer, William G. Allen, married a white woman, Mary King, in New York City in 1853, the couple was forced to flee to England to escape a mob that threatened to tar and feather Allen.[36]

The Allens never returned to America, and throughout the 1850s, many other northern African Americans began to wonder if emigration was the real answer. In 1852, Martin R. Delany, a black physician in Pittsburgh and one-time associate of Frederick Douglass, led an exploration party up the Niger River in west Africa, hoping to find a useful location for an expatriate black settlement. Henry Highland Garnet, a black minister, organized the African Colonization Society in 1858 to begin another emigré settlement in Africa, and in 1859, James T. Holly and James Redpath founded a Haytian Emigration Bureau to promote black movement to Haiti. Even Frederick Douglass was swayed by the appeal of emigration. He sup-

[35]"The First Joint Debate at Ottawa" [August 21, 1858] in *Lincoln-Douglas Debates*, Holzer, ed., pp. 54, 66.

[36]George A. Levesque, "Boston's Black Brahmin: Dr. John S. Rock," in *Civil War History* 26 (December 1980), pp. 326–346; R. J. M. Blackett, "William G. Allen: The Forgotten Professor," in *Civil War History* 26 (March 1980), pp. 39–52.

ported the Republicans in 1856, and cautiously endorsed Lincoln in 1860. But Lincoln's mild-tempered inaugural in 1861 caused Douglass to dismiss him as "the most dangerous advocate of slave-hunting and slave-catching in the land," and the bombardment of Fort Sumter actually found Douglass about to leave for Haiti on a two-month fact-finding mission.[37]

The outbreak of the war rallied Douglass's optimism, and he hoped that the war might shift the earth out from under the caution and hesitancy that had stymied all real movement toward the elimination of slavery. White Northerners must awake, Douglass pleaded, to the new reality that war "bound up the fate of the Republic and that of the slave in the same bundle."[38] But neither Lincoln nor the federal government gave Douglass much hope to think that the northern war effort was really going to make the destruction of slavery its true object. As much as Lincoln might have wanted to free all the slaves, he consistently declared that the war was being fought to preserve the Union, not to abolish slavery, and the political realities of wooing both southern Unionists and northern Democrats during the summer and fall of 1861 convinced Lincoln that the road of compromise and evasion was, as it had been on the court circuit, the only safe course to take.

And yet, almost from the first, Lincoln found himself under pressure to move black freedom to the front of the wartime agenda. Part of the pressure came from the radical wing of his own Republican party—from senators like Charles Sumner of Massachusetts, Zachariah Chandler of Michigan, and Ben Wade of Ohio, and Thaddeus Stevens, George Julian, and James Asbury in the House—who pressed Lincoln from the beginning of the war to call slavery the real cause of the conflict. "The occasion is forced upon us and the invitation presented to strike the chains from four millions of human beings and create them men," argued the hot-tempered and impatient Stevens, "to extinguish slavery on this whole continent; to wipe out so far as we are concerned the most hateful and infernal blot that ever disgraced the escutcheon of man; to write a page in the history of the world whose brightness shall eclipse all the records of heroes and sages." More pressure came from Lincoln's generals and administration. In July, 1861, the former Republican presidential candidate, John Charles Frémont, was appointed commander of the federal troops in the wavering border state of Missouri. On August 30th, Frémont imposed martial law on Missouri and unilaterally freed all slaves within the state. Alarmed lest Frémont's proclamation should set off a proslavery uprising in Missouri, Lincoln revoked Frémont's order and relieved him of command. Then, in December, Lincoln's secretary of war, Simon Cameron, used the department's annual report to urge the president to punish the "rebel traitors" by emancipating as many slaves as he could find, enlisting them in the Union army, and sending them off to fight their

---

[37]David W. Blight, *Frederick Douglass' Civil War: Keeping Faith in Jubilee* (Baton Rouge, 1988), pp. 128–134.

[38]"Nemesis," in *The Life and Writings of Frederick Douglass*, ed. Philip S. Foner (New York, 1950), vol. 3, p. 99.

former masters. That, together with Cameron's shady dealings with contractors and cronies, got him sacked by Lincoln a month later and packed off safely to St. Petersburg as the American minister to Russia. Still, even though Lincoln publicly insisted that neither of these men spoke for his administration in word, thought, or deed, Lincoln coyly admitted to Charles Sumner that he thought the policy of emancipation, if not these would-be emancipators, was right. "Between you and me on this subject," Lincoln whispered, "is a difference of a month or six weeks' time."[39] If the time or the situation allowed, Lincoln was more willing than he gave evidence to press for the end of slavery.

But the most significant pressure on Lincoln to make black freedom a war issue came from the blacks themselves, and not necessarily from the free blacks of the North. Whatever disclaimers Lincoln might make about the war not being fought against slavery, the slaves themselves knew better. When Du Pont's flotilla steamed into Port Royal Sound in November, 1861, the slaves on the Sea Islands in the sound knew exactly what the rumble of the federal naval guns meant. "Son, dat ain't no t'under," whispered one slave boy's mother, "dat Yankee come to gib you Freedom."[40] Soon, federal garrisons and commanders found themselves besieged by runaways who expected that having found the federal army, they were now free. In May of 1861, three runaways showed up at Fortress Monroe, the solitary outpost of federal authority left in Confederate Virginia, and they appealed to the commander, Benjamin Butler, for protection. The next day, their master showed up at Fortress Monroe to demand the return of his slaves under the terms of the Fugitive Slave Law. But Butler, a Massachusetts Democrat who had promptly offered his services to Lincoln after Fort Sumter, smartly informed the master that since Virginia had seceded from the Union, it had forfeited all the benefits of the Fugitive Slave Law. Of course, Butler did not exactly have the power to declare the three runaways free, but when he learned that they had been assigned to dig Confederate fortifications, he decided that they were certainly "contraband of war," and therefore liable to seizure by the federal government as enemy property. Butler put them to work at Fortress Monroe; by July, a thousand such "contrabands" had presented themselves for "seizure" by Butler.

This situation presented Lincoln with a dilemma: Like Butler, he had no constitutional power to make slaves free, but he certainly had no desire to make runaways slaves again. Therefore, Lincoln endorsed Butler's action, and in order to back him up, Congress passed a Confiscation Act in August, 1861, that permitted federal commanders to seize the slaves of anyone proven to be in arms against the federal government. The Confiscation Act was not a popular measure—the vote in Congress had gone almost straight down party lines—but its success encouraged Lincoln to believe that black freedom really could be made a viable part of his war program. On March 6, 1862, Lincoln proposed to Congress that the federal govern-

[39]David Donald, *Charles Sumner and the Rights of Man* (New York, 1970), p. 48.
[40]Willie Lee Rose, *Rehearsal for Reconstruction: The Port Royal Experiment* (New York, 1964), p. 12.

ment conduct an experiment in gradual emancipation of the slaves in the border states, with Congress offering compensation to any slave-owners who liberated their slaves. It was purely a voluntary program, and Lincoln was careful to justify it as a way of further detaching the border states from their connections to the slave South. Too careful, in fact, according to the abolitionist Republican Thaddeus Stevens, who contemptuously referred to the compensated emancipation scheme as "the most diluted milk and water gruel proposition that was ever given to the American nation." But Lincoln believed that his scheme actually represented a very different form of liquor. To the abolitionist orator Wendell Phillips, Lincoln confided that his real motive was not unlike the Irishman in the prohibitionist state of Maine, who asked for a glass of soda water "with a drop of the creature [put] into it unbeknownst to myself." Lincoln had asked for the soda water of limited emancipation, but with the real liquor of black freedom poured in "unbeknownst to myself." The principle of emancipation had been put forward, no matter how low its profile.

Lincoln hoped that compensated emancipation would begin a soft and unoffending abolition of slavery in the border states. But in the spring of 1862, as the debacle on the peninsula showed Lincoln that the southern states had no intention of being wooed by gentle handling either out of slavery or back into the Union, Lincoln began to reach for the unmentionable weapon of outright emancipation in the rebellious Confederacy. On July 12, 1862, as Congress was preparing to vote on an even more sweeping Confiscation Act, Lincoln warned the border states' congressional delegations to expect more and more dramatic antislavery measures from him. "Our country is in great peril," Lincoln argued, "demanding the loftiest views and boldest actions to bring it speedy relief." If they did not take action on their own "to emancipate gradually," then the "friction and abrasion" of war would do it for them. It was time, he said, referring to a biblical metaphor of cataclysm, to read "the signs of the times."[41]

In the event, the border states were not willing, and their congressional caucus voted to reject Lincoln's scheme. What was worse, General McClellan now chose this moment to lecture Lincoln on the unwisdom of dragging slavery into the war. This "should not be a War looking to the subjugation of the people of any state," nor should the "entire confiscation of property, political executions of persons, territorial organization of states or forcible abolition of slavery . . . be contemplated for a moment."[42] But Lincoln was long past caution on this point. On July 13th, Lincoln confided to Secretary of the Navy Gideon Welles that if the southern states persisted in their rebellion, it would be "a necessity and a duty on our part to liberate their slaves." Four days later, Congress passed the Second Confiscation

[41]Lincoln, "Appeal to Border State Representatives" [July 12, 1862], in Collected Works, vol. 5, pp. 318–319.
[42]"To Abraham Lincoln," in The Civil War Papers of George B. McClellan, Stephen W. Sears, ed. (New York, 1989), p. 344.

Act, which freed any and all slaves who came within the lines of the Union forces, no matter whether their masters were Unionists or seceders. Then, on July 22nd, Lincoln read to an astounded Cabinet a preliminary draft of an Emancipation Proclamation that would free all the slaves in the rebel states.[43]

As with the compensated emancipation proposal, Lincoln's proclamation sounded like a good deal less than the radical Republicans and the old-line abolitionists wanted. It provided only for the emancipation of slaves still inside Confederate territory, and left untouched slaves in the border states and in areas of the South already occupied by federal forces. Furthermore, emancipation was justified strictly as a military measure to further weaken the South internally, rather than as a stroke of political and moral justice. But, just like the compensated emancipation scheme again, there was more of the "creature" in it than met the eye. It was, in fact, a revolutionary gesture: It declared that slavery was the real danger to the republic, and promised that the war was now to be fought as a moral revolution to overturn the entire social and economic order of the South. Above all, it announced to whatever slaves might hear it that the federal army was now the jubilee in motion, with the proclamation acting as a standing invitation for slaves to flee to the safety of the federal army and navy to achieve their freedom. From 1863 onwards, up to 20 percent of the southern slave population deserted to the Union lines. The spirit of John Brown stalked the land again.

And yet the language of the proclamation that Lincoln was contemplating was couched in anything but revolutionary language. Lincoln's preliminary draft was a lawyer's brief, with all the emotional impact (as Richard Hofstadter once put it) "of a bill of lading," and the text of the proclamation was preoccupied with establishing the military necessities that formed the justification for it. Furthermore, Lincoln kept the discussion of the proclamation quiet, feeding the restlessness of antislavery Northerners like Horace Greeley, who could not understand why Lincoln was dragging his heels. Lincoln's public response to Greeley's "Prayer of Twenty Millions" in August was, in large measure, intended to soften the blow of the proclamation on unsympathetic Northerners; but it was also his way of underscoring that he had no Constitutional authority, apart from his place as commander in chief of the federal armed forces, to do anything about slavery. As a lawyer, Lincoln knew that only by offering a military justification for the Emancipation Proclamation, and limiting it to a military application (only the slaves in the Confederate states), could he secure emancipation from future constitutional challenges. Considering that Roger B. Taney was still the chief justice of the United Sates, security was no ignoble justification.

On the advice of his cabinet, Lincoln waited to publish the preliminary proclamation until the federal armies had won some significant victories so that the proclamation would not appear as a counsel of despair on Lincoln's part. Antietam gave

---

[43]Stephen B. Oates, "Lincoln's Journey to Emancipation," in *Our Fiery Trial: Abraham Lincoln, John Brown, and the Civil War Era* (Amherst, MA, 1979), pp. 80–85.

Lincoln all he needed in the form of a victory. On September 22, 1862, Lincoln released the text of the proclamation with the warning that, unless southern resistance ceased before January 1st, the terms of the proclamation would automatically go into effect on that date. The Confederates did little more than rain curses on Lincoln's head, and on January 1, 1863, the proclamation became official.

Northern Democrats were aghast, and in the Army of the Potomac, there were ugly mutterings among McClellan's old officers about not wanting to fight a war just to liberate the slaves. "The Democrats are bold in their treason & [we] may have civil war in Indiana in six months," wrote one Ohio Republican in Congress, who also heard it darkly "asserted that the Army of the Potomac had been drilled into an anti-Republican engine. . . ."[44] Lincoln told his secretary, John Hay, that he had heard of a "McClellan conspiracy" that aimed to thwart emancipation by avoiding "any decisive victory . . . to keep things running on so that they, the Army, might manage things to suit themselves."[45] But in the end, no significant opposition to the proclamation emerged from the North or from its armies. The November congressional elections brought the Republicans a gain of five seats in the Senate; and although the Democrats sent thirty-five new Congressmen to Washington, the Republicans held on to a twenty-five-seat majority in the House. As for the Army of the Potomac, McClellan's officers might mutter as they liked: The ordinary soldiers had seen enough of what slavery really was along the peninsula to change even the most self-interested Yankee into a hardened and abolitionist. "To magnify & Perpetuate Slavery the slave holders brought on this war," wrote Theodore Gates, the colonel of the 20th New York, the week after the proclamation became official. "It will be but a just retribution that slavery dies by the war."[46] The soldiers of the 150th Pennsylvania actually held a political rally in March, 1863, to declare their support for the proclamation and their anger at Democratic or McClellanite dissension:

> . . . we believe that "fighting for Southern rights" means nothing more than warring for the extension of slavery, which we regard alike as a *curse to the land,* and a *great moral wrong.* . . . [and] we hail with joy the President's proclamation doing away with that institution in every State in which rebellion exists, and hope soon to see it forever blotted from our soil.[47]

Thus Lincoln and the United States at last arrived at the goal of black freedom. But this only extended to the slave the goal of natural rights, to life and liberty; nothing had as yet been said by Lincoln about black political equality. The Emanci-

---

[44]Allan G. Bogue, "William Parker Cutler's Congressional Diary of 1862–63," in *Civil War History* 33 (December 1987), pp. 322–323.

[45]*Lincoln and the Civil War in the Diaries and Letters of John Hay,* Tyler Dennett, ed. (1939; rept. Westport, CT, 1972), pp. 50–51.

[46]*The Civil War Diaries of Col. Theodore B. Gates, 20th New York State Militia,* Seward R. Osborne, ed. (Hightstown, NJ, 1991), p. 60.

[47]"Resolution of Soldiers of the 150th Pennsylvania Volunteers, March 11, 1863," in *The Radical Republicans and Reconstruction, 1861–1870,* Harold M. Hyman, ed. (Indianapolis, IN, 1967), pp. 108–109.

pation Proclamation only brought all African Americans up to the level where Lincoln had left Douglas in the 1858 debates. The question remained whether the next step, which Lincoln had denied in 1858 as a necessary consequence, had to be taken after all. Lincoln, still hoping to evade a political gauntlet, at first hoped that he could dodge the question by promoting several schemes for colonizing emancipated blacks elsewhere—in effect, suggesting that they find political equality someplace other than the United States. Colonization had been one of the pet solutions of the Whigs ever since the days of Henry Clay, and in August, 1862, Lincoln the ex-Whig tried to persuade a delegation of free black leaders led by Edward M. Thomas that it would be all for the best if African Americans could create a new life for themselves in Liberia, or Central America, or the Caribbean, rather than trying to raise themselves to political equality in white America. But few black leaders saw any reason why they should have to abandon the only country they had known. Frederick Douglass was outraged when he heard of Lincoln's plans for colonization. "Mr. Lincoln assumes the language and arguments of an itinerant Colonization lecturer," Douglass stormed on the pages of his newest publication, *Douglass's Monthly* in September, 1862, "showing all his inconsistencies, his pride of race and blood, his contempt for Negroes and his canting hypocrisy." A mass meeting of free blacks in Philadelphia denounced the colonization plans: "Shall we sacrifice this, leave our homes, forsake our birthplace, and flee to a strange land to appease the anger and prejudice of the traitors now in arms against the Government?"[48] Obviously not, unless Lincoln was prepared to force them at gunpoint. So, in the end, it came back to Lincoln to persuade a nation whose basic racial theories were usually little more than variations on bigotry that they were going to have to accept African Americans as their political and social equals, as well as their natural equals.

The resentment Lincoln stirred over the colonization scheme seems to have marked something of a turning point in terms of his own racial prejudices. In August, 1863, when Frederick Douglass came to the White House to meet Lincoln for the first time, he was sure that he would still meet a president who was "preeminently the white man's president, entirely devoted to the welfare of white men." But he came away with a very different view of Lincoln than he had expected. Lincoln was "the first great man that I talked with in the United States freely who in no single instance reminded me of the difference between himself and myself, or the difference of color."[49] Nor did Lincoln mean to allow others to remind Douglass of the issue of color, and Lincoln was soon implementing a series of measures that would at least bring African Americans closer to the mainstream of American life. The first of these measures came in the form of an economic experiment. When the federal navy seized the islands in the Port Royal Sound in the fall of 1861, the navy expected only to use the islands as a coaling station for the federal navy's blockade

---

[48]Blight, *Frederick Douglass' Civil War: Keeping Faith in Jubilee*, pp. 138–140.
[49]Douglass, *Life and Times of Frederick Douglass, Written By Himself* (New York, 1941), pp. 347–349.

of the Carolina coast. But slaveowners on the islands fled from the northern occupation, leaving their plantations, and in many cases their slaves, behind. Since the slaves could now be deemed "contraband," Treasury officials at Port Royal began putting the slaves to work harvesting the cotton on the abandoned plantations. Then, with the backing of antislavery societies in Boston, New York, and Philadelphia, a small army of white civilian "Gideonites" descended upon Port Royal with evangelical fire in their hearts and schoolbooks in their hands to preach, to teach, to heal, and to divide up the old plantations into farm plots for the newly free slaves to manage as their own property. The results were extremely gratifying— one of the new cotton-planting operations easily cleared $80,000 in one year—and they demonstrated that free blacks had the full capacity to compete equally with whites on national markets and without having to displace northern workers.[50]

The second measure was military in nature. At the beginning of the war, thousands of free blacks volunteered to serve in the Union army. But the regular army had a long-standing policy of refusing to take black soldiers, and the state volunteers excluded blacks under the terms of the 1792 federal militia act. However, a new militia act in July of 1862 gave the president discretion to enlist black soldiers as he saw fit, and after the Emancipation Proclamation became official, the doors to black enlistment were gradually swung open. "The bare sight of fifty thousand armed and drilled black soldiers on the banks of the Mississippi would end the rebellion at once," Lincoln wrote to Andrew Johnson, a Tennessee Unionist, "And who doubts that we can present that sight if we but take hold in earnest."[51] Eventually, 178,000 African Americans enlisted in the Union army, and almost 10,000 served in the navy.

Most of the black recruits were organized into segregated regiments commanded by white officers, and sworn directly into federal service (and numbered as the 1st through the 138th United States Colored Troops, along with six regiments of cavalry, fourteen of heavy artillery, and 10 batteries of light artillery). Several other regiments, like the 5th Massachusetts Colored Cavalry, the 29th Connecticut Colored Infantry, and the 54th and 55th Massachusetts Infantry were raised as state volunteers (although in the case of the 54th Massachusetts, recruits were enlisted from all over the North, rather than just Massachusetts). In whatever form, they shocked a number of white soldiers out of their smug bigotry. "I never believed in niggers before," wrote one Wisconsin cavalryman, "but by Jesus, they are hell in fighting."[52] That, in turn, forced on the federal government the burning question how African Americans who fought to defend the Union could any longer be denied full political equality, and with it the right to vote, in that Union. "Once let a black man get upon his person the brass letters U.S.," said Frederick Douglass,

[50]Willie Lee Rose, *Rehearsal for Reconstruction: The Port Royal Experiment* (New York, 1964), p. 306.
[51]Lincoln, "To Andrew Johnson" [March 26, 1863], in *Collected Works*, vol. 6, pp. 149–150.
[52]Randall Jimerson, *The Private Civil War: Popular Thought during the Sectional Conflict* (Baton Rouge, 1988), p. 106.

"let him get an eagle on his button, and a musket on his shoulder and bullets in his pockets, and there is no power on earth which can deny he has won the right to citizenship in the United States." For Douglass, that claim had a personal tinge: Two of his sons, Claude and Lewis, enlisted in the army, and a third, Frederick, Jr., worked as a recruiter for the black regiments among freed slaves in Mississippi.

Ultimately, it was up to Lincoln to answer Douglass's challenge, and he began to work on the extension of voting rights to freed slaves as early as 1863. There was, at first, some difficulty in determining where that experiment ought to take place, especially since a number of the free states still denied free blacks the right to vote. That problem was solved for Lincoln by the federal navy, which seized the port city of New Orleans in April of 1862 and opened most of southern Louisiana to federal occupation by the end of the year. In the summer of 1863, Lincoln approved a plan for occupied Louisiana for electing a state legislature that would rescind the state secession ordinance and adopt a new state constitution. In December, Lincoln issued an amnesty proclamation offering pardon to any rebels who took an oath of allegiance to the United States—and who swore to uphold all wartime policies concerning emancipation. In March, 1864, Lincoln urged the new governor of Louisiana, Michael Hahn, to make some limited provision in the new state constitution for black voting rights. "I barely suggest for your private consideration," Lincoln suggested softly, "whether some of the colored people may not be let in—as, for instance, the very intelligent, and especially those who have fought gallantly in our ranks. They would probably help, in some trying time to come, to keep the jewel of liberty within the family of freedom."[53] In the event, Hahn's constitutional convention balked at granting full voting rights to blacks, and would only concede "permission" to the legislature to extend the vote to blacks if it later saw fit. But the principle of political equality had at least been granted, even if grudgingly and of necessity, and in 1865, Lincoln would make full voting rights for blacks a necessary part of the reconstruction of the southern states.

Lincoln was fully conscious when he issued the Emancipation Proclamation that he was sending the war and the country down a very different road from the one people had thought they would go. If he seems to have taken an unconscionably long time about taking that turn, and if he made a number of ambiguous utterances about the relationship of the war and slavery beforehand, it was largely because all of Lincoln's instincts led him to avoid tumultuous challenges over issues and seek evasions or compromises that would allow him to get the decision he wanted without paying the costs. He had yet to confront for himself the full implications of some of the issues of black freedom and black equality, and he knew that the North was even further from having come to grips with them. "No human power can subdue this rebellion without using the Emancipation lever as I have done," Lincoln realized. But to bring African Americans out of slavery and into the war to save the Union meant that the Union, if victorious, had an immense

[53]Lincoln, "To Michael Hahn" [March 13, 1864], in *Collected Works*, vol. 7, p. 243.

obligation to grant them full political equality as Americans. "If they stake their lives for us, they must be prompted by the strongest motive . . . and the promise, being made, must be kept." If he failed to honor that promise, Lincoln ruefully acknowledged, "I should be damned in time & in eternity for so doing."[54]

The problem Lincoln would now face would be finding a general for the Army of the Potomac with a similar vision for the war. And when he finally dismissed George B. McClellan in November, 1862, he had no idea that it would take another bloody year before he would find one.

Further Reading

The military history of the American Civil War has been so much the object of the military "buff" that it is sometimes difficult to disentangle faddism and hobby writing from the serious history of Civil War combat. Among the finest new approaches have been Herman Hattaway and Archer Jones, *How the North Won: A Military History of the Civil War* (Urbana, IL, 1983) and Richard E. Beringer, Herman Hattaway, Archer Jones, and William Still, *Why the South Lost the Civil War* (Athens, GA, 1986). Two specific studies that touch on the theoretical aspects of Civil War strategy and tactics are Edward Hagerman's *The American Civil War and the Origins of Modern Warfare: Ideas, Organization, and Field Command* (Bloomington, IN, 1988) and Paddy Griffith's *Battle Tactics of the Civil War* (New Haven, 1987), both of which I have borrowed from with great delight. One fairly eccentric but highly informative interpretation of Civil War combat is Grady McWhiney and Perry D. Jamieson, *Attack and Die: Civil War Military Tactics and the Southern Heritage* (University, AL, 1982). The structure of the prewar U.S. Army is covered in George Ness, *The Regular Army on the Eve of the Civil War* (Baltimore, 1990), while the tiny and all-but-forgotten Confederate regular army has found a remembrance in Richard Weinert and his *The Confederate Regular Army* (Shippensburg, PA, 1991).

The opening campaigns of the war mentioned in this chapter can be traced in greater detail in a plethora of battle histories, beginning with William C. Davis's *Battle at Bull Run: A History of the First Major Campaign of the Civil War* (New York, 1977). George McClellan has enjoyed a highly interesting biography in Stephen W. Sears, *George B. McClellan: The Young Napoleon* (New York, 1987), which should be read in conjunction with Sears's 1983 book on the Antietam campaign, *Landscape Turned Red: The Battle of Antietam* (New York, 1983) and a more recent history of the peninsula, *To The Gates of Richmond: The Peninsula Campaign* (New York, 1992). Rowena Reed's *Combined Operations in the Civil War* (Annapolis, 1978) is a highly innovative work that touches on technical aspects of the peninsula campaign. The peninsula brought Robert E. Lee to the forefront of the Civil War, and the four volumes of Douglas Southall Freeman's *R. E. Lee* (New York, 1936) remain the place to begin with the great Virginia general. John Hennessy's *Return to Bull Run: The Campaign and Battle of Second Manassas* (New York, 1993) offers a particularly good account of this long-neglected battle. The literature on Antietam is particularly rich in new works. The long-time standard, James V.

---

[54]Lincoln, "Interview with Alexander W. Randall and Joseph T. Mills" [August 19, 1864], in *Collected Works*, vol. 7, p. 507.

Murfin's *The Gleam of Bayonets: The Battle of Antietam and Robert E. Lee's Maryland Campaign, September, 1862* (New York, 1965), has found new company in Stephen Sears's Antietam book and in John Priest, *Antietam: The Soldiers' Battle* (Shippensburg, 1989).

The final object of the battles came back to the question of slavery and its future, and for understanding the agonizing position of blacks who wanted the war for the Union to become a war of freedom, James M. McPherson's *The Struggle for Equality: Abolitionists and the Negro in the Civil War and Reconstruction* (Princeton, 1964) and the works of Benjamin Quarles, *The Negro in the Civil War* (New York, 1953) and *The Black Abolitionists* (New York, 1969) are still important starting places. The centrality of Frederick Douglass in this regard is attested to by a number of fine studies of Douglass and his writings, including Waldo E. Martin, *The Mind of Frederick Douglass* (Chapel Hill, NC, 1984) the authors of the essays in *Frederick Douglass: New Literary and Historical Essays* (New York, 1990) edited by Eric J. Sundquist, and D. J. Preston, *Young Frederick Douglass: The Maryland Years* (Baltimore, 1980). Benjamin Quarles's *Frederick Douglass* (New York, 1948) remains an important landmark in interpreting Douglass, but it now has to be read in the light of two important new works, William S. McFeely's biography *Frederick Douglass* (New York, 1991) and David W. Blight's study of the wartime Douglass, *Frederick Douglass' Civil War: Keeping Faith in Jubilee* (Baton Rouge, 1989).

The controversial question of Lincoln's motives and intentions in issuing the Emancipation Proclamation has been handled from opposing angles by Don D. Fehrenbacher, "Only His Stepchildren: Lincoln and the Negro," in *Civil War History* 20 (December 1974), pp. 293–310, and George M. Frederickson, "A Man But Not a Brother: Abraham Lincoln and Racial Equality," in the *Journal of Southern History* 61 (February 1975), pp. 39–58. One of the most negative portrayals of Lincoln and emancipation is contained in Frederickson's, *The Black Image in the White Mind: The Debate on Afro-American Character and Destiny, 1817–1914* (New York, 1971), but many of Frederickson's conclusions were challenged in the 1980s, and Lawanda Cox's *Lincoln and Black Freedom: A Study in Presidential Leadership* (Urbana, IL, 1985) offers a considerably more sympathetic portrayal of Lincoln's intentions, especially in the context of Lincoln's early reconstruction plans for Louisiana. Louis S. Gerteis's *From Contraband to Freedman: Federal Policy Toward Southern Blacks, 1861–1865* (Westport, CT, 1973) and William A. Gladstone's profusely illustrated *United States Colored Troops, 1863–1867* (Gettysburg, PA, 1990) offer two glimpses of the ways in which the Union stumbled awake to its obligations to the freed slave.

CHAPTER 5

Elusive Victories

East and West: 1862–1863

"The Mississippi is well worth reading about," wrote Mark Twain in the opening lines of *Life on the Mississippi*. "It is not a commonplace river, but on the contrary is in all ways remarkable." For Twain, who was born beside it and worked upon it, most of that remarkableness was a matter of the colorful characters who populated the river, the clusters of peculiar towns along its banks, and the eccentricities of the broad, slow-winding river itself. For foreign travelers in the South, it was the vast cross-section of life it contained that regularly left their mouths agape. When William Howard Russell arrived in Memphis, he was bewildered by how the river embraced "this strange kaleidoscope of Negroes and whites, of extremes of civilisation in its American development . . . of enormous steamers on the river, which bears equally the dug-out or canoe of the black fisherman" and "all the phenomena of active commercial life . . . included in the same scope of vision which takes in at the other side of the Mississippi lands scarcely settled."[1] The Mississippi was almost more than a river: As Twain remembered it, the Mississippi was "the great Mississippi, the majestic, the magnificent Mississippi, rolling its mile-wide tide along, shining in the sun."

Twain and Russell were not the only ones in 1862 concerned with the grandeur of the Mississippi River. Both Jefferson Davis and Abraham Lincoln had traveled, worked, and lived on the Mississippi and knew it well. Lincoln had grown up in Indiana and Illinois with the talk of the river and its great tributaries all around him, and in his youth, he had flat-boated cargoes of goods downriver for sale. Jefferson Davis's sprawling plantation, Brierfields, occupied a portion of Davis Bend, eighty miles on the river above Natchez, Mississippi. But the immediate concern of both Davis and Lincoln with the river in 1862 was commercial, not aesthetic or romantic. Whatever else the river was to Americans, it was the great commercial highway of the American republic. Before the Revolution, the econ-

[1]Russell, *My Diary North and South*, Fletcher Pratt, ed. (New York, 1954), pp. 139, 161.

omy of Britain's North American colonies was hooked into Britain's transatlantic trading networks, and the economic geography of that trade ran eastward, to the Atlantic seaboard. With the creation of the United States, and Britain's surrender of all of its former colonial territory over the Appalachian mountains, white settlers poured over the mountain passes into Kentucky, Tennessee, the Northwest territories, and eventually (after Andrew Jackson had ruthlessly cleared out the Cherokee, Creek and Seminole Indians) the Alabama and Mississippi territories. But rather than attempting to trade their agricultural surpluses back over the Appalachians, the new settlers discovered instead that it was much easier to trundle their goods down to the broad navigable rivers that drained the trans-Appalachian territories— the Ohio River, the Cumberland River, the Tennessee River. All of those rivers flowed west or south, away from the old Atlantic seaboard trading centers, and all of them emptied into the even broader southward flow of the Mississippi.

With the addition in 1803 of the Louisiana Purchase territory, the republic acquired undisputed title to the entire Mississippi River valley, plus its great western tributaries, the Red and Missouri Rivers. Taken together, the entire Mississippi River system pulled into itself the commerce of 1.25 million square miles in a gigantic net that stretched to include Pittsburgh on the east and St. Louis on the west, and it tied Westerners and Southerners into closer economic units than Westerners enjoyed with the old east coast. It was the river, too, that helped to throw Southerners into the lap of the Democratic party in the 1830s and 1840s, since they had no wish to help the Whigs build canals and highways in the North when the river brought the nation's commerce their way simply by force of nature.

If the river provided the means for getting the agricultural commerce of the west to market, it was the port of New Orleans that provided the marketplace— provided, in fact, one of the great international entrepôts of the world. Down the long river network to New Orleans went most of the grain, hogs, cattle, cotton, goods, and produce of Ohio, Minnesota, Missouri, Indiana, Kentucky, Mississippi, Illinois, and Louisiana; and then, in the 1850s, as Tennessee and the border states developed new iron and textile industries, the South's infant industrial potential poured out onto the rivers and down to New Orleans, as well. Up the river from New Orleans, beating against the sluggish brown current of the Mississippi, came the imported goods and manufactures that southern and western agriculture depended on. In 1814, New Orleans welcomed twenty-one steamboats and 67,560 tons of freight to its river docks; by 1830, 778 steamboats snuffled into place along the ever-expanding docks, bearing over 260,000 tons of freight and agricultural produce worth over $26 million; by 1860 and the outbreak of the Civil War, New Orleans had to accommodate over 3,500 steamboat arrivals during the year, with over 2 million tons of freight and cotton, wheat, and other agricultural goods that earned over $185 million. It was from New Orleans that William Howard Russell could see "a grand slave confederacy enclosing the Gulf in its arms, and swelling to the shores of the Potomac and Chesapeake, with the entire control of the Mississippi and a monoply of the great staples on which so much of the manufacture and commerce of England and France depend."[2] If cotton was king, then New Orleans was its prophet.

It was scarcely noticed that, by 1860, some of the Mississippi River system's grand predominance over the west was already beginning to slip away. Southerners in Congress could block the massive appropriations needed for building the rival systems of national roads and canals that would divert western trade back toward eastern markets, but they could not prevent state legislatures in the North from building canals of their own, like New York's Erie Canal, which linked the entire Great Lakes water system with the Hudson River and New York City. Nor could they prevent private railroads—the steam-powered mate of the riverboat—from extending their fingers over the Alleghenies into Ohio and Illinois and across the Mississippi into Missouri. The knell for New Orleans' slipping control over the commerce of the continent rang in 1856, when the steamboat *Effie Afton* rammed a railroad bridge over the Mississippi at Rock Island, Illinois. The boat burned and sank, and the vessel's owners sued the owners of the bridge—the Rock Island Bridge Company—on the grounds that the bridge was a hazard to navigation. The real question was whether New Orleans river traffic deserved a better right-of-way than a Yankee railroad, and in the event, the steamboat (and New Orleans) lost the case.

One of the lawyers for the railroad was Abraham Lincoln.

1. The War on the Border

At the outbreak of the war, the importance of controlling the Mississippi River and its vast system of tributary rivers was obvious to both the Union and the Confederate governments. Indeed, the only really aggressive feature of General Winfield Scott's "Anaconda Plan" had been its insistence on redeeming the Mississippi River valley for the Union. So long as the Confederacy controlled the lower Mississippi River and New Orleans, the prevailing wisdom dictated that northern farmers everywhere west of the Appalachians would suddenly face ruin, and angered farmers were very likely to take their anger with them to the ballot box at the next congressional by-elections unless Lincoln and his soldiers did something about it very quickly. By the same token, Jefferson Davis realized that the Confederacy would never be secure unless it could control not just New Orleans and the lower Mississippi, but also the great tributaries, the Ohio and the Missouri.

The Ohio was, in Davis's judgment, the natural northern boundary of the southern Confederacy. The Ohio would offer a natural defensive moat for southern armies to resist federal invasion. Also, Confederate presence on the south bank of the Ohio would further paralyze northern commerce and force the Lincoln govern-

[2]Russell, *My Diary*, p. 137.

ment to the negotiating table. But most important of all, the Ohio was fed, near its confluence with the Mississippi, by two vital rivers, the Tennessee and the Cumberland, which led deep into Tennessee, Mississippi, and Alabama. Unless the south bank of the Ohio was firmly in Confederate hands federal steam-powered transports, supply ships, and gunboats could enter the Tennessee and Cumberland Rivers without obstruction and use them as easy invasion routes into the Confederate heartland. But in order to control the Ohio, the Confederates needed to control the border states, especially Kentucky and Missouri, and that was precisely what Abraham Lincoln was determined to prevent. He still hoped, well into 1862, that Confederate control of the upper South could be disrupted by appealing to pro-Union sentiment in eastern Tennessee, western Virginia, and northern Alabama and Arkansas. But none of that would be possible if Kentucky and Missouri, by falling into Confederate hands, stood in the way. "To lose Kentucky is nearly the same as to lose the whole game," Lincoln wrote to Orville Browning in September, 1861, "Kentucky gone, we cannot hold Missouri, nor, as I think, Maryland. These all against us, and the job on our hands is too large for us."[3]

Thus, the political race to woo the border states became the first round of the Civil War in the west, and in the case of both Missouri and Kentucky, it was a round won largely by the Union. At first, all the advantages in the race seemed to belong to the Confederacy. Both Missouri and Kentucky were slave states, and had important social and economic ties to the South, and every natural appearance indicated that they would join the Confederacy. But the appearances proved deceiving, and for two reasons. The first was Lincoln's carefully cultivated assertions that he had no intention of touching slavery in the states where it was sanctioned by the Constitution. Those assurances, however much they grated on the ears of abolitionists, persuaded border state Unionists not to risk their slave property on the shaky chances of a rebellion. Second, in both states, slavery was not nearly as powerful an institution as in the lower South, and slaveholding and strong Unionist sentiments often existed hand-in-hand. Missouri quickly became a case in point. Although Missouri had been a slave state since the days of the Missouri Compromise, slavery had actually flourished there only along a fairly narrow belt of counties stretching across the center of the state. In St. Louis, Missouri's principal Mississippi River town, the population was increasingly taking on a free-soil flavor from immigrants from across the Mississippi River in Illinois, and from a flourishing community of German refugees and exiles who found their home there after having fled political oppression in Germany following the revolutions of 1848, and who had no sympathy at all with slavery. As the lower South began to secede from the Union, the proslavery governor of Missouri, Claiborne F. Jackson, strong-armed the state legislature into calling a secession convention. But not a single one of the delegates elected to the convention favored secession for Missouri, and it adjourned in February, 1861, leaving Missouri still in the Union. Lincoln's call for volunteers

[3]Lincoln, "To Orville H. Browning" [September 22, 1861], in *Collected Works*, vol. 4, p. 532.

after Sumter set off another call for a secession convention in April, and as an extra measure to support secession, Governor Jackson called out the state militia and Missouri Unionists believed that he was ready to seize the federal arsenal in St. Louis. But Jackson and the militia had not reckoned with the boldness of the arsenal's commander, Captain Nathaniel Lyon. On May 10th, Lyon surrounded a state militia encampment at Lindell's Grove with 7,000 regulars and pro-Union volunteers and captured the entire encampment without a shot. But when Lyon attempted to parade his prisoners through the streets of St. Louis to the arsenal, he was attacked by a prosecession mob and his men opened fire. Twenty-eight people, including many innocent bystanders, were killed.

Lyon's preemptive strike at the militia had been unauthorized and even reckless, but it successfully stunned the secession movement in Missouri before it had barely gotten under way. After a month of fruitless political jockeying between himself and Lyon, Jackson fled to southwestern Missouri with a proslavery remnant of the legislature, and there declared Missouri out of the Union. But the Unionists organized their own ad hoc legislature, the "Long Convention," and Jackson's rump assembly never really amounted to more than a government-in-exile. Although Missouri would be repeatedly invaded by Confederate forces loyal to Jackson, and large areas of the backcountry were turned by Confederate guerillas into no-go areas for federal troops, they never seriously threatened the hold that Missouri Unionists retained on St. Louis and the strategic dock-and-riverbank areas along Missouri's stretch of the Mississippi.

The story in Kentucky was fundamentally the same. The governor, Beriah Magoffin, was proslavery and called the Kentucky legislature into special session to arrange for a state secession convention. But when the legislature met on January 17, 1861, it turned down Magoffin's request and instead chided the southern states for reacting too hastily to Lincoln's election. After Lincoln's call for volunteers, Magoffin again begged the legislature to call for a secession convention; again the legislature refused, and Magoffin was forced to resort to the unusual expedient of declaring Kentucky "neutral."[4] Both Lincoln and Davis were anxious not to push the Kentuckians too hard. Davis, like Lincoln, wanted "to treat Kentucky with all possible respect." And so, for several months, Union forces on the other side of the Ohio and Confederate forces below the Kentucky border fumed and waited. In August, however, the Kentucky legislative elections gave a resounding majority to pro-Union delegates. Reading what he presumed was Union-slanted handwriting on the wall, the Confederate commander in western Tennessee, Major General Leonidas Polk, decided that the Confederacy could wait no longer to secure the Ohio River line, and on September 3, 1861, Polk's troops moved into Kentucky and occupied Columbus. Jefferson Davis supported Polk's action, and Confederate troops moved over into Kentucky to occupy Bowling Green. As a result, the Kentucky legislature angrily voted to end state neutrality and reconfirm its alle-

4William B. Hesseltine, *Lincoln and the War Governors* (New York, 1948), pp. 209–210.

giance to the Union. The unhappy Governor Magoffin resigned his office in August, 1862, and retreated into private law practice.

Keeping Kentucky and Missouri in the Union saved the Ohio River line for the North by the end of 1861. The question now, however, would be what the federal government proposed to do next about it, and on that score both President Lincoln and his new general-in-chief, George B. McClellan, both had very clear ideas. Lincoln wanted Kentucky occupied at once and cleared of Confederates, followed by a thrust into eastern Tennessee that would rally Tennessee Unionists to the federal armies. McClellan also advocated a movement into Kentucky and eastern Tennessee in the spring of 1862 as part of his overall plan to move on Virginia and the Carolina coast. Unfortunately, the federal forces along the Ohio River line were badly organized and equipped, and, what was more, the length of the Ohio River was divided between two military departments whose commanders were either unwilling or unable to cooperate. The first of these departments, the Department of the Ohio, running from western Virginia to the mouth of the Cumberland River, consisted of about 45,000 men commanded by Brigadier General Don Carlos Buell. It was to Buell that McClellan looked to spearhead the drive into eastern Tennessee. In January of 1862, he wrote anxiously to Buell that "my own advance cannot, according to my present views, be made until your troops are soundly established in the eastern portion of Tennessee."[5] But Buell was badly hampered by the rawness of his men, his lack of experienced officers, and by the difficulties of the terrain that lay before him. Although he defeated a small Confederate force at Logan's Crossroads, in southern Kentucky, on January 19, 1862, Buell's men had neither roads nor railroads to operate upon, and they proceeded to bog themselves down in the impenetrable wild mountains north of Knoxville.

This provided an unlooked-for opportunity to Buell's neighbor, Major General Henry Wager Halleck, the commanding general of the Department of Missouri, whose military jurisdiction stretched from the Cumberland River into Missouri itself. An aloof, forbidding officer, Halleck was an 1839 graduate of West Point, and one of the prizes of the Corps of Engineers. He was also a clear-thinking and capable administrator, and after leaving the army as a captain in 1854, he served as secretary of state for California, practiced law in San Francisco, and wrote several outstanding textbooks on legal and military affairs. The outbreak of the war brought him back to the army as a major general, and in November, 1861, he inherited the troubled Department of Missouri. His appointment as the department head was largely prompted by Halleck's considerable administrative skills, since Missouri in 1862 was still a large political black hole, and no one expected much from him in the way of fighting.

But Halleck had no intention of playing second fiddle to Buell. In January, 1862, Halleck suggested to McClellan that a more direct route into the southern

[5]McClellan to Buell [January 6, 1862], in The Civil War Papers of George B. McClellan: Selected Correspondence, 1860–1865 (New York, 1989), p. 148.

heartland lay in western, rather than eastern, Tennessee. There, Halleck pointed out, an army willing to borrow the steamboats that carried the river commerce could use the broad, navigable Cumberland and Tennessee Rivers to move upon instead of getting as bogged down as Buell was in eastern Kentucky. What was more, the Tennessee River was navigable to steam-powered transports and gunboats all the way south through Tennessee into Alabama, while the Cumberland wound eastward into the eastern Tennessee mountains. An army that controlled these rivers could, just by sitting along them, force three things to happen. First, using steamboats to seize control of the Tennessee River would isolate the occupation force that the Confederates had installed at Columbus, Kentucky, and compel them to retreat in order to keep their lines of supply open. That could clear all of western Kentucky of rebels at one stroke. Second, a similar steamboat movement up the Cumberland would turn the flank of whatever Confederate forces were in the eastern mountains of Kentucky and force them to withdraw into middle Tennessee and abandon eastern Tennessee without a battle. And third, such an operation would have the additional advantage of severing the Memphis & Ohio Railroad, one of the Confederacy's two east-west railroad lines, because the Memphis & Ohio relied on bridges over the Tennessee River, as well as the Cumberland River at Clarksville, which gunboats could easily destroy. By moving into western Kentucky and Tennessee on the rivers, rather than marching overland through eastern Kentucky and Tennessee, a federal army could easily peel open the upper South like ripe fruit.

It went without saying, of course, that both the Cumberland and Tennessee Rivers flowed through Halleck's rather than Buell's department, and that any such operation would be under Halleck's and not Buell's command. But even considering the element of personal ambition lurking within this plan, Halleck had a point. Even Buell conceded that it might be a wise move to try to crack the Confederacy's shell further to the west than he himself was operating. So, in January, 1862, even while he was still haranguing Buell to move into eastern Tennessee, McClellan acceded to Halleck's proposal to push up the two rivers into western Tennessee, with Nashville as the ultimate objective.

Halleck's plan succeeded beyond anyone's wildest dreams, and that was chiefly because he enjoyed two advantages that, it is safe to say, no one else in the world possessed. The first was a fleet of ironclad gunboats ideally designed for river warfare. Prior to the 19th century, and for almost as long as ships had been used as weapons of war, navies had been content to build their warships—and all their other ships—of wood, and relied on lofts of sail to move them. Even if the navies of Europe had seriously desired to plate their wooden ships with protective iron, the technology of ironmaking was too primitive and too expensive before the 19th century to provide iron that would not shatter upon impact, while the inability of sail to move ships weighted down with iron armor would leave an ironclad warship almost dead in the water. But in 1814, at about the same time that steam-powered river boats first appeared on the Mississippi River system, the British navy began experimenting with steam propulsion in its warships, first in the form of paddlewheel steamers, and then using ships which employed steam-driven screw propellers. Then, in the 1820s, the French navy began developing explosive shells for use by its warships, so that even the best-built wooden warship could be turned into a roaring holocaust with only one hit by a naval gun. With steam propulsion at last available to move heavier and heavier ships, and pressed with the urgent necessity of protecting their wooden warships from the fiery impact of explosive shells, both the French and the British navies began tinkering with the use of protective iron armor. The Crimean War of 1854–1856, in which France and England were allied against Russia, gave the two navies the chance to try out their ideas under fire. They constructed five "floating batteries," awkward and unseaworthy monstrosities that were little more than large wooden packing cases with sloping sides sheathed in wrought iron, four-and-one-half inches thick. Although these gunboats could only crawl along at the antediluvian speed of 4 knots, their iron sides proved invulnerable to anything the Russian artillery could do to them, and they were a tremendous success. When in 1859 the British launched the first full-size, sea-going ironclad warship, *Warrior*, a new age in naval warfare had at last arrived.

The lessons taught by the "floating batteries" were not lost on American designers, and in August, 1861, the War Department contracted with John B. Eads to build seven ironclad gunboats for use on the western rivers. Eads and his chief designer, Samuel Pook, built what amounted to a series of 512-ton "floating batteries" like those used in the Crimea, with flat bottoms, slanting armored sides of two-and-a-half inches of iron plate, and an assortment of cannon. Known as "Pook's Turtles," the gunboats were awkward to handle, badly overweight, and (since no one seems to have thought of who was going to operate them) had no crews. But the naval officer detached to bring them into service, a stern antislavery Connecticut salt named Andrew Foote, managed to get the boats finished and launched, rounded up crews (with Halleck's authorization), and otherwise provided Halleck with an armored naval flotilla. "Pook's Turtles" were far from being great warships, but they were more than anything the Confederates had on the Tennessee or the Cumberland.

Nothing that Foote or the gunboats achieved along the rivers would have amounted to much if Halleck had not also possessed another less obvious advantage, and that was an officer who could take command of the Union land forces, work in tandem with Foote, and win Halleck's campaign for him. The name of that officer was Ulysses Simpson Grant.

No one in American history has ever looked less like a great general than Ulysses Grant, and there had been nothing in his life up to this point that in any way suggested he was ever going to be a great general. Born in Ohio in 1822 as Hiram Ulysses Grant, his father managed to wangle an appointment for him to West Point in 1839 (the congressman who made out the appointment papers somehow confused Grant's name with the names of some of Grant's relatives and this turned him into Ulysses Simpson Grant). No brilliant student, Grant graduated in 1843, the 21st in a class of 39 cadets, and although he was a talented horseman with a penchant for mathematics, he was shunted off as a lieutenant to the 4th U.S. Infantry. The Mexican-American War brought him his first action and first promotion to captain. But after the war, peacetime boredom and separation from his family drove him to alcohol, and in July, 1854, he resigned from the army.

For the next seven years, Grant failed at nearly everything he tried, until his father finally gave him a job as a clerk in a family leather-goods store in Galena, Illinois. Having been in the army most of his life, and with simple economic survival occupying all of his attention since leaving the army, Grant "had thought but little about politics." Although he was (like Lincoln) "a Whig by education and a great admirer of Mr. Clay," the disintegration of the Whigs left him with no one to vote for in 1856, and for a while he indulged a brief fling with the Know-Nothings. He soon enough grew weary of the Know-Nothings' ethnic hate-mongering, but his fear that a Republican presidential victory in 1856 would trigger civil war threw him to the Democrats. He had not lived in Galena long enough to register to vote in the 1860 election, which (he reflected later) was just as well, for if he had voted, it would have been for Douglas.[6] But when the war broke out, Grant unhesitatingly wrote to the War Department to try to get a commission in the regulars to fight secession. He never received a reply (the letter was found years later in "some out-of-the-way place" in the adjutant-general's office), but a month later, the governor of Illinois appointed Grant colonel of the 21st Illinois Volunteers, and from then on, Grant went nowhere but up. In September, a friend in Congress obtained a brigadier general's commission for him, and in November, he found himself under Halleck's command in the Department of Missouri.

Grant and Halleck had both seen the opportunity the Tennessee and Cumberland Rivers presented at virtually the same time. However, the Confederates in Kentucky also realized the vulnerability of the river lines and had constructed two forts at points on the rivers just below the Kentucky-Tennessee border—Fort Henry on the Tennessee River and Fort Donelson on the Cumberland. Both were in good position to bottle up the rivers pretty securely. But Flag Officer Foote was confident that his gunboats could beat down the fire of the forts if Grant could bring along enough infantry to take the forts from their landward sides. So, Halleck gave Grant 18,000 men, and on February 3, 1862, he put them onto an assortment of steamboats and transports, and along with Foote's gunboats, entered the Ohio and then the Tennessee River for the turn down to Fort Henry. As it turned out, heavy early-spring rains put Fort Henry's parade ground under two feet of Tennessee River overflow. Unable to return the fire of Foote's gunboats, the Confederates hurriedly abandoned Fort Henry on February 6th.

Almost any other federal commander in 1862 would have sat down at once and begged alternately for reinforcements, more supplies, and a promotion. But Grant

[6]Grant, "Personal Memoirs," in *Memoirs and Selected Letters*, M. D. McFeely and W. S. McFeely, eds. (New York, 1990), pp. 142, 144–145.

now began to demonstrate to what degree he resembled no other federal general in 1862 or any other year, for as soon as Fort Henry had surrendered, he sent one gunboat downriver to destroy the Memphis & Ohio Railroad bridge over the Tennessee, and he then casually telegraphed Halleck that he was going to move over to Fort Donelson at once.

Although Fort Donelson was really little more than a stockade with some particularly nasty gun emplacements overlooking the Cumberland, it proved a harder nut to crack than Fort Henry. Fort Donelson had a combined garrison of some 19,000 men, and its river batteries badly damaged Foote's gunboats when they tried to duplicate their earlier success at Fort Henry. But the Confederate command at Fort Donelson was divided unevenly between two incompetents, former Secretary of War John B. Floyd and Gideon Pillow, and even more badly divided over its options. Floyd and Pillow threw away, by inaction, an opportunity to beat Grant piecemeal while his troops were still strung out on the roads between the two forts. They then threw away an opportunity to evacuate Fort Donelson on February 15th when they punched an escape hole through Grant's lines and then turned about and walked back to their entrenchments. The next day, Fort Donelson finally surrendered to Grant. About 5,000 Confederates (including Floyd and Pillow) made off in the night, leaving another 14,000 to fall into Union hands.

Little more than a single week's campaigning had driven an ominous wedge into the upper South. It also made Grant a national hero, for when the last Confederate commander at Donelson sent out his white flag, suggesting that he and Grant negotiate for terms of surrender, Grant had bluntly replied that he would consider "no terms at all except immediate and unconditional surrender." It was with a genuine sense of relief that the northern public at last heard of a general who was concerned merely with winning, simply winning.

2. From Shiloh to Vicksburg

When the news of the surrender of Forts Henry and Donelson struck Washington, the victory-starved capital went berserk with joy. Guns boomed all day, and the Senate violated its own procedural rules by cheering and applauding like schoolboys. Grant suddenly found himself a man with a reputation for fighting, and on March 7th, he was rewarded with a promotion to major general, while Foote won promotion to rear admiral when Congress created the new rank that summer. Grant's aggressiveness was certainly a welcome departure from the attitude that other northern generals had brought to the battlefield, an attitude that may owe something to the fact that Grant had been a terrible student under Mahan at West Point and (unlike McClellan) had failed to win one of the much-coveted postings to the Corps of Engineers after graduation. Grant himself ruefully admitted that he "had never looked at a copy of tactics from the time of my graduation," and even then, "my standing in that branch of studies had been near the foot of the class." But in this case, Grant's ignorance only meant that he had less to unlearn and more readiness to adapt to the realities of his situation as a commander. "War is progressive," Grant wrote in his *Memoirs*, and as military historian John Keegan has pointed out, Grant showed a remarkable capacity to understand the ways in which this war would defy the tactical and strategic lessons inculcated by the West Point engineers.[7]

One way in which Grant's flexibility came immediately to his service was his appreciation for the telegraph as a means of strategic communication. Electrical telegraphy was only seventeen years old at the outbreak of the Civil War, and had never before been put to any serious military uses. But Grant understood at once the capacity of the telegraph to concentrate and transmit information and to allow generals to coordinate and redeploy scattered forces. He stayed in constant telegraphic communication with Halleck all during the Henry-Donelson campaign, laying down miles of telegraph wire as he advanced, and in later campaigns Grant stayed in constant touch with his subordinates over telegraph networks as long as 1,500 miles. Grant also possessed an advantage over other old regulars like Winfield Scott in his tolerance of the vagaries of the volunteer army. Although Grant was a West Point man and an ex-regular himself, he conceded from the start that the real burden of the war was going to have to be carried by the volunteers—by civilians in uniform who remained civilians in temperament even after they donned their uniforms. Unlike the regulars, the volunteers could not simply be expected to shoot straight, keep clean, and obey orders. They would have to be reasoned with, sorted out gently, and kept from turning a parade ground into a debating society. And yet, as Grant quickly realized, for all his pigheaded independence the volunteer soldier really wanted to fight, and he would do so if only he could be put into the right hands. When Grant was made colonel of the 21st Illinois, he learned that he had been put there to replace an earlier colonel, foolishly elected by popular ballot of the regiment, who had done nothing to teach them anything useful. To bring the regiment around, Grant was careful to appeal to the volunteer's own desire to be led, and not driven, into battle. "My regiment was composed in large part of young men of as good social position as any in their section of the State," Grant wrote, "It embraced the sons of farmers, lawyers, physicians, politicians, merchants, bankers, and ministers, and some men of maturer years who had filled such positions themselves." These men knew nothing of military discipline, and in their own republican way, they all imagined that they were the equal of any officer. Grant "found it very hard work for a few days to bring all the men into anything like subordination." But once Grant made it clear that discipline in battle was what saved lives and won wars—and that discipline was not the humiliating business of kowtowing to some idiot in shoulder straps—then "the great majority favored discipline, and

[7]Edward Hagerman, *The American Civil War and the Origins of Modern Warfare*, (Bloomington, IN, 1988), p. 169; Grant, "Personal Memoirs," p. 166.

by the application of a little regular army punishment all were reduced to as good discipline as one could ask."[8]

There was one thing more that set Grant off from his contemporaries in the army, and that was his willingness to gamble on combined army-navy operations. Of all the major commanders in the Civil War, only Grant and McClellan seem to have had much understanding of how to use the navy and other forms of water-borne supply in conjunction with the army. And it is safe to say that if only McClellan had also had a little of Grant's combativeness, it would have been McClellan who ended the war in 1862, and McClellan's name rather than Grant's would be the one celebrated in the textbooks. As it was, however, McClellan botched all the advantages that the use of combined navy-army operations gave him on the peninsula, while Grant's cooperation with Foote in the movement down the Tennessee and Cumberland was so smooth that the sheer innovation of using the navy to transport troops on the inland rivers often gets overlooked. Nevertheless, it is vital for comprehending Grant's success to understand that Grant was a mover—indeed, hardly anyone in the Civil War demonstrated a greater skill in swiftly moving large bodies of infantry from one place to another—and he eagerly seized on the river lines as a rapid way of overcoming the Confederacy's advantage of interior lines.

The question now for Grant was whether his immediate superior in St. Louis, Henry Wager Halleck, would let him keep on moving, for in this early spring of 1862, Grant was as optimistic as nearly everyone else in the North that with a little energy the war could be wrapped up right then, and especially on the rivers. " 'Secesh' is about on its last legs in Tennessee," Grant calmly predicted, and he clearly remembered twenty-five years later the confidence he had then that "after the fall of Fort Donelson the way was opened to the National forces all over the South-west without much resistance."[9]

Meanwhile, the Confederate forces in the West were thrown into a panic by the speed of Grant's movement and the embarrassing loss of Forts Henry and Donelson. The Confederates had pinned their hopes on using the Ohio River as their northern line of defense, and their eagerness to stake out the Ohio line as a Confederate moat was what had led them to take the risk of violating Kentucky's neutrality in 1861. Once having invaded Kentucky, the Confederates tried to make sure they could hold it. All Confederate forces between the Mississippi and the Appalachians were consolidated into one department, and overall command of that department was given in September, 1861, to Albert Sidney Johnston, one of the most highly regarded officers of the old regular army and one of the dearest military friends of Jefferson Davis. With 43,000 men at his disposal, with the two forts,

[8]John Keegan, The Mask of Command (New York, 1987), pp. 187–194, 210–211; Grant, "Personal Memoirs," pp. 160–161.

[9]Grant to Julia Dent Grant [March 21, 1862], in The Papers of Ulysses Simpson Grant, John Y. Simon, ed. (Carbondale, IL, 1972), vol. 4, p. 406; Grant, "Personal Memoirs," p. 214.

Henry and Donelson, on the Tennessee and Cumberland, with another fort on Island No. 10 in the Mississippi, with Confederate forces already holding the Ohio River line at Columbus, and with convenient railroad links along the Memphis & Ohio to assure him of the advantage of interior lines—with all this, Johnston certainly began the war in the west holding what appeared like the all the best strategic cards.

The problem was that Johnston's cards were actually of less value than they seemed. Johnston's forts were either incomplete or poorly constructed, his men and his officers were badly undertrained and underequipped, and Johnston himself turned out to be something less of a general than his reputation had suggested. He failed utterly to anticipate Grant's strike at Henry and Donelson, and by the time Johnston realized what had happened, federal gunboats were controlling the Tennessee and Cumberland, the Memphis & Ohio had been cut, and Johnston had lost all ability to concentrate his troops anywhere in Kentucky or Tennessee. Recalling the garrisons at Columbus and Bowling Green, and hastily gathering what forces he could lay his hands on, Johnston abandoned all of Kentucky and what remained to him of Tennessee, and selected as a concentration point the town of Corinth, a railroad junction just below the Tennessee-Mississippi border on the other remaining east-west Confederate rail line, the Memphis & Charleston. The other Confederate outposts left in Tennessee, including Island No. 10 in the Mississippi River, simply dropped into the hands of Halleck's other forces. "Secession is well-nigh played out—the dog is dead," trumpeted "Parson" Brownlow, who defied Confederate authorities in Tennessee to stop publication of his pro-Union newspaper, the Knoxville *Whig*. "Their demoralized army is on their way back to the Cotton States."[10]

The jubilation Halleck felt at these successes was matched only by the pleasure of the rewards he reaped. The afternoon after Fort Donelson surrendered, Halleck wired McClellan: "Give me command in the West. I ask this for Forts Henry and Donelson."[11] The War Department did even better: It promoted Halleck to top federal command in the West *and* demoted McClellan to field command in the East. Don Carlos Buell, who was supposed to be carrying the real war in the West into eastern Tennessee, suddenly became Halleck's subordinate, and Halleck was now set free to prosecute the western war as he wished—not by invading the mountains of eastern Tennessee and rallying some vague body of Tennessee Unionists, but by pursuing the Confederacy's western army down to Corinth and smashing it up for good. With that tantalizing object in mind, Halleck ordered Grant to push south along the Tennessee River toward Corinth with the force he had used to capture Henry and Donelson. At the same time, and with ill-concealed satisfaction, Halleck ordered Buell to bring his men down to the Tennessee River for a

[10]William G. Brownlow, *Sketches of the Rise, Progress, and Decline of Secession* (Philadelphia, 1862), pp. 388–389.

[11]Halleck to McClellan [February 17, 1862], in *Official Records*, series 1, vol. 7, p. 628.

rendezvous with Grant. By the time the two forces had rendezvoused on the Tennessee, Halleck would have come up the river by steamboat to take personal command and push on overland to Corinth.

The federal army began moving up the Tennessee River on March 5th, unloading first at Savannah, Tennessee, on the east bank of the river. On March 17th, Grant began moving them again and steamed nine miles farther upstream to a scrawny little steamboat tie-up called Pittsburg Landing on the west bank of the Tennessee, which Halleck had designated as the rendezvous point with Buell and the forward depot for the big push on Corinth. And there Grant sat, waiting for Halleck to come up from departmental headquarters in St. Louis, and waiting for Buell (who spent twelve days building a bridge across a creek) to make it to the ferry-over at Savannah. In the meantime, Grant's 33,000 men were allowed to sprawl out from the river landing, in no particular order, for almost three miles (all the way to a little log meeting house innocently known as Shiloh Church), just as though there were no Confederates worthy of notice within a thousand miles.

Tragically for Grant, he was wrong. In fact, he had committed the worst error in strategic judgment he would ever make during the war, for Grant and Halleck alike had sadly underestimated Albert Sidney Johnston's determination to win back what he had lost in Kentucky. The ease with which Grant had walked over Fort Henry and Fort Donelson and put half of Johnston's western army out of commission and galvanized the Confederates into frantic action. Jefferson Davis hurriedly stripped every Confederate garrison along the Gulf coastline, and all other points between there and Corinth, of every soldier he could lay hands on, and concentrated them at Corinth until Johnston had an army of about 40,000 men at his disposal. Additionally, Davis sent Johnston the Confederacy's most successful general to date, Pierre Beauregard, as a sort of auxiliary commander to help plan a counterblow at the federal forces.

Downriver on the other hand, Grant's victories bred a slaphappy complacency. That complacency allowed Grant to sit motionless at Pittsburg Landing until the morning of Sunday, April 6th, when Johnston's army came crashing through the underbrush around Shiloh Church and rolled up to within half a mile of destroying an entire federal army, not to mention the future military career of U.S. Grant.

What happened over the next forty-eight hours has been sufficient to give the name *Shiloh* an eerie, wicked ring that still sends shivers into the American spine. In some respects, it was hardly a battle. Johnston had only the barest hold over his green and undisciplined rebel soldiers, and it is one of the great marvels of military history that he ever managed to assemble them at Corinth, get them over the flood-soaked Tennessee roads to Pittsburg Landing, and do it all without attracting any attention from the federals, from Grant on down to the lowliest cavalry pickets. But Johnston was a desperate man in a desperate strategic situation, and marvels are sometimes what desperation is capable of conjuring up. The exact obverse of Grant's optimism, Johnston was convinced that unless he got to Grant before Buell and Halleck did, then the war in the West was as good as over. And so desperation as much as anything else got Johnston moving and got him to Shiloh Church that morning, while the federal army was still rubbing sleep from its eyes. That, and the stupendous indifference of the federals (Grant was actually downriver at Savannah, sitting down to breakfast) gave the Confederacy its best and biggest chance of evening up, and maybe bettering, the scores set at Henry and Donelson.

Once the battle began, however, the terrain, the rawness of his troops, and Johnston's own fatal streak of hesitancy took matters out of his hands. Shiloh became a huge grappling match, with disconnected pieces of each army standing, breaking, and running in almost every direction. By nightfall, Albert Sidney Johnston himself was dead, killed by a stray bullet that severed an artery and left him to bleed to death, and the two bleary, punch-drunk mobs of soldiers that had been armies that morning faced each other around the river landing without much idea of what was coming next. More than one high-ranking Union officer thought it was the end and counseled a retreat across the Tennessee. Grant, who raced upriver to Pittsburg Landing by steamboat at the first faint thump of artillery, saw at once that it was the Confederates who had failed, not the federals. So long as they held the landing, the federals still held the key to the Shiloh battlefield; and it was plain to Grant that the Confederates had spent their last strength just getting that far. One of Grant's officers, an Ohioan named William Tecumseh Sherman, found Grant that night in the pouring rain, standing under a tree with a cigar clenched between his teeth. Sherman had lost most of his division that morning, and he had come to advise Grant that a pullout was the only hope. But Sherman, whose years at West Point had overlapped Grant's, sensed something in Grant's brooding imperturbability that prompted him to change his tune. "Well, Grant," Sherman said, "we've had the devil's own day, haven't we." "Yes," Grant replied, "Yes. Lick 'em tomorrow, though."[12]

By the next morning, Grant had reorganized his forces (as best he could), called in reinforcements (Buell chose just this moment to arrive at Savannah), and proceeded to shove back at the battered Confederates. By 3:00 P.M. on April 7th, Beauregard, who had taken over command from the fallen Johnston, had pulled the remains of the Confederate army back onto the road to Corinth. Four days later, Halleck arrived at Pittsburg Landing to take command of Grant's and Buell's newly combined armies, and to find out exactly what had happened.

The most obvious fact was the casualty list: Grant's army had lost almost 13,000 men killed, wounded, or missing, almost a third of his force, while the Confederates had lost 10,000 of their own. Wits as well as lives had been lost, as the untested soldiers of both armies were unhinged by the appalling and concentrated carnage. "I have heard of wars & read of wars," wrote George Asbury Bruton of the 19th Louisiana two days after the battle, "but never did I think it would be my lot to participate in such a horrible scene. . . . I never want to witness any other such scene. It seems as if I can hear the goans of the dying & wounded men and the cannons roaring all the time worse than any thunderstorms that ever was heard." A

---

[12]Bruce Catton, *Grant Moves South* (Boston, 1960), p. 242.

sergeant from the 9th Indiana named Ambrose Gwinnett Bierce went cold with horror when he found that gunfire had ignited the underbrush where part of the battle had raged and incinerated dead and wounded alike: "at every point . . . lay the bodies, half-buried in the ashes; some in the unlovely looseness of attitude denoting sudden death by the bullet, but by far the greater number in postures of agony that told of the tormenting flame." Bierce stumbled over another federal sergeant, shot in the head but still alive, "taking in his breath in convulsive, rattling snorts, and blowing it out in sputters of froth which crawled creamily down his cheeks" while "the brain protruded in bosses, dropping off in flakes and strings."[13]

Most of the loss was blamed squarely on Grant's lack of preparedness. Not only had Grant not organized his camp for defense, but he himself was nowhere near it when the fighting began, and at that point the old story of Grant's alcohol problems in the old army resurfaced and the word began to circulate that Grant had been drunk. Actually, Grant had been stone sober, and he had been at Savannah for the very good reason that he would be needed there when Buell's column finally arrived on the Tennessee. Although it was true he had been caught dangerously by surprise, he had nevertheless managed to pull victory out of the jaws of defeat. And Shiloh had taught Grant a very effective lesson about the war, the same lesson that Lincoln was shortly to learn on the peninsula, and that was that the Confederates were deadly in earnest about winning this war and were not going to go away merely because a federal army and a gunboat or two showed up to remind them who was supposed to be in charge. "Up to the battle of Shiloh, I, as well as thousands of other citizens, believed that the rebellion against the Government would collapse suddenly and soon if a decisive victory could be gained over any of its armies," Grant recollected, but after Shiloh, "I gave up all idea of saving the Union except by complete conquest."[14]

At the same time, however, Halleck would be taking no more chances. Now that Halleck and Buell were on the scene, Grant ceased to be a semi-independent operator, and became just another part of Halleck's command along with Buell, and the dazzling thrust that had brought a Union army to the Mississippi border in two months slowed to a crawl. Turning inland from the river toward Corinth, Halleck's advance took a month and a half (during which he stopped every night to entrench) to move over to Corinth, and when Halleck finally arrived there on May 29th, Beauregard took counsel of prudence and abandoned Corinth without a fight. With the fall of Corinth into federal hands, the Confederacy's last direct east-west rail line, the Memphis & Charleston Railroad, was cut, and in June, the outflanked Confederate garrisons along the Mississippi at Fort Pillow and Memphis collapsed. The Mississippi (at least down to Vicksburg), the Tennessee, and the Cumberland Rivers were all now securely under Halleck's control.

[13]Allen C. Guelzo, "Ambrose Bierce's Civil War," in Civil War Times Illustrated 20 (November 1981), pp. 36–45.

[14]Grant, "The Battle of Shiloh," in Battles and Leaders of the Civil War, C. C. Buel and R. U. Johnson, eds. (rept. New York, 1956), vol. 2, pp. 485–486.

And at that point the Union army in the West ran out of steam, and for several reasons, the first and most important of which had to do with the Confederates. In June, the luckless Beauregard fell ill—or at least claimed to be feeling unwell—and departed from the army on sick leave. Jefferson Davis, who had grown increasingly unhappy with the Confederacy's first military hero, gladly replaced Beauregard with a scrappy, hot-tempered regular army veteran Braxton Bragg. To Davis's delight, Bragg immediately determined to regain the initiative in the West. Commanding a force of about 30,000 men, Bragg swung around the edges of the federal penetration into Tennessee and raced up through eastern Tennessee, where he picked up another 18,000 reinforcements under Edmund Kirby Smith. By the end of August, Bragg was aiming at the Kentucky border and he stood in a fair way to undo everything that had been won by the Union since February.

Halleck immediately detached Buell's troops to try to head off Bragg. But Buell was no faster a mover in the summer of 1862 than he had been the previous winter, and instead of pursuing Bragg pell-mell, Buell proceeded to retrace his original path through Tennessee, rebuilding the Nashville & Chattanooga Railroad as he went. That was slow enough work on its own terms, but it was made slower by the activities of two of the Confederacy's most notorious raiders, John Hunt Morgan and Nathan Bedford Forrest. Bragg had given both Morgan and Forrest cavalry brigades and orders to create as much havoc as possible in between himself and Buell. This, Forrest and Morgan did effortlessly. Forrest, a former millionaire slave trader, was a natural military genius who possessed the killer instinct in spades, and in the middle of July, Forrest's raiders struck at Buell's patiently rebuilt railroad line at Murfreesboro, Tennessee, and put it out of commission for two weeks. Meanwhile, Morgan swept up through Nashville in August, destroying rail lines and a railroad tunnel and further delaying Buell. Cloaked by these distractions, Bragg rolled into Kentucky and occupied Glasgow, Kentucky, on September 14th. He then began recruiting volunteers for the Confederate army, and commenced a leisurely move on Frankfort, the capital of Kentucky, where he scattered the Unionist legislature and inaugurated a Confederate governor at point of bayonet on October 4, 1862.

But by that time, Buell had finally managed to catch up with Bragg, and on October 8th, the two armies collided near Perryville, Kentucky. The battle that resulted was a happenstance affair like Shiloh, with neither Bragg nor Buell fully in control of the day's events. After a day of pitiless slugging, the battle of Perryville ended with Buell in command of the field, while Bragg withdrew into Tennessee. Buell had saved the Ohio River for the Union, but he received small thanks for it. Like McClellan, he failed to pursue the fleeing Confederates, and on October 24, 1862, he was relieved of his command.

If the distraction afforded by Bragg's abortive offensive into Kentucky was one reason why the federal offensive in the west came to halt, then the other reason was Halleck himself. Halleck had not been happy about the need to divide his forces and send Buell off after Bragg, and he now began to entertain visions of Confederate raiders chopping at the railroads and bridges behind him. Halleck dug himself into Corinth, determined not to risk the troops he had left under his command on further offensive moves, and began parceling up Grant's men into small garrisons to keep the likes of Forrest and Morgan away from his supply lines. Grant fumed and sputtered in frustration, and in May he would have resigned his commission had not Sherman talked him out of it. In July, 1862, Halleck was called to Washington to assume the post of general-in-chief of the federal armies, the job Lincoln had taken away from McClellan in March. But far from being relieved to get Halleck off his back, this only meant that Grant had lost his only connection with the military powers-that-be. Grant settled into command of the new military district of Cairo and the Mississippi (effectively this meant that Grant was responsible for policing all the newly occupied Confederate territory between the Tennessee and Mississippi Rivers), with sufficient men to fend a serious Confederate attempt to retake Corinth in October, but without quite enough to do much on his own.

But Grant's mind never stayed still for long, and by the end of 1862, he was ready to approach Halleck with a proposal for a new campaign. During the spring campaign down the Tennessee, the upper stretches of the Mississippi River had fallen into Union hands simply because the Confederates could no longer hold them once they had lost the Tennessee River. What was worse for the Confederates was that they had also lost New Orleans. The federal navy had been planning its own operation against New Orleans as early as November, 1861, and in February, 1862, command of an assault flotilla was given to a hard-eyed and aggressive fleet captain named David Glasgow Farragut. With four big steam-powered frigates and a collection of small 500-ton gunboats and mortar-schooners, Farragut began the ascent of the Mississippi on April 16th, stopping below New Orleans on the 18th for six days so that his mortar-schooners could pound the two forts that guarded the river. Impatient with the results of the bombardment, at 2 AM on the morning of the 24th Farragut arranged his ships in two columns and swept up the river past the fire of the forts. Farragut anchored for the day just above the forts, and the next morning ran his ships past the last small Confederate batteries below New Orleans. At noon on April 25th, Faragut dropped anchor in the river by the city and sent ashore an officer to raise the United States flag over the New Orleans mint. The downriver forts, abandoned by most of their disheartened garrisons, surrendered on April 28th.[15]

The fall of New Orleans was probably the severest single blow the Confederacy sustained in the war. New Orleans was the Confederacy's great port, its doorway to the rest of the world, and its commercial and financial equivalent of New York City. In addition to losing the city itself, 15,000 bales of cotton (worth over $1.5 million) were burned by the retreating Confederates, along with more than a dozen river steamboats, a half-completed ironclad gunboat, and the entire city dock area. "The extent of the disaster is not to be disguised," wrote Edward Pollard of the Richmond *Examiner*. "It annihilated us in Louisiana . . . led by plain and irresist-

---

[15]Alfred Thayer Mahan, *The Gulf and the Inland Waters* (1883; rept. New York, 1970), pp. 73–88.

ible conclusion to our virtual abandonment of the great and fruitful Valley of the Mississippi," and cost the Confederacy "a city which was the commercial capital of the South, which contained a population of one hundred and seventy thousand souls, and which was the largest *exporting* city in the world."[16] Serious though the loss of Tennessee was that spring, the Confederacy could have survived that loss so long as it held New Orleans and the lifeline New Orleans offered to the outside world. But Albert Sidney Johnston had convinced Jefferson Davis that the real threat to New Orleans was from the Yankees on the Tennessee River and the upper Mississippi, and Johnston's determination to throw Grant and Halleck out of Tennessee had led Davis to strip all the Gulf coast garrisons, including New Orleans, of men and equipment, including a squadron of river gunboats that might have made a significant difference in Farragut's ability to maneuver upriver. When the federal navy burst through the back door into New Orleans only two weeks after Shiloh, the city was simply too weak to defend itself.

With the Union suddenly holding both the upper and lower ends of the river, it seemed to Ulysses Simpson Grant a worthwhile effort to move over and seize and remaining parts in the middle, around the fortified town of Vicksburg, Mississippi. Grant could not have known it, but at that very moment, Halleck was already under pressure from Lincoln to make precisely that kind of move. The November by-elections would soon be upon Lincoln, and the farmers of the Union west were restless at the prospect of a longer and longer war that kept the Mississippi shipping network closed to them. John A. McClernand, a powerful Illinois Democrat and now major general of volunteers in Grant's district, had gone off on his own to Washington and demanded that Lincoln let him recruit his own army to take down the Mississippi and blow open the Vicksburg bottleneck. To placate the northern Democrats, Lincoln had given him a curiously worded authorization in October to raise a force of volunteers. Halleck looked upon McClernand as a nuisance, but rather than take the risk that Lincoln would actually allow an inexperienced politician to take a federal army on a joyride down the Mississippi, Halleck sanctioned Grant's plan to move on Vicksburg, with McClernand parked safely under Grant's command.

This time, almost nothing went right for Grant. At first, Grant hoped simply to march overland from Corinth with a force of 72,000 men and quickly seize Vicksburg and its garrison; but once under way in November, Grant changed his mind and detached Sherman and 32,000 men to advance down the Mississippi in another combined army-navy operation. He might have saved himself the trouble: Confederate raiders under Earl Van Dorn struck at Grant's supply base at Holly Springs, Mississippi, on December 20th, destroying the bulk of Grant's supplies and stopping his overland march in its tracks. Meanwhile, Sherman's men arrived opposite Vicksburg on December 26th to find that the Confederate garrison at

[16]Pollard, *Southern History of the War* (New York, 1866), vol. 1, pp. 326–327.

Vicksburg had been reinforced to meet him. After a series of futile attacks on December 29th, Sherman withdrew and the whole endeavor went up in smoke.

But Grant would not give up on Vicksburg that easily. He would admit only that the idea of an overland march on Vicksburg from above the city was impractical, and during the winter of 1862–1863, he mounted no less than four attempts to move his men downriver, past Vicksburg, and land them on the other side of the city, where he could cut off supplies and reinforcements from points south and east. But none of his ideas (which included schemes to dig canals around Vicksburg, to navigate the back bayous, to reroute the Mississippi) worked, and by March, 1863, he was no closer to taking Vicksburg than ever. Finally, in April, Grant decided to gamble on the riskiest of all the possible approaches to Vicksburg. He ferried his men across the Mississippi, marched them down below Vicksburg on the opposite shore, and on the moonless night of April 16, 1863, ran a fleet of twelve navy gunboats past the four-mile-long line of Confederate naval artillery on the Vicksburg waterfront. Every one of the gunboats was hit, but only one was sunk, and once below Vicksburg, they provided cover for Grant to safely ferry his men back across the Mississippi, this time *below* Vicksburg. Within a month, Grant had cut off all of Vicksburg's outside communications and had bottled up the city's 30,000 Confederate soldiers into an airtight siege. After six weeks, the Confederates were reduced to near-starvation, and on July 4, 1863, Vicksburg surrendered to Grant.

With it the Confederacy had lost a citadel, an army, and an additional measure of its self-confidence; with it, Ulysses Simpson Grant had redeemed a reputation. And he also set a president to wondering whether he had at last found a general who could win his war for him.

3. The Politics of War

At the beginning of the Civil War, Abraham Lincoln was fifty-two years old, and the numerous photographs taken of him during his first year as president reveal a man thin and spare, but erect and powerful, with a strongly etched face and the familiar whiskers (which he had grown as a fashionable whim shortly after his election) encircling his jaw. But by the end of the war, Lincoln's face had grown aged and care-worn, his cheeks sunken into ashen hollows, his coarse black hair showing strands of white, and his beard shrunken to a pitiful tuft at the chin. As the conflict dragged on and the casuality lists began to lengthen, Lincoln descended deeper into a peculiar blend of religious mysticism and fatalism in which he began to view himself as merely "an instrument of Providence," powerless to guide events on his own terms.[17]

[17]William J. Wolf, *The Almost Chosen People: A Study of the Religion of Abraham Lincoln* (New York, 1959), pp. 36–37, 77–78, 147.

Other burdens conspired to further drain Lincoln's energies and blacken his impenetrable moods. He received a glut of hate mail, much of it threatening him with various kinds of death, which he filed in an envelope marked "Assassination." "Soon after I was nominated in Chicago," Lincoln told his friend Ward Hill Lamon, "I began to receive letters threatening my life. The first ones made me feel a little uncomfortable; but I came at length to look for a regular installment of this kind of correspondence in every mail." Eventually, the threats preyed so much on his mind that he began to dream of assassination and funerals in the White House. His secretaries began to hide the hate mail from him, and Lamon pestered him so badly to protect himself that Lincoln made him federal marshal of the District of Columbia and let Lamon and Stanton provide regular guards. But Lincoln himself made no attempt at protection. As he explained resignedly to Francis Carpenter, there was no protection in this life from fate: "If . . . they wanted to get at me, no vigilance could keep them out." Besides, Lincoln added, the politics of republicanism required a certain amount of risk from its leaders. "It would never do for a President to have guards with drawn sabres at his door, as if he fancied he were, or were trying to be, or were assuming to be, an emperor."[18]

But, as it turned out, it was not for Lincoln that the bell tolled. In February of 1862, Lincoln's second son, William Wallace Lincoln, died of typhoid fever in the White House, and grief over the boy's death nearly tipped Mary Todd Lincoln over the brink into insanity. Lincoln, himself "worn out with grief and watching," could only explain the death as yet another visitation of that inscrutable power that held human destinies in a powerful and inescapable grip. After Willie Lincoln's death, Lincoln's own health began to suffer. Unable to sleep, he paced the White House through the night, or sat up into the wee hours of the morning in the telegraph room of the War Department to receive the latest news of the war. He gradually began to lose weight, until his clothes seemed to hang from him, and in the summer of 1863, he contracted a mild form of smallpox. There was, he complained, a tired spot in him that no rest could ever touch.

But over and above all these reasons for the haggard look of Lincoln's face was the crushing weight of having to conduct what amounted to two separate wars. In addition to the shooting war, Lincoln was also compelled to wage a political war behind the lines to keep up civilian support and morale, and to enable the armies to keep on fighting. And the general consensus of the day was that Lincoln was thus far no more successful in winning the political war than he was in winning the military one. "My opinion of Mr. Lincoln," wrote Orestes Brownson to Charles Sumner at the end of 1862, "is that nothing can be done with him. . . . He is wrong-headed . . . the petty politician not the statesman & . . . ill-deserving the sobriquet of Honest." The New York lawyer, George Templeton Strong, confided to

---

[18]Francis B. Carpenter, *Six Months at the White House with Abraham Lincoln* (New York, 1867), pp. 65–67; Stephen B. Oates, *With Malice Toward None: The Life of Abraham Lincoln* (New York, 1977), p. 416.

his diary in 1862, "Disgust with our present government is certainly universal. Even Lincoln himself has gone down at last. Nobody believes in him any more."[19]

Of course, the benefit of hindsight suggests that Lincoln's critics were wrong, and that Lincoln eventually succeeded in rallying the political morale of the North around even the most radical of his policies, emancipation. But it is also true that Lincoln only accomplished that goal very slowly, and at the cost of terrific political turmoil. The reasons lying behind that turmoil are twofold. The first is bound up with Lincoln's inexperience in national politics. Although Lincoln had been involved in state and local politics for almost his entire adult life, he had never actually been elected to an office of any consequence in Illinois beyond the state legislature, and his only experience on the national level before 1861 consisted of his solitary and undistinguished term as a Representative from Illinois's 7th District. His work habits had been shaped by the experience of local politics and a two-man law practice, and as a result Lincoln only grudgingly delegated even routine correspondence to his secretaries. "His methods of office working were simply those of a very busy man who worked at all hours," Robert Todd Lincoln recalled,

> He never dictated correspondence; he sometimes wrote a document and had his draft copied by either [John] Nicholay or [John] Hay [Lincoln's secretaries]; sometimes he himself copied his corrected draft and retained the draft in his papers. . . . He seemed to think nothing of the labor of writing personally and was accustomed to make many scraps of notes or memoranda. In writing a careful letter, he first wrote it himself, then corrected it, and then rewrote the corrected version himself.[20]

These workaholic habits, combined with the demands of superintending the war effort, left Lincoln with little time or attention for direct management and manipulation of Congress. Even though Lincoln enjoyed substantial Republican majorities in both the 37th Congress (elected with him in 1860) and the 38th Congress (elected in the congressional by-election in 1862), he made little effort to give legislative direction to Congress, and let the powerful Republican party caucus run the legislative branch while he threw his presidential energies into managing the war effort. Only when the Republicans tried to pry their way into the operation of the Cabinet did Lincoln even bother to meet with the caucus, much less use them as his legislative surrogates.[21] In fact, Lincoln showed only marginally more interest in the day-to-day operations of the Cabinet. Secretive and closemouthed by nature, Lincoln hardly ever involved his Cabinet secretaries in policymaking decisions,

[19]J. G. Randall, *Lincoln the President* (New York, 1945), vol. 2, p. 241; *The Diary of George Templeton Strong,* Allan Nevins and Milton Halsey Thomas, eds. (New York, 1952), vol. 3, p. 256.

[20]Robert Lincoln to Isaac Markens [February 13 and June 18, 1918] in *A Portrait of Abraham Lincoln in Letters by His Oldest Son,* Paul Angle, ed. (Chicago, IL, 1968), pp. 56, 62; Helen Nicolay, *Personal Traits of Abraham Lincoln* (New York, 1912), pp. 189–190.

[21]Allan G. Bogue, *The Congressman's Civil War* (Cambridge, 1989), pp. 44–59, 63, 74–88, 114, 118, 121–132.

except to confirm a conclusion he had already reached. Instead, he preferred to assign them areas of responsibility that he did not want to be bothered with, and though he gave his Cabinet secretaries wide enough room to use their own talents in managing those responsibilities, it was plain that Lincoln regarded them as little more than clerks rather than partners in the great business of managing the war.

A deeper reason for Lincoln's apparent inattentiveness to running a wartime government lay in the politics of Whiggery. Although Lincoln was elected president as a Republican, he still carried over into the Republican party many of the political principles of the old Whigs, and chief among those principles was the Whiggish suspicion of putting too much power into the hands of the national president.[22] The symbolic archenemy of Whiggism was Andrew Jackson, and the incessant complaint of Whigs during and after Jackson's presidency was that Jackson was a high-handed tyrant who converted the presidency and the Democratic party into a personal government.[23] After his own election as president, Lincoln insisted in consistently Whiggish terms that he intended to take a back seat to Congress in running the country. "My political education strongly inclines me against a very free use of . . . the Executive, to control the legislation of the country," Lincoln declared in 1861. "As a rule, I think it better that congress should originate, as well as perfect its measures, without external bias."[24] With such a minimalistic view of the presidency in hand, Lincoln had no intention of giving authoritarian direction to Congress. Only on the subject of war powers did the Whigs make significant concessions to the powers of the presidency; and Lincoln was careful, whenever he did proclaim some dramatic new policy or claim to authority, to justify it on the basis of the powers given him by the Constitution in time of war.

There are few better illustrations of this executive Whiggism than Lincoln's deliberate indifference to the need for financing the war, and the impact it might have on the northern economy. From the first call for volunteers, it was clear that some way had to be found to harness the North's unquestioned industrial and financial superiority to the task of winning the war. Lincoln, however, refused to take responsibility for fiscal and revenue policy, turning the problem over instead to Salmon Chase, his secretary of the treasury. "Money," exclaimed Lincoln, when Chase brought a group of New York bankers to the White House to discuss war finance, "I don't know anything about 'money.' I never had enough of my own to fret me, and I have no opinion about it any way."[25] But Chase did not have much more experience in fiscal matters than Lincoln. In fact, Chase was an ex-Democrat

[22]David Donald, "Abraham Lincoln: A Whig in the White House," in Lincoln Reconsidered: Essays on the Civil War Era (New York, 1947, 1956), pp. 187–208.

[23]J. P. Kennedy, "A Defence of the Whigs," in Political and Official Papers (New York, 1972), pp. 320–321.

[24]Lincoln, "Speech at Pittsburgh, Pennsylvania" [February 15, 1861], in Collected Works, vol. 4, pp. 214–215.

[25]Carpenter, Six Months at the White House, p. 252.

who had thrown his allegiance to the Republicans over slavery and Kansas-Nebraska, and he had never fit comfortably with the Whigs or the Whiggish economic views that abounded in the new party. Chase was skeptical on tariffs, hesitant about the virtues of federally financed "internal improvements," and was so resolutely set against banking networks that in 1853 he had actively supported a restructuring of the Treasury Department to prevent it from borrowing money (Congress reserved the sole right to authorize borrowing), to set interest rates on Treasury securities, or to use commercial bank accounts for government payables or receivables.

Of course, part of the rationale for appointing Chase as secretary of the treasury was precisely because he was a former Democrat, and so could assuage the fears of other Democrats that the Republicans were going to reverse six decades of Democratic rule over the nation's fiscal policy. But that did nothing to ease the pain of Chase's inexperience or distaste for such responsibilities, or the flimsy structures of government finance that he inherited from his erstwhile Democratic friends. The nation's financial and banking system was in 1861 still very largely what Andrew Jackson and the Democrats had made it in the 1830s. Suspicious of the market revolution and of finance capitalism, Jackson demolished the federally sponsored Bank of the United States and effectively took the federal government out of the national money system. The Treasury Department became little more than a warehouse for government cash and customs receipts. This meant that banking became a local enterprise for individual state governments to charter, which each state did mostly by its own lights. Jackson also took the added precaution of restricting all federal government monetary transactions to hard coin, or *specie* (which the Democrats regarded as the only real money), so that the Treasury would neither accept paper money for itself nor print its own. But no such restriction applied to the state-chartered banks, and so by 1861, the American economy was riding on a crazy quilt of state bank notes and bonds whose real value sometimes had only the faintest connection to the numbers printed on their faces.

The great virtue of this system in Democratic eyes was that it kept the national government small and fiscally weak. However, whatever that might have meant as an asset in peacetime politics, it became another matter entirely in war. Northern banks that had acted as the South's financial brokers for decades often had nothing more than southern bank notes and bonds in their vaults as backing for their own accounts and bank notes, and with the secession of the southern states, northern bankers suddenly found that they no longer had any guarantee that southerners would stand by those notes and bonds, or redeem them with specie. Southern bond prices in New York City plummeted like dead pigeons; of the 913 mercantile and banking firms in New York at the beginning of 1861, only 16 were still in business by year's end. The unlooked-for blessing in this disaster was that the collapse of southern bonds and notes wiped out any fiscal leverage the Confederates might have had on the northern financial markets in 1861, and northern businessmen who might otherwise have hesitated to support Lincoln in making what amounted to war on their investments now swung behind the war as the only hope of reclaiming what the Southerners owed them. At the same time, European finance capitalists who had invested in American bonds and notes now hurriedly unloaded them for whatever they could get on the open market, thus telescoping American foreign indebtedness and leaving American businesses with more unobligated gold in their reserves than they had expected.[26]

All of this was a voyage of discovery for Chase, and notwithstanding Lincoln's confidence that Chase knew his way around fiscal matters, it took Chase time to figure out what was happening, how much money he would have to get to pay for the war, and where (and in what form) he was going to get it. At the very beginning, Chase greatly underestimated the amount of money needed to fund the war (he thought $328 million ought to do the job), and he was reluctant to ask Congress to raise it by direct taxation, which in Democratic eyes was the unpardonable political sin. But Chase soon found that the war was costing the federal government $1 million a day, and by the end of 1861, he could foresee the pricetag on the war hitting $500 million for 1862. As he did so, Chase found himself in the peculiarly un-Democratic posture of supporting Republican Senator John Sherman's Omnibus Revenue Act in August of 1861, which allowed the levying of a direct income tax and the issue of $150 million in short-term Treasury notes and another $100 million in long-term bonds.

But the old Democratic insistence that Treasury transactions take place only in gold hobbled the sale of these notes, and what was actually raised from the marketing of these securities turned out to be hopelessly inadequate. By February of 1862, all the proceeds had been spent away, and a further issue of bonds and notes would be taken by the financial markets as a confession of desperation. At this point Congress stepped in with its own measures for war finance, and on February 25, 1862, Congress passed the Legal Tender Act, which authorized Chase to print $150 million in paper money to pay government debts. The issue of paper money was a particularly difficult pill for northern Democrats to swallow, since Jacksonian economics confidently predicted that the use of notes, bonds, and especially unsecured paper money rather than specie would destroy public confidence in the economy, feed financial speculation on the money markets, and send prices through the roof. And in fact, successive issues of another $300 million of legal tender notes (or "greenbacks," from the green ink used to print their reverse sides) helped to inflate prices in the North by almost 80 percent during the war. But in July, at the prompting of Thaddeus Stevens as chair of the House Ways and Means Committee, Congress carefully propped up the Treasury's paper issues with the Internal Revenue Act of 1862, which used a graduated income tax to bring in $600 million in new revenue and take the inflationary steam out of the greenbacks. In fact, Congress eventually began to take its financial cues more from Stevens (a long-time Whig)

---

[26]Richard F. Bensel, *Yankee Leviathan: The Origins of Central State Authority in America, 1859–1877* (Cambridge, 1990), pp. 243–254.

and William P. Fessenden than Chase. Congress took one further step away from
the era of Jacksonian finance in 1863 when it passed the National Banking Act.
The act resurrected the issuance of federal charters for banks, a policy which had
been killed when Jackson destroyed Nicholas Biddle's Second Bank of the United
States in the 1830s, and created a national banking system that effectively turned
private banks into depositories and receivers for federal funds. The new national
banking system relied on the greenbacks and national bank notes, and Congress
drove the old state bank note issues permanently out of existence by slapping a
ruinous 10 percent tax on their use.

For long-term borrowing, Chase washed his hands of the un-Jacksonian chore
of hawking government securities through the Treasury by designating a fellow-
Ohioan, Jay Cooke, as the Treasury's bond agent. Cooke, a natural-born financier,
had made his fortune in banking before retiring at the tender age of 37. But in 1861,
restless for new challenges, Cooke opened a new brokerage house in Philadelphia,
Jay Cooke & Company, and in the summer of 1861, Cooke put into Chase's hands
an ambitious proposal for funding the war through the sale of a new and complicated series of government securities. With Chase's hestitating approval, Cooke
oversaw the issuing of a bewildering variety of government bonds and notes, carrying variable interest rates over varying terms. The most popular of these securities
was the "5–20" bond (rather like modern federal savings bonds, these were discounted bonds that were redeemable at a minimum of five years, but which came to
full maturity in twenty years), and through his network of 2,500 subagents, Cooke
was able to sell $362 milion of them in their first year of offering. Not only were the
redemption dates reasonable and the minimum purchase low (anyone with $50
could purchase 5–20s with interest rates as high as 7.5 percent), but the direct taxes
enacted by Congress assured investors that the Treasury would have the money in
hand to redeem the bonds at time of maturity. By skillfully juggling the dynamic of
notes, bonds, paper money, and taxation, Chase, Cooke, and Congress succeeded
in raising the money needed for the war without sapping the northern economy.
They also hooked the nation's private finance capital to the interests of the federal
government, for as private investors bought the new securities, they were also
buying an interest in the success of the North in the war (after all, if Lincoln and
Chase failed, investors would probably never recover their investments). And in
return, as the federal government inched toward victory, northern financiers like
Cooke, J. Pierpont Morgan, and A. J. Drexel found themselves mounting a rising
tide of financial power and experience. Over the 1860s, the number of New York
City banking houses would leap from 167 in 1864 to 1,800 in 1870, and the New
York Stock Exchange would open its own building in 1863. The war would thus
mean an unprecedented transfer of the nation's private capital into government
hands (the nightmare of the old Jacksonians) and the rise of a new class of American finance capitalists who brokered this transfer.[27]

27Bensel, *Yankee Leviathan*, pp. 251–252.

Successful though these fiscal measures were, there remained some question as to whether they were actually constitutional, and the need to deal with the constitutionality of a broad spectrum of wartime policies soon became a major headache for Lincoln. At the very beginning of the war, on April 27, 1861, Lincoln authorized General-in-Chief Scott to suspend the writ of habeas corpus along the insecure railway lines running into Washington through Maryland, and to imprison anyone suspected of threatening "public safety" there. Roger Taney, who was still sitting as the chief justice of the United States despite his eighty-four years, was convinced that Lincoln had no authority to repress secession; and he now looked for an opportunity to stymie Lincoln's self-claimed war powers by contesting the suspension of the writ in Maryland. Taney got his chance in the case of John Merryman, a Confederate sympathizer arrested in Baltimore on May 25, 1861, and imprisoned without a warrant in Fort McHenry. On May 26th, Taney issued a writ to free Merryman, and for several days it seemed that Lincoln might be legally incapable of keeping prosouthern agitators off the streets. But Lincoln argued that there was a thin line between legitimate political dissent and the kind of inflammatory political rhetoric that could be used to cripple the Union's ability to wage war, and he insisted that the authority to make such a distinction lay fully within his war powers under Article I, Section 9 of the Constitution. "Ours is a case of Rebellion," Lincoln argued, "in fact, a clear, flagrant, and gigantic case of Rebellion; and . . . in such cases, men may be held in custody whom the courts acting on ordinary rules, would discharge."[28] In the end, Lincoln ignored Taney's writ, and the case of *ex parte Merryman* became a dead letter.

Lincoln's wartime authority suffered two other major legal challenges in the *Prize Cases* of 1863 and *ex parte Milligan*. *Prize Cases* was actually a collection of suits brought against the federal government by the owners of four ships and cargoes stopped by the federal blockade of southern ports in May, June, and July of 1861 and turned over to federal prize courts to be auctioned off. *Prize Cases* questioned the legality of the blockade, for if (as Lincoln claimed) the southern states were not in fact a belligerent nation but only an insurrection, then a blockade of international commerce had no legal standing, and ships seized by such a blockade could not be turned over to the prize courts. The case was decided by the Supreme Court on May 10, 1863, with a bare five-to-four majority deciding that, although the Confederacy could not be recognized as a belligerent nation on its own, the federal government could still claim belligerent rights for itself in attempting to suppress the Confederacy. Writing for the majority, Justice Robert C. Grier agreed with Lincoln that "It is not necessary that the independence of the revolted province or State be acknowledged in order to constitute it a party belligerent in a war according to the law of nations." But Chief Justice Taney wrote a blistering dissent for the minority, arguing that "the President does not possess the power under the Constitution to declare war . . . within the meaning of the law of nations . . . and thus change the country

---

[28]Lincoln, "To Erastus Corning and Others" [June 12, 1863], in *Collected Works*, vol. 6, p. 264.

and all its citizens from a state of peace to a state of war." Nothing would have pleased Taney more, or more quickly have struck a major strategic weapon from Lincoln's hand, than if the Court had agreed with Taney's passionate contention that the blockade's "capture of the vessel and cargo in this case, and in all cases before us . . . are illegal and void. . . ."[29]

The Republicans were shocked by how easily the change of one vote on the high court could have undercut the operation of the blockade, and calls began to go up in Congress for either a new court or the replacement of the current justices. Most of this criticism was aimed at Roger Taney, who insisted on holding onto his seat on the Court despite his poor health in an undisguised search to find more ways of checking Lincoln's "excesses." Taney especially yearned to hear an appeal that would have given him the opportunity to issue an opinion on emancipation, which Taney denounced as an unconstitutional interference with property rights. But death came to Taney before an appeal did, and when Taney died in Washington on October 12, 1864, Lincoln quickly replaced him with Salmon Chase. The high court gave Chase's old Democratic inclinations freer rein than his Cabinet post, and his opinions did not actually greatly differ in substance from Taney's, although they lacked Taney's burning hostility to Lincoln's administration. In the case of *ex parte Milligan*, the Chase court ruled that Lambdin Milligan, an Indiana Democrat and southern sympathizer could not be arrested and tried by a military commission in places like Indiana, where legitimate civil courts were still operating. In the *Legal Tender* cases, Chase actually ruled that Congress had no authority to issue paper money as legal tender and that he had been wrong as treasury secretary to issue it. But both *ex parte Milligan* and the *Legal Tender* cases were not finally decided until long after the close of the war, and had no impact on the subsequent course of the wartime policy.

The Milligan case, however, does point to a third area of political difficulty Lincoln encountered, and that was the ever-increasing opposition of the northern Democrats to the war. From the beginning of the secession crisis, pro-Union northern Democrats had strained to support the Union cause and distance themselves from their southern counterparts, whom they denounced as the cause of so much of the secession trouble. Stephen Douglas, who wore himself into an early grave in June, 1861, stumping against secession, declared that "There are but two parties, the party of patriots and the party of traitors. [Democrats] belong to the first." And Lincoln, recognizing that the Democrats had garnered a healthy 44 percent of the vote in a three-way race in 1860, struggled to appease them with political and military appointments.

But the spirit of Democratic-Republican bipartisanship lasted only a short while. The northern Democrats' view of the war was summed up in their slogan, "The Constitution as it is; the Union as it was"—and, some of them were inclined

---

[29]*Reports of Cases Argued and Determined in the Supreme Court of the United States at December term 1862* (Washington, DC, 1863), vol. 2, pp. 669, 698–699.

to add, "the Negroes where they are." As the Republican-dominated Congress began to impose direct taxes, to issue unsecured "greenback" currency, and gradually move toward emancipation and abolition—to enact, in other words, the Whig domestic agenda—Democratic support began to crumble. The fragments fell into two basic piles. The first, known as the "War Democrats," had no real organized leadership after the premature death of Stephen Douglas, but War Democrats like Edwin Stanton, Benjamin Butler of Massachusetts, and Andrew Johnson of Tennessee, were as forward as any Republican in their support for the war. However, many of them carefully defined the war they were supporting as a war to reunite the nation and suppress treason, not a war against slavery to revolutionize society. Robert C. Winthrop, a Massachusetts independent who ended up siding with the Democrats during the war, protested that

> I, for one, have never had a particle of faith that a sudden sweeping, forcible emancipation could result in anything but mischief and misery for the black race, as well as the white. . . . The idea that the war is not to be permitted to cease until the whole social structure of the South has been reorganized, is one abhorrent to every instinct of my soul, to every dictate of my judgment, to every principle which I cherish as a statesman or as a Christian. It is a policy, too, in my opinion, utterly unconstitutional; and as much in the spirit of rebellion as almost anything which has been attempted by the Southern States. . . . We are not for propagating philanthropy at the point of the bayonet. We are not wading through seas of blood in order to reorganize the whole social structure of the South.[30]

But it became increasingly difficult for many War Democrats to keep that line up: Stanton and Butler both moved over to the Republicans at a very early stage of the war and became ardent supporters of emancipation. Increasingly, political momentum in the party passed to the "Peace Democrats." Rallying around prominent Democrats like Samuel Tilden, Horatio Seymour, and Fernando Wood of New York, the Peace Democrats reversed the War Democrats' order of priorities: End Lincoln's war first, before it destroys the country, even if it means conceding southern independence.

The Republicans looked on the agitation of the Peace Democrats as just more evidence of the same Democratic policies that had brought on the war in the first place, and so it was not long before partisanship yielded to howling accusations of treason. At first it was only a matter of name-calling: In the fall of 1861, Ohio Republicans began comparing leading Peace Democrats to copperhead rattlesnakes, and the term "Copperhead" became the standard Republican way of talking about Democrats. Resentment of dissent soon yielded to fear that Confederate agents would manipulate the "Copperheads" into a dangerous fifth column, and so army generals began removing Democratic judges from their benches, Democratic preachers from their pulpits, and Democratic newspapers from the mail. Estimates of the

[30]Winthrop, "Great Speech of Hon. Robert C. Winthrop at New London, Conn." in *Union Pamphlets of the Civil War, 1861–1865* (Cambridge, MA, 1967), vol. 2, pp. 1098, 1101.

actual number of arrests by military authorities vary, from only about 4,400 all the way up to 35,000. But each one of these was treated as an insufferable violation of civil liberties, and each one only heightened Democratic resentments at Lincoln's administration.

The most sensational and illuminating of these civil-liberties cases concerned the Democratic candidate for governor of Ohio in 1863, Clement Laird Vallandigham. Forty-three years old and probably the most handsome politician in America, Vallandigham sat in Congress from 1858 until 1863, when Republicans in the Ohio legislature successfully gerrymandered his district out from under him. It was not hard to see why. Vallandigham wore the "Copperhead" tag as a badge of honor, even to the point of fashioning a lapel pin made from the head of a copper penny. In January of 1863, Vallandigham decided to run for governor of Ohio, and thereupon he ran afoul of Major General Ambrose Burnside. A thoroughgoing War Democrat and now commander of the federal Department of Ohio, Burnside issued a general order that forbade "the habit of declaring sympathy for the enemy" and promised as punishment either arrest or exile through the Confederate lines. Vallandigham became an obvious target for Burnside's order, and on May 1, 1863, Burnside planted several spies in an election crowd that Vallandigham was due to address. Vallandigham made a few incautious remarks about "King Lincoln" and the "wicked, cruel and unnecessary" war he was waging, all of which was enough for Burnside. Four days later, a company of federal soldiers broke down the door of Vallandigham's house and hauled him off to Cincinnati for a military trial.

Vallandigham was no fool: Though a military commission easily found him guilty of violating Burnside's general order, he appealed for a writ of habeas corpus and cast himself as a martyr in the cause of the Constitution. Sensing the political Pandora's box that Vallandigham's arrest could easily open, Lincoln changed his sentence from imprisonment to banishment to the Confederacy. But Lincoln was unable to escape the eruption of attack and abuse from northern Democrats that followed in Vallandigham's wake, and when the Ohio Democrats met in Columbus in June to select a nominee for the Ohio governorship, a crowd of as many as 100,000 showed up to demand Vallandigham's nomination. But Vallandigham's absentee campaign slowly evaporated without his magnetic presence, and a daring Confederate raid into Ohio under John Hunt Morgan frightened Ohioans into a clearer sense of their wartime priorities. When the votes were tallied in the fall elections, Vallandigham lost his long-distance bid for the governorship by 100,000 votes. Relieved, Lincoln turned his attention to other matters than Vallandigham, and when he was advised in the summer of 1864 that Vallandigham had slipped back into Ohio, disguising himself with set of false whiskers and a pillow under his suit, Lincoln merely advised the new departmental commander to leave Vallandigham alone.

The oddity of the Democratic protests over Lincoln's suspension of the writ of habeas corpus and the Vallandigham arrest was how atypical the Vallandigham, Merryman, and Milligan cases were. When the record of civil arrests under Lincoln's administration has been looked at closely, most of them have turned out to be arrests for wartime racketeering, the imprisonment of captured blockade runners, deserters, and the detention of suspicious Confederate citizens, and not the imprisonment of political dissenters; most of the cases dealt with, like Vallandigham's, by military commissions occurred in areas of the occupied Confederacy, not in the North.[31] The Vallandigham case notwithstanding, Lincoln turns out to have been as undisposed to erect a political despotism over the North as he was to fashion a legislative despotism over Congress. When measured against the far vaster civil-liberties violations levied on German-Americans and Japanese-Americans in America's two 20th-century world wars, Lincoln's treatment of Vallandigham appears almost casual.

But if Lincoln found himself, for one reason or another, unable or unwilling to run Congress, the courts, or the Democratic party after the Jacksonian pattern, that did not mean that he was without any power to give the war direction. Lincoln chose in good Whig fashion to give shape to the war more by military rather than political means while allowing a Republican Congress to strike down the political legacy of passive national government that had been built up since 1800 by successive Democratic administrations rather than trying Jackson-style to do it himself. Lincoln, as a war president, managed to expand and, at the same time, shrink the effective powers of the presidency. And by juggling both, he succeeded simultaneously in being consistent with his own Whiggism and in giving the war the kind of direction it most needed.

Further Reading

The intricate story of the political compromises that kept Kentucky and Missouri from joining the Confederacy has been told in several venerable but still important studies, including E. Merton Coulter, *The Civil War and Readjustment in Kentucky* (Chapel Hill, NC, 1926), Edward C. Smith, *The Borderland in the Civil War* (New York, 1927), and William E. Parrish, *Turbulent Partnership: Missouri and the Union, 1861–1865* (Columbia, MO, 1963). The most important figure in the subsequent campaigning across Kentucky and Tennessee in early 1862 is Ulysses S. Grant, whose *Personal Memoirs* are among the mainstays of Civil War literature. Almost as fascinating a literary monument to Grant is the three-volume biography of Grant begun by Lloyd Lewis in *Captain Sam Grant* (Boston, 1950) and finished by Bruce Catton in *Grant Moves South* (Boston, 1960) and *Grant Takes Command* (Boston, 1968). Grant's most recent biographer has been William S. McFeely, in *Grant: A Biography* (New York, 1981). McFeely's portrait of Grant is not at all flattering, and has been critiqued by Brooks Simpson in "Butcher? Racist? An Examination of William S. McFeely's *Grant: A Biography*" in *Civil War History* 33 (March 1987), pp. 63–83. Simpson's own study of Grant's military and political career, *Let Us Have Peace: Ulysses S. Grant and the Politics of War and*

---

[31]Mark E. Neely, Jr., *The Fate of Liberty: Abraham Lincoln and Civil Liberties* (New York, 1991), pp. 24–28, 60, 98, 133–137.

Reconstruction, 1861–1868 (Chapel Hill, NC, 1991), adopts a much more favorable interpretation, especially of Grant's postwar political career. Grant's personal and official papers and letters have been made available through John Y. Simon's immense project of *The Papers of Ulysses S. Grant* (Carbondale, IL, 1967–).

Among the best books on the early western military campaigns is the first volume to offer a comprehensive account of them, Manning Ferguson Force's *From Fort Henry to Corinth* (1881; rept. Wilmington, NC, 1989). Among the more recent accounts of the operations on the Tennessee and Cumberland Rivers are James Hamilton, *The Battle of Fort Donelson* (New York, 1968) and Benjamin F. Cooling, *Forts Henry and Donelson* (Knoxville, TN, 1988). The fall of New Orleans has generated curiously little literary attention, which leaves Alfred Thayer Mahan's rather dry but technically faultless description of New Orleans in *The Gulf and the Inland Waters* (1883; rept. Freeport, NY, 1970) as the best account of Farragut's great triumph. The overall shape of Confederate decision making in the west in 1862–63 is covered in Archer Jones, *Confederate Strategy from Shiloh to Vicksburg* (Baton Rouge, 1961), while Thomas L. Connelly offered a collective biography of the Confederacy's western army in *Army of the Heartland: The Army of Tennessee, 1861–1862* (Baton Rouge, LA, 1967), and joined together with Archer Jones to write *The Politics of Command: Factions and Ideas in Confederate Strategy* (Baton Rouge, 1973). The first great battle in the west to result from those decisions has been covered with marvelous narrative skill by Wiley Sword in *Shiloh: Bloody April* (New York, 1974) and by James Lee McDonough in *Shiloh—In Hell Before Night* (Knoxville, TN, 1977). Kenneth Hafendorfer rescues *Perryville: Battle for Kentucky* (Louisville, 1991) from its undeserved neglect, while Edwin Bearss's *The Vicksburg Campaign* (three volumes, Dayton, OH, 1991) covers nearly every conceivable detail of the lengthy and varied operations that finally resulted in the capture of the great Confederate outpost on the Mississippi.

The mechanics of running a war have not usually generated either the excitement or the book-length narratives that the battles and leaders have, which is a pity since the politics and economics of war create the stages upon which the generals and their armies strut their little hour. Nevertheless, a number of published papers and diaries of Lincoln's Cabinet secretaries offer critical glimpses into the operation of wartime politics at the highest levels in the North, beginning with David Donald's edition of Salmon Chase's wartime diaries, *Inside Lincoln's Cabinet: The Civil War Diaries of Salmon P. Chase* (1954). The three volumes of Howard K. Beales's edition of *The Diary of Gideon Welles* (New York, 1960) are, if anything, even richer in first-hand observations of the politics of the war, while the diaries kept by Lincoln's secretary, John Hay and edited by Tyler Dennett as *Lincoln and the Civil War in the Diaries and Letters of John Hay* (1939; rept. New York, 1972) also offer a multitude of insights. Chase's decision to invite Jay Cooke to act as the Treasury's wartime agent was of greater significance to the long-term Union victory than a number of battles, and is described in detail by Ellis Oberholtzer in *Jay Cooke: Financier of the Civil War* (two volumes, New York, 1970). The war involved not only economic and political, but also legal and constitutional problems for the Union, most of which are surveyed in J. G. Randall, *Constitutional Problems Under Lincoln* (Urbana, IL, 1951) and Harold Hyman, *A More Perfect Union: The Impact of the Civil War and Reconstruction on the Constitution* (New York, 1973). The particular problems posed by the blockade have been searchingly analyzed by Ludwell H. Johnson, "The Confederacy: What Was It? A View from the Federal Courts," in *Civil War History* 32 (March 1986), and Johnson's article on the *Prize Cases*, "Abraham Lincoln and the Development of

Presidential War-making Powers: Prize Cases (1863) Revisited," in *Civil War History* 35 (September 1989).

The fires set in the rear of the Union cause by Democratic and Copperhead dissent have been the particular object of Frank L. Klement's attention in a series of volumes, *The Copperheads in the Middle West* (Chicago, 1960), *The Limits of Dissent: Clement L. Vallandigham and the Civil War* (Lexington, KY, 1970), and *Dark Lanterns: Secret Political Societies, Conspiracies, and Treason Trials in the Civil War* (Baton Rouge, 1984). Despite Klement's exhaustive review of the various conspiratorial movements, it is still possible to argue with his optimistic conclusion (especially in *Dark Lanterns*) that these conspiracies were mostly the opportunistic fantasy of the Republicans or the northern military. By contrast, Mark Neely's Pulitzer Prize-winning *The Fate of Liberty: Abraham Lincoln and Civil Liberties* (New York, 1991) offers a comprehensive rebuttal to wartime charges that Lincoln wantonly disregarded the civil rights of dissenters and Democrats and imposed a quasi-dictatorship on the North.

CHAPTER 6

The Soldier's Tale

The ordinary soldier of the Civil War was usually a temporary volunteer. Unlike most of the European nations, which used either a universal military draft or relied upon an army of long-service professionals, the armies of the American Civil War were filled with untrained amateurs who had left their plows in their fields or their pens by their inkwells, and who fully expected to return to them as soon as the war was over. Although both the Union and the Confederacy eventually resorted to a compulsory draft to keep their ranks filled, right down to the end of the war it was mostly the volunteer, signing the enlistment papers of his own volition, who shouldered the burden of war.

These volunteers had almost as many reasons for enlisting as there were ordinary soldiers to volunteer. When asked why he had enlisted, Douglas J. Cater, a musician in the 3rd Texas Cavalry, "thought of the misguided and misinformed fanatical followers of Wm. Lloyd Garrison and Harriet Beecher Stowe" who had driven the issue of slavery through Congress until the southern states "saw no other solution than a peaceful withdrawal and final separation." Cater owned no slaves himself, but he was convinced that slavery was the right condition for blacks. Northerners "had now become fanatical, and wrote and preached about it, without considering the condition of the Negro in the jungles of Africa as compared to his happy condition (of course there were exceptions) with his master in the cultivation of the fields of the southern states." As a result, secession was merely the South's "exercise of Constitutional rights in their desire for harmony and peace. . . ."[1]

But for many more Southerners, it was individual local patriotisms rather than the defense of slavery or even the Confederacy that tipped the balances toward enlistment. Patrick Cleburne, a well-born Protestant immigrant from Ireland, owned no slaves and had no interest in slavery, but he enlisted in the 1st Arkansas regiment in 1861 because "these people have been my friends and have stood up to me on all occasions." Philip Lightfoot Lee, of Bullitt County, Kentucky, offered a whole calendar of local loyalties as his reason for joining a rebel Kentucky brigade.

[1]Douglas John Cater, *As It Was: Reminiscences of a Soldier of the Third Texas Cavalry and the Nineteenth Louisiana Infantry*, T. Michael Parrish, ed. (Austin, TX, 1990), pp. 67–68, 69, 173.

At first, he explained, he was for the Union; if that split apart, he was for Kentucky; if Kentucky failed, he would go for Bullitt County; if Bullitt County collapsed, he would fight for his home town of Shepardsville; and if Shephardsville were divided, he would fight for his side of the street.[2]

Northern soldiers found themselves enlisting for an equally wide spread of reasons. For some Northerners, the war was a campaign to keep the American republic from being torn in two and made vulnerable to the hungry ambitions of foreign aristocracies. Walt Whitman, who found part-time government work in Washington so that he could volunteer as a nurse in the army hospitals, wrote in 1863 that a divided America would reduce the world's greatest republican experiment to the level of a third-rate power that would then lie prone at the feet of England and France. "There is certainly not one government in Europe but is now watching the war in this country, with the ardent prayer that the United States may be effectually split, crippled, and dismember'd by it." The war not only endangered the possibility of republican government by inviting foreign intervention, but it also raised the question of whether, if the Confederacy succeeded, republican government could ever be made to work again at home. "If the ground assumed by the States in revolt is yielded, what bond is there to hold together any two States that may remain—North or South, East or West?" asked Ezra Munday Hunt, a surgeon in the 19th New Jersey. "What becomes of our national power, or title to respect? In such an event, must not the wealth and enterprise and energy of this young nation become the prey of contending factions, and our very name be a hissing and a byword among other nations?" On the other hand, declared one Union colonel at a mass Union rally in Indianapolis in February, 1863, if the Union was saved, it would keep the principle of republican government alive for the benefit of every other nation yearning to throw off the shackles of aristocracy. It "would be to not only strengthen our own government, but to shed a radiating light over all the other nations of the world by which the down-trodden people could see their way to liberty."[3]

Few of the white Union recruits listed any interest in destroying slavery as a motivation for enlistment. "If *anyone* thinks that this army is fighting to free the Negro, or that that is any part of its aim, they are *terribly mistaken*," declared Massachusetts Sergeant William Pippey. "I don't believe that there is *one abolitionist* in *one thousand*, in the army." Indiana Sergeant Samuel McIlvaine wrote his parents

[2]Howell and Elizabeth Purdue, *Pat Cleburne: Confederate General* (Hillsboro, TX, 1973), p. 74; Randall Jimerson, *The Private Civil War: Popular Thought during the Sectional Conflict* (Baton Rouge, LA, 1988), pp. 24–25; William C. Davis, *The Orphan Brigade: The Kentucky Confederates Who Couldn't Go Home* (New York, 1980), pp. 1, 29, 57.

[3]Whitman, "Attitude of Foreign Governments During the War," in *The Portable Walt Whitman*, Mark Van Doren, ed. (New York, 1945, 1969), pp. 562–563; Hunt, "About the War" and "The Great Union Meeting Held in Indianapolis, February 26th, 1863," in *Union Pamphlets of the Civil War*, Frank Freidel, ed. (Cambridge, MA, 1967), vol. 1, p. 562 and vol. 2, p. 602; Bell I. Wiley, *The Life of Billy Yank: The Common Soldier of the Union* (1952; rept. Baton Rouge, LA, 1978), p. 39.

to explain that he had enlisted to defend "this Government, which stands out to the rest of the world as the polestar, the beacon light of liberty & freedom to the human race." And so in February, 1862, Sergeant McIlvaine made no effort to stop "three or four slave hunters" from entering the regiment's campsite and seizing two runaway slaves who "got mixed with the Negro cooks and waiters and were thus endeavoring [to] effect their escape to the North." Even though the runaways had armed themselves with a pistol and a butcher knife, "they had evidently counted on being protected in the regiment but they were sadly disappointed, as they were disarmed by their pursuers and taken back without molestation on our part."[4] Even William Tecumseh Sherman was indifferent at best to making the war a crusade against slavery. "I would prefer to have this a white man's war and provide for the negroes after the time has passed," Sherman wrote to his wife, Ellen Ewing Sherman, "but we are in revolution and I must not pretend to judgment. With my opinion of negroes and my experience, yea, prejudice, I cannot trust them yet."[5]

But as the war brought more and more Northerners into close contact with the brutal realities of the slave system, the urge to destroy slavery gradually became an important part of the soldier's motivations. "I had thought before that God had made the Negro for a slave for the whites," Elisha Stockwell of the 14th Wisconsin recalled, but after seeing one slaveowner abuse two female slaves, "my views on slavery took a change." Marcus Spiegel, a German Jew who rose to command an Ohio regiment before his death in battle in 1864, enlisted as a pro-Union Democrat, believing that "it is not necessary to fight for the darkies, nor are they worth fighting for." But by early 1864, Spiegel had seen enough of slavery in Louisiana to change his mind. "Since I am here I have learned and seen more of what the horror of Slavery was than I ever knew before." Never again would Spiegel "either speak or vote in favor of Slavery; this is no hasty conclusion but a deep conviction." Later in the war, a white Iowa regiment captured twenty-three prisoners from a Confederate unit that had participated in the massacre of black federal soldiers at Fort Pillow; the angry whites interrogated the prisoners, asked them if they remembered Fort Pillow, and then shot them all.[6]

Sometimes, both Union and Confederate volunteers would be led by more pragmatic motives to join the armies. Some simply wanted to get away from home. The federal army set eighteen as the minimum age for its recruits, but recruiting officers didn't mind winking at restless teenagers in order to fill a recruiting quota. Henry C. Matrau was only fourteen when he joined Company G of the 6th Wiscon-

---

[4]McIlvaine, *By the Dim and Flaring Lamps: The Civil War Diaries of Samuel McIlvaine*, C. E. Cramer, ed. (Monroe, NY, 1990), pp. 32, 147.

[5]Jimerson, *The Private Civil War*, pp. 41, 43; Lloyd Lewis, *Sherman: Fighting Prophet* (New York, 1932), p. 303.

[6]*Your Own True Marcus: The Civil War Letters of a Jewish Colonel*, Frank L. Byrne and Jean Soman, eds. (Kent, OH, 1984), pp. 62, 315–316; Marvin R. Cain, "A 'Face of Battle' Needed: An Assessment of Motives and Men in Civil War Historiography," in *Civil War History* 28 (March 1982), p. 23.

sin in 1862, but the mustering officer simply treated the boy's presence on the line as a pleasant joke.

> More than a hundred men who had become interested in the little chap stood around to see if he would pass muster. He had picked out a pair of large shoes into which he stuffed insoles that would raise him up a half inch or more, higher heels and thicker soles had been added to the shoes. The high crowned cap and the enlarged shoes lifted the little fellow up. . . . I can see him as he looked when he started to walk past the mustering officer. I can see Captain McIntyre of the Regular Army, who mustered our regiment. The minute the boy started down the line, his eyes were fixed upon him, and he watched him until he reached the left of the company. I can see the captain's smile of approval as the little fellow took his place. He had won the day. He was mustered into Uncle Sam's service for three years or during the war.[7]

As many as 10,000 boys below the age of eighteen managed to join the army legally, as drummer boys or musicians, but it is entirely possible that as many as 800,000 underage soldiers, many as young as fifteen, illegally slipped past cooperative recruiters. Elisha Stockwell was one of these fifteen-year-olds when he signed up to join Company I, 14th Wisconsin Volunteers, and though his father successfully voided the enlistment, the boy took the first chance he had in February, 1862, and ran away to join the regiment. Stockwell admitted that he thought of politics as "only for old men to quarrel over." He just wanted to get off the farm and see the wider world.[8]

Whatever the reason for enlisting, by 1865, the Union had sworn in 2,128,948 men—approximately one-fifth of the white adult male population of the northern states—while the Confederacy probably enrolled a little under 1 million men, about one-third of its white adult male population. And they represented not simply a statistical percentage of the American population, but also a healthy cross section of classes and occupations. The Civil War was by no means merely a "poor man's war." The Virginia brigade first commanded by "Stonewall" Jackson at Bull Run in 1861 carried on its rolls 811 farmers, 477 ordinary laborers, 107 merchants, 41 lawyers, 26 printers, 142 students, 75 blacksmiths, six bakers, five distillers, two dentists, and four "gentlemen."[9] The 11th Ohio boasted that it had enlisted workmen from approximately 100 trades and occupations, "from selling a paper of pins to building a steamboat or railroad." The 19th Massachusetts had six Harvard graduates in its ranks, while the 23rd Ohio carried two men on its regimental rolls who would later be presidents of the United States, Rutherford B. Hayes and William McKinley. One study of 1,337 Union recruits from Newburyport, Massachusetts, has shown that high-status skilled workers and professionals were actually

---

[7] L. J. Herdegen and W. J. K. Beaudot, *In the Bloody Railroad Cut at Gettysburg* (Dayton, OH, 1990), p. 65.

[8] *Private Elisha Stockwell, Jr., Sees the Civil War*, Byron R. Abernathy, ed. (Norman, OK, 1985), p. 15.

[9] James I. Robertson, *The Stonewall Brigade* (Baton Rouge, 1963), pp. 15–16.

over-represented in the Union army; the rates of enlistment for those in the poorest and wealthiest categories among the Newburyport troops was almost even. [10] Similar studies of Concord, Massachusetts, and Claremont and Newport, New Hampshire, have also shown that white-collar workers and independent artisans (the segments of the northern population with the greatest openness to the Whig-Republican ideology) formed the largest segment of recruits, while soldiers from the lowest and highest wealth categories enlisted at approximately the same rates. [11]

Taken as a whole, skilled laborers and professionals made up approximately 25 percent and 3 percent (respectively) of the Union army, which works out to almost exactly the same proportions these groups occupied in the entire male population of the North in the 1860 census. Unskilled laborers made up about 15 percent of the federal recruits, which means that poor workers were actually slightly under-represented in the Union army. As for the Confederates, unskilled laborers composed only 8.5 percent of the recruits, a substantial under-representation of this group, which otherwise comprised almost 13 percent of the white Southern population. [12]

1. The Making of the Volunteers

Since so much of the responsibility for recruitment fell upon the individual states, and since so few of the states were really equipped to handle recruitment in any systematic fashion, the actual process of raising and organizing a regiment often became a matter of local or personal initiative. Recruitment rallies were a ritual of the early days of the war, and like religious revivals, they had the capacity to bring the full social pressure of local communities to bear on potential recruits. John D. Billings, who served in the 10th Massachusetts Artillery, came to recognize a fairly predictable pattern in recruitment rallies that appealed to the social self-definition of white males. "The old veteran of 1812 was trotted out, and worked for all he was worth, and an occasional Mexican War veteran would air his non-chalance at grim-visaged war," Billings remembered, but the clearest challenge of all would come from "the patriotic maiden who kept a flag or handkerchief waving with only the rarest and briefest of intervals, who 'would go in a minute if she was a man.' " To be a man, or to avoid becoming a "woman" while women were becoming "men," put a

[10]Maris A. Vinovskis, "Have Social Historians Lost the Civil War? Some Preliminary Demographic Speculations," in Toward a Social History of the American Civil War: Exploratory Essays, Maris A. Vinovskis, ed. (New York, 1990), pp. 1–30.

[11]William J. Rorabaugh, "Who Fought for the North in the Civil War? Concord, Massachusetts, Enlistments," in Journal of American History 73 (December 1986), pp. 695–701; Thomas R. Kemp, "Community and War: The Civil War Experience of Two New Hampshire Towns," in Toward a Social History of the American Civil War, pp. 31–77.

[12]See the tables that James M. McPherson created from data on Union enlistees and on Confederate soldiers (based on profiles assembled by Bell I. Wiley) in Ordeal By Fire: The Civil War and Reconstruction, p. 359.

substantial squeeze on any townsman's reluctance to enlist. At other points, the recruitment meeting would mimic the fervor, as well as the structure, of an evangelical revival:

> . . . Sometimes the patriotism of such a gathering would be wrought up so intensely by waving banners, martial and vocal music, and burning eloquence, that a town's quota would be filled in less than an hour. It needed only the first man to step forward, put down his name, be patted on the back, placed upon the platform, and cheered to the echo as the hero of the hour, when a second, a third, a fourth would follow, and at last a perfect stampede set in to sign the enlistment roll, and a frenzy of enthusiasm would take possession of the meeting.[13]

To enlist was a conversion to true manhood; to skulk was a fall from social grace.

Recruits usually moved from the recruiting meeting or office to a "camp of rendezvous," which would be almost anything from a city park to a county fairground. Since most recruits in the early stages of the war joined local companies rather than fully formed regiments, the "camp of rendezvous" was the place where the plethora of local companies were sorted out into regiments for the first time. The largest of these camps in the North was Camp Curtin, outside Harrisburg, Pennsylvania. Harrisburg was the most important east-west junction point for the northern railroad system, and Camp Curtin's location one mile north of the Pennsylvania Railroad's main Harrisburg depot made it the prime location for the organization of Pennsylvania troops as well as a major supply dump for military equipment for the Army of the Potomac. In all, 106 regiments were organized at Camp Curtin; but close behind Curtin in organizational numbers were Camp Chase at Columbus, Camp Morton in Indianapolis, Camp Butler in Springfield, and Camp Harrison and Camp Dennison in Cincinnati.[14]

At camps like these, North and South, recruits were issued blankets, tin plates and cups, forks and knives and, once they had been officially mustered into United States or Confederate States service, uniforms. The official uniform of the United States Army in 1861 included a long, dark-blue frock coat, with matching wool pants, and a tall-crowned broad-brimmed black felt hat known by the name of its designer as the "Hardee." There were few enough of these available in 1861 to issue to the volunteers, who preferred to show up in their own homegrown varieties of uniforms anyway. But the gaudier the uniform or the less in conformity it was to regulations, the less likely it was to win favor in the eyes of army quartermasters or West Point regulars, and the harder it was to replace them when, after a few months, they wore out. By the spring of 1862, the general uniform pattern of the Union armies had settled into the use of a navy-blue frock coat or sack coat, with sky-blue or robins-egg-blue trousers, and either a black felt slouch hat or a baggy-

---

[13]John D. Billings, *Hardtack and Coffee, Or The Unwritten Story of Army Life* (1887; rept. Williamstown, MA, 1973), pp. 38, 41.

[14]William J. Miller, *The Training of an Army: Camp Curtin and the North's Civil War* (Shippensburg, PA, 1990), pp. 237–238.

looking, flat-topped forage cap sometimes called (after its French pattern) a *kepi*. Only four sizes of this standard uniform were manufactured for Union army use, which compelled most soldiers to develop some kind of crude sewing skills in order to make them fit. Shoes were simply hard leather brogans, square-toed and ill-fitting at best. "My first uniform was a bad fit," remembered Warren Lee Goss, a Massachusetts volunteer:

> My trousers were too long by three or four inches; the flannel shirt was coarse and unpleasant, too large at the neck and too short elsewhere. The forage cap was an ungainly bag with pasteboard top and leather visor; the blouse was the only part which seemed decent; while the overcoat made me feel like a little nubbin of corn in a large preponderance of husk.[15]

The Confederate dress regulations adopted in September, 1861, specified a uniform of similar design, but adopted cadet gray as the official uniform color, largely since so many state militia units were already clothed in gray uniforms of their own design and purchase. As the blockade progressively cramped Confederate supplies, Confederate uniforms became shabbier and more improvised; by the end of the war, some Confederate soldiers were dressed in old farm clothes and captured federal uniforms. What was worse, supplies of chemical dye had become so scarce that Southerners were forced to resort to common vegetable dyes to color what uniforms they could make, and so produced frocks and trousers, not in gray, but in a brownish, mousy color nicknamed "butternut."

If the "camp of rendezvous" was too small, then the next stop for a newly organized regiment would be a larger "camp of instruction," where the volunteer was supposed to learn the basics of drill and discipline. At the beginning of the war, the "camp of instruction" frequently turned into a local entertainment. "Crowds of ladies and gentlemen repair every afternoon to the 'Camp of Instruction' of the Virginia Volunteers, at the Hermitage Fair Grounds," reported one Richmond newspaper. "The proficiency of the Lexington Cadets . . . is something wonderful to behold, and worth going a long distance to see."[16] Unfortunately, since the United States had fought its last major war over thirteen years before in Mexico, and had kept up only the tiniest regular army since then, most young Americans of military age had never in their lives encountered the reality of military life, and knew next to nothing of military drill and discipline, and everything had to be taught from the very beginning, including something as simple as how to stand at attention. Moreover, as volunteers, few them seemed inclined to take drill and discipline or the military itself with the spit-polish seriousness it demanded. The volunteer never ceased to think of himself as an independent American, and

[15]Goss, "Going to the Front," in *Battles and Leaders of the Civil War*, C. C. Buel and R. U. Johnson, eds. (rept. New York, 1956), vol. 1, p. 152.

[16]Richmond *Daily Whig*, May 22, 1861, in *Richmond in Time in War*, W. J. Kimball, ed. (Boston, 1960), p. 8.

experienced a good deal of confusion and irritation at being made to obey orders he could see no sense in. Michigan Lieutenant Charles Haydon was annoyed to find that "many of the men seem to think they should never be spoken to unless the remarks are prefaced by some words of deferential politeness. Will the gentlemen who compose the first platoon have the kindness to march forward, or will they please to halt, &c. is abt. what some of them seem to expect."[17]

Discipline in the Confederate armies was, if anything, even worse. One major difficulty in imposing discipline on southern soldiers was that the discipline, regimentation, and authoritarianism of camp life was very nearly identical to that of the plantation, and southern whites resented and resisted efforts to impose on them what looked for all the world like the discipline they imposed at home on black slaves. One Georgia private insisted that "I love my country as well as any one but I don't believe in the plan of making myself a slave. . . ." And when he wrote home, he did not hesitate to compare military life with plantation slavery: "A private soldier is nothing more than a slave and is often treated worse. I have during the past six months gone through more hardships than anyone of ours or Grandma's negroes; their life is a luxury to what mine is sometimes." This situation was all the more galling to nonslaveholding whites, who had grudgingly supported the slave system precisely because black slavery was the one social fact which gave them any sense of equality with white planters. Military life forced slaveholders and nonslaveholders into precisely the relationship of class and command that denied *herrenvolk* equality among whites. Frank Robinson, a Louisiana soldier, complained that "the life of a common soldier . . . is a great deal worse than that of a common field hand." But even worse, "those commissioned officers . . . are just like the owners of slaves on plantations, they have nothing to do but strut about, dress fine, and enjoy themselves."[18]

In many cases, the discipline problem lay not so much with the volunteer soldier as with the volunteer system itself, since volunteer regiments were usually allowed to elect their own officers from among themselves, officers who might be popular as good fellows but who knew neither how to give orders and get them obeyed, nor even what kind of orders to give. Charles Wainwright, a regular artillery officer, was more exasperated at the officers the volunteers elected than at the volunteers themselves. "Their orders come out slow and drawling, then they wait patiently to see them obeyed in a laggard manner, instead of making the men jump to it sharp. . . ." This was because, as Wainwright realized, the officers had "raised their own men and known most of them in civil life." A northern missionary at Port Royal was shocked to see "officers and men . . . on terms of perfect equality socially" in the Union army. ". . . Off duty they drink together, go arm

---

[17]Jimerson, *The Private Civil War*, p. 201.

[18]James I. Robertson, *Soldiers Blue and Gray* (Columbia, SC, 1988), p. 124; Jimerson, *The Private Civil War*, p. 206.

in arm around the town, call each other by the first name, in a way that startles an Eastern man."[19]

Time and the Confederate and federal governments eventually weeded out the worst of the incompetent officers. The federal army imposed qualifying exams for commissioned officers after First Bull Run, and the Confederacy followed in 1862. But even then, the qualifying exams were woefully easy to pass. Dillon Bridges of the 13th Indiana Cavalry was examined by a three-man board after being elected captain of Company M in 1864, and failed to answer some of the most obvious of the 39 questions on the exam:

> Q. How are battalions placed?
> A. Can't tell. . . .
>
> Q. Moving in column of fours and you wish to form platoons, what command?
> A. Can't tell. . . .
>
> Q. What course would you pursue in sending or receiving a flag of truce?
> A. I do not know. . . .
>
> Q. Have you ever studied the tactics or Army regulations?
> A. Not half an hour. All I have learned has been from observation.

Bridges was eventually prevailed upon to resign his captaincy. But Company M's second lieutenant, John A. Chapman, who confessed that he was "not capable of standing an examination," was passed by the examining board after a few perfunctory questions about picket duty.[20]

Even if Dillon Bridges had studied "the tactics or Army regulations," none of that might have made him a more effective officer. The prevailing tactics books—Scott, Hardee, and after 1862, Silas Casey's System of Infantry Tactics—were long on the technicalities of drill, such as basic weapons-handling and movement in and out of formations, but painfully short on real instruction for combat. One Ohio colonel, Jacob Ammen, recorded how he handled and instructed both his volunteer officers and men: "Daily drills—daily recitations in tactics—take the starch out of some, and others are learning fast. And now I superintend—select an officer to drill the others in the morning, one squad drill, company drill, and Battalion drill in the afternoon. . . . I drill the sergeants daily, in length of step, time and preserving distance."[21] All of this was effective for bringing large and unwieldy bodies of men to the battlefield itself, but it generally turned out to be useless once the shooting started, as units lost cohesion and started to take casualties. "Instead of practising

---

[19]Wainwright, A Diary of Battle: The Personal Journals of Colonel Charles S. Wainwright, 1861–1865, Allan Nevins, ed. (New York, 1962), p. 27. Joseph T. Glathaar, The March to the Sea and Beyond: Sherman's Troops in the Savannah and Carolinas Campaigns (New York, 1985), p. 26

[20]John W. Powell, "How to Pick Out Bad Officers," in Civil War Times Illustrated 30 (March/April 1991), pp. 46–49.

[21]T. Harry Williams, Hayes of the Twenty-Third: The Civil War Volunteer Officer (New York, 1965), pp. 30–31.

the men in the simple flank and line movements used in battle, or at targets, or in estimating distances," complained Union artilleryman Frank Wilkeson, "they were marched to and fro and made to perform displayful evolutions," which would have been commendable if war had been a "competitive drill for a valuable, and maybe, sacred prize," but which were worse than useless "in a rugged, wooded country where the clearings were surrounded by heavy forests . . . and where practice and practice and still more practice in estimating distances was required, if we were to fire accurately and effectively."[22] Confederate General Daniel Harvey Hill put the matter even more simply: "Whoever saw a Confederate line advancing that was not crooked as a ram's horn? Each ragged rebel yelling on his own hook and aligning on himself." Fewer still were even trained in how to fire. Target practice was almost unknown in both armies, and when it was tried, the results were usually too pitiful to be encouraging. The 14th Illinois tried to practice target shooting at a barrel set up 180 yards away from the firing line: Out of 160 tries, only four shots hit the barrel. George Eminhizer of the 45th Pennsylvania received no weapons training at all at Camp Curtin in 1862, and was greatly embarrassed by the command to load his rifle. "I did not know how," Eminhizer recalled. "I turned to my comrade on the right and said: 'Can you tell me which end of the cartridge I must put in first?' He loaded the gun for me." At least Eminhizer did not have to learn his lesson under fire. Ulysses Grant remembered seeing raw federal soldiers coming under attack at Shiloh who had only been issued weapons on the way down the Tennessee "and were hardly able to load their muskets according to the manual." Their officers knew no better, and Grant could only concede that it was perfectly natural "that many of the regiments broke at the first fire."[23]

The weapon the volunteer was expected to master, on his own or otherwise, would depend largely on which branch of the service he volunteered to serve in— the *infantry*, the service of the common foot soldier, the *cavalry*, the horse-mounted soldier, or the *artillery*, which serviced the various sizes and shapes of cannon that supported the infantry or protected fortifications. Both armies also recruited engineering and medical services, and attracted a plethora of chaplains, clerks, and civilian sutlers who accompanied the combat soldiers on campaign. But the infantry was the backbone of the army, and the burden of winning a battle or a campaign invariably rested on the skills and endurance of the infantryman. Approximately 80 percent of the combat strength of the Union army was infantry, with 14 percent serving in the cavalry and 6 percent in the artillery. In the Confederate army, the differential was much the same: 75 percent served in the infantry, with another 20 percent in the cavalry and the remaining 5 percent in the artillery.[24]

The basic infantry weapon was the Model 1861 United States Rifle Musket,

[22]Wilkeson, *Recollections of a Private Soldier of the Army of the Potomac* (New York, 1887), pp. 21–22.
[23]Bell I. Wiley, *The Life of Billy Yank*, p. 51; Miller, *Training of an Army*, p. 115; Grant, "The Battle of Shiloh," in *Battles and Leaders*, Buel & Underwood, eds., vol. 1, p. 473.
[24]Robertson, *Soldiers Blue and Gray*, p. 19.

frequently know as the "Springfield" rifled musket (so named from the Springfield, Massachusetts, armory where most of them were made), a 58-½-inch-long, single-shot, muzzle-loading rifle, weighing 9¼ pounds and fitted to carry a 21-inch-long triangular socket bayonet for use in hand-to-hand fighting. The Springfield rifle was, in its time, something of an innovation over the inaccurate and shortsighted smoothbore muskets used from the time of the Revolution up through the Mexican War, and the earliest version of the Springfield had been introduced to the army in 1855 by no one less than then-Secretary of War Jefferson Davis. Firing a conical, soft-lead .58 caliber slug (hilariously misnamed the "minnie ball" after its designer, French Captain Claude-Étienne Minié) the Springfield could hit an 11-inch bull's-eye at 350 yards, and, due to the deadly slow spin of its high-caliber rifling, it could also penetrate 6 inches of pine board at 500 yards. It was, nevertheless, slow to load, and required a sequence of nine separate steps (known as "load in nine times"). Each minié ball, packed into a cigar-shaped paper tube along with 60 grains of black powder, had to be removed from the soldier's cartridge box, torn open with the teeth, emptied into the musket's barrel, and rammed home with a ramrod. Then the infantryman would have to raise the musket, fit a percussion cap onto the nipple of the lock-plate above the trigger, and pull the trigger—exploding the percussion cap and igniting the powder charge in the paper tube. At best, a well-trained infantryman could load and fire three times in a minute.

Federal arsenals manufactured almost 700,000 of the Model 1861 Springfields for use during the war, while 20 private northern arms manufacturers supplied 450,000 more. But the Springfields were by no means the only weapons soldiers favored. The British army's .577 caliber Enfield rifle was another highly popular muzzle-loader, and approximately 400,000 Enfields were run through the blockade to equip the Confederate armies, who had no access to the Springfield rifle beyond what could be scavenged from battlefields. The federal government, itself short on weapons for the volunteers, bought up 500,000 Enfields for Union army use. The Sharps rifle, a single-shot, breech-loading .52 caliber rifle invented by Christian Sharps in 1844, was favored as a sharpshooter's rifle, and a variety of imported muzzle-loaders, such as the Austrian Lorenz rifle and the French-designed Belgian rifle, found their way into Union and Confederate hands. Ironically, the Sharps, the Enfield, and the Springfield were already on the road to obsolescence by 1861. Christopher Miner Spencer, a Connecticut inventor, had developed a seven-shot repeating rifle that fired manufactured brass cartridges from a magazine in the stock of the rifle, and Spencer personally demonstrated its usefulness to President Lincoln at a special target shooting at the White House on August 17, 1863. Alongside Spencer's rifle, the Colt Patent Firearms company introduced a repeating rifle with a peculiar five-chambered revolving cylinder, while the New Haven Arms Company's Henry repeating rifle could carry fifteen rounds in its magazine, and could reload a new cartridge and eject a spent one with a single lever motion.

Oddly, the repeating rifles failed to get the critical approval of the chief of the army ordnance bureau, James Wolfe Ripley, an old army regular who distrusted the repeaters. Part of this distrust may have been simple obstinacy on the part of the sixty-seven-year-old Ripley. But Ripley had at least some justification in fearing that the move to rapid-fire repeating rifles would put too much stress on the federal arsenals' ability to supply ammunition in sufficient quantities to the Union armies. Repeating rifles encouraged soldiers to blaze away without regard for supply, and Ripley had enough trouble supplying soldiers with muzzle-loading ammunition without having to think of the quantities of expensive, brass-encased repeating cartridges he would have to supply for an army full of repeaters (Spencer cartridges cost over $2 apiece). Ripley was also wary of committing the army to the use of weapons that, in 1861, were largely the brain-children of commercial manufacturers, and whose models used widely competing calibers of ammunition and involved complicated assortments of moving parts that were not interchangeable. As it was, an early government contract for 10,000 Spencer repeaters was nearly lost by Spencer when his small factory was unable to keep up a supply of the weapons or their ammunitions. Whatever else was wrong with the Springfield, it was a simple and durable weapon and cost little more than half the price of a Henry repeater or a Spencer, while the Enfield and Springfield accepted the same standardized minié ball.

These arguments were perfectly plausible to an army bureaucrat; they meant a good deal less to the soldier in the field. In 1861, Colonel Hiram Berdan went over Ripley's head to the president to get authorization to arm his two regiments of United States Sharpshooters with the Sharps breechloading rifle; and in 1863, Colonel John T. Wilder offered to buy Spencer repeating rifles for his brigade out of the contributions of the men themselves (Ripley relented on this occasion and refunded the cost of purchase to Wilder's men). Wilder's men got the first test of their repeaters in June, 1863, when they easily outshot both Confederate cavalry and infantry at Hoover's Gap, Tennessee. In August, Spencer got his opportunity to display his repeating rifle before Abraham Lincoln, and on September 15th, Ripley was officially retired. By January of 1865, the ordnance bureau was no longer even considering new models of muzzle-loaders. By contrast with Union hesitancy, the Confederates were much more willing to experiment with new weapons, and were happy to capture as many Spencers as they could. But the South lacked the technology to manufacture its own copy of the Spencer, and it had no way to manufacture the special cartridges used by the captured rifles.

Despite the improvements in sheer killing power represented by the rifled musket and the repeating breechloader, British military historian Paddy Griffith has pointed out that the overall impact of the new firearms technology was comparatively limited on the Civil War battlefield. Although the rifle could bring down a target at three times the range of an old smooth-bore musket, the difficulties posed by the inexperience of Civil War officers, the poor training in fire offered to the Civil War recruit, and the obstacles created by the American terrain generally cut down the effective range of Civil War fire combat to little more than eighty yards, where the technological advantage of a rifle over a smooth-bore musket shrank to the vanishing point. Poor combat training and even poorer instruction in the use of the rifle resulted instead in large masses of drilled soldiers being maneuvered into close firing positions to each other, where they proceeded to blaze away for prolonged periods of time. Officers and men who were unschooled in the need to close with the enemy ended up slugging matters out in close-range, stand-up firefights, piling up bullet-riddled corpses until one side or the other collapsed and retreated.[25] The immense casualty lists piled up at Antietam and Shilo had less to do with the new weapons and more to do with the sheer stumbling inability of the armies to do anything with them. And that, in turn, was what made so many of the immense and bloody battles of the Civil War so surprisingly resultless. Elisha Paxton, a lieutenant in "Stonewall" Jackson's brigade, complained in 1862 that "our victories . . . seem to settle nothing; to bring us no nearer the end of the war. It is only so many killed and wounded, leaving the work of blood to go on with renewed."[26] Unlike the sweeping winner-take-all Prussian victories at Königgrätz in 1866 and Sedan in 1870, Civil War battles resembled endless rounds in a boxing match. Not until the last year of the war did Civil War field officers acquire sufficient experience and confidence to begin experimenting with French-style "shock tactics" concentrating on rapid movement across battlefields and into personal encounter with the enemy and eliminating the costly and indecisive firefights that had dominated the Civil War battlefield up until then.[27]

Until that time, battlefield maneuvers in the Civil War floundered onward in blood, guided in their floundering by inadequate training and the popular images mid–19th-century Americans had of the Napoleonic wars. The most common tactical formation the volunteer infantryman fell into was the line of battle: a regiment drawn up in two lines, one behind the other, with a thin curtain of skirmishers in front to clear the advance and another thin curtain of sergeants and lieutenants in the rear to give orders and restrain cowards and shirkers. Alignment was maintained by sergeants and corporals on the flanks of the lines, bearing small flags called *guidons* in their musket barrels; and by a color guard in the center of the front line, bearing the regiment's national and state flag. In the midst of movement and battle (and Civil War battlefields were notoriously smoky, due to the billows of black-powder smoke drifting over friend and foe alike), these regimental colors could be the most important markers and pointers of all, since they could be seen and followed when drums and orders could not be heard. The position regimental colors occupied in battle also made them the most potent emotional symbol of the Civil War soldier's group identity. When the colonel of the 51st New York asked his regiment "if they would exchange" their old bullet-shredded state color for a new one, "the boys let up such a yell as convinced the Colonel that the City would

[25]Paddy Griffith, *Battle Tactics of the Civil War* (New Haven, 1987), p. 111.

[26]Gerald F. Linderman, *Embattled Courage: The Experience of Combat in the American Civil War* (New York, 1987), p. 250.

[27]Griffith, *Battle Tactics of the Civil War*, pp. 137–150.

have a good time getting that old Flag." Lieutenant George Washington Whitman of the 51st (Walt Whitman's brother) added, "it has 15 or 20 bullet holes in it and the staff was shot in two at New Bern, and we think a great deal of it." James Madison Williams had a similar reaction when the 21st Alabama was sent a new flag to replace the one damaged at Shiloh: "I like the ragged old flag torn with the enemy's shot, that we carried through the fight, better than all the flags in the Confederacy. . . ."[28]

Under these circumstances, infantry movement on Civil War battlefields remained largely what it had been in the Revolution and the Mexican-American War—large, rigid formations of men, moving slowly over open ground toward other large, static formations of men, until both were near enough to each other to inflict the level of casualties that would make the other formation break, or else near enough to close with the bayonet. The end result was often carnage. The 1st Texas Volunteers lost 82.3 percent of its men at Antietam; the 1st Minnesota lost almost as much in the first two days of action at Gettysburg. All in all, as many as one out of every sixteen men in both armies may have died in battle, and largely because the Civil War armies were, as Prussian Field Marshal Helmut von Moltke was gracelessly said to have observed, little better than two armed mobs chasing each other around the countryside.

The terrific rates of death in the infantry might have persuaded more men to seek service in the cavalry or artillery, had they not had their own problems, too. Artillery in the 19th century could be roughly divided into two groups, field artillery and heavy artillery. The field artillery was organized into regiments composed of ten batteries, with each battery made up of six cannon (although on campaign, most artillery batteries were split off from their administrative regiments and parceled up among infantry battalions and brigades to supply supporting fire to the infantry); the heavy artillery was mainly distributed in permanent field fortifications. The weapons these batteries employed varied almost as much as the infantry's weapons, but the most popular field gun was the easily handled 12-pounder smooth-bore, muzzle-loading Napoleon, which could throw a projectile with reasonable accuracy up to 1,600 yards. The kinds of ammunition used varied as well, depending on the need of the moment. Most Civil War field batteries fired four basic kinds of shot. The artillery man's standby was *solid shot*, a solid iron ball, either wrought or cast iron, that relied on its weight and the speed of its impact to destroy a target. Civil War artillery also turned to *shell*, a hollow sphere or cone containing powder or other explodables that were ignited by a fuse charge in the base of the shell, with the fuse cut to a predetermined length to ensure the shell enough flying time to reach its target before exploding and blowing whatever was near it to pieces. The artillery also employed *case*, another version of shell that contained seventy-six musket balls, similar to what the

[28]*Civil War Letters of George Washington Whitman*, Jerome M. Loving, ed. (Durham, NC, 1975), p. 56; *From That Terrible Field: Civil War Letters of James M. Williams, Twenty-first Alabama Infantry Volunteers*, John Kent Folmar, ed. (University, AL, 1981), p. 60.

British called *shrapnel.* The most fearsome load in the artillery limber was *canister,* a lethal tin cylinder packed with balls or slugs that could turn a cannon into a giant sawed-off shotgun. Case and canister were short-range items, and specifically used as antipersonnel ammunition. Canister used on masses of infantry at close ranges could be hideous in its effect. A Napoleon, triple-shotted with canister tins, could blow 650 lead balls into an oncoming enemy unit, equivalent to the fire of an entire infantry regiment. But in general, artillery was used in the Civil War mostly to disorganize and disrupt attacking infantry formations, rather than actually to kill or maim individuals, and it served its purpose best by preventing enemy formations from getting close enough to do damage to one's own infantry.

The Union's industrial resources gave it the technical edge in artillery all through the Civil War. However, the rural and agrarian structure of southern society gave the Confederacy an equal edge in terms of cavalry. The Confederacy also possessed several great natural cavalry leaders: In the West, Nathan Bedford Forrest used his cavalry to burn and pillage Union supply lines with virtual impunity; in the East, J. E. B. Stuart, the twenty-eight-year-old commander of Lee's cavalry, easily rode circles around McClellan's clumsy northern cavalrymen—on the peninsula, he *literally* rode around McClellan's entire army—and created an image of the Confederate cavalry as banjo-strumming knights-errant, dressed in plumes and capes. The great difficulty with cavalry was that it was expensive, and the South was forced to restrict the size of its cavalry arm simply through its inability to provide mounts (much of the Confederate cavalry was actually mounted on horses owned by the troopers themselves). And if the combat training of Civil War volunteer infantry left a great deal to be desired, the training of Civil War cavalry was even worse. "The difficulty of converting raw men into soldiers is enhanced manifold when they are mounted," complained Confederate Lieutenant General Richard Taylor, who rose to command the Confederate department of East Louisiana, Mississippi, and Alabama, and this seemed especially and painfully true when it came to dealing with Taylor's own Confederate cavalry.

> Living on horseback, fearless, and dashing, the men of the South afforded the best possible material for cavalry. They had every quality but discipline, and resembled Prince Charming, whose manifold gifts, bestowed by her sisters, were rendered useless by the malignant fairy. Scores of them wandered about the country like locusts, and were only less destructive to their own people than the enemy. . . . Assuredly, our cavalry rendered much excellent service, especially when dismounted and fighting as infantry. Such able officers as Stuart, Hampton, and the younger Lees in the east, Forrest, Green, and Wheeler in the west, developed much talent for war; but their achievement, however distinguished, fell far below the standard that would have been reached had not the want of discipline impaired their efforts and those of their men.[29]

[29]Taylor, *Destruction and Reconstruction: Personal Experiences of the Late War,* Charles P. Roland, ed. (Waltham, MA, 1968), p. 53.

North Carolina Governor Zebulon Vance grew so exasperated with the indiscipline of Confederate cavalry wandering through his state that he cried out in 1863: "If God Almighty had yet in store another plague worse than all others which he intended to have let loose on the Egyptians in case Pharaoh still hardened his heart, I am sure it must have been a regiment or so of half-armed, half-disciplined Confederate cavalry."[30]

If the Civil War departs from the pattern of the Napoleonic wars at any major point, it is in its failure to use cavalry to achieve decisive victory on the battlefield. Instead, Civil War cavalry spent most of the war on raiding and scouting duties. At Gettysburg, the federal cavalry performed the vital service of delaying the Confederate infantry long enough to allow the slower-moving federal infantry to reach the battlefield. But few cavalry units in the Civil War ever got the chance to play the classical role of cavalry, carved out by European horse soldiers since the 1600s, as the deliverer of the finishing blow to enemy infantry, routing and dispersing enemy foot soldiers into irreversible panic. Part of this was because cavalry training was no better than the training offered to Civil War infantry; but another part was simply that Civil War infantry combat usually failed to reach those moments of overwhelming battlefield crisis when the table would be set for the cavalry to annihilate the enemy with a single crushing blow. It was not until the closing campaigns of the war in northern Alabama and in Virginia that Civil War cavalry finally established a clear tactical role for itself and emerged as a critical factor in pursuing and demoralizing defeated infantry.[31] By then, the introduction of the Spencer repeating carbine (the downsized version of the rifle issued for cavalry use) had made the classical cavalry sidearm, the saber, useless as a field weapon. On the occasions when cavalrymen actually engaged enemy infantry, they usually dismounted and fought on foot with their carbines.

2. The Making of the Armies

The volunteer who mastered the intricacies of his weapon and drill would leave his "camp of instruction" with the rest of his regiment and be shipped off to wherever the main armies might be at that moment. From that point on, the basic organizational unit, and the unit that most soldiers were most liable to use to identify themselves, was the regiment. Unlike the regimental system of the British army, the volunteer regiments of the Civil War had no previous history. They were the creations of 1861, with no existing traditions or institutions with which to shelter and socialize the new recruit, and no already existing cadres of officers or noncommissioned officers or permanent barracks or recruiting depots. It fell on the volunteers themselves to turn their regiments into either liveable facsimiles of home life,

[30]Vance to James Seddon [December 21, 1863], in *Official Records*, series 4, vol. 2, pp. 1061–1062.
[31]Griffith, *Battle Tactics of the Civil War*, pp. 181–186.

or freewheeling moral carousels. Some units, like the two regiments of Hiram Berdan's United States Sharpshooters, prided themselves on living "like a band of brothers, imbued with the one feeling of patriotism in their voluntary enlistment for three years." St. Clair A. Mulholland described the camp of his 116th Pennsylvania as a religious idyll where "seldom was an obscene word or an oath heard in the camp" and "meetings for prayer were of almost daily occurrence, and the groups of men sitting on the ground or gathered on the hill side listening to the Gospel were strong reminders of the mounds of Galilee when the people sat upon the ground to hear the Savior teach."[32] But in other regiments, the abrupt transition from domestic routine to the poorly structured life of an army camp meant crossing over a social line where the customary behavioral restraints might mean very little. Prostitution, drunkenness, gambling, and thievery were rife in both federal and Confederate regiments. Edward King Wightman of the 9th New York found that "most of our common soldiers are scarcely above brutes by nature."

> The privates, of course, are not such people as you or any sensible man would choose, or perhaps I should say could endure, as associates. As a mass, they are ignorant, envious, mercenary, and disgustingly immoral and profane. Being as they are here free from the restraints of civil law, they give loose rein to all their vices and make a boast of them. In our whole regiment, I know no private who will not curse and swear and but few who will not, when circumstances favor, rob and steal or, as they more euphoneously style the operations, "briz things."[33]

On paper, Civil War regiments were supposed to contain eight to ten companies of approximately 100 enlisted men and officers each, commanded by a colonel, so that the full strength of a regiment ought to have been approximately 1,000 men. In the Union army, however, regiments were often allowed to dwindle down to between 200 and 300 men, as the ranks were thinned by sickness and casualties. The reason for this queer practice was nakedly political. Since the volunteer regiments were raised by the states, it was easier for many northern governors to create new regiments, and thus create new openings for cronies whom they wished to reward with officers' commissions, than to keep refilling the old regiments. The result was an army of shadow regiments. When Union General John A. Dix reviewed George Washington Whitman's 51st New York at Newport News, Virginia, in February, 1863, the 51st "could only muster 140 men," and "when we came along with our old flag all torn to pieces, I saw the old. Gen. eye the flag and Regt. and shake his head."[34] In many cases, it was up to the regimental commanding officer to keep up a supply of new enlistments from back home for his regiment,

[32]Charles A. Stevens, *Berdan's United States Sharpshooters in the Army of the Potomac* (1892; rept. Dayton, OH, 1984), p. 20; Mulholland, *The Story of the 116th Regiment, Pennsylvania Infantry* (1895; rept. Baltimore, MD, 1991), p. 184.

[33]Wightman, *From Antietam to Fort Fisher: The Civil War Letters of Edward King Wightman, 1862–1865,* E. G. Longacre, ed. (Madison, NJ, 1985), pp. 74, 97.

[34]Whitman, *Civil War Letters of George Washington Whitman,* p. 88.

but most commanders could ill afford to detail their precious supply of junior officers for recruiting duty behind the lines. The Confederate armies, on the other hand, recognized the value of integrating new recruits and replacements with veteran combat regiments, and so the Confederate regiments were more likely to maintain their organizational integrity throughout the war than Union regiments.

If the regiment was the basic unit of identity, the brigade was soon recognized as the basic unit of maneuver on the Civil War battlefield, and most of the movement and action in Civil War combat occurred in groups of brigades. The average brigade consisted of four or five regiments, commanded by a brigadier general, and sometimes they acquired an identity of their own to rival the individual regimental identities. The Iron Brigade of the Army of the Potomac was composed of five western regiments who retained the use of the black "Hardee" hat as their badge. The Irish Brigade, another Army of the Potomac unit, was composed of an odd amalgam of Irish-born New Yorkers and Protestant Pennsylvanians who carried a green flag emblazoned with a gilded harp into battle. The Philadelphia Brigade, which was yet another Army of the Potomac unit, was the only brigade in either army that took its name from its hometown.

Brigades were themselves usually organized into divisions, comprising two or three brigades, and commanded by a either a senior brigadier general or a major general. Finally, the divisions were organized into corps, with both armies making up a corps from two or three divisions. Confederate corps were generally identified by the name of their commanding general, while Union corps were assigned numbers. The corps commanders, usually senior major generals, were the brains of an army, and the measure of any army's effectiveness could be reliably prophesied from the quality of its corps commanders. In Lee's army in 1863, the corps commanders—which over the course of the year included James Longstreet, "Stonewall" Jackson, and Ambrose Powell Hill—were probably the best assemblage of military talent and daring on the North American continent. But the Army of the Potomac also boasted three equally outstanding combat soldiers in the commanders of the 1st Corps (John F. Reynolds), the 2nd Corps (Winfield Scott Hancock) and the 6th Corps (John Sedgwick).

To the ordinary volunteer, however, the principal concern was not with generals, or even weapons, but with the experience of war service itself. Much as enlistment propaganda might have initially convinced the volunteer that the Rebel or the Yankee was his sworn enemy, the volunteer soon recognized that the soldier opposite him was an American like himself, and soldiers from both armies often indulged in surprising amounts of fraternization in the quiet periods between battles. Edward King Wightman described such a meeting near Fortress Monroe in May, 1863, with a "Johnny Reb" who had "laid aside his piece and crossed over in a skiff to exchange papers with our pickets." Wightman looked over this "very lean black-eyed fellow with long straight hair," and noticed that he "was well clothed in a gray jacket and pants and so forth." Wightman "bantered him the best I knew how, but he took it very well." A year later, Wightman saw a more general truce break out on the James River between Confederates and federals who created a temporary market for swaps of goods. "One of our men, laying aside his rifle, would walk out boldly half-way to the enemy's line, leave a little bag of coffee on a stump, and return," while "Johnny Reb would then issue forth, take the coffee and substitute in its place a big plug of tobacco, which was speedily secured for the service of the Union." Eventually the "ballygogging" attracted the notice of a Confederate officer who "determined to make a demonstration."

> All at once the rebs started for cover, but not before they had called out warn-ingly, "Take care, Yanks, we're going to shell ye." To this our boys replied by flopping into pits, leaving but one eye exposed and crying with equal friendship, "Lay low, Rebs!" The artillery fire opened on the right, intermingled with rapid volleys of musketry, and worked gradually around to us. In our immediate neigh-borhood shells were dropped in profusion, spiced with a few rifle balls; but no advance was made and no one was hit. In an hour everything was quiet again, and we all came forth whistling and laughing as before, to cook our supper. The rebs did likewise.[35]

Soldiers like Wightman soon learned that the real enemy in the war was not the other soldier, but rather disease, wounds, and the fear of wounds. Disease, in fact, turned out to be the real killer of the Civil War. For every soldier who died in battle, another two died of disease in camp, and overall, over 10 percent of the Union army, and 18 percent of the Confederate army, were killed off by disease rather than by bullets. One principal cause for the ravages of disease was the nature of military camp life in the 19th century, which in clinical terms acted as little better than a disease funnel. Americans of the Civil War era knew little or nothing of bacteriology, and so neither the volunteer nor his officers had any idea of the communicative and infectious nature of malaria, typhus, bronchitis, or pneumonia. As a result, men were taken into the armies carrying a number of diseases with them, and then packed into teeming military camps where they could easily spread a vast sampling of pathogens among themselves. The volunteers unwittingly added to the odds against them by responding to sanitary discipline with the same con-temptuous independence they displayed towards military discipline, and they could be persuaded to take appropriate health precautions only with the greatest diffi-culty. Camp life, for white American males in the 19th century, created an inver-sion of social roles, since male soldiers now found themselves responsible for a range of domestic labors—sewing clothes, cooking meals, cleaning—that were normally assigned at home to women, and many soldiers were unable to make the cognitive adjustment to the performance of these tasks even when their lives depended on it. "I am most heartily sick of this kind of life," wrote Jacob W. Bartness, an Indiana soldier, to his wife in 1865, "Oh, what a pleasant retreete from the repulsive scenes

---

[35]Wightman, *From Antietam to Fort Fisher*, pp. 132, 196–197.

of this man-slaughtering life, would be the society of my family in some secluded spot, shut out from the calamities of war."[36]

On campaign, the constant exposure to all varieties of weather, and the vulnerability of northern-bred systems to the ecological differences of the southern climate and environment, made northern soldiers particularly vulnerable to sickness. Furthermore, the impossibility of washing and cleaning on long marches made the volunteer an easy target to infestations of lice, fleas, ticks, and other body pests. For John Billings, the constant presence of lice was a great leveler of pretensions, the butt of a good soldiers' joke. "Like death," Billings wrote, lice were "no respecter of persons." The army *grayback* "inserted its bill as confidingly into the body of the major-general as of the lowest private. I once heard the orderly of a company officer relate that he had picked *fifty-two graybacks* from the shirt of his chief at one sitting."[37] Few soldiers suspected that these pests also helped to transmit disease through bites and open sores. In camp, the volunteers carelessy continued to make their own trouble for themselves. Water contaminated by poorly dug latrines, along with piles of waste and garbage left to attract flies and rodents, brought on waves of dysentery, diarrhea, and typhoid, but did little to convince the volunteer to protect himself. "Our poor sick, I know, suffer much," complained Lee, but "they bring it on themselves by not doing what they are told. They are worse than children, for the latter can be forced."

The army medical services compounded these problems instead of curing them. Like the army itself, army medical practice, at the outbreak of the war, was almost nonexistent. In 1861, the Union surgeon general was Colonel Thomas Lawson, an eighty-four-year-old veteran of the War of 1812 who had only 113 other surgeons on the army rolls to assist him (and 26 of them resigned to join the Confederacy). No provision had been made for a system of army general hospitals, and those surgeons and doctors who were on hand were liable to make matters worse instead of better. Not only were they necessarily as ignorant as everyone else of the most basic notions of bacteriology, but they relied on cures that were often worse than the disease. In addition to alcoholic stimulants, opium-based painkillers were unwisely ladled out in fantastic amounts: One estimate suggests that over 10 million opium pills, plus 2.8 million ounces of opium-related medicines, were handed out by federal medical officers during the war. The result was widespread addiction, either to opiates or to alcohol, in order to cope with pain and illness, and in some cases, with battle fatigue and anxiety. Braxton Bragg's erratic behavior as a Confederate field commander may have been related to opium addiction; John Bell Hood, an aggressive Confederate field general who lost both an arm and a leg in combat, sustained himself on alcohol and opiates, and they in turn probably helped him lose

[36]Glathaar, *The March to the Sea and Beyond*, p. 43.
[37]Billings, *Hardtack and Coffee*, p. 80.

his luckless campaign in Tennessee in 1864 by sapping his strength and deadening his judgment.[38]

What made all of this worse was the reluctance of the army medical services to issue medical discharges. Fearing abuse of the discharge system by conniving soldiers, regimental surgeons in the Civil War turned themselves into the first line of defense against military "malingering." William Fuller, second assistant surgeon of the 1st Michigan Volunteers, seems to have treated men who reported on sick call to a classic case of military Catch-22—the more serious an illness, Fuller reasoned, the more likely it was faked. "Vast strides have been made in the proficiency of malingering in this country since the first year of the war," Fuller intoned solemnly. "When a surgeon has reason to think that a man has an object or a motive for feigning, no statement of his should be accepted as true. . . ."[39] The result of Fuller's zeal, however, was that sick men were sent back into camp or onto the march, where they only managed to infect other men and further spread sickness.

Eventually, much of the neglect and malpractice in both the federal and Confederate army medical systems was ironed out. A new federal surgeon-general, Brigadier General William A. Hammond, was appointed in 1862, and soon Union army medical care drastically improved: 190 new army hospitals were established under Hammond's aegis with 120,000 beds, and 15,000 new surgeons were recruited. Even the Confederates, shorthanded and undersupplied as they were, built thirty-four military hospitals in and around Richmond, the largest of which could hold 4,300 men. Additionally, the federal War Department authorized the operation of the civilian-run United States Sanitary Commission and the Christian Commission to act as voluntary auxiliaries for providing nursing and hospital care. As a result, the actual disease mortality rates fell from 73 percent of all wartime deaths in the Revolution and 86 percent of all war-related deaths during the Mexican-American War to little more than 61 percent in the Civil War (the rates of death from disease would actually go back up in the Spanish-American War to over 84 percent of all wartime deaths among American soldiers). But the disease statistics are appalling all the same, and sickness often decimated a regiment long before it ever fired a gun in anger.

The greatest damage to the volunteer's health was usually done by the soldier's diet. Food preservation was only in its infancy in the 1860s, and as a result, the soldier on campaign was issued only the most portable—and most indigestible—of rations. The marching ration of the federal soldier in the Army of the Potomac was "one pound of hard bread; three-fourths of a pound of salt pork, or one and one-fourth pounds of fresh meat; sugar, coffee, and salt." The hard bread was, in the most literal sense of the word, *hard,* and so it went in the Army of the Potomac by

[38]David T. Courtwright, "Opiate Addiction as a Consequence of the Civil War," in *Civil War History* 24 (June 1978), pp. 101–111; James Street, "Under the Influence," in *Civil War Times Illustrated* 27 (May 1988), pp. 30–35.

[39]Albert Castel, ed., "Malingering," in *Civil War Times Illustrated* 26 (August 1977), pp. 29–31.

the name of *hardtack*. John Billings described it as "a plain flour-and-water biscuit" measuring "three and one-eighth by two and seven-eights inches, and . . . nearly half an inch thick." Hardtack resembled a large, hard cracker more than anything that could be called bread, and "they may have been so hard that they could not be bitten" and "required a very strong blow of the fist to break them." On the other hand, Billings admitted that "hardtack was not so bad an article of food . . . as may be supposed," and devising ways of eating it stretched the soldier's imagination in odd ways. "Many of them were eaten just as they were received—hardtack *plain,*" while others were "crumbed in coffee" and "furnished the soldier his breakfast and supper." Others "crumbled them in soups for want of other thickening" or "crumbed them in cold water, then fried the crumbs in juice and fat of meat," and still others simply "liked them toasted, either to crumb in coffee or . . . to butter." The invariable accompaniment to hardtack, and to any other circumstances, was the soldier's coffee.

> One of the most interesting scenes presented in army life took place at night when the army was on the point of bivouacking. As soon as this fact became known along the column, each man would seize a rail from the nearest fence, and with this additional arm on the shoulder would enter the proposed camping-ground. In no more time than it takes to tell the story, the little camp-fires, rapidly increasing to hundreds in number, would shoot up along the hills and plains, and as if by magic acres of territory would be luminous with them. Soon they would be surrounded by the soldiers, who made it an almost invariable rule to cook their coffee first, after which a large number, tired out with the toils of the day, would make their supper of hardtack and coffee, and roll up in their blankets for the night. If a march was ordered at midnight, unless a surprise was intended, it must be preceded by a pot of coffee; if a halt was ordered in mid-forenoon or afternoon, the same dish was inevitable, with hardtack accompaniment usually. It was coffee *at* meals and *between* meals; and men going on guard or coming off guard drank it at all hours of the night, and to-day the old soldiers who can stand it are the hardest coffee-drinkers in the community, through the schooling which they received in the service.

Last in the soldier's estimate was the army's standard meat ration, salt pork, which Billings found "musty and rancid . . . flabby, stringy, 'sow-belly' " that was frankly indigestible to anyone but a hungry soldier.[40] There were, at times, exceptions to this diet. In the Union army's winter camps, the soldier's ration was usually expanded to add vegetables and fresh meat. Occasionally, the armies would drive their own beef herds along with them on the march to provide more fresh beef. And there were always boxes and packages from home with varieties of good things that the government had no interest in issuing. But even with these additions, the average soldier's diet did little except further reduce his resistance to infection and exhaustion, and wreak unmeasurable havoc with his digestive system.

[40]Billings, *Hardtack and Coffee*, pp. 113–114, 116–117, 129–130.

As for the Confederate armies, the food was not only bad, but sometimes nonexistent. The impact of the blockade and the breakdown of the Confederacy's internal transportation system meant that its volunteers frequently went hungry on campaign, and it could be said without the guilt of exaggeration that through most of the Civil War, the average Confederate soldier lived on raw courage and endurance more than on food and drink. George Asbury Bruton wrote to his brother and sister in 1864 that "Our rations is small. We get ¼ pound of bacon per day and 1 pound of corn meal. Sometimes we get a little rice & sometimes we get a spoon full of soap to wash our hands." Seven months later, Bruton lectured his brother James for not appreciating "home as you ought." At home, "you have good clothes to put on and good socks to put on before you put on your clothes & best of all a good hot breakfast with plenty of ham & eggs, potatoes, & butter & milk." Unlike brother James, George Bruton and the 19th Louisiana were living on "a little piece of half-cooked beef about as big as my 3 fingers for a days ration and 4 doggers of corne bread about the size of a grand mother biscuit. . . ." In addition to poor rations, there were "thousands without a blanket & more bairfotted & all without socks." Mary Bedinger Mitchell, a Virginia woman, watched in disbelief as Lee's army passed by her house in September of 1862, on its way to Antietam:

> When I say that they were hungry, I convey no impression of the gaunt starvation that looked from their cavernous eyes. All day they crowded to the doors of our houses, with always the same drawling complaint: "I've been a-marchin' an' a-fightin' for six weeks stiddy, and I ain't had n-a-r-thin to eat 'cept green apples an' green cawn, an' I wish you'd please to gimme a bite to eat." . . . I know nothing of numbers, nor what was or was not engaged in any battle, but I saw the troops march past us every summer for four years, and I know something of the appearance of a marching army, both Union and Southern. There are always stragglers, of course, but never . . . were want and exhaustion more visibly put before my eyes, and that they could march or fight at all seemed incredible.[41]

The most fearsome thing the volunteer faced, however, was actual combat. The Civil War battlefield presented the volunteer with a frightening variety of sensations, the first of which was the sheer unfamiliarity of the ground he was fighting on. Soldiers' accounts of Civil War battle are notorious for their uncertain geographical references. Robert Lewis Dabney's memoir of his commander, "Stone-wall" Jackson, is peppered with bland descriptions of terrain—"alternate woods and fields," "abrupt little ravines," "a wide expanse of fertile meadows"—which betrayed how utterly unfamiliar Dabney was with the Shenandoah Valley territory he was fighting over. The noises of the battlefield were even more disorienting, since the concussive impact of artillery and massed rifle fire created an amphitheater of noise unlike anything within the experience of any 19th-century American. The low velocity of the minié ball gave it a peculiar and noticeable humming whir, and

---

[41]M. B. Mitchell, "A Woman's Recollections of Antietam," in *Battles and Leaders,* Buel & Johnson, eds., vol. 2, pp. 687–688.

soldiers devoted considerable time to trying to explain the sound of rifle fire in letters and diaries. "You never heard such whooping," wrote private Bruton after Shilo, "the bullets whistled worse & faster than pouring peas on a dry cow hide." Another Confederate soldier at Shiloh wrote that rifle bullets sang angrily around him "worse than ever bees was when they swarm." When a bullet struck a man, it made what Amos Currier of the 8th Iowa called "a peculiar spat." For others, the sheer volume of unlooked-for terror and confusion in the environment of 19th-century battle was so vast that the provincial and localized vocabulary of most Americans was simply beggared by it. "I have not time nor disposition to attempt a description," wrote James Madison Williams of the 21st Alabama after Shiloh, "when I go home it will take me months to describe what I saw on that terrible field."[42]

But the most frightening aspect of combat was the chance of being seriously or mortally wounded. Not only was the general inexperience of the volunteer officer more likely to expose a soldier to lethal amounts of fire for longer periods of time than in any other 19th-century war, but the soft lead minié ball (unlike the steel-jacketed bullets of later wars) spread and mushroomed upon impact, smashing up bones and cartilage, and making dreadful exit wounds. "Often did I see a simple gunshot wound," wrote one surgeon, "scarcely larger than the bullet which made it, become larger and larger until a hand would scarcely cover it, and extend from the skin downward into the tissues until one could put half his fist into the sloughing wound." Artillery rounds could deliver even more horrifying forms of death, adding to the terror of every soldier nearby. A shell plowed through Company E of the 9th Vermont during an attack on Confederate entrenchments below Richmond in 1864, and Colonel Edward H. Ripley looked over to see a favorite corporal "lying on his side and face . . . his buttocks clear to the thigh bones were both carried away, showing a raw mass of torn flesh with the crushed bones protruding. He was alive, conscious, and brave." A few moments later another shell crashed near Ripley and "I was dashed in the face with a hot streaming mass of something horrible which closed my eyes, nose and mouth. I thought my head had gone certainly this time." It hadn't; instead, it was the "brains, skull, hair and blood" of an artilleryman who had been standing nearby. Ripley had to be cleaned off by a staff officer who "just then came up and happened to have a towel in his boot leg."[43]

Nothing in Civil War field medicine was able to deal with the wounds or the trauma that the rifles and artillery of the era inflicted, and not until after the turn of the century would surgical skill develop to the point where gunshot wounds to main body parts could even become routinely operable. This meant that, for the badly

[42]Bell I. Wiley, *The Life of Johnny Reb: The Common Soldier of the Confederacy* (1943; rept. Baton Rouge, LA, 1982), p. 34; J. A. Frank and G. A. Reaves, *Seeing the Elephant: Raw Recruits at the Battle of Shiloh* (Westport, CT, 1989), p. 105; Williams, *From That Terrible Field*, p. 53.

[43]"Charging New Market Heights: Edward Ripley Recalls," Edward Longacre, ed., in *Civil War Times Illustrated* 20 (February 1982), p. 42.

wounded soldier, the common regimental surgeon was little better than death itself. Wounds to the extremities could only be treated by amputation, in order to head off the onset of gangrene and blood poisoning, and at the height of any major battle, a surgeon's field or division hospital would resemble nothing so much as a butcher's shop on market day—an unventilated tent or barn, with an old door set up on two barrels for an operating table, an unending line of wounded men in various degrees of shock, a pile of amputated limbs that reminded observers of a cord of wood, and a corner full of men with wounds to the abdomen or chest who had simply been set aside as surgically hopeless. "I am not out of [hearing] much of the groans of the wounded from morning till night," wrote Claiborne Walton, a surgeon with the 21st Kentucky, in 1864:

> My hands are constantly steaped in blood. I have had them in blood and water so much that the nails are soft and tender. I have amputated limbs until it almost makes my heart ache to see a poor fellow coming in the Ambulance to the Hospital. . . . I could tell you of many yes—of the [most] distressing cases of wounds. Such as arms shot off—legs shot off. Eyes shot out—brains shot out. Lungs shot through and in a word *everything* shot to pieces and totally maimed for all after life. The horror of this war can never be half told.[44]

Most of the soldiers who arrived on surgeon Walton's table probably knew what the result of their wounds would be long before they actually made it to a field hospital. As Frank Wilkeson, an artilleryman in the Army of the Potomac, observed in 1864, the Civil War soldier became a quick study in analyzing what wounds meant:

> Wounded soldiers almost always tore their clothing away from their wounds, so as to see them and to judge of their character. Many of them would smile and their faces would brighten as they realized that they were not hard hit, and that they could go home for a few months. Others would give a quick glance at their wounds and then shrink back as from a blow, and turn pale, as they realized the truth that they were mortally wounded. The enlisted men were exceeding accurate judges of the probable result which would ensue from any wound they saw. They had seen hundreds of soldiers wounded, and they had noticed that certain wounds always resulted fatally. They knew when they were fatally wounded, and after the shock of discovery had passed, they generally braced themselves and died in a manly manner. It was seldom that an American or Irish volunteer flunked in the presence of death.[45]

Perhaps not. But a large number of Civil War soldiers certainly quailed at the prospect of combat, and they deserted the Union and Confederate armies in droves. Over 200,000 federal soldiers deserted during the war, nearly 12 percent of the entire total of Union enlistments, while 104,000 Confederates, as much as 16

---

[44]"One Continued Scene of Carnage: A Union Surgeon's View of War," in *Civil War Times Illustrated* 15 (August 1976), pp. 34, 36.

[45]Wilkeson, *Recollections of a Private Soldier*, pp. 206–207.

percent of the Confederate armies, took French leave of their units.[46] Others who might have lacked the will to face enemy fire were set up on their legs by the free use of alcohol. Many of the Civil War's legendary charges into the face of the enemy were made by soldiers who had been drugged into near-insensibility by the liberal dispensing of hard liquor before battle. The 16th North Carolina went into action at Seven Pines after the company commissary "hobbled down with several canteens of 'fire water' and gave each of the men a dram. He knew we needed it, and the good angels only smiled." Confederate prisoners taken by Berdan's Sharpshooters at Malvern Hill had been "unduly excited by frequent rations of whiskey . . . their canteens, some half full of this stimulant." Members of Confederate General George Pickett's staff, and even one of his brigadiers, downed a bottle of whiskey over a lunch of cold mutton just before Pickett's famous charge at Gettysburg.[47] On the other hand, officers who prodded men too hard into battle were likely to become targets for disgruntled enlisted men, especially on a battlefield where it was difficult to establish whether an officer's death was a normal combat fatality or a covert assassination. It was not at all unusual, wrote New Jersey Private Alfred Bellard, for overbearing Yankee martinets to receive "a stray ball occasionally on the field of battle."[48]

The most obvious evasion of combat was simple flight. "The *sneaks* in the army are named *Legion*," remarked Edward King Wightman, "When you read of the number of men engaged on our side, strike out at least one third as never having struck a blow." Oliver Wendell Holmes reminded his fellow veterans of the 20th Massachusetts years after the war that "We have stood side by side in a line, we have charged and swept the enemy—and we have run away like rabbits—all together." Sometimes, the "sneaks" did not need to resort to the humiliation of running in order to evade battle. Any wounded comrade in a fight became an excuse for one or two others to break ranks and assist the wounded man to a field hospital; and unless a brigade or division commander was unusually diligent in posting a provost guard in the rear of his units, a wounded man's helpers would simply remain out of sight and sound of the action for the rest of the day. Only by 1864 were serious efforts to keep able-bodied men from leaking rearwards out of a fight really working, as Frank Wilkeson discovered when he strolled too far away from his artillery unit in the Wilderness, and was prodded into frontline infantry combat by a provost guard who demanded that he "show blood" before being allowed to move to the rear. And yet, however easy it may be to point out the failings of the volunteer under fire, it is also

[46]Vinovskis, "Have Social Historians Lost the Civil War?" in *Toward a Social History of the American Civil War*, Vinovskis, ed., p. 10.

[47]George Henry Mills, *History of the 16th North Carolina Regiment in the Civil War* (1903; rept. Hamilton, NY, 1992), pp. 14–15; C. A. Stevens, *Berdan's United States Sharpshooters*, p. 151; George R. Stewart, *Pickett's Charge: A Microhistory of the Final Attack at Gettysburg, July 3, 1863* (2nd ed., Dayton, OH, 1980), p. 106.

[48]Alfred Bellard, *Gone For a Soldier: The Civil Memoirs of Private Alfred Bellard*, David Donald, ed. (Boston, 1975), p. 188.

true that the volunteer in the Civil War—Union or Confederate, black or white, however untrained or uncomprehending he might be of the niceties of military life—was being asked to stand up to some of the most savage combat ever met by soldiers in the 19th century. War would be easy, Holmes wrote before Antietam, if one could "after a comfortable breakfast . . . come down the steps of one's home, putting on one's gloves and smoking a cigar, to get on a horse and charge a battery up Beacon Street." The reality, however, was that the soldier faced "a night on the ground in the rain and your bowels out of order and then after no particular breakfast to wade a stream and attack an enemy."[49] If Holmes and his companions sometimes ran "like rabbits," they had more than enough incentives.

What, then, accounts for the "will to combat" among the green volunteers at a place like Shiloh, where individual groups of raw soldiers continued to fight on and on despite the dissolution of all command control from above? There were some soldiers who found that they were enthralled by war, and the exhilaration of combat. "I love war," wrote Philip Kearney, one of the most combative of the Army of the Potomac's generals. "It brings me indescribable pleasure, like that of having a woman." For more than a few, combat was simply a risk to be exchanged for the chance to loot. One officer of the famed Louisiana Tiger battalion was shocked after First Bull Run to find "30 or 40" of his men "marching up with new uniforms on, gold rings on their fingers, and their pockets filled with watches and money that they had stolen." For others, a willing entrance into battle was due to the bravery and example of a regimental or company leader; sometimes it was the powerful incentive of following the colors forward. At other times, a strange, hysterical killer instinct took over and banished any consideration of personal safety. Colonel Rufus Dawes of the 6th Wisconsin spoke of seeing men at Antietam "loading and firing with demoniacal fury and shouting and laughing hysterically," while David Thompson wrote of the "mental strain" of combat in which "the whole landscape for an instant turned slightly red." Michael Hanifen of the 1st New Jersey Artillery, remembered that "it is a terrible sight to see a line of men, two deep, coming up within 300 or 400 yards of you, with bayonets flashing and waving their colors, and you know that every shot you fire into them sends some one to eternity, but still you are prompted by a devilish desire to kill all you can."[50]

For Amos Judson, a captain in the 83rd Pennsylvania, the ultimate answer to the murderous question of courage in battle lay hidden within each soldier. "In my opinion, what is called courage is very much a matter of pride or principle with others, and a compound of both with all men." Sometimes it was a result of fear, sometimes a result of being fed sufficiently, and sometimes it was really no more

[49]Wightman, *From Antietam to Fort Fisher*, p. 91; Liva Baker, *The Justice from Beacon Hill: The Life and Times of Oliver Wendell Holmes* (New York, 1991), pp. 131–132.

[50]Linderman, *Embattled Courage*, p. 74; "The Diary of Corporal Westwood James," Michael Musick, ed., in *Civil War Times Illustrated* 17 (October 1978), p. 35; Thompson, "With Burnside at Antietam," in *Battles and Leaders*, Buel and Johnson, eds., vol. 2, pp. 661–662; Hanifen, *History of Battery B, First New Jersey Artillery* (1905; rept. Highstown, NJ, 1991), p. 53.

than "a proper sense of duty on the field of battle, and you will consequently find men of the most quiet and apparently timid dispositions at home, to be the most resolute and reliable men in action."[51] The only thing, said Judson, that he had never seen in the war was "any manifestations of absolute fear of trepidation or trembling during a fight, or during even the anticipation of one." Judson was, of course, telling less then he knew. It might have been more accurate to say that the only shame that the American volunteer of 1861 to 1865 had to endure was that his enemy was another American.

Further Reading

In 1886, former federal artilleryman Frank Wilkeson was growing disgusted with the flood of Civil War memoirs flowing from the pens of former generals who sought chiefly "to belittle the work of others, or to falsify or obscure it. . . ." He sat down to write his own recollections of service in the Army of the Potomac in 1864 and 1865 to give a voice to "the private soldiers who won the battles, when they were given a fair chance to win them" and who "have scarcely begun to write the history from their point of view." The result of Wilkeson's recollections was one of the early classics of Civil War memoir literature, the gritty and realistic *Recollections of a Private Soldier in the Army of the Potomac* (New York, 1887), and it has been followed since Wilkeson's time by a seemingly unending flood of regimental histories, published diaries, and collections of private letters edited by descendants and scholars of the Civil War soldier.

The most obvious primary source for the ordinary life of the Civil War soldier is the regimental history, which developed between 1885 and 1910 into what amounts to a major genre of American literature. The earliest, and arguably the liveliest, of these "regimentals" is Amos Judson's *History of the Eighty-Third Regiment, Pennsylvania Volunteers* (1865; rept. Dayton, OH, 1986), which was published shortly after the end of the war. Free from many of the conventions that later shackled and then strangled the regimental history, Judson's volume bristles with cracker-barrel wit and a keen reporter's eye for the foibles of the American character. After Judson have come a string of regimental histories, running out to nearly 800 volumes. Until 1910, when the soldiers of the Civil War generation began passing swiftly from the scene, most regimental histories were written by survivors of the regiments themselves. But since the Civil War Centennial in the 1960s, the regimental history has been generously reborn as a vehicle of Civil War history. A forerunner of this rebirth was John J. Pullen's *The Twentieth Maine: A Volunteer Regiment in the Civil War* (Philadelphia, 1957). This regeneration blossomed into several great unit histories, such as James I. Robertson's *The Stonewall Brigade* (Baton Rouge, 1963), Alan Nolan's *The Iron Brigade: A Military History* (New York, 1961), William C. Davis's *The Orphan Brigade: The Kentucky Confederates Who Couldn't Go Home* (New York, 1980), Warren Wilkenson, *Mother, May You Never See the Sights I Have Seen: The Fifty-seventh Massachusetts Veteran Volunteers in the Last Year of the Civil War* (New York, 1990), and more recently, Richard

---

[51]Judson, *History of the Eighty-Third Regiment, Pennsylvania Volunteers* (1865; rept. Dayton, OH, 1986), pp. 186–187.

Moe's *The Last Full Measure: The Life and Death of the First Minnesota Volunteers* (New York, 1993).

Another genre closely related to the regimental history is the volume of collected war letters. Oliver W. Norton's *Army Letters, 1861–1865* (Chicago, 1903) is one of the best examples of such collections, coming directly from the editorial hand of the soldier who wrote them. Most often, however, these collections have been discovered in archives or among family heirlooms, and have been reconstructed and edited by modern scholars or archivists. A model for such a modern collection is the assemblage of letters of Edward King Wightman in *From Antietam to Fort Fisher: The Civil War Letters of Edward King Wightman*, edited by E. G. Longacre (Madison, NJ, 1985). Sometimes, soldiers kept their opinions to themselves, or at least to their diaries, and several memorable soldiers diaries have survived to be republished in scholarly editions. The most outstanding examples of this sort are Allan Nevins's edition of the diary of the upper-class New York artillery chief, Charles S. Wainwright, in *A Diary of Battle: The Personal Journals of Col. Charles S. Wainwright, 1861–1865* (New York, 1962) and K. Jack Bauer's edition of *The Civil War Diary of Rice C. Bull, 123rd New York Volunteer Infantry* (San Rafael, CA, 1977).

Some veterans of the war chose to pour their experiences into a third genre, the personal memoir. The outstanding example of the Civil War memoir is Ulysses S. Grant's *Personal Memoir*, but the common soldiers also produced memoirs of their service that match Grant's for interest if not eloquence. Foremost among these soldier memoirs must be Wilkeson's *Recollections of a Private Soldier* and the far sunnier *Hard Tack and Coffee: The Unwritten Story of Army Life* (1887; rept. Williamstown, MA, 1973) by John D. Billings. From the Confederate side, Henry Kyd Douglas's *I Rode with Stonewall* (Chapel Hill, NC, 1940) is the most famous, but it should not eclipse the new edition of the full text of E. P. Alexander's memoirs, *Fighting for the Confederacy: The Personal Recollections of General Edward Porter Alexander*, Gary W. Gallagher, ed. (Chapel Hill, NC, 1989).

Not every memoir or regimental history necessarily took the form of a book. Civil War veterans organizations, such as the Military Order of the Loyal Legion of the United States, regularly met to hear members read papers related to their wartime experiences, and an almost-bottomless well of material on the common soldier can be found in the seventy-two volumes of MOLLUS Papers, the fifty-five volumes of the Southern Historical Society Papers, the forty-three volumes of the *Confederate Veteran* magazine, and the nineteen volumes of the *Confederate Military History*. In another postwar contribution to the history of the common soldier, the adjutants general of many of the northern states issued comprehensive volumes of rosters and unit histories of their state volunteer regiments, the most striking of which are the five volumes of Samuel P. Bates's *History of Pennsylvania Volunteers, 1861–65* (Harrisburg, PA, 1869). Additionally, current popular Civil War periodicals, such as the standard-bearer *Civil War Times Illustrated*, feature previously unpublished military and civilian accounts of the war.

A number of important studies of the Civil War soldier have attempted to synthesize the vast array of materials available in the regimental histories, letters, diaries, and memoirs into a comprehensive portrait of Wilkeson's "private soldier." The most famous of these synthetic studies are Bell I. Wiley's *The Life of Johnny Reb: The Common Soldier of the Confederacy* (1943; rept. Baton Rouge, LA, 1978) and *The Life of Billy Yank: The Common Soldier of the Union* (1952; rept. Baton Rouge, LA, 1991). These two works have been supplemented by James I. Robertson's *Soldiers Blue and Gray* (Columbia, SC, 1988). Specific aspects of the soldier's experience in combat have been skillfully analyzed in Gerald Linderman's *Embattled Courage: The Experience of Combat in the Civil War* (New York, 1987), which traces the predominance and the ebbing of the idea of "courage" as an animating principle in the Civil War soldier's "will to combat." On a par with Linderman, Wiley, and Roberton are Joseph T. Glathaar's *The March to the Sea and Beyond: Sherman's Troops in the Savannah and Carolinas Campaigns* (New York, 1985), and Reid Mitchell's *Civil War Soldiers: Their Expectations and Their Experiences* (New York, 1988), while Randall Jimerson's *The Private Civil War: Popular Thought during the Sectional Conflict* (New York, 1988) offers a mix of soldier and civilian responses to the war. The essays in Maris Vinovskis's *Toward a Social History of the American Civil War: Exploratory Essays* turn the attention of the "new social history" onto the lives of northern Civil War soldiers, especially concerning their recruitment and postwar experiences. A shorter example of social-history analysis, based on regimental order and letter books, is Stephen Z. Starr's "Hawkeyes on Horseback: The Second Iowa Volunteer Cavalry," in *Civil War History* 23 (September 1977), but Starr's exhortation to use the treasure trove of material contained in these sources has gone, for the most part, unheeded.

The Civil War field officer has attracted comparatively less notice in the current literature than Wilkeson's "private soldier," although T. Harry Williams's *Hayes of the Twenty-Third: The Civil War Volunteer Officer* (New York, 1965) is a wonderful reminder that even the officer was a common soldier in the Civil War. James A. Garfield, an Ohio officer who later rose to become president of the United States (along with two other Ohio veterans of the Civil War, Hayes and McKinley) left intriguing examples of both diaries and letters, which have been edited and published as *The Wild Life of the Army: Civil War Letters of James A. Garfield*, edited by F. D. Williams (East Lansing, MI, 1964) and *The Diary of James A. Garfield*, edited by H. J. Brown and F. D. Williams (East Lansing, MI, 1967). A particularly useful officer memoir is Jacob Dolson Cox's *Military Reminiscences of the Civil War* (two volumes, New York, 1900). One grade of officer that has attracted an exceptional amount of notice has been the Civil War surgeon. George Worthington Adams's *Doctors in Blue: The Medical History of the Union Army in the Civil War* (New York, 1952) and H. H. Cunningham's *Doctors in Gray: The Confederate Medical Service* (Baton Rouge, LA, 1958) make the very best of what could hardly help being an appalling story. Likewise, Civil War diseases have had their biographers: Paul E. Steiner's *Disease in the Civil War: Natural Biological Warfare in 1861–1865* (Springfield, IL, 1968) and David T. Courtwright's *Dark Paradise: Opiate Addiction in America before 1940* (Cambridge, MA, 1982) illustrate the terrible toil that both camp diseases and their cures took on the Civil War soldier.

And even the regimental colors have biographies. Richard Sauers's two-volume illustrated history of the flags carried by Pennsylvania's volunteer regiments, *Advance the Colors* (Harrisburg, 1987, 1992) photographs and documents every Pennsylvania regimental color, along with a brief history and bibliography for the units that carried them. Those who fled from the colors also have a remembrancer in Ella Lonn's *Desertion During the Civil War* (New York, 1928).

Abraham Lincoln (1809–1865), sixteenth president of the United States. His ambition was a "little engine" that drove him to success as an Illinois lawyer and finally to the presidency in 1860. Lincoln's antislavery beliefs convinced Southerners that the time had come for their states to secede from the Union. *Portrait, Edward Marchant; the Union League of Philadelphia.*

Jefferson Davis (1808–1889), president of the Confederate States of America. A Democrat and southern sectionalist, he struggled to create a genuine Confederate nationalism from the conflicting political passions of states' rights and the defense of slavery. *Library Company of Philadelphia.*

A "contraband." As early as the summer of 1861 thousands of slaves fled to Union forts and encampments, where sympathetic northern officers declared them "contraband of war" and refused to return them to their owners. *Henry Deeks.*

Frederick Douglass (1817–1895), African-American abolitionist, orator, and newspaper publisher. Born in Maryland of a slave mother and white father, he fled slavery in 1838 and settled in the North. In 1847 he founded an antislavery newspaper, *North Star*. During the Civil War, Douglass called for making abolition a war aim and for enlisting black soldiers in the Union armies. *Massachusetts Historical Society.*

A *Harper's Weekly* cover in 1861 depicting the bombardment of Fort Sumter as seen from the housetops of Charleston, South Carolina. The decision of the Confederates to force federal troops to surrender Sumter triggered the outbreak of the war.

Confederate faces: Major W. P. Parks (*left*) and Lieutenant E. R. Ward (*right*). The ordinary soldiers of the Civil War were usually untrained civilians who volunteered for war service confident that the war would last only a short time. Army life weighed heavy on Southerners, who found that the constraints of army discipline often reminded them of the discipline imposed on black slaves. Desertion rates were high, but southern soldiers fought to the end with courage and determination despite crippling shortages of clothing, food, and supplies. *Henry Deeks.*

Union faces: 1st Lieutenant Emory Upton, a West Point graduate of 1861, in the formal full-dress uniform of the U.S. Artillery (*left*) and an unidentified infantryman of the 72nd Pennsylvania Volunteers uniformed in the "Zouave" style, in imitation of an elite French Algerian colonial troop (*right*). The federal army numbered little more than 16,000 men at the beginning of the war, and so the government turned to civilian volunteers to fill most of its wartime personnel needs. Although the Union soldier was better equipped and supplied than his Confederate counterpart, he was often poorly led and showed the same streak of independence and resistance to army discipline. Not even federal uniforms were completely standardized. In the first two years of the war, the restoration of the Union was a larger issue to many of these volunteers than slavery, but their exposure to the slave system as they invaded the South convinced many of them that the elimination of slavery had to be the principal aim of the war. *Henry Deeks (Upton); Herbert Peck (unidentified Zouave).*

Robert E. Lee (1807–1870), Confederate general and commander of the Army of Northern Virginia. He took command of Confederate forces in Virginia in 1862 and scored a series of brilliant victories until meeting defeat at Gettysburg in 1863. An aggressive and combative battlefield commander, Lee was courtly and gentlemanly in person and was generally beloved by his soldiers. *Civil War Library and Museum.*

George B. McClellan (1826–1885), Union major general and commander of the Army of the Potomac. A gifted organizer, he was unable to turn the Union's advantages in numbers into victories. He fought the Confederate army to a draw at Antietam in 1862, but his political opposition to Lincoln's decision to emancipate southern slaves forced the president to dismiss him from command. He unsuccessfully ran against Lincoln as the Democratic candidate for president in 1864. *Civil War Library and Museum.*

The Trossell farm on the Gettysburg battlefield, July, 1863. Civil War combat was often managed by inexperienced officers who had been trained to give preeminence to defensive rather than offensive warfare. Battlefields frequently became theaters of stalemate, where indecisive short-range confrontations littered the field with corpses and wreckage. *Civil War Library and Museum.*

Ulysses S. Grant (1822–1885), Union lieutenant general. At the outbreak of the Civil War he was commissioned a colonel in the Volunteers and immediately ascended to the command of federal forces in the West. His spectacular victories at Forts Henry and Donelson and at Vicksburg and Chattanooga paved the way for Grant's transfer to the east, where he spearheaded the year-long campaign that finally forced the surrender of the Army of Northern Virginia in 1865. *David Charles.*

The Confederate blockade runner *Teaser*. The federal navy's blockade of the southern coastline forced the Confederates to develop special blockade runners that could slip through and bring supplies into the beleaguered Confederacy. Early blockade runners easily escaped the federal navy's clutches, but the risks became much higher as federal ships became more skilled and as more Confederate ports fell to Union forces. *Civil War Library and Museum.*

A *Harper's Weekly* cover of 1863 showing the training of black recruits. The use of African Americans in the Union army was a hotly debated issue. The willingness of African Americans to enlist and fight for the Union paved the way for free blacks and former slaves to claim great civil rights in American society.

THE LADIES OF NEW ORLEANS before GENERAL BUTLER'S Proclamation.   After GENERAL BUTLER'S Proclamation.

Southern women initially supported the Confederacy, but as federal armies and navies occupied southern territory, they arranged their own private defiance of the "Yankees" or turned their frustration on Confederate men who had failed in their roles as "protectors." In this cartoon, New Orleans women step outside conventional women's roles to spit on federal officers occupying their city; in the matching panel, federal General Benjamin Butler's notorious "Woman Order" forces them to adopt more "ladylike" behavior. *Harper's Weekly*, 1862.

David G. Farragut (1801–1870), Union naval commander. Farragut commanded the federal naval flotilla that captured New Orleans in April, 1862. The fall of New Orleans cost the Confederacy its major cotton-exporting center and may have been the single greatest economic and military catastrophe the South suffered. *David Charles.*

Sara Emma Edmonds (1842–1898), Union nurse, soldier, and spy. Defiant, independent, and unwilling to concede soldiering as an exclusively male preserve, Edmonds enlisted in disguise as a male nurse in 1861, served in combat with the 2nd Michigan Volunteers, and disguised herself as an African-American washer woman to spy on rebel fortifications.

"Colored Troops Liberating Slaves in North Carolina " (*Harper's Weekly*, 1864). Nearly 200,000 African Americans served in Union land and sea forces during the war and played an active role in putting an end to slavery.

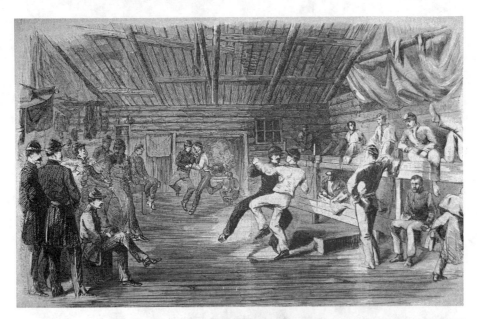

"The Stag Dance" (*Harper's Weekly*, 1864). Male soldiers found that army life forced them to redefine the traditional sexual division of labor as well as to improvise male relationships to preserve a sense of connection to civilian life.

Dr. Mary Walker (1832–1919), Union contract surgeon. One of the first American women to enter the medical profession, she eventually served with the federal Army of the Cumberland in 1864 and directed the infirmary of a military prison for women in Cincinnati. Although never actually commissioned by the federal government, she claimed the rank of major and was awarded the Congressional Medal of Honor for her service. *Amy Carroll Deeks.*

The 63rd New York Volunteers, with regimental band. The ordinary soldier was offered only meager combat training. With most training focusing on formal drill, battles often resembled slow-moving ballets performed by large groups of static men blazing away at close range with rifle fire. *Civil War Library and Museum.*

George G. Meade (1815–1872), Union major general. He inherited command of the Army of the Potomac from Joseph Hooker and successfully defended Gettysburg in the war's most famous battle, forcing Robert E. Lee and the Army of Northern Virginia to abandon its invasion of the North in 1863. *Portrait, Daniel R. Knight; Civil War Library and Museum.*

William Tecumseh Sherman (1820–1891), Union major general. He successfully captured Atlanta and launched a "March to the Sea" that disrupted Confederate supplies and rail lines and led to the capture of Savannah. Sherman gained renown as a fierce commander, although the actual destruction he brought to Georgia and the Carolinas was considerably less severe and systematic than that of modern warfare. *Portrait, James R. Lambdin; Union League of Philadelphia.*

Philip H. Sheridan (1831–1888), Union major general. An aggressive and successful infantry commander in the West, Sheridan was put in charge of federal forces in the Shenandoah Valley in 1864 and cleared it of Confederate troops under General Jubal Early. *Portrait, James R. Lambdin; Union League of Philadelphia.*

The Wilmer McLean house, Appomattox Court House, Virginia. McLean, who owned a farm on the site of the first Bull Run battlefield, moved his family to Appomattox Court House to avoid further involvement in the war. However, after Lee's retreating army was cornered nearby in 1865, Lee and Grant met in the McLean home to formalize the Confederate surrender. *Civil War Library and Museum.*

Confederate barracks. The onset
of winter generally forced an end
to open-air campaigning, as soldiers constructed crude winter
quarters that soon resembled
large shacks or hut cities. In the
absence of effective medical
knowledge of communicable diseases, Civil War soldiers easily
contracted numerous lethal ail-
ments at these encampments.
Civil War Library and Museum.

Edwin M. Stanton (1814–1869),
Lincoln's secretary of war. Although aligned with the Democratic party, Stanton joined Lincoln's cabinet in 1862 and
promptly became indispensable.
After Lincoln's death, Stanton
became a rallying point for resistance to President Andrew Johnson's attempts to create a more
lenient peace for the South. *David Charles.*

THE REISSUE OF

HARPER'S WEEKLY.
A
JOURNAL OF CIVILIZATION

VOL. IX.—No. 425.]   NEW YORK, SATURDAY, FEBRUARY 18, 1865.   [SINGLE COPIES TEN CENTS. $4.00 PER YEAR IN ADVANCE.

SCENE IN THE HOUSE ON THE PASSAGE OF THE PROPOSITION TO AMEND THE CONSTITUTION, January 31, 1865.

"Passage of the Thirteenth Amendment in the House of Representatives" (*Harper's Weekly,* 1865). Lincoln's determination to use the war to end slavery was qualified by the realization that he had no constitutional authority to abolish it. Knowing that postwar legal challenges to abolition could easily arise, Lincoln sought a permanent end to slavery by amending the Constitution. The Thirteenth Amendment, banning slavery, passed the House of Representatives on January 31, 1865, and was ratified by the states the following December.

CHAPTER 7

The Manufacture of War

The thin winter sunlight was fading rapidly over the outer sand islands of the Cape Fear River when an iron-hulled side-wheel steamer slipped slowly away from the dark protection of the river inlet. As the moon rose, the steamer nudged cautiously down into the ship channel that broadened toward the Atlantic Ocean, and her master anxiously scanned the dark horizon of the moonlit waters.

Beyond the bar, the masts of ships poked up in the silvery light, ships that wanted nothing so much as to run down the slender steamer, her master and her crew, and put them as long under lock and key as the law of the sea would allow. For the steamer's name was *Cecile*, and she was the property of John Fraser & Company, who had fitted her out on behalf of the Confederate States of America to run war supplies through the U.S. Navy's blockade of southern ports and rivers. And her master was Lieutenant John Newland Maffitt, a 42-year-old North Carolinian and former U.S. Navy officer whose 15 years of duty with the United States Coastal Survey had made him the master of virtually every shoal, sandbar, and inlet on the Gulf and Atlantic coastlines of North America. On board the *Cecile* were 700 fat bales of southern cotton that would buy the Confederacy rifles, shoes, clothing, and food for its armies. Maffitt and the *Cecile* were vital strands in the Confederacy lifeline to the outside world, and the federal navy hung close to the mouth of the Cape Fear River, hoping to choke Maffitt and his ship and the future of the Confederacy all at once.

The moon sank, and Maffitt urged the *Cecile* over the bar and out to sea, counting on the now-inky darkness to cloak her stealthy passage through the net of the federal blockade. Every light had been extinguished, every command was whispered, even the white paint on the steamer's upper works had been repainted in drab or dark colors. But Maffitt could not disguise the splashing of the steamer's side-wheel paddles, and as he crept past the federal ships, a large gas-fired spotlight shot a beam of light across the *Cecile*. There was no need for stealth now. Maffitt roared for full speed as the guns of the blockade ships leapt to life, throwing shells over the *Cecile* and striking her a glancing blow that knocked several bales of cotton into the sea.

The federal ships had the guns and the spotlights, but Maffitt had the advantage of speed and surprise, and together Maffitt and the *Cecile* slithered away into the night. The next afternoon, another U.S. Navy warship appeared over the horizon and set off after the *Cecile*. This one gained on the *Cecile*, and while he prayed for the coming of darkness, Maffitt had his chief engineer feed coal dust into the engines. The coal dust sent up a thick sooty cloud of smoke from the *Cecile*'s funnel, trailing behind the steamer in a fat black plume. Once the smoke screen was thick enough to conceal him, Maffitt switched back to clean-burning anthracite coal and changed course, leaving his befuddled federal pursuer chasing the smoke. The next day, Maffitt and the *Cecile* were in Nassau.

Lying only 570 miles from Wilmington, North Carolina, Nassau was the chief port-of-call on the British-held Bahama islands. There, agents, brokers, importers, and exporters flocked from England and the Confederacy to set up offices and warehouse stocks of weapons and supplies to be run through the blockade. There, too, southern cotton could be transshipped to British steamers to be ferried to England or France to pay for the Confederacy's purchases and feed Europe's cotton-hungry textile mills. In the heydey of blockade-running in 1863, a blockade-runner would clear Nassau on an average of every other day, while St. George in Bermuda, the Spanish-held port of Havana, and the Danish island of St. Thomas would all contribute their share of low-slung, quick-driving steamers to pierce the federal blockade. Meanwhile, federal navy vessels could only hover impotently off the limits of British territorial waters in the Bahamas or Bermuda, or off the Spanish or Danish Caribbean islands, while the Confederate agents wheeled and dealed for the weapons that would be used against the federal armies.

Once emptied of his cotton cargo, Maffitt was ready to take on military freight from John Fraser & Company's agents for the return run to Wilmington. In this case, he would carry 900 pounds of gunpowder, purchased in England through John Fraser & Company's partner firm, Fraser, Trenholm & Company. As Maffitt realized, it was a cargo that required only one well-placed shell from a federal blockader "to blow our vessel and all hands to Tophet." Maffitt, however, was unworried. Under cover of night, the *Cecile* glided out of Nassau. At daybreak, three federal ships were waiting for her, and sent several shells screaming through her rigging. But the *Cecile*'s superior speed soon left them far behind. Sixty miles from Wilmington, Maffitt slackened speed to take his bearings on the coastline he knew so well, and in a final burst of the *Cecile*'s engine power, he boldly stormed through the blockade line outside Wilmington at 16 knots, with federal shells dropping around him. Nothing touched the *Cecile* and the ship crossed the bar at Wilmington with her precious cargo, which would soon be headed for Albert Sidney Johnston's waiting soldiers in the west.[1]

The *Cecile* was only one of 286 blockade-runners that cleared the port of

---

[1] E. C. Boykin, *Sea Devil of the Confederacy: The Story of the Florida and her Captain, John Newland Maffitt* (New York, 1959), pp. 3–9.

Wilmington during the Civil War. Taken together, blockade-runners like the *Cecile* brought out 400,000 bales of cotton, which the Confederate government and private southern entrepreneurs parlayed into loans, purchases, and acquisitions that helped keep the southern war effort running long after southern sources of supply had been depleted or out-run. These same blockade-runners brought 400,000 rifles into the Confederacy, along with 2.25 million pounds in ingredients for gunpowder and 3 million pounds of lead for bullets, in addition to clothing, blankets, shoes, and medicines. The blockade runners also kept Great Britain and the markets of Europe bound into a tight web of finance and diplomatic intrigue with the Confederacy, and kept the threat of European intervention in the war hanging like a sword over the head of the Union.[2]

Lieutenant Maffitt continued to run the *Cecile* into Nassau and Wilmington for the next three months. In May, Maffitt was posted to a twin-screw steamer that he would use to raid and burn Yankee commercial shipping. He would never be caught by the U.S. Navy.

The *Cecile* ran aground on the Abaco reef in the Bahamas on June 17, 1862, and was abandoned.

1. The Watchers Overseas

Five days after the surrender of Fort Sumter, President Lincoln tried to nudge southern secessionists a little harder into second thoughts by proclaiming a blockade of all Confederate ports. "Whereas an insurrection against the Government of the United States has broken out in the States of South Carolina, Georgia, Alabama, Florida, Mississippi, Louisiana, and Texas," Lincoln declared, it was now "advisable to set on foot a blockade." Any ships—and this included ships flying a foreign flag, and not just ships registered as Confederate vessels—attempting to penetrate the blockade "will be captured and sent to the nearest convenient port, for such proceedings against her and her cargo as prize, as may be deemed advisable."[3] Still convinced at that early stage in the war that a firm hand and firm gestures by the federal government would be all the situation would require to deflate the upstart Confederate regime, Lincoln announced the measure only as a military necessity. Nevertheless, the blockade immediately embroiled both the Union and the Confederacy in an ongoing battle of international diplomacy that lasted for the length of the war and for years beyond.

This diplomatic tangle persisted for the Union because, whether Lincoln had clearly recognized it or not in 1861, imposing a blockade created three thorny and potentially disastrous foreign policy problems for the blockaders. In the first case, a naval blockade of the South might anger the South's major trading partners, who in

[2]Stephen R. Wise, *Lifeline of the Confederacy* (Columbia, SC, 1988), pp. 59–60, 166, 180, 221, 226.
[3]"Proclamation of a Blockade," April 19, 1861, in *Collected Works*, vol. 4, pp. 338–339.

turn might decide to break the blockade by force. Any attempt to disrupt the transatlantic flow of cotton might, for instance, easily invite Britain to conclude that its national interests were at stake, and that might provoke the British into either breaking the blockade by force (at the least), or (at worst) actively intervening in the course of the war to secure southern independence and bring the war and the blockade to an end. For their part, the Confederates were fully aware of the value of the cotton export trade, and they expected that the loss of cotton would compel Britain, and perhaps France, to intervene before a few months had passed. A week-and-a-half after Lincoln's blockade proclamation, the English newspaper correspondent William Howard Russell noticed an advertisement in a Charleston merchant's office for direct sailings between Charleston and Europe, and when Russell wondered whether that might be a little premature due to the blockade, he was quickly told that cotton would solve that problem in a short while.

> "Why, I expect, sir," replied the merchant, "that if those miserable Yankees try to blockade us, and keep you from our cotton, you'll just send their ships to the bottom and acknowledge us. That will be before autumn, I think." It was in vain I assured him he would be disappointed. "Look out there," he said, pointing to the wharf, on which were piled some cotton bales; "there's the key that will open all our ports, and put us into John Bull's strong box as well."[4]

Southerners were also convinced that it was worth Britain's while to remember that the South, which had always needed to import British manufactured goods as badly as Britain had needed to import southern cotton, would continue to be an important market for the sale of British exports. The Confederate states, freed from the high import tariffs of the federal Union, would be in an even better position to buy British goods than they had been in the Union.

Entirely apart from the realpolitik of cotton, the status of blockades in international law was a highly technical and tricky affair that posed problems of its own. Lincoln insisted from the beginning of the war that the southern states had no constitutional right to secede from the Union, and when the Confederates insisted that their republic was a legitimate and independent nation, and the Civil War a conflict of two belligerent nations, Lincoln would declare that it was really only an insurrection against federal authority. By the terms of the 1856 Declaration of Paris, which defined the conditions of blockade in times of war, a blockade made any ships and cargoes attempting to run through it liable to immediate seizure and sale in a prize court; but such a blockade could only legally exist between two belligerent powers, which was precisely the legal condition Lincoln wanted most to avoid. If Lincoln had wished to take the example of other civil wars as his guide, then the granting of belligerent rights to the Confederacy might not have seemed as awful as it appeared in the spring of 1861, since in other cases of civil war, the warring interests had generally conceded de facto belligerent status to each other without

[4]Russell, *My Diary North and South*, Fletcher Pratt, ed. (New York, 1954), p. 69.

that impinging on the ultimate political settlement of the war. But even de facto recognition of belligerency still would have accorded the Confederacy rights on the international stage that Lincoln would have preferred they do without—the right to raise money on foreign exchanges, to capture United States ships and raid United States commerce without either being classified as piracy, and to enlist or hire foreign troops and shipping for the Confederate cause in other countries (so far as the domestic laws of those countries permitted). Even worse, Lincoln was fearful that de facto recognition of the Confederacy as a legitimate belligerent would open the door for foreign powers to recognize the Confederacy as a de jure belligerent and an independent nation, and open yet another door toward international intervention and mediation.

In the end, Lincoln attempted to have matters both ways. His blockade declaration carefully avoided any use of the terms "civil war" and described the Confederacy only as a "combination" that federal authority found "too powerful to suppress" by normal police action, all of which was designed to authorize an international blockade but to do so without relying on the customary procedures (or the customary consequences) of international law. But in the eyes of the European powers, a blockade was a blockade, and a blockade meant the concession of belligerent rights. After all, in the 1820s, the United States itself had practiced what Lincoln was trying not to preach by conceding belligerent rights to Spain's rebellious colonies in South America. The British government took swift advantage of this on May 13, 1861, when in the course of proclaiming its neutrality in the American conflict, Great Britain also extended de facto recognition to the Confederacy as a belligerent nation. When the American minister in London, Charles Francis Adams, protested to the British foreign minister, Lord John Russell, the British minister had only to point out that "It was . . . your own government which, in assuming the belligerent right of blockade, recognized the Southern states as belligerents. Had they not been belligerents, the armed ships of the United States would have had no right to stop a single British ship upon the high seas."[5]

Lincoln was not happy with the British decision, but he was unhappier still with the unsolicited attempts of his secretary of state, William Henry Seward, to respond to that decision on his own. Before his inauguration, Lincoln had been confronted with the need to placate the major Republican front-runners who had been passed over by his nomination, which was why he handed the Department of the Treasury to Salmon P. Chase, and why he gave the Department of State to William H. Seward, the most famous political name in the Republican party. Seward had been the most prominent voice among the antislavery Whigs long before Lincoln was heard of outside Illinois, and in 1860 he had confidently expected to win the Republican party's nomination without much contest. Of course he hadn't, but when Lincoln offered the State Department to Seward as a sop to

[5]Ludwell H. Johnson, "The Confederacy: What Was It? The View from the Federal Courts," in *Civil War History* 32 (March 1986), p. 6.

Seward's political vanity the New Yorker interpreted the proposal as a concession of weakness on Lincoln's part. Seward promptly cast himself in the role of a grand secretary, on the model of John Quincy Adams, James Monroe, and Henry Clay. That led him to make on-the-spot decisions and bottomless promises that he had no real authority to make: On April 1, 1861, Seward actually presented a memorandum to Lincoln, seriously urging the president to provoke a war with France and Spain in the Caribbean as a way of reunifying the states in the face of a foreign threat. Lincoln ignored Seward's proposal, and made it clear that, so far as the war was concerned, the president would be responsible for foreign policy, not Seward.[6] But Lincoln did not anticipate Seward's penchant for composing incontinent dispatches and firing them off to American diplomats to present to other governments, and the worst of them went out to Charles Francis Adams a week after the British neutrality proclamation.

Seward entertained little affection for Great Britain, and British recognition of Confederate belligerancy brought out the worst in him. On May 21st, Seward drafted a violent protest against the British action that actually threatened the British with war if they made any attempt to intervene in the blockade or the American conflict. The Confederacy was "a Power existing in pronunciamento only," Seward announced, and British recognition of belligerent rights would have no effect unless the British also meant to intervene to "give it body and independence by resisting our measures of suppression." In that case, Seward trumpeted, "we, from that hour, shall cease to be friends and become once more, as we have twice before been . . . forced to become, enemies of Great Britain." Seward's little manifesto might have been enough, all by itself, to bring on a war, had not Charles Francis Adams took it upon himself to delete the most provocative passages in the document before reading it to Lord Russell. Russell merely pointed to what Adams already knew, that the United States itself had granted belligerent status to the Latin American republics when they rose in rebellion against their Spanish colonial masters, and added the reminder that the United States had tried to extend similar status to French Canadian rebels in a revolt against British authority in Canada in 1837. As for the belligerent status of the Confederacy, the Lincoln government might claim as it liked that the Confederacy was merely an insurrection; to British eyes, the Confederacy was an organized government with its own constitution, congress, and president, with an army and nine million people behind it. In the end, all that Seward's note served to create was a dangerous and highly charged diplomatic atmosphere requiring only a small spark to explode it.[7]

In the end, the greatest difficulty that the imposition of a blockade posed for Lincoln was a practical one: How was the United States Navy to enforce it? On the

---

[6]Seward, "Some Thoughts for the President's Consideration," in *Dear Mr. Lincoln: Letters to the President,* ed. Harold Holzer (New York, 1993), p. 239; Lincoln, "To William H. Seward," in *Collected Works,* volume four, pp. 316–318.

[7]Brian Jenkins, *Britain and the War for the Union,* (Montreal, 1974, 1980), vol. 1, pp. 104–109.

day Lincoln proclaimed the blockade to be in effect, the United States Navy listed only forty-two ships in commission, and of them only twenty-four were modern steam-powered vessels (and only three of those were in northern ports at the outbreak of the war and thus available immediately for blockade duty). Before them stretched 3500 miles of southern coastline, with more than 180 openings for commerce and 9 fairly sizable ports—Charleston, Wilmington, Mobile, Galveston, New Orleans, Savannah, Pensacola, Norfolk, and Jacksonville. On the surface, the suggestion that a blockade of the Confederacy now existed with these ships seemed preposterous. But in short order, the aggressive secretary of the navy, Gideon Welles, chartered or commissioned 200 vessels of various sizes and descriptions, while 23 specially de-signed steam-powered blockade gunboats (which became known as the ingenious "ninety-day gunboats") were laid down and completed by March, 1862. On April 30, Norfolk was officially blockaded, followed by Charleston on May 28th, New Orleans on May 31st, and Wilmington on July 21st.[8]

The speed of the navy's mobilization was a major accomplishment, but it also presented a major problem for the federal navy, too, for in addition to the logistical problems of supplying and organizing these vessels, few federal navy officers were prepared to deal with the difficulties in international diplomacy that blockade duty might present. And in November, 1861, one of those officers struck off the spark that almost created war between the United States and Great Britain.

On November 8, 1861, the federal steam sloop, San Jacinto, stopped a British mail steamer, the Trent, en route from Havana, Cuba, to St. Thomas in the West Indies. The San Jacinto's master, Captain Charles Wilkes, had learned in Havana that two Confederate commissioners, James Mason and John Slidell, had slipped through the blockade to Nassau and from there to Cuba. They had then purchased passage on board the British mail packet Trent for St. Thomas, where they planned to board yet another steamer for England, where they would set up shop to appeal for British diplomatic recognition and military aid. The vision of the Confederate diplomats sailing serenely to England to plot the destruction of the Union alter-nately maddened and excited Wilkes, who pulled down every book on the law of the sea in his possession, pored over them in his cabin, and decided that the presence of the Confederates on the Trent provided sufficient reason for stopping and searching an unarmed neutral ship. Wilkes waited for the Trent in the Bahama Channel, and when it hove into view, Wilkes fired two shots across its bow to stop the ship. He then boarded it and took off Mason and Slidell and their secretaries and brought them as prisoners to Boston.

Northern public opinion was at first jubilant at Wilkes's daring pinch of the two Confederate emissaries, and Congress voted to grant Wilkes a gold medal. But the British government was substantially less enthused: An unarmed British ship, flying the British flag under a declaration of British neutrality, and carrying British

[8]Donald L. Canney, The Old Steam Navy: Volume One, Frigates, Sloops, and Gunboats, 1815–1885 (Annapolis, MD, 1990), pp. 91–94.

mail, had been fired upon, stopped, and boarded by an American war vessel, and had four civilian passengers hauled off without so much as a by-your-leave. When news of the *Trent* boarding reached Britain on November 27th, the prime minister, Lord Henry Palmerston, immediately drafted an ultimatum and ordered a squadron of steamers and 7,000 troops readied to send to Canada. On December 23rd, the British ambassador, Lord Richard Lyons, handed Seward a note demanding the release of Mason and Slidell and an official apology, or else Lyons would break off diplomatic relations and return to London.

Seward was always happy to talk about war with Britain, but with the reality of the situation staring him in the face, he proceeded to eat his words. Seward consulted with McClellan, who advised him that the United States was in no position to fight the Confederates along the Ohio and the Potomac, and then simultaneously fight a British army along the St. Lawrence. And there was no doubt that the British could muster more than sufficient forces in Canada to cause serious trouble. Up until the 1840s, the British government left the defense of Canada largely in the hands of local militia, and much of that militia was as disorganized and ragtag as its counterparts across the border. But in 1855, a Canadian Militia Act allowed the governor-general of Canada to reorganize the Canadian militia around a core of 5,000 volunteers who were to be armed and uniformed on a par with British regulars. When the *Trent* affair exploded, the Canadian volunteer militia was immediately called out, and Palmerston's troops were shipped to New Brunswick; another 35,000 Canadian volunteers were called up, and another 11,000 British regulars were soon on their way across the Atlantic. These were not forces that either Lincoln or Seward wanted to tangle with, and on December 25th, Lincoln met with his Cabinet and, at Seward's urging, they decided to swallow their humiliation. Mason and Slidell were released and placed on board a ship bound for Southampton, England, Wilkes was made to bear the blame for the seizure of the *Trent* for having acted "upon his own suggestions of duty," and the crisis relaxed. But it had been a near thing.[9]

The international ill-temper created by the federal blockade and its problems seemed to set every diplomatic wind blowing in the Confederacy's favor. The landed English aristocracy sympathized with what they saw as a corresponding plantation aristocracy in the South, and they were not sad at the prospect of the American republic demonstrating what they had all along insisted was the inevitable fate of republics—instability, faction, division, civil war, and dismemberment. In the House of Commons, Sir John Ramsden happily greeted the American Civil War as the bursting of "the great republican bubble," and the *Times* of London, the great mouthpiece of Tory reaction, offered its considered opinion that the self-destruction of "the American Colossus" would be the "riddance of a nightmare" for

[9]Virgil Carrington Jones, *The Civil War at Sea: The Blockaders, January 1861–March 1862* (New York, 1960), pp. 292–310; John A. Williams, "Canada and the Civil War," in *The Shot Heard Round the World: The Impact Abroad of the Civil War,* Harold Hyman, ed. (New York, 1969), p. 269.

all monarchies.[10] Similarly, British soldiers, among them Lieutenant-Colonel Garnet Wolseley (who would eventually rise to become the most famous British general of the Victorian age) and Lieutenant-Colonel Arthur Fremantle, slipped through the Union blockade to attach themselves to the Confederate army as military observers. There, they came to admire the lofty and chivalric principles of war they saw practiced by the southern generals. Fremantle found Robert E. Lee the very embodiment of a proper British officer, even down to his religion. "General Lee is, almost without exception, the handsomest man of his age I ever saw. . . . He is a perfect gentlemen in every respect" and, added Fremantle with evident gratification, "is a member of the Church of England." Wolseley, too, was struck with admiration for Lee, and one of Wolseley's aides described Lee in terms that bordered on beatification:

> Every one who approaches him does so with marked respect, although there is none of that bowing and flourishing of forage caps which occurs in the presence of European generals; and, while all honor him and place implicit faith in his courage and ability, those with whom he most intimate feel for him the affection of sons to a father. . . . When speaking of the Yankees he neither evinced any bitterness of feeling nor gave utterance to a single violent expression, but alluded to many of his former friends and companions among them in the kindest terms. He spoke as a man proud of the victories won by his country and confident of ultimate success under the blessing of the Almighty, whom he glorified for past successes, and whose aid he invoked for all future operation.

Fremantle, after leaving the Confederacy in 1863, happily declared that "a people which in all ranks and in both sexes display a unanimity and a heroism which can never have been surpassed in the history of the world is destined sooner or later, to become a great and independent nation."[11]

But it was not just the aristocrats and generals who sympathized with the Confederacy. So long as Lincoln explained the federal government's aims in the war solely in terms of reuniting the Union or of deposing conspiratorial regimes of secessionists in the southern states, the Union cause seemed legalistic and lackluster, while the Confederacy could claim that its war was being waged on the basis of national independence and free trade, which had been the cornerstones of Manchester liberalism since the repeal of the Corn Laws in the 1830s. As a result, some English liberals admired the South's fight as a struggle against money-grubbing Yankee overlordship and high protective tariffs. The Liberal stalwart and Chancellor of the Exchequer William Ewart Gladstone told a political rally in October of 1862 that "Jefferson Davis and the other leaders of the South have made an army;

[10]Martin B. Duberman, *Charles Francis Adams, 1807–1886* (Boston, 1961), p. 264; Frank Lawrence Owsley, *King Cotton Diplomacy: Foreign Relations of the Confederate States of America* (Chicago, 1959), p. 186.

[11]Fremantle, *The Fremantle Diary,* Walter Lord, ed., (New York, 1954), pp. 197–199; J. R. Jones, *Life and Letters of Robert Edward Lee: Soldier and Man* (1906; rept. Harrisonburg, VA, 1978), pp. 203–204.

they are making, it appears, a navy; and they have made what is more than either; they have made a nation." The English working class, and particularly those who had lost their jobs in textile mills that had run out of cotton to spin, also had reason to wish for Confederate victory. "I need hardly say that now there is great distress from want of employment—the result of your horrid war," a Methodist preacher wrote to the American evangelist, Charles Grandison Finney. Another English friend advised Finney, "We have been working short time at the mill . . . & we seem to get worse & worse weekly & from all human appearances we can see no end to it after all." By December, 1862, almost 15 percent of English textile workers were out of work entirely, and another 70 percent were working reduced shifts. "Better fight Yankees," read one workers' newspaper, "than starve operatives."[12]

The blockade inflicted damage on the French economy, too, and with some of the same results in French public opinion. The French emperor, Napoleon III, also had reasons based on colonial ambition for preferring an independent southern Confederacy. In late 1861, England, France, and Spain sent troops into Mexico to enforce the collection of debts owed by the bankrupt Mexican republic. The English and the Spanish soon withdrew, but the French stayed, for Napoleon intended to use the debt crisis as a pretext for deposing the Mexican president, Benito Juárez, and installing a French puppet ruler who would govern Mexico, for all intents and purposes, as a French colony. The chief threat to this scheme was the United States, which publicly warned Napoleon not to intervene in Mexican affairs. But by 1862, the United States was in no position to obstruct Napoleon's ambitions in Mexico, and Napoleon hoped that the division of the American republic and the creation of an independent southern Confederacy would permanently eliminate the United States as an obstacle to French colonization in Central America. The Confederate agents in Europe, headed by John Slidell, decided to play on Napoleon's desires, and offered Confederate support for his Mexican adventure, plus a renewed supply of cotton, if the emperor would grant French diplomatic recognition to the Confederacy and aid the Confederates in breaking the blockade. Napoleon pulled shy of accepting the Confederate offer, but he did create a favorable climate in France for Confederate agents to obtain loans and other assistance. The French banking house of Emile Erlanger underwrote the sale of $14.5 million of Confederate bonds in March, 1863, and Confederate purchasing agents were able to buy up substantial amounts of war supplies to be run through the blockade.

The most damaging pieces of war equipment the British and French allowed the Confederates to buy from them were ships, especially commerce raiders. In March, 1861, the Confederate government appointed a former U.S. naval officer named James Bulloch as its civilian naval agent, and by June, Bulloch had set himself up in Liverpool to arrange contracts for building or buying ships for the

---

[12]Allan Nevins, *The War for the Union: War Becomes Revolution, 1862–1865* (New York, 1960), p. 264; Phillip Shaw Paludan, *"A People's Contest": The Union and the Civil War, 1861–1865* (New York, 1988), p. 269.

Confederacy. Bulloch turned out to be an extremely adroit and successful bargainer, as well as a careful reader of the terms of Britain's Foreign Enlistment Act of 1819, which forbade the building and arming of warships for foreign belligerents in British shipyards. The act threatened violators of the law with seizure of these vessels, but the law also provided little in terms of the proof required beforehand to demonstrate that a ship was being built or fitted out with belligerent intent. It became easy, therefore, for Bulloch to build or purchase English ships through registered agents or English partners, sail them out of British waters, and then outfit them for their real military purposes somewhere else. Bulloch's first commission, a steamer named *Oreto*, sailed from Liverpool in March of 1862 as a merchant ship with what appeared on the records as an English captain and crew, and registry with the tiny Kingdom of Palermo. Having fulfilled the letter of British neutrality, Bulloch then ordered the *Oreto* to a rendezvous on a deserted island in the Bahamas, where she was equipped with naval guns, a Confederate crew, and a new name, C.S.S. *Florida*. The *Florida* then set off on a two-and-a-half-year career of commerce raiding that sent thirty-seven Yankee merchant ships to the bottom or into prize courts.

The *Florida* was not the only ship Bulloch would slip out of England through the cracks in the laws. In the summer of 1861, Bulloch had negotiated with another firm, Laird Brothers, for the construction of a sleek steam cruiser known only by its yard number, *290*. The U.S. consul in Liverpool suspected from the beginning that Bulloch was planning another *Oreto*, and gathered considerable evidence that *290* was intended for purposes other than peaceful trade. But the British government was slow to follow up on the charges, and by the time an order was issued in July, 1862, to impound the ship, Bulloch had already bundled it out to sea. The *290* sailed blithely to the Azores, where it, too, was outfitted with guns and stores and took on the most dreaded name in the entire gallery of American ships—C.S.S. *Alabama*.

By the autumn of 1862, the Confederacy seemed to be as close as it was ever to come to obtaining outright cooperation and recognition from France and Britain. The effects of the cotton blockade, the unpleasant consequences of the *Trent* affair and other blockade incidents, and especially the surprising success of the Confederate armies under Lee and Bragg in Virginia and Kentucky, suggested to both Lord Palmerston and Napoleon III that perhaps the time had at last arrived to intervene in the American mess. Palmerston knew that recognition of the Confederacy could easily bring on the war with the United States that he had avoided in 1861, since the Confederacy would not be "a bit more independent for our saying so unless we followed up our Declaration by taking Part with them in the war."[13] But by late summer, 1862, the North appeared too exhausted to support a second war. In June, Palmerston had surprised Charles Francis Adams with a savage note, denouncing Union occupation practices in New Orleans, and Adams took the note as a signal that the Palmerston government was about to open a campaign for intervention and

---

[13]Jenkins, *Britain and the War for the Union*, vol. 2, p. 66.

mediation. Later in June and again in July, debate erupted in Parliament over southern recognition, with two prosouthern members loudly demanding that Britain step in and mediate a settlement between the Confederacy and the United States. In August, Earl Russell began sounding out the French about the possibility of a joint Anglo-French intervention to stop the war. Finally, on September 14, 1862, Palmerston drafted a short note to Russell that asked whether it might not "be time for us to consider whether . . . England and France might not . . . recommend an arrangement upon the basis of separation?" Three days later, Russell responded favorably to Palmerston's suggestion, observing that "the time is come for offering mediation to the United States Government, with a view to the recognition of the Independence of the Confederates." Palmerston agreed with Russell's call for a cabinet meeting to discuss the offer, adding that "if the Federals sustain a great defeat, they may be at once ready for mediation. . . ."[14]

But in fact, the federals did not sustain a great defeat. On the same day that Russell yielded to Palmerston's suggestion about recognizing southern independence, Lee and McClellan fought each other to a bloody standstill at Antietam. When Lee later retreated, Palmerston decided to shelve his proposal. And there the matter rested, for whatever abstract or emotional sympathies the British might feel for the Confederacy, none of them was so burning that Palmerston would commit his government to backing a sinking horse. Although Seward and Lincoln had come out of the *Trent* affair in 1861 in what looked like humiliation, the fact that they had survived a diplomatic blunder of that proportion without triggering war, meant that the Confederates had been the real diplomatic losers. After the *Trent* affair, there is no evidence that the British government ever seriously planned to use force to get the North to the peacetable, and even Russell and Palmerston talked about intervention only if it could be jointly arranged with the French and the Russians.[15] Despite the effect of the cotton blockade in 1862, British textile merchants soon found new sources of cotton in Egypt and India, and the British economy gradually recovered, thus removing a major agitation for intervention. Also, as Palmerston acknowledged, recognition could very likely mean war with the United States, and that would principally mean a war at sea. While the British navy was undoubtedly the most powerful in the world at that time, the American navy had grown by leaps and bounds since 1861, and the example of the *Florida* and the *Alabama* demonstrated how easily even a few American warships could create serious trouble for British commerce, sending insurance rates as well as losses in ships and cargoes beyond acceptable limits. And, in the event of armed intervention, the British army would be compelled to operate from the Canadian border,

[14]The Palmerston-Russell correspondence is contained in Appendix E of James V. Murfin, *The Gleam of Bayonets: The Battle of Antietam and the Maryland Campaign of 1862* (New York, 1965), pp. 394, 396–397, 399–400.

[15]Howard Jones, *The Union in Peril: The Crisis Over British Intervention in the Civil War* (Chapel Hill, NC, 1992), pp. 210–226.

and to do so under the disadvantage of having to supply it across 3,000 miles of Atlantic Ocean.

But even if the military situation had not been enough to give the British pause, there was the business of President Lincoln's preliminary Emancipation Proclamation, issued a week after Antietam. Lincoln's decision to make even partial abolition of slavery a stated aim of the war altered the British public's view of intervention as decisively as Antietam or Perryville. No matter what opinion an English aristocrat had of southern planters, or what opinion English merchants or workingmen had of tariffs or cotton, few Englishmen wanted to set themselves up as the enemies of a war against slavery. One week after the preliminary proclamation was issued, a meeting staged by pro-Confederate British sympathizers at Staley-bridge, outside Manchester, was broken up by a pro-Union workers' group; in Manchester, a New Year's Day workers' meeting forwarded to Abraham Lincoln a series of resolutions affirming that "since we have discerned . . . that the victory of the free north, in the war which has so sorely distressed us as well as afflicted you, will strike off the fetters of the slave, you have attracted our warm and earnest sympathy"; on January 29th, a mass pro-Northern meeting at Exeter Hall in London drew overflow crowds that spilled out into the streets and snarled traffic. Great as the suffering of the unemployed mill workers was, they saw in the Emancipation Proclamation an unambiguous blow against oppression and tyranny of every kind. "The distress in Lancashire is & has been very great," admitted one of Charles Grandison Finney's correspondents in March, 1863, but all the same, "I would be very sorry & so I am persuaded would the bulk of our Lancashire people to see you patch up a peace with the South upon the basis of protection of slavery."

> We are Sure the mass of our people [are] Sympathetic with the Northern interest, especially since the Emancipation Policy has been adopted. I cannot tell you how glad I felt & how I shouted Hurrah for Lincoln when news reached here that he had confirmed that Proclamation on the 1st Jan[uar]y. . . . The reason why many of our people did not sooner sympathize with the North was a feeling that they were not fighting for the destruction of slavery but merely for the Union with or without slavery.

When Gladstone attempted to raise the subject of Confederate recognition in a cabinet meeting in October, 1862, Palmerston quashed the motion and leaked a "semi-official" disavowal of Gladstone's they-have-made-a-nation speech to the press. In September, 1863, Russell stepped in and seized two powerful ironclad warships that Bulloch had contracted for at Laird Brothers and appropriated them for the British navy.

There was, of course, still the French. Napoleon III was less moved by the Emancipation Proclamation than Palmerston, and he continued to make hopeful noises about European support and recognition for the Confederacy. The negotiation of the Erlanger loan in March of 1863, and the emperor's private approval of a plan by Bulloch to build two ironclads and two wooden steam cruisers in France, gave further encouragement to Confederate agents to hope that Napoleon III might yet act on his own. But Napoleon was unwilling to act for the Confederacy without British support, and that support never had much hope of materializing after September, 1862, if it ever had at all. On November 10, 1862, Napoleon proposed to Palmerston that Britain, France, and Russia impose a six-month armistice in America, along with a lifting of the blockade—but Palmerston's cabinet rejected it. In June, 1863, the emperor met with John A. Roebuck, a pro-Confederate member of Parliament, and made veiled suggestions about another cooperative intervention to end the war—but Parliament refused to listen. And with that, the emperor's interest in American affairs wandered, and by 1866, he would even abandon his luckless puppets in Mexico. In January, 1864, the French government withdrew permission for the construction of Bulloch's ships, and only a phony sale of one of the ironclads to Denmark allowed Bulloch to salvage at least one of his prizes. By the time the ship (named C.S.S. Stonewall) could be repurchased from the Danes, fitted for service, and sailed to the West Indies, the war was over.

By the end of 1863, the once-bright confidence of the Confederacy that Europe would be forced by economic necessity to step in and guarantee southern independence lay in the dust. In August, 1863, the Confederate government recalled John Mason from London, effectively conceding the hopelessness of winning over British opinion; in October, Jefferson Davis and the Confederate cabinet concurred in expelling all British consuls from southern ports on the grounds that the consuls had been obstructing southern military draft laws.

Much of the credit in frustrating Confederate foreign policy lies with the American minister to Britain, Charles Francis Adams. The perfect statesman, Adams not only tirelessly represented the Union cause to the British government and the British people, but financed an active network of spies and agents who relentlessly exposed Confederate violations of the British neutrality laws and hobbled Confederate efforts to raise money and buy arms. William L. Dayton, the American ambassador to France, was equally active in pushing the French to stay within their own neutrality laws, and Dayton's shrewd exposures of the shakiness of Confederate finance critically depressed the value of the Confederate bond sale by the Erlangers. But the two rocks on which Confederate hopes for foreign intervention unavoidably foundered were the fatal timing of its military defeats in 1862, and the moral capital Lincoln earned for the Union with the Emancipation Proclamation. After Antietam, and after Emancipation, the Confederacy was simply no longer believable.

2. The War at Sea

Lincoln's decision to impose a naval blockade of the Confederacy infinitely broadened, at one stroke, the entire scope of the Civil War. The simple fact of the blockade committed the Union to waging a war beyond the local boundaries of states and the lines of railroad and rivers, and out along the whole stretch of the southern coastline and the high seas. By the same token, the Confederacy could ill aford to stand by and allow the federal navy to puts its hands around its neck and wring it without doing something. And so, between the federal navy's determination to choke the Confederates inside their own harbors, and the Confederacy's desperation to find some way of forcing the navy to loosen its grip, the civil war spread outwards from land to sea, and from there, around the world.

Unhappily for Lincoln's plans, the federal navy was only slightly better equipped to wage this kind of war than the regular army had been for the war on land. In 1861, the cream of the fleet were the six big 5,000-ton steam frigates, *Niagara, Roanoke, Colorado, Merrimack, Minnesota,* and *Wabash,* launched in 1855 and carrying batteries of up to forty 9-inch, 10-inch, and 11-inch smooth-bore cannon (and with room for some specialty armament as well, like the *Minnesota*'s 150-pound Parrott rifle and the *Niagara*'s twelve 12-inch shell guns). Following the steam frigates were the twelve steam sloops of 1857 and 1858, the biggest of which—*Hartford, Brooklyn,* and *Richmond*—displaced 2,500 tons and carried sixteen to twenty 9-inch guns.

None of these ships, however, had been designed for blockade duty. As it was, the outbreak of the war found all of the frigates in various navy yards undergoing all sorts of refitting and overhaul. One of them, the *Merrimack,* suffered from chronic engine trouble and was in drydock for machinery repairs at Gosport Navy Yard at Norfolk when Virginia passed its secession ordinance. Despite the entreaties of Benjamin Isherwood, an army engineer sent expressly to Norfolk to get the *Merrimack* out of danger, the commandant of the yard ordered the frigate burnt and scuttled to prevent it from falling into the hands of the rebels. As with the ships, there was also some question about the reliability of the navy's officers. Although only 237 of the navy's officer corps resigned and went south at the beginning of the war (about 15 percent of the navy's officers, as compared to the 28 percent of the army's officers who joined the Confederacy) federal Admiral Samuel F. Du Pont was keenly aware of the fact that "not a single officer" in his South Atlantic Blockading Squadron in 1862 had "voted for Lincoln." But at the same time, Du Pont was also aware that "there is not a proslavery man among them," and the officers who had some chance ashore to see the remains of the slave system for themselves experienced great awakenings. The aristocratic Du Pont, whose home was in the border slave state of Delaware, confessed that he had "been a sturdy conservative on this question, defended it over the world, argued for it as partriarchal in its tendencies." But he was horrified by the conditions he found on the coastal plantations. Having seen "the *institution* 'de pres'," Du Pont wrote feelingly to a friend in Philadelphia, "May God forgive me for the words I have uttered in its defense as intertwined in our Constitution."[16]

---

[16]Du Pont to Mrs. Du Pont, April 10–13, 1862, and Du Pont to James Stokes Biddle, December 17, 1861, in *Samuel Francis DuPont: A Selection from His Civil War Letters,* John D. Hayes, ed. (Ithaca, NY, 1969), vol. 1, pp. 281, 413.

In terms of both ships and personnel, it was clear that the federal government was going to have to find ways to improvise a navy, as much for the blockade as to maintain the navy's high-seas profile. That the government did, in fact, manage to improvise such a navy is largely due to Gideon Welles, the secretary of the navy, an ex-Democrat and former naval bureau chief. Welles and his assistant secretary, Gustavus Fox, realized from the beginning that it was much more important to put ships of any size or description outside a southern port as soon as possible to make the blockade visible than to wait until a specially designed blockading fleet could be built. So Welles chartered one of almost everything that could float, armed them in makeshift fashion, and sent them off to pound a beat outside southern rivers and harbors. By July, 1861, Welles had organized four blockading squadrons, two along the Gulf and two along the Atlantic, to guard the Confederate coastline; and by the end of the war, he would have bought, borrowed, deployed, and built over 600 warships, merchant vessels, steamboats, and ordinary tugs, and turned them into a blockading fleet.

The principal objective of the blockade was to prevent any shipping, southern or otherwise, from entering or leaving the Confederacy. That meant, for much of the time, that blockade duty was an incessant string of empty, passive, and depressingly boring days, waiting for the possible blockade-runner to appear over the horizon. "Dull! Dull! Dull! is the day," wrote the surgeon of the federal blockader *Fernandina* in his diary, "Nothing to do." One sailor stationed off Wilmington, North Carolina, explained in his diary how adventurous blockade duty really was.

> I told her [his mother] she could get a fair idea of our 'adventures' if she would go on the roof of the house, on a hot summer day, and talk to half a dozen hotel hallboys, who are generally far more intelligent and agreeable than the average 'acting officer.' Then descend to the attic and drink some tepid water, full of iron rust. Then go on the roof again and repeat this 'adventurous process' at intervals, until she has tired out and go to bed, with every thing shut down tight, so as not to show a light. Adventure! Bah! The blockade is the wrong place for it.[17]

And yet, for all its discomforts, blockade duty was still preferred over service on the inland rivers or on foreign stations, chiefly because blockade duty offered the prospect of prize money to any ship's crew who captured a merchant ship trying to run the blockade. When the ninety-day gunboat *Kennebec* could lap up over $1.5 million in prize money for its 100 officers and crewmen, and when Rear Admiral Samuel Phillips Lee could pocket between $110,000 (Lee's reported figure) and $150,000 (what Gideon Welles believed he had raked in) in prize money over the two years he commanded the North Atlantic Blockading Squadron, blockade duty could suddenly seem inexplicably appealing after all.[18]

---

[17]William Still, "The Common Sailor: The Civil War's Uncommon Man," in *Civil War Times Illustrated* 23 (Februaury 1985), pp. 38–39.

[18]Canney, *The Old Steam Navy*, p. 94; Virginia Jeans Laas, " 'Sleepless Sentinels': The North Atlantic Blockading Squadron, 1862–1864" in *Civil War History* 31 (March 1985), p. 33.

But the blockade came to involve more than merely sitting in ambush for Confederate blockade-runners. A surprisingly large proportion of blockade seizures were made by the little Potomac Flotilla, which ran small aggressive expeditions up the Potomac and the other Chesapeake Bay rivers to disrupt Confederate coastal trade and the smuggling of medicines and weapons through Confederate lines in Virginia. At the other end of the scale, the navy also aimed to shut down as many major southern ports as it could. In November, 1861, the navy seized Beaufort and the Carolina Sea islands, and in the following January, the army and navy together seized a foothold on the North Carolina coast. In April, 1862, another joint army-navy operation recaptured Fort Pulaski on the Savannah River, and closed the Georgia coastline to blockade running, and a few weeks later Farragut and his steam sloops shouldered their way past the Confederacy's Mississippi River forts and steamed up to New Orleans. Farragut also sealed off Mobile Bay in August, 1864, and in January, 1865, Wilmington surrendered to yet another joint expedition led by Farragut's stepbrother, Rear Admiral David Dixon Porter. Only Charleston managed to hold out against the federal navy. Throughout the summers of 1863 and 1864, both the army and navy attempted to capture the Charleston harbor defenses and bombard Fort Sumter (now in Confederate hands) into submission. But Sumter, and the rest of Charleston harbor, survived until February of 1865, when the approach of a federal army from Georgia finally forced the Charleston garrison to evacuate the city.

The Confederates had been aware from the beginning of the war that the blockade represented a noose that would strangle them if they could not first find a way to cut through it. And so, if maintaining the blockade was the item of first importance for the federal navy, then breaking it immediately became a top priority for the Confederates. "The blockade is breaking up the whole South," wrote "Parson" Brownlow, the Unionist Tennessean in the spring of 1862, "It has been remarked in the streets of Knoxville that no such thing as a fine-toothed comb was to be had, and all the little Secession heads were full of squatter sovereigns hunting for their rights in the territories."[19] Unfortunately, the Confederates had very little at hand to use as a weapon against the federal ships. At least the Union started out with *some* kind of a navy; the Confederates had none, except for a few small sloops and revenue cutters they were able to seize at the time of secession. By February of 1862, the Confederate navy still only amounted to thirty-three ships. Nor did the Confederates have much to build with. The South had little or nothing in the way of a shipbuilding industry: It possessed few of the raw materials or manufacturing plants for fitting and arming warships, and lacked building and repair facilities. Of course, Virginia had occupied the federal navy yard at Norfolk in April, 1861, but the Norfolk yard could easily be sealed off by federal blockading ships in Hampton Roads and at the mouth of the Chesapeake. If the South had any hope for breaking

---

[19]Brownlow, *Sketches of the Rise, Progress, and Decline of Secession* (Philadelphia, 1962), p. 423.

the blockade, it was going to have to be by some pretty unexpected and unconventional means.

However, the unexpected and unconventional seem to have come naturally to the Confederate secretary of the navy, Stephen R. Mallory, whose technical ingenuity single-handedly created a Confederate navy and almost broke up the blockade with it. Mallory laid hands on any possible weapon, any proposed invention, no matter how unlikely—mines made from beer kegs, submarines made from boiler-plate, gunboats laminated with railroad iron—and floated them out to do battle with the federal steam frigates. It was in that last category—ironclads—that Mallory came the nearest to succeeding in his schemes. A former U.S. Senator from Florida and formerly the chairman of the Senate Naval Affairs Committee, Mallory was fully abreast of the latest developments in building ironclad gunboats and warships. However imposing the federal steam frigates and steam sloops might seem, Mallory was aware that not a single one of them was ironclad; and the federal ironclad gunboats being built for use on the Mississippi were strictly river boats, too small to venture out on the ocean. Let the Confederacy manage, somehow, to construct even one ironclad warship capable of steaming on the high seas, then that one ship would be more than a match for each and every one of the federal frigates.

The difficulty, for Mallory, was that nowhere in the Confederacy was there the capability of building such a ship, even if he could find enough iron plate to armor her. And then, on June 25, 1861, two of Mallory's lieutenants at Norfolk reminded Mallory about the scuttled steam frigate *Merrimack* in Norfolk navy yard. They pointed out that the hull and boilers of the *Merrimack* were still relatively intact, and if the ship could be pumped out and refloated, it would be possible to cut away her burnt-over masts and charred upper decks, build an iron casemate over the hull, and arm it with enough guns to sink anything the federal navy could send against the ship. Mallory bought the idea at once: He had the sunken frigate raised and inspected, and in July, 1861, work began on reconstructing the *Merrimack* as a seagoing ironclad warship. On February 17, 1862, the rebuilt *Merrimack* was launched and commissioned—and given a new name, *Virginia*. The reborn steam frigate now looked nothing like its first form—or for that matter like anything else afloat. Cut down to the waterline of its hull, the Confederate engineers had erected a twenty-four-foot high iron-plated casemate on top of the hull, rounded at each end, and with sides sloping outwards at a 36° angle. Four gunports with iron shutters gaped in each side, and at each rounded end of the casemate were three more gunports, and just beneath the waterline at her bow was a fifteen-hundred-pound cast iron ram, which the iron-clad could use to smash in the timber hulls of the federal blockading fleet. On February 24th, the *Virginia* was given a master, Franklin Buchanan, and on March 8th, Buchanan nosed the makeshift ironclad's way out of Norfolk and downstream into Hampton Roads.

Standing out in the Roads, sealing off Confederate access to the Chesapeake Bay and the Atlantic, were seven ships of the North Atlantic Blockading Squadron—the prize steam frigates *Minnesota* and *Roanoke*, the 24-gun sail-powered sloop *Cumber-*

land, an obsolete 44-gun sail frigate named *Congress,* and an assortment of supporting craft. Shortly after 1:00 P.M., the *Virginia* bore down on them, selecting the *Cumberland* as its first target. The startled federals beat-to-quarters and opened fire on the *Virginia,* only to watch their solid iron shot bounce harmlessly off the *Virginia*'s iron-plated sides. The *Virginia* returned the fire, and then drove directly at the *Cumberland,* smashing its ram into the *Cumberland*'s side. The stricken sloop sank bow first, its gun crews still trying to bang shot off the *Virginia*'s sides, until the water closed over the ship's unlowered flag.

The rest of the federal squadron, having watched the easy destruction of the *Cumberland,* attempted to escape. But the *Congress, Minnesota,* and *Roanoke* all managed to run aground in the shallow waters of the Roads. The *Virginia* drew up behind the old frigate *Congress* and pounded it into a blazing shambles in half an hour, and would probably have done the same to the rest of the federal ships had not the tide started to ebb. Anxious not to be caught aground themselves, the Confederates turned their triumphant experiment around and the *Virginia* slowly steamed back up the Roads, intending to finish off the stranded *Minnesota* the next morning. And then what? In a confidential letter to Franklin Buchanan on March 7th, Mallory grandly suggested that once the *Virginia* finished off the federal ships in Hampton Roads, Buchanan should steam out into the Chesapeake, and then up the Potomac to bombard Washington. Buchanan could then continue on to New York and "burn the city and the shipping." With that, "peace would inevitably follow. Bankers would withdraw their capital from the city. The Brooklyn navy yard and its magazines and all the lower part of the city would be destroyed, and such an event, by a single ship, would do more to achieve our independence than would the results of many campaigns." Whether the *Virginia*'s unwieldy bulk could ever have really survived the first pitch and roll of the open ocean is debatable; but Mallory *thought* she could, and what was more, so did Lincoln's Cabinet.

The next morning, the *Virginia* steamed back down the Roads to destroy the *Minnesota* and perhaps put an end to the war. But as the Confederate ironclad bore down on the stranded *Minnesota,* the officers of the *Virginia* noticed that the federal ship was not alone. At first, they thought a raft had been brought alongside the *Minnesota* to take off the steam frigate's crew. But then the raft began to move, and as it did, the Confederate sailors and gunners got their first good look at what they could only describe as "a tin can on a shingle." It was in fact a federal warship, an ironclad that floated almost flush on the surface of the water except for a single round gun turret in the middle. Its name was *Monitor.*

The federal navy had actually found out about the Confederate plans to rebuild the *Merrimack* as early as August, 1861. Although Navy Secretary Welles himself was skeptical of the usefulness of ironclads on the high seas, the threat of what the *Merrimack* might be turned into forced him to ask Congress for an appropriation of $1.5 million to experiment with three ironclad designs. Two of the designs Welles commissioned were little more than customary steam frigates with various kinds of armor plating; the third prototype came from a Swedish inventor named John

Ericsson, and it was so bafflingly different that one officer told Ericsson to take his model of the ship home and worship it. "It will not be idolatry," the officer quipped. "It is the image of nothing in the heavens above, or the earth beneath, or the waters under the earth." Certainly it was peculiar: Ericsson's plans called for an iron-plated raft 172 feet long and 41 feet wide, with a small armored pilot house at the bow, two portable smokestacks that could be taken down for combat purposes, and, in the center, a revolving gun turret (with two 11-inch naval cannon) which could be turned to face in any direction. The turret was the greatest marvel in this little ship of marvels, and it took the fancy of both Welles and Lincoln. On October 4, 1861, Welles and Ericsson signed the contract for the weird little ironclad, and little less than four months later, Ericsson launched the vessel from a private shipyard at Greenpoint, Long Island. At the invitation of Assistant Navy Secretary Fox, Ericsson named the ship *Monitor*. Formally commissioned on February 25, 1862, at the Brooklyn Navy Yard, the *Monitor* sailed down the East River on March 4th, bound for Hampton Roads to search out and destroy the rebuilt *Merrimack* before the Confederates could turn their ironclad loose.

The *Monitor* arrived one day too late. But for the *Minnesota*, and the rest of the federal blockade, she had come just in time. For the next three hours, the two strangest ships in the world battered at each other with their guns, each mutually unable to hurt the other. The captain of the *Minnesota* watched in a mixture of delight and disbelief as the little *Monitor*, "completely covering my ship as far as was possible with her dimensions . . . laid herself right alongside of the *Merrimack*, and the contrast was that of a pigmy to a giant."

> Gun after gun was fired by the *Monitor*, which was returned with whole broadsides from the rebels with no more effect, apparently, than so many pebblestones thrown by a child. After a while they commenced maneuvering, and we could see the [*Monitor*] point her bow for the rebels, with the intention . . . of sending a shot through her bow porthole; then she would shoot by her and rake her through her stern. In the meantime the rebel was pouring broadside after broadside, but . . . when they struck the bomb-proof tower [the *Monitor*'s turret] the shot glanced off without producing any effect, clearly establishing the fact the wooden vessels can not contend successfully with ironclad ones; for never before was anything like it dreamed of by the greatest enthusiast in maritime warfare.[20]

And then both, baffled at the other's invincibility, drew off. The *Virginia*'s plans to burn Washington and New York had been stymied by the surprise appearance of the *Monitor*, the *Minnesota* had been saved, and so had every other wooden warship in the federal fleet.

The two ironclads never fought again; in fact, neither of them survived the year. When McClellan began his movement up the James River peninsula later in April, the Confederates were forced to evacuate Norfolk. The *Virginia*, drawing too

---

[20]"Report of Captain Van Brunt, U.S. Navy, commanding U.S.S. Minnesota," in *Official Records/ Navies*, series 1, vol. 7, p. 11.

much water to retreat up the James River, had to be blown up on May 11th to keep it from capture. The *Monitor* remained on station in Hampton Roads until November, 1862, when it was ordered to join the blockading squadron off Beaufort, North Carolina, where it was rumored that the Confederates were constructing another blockade-breaking ironclad. But on December 30th, in treacherous water off Cape Hatteras, the *Monitor* was caught in a severe storm and sank with the loss of four officers and twelve men.

Despite their short lives, the *Monitor* and the *Virginia* had written their own chapter in naval history, since their combat was the first occasion in which ironclad warships fought each other. Both ships also became the model for further experiments in building ironclads. The success of *Monitor*'s design induced the U.S. Navy to build sixty *Monitor*-type vessels, some of them big enough to carry two turrets, and even one, the *Roanoke*, with three, and from that point until after the Second World War, the turret's design would dominate naval ship building. The Confederates clung to the casemate design of the *Virginia*, and with its limited resources, the Confederate navy scraped together enough men and material during 1862 to have four large ironclads built by private firms on the Mississippi River, the *Arkansas*, the *Tennessee*, the *Mississippi*, and the *Louisiana*. None of them, however, was used well or wisely by the Confederate navy, and all of them were eventually destroyed by the Confederates to avoid federal capture.[21] Undaunted, the Confederate navy laid down twenty more casemate-style ironclads, and three new facilities for rolling iron plate were developed in Richmond, Atlanta, and northern Alabama. But the overall scarcity of materials in the Confederacy, and the inadequacy of even three new mills in rolling enough iron, doomed most of these ships to rot on the stocks. One of the most fearsome of them, the *Albemarle*, was sunk at her moorings in the North Carolina sounds by a daring nighttime federal raid, while the 216-foot *Tennessee* (the second rebel ironclad to bear that name) was pounded into surrender by the combined gunnery of Farragut's fleet at Mobile Bay in 1864.

The Confederates continued to experiment with a variety of exotic naval weapons. Commander Matthew F. Maury developed the first electrically detonated harbor mines, and between electric mines and other improvised naval explosives, the Confederates sank thirty-seven federal ships, including nine ironclads, on the waters of the Confederacy's rivers and harbors. A four-man "torpedo-boat," appropriately named the *David* and closely resembling a floating tin cigar, puttered out of Charleston on the night of October 5, 1863, with 100 pounds of high explosive rigged on a ten-foot spar that jutted out from the little metal boat's bow. Lieutenant William Glassell maneuvered the *David* up to the side of one of the federal blockade ships—which just happened to be one of the other federal ironclad prototypes, the *New Ironsides*—and detonated the spar "torpedo." The explosion cracked iron plates and struts in the *New Ironsides'* hull, while the wash from the detonation

[21]William N. Still, *Iron Afloat: The Story of the Confederate Armorclads*, 2nd ed. (Columbia, SC, 1985), pp. 41–61.

swamped the *David* and drowned its small boiler fire. But a quick-thinking engineer relit the boiler and navigated the unlikely little vessel back into Charleston harbor. Far stranger than the *David* was the unlikely brainchild of a civilian, Horace F. Hunley, who built a primitive submarine (which he named *Hunley*) that successfully destroyed the federal sloop *Housatonic* on February 17, 1864. Unfortunately, the *Hunley* destroyed itself along with the *Housatonic,* and any serious further Confederate interest in submarines went up in the same explosion.

Even with all the inventiveness in the world at its disposal, it was apparent, after the failure of the *Virginia* to disrupt the blockade, that the Confederacy could not wait for the development of some other secret weapon to pry the blockade ships loose. And so, unable to break the federal navy's hold on the Confederate throat, the Confederates responded by trying to get their own grip around the federal throat by sending out commerce raiders to prey on northern shipping. The chief problem Secretary Mallory had to resolve before unloosing a fleet of Confederate commerce raiders was the same one he had encountered over the ironclads—where to get them. That problem was solved in large measure by the ingenuity of Confederate agents abroad, like James Bulloch, who contracted in Britain for the construction of the raider commissioned in 1862 as the *Florida.* Under the command of the veteran blockade-runner John Maffitt, the *Florida* captured or sank thirty-seven United States merchant ships, including the richest prize taken by a Confederate commerce raider,, the *Jacob D. Bell,* the worth of whose cargo was conservatively estimated at $1.5 million. The *Florida* was finally captured by federal subterfuge in Brazilian waters in October of 1864, but it had set the pattern that other Confederate raiders would happily follow.

The most famous of the Confederate raider captains was Raphael Semmes, a 52-year-old lawyer and ex-navy officer. Semmes was a strong advocate of the use of commerce raiders, and even took it upon himself in 1861 to convert an old New Orleans steamer into the *Sumter.* Over the next six months he captured or burned eighteen United States merchant ships. Cornered in the British outpost of Gibraltar in January, 1862, Semmes simply sold the *Sumter* to the British, paid off his crew, and disappeared. Six months later, Semmes turned up in the Azores, where he took command of Bulloch's newest purchase from British shipbuilders, a sleek, deadly 1,000-ton cruiser that Semmes named the *Alabama.* Over the next two years, Semmes sailed his beautiful ship across the Atlantic and Indian oceans, never calling at a Confederate port, always replenishing his supplies from captured Yankee ships or from stores purchased by Confederate agents in Cape Town, Singapore, and the French port of Cherbourg. By the time Semmes brought the *Alabama* into Cherbourg for a badly needed refitting in June of 1864, he had sunk or captured sixty-four Union merchant vessels worth more than $6.5 million, and had even sunk a federal blockade ship, the *Hatteras.* But while anchored in Cherbourg harbor, the *Alabama* was trapped by the federal steam sloop *Kearsarge,* and when Semmes and the *Alabama* attempted to fight their way free, the *Kearsarge*'s two 11-inch pivot guns sent the *Alabama* to the bottom. Semmes was rescued by an English yacht, and managed to make his way back to the Confederacy, where he was promoted to rear admiral and, ironically, given river-defense duty below Richmond.

The *Alabama* and *Florida* were only the most successful of the southern commerce raiders. Together with some twenty smaller cruisers, the Confederate commerce raiders accounted for the destruction of at least 257 United States–registered ships. After the war, the United States demanded that the British government take responsibility for the raiders its shipyards had built by paying reparations, and in 1872, the British settled the so-called "*Alabama* claims" for $15.5 million. But that figure cannot begin to account for millions expended in chasing the raiders down, or for the trade that was frightened off the seas by the Confederate raiders, or for the 1,000 other American vessels that were transferred (either for safety or for the opportunity to evade federal prohibitions on trade with the Confederacy) to other flags.[22] The American merchant marine, which before 1861 had held first place in the Atlantic carrying trade, was toppled from its preeminence, and has, to this day, never recovered from the blows dealt it by the *Alabama* and the Civil War.

But for all the destruction wrought by the commerce raiders, the one thing they failed to do was force any lightening in the pressure the federal blockade was gradually twisting around the Confederacy. And that meant that, in the end, the most effective way of dealing with the federal blockade was to evade it. At the beginning of the war, the creation of a special blockade-running flotilla was beyond the power of the Confederacy, which had all it could do to build its few ironclads and buy its handful of commerce raiders. Instead, the Confederate government designated the Charleston firm of John Fraser & Company (and its Liverpool branch, Fraser, Trenholm & Company) as its European financial agents and left blockade-running up to the entrepreneurial ingenuity of the company. This meant that Fraser, Trenholm & Company assumed all the risks of hiring their own ships (like the *Cecile*) and their own crews to run the blockade with southern cotton or European weapons, but it also allowed the company to make immense profits.

The example of Fraser, Trenholm & Company soon showed other British and southern entrepreneurs how quickly a path to wartime fortunes could be blazed, and a series of private import-export firms based either in England or Nassau sprang up to run cotton, weapons, supplies, and costly consumer goods in and out of southern ports. The Importing and Exporting Company of South Carolina was created by a consortium of Charleston businessmen and run by William C. Bee and Charles T. Mitchell, who bought up two blockade runners, the notorious *Cecile* and the *Edwin* from the Fraser firm in March 1862 to make the company's first dash through the blockade. The *Cecile* made a successful roundtrip from Charleston to Nassau and back, but the *Edwin* ran aground outside Charleston harbor on its way back from Nassau and had to be abandoned. Nevertheless, the venture was a smashing success for the company. The Charleston cotton the two vessels dropped in Nassau netted

[22]Kenneth J. Blume, "The Flight from the Flag: The American Government, the British Caribbean, and the American Merchant Marine, 1861–1865," In *Civil War History* 32 (March 1986), pp. 44–55.

the company $18,000, while the goods that were brought back were either sold to the Confederate government or auctioned off to the public for $90,000. The company had no trouble recovering its expenses (or the stockholders their investment), and it paid Bee and Mitchell a handsome commission of $5,000. On its next voyage, the *Cecile* brought 2,000 Enfield rifles through the blockade, along with a rich cargo of private goods that netted the company another $100,000.[23]

One reason why private entrepreneurs were willing to risk their necks and their ships in this way is because, at first, there was comparatively little neck to risk in running the blockade. In 1861, the Union navy still had only a few ships on blockade duty, and not many of them knew much of what they were doing, and as a result at least nine out of ten blockade runners made it through. But by the end of 1862, the only major ports still open to blockade runners were Mobile, Charleston, and Wilmington, and federal sailors (with visions of prize money dancing through their heads) had become more skilled at ship catching. Of course, as the risks went up, so did the costs, and in the interests of maintaining their profit margins, the entrepreneurs turned to the design and construction of long, lean, rakish ships, burning smokeless coal, and specially designed for fooling federal navy observers. But the longer and leaner the ships, the less capable they were of carrying heavy war materials as cargo, and since the entrepreneurs mistrusted the Confederate government's procurement policies anyway, the hulls of the purpose-built blockade-runners filled up with luxury goods that commanded fairy-princess prices on the consumer markets, but which did little or nothing to support the Confederate war effort.[24] Eventually, this forced the Confederate government to begin operating its own line of blockade runners to ensure the flow of badly needed war material to the front lines, and in 1864, the Confederate Congress imposed a series of new regulations that forbade the import of high-cost luxuries and forced private shippers to yield one-half of their cargo space to government use.

But neither private ventures nor government regulations were ever able to deliver to the South the kind of triumph over the blockade that the Confederacy needed. In terms of simple numbers, the successes of the blockade-runners appear impressive: Over the course of the war, some 300 blockade-running steamers made approximately 1,300 attempts to run the blockade, and made it through unscathed over 1,000 times.[25] But that impression fades when placed beside the hidden cost of the blockade. The real success of the blockade has to be measured, not in terms of how many cleverly designed blockade-runners squeezed through it, but by how many ordinary ships from around the world never tried it at all. By comparison with

[23]Wise, *Lifeline of the Confederacy*, pp. 69–70.

[24]Robert B. Ekelund, Jr., and Mark Thornton have dubbed this trend "the Rhett Butler effect," after the self-centered blockade-running hero of Margaret Mitchell's *Gone With the Wind* (see "The Union Blockade and Demoralization of the South: Relative Prices in the Confederacy," in *Social Science Quarterly* 73 [December 1992], pp. 891–900).

[25]Wise, *Lifeline of the Confederacy*, p. 221.

the South's prewar import-export trade, the blockade-runners amount to little more than a trickle. The South exported ten times as much cotton in 1860 as it passed through the blockade during all four years of the war; nearly five times as many ships called at southern ports in 1860 as made it through four years of blockade. And although the blockade, by itself, may not have exactly won the war for the Union, there is no question that it seriously constricted the South's ability to make war, much less to win it.

3. Supplying the War

Nothing that the northern or southern volunteer was naturally endowed to do or suffer would have amounted to much if he had not been constantly supplied and supported with weapons, food, ammunition, and clothing from far behind the lines. Even if the volunteer was not always as well supplied as he thought he ought to have been, it has to be remembered that American society and government before 1861 was utterly unprepared for the organizational demands placed upon it by a major war. As late as 1830, the entire federal bureaucracy in Washington consisted of exactly 352 people, and in 1861 the total number of government employees (including non-Washingtonians like postmasters and customs officers) numbered no more than 40,651. The same was true on the local level. Up until 1854, the city of Philadelphia was still governed as a collection of twenty-seven separate colonial-era municipalities; until 1848, it still pumped its city water through wooden pipes, and pigs were still scavenging in the city streets in the 1860s. Backyard trenches served as toilets for much of New York City, and garbage and waste water ended up in street gutters where it bred cholera, typhus, and other contagious diseases. Until 1861, Louisiana did not possess a single macadamized road.[26] The Civil War suddenly threw into the laps of the Richmond and Washington governments an immense and hitherto inconceivable problem in management, and there were very few people in either capital who knew how to impose organizational management on the resources needed to win such a war. "We have more of the brute force of persistent obstinacy in Northern blood than the South has," Frederick Law Olmstead wrote hopefully, "if we can only get it in play. . . ."[27]

The ultimate means for getting a federal supply system "in play" was the secretary of war, Edwin McMasters Stanton. A heavy-set Ohio lawyer and former attorney general (in the closing months of the Buchanan administration), Stanton possessed an immense coarse black-and-white beard, rude and dictatorial manners,

[26]Elizabeth M. Geffen, "Industrial Development and Social Crisis, 1841–1854" and Russell F. Weigley, "The Border City in the Civil War, 1854–1865," in *Philadelphia: A 300–Year History*, Russell F. Weigley, ed. (New York, 1982), pp. 317, 373; Ernest A. McKay, *The Civil War and New York City* (Syracuse, NY, 1990), p. 217.

[27]Olmstead to Oliver Wolcott Gibbs [January 31, 1863], in *The Papers of Frederick Law Olmstead: Volume IV, Defending the Union*, Jane Turner Censer, ed. (Baltimore, 1986), p. 505.

and "a perpetually irritable look in his stern little eyes."[28] His appointment as secretary of war on January 20, 1862, to replace Simon Cameron came as a surprise, and to no one more than Stanton. Not only was he a lifelong Democrat, but in 1855, he had personally snubbed Lincoln as "that giraffe" and that "creature from Illinois" when both were retained as counsel in a patent case for the McCormick Reaper Company. But Stanton was a solid Union man, and heartily antislavery. The fact that he was a Democrat could actually have been considered an advantage to Lincoln in trying to garner increased Democratic support for the war. And he had what few of the Republicans had, and that was experience in the inner workings of national government. Whatever Lincoln's reasons were, time soon justified them, for Lincoln could not have chosen a better foreman to run his wartime workshop. Within a week of assuming office, Stanton wrote to Charles A. Dana that as soon as he could "get the machinery of the office working, the rats cleared out, and the rat holes stopped we shall *move.*" And *move* is precisely what Stanton did. He drove himself and his staff of undersecretaries with maniacal fury and animation, auditing government contracts, reviewing and digesting military data for Lincoln's use, intimidating army contractors, barking orders, and banging on his stand-up writing desk to make his point. He also took it as his duty to keep the Union army's generals in line with administration policy. Where they did not, as in the East, they found Stanton an implacable and unforgiving enemy, and sooner or later he had them sacked; where they did, as in the West, they found themselves promoted. It was Stanton more than anyone else who would help bring Ulysses Simpson Grant to the command of all the Union armies in 1864; it was also Stanton who helped destroy George Brinton McClellan. "This army has to fight or run away," Stanton wrote to Dana, and Stanton took it upon himself to ensure that "while men are striving nobly in the West, the champagne and oysters on the Potomac must be stopped."[29]

Determined to sweep up the entire War Department as his private fiefdom, Stanton began welding the various parts of the department together into a unified and coherent staff. His first move in that direction was to depose McClellan as general-in-chief of the federal armies in March, 1862, and to replace him in July with Henry Wager Halleck. In the process, Stanton sharply redefined the job of general-in-chief, so that Halleck spent the rest of the war as little more than the means of transmitting Stanton's policy directives down to federal commanders in the field. But, to be fair to Halleck, there really was a need, in a civilian-run republic, for a reliable and competent organizer who could perform that kind of liaison between the civilian leadership at the War Department and the military at the front, and Halleck performed the job superbly throughout the war. "Halleck was not thought to be a great man in the field," wrote Charles A. Dana, who joined the

[28]George S. Bryan, *The Great American Myth* (New York, 1940), pp. 129–130.

[29]Benjamin P. Thomas and Harold Hyman, *Stanton: The Life and Times of Lincoln's Secretary of War* (New York, 1962), pp. 63–66, 141–168.

War Department as one of Stanton's assistant secretaries of war, "but he was never-theless a man of military ability, and by reason of his great accomplishments in the technics of armies and of war was almost invaluable as an adviser to the civilian Lincoln and Stanton."[30]

In addition to the general-in-chief, Stanton next brought securely under his dictate the heads of the three most important War Department supply bureaus, Quartermaster-General Montgomery C. Meigs, Commissary-General Joseph P. Tay-lor, and the Chief of Ordnance James W. Ripley. None of these men was more important to Stanton than Meigs, a 46-year-old Georgian who had been promoted to brigadier general only in 1861. As quartermaster-general he was responsible for supplying the federal armies with all of their basic hardware, including uniforms, tents, ambulance wagons, supply wagons, mules, cavalry and transport horses, and the forage to feed them—everything from hospitals to tent pins. But supplying the immense variety of the army's goods was only half the challenge. The sheer volume of what was required of each of these items was what really staggered belief. Already in September, 1861, the Army of the Potomac needed 20,000 cavalry horses and a further 20,000 transportation horses just to do its daily business. On the peninsula, the Army of the Potomac needed 25,000 horses and mules (along with forty-five wagons for every 1,000 men) to haul baggage and supplies. By the middle of 1862, that requisition had swollen to 1,500 horses weekly, and by 1864, the demand had risen to 500 horses a day, with the government shelling out $170 each. Outfitting a regiment with uniforms cost $20,000 per regiment, and the uniforms could easily be worn out by three months of campaigning. Shoes were by far the worst problem, since the army could scarcely move without them, and then, when it did move, it consumed them at a rate of 25,000 weekly.[31] Since so much of this had to be done virtually at once, and by officers and clerks who had never before in their lives administered anything like it, the opportunities for mistake and oversight were legion. It also went without saying that, under these circumstances, the opportuni-ties for fraud, kickbacks, and corruption were even greater. Nevertheless, Montgom-ery Meigs proved to be both tireless and incorruptible as the quartermaster-general. Meigs's expenditures rose over the course of the war from $40,631,000 in 1861–1862 to $226,199,000 in 1864–1865, and by the end of the war, his department had spent nearly $1.5 billion. But despite the gargantuan size and the frantic demands of his department, a Congressional audit could not find so much as one penny unaccounted for in any major contract authorized by Meigs.[32]

Keeping the federal armies clothed and equipped was one thing. Keeping them

---

[30]Charles A. Dana, *Recollections of the Civil War With the Leaders at Washington and in the Field in the Sixties* (New York, 1898), p. 187.

[31]Hagerman, *The American Civil War and the Origins of Modern Warfare*, p. 45; Nevins, *The War for the Union: War Becomes Revolution*, pp. 475–476.

[32]Russell F. Weigley, *Quartermaster General of the Union Army: A Biography of M. C. Meigs* (New York, 1959), pp. 317, 358; Herman Hattaway and Archer Jones, *How the North Won: A Military History of the Civil War* (Urbana, IL, 1983), pp. 120–124.

fed and armed was quite another, and those responsibilities fell to the commissary-general, Colonel Joseph P. Taylor, and the chief of ordnance, Brigadier General James Wolfe Ripley. Neither Ripley nor Taylor ever won the praise awarded to Montgomery Meigs—Ripley, because of his stubborn refusal to permit the introduction of the breechloading repeating rifle into the war, and Taylor, because Union army food was so consistently bad by civilian standards. But Taylor was up against the fact that the technologies of food preservation, including meat-packing, canning, and condensed liquids, were still relatively new. What critics missed was the happier fact that, although army food was bad, the Union armies rarely lacked for sufficient quantities of it. Something of the same could be said about Ripley. The ordnance chief's insistence on sticking by the muzzle-loading rifle as the standard infantry arm, rather than introducing the breechloading repeating rifle, was one of the most wrongheaded administrative decisions of the war. But in spite of this one majestic failure of judgment, Ripley turned into a surprisingly competent administrator. Once having made up his mind against the breechloading repeaters, Ripley never failed to deliver sufficient supplies of muzzleloaders or their ammunition to the Union army, and that was no small accomplishment.

At the beginning of the war, Ripley had only about 437,000 muskets and rifles in his inventory of government weapons, with only 40,000 being of any recent vintage, and he could count on only two federal armories capable of manufacturing arms, one at the Harpers Ferry arsenal and the other at the Springfield, Massachusetts, arsenal. The Springfield arsenal could be pushed to manufacture 3,000 rifles a month, but the Harpers Ferry arsenal (with most of its manufacturing equipment) had to be abandoned to the Confederates after the secession of Virginia from the Union. With no other alternative but outside contracting and foreign purchases, Ripley managed to acquire 727,000 arms from foreign dealers over the next year, and let out contracts to a variety of smaller arms manufacturers who subsequently built their fortunes on wartime government purchases—Remington, New Haven Arms (which in 1866 changed its name to Winchester), Smith & Wesson, and Samuel Colt. Ripley also expanded the armory at the Springfield arsenal to a production level of 300,000 weapons a year, and opened or enlarged nine other arsenals across the North. By the end of 1862, the federal government was making enough weapons to meet its own needs without more foreign imports, and by September, 1863, Ripley was able to report that the Springfield arsenal was now actually stockpiling surplus rifles.

None of these success stories about the supply of weapons or clothing or food might have amounted to much if the War Department had had no way of moving them to where they were needed. As it was, though, the greatest administrative success story of them all was Stanton's shrewd manipulation of the northern railroad system. The North began the war with 22,000 miles of railroads compared to the Confederacy's 9,000, and they carried with them the capacity to transport men and supplies at almost ten times less the cost of horse-and-wagon transport. Although Congress initially gave Lincoln authority to seize control of the northern railroads in 1862, Stanton instead set about striking a deal with the major rail operators, and less than a month after taking over the War Department, he sat down in a Washington hotel room with McClellan, Meigs, and the most important northern railroad presidents. They set a basic troop transportation rate (they agreed on two cents per mile per soldier, with eighty pounds of baggage each), and agreed on standardizing gauges among the lines (they settled for the English gauge of 4 feet, 8-½ inches), signaling systems, and freight. These arrangements effectively discouraged the disruption of rate wars by guaranteeing full-time operations to the rail lines, kept the military out of the railroad business by leaving all of the railroad company's offers in place to direct operations as normal, and moved the Union army and its supplies around the frontiers of the Confederacy fast enough to overcome the Confederacy's advantage of interior lines. By 1865, Stanton's deal with the railroads was moving 410,000 horses and 125,000 mules each year, plus 5 million tons of quartermaster, ordnance, and commissary stores.[33]

Together with the successful creation of a working staff within the War Department, and the extraordinary accomplishments of Meigs, Ripley, and Taylor as the major department heads, the Union forces never seriously lacked for the materials necessary to win the war. On the Confederate side of the ledger, however, the case was less happy. In a March 4, 1862, address to the Confederate congress, Jefferson Davis estimated that the Confederate armies would need 300,000 more men than they then had enlisted, 750,000 rifles, 5,000 cannon, and 5,000 tons of gunpowder, but at the same time he had to admit that he had no idea how the Confederacy was going to obtain them. The Confederacy had only one-ninth of the industrial capacity of the North, and only a relative handful of major industrial plants—the Tredegar Iron Works in Richmond, employing some 700 hands, the Shelby Iron Works and the Brierfield Furnace in northern Alabama, and the complex of iron works begun in Selma, Alabama, later in 1861. The Confederacy might have drawn some consolation from the fact that its lack of industrial promise was compensated for by the South's substantial agricultural resources. But even then, much of the South's agricultural produce was committed to cotton in order to pay for the Confederacy's foreign imports, and its principal grain-growing and meat-producing areas lay in the upper Confederacy, which fell into Union hands early in the war.

Not only was the Confederacy seriously deficient in railroad mileage at the onset of the war, but the two east-west rail systems that did manage to offer a fairly direct route across most of the Confederacy were both cut by the Union army before the summer of 1862. Furthermore, since so many of these lines had only been built with limited uses in view, they had been allowed to make do with poor sidings and fuel facilities and even poorer quality track, and by 1863, the excessive wear of wartime rail movement was chewing the southern rail lines up. But with the southern iron works already fully committed to manufacturing weapons, there were

[33]Paludan, *A People's Contest*, pp. 141–143; Nevins, *The War for the Union: The Organized War, 1863–1864* (New York, 1971), p. 301; Thomas Weber, *The Northern Railroads in the Civil War, 1861–1865* (New York, 1952), pp. 129–130, 223–224.

no means of also manufacturing new rail iron. Confederate officials were reduced to cannibalizing iron from unused branch lines to make repairs.

These problems were exacerbated by a sheer lack of organizational talent in the upper echelons of the Confederate government. As a former soldier and secretary of war himself, Davis was easily the superior of Lincoln in simple military experience. But Davis found it difficult locate competent officers and cabinet secretaries on the scale of Stanton or Meigs. Davis ran through four secretaries of war by November, 1862, and the personal military acquaintances whom Davis appointed to the quartermaster's and commissary departments were far from the standards set by their federal counterparts. By the spring of 1862, the Confederate commissary general, Lucius B. Northrop, was forced to start cutting the standard rations of the Confederate volunteer, and by the fall of 1864, it had fallen to one-third of a pound of meat and a pound of bread a day; and even with this reduction, the commissary's main depot in Richmond was often as low as only nine days' supply for the army. Northrop himself was forced to bear most of the blame for this situation as "the most cussed and vilified man in the Confederacy," and the vilification was aggravated by his enforcement of an impressment act in 1863 that authorized his agents to seize food supplies when farmers refused to sell them at the government rate.[34] But even taking Northrop's critics at face value, the fundamental cause of the shortages lay less with Northrop than with the deficiencies of the Confederate rail system. The Confederacy did not so much lack food supplies—both Grant and Sherman found plenty of food to pillage in their invasions of Mississippi and Georgia in 1863 and 1864—as it lacked easy means for getting them and then moving them where they were needed. The unhappy Northrop was driven to distraction in August of 1862 when he discovered that a shipment of meat from Nashville to Richmond had been delayed on the railroads by twenty days, during which the meat slowly spoiled into uselessness. By 1865, he had managed to bring 2.5 million rations of meat (most of it run through the blockade) and 700,000 rations of bread into Richmond. But little of it ever got into the haversacks of Lee's army.[35]

The one major exception to this gloomy schedule of inability in Davis's war administration was the aloof, hard-driving chief of ordnance, Josiah Gorgas. A northerner by birth and director of the Frankford Arsenal in Philadelphia, Gorgas had married a daughter of the governor of Alabama and threw in his hat with the southern cause. Resigning his commission in the U.S. Army, Gorgas took over the gun manufacturing machinery captured at Harpers Ferry, seized the cannon abandoned at the Norfolk Navy Yard, and proceeded to build a Confederate ordnance supply from scratch. He hired agents to scour Europe for weapons, and successfully ran 600,000 arms through the blockade on ships he had either bought or subsidized for the Confederate war department. Gorgas also established new armories across the South, built a chemical laboratory, a major gunpowder factory, and a new

[34]Chesnut, Mary Chesnut's Civil War, C. Vann Woodward, ed. (New Haven, CT, 1981), p. 124.
[35]Clement Eaton, A History of the Southern Confederacy (New York, 1954), p. 143.

cannon foundry in northern Georgia, and organized a string of eight new arsenals from Richmond to Selma, along with several other smaller gunworks in the Carolinas. Together, the new plants were manufacturing 170,000 rifle cartridges a day, and his gunpowder factory produced 2.7 million pounds of gunpowder over the course of the war.[36] By 1864, Gorgas was the only member of the Confederate war department who could really describe himself as an unqualified success—which he did not hesitate to do.

But Gorgas's successes also contained the basic germ of Confederate failure, for running through all of Gorgas's endeavors was the common fact that, as the chief of ordnance, Gorgas found himself directly intervening in the production as well as the administration of war material. Edwin Stanton, for all his driving determination to get the war moving, was respectful and cautious in dealing with the North's industrial potential. As a former corporate lawyer (like Lincoln), Stanton wanted "the aid of the highest business talent . . . this country can afford," and his arrangements with the northern railroads were carefully constructed to harness the military power of railroad technology, while leaving the actual direction of the railroads to the private sector.[37] Similarly, Stanton's quartermaster and commissary heads contracted out much of their needs for weapons, horses, and clothes by bid on the open market, rather than by appropriating existing industries for government use. By contrast, the Confederate war department moved to nationalize Confederate industry and develop state-sponsored enterprises, intervening dramatically in the Confederate economy by setting official prices for goods and even competing against its own citizens with government-owned blockade runners. Although this control fell considerably short of what some historians of the Confederacy have called "state socialism," it still meant that the Confederate government came to exercise substantial control over southern industrial production and prices. The South was, in fact, torn between its rhetorical approval of the planter aristocrat and its admiration for the cotton capitalist, and so the Confederacy's attempt to create an industrial base for its war effort by state subsidy and control was qualified, and often paralyzed, by a deep ambivalence about the marriage of war and market.[38]

Nothing illustrates better this hesitation between the ideology of the plantation and the ideology of the market than Confederate railroad policy. In 1861, then–Secretary of War Leroy Walker attempted to bargain with southern railroad presidents for a quid pro quo arrangement not unlike the one Stanton hammered out with the northern railroads a year later. But in February, 1862, the Confederate quartermaster department urged Jefferson Davis to disregard Walker's initiative and militarize the railroads "under the direction of an efficient superintendent, free from

[36]Eaton, *History of the Southern Confederacy*, p. 135; Frank E. Vandiver, *Their Tattered Flags: The Epic of the Confederacy* (New York, 1970), pp. 240–242.

[37]Hattaway and Jones, *How the North Won*, p. 121.

[38]Richard E. Beringer, Herman Hattaway, Archer Jones, and William Still, *Why the South Lost the Civil War* (Athens, GA, 1986), pp. 213–221.

local interests, investments, or connection with special railroads," and in March, the Confederate congress authorized Davis to take "absolute control and management of all railways and their rolling stock." But Davis, a cotton capitalist himself, hesitated to seize control of the railroads outright, and railroad presidents begged and parried for exemptions, advantages, and special orders prohibiting military interference with their railroads.[39] This muddle of directives served no real purpose except to signal departmental Confederate military commanders that there was no coherent railroad policy, and that they were free to offer abysmally low rates for transportation, disrupt freight schedules with claims for military priority, and generally run the South's limited supply of locomotives and boxcars until they fell apart. By the end of the war, the feeble southern railway system had been run into the ground by the unsure policies of the Confederate government and military.[40]

The struggle of the Union and Confederacy economies to supply and support their armies thus became a reflection of the prewar republic's ideological struggles over the market revolution, and in that respect the Civil War assumed many of the tones of the old debate about the nature of republicanism itself. The "free labor" ideology of the Republican party, with its confidence that a "harmony of interests" naturally existed between capital and labor, found convenient expression in Stanton's decision to step back from drastic economic interventions and allow the northern capitalism to lay its golden eggs for the war effort. The Confederacy, torn between the urgings of an authoritarian labor system and the lure of the markets, was no less torn between sanctioning wildcat entrepreneurism and imposing state-ordered controls. And in that indecision lay many of the seeds of the Confederacy's destruction.

Further Reading

The Confederacy's attempts to draw France and England into the war as mediators or belligerents has received surprisingly good coverage from both English and American sources, although the consensus that has emerged from that literature leans toward the opinion that the Confederacy never really had much serious prospect of being actively protected by either European power. Howard Jones's *Union in Peril: The Crisis Over British Intervention in the Civil War* (Chapel Hill, NC, 1993) makes it clear how limited British enthusiasm for the Confederacy really was, and also how differently the Emancipation Proclamation was read at the various levels of British government and society. J. M. Hernon, in "British Sympathies in the American Civil War," *Journal of Southern History* 33 (August 1967) and Philip Foner's *British Labor and the American Civil War,* (New York, 1981) argue that the British working classes were never really sympathetic to the Confederacy despite their sufferings, but an entirely opposite case is

---

[39]Mary A. DeCredico, *Patriotism for Profit: Georgia's Urban Entrepreneurs and the Confederate War Effort* (Chapel Hill, NC, 1990), pp. 76–90.

[40]Turner, *Victory Rode the Rails,* p. 172; Jeffrey N. Lash, *Destroyer of the Iron Horse: General Joseph E. Johnston and Confederate Rail Transport, 1861–1865* (Kent, OH, 1991), p. 186

made by Mary Ellison's *Support for Secession: Lancashire and the American Civil War* (Chicago, 1972). Henry Blumenthal's *France and the United States: Their Diplomatic Relations, 1789–1914* (Chapel Hill, NC, 1970) and Lynn Case and Warren Spencer's *The United States and France: Civil War Diplomacy* (Philadelphia, 1970) draw some of the same conclusions from an examination of Franco-American diplomacy. The Confederacy's one major French success, the Erlanger loan, is explained in J. F. Gentry, "A Confederate Success in Europe: The Erlanger Loan," in *Journal of Southern History* 26 (May 1970).

The story of the blockade runners themselves has been told best in Stephen R. Wise's *Lifeline of the Confederacy: Blockade-Running During the Civil War* (Columbia, SC, 1988), but Frank Owsley's *King Cotton Diplomacy: Foreign Relations of the Confederate States of America* (Chicago, 1931) is still a useful survey of blockade running, although Owsley's thesis that the blockade was easily outwitted and played little role in the Confederacy's defeat is dubious. The ingenuity with which the Confederates fashioned a fleet of ironclad warships has been told by veteran naval historian William N. Still in *Iron Afloat: The Story of the Confederate Armorclads* (1971; rept. Columbia, SC, 1985). The Confederate secretary of the navy who was the spark for much of that ingenuity awaits a modern biography, but Joseph T. Durkin's *Stephen R. Mallory* (Chapel Hill, NC, 1938) is still a worthy account of Mallory's life. The diplomatic intrigues, the blockade runners, and the commerce raiders have distracted attention from the story of gunboat warfare on the Mississippi, which has been studied in fine detail by James M. Merrill, *Battle Flags South: The Story of the Civil War Navies down the Mississippi* (Rutherford, NJ, 1970).

Stephen Mallory's opposite number in Lincoln's cabinet has also enjoyed outstanding biographical treatment from John Niven in *Gideon Welles: Lincoln's Secretary of the Navy* (New York, 1973) and Richard S. West, Jr., in *Gideon Welles: Lincoln's Navy Department* (Indianapolis, IN, 1953), and Welles's famous diaries have been edited by Howard K. Beale in three volumes as *The Diary of Gideon Welles, Secretary of the Navy Under Lincoln and Johnson* (New York, 1960). The momentous combat of the *Monitor* and *Virginia* has never been better told than in William C. Davis's lively and detailed *Duel Between the First Ironclads* (New York, 1975). Seward's diplomatic *faux pas* in the first year of the war have been dealt with in a more positive fashion by Norman Ferris in his aptly titled *Desperate Diplomacy: William Henry Seward's Foreign Policy, 1861* (Knoxville, TN, 1977) and in *The Trent Affair* (Knoxville, TN, 1975). Managing the war feil in large measure to Stanton, whose biography by Harold Hyman and Benjamin P. Thomas, *Stanton: The Life and Times of Lincoln's Secretary of War* (New York, 1962) is one of the models of Civil War biographical literature. An outstanding general survey of the organization of the North's economic resources during the war is Philip Shaw Paludan's *A People's Contest: The Union and the Civil War* (New York, 1988).

Under the Confederate flag, *Confederate Supply* (Durham, NC, 1969) has been surveyed by Richard D. Goff. However, none of the Confederacy's supply managers has received as much praise or attention as Josiah Gorgas. Frank Vandiver not only provided a biography of Gorgas in *Ploughshares into Swords: Josiah Gorgas and Confederate Ordnance* (Austin, TX, 1952) but also edited and published Gorgas's diary as *The Civil War Diary of General Josiah Gorgas* (University, AL, 1947). The Confederate rail system and its eventual breakdown has been chronicled in Robert C. Black, *The Railroads of the Confederacy* (Chapel Hill, NC, 1952).

The argument that the Confederacy adopted a form of "state socialism" in order to meet the war's industrial needs grows out of the increasing control that the Confederate government exercised over the southern economy during the war. This argument was first put forward by Louise Hill in *State Socialism in the Confederate States of America* (Charlottesville, VA, 1936), and received a more recent restatement in Raimondo Luraghi's article, "The Civil War and the Modernization of American Society," in *Civil War History* 18 (September 1972) and Luraghi's subsequent book, *The Rise and Fall of the Plantation South* (New York, 1978). The "state socialism" thesis has some attraction, especially for those who interpret the Civil War as a struggle by northern capitalism to impose a liberal industrial order on America, but it has to be seriously qualified by the halfhearted ways in which the Confederate government imposed state control over private industry, and the ways in which Mary A. DeCredico has shown in *Patriotism for Profit: Georgia's Urban Entrepreneurs and the Confederate War Effort* (Chapel Hill, NC, 1990) that individual entrepreneurship continued to flourish during the war. Richard F. Bensel has presented a similar case for interpreting the Confederacy as a remarkable example of state centralization in *Yankee Leviathan: The Origins of Central State Authority in America, 1859–1879* (Cambridge, 1990), although less with a view toward portraying the Confederacy as a precapitalist state and more toward seeing the war as an experiment in the centralization of state power for both North and South.

CHAPTER 8

Year That Trembled

East and West: 1863

Early on the morning of April 1, 1863, an angry group of women gathered in the small, squat brick building of the Belvidere Hill Baptist Church in the Oregon Hill section of Richmond. They met for complaint, not for prayer. Some of the women had husbands in the Confederate army and were fending for themselves on the pittances they could earn and the unkept promises of assistance made by the Confederate government. Others had husbands in the Tredegar Iron Works whose pay fell woefully short of what was needed to keep soul and body together. Food supplies in the Confederate capital were dwindling as the fruits of the last year's harvest were drawn down by Robert E. Lee's army and the civilian population of the city, and what was now offered for sale by Richmond's merchants, bakers, and butchers was going for astronomical prices. One woman, Mary Jackson (who was variously described as a farmer's wife, a sign-painter's wife, and the mother of a soldier), stood up behind the pulpit of the church and demanded action: Let the working-class women of Richmond assemble the next day and march to Governor John Letcher's mansion on Capitol Square, and force the governor to make good on the promises of assistance. And if assistance was not forthcoming, then let them turn on the "extortioners" in the shops and levy their own brand of fairness by ransacking the bakeries and stalls for what they needed.

The next morning, a crowd of 300 women joined Mary Jackson at a city marketplace four blocks from Capital Square. Armed with a Bowie knife and revolver, Jackson led a seething procession through the streets to the state capitol, where Letcher met them on the front steps. The governor, however, had nothing to offer them but a few expressions of personal concern, and after a short speech, he retreated to his office and left the dissatisfed crowd milling around in capitol square. Another woman named Mary Johnson, "a tall, daring Amazonian looking woman" with a "white feather, standing erect from her hat," took the lead of the crowd and pointed them down Richmond's Main Street. Knives, guns, and hatchets appeared and the crowd surged down the street toward Richmond's shops.[1]

Over the next several hours, all semblance of order disappeared in Richmond's commercial district as the enraged women broke down doors and windows, seized bread and meat, and then went on to loot jewelry, clothing, and hats. The hapless Governor Letcher and Richmond's mayor, Joseph Mayo, appeared on the scene to calm the mob, but the women were beyond the calm words of the politicians. At last, the Richmond Public Guard, called out by Governor Letcher, filed into Main Street. Someone or some people in the crowd pulled a wagon into the street as a hasty barricade, and at that moment, all that was needed for Confederate soldiers to begin shooting down Confederate women in the streets of Richmond was one reckless gesture, one careless word.

No one had ever thought of Jefferson Davis as possessing a dramatist's sense of timing, but on this occasion, the president of the Confederacy appeared at precisely the right moment. It is not clear who summoned Davis, or whether Davis (who lived only a few blocks away) was simply following his own ear for trouble, but he found the mob and the soldiers at the point where each was ready to begin shooting. Coolness under pressure had been Davis's long suit ever since his army days, and he quickly mounted the barricade wagon and began to speak. His speech was conciliatory, reproachful, and threatening by turns. He knew they were hungry, but he pointed out that farmers in the countryside would only be more unwilling to bring their produce to market in Richmond if they knew that it would be stolen by rioters there. He shamed them by pointing to the stolen jewelry and clothing in their hands when their protest was supposed to be for bread. He even offered them money from his own pockets. But he closed by taking out his pocket watch and announcing that if the crowd had not dispersed in five minutes, he would order the soldiers to open fire. A minute or two crawled past, and then the crowd slowly began to break up and drift away. Eventually forty-four women and twenty-nine men were arrested on theft and riot charges.[2]

The Richmond bread riot was not an isolated case. During 1863, similar riots broke out in Georgia, North Carolina, and Alabama; in Mobile, a crowd of women carrying banners with slogans like *Bread or Blood* and *Bread and Peace* marched down Dauphine Street, smashing shop windows as they went. The war Southerners had entered so confidently two years before was now imposing strains on southern society that few could have imagined. The creation of a workable southern nation required more than enthusiasm. It required time to make a compelling case for the secession that had led to this war, and still more time in which to sort out the ambivalences and tensions in southern society—tensions between slaveholders and nonslaveholders, between the lovely image of the South as a society of plantation aristocrats and the grubbier realities of cotton capitalism, between the democratic model of personal independence and states' rights and the need to centralize every

[1]Michael B. Cresson, "Harlots or Heroines? A New Look at the Richmond Bread Riot," in *Virginia Magazine of History and Biography* 92 (April 1984) pp. 131–175.
[2]William C. Davis, *Jefferson Davis: The Man and His Hour* (New York, 1991), pp. 497–498.

southern resource in order to win the war. Unfortunately, time was in short supply in the Confederacy. Southern armies were losing territory, southern men were avoiding war service, southern families were going hungry, and even great southern planters found themselves at the mercy of crafty financial "extortioners." If Southerners were ever to have the time needed to understand why they were fighting this war, then the Confederate armies must strike and strike quickly to secure Confederate independence, or else the stress of performing this experiment in nation building under the sword of war would push the southern nation into collapse.[3]

The day after the Richmond bread riot, the lead editorial in the Richmond *Dispatch* was resolutely headlined, "Sufferings In The North."

1. Someone More Fit to Command

On November 7, 1862, President Lincoln finally dismissed George Brinton McClellan from command of the Army of the Potomac. The immediate reason for McClellan's dismissal was his slowness in pursuit of Lee's battered Army of Northern Virginia after its hammering at Antietam. But looming behind that was the larger conflict between Lincoln and McClellan over the president's new war policy goals on slavery and emancipation, goals that McClellan most emphatically did not share. Getting rid of McClellan only solved half the problem; it now became necessary for Lincoln to find a replacement who would be willing to carry out faithfully the president's war aims, and be aggressive enough to pursue and bring to battle the Army of Northern Virginia. At first, Lincoln thought he had found such a man in one of McClellan's corps commanders, Major General Ambrose Burnside. A florid, six-foot Rhode Islander, with a pair of immense muttonchop whiskers, Burnside was admired by one reporter as "the very *beau ideal* of a soldier." A West Point graduate of 1847, Burnside had served briefly in the Mexican War, and then resigned from the Army in 1852 to go into the arms business, where he successfully patented a single-shot breechloading rifle known as the Burnside carbine. When the war broke out, he personally raised the 1st Rhode Island Volunteers and commanded the expedition that captured Roanoke Island in February of 1862. The Roanoke Island expedition made Burnside's reputation as an aggressive combat soldier, and when McClellan's Peninsula campaign collapsed that July, Lincoln offered Burnside command of the Army of the Potomac on the spot. But Burnside felt too much personal gratitude to McClellan for past favors to take advantage of McClellan's failure, and he instead chose to serve under McClellan as commander of the 9th Corps of the Army of the Potomac. By November, however, there was no question that McClellan had to leave the army, and Burnside reluctantly obeyed Lincoln's summons to replace him.

That reluctance should have warned Lincoln that all was not what it seemed

---

[3]Drew G. Faust, *The Creation of Confederate Nationalism: Ideology and Identity in the Civil War South* (Baton Rouge, LA, 1988), pp. 49–57.

with Burnside. Despite the reputation he had won as a fighter in the Roanoke expedition, Burnside was actually hesitant and unsure of himself as a general, and the higher he ascended the ladder of command responsibilities, the more hesitant and unsure he grew. At Antietam, McClellan had ordered Burnside to throw his corps across a bridge on the Antietam Creek and attack Lee's right flank. Instead, fearing that the Confederates on the other side of the bridge were too many for his corps to push past, Burnside dallied for almost the entire afternoon of the battle. When he finally mustered enough resolve to attack across the bridge, he discovered that only a thin curtain of Confederate skirmishers had been defending it. By his hesitation and caution, Burnside was a major part of the failure to crush Lee's army, and he escaped criticism only because so much of Lincoln's disappointed wrath after Antietam was poured out on McClellan's head instead.

Burnside also had two other weights on his shoulders beside those of the Army of the Potomac and his purported reputation as a fighter. First, he was aware that despite the lateness of the year, Lincoln and the War Department would expect him to mount a campaign as soon as possible to make up for the time McClellan had wasted in the fall. Second, there would be no patience with further plans for an indirect campaign down to the James River peninsula, with a careful and bloodless siege of Richmond. Lincoln wanted confrontation, not turning movements, and that meant making Lee and the Army of Northern Virginia the real object of attack, not the city of Richmond. So, within a week of taking over the Army of the Potomac, Burnside called his seven corps commanders together and unveiled his plan—abandoning the James River route, he would march overland, cross the Rappahannock River at Fredericksburg, and draw Lee into a knock-down-drag-out fight in the flat country somewhere between Fredericksburg and Richmond. Since the bridges across the Rappahannock at Fredericksburg had been destroyed, Burnside would surprise Lee by building a bridge of pontoon boats there, and be on the south side of the Rappanhannock before Lee knew what was happening.

The critical point in this plan was getting across the Rappahannock quickly, for if Lee got wind of what was happening, and moved the Army of Northern Virginia to Fredericksburg first, the Army of the Potomac would have to fight its way across the Rappahannock and out of Fredericksburg at a decided disadvantage. And unhappily for Burnside, this was precisely what happened. Although Burnside took only three days, from November 14 to November 17, to march the Army of the Potomac down to the Rappahannock opposite Fredericksburg, his pontoons were nowhere to be found. And by the time that the pontoon train finally arrived from Washington on November 25, Lee had frantically assembled the scattered corps of the Army of Northern Virginia and dug them in along a ridge known as Marye's Heights, overlooking Fredericksburg. The advantage of surprise had been lost.

In any other circumstances, a commander of the Army of the Potomac would have been well advised to give up the campaign as lost at that moment and gone into winter quarters until spring brought fairer weather. But Burnside was under too much pressure from Washington to stop now, and he ordered the river crossing forced and the pontoon bridges built under fire. Remarkably, his soldiers and engineers pulled it off, and by December 12, 1862 a shaky bridge had been floated across the Rappahannock and the town of Fredericksburg secured. But there still remained the Confederates on the heights beyond the town, and on December 13th, as if to annihilate all memory of his hesitancy at Antietam, Burnside threw the Army of the Potomac at the Confederates in, not one or two, but six formal, perfectly drilled but ghastly frontal assaults. From behind a stone wall at the foot of Marye's Heights, the Confederates mowed down the thick, slow-moving federal formations all day, until more than 12,000 Union soldiers were dead or wounded, 6,000 of them alone piled in front of Marye's Heights. "We had to advance over a level plane, and their batteries being on high ground and they being behind breastworks, we had no chance at them, while they could take as deliberate aim as a fellow would at a chicken," wrote George Washington Whitman to his brother three weeks after the battle, "The range was so short, that they threw percussion shells into our ranks that would drop at our feet and explode, killing and wounding Three or four every pop."[4] The next day, Burnside wanted to make one more attack, led by himself personally, but his disgusted corps commanders talked him out of it.

Burnside withdrew to the north bank of the Rappahannock, hoping for a second chance to get at Lee. But when he started a new campaign on January 19, 1863, to get across the Rappahannock several miles further west, winter rains turned the roads into bottomless morasses, and Burnside's infamous "Mud March" slopped to a halt. With the soldiers of the Army of the Potomac demoralized and deserting in record numbers, with most of Burnside's corps commanders publicly criticizing his ineptitude, Lincoln had no choice but to relieve him.

Lincoln's second choice for a general for the Army of the Potomac was yet another soldier with a reputation for aggressiveness, Major General Joseph Hooker. A handsome, happy-go-lucky brawler with an alcoholic red nose and an awesome command of old army profanity, Hooker had the added advantage (as far as Lincoln was concerned) of being one of the few anti-McClellan officers in the upper echelons of the Army of the Potomac. He was also a surprisingly good administrator, and he spent the first three months of 1863 restoring shattered morale and organization until, by April, 1863, Hooker was able to invite Lincoln down to the army's camps on the Rappahannock for a grand review. But while Hooker was an uncommon organizer and a popular division and corps commander, there was some question about whether he possessed "the weight of character" needed to "take charge of that army." Hooker was, in fact, a bragger and a show-off. He deliberately played up to the press to swell his image as a stern, remorseless campaigner, and he reveled in the nickname the newspapers happily bestowed upon him, "Fighting Joe Hooker." But despite the image, Hooker grew unsteady and unsure under pressure. "He could play the best game of poker I ever saw," commented Hooker's chief of cavalry, George Stoneman, "until it came to the point where he should go a thousand better, and

---

[4]Civil War Letters of George Washington Whitman, Jerome M. Loving, ed. (Durham, NC, 1975), p. 78.

then he would flunk."[5] But far worse, Hooker was also grasping and unscrupulous, loyal only to his own ambitions. He had privately damned McClellan behind the general's back to members of the Cabinet, and undercut Burnside's authority so often by criticism and innuendo that the normally placid Burnside beseeched Lincoln to have Hooker court-martialed for insubordination. "Gen. Hooker," wrote Colonel Theodore Gates of the 20th New York, "is reputed a very ambitious & some what unscrupulous man."[6] It was an open secret that Hooker had even taken it upon himself to criticize Lincoln, and Lincoln bluntly informed Hooker that he had only appointed him to command the Army of the Potomac with serious reservations. "I have heard, in such way as to believe it, of your recently saying that both the Army and the Government needed a Dictator," wrote Lincoln in a letter he quietly handed to Hooker after summoning the general to the White House to appoint him as commander of the Army of the Potomac:

> Of course it was not *for* this, but in spite of it, that I have given you the command. Only those generals who gain successes, can set up dictators. What I now ask of you is military success, and I will risk the dictatorship. . . . I much fear that the spirit which you have aided to infuse into the Army, of criticizing their Commander, and withholding confidence from him, will now turn upon you.[7]

Hooker now proceeded to confirm every one of the worst of those reservations. To begin with, his plans were little more than a variation of Burnside's: the Army of the Potomac would again attempt to cross the Rappahannock and force a fight with the Army of Northern Virginia above Richmond. Since the Fredericksburg crossing was obviously too dangerous, Hooker left two of his infantry corps opposite Fredericksburg as decoys, while actually crossing the Rappahannock about twelve miles to the west. In theory, this would bring the bulk of the Army of the Potomac across the Rappahannock and down onto Lee's left flank at Fredericksburg before the Confederates could act; Lee would be forced to fight, pinned against the Rappahannock, or to fall back on Richmond. Unhappily for Hooker, the country on the other side of the Rappahannock where he proposed to cross was a dark, unsettled tangle of woods and scrub underbrush, crisscrossed by few usable roads, and known only as the Wilderness. And when, on May 1st, Hooker got his corps around and over the Rappahannock and into the Wilderness, its impassable and spooky terrain caused the general's aggressiveness to falter. Rather than advance, Hooker decided over the protests of his corps commanders to entrench the army around a little country crossroads called Chancellorsville, and wait to see what would happen, which was usually a fatal thing to do in the vicinity of Robert E. Lee.

As it was, Lee had been as surprised by Hooker's move as by Burnside's back in

---

[5]Alexander K. McClure, *Recollections of Half a Century* (Salem, MA, 1902), p. 348.

[6]*The Civil War Diaries of Col. Theodore B. Gates, 20th New York State Militia*, Seward R. Osborne, ed. (Hightstown, NJ, 1991), p. 60.

[7]Lincoln, "To Joseph Hooker" [January 26, 1863], in *Collected Works*, vol. 6, pp. 78–79.

December, but he took as full advantage of Hooker's hesitancy as he had of Burnside's difficulty with his pontoon bridges. While the Army of the Potomac entrenched, Lee left only a thin line of Confederate troops to guard Fredericksburg, and pulled the rest over to confront Hooker in the Wilderness. He had only 43,000 men (one entire corps of the Army of Northern Virginia was absent on detached service) to face Hooker's 73,000. And yet, shrewdly sensing that Hooker was already losing his nerve, Lee threw the single most dramatic gamble of the Civil War. Dividing his already under-strength army into two parts, he ordered "Stonewall" Jackson to march his 26,000-man corps entirely around the right flank of Hooker's army and use the advantage of surprise to crumple Hooker's line like a piece of paper. Jackson began his flank march at 6:00 A.M. on May 2, 1863, and after twelve hours of marching, his men were in position on the edge of the unsuspecting 11th Corps of the Army of the Potomac. Near 6:00 P.M. Jackson sent his men screaming through the woods, and just as Lee had guessed, the unprepared federals fell to pieces. Only the fall of darkness prevented Jackson from rolling right over Hooker's headquarters. Over the next two days, Lee pressed home his attack again and again, while the bewildered and paralyzed Hooker simply drew his lines in tighter. Finally, on May 5th, Hooker had had enough and pulled his army back over the Rappahannock. He had lost nearly 17,000 men and a major battle, and what was more, had lost them to a force nearly half the size of his own, and had done it while nearly one-third of his own army stood idle for want of orders from its confused and vacillating commander. It was now Hooker's turn to fall prey to the same rumor mill he had so often turned himself, and on May 13th, Lincoln informed Hooker that his corps and division commanders were already muttering loudly behind the general's back. Not that Lincoln intended to do anything about it: He vetoed a proposal for a new crossing of the Rappahannock that Hooker telegraphed to him on May 13th, and the following month, seeing the handwriting on the wall, the exasperated Hooker resigned.

By this time a certain paranoia had begun to set in among the officers of the Army of the Potomac: Could the Army of Northern Virginia ever be beaten? By the summer of 1863, it seemed not. "Everywhere but here success crowns our arms," complained Theodore Gates. "The Army of the Potomac which has been petted & lauded ad nauseum & drilled & dressed more and better than any other in the service has accomplished absolutely nothing. . . . So our Generals rise & fall one after another."[8] Even the Army of Northern Virginia was becoming convinced of its own invincibility. George Henry Mills of the 16th North Carolina went cheerfully into camp with his regiment after Chancellorsville, "where we put in the time drilling on the beautiful fields of the Rappahannock and waiting for Halleck to put up another General for us to whip."[9] The magnetic pole of that confidence, beyond any question, was the figure of Lee, and by the summer of 1863, Lee enjoyed a

[8]*Civil War Diaries of Col. Theodore B. Gates,* pp. 60, 63.
[9]Mills, *History of the 16th North Carolina Regiment in the Civil War* (1903; rept. Hamilton, NY, 1992), p. 33.

degree of adulation from his own army that few generals have ever seen. Lieutenant Wesley Lewis Battle of the 37th North Carolina watched Lee return the salute of his regiment at a review on May 29, 1863, and Lieutenant Battle's reaction surprised even himself:

> After the review was over & we were marching back to Camp, Gen. A. P. Hill rode up to Col. Barbour & told him to make his Regt. give three cheers for Gen. Lee. It is impossible for me to describe the emotions of my heart as the old silver-headed hero acknowledged the salute by taking off his hat, thereby exposing the most noble countenance I ever beheld. I felt proud that the Southern Confederacy could boast of such a man. In fact I was almost too proud for the occasion, for I could not open my mouth to give vent to the emotions that were struggling within.[10]

Actually much of Lee's success as a commander was a result of three unrelated factors. The first was clearly his adroit choice and management of his subordinate officers. Lee succeeded in gathering around him a remarkable collection of military talent, especially "Stonewall" Jackson and James Longstreet, with whom he communicated on an almost intuitive level. With officers like this on hand, it became Lee's style only to give general shape to plans for a campaign or battle, and to leave the actual execution to his subordinates, confident that they understood his intentions so perfectly that on-the-spot decision-making could be left entirely to their own discretion. It was just as well that he enjoyed that rare sense of cooperation with his subordinates, for none of Lee's major corps commanders—Jackson, A. P. Hill, Longstreet, Richard Ewell—showed much capacity to get along intuitively or otherwise with each other. Jackson and Hill in particular carried on a spiteful and venomous vendetta against each other, culminating in 1863, when Jackson attempted to have Hill cashiered.[11]

Lee alone seemed exempt from the friction of the talented and prickly personalities in the upper command levels of the Army of Northern Virginia, partly because of his own personal reticence and partly because he could rely on the social aura with which his place at the apex of southern plantation society surrounded him. For Lee, unlike his senior officers, was the only major representative of the slaveholding planter class in the top hierarchy of the army. "Stonewall" Jackson was an orphan, raised in the yeoman farmer counties of western Virginia, and most observers were struck by how much he looked like a farmer rather than a general. Captain William Seymour of the Louisiana Tiger battalion noticed that Jackson regularly wore nothing more impressive than "an old rusty, sunburnt grey coat and a faded blue cap of a peculiar pattern, the top of which fell forward over his eyes." From his appearance, wrote George Henry Mills, "no one would have suspected that he was more than a

[10]"In the Words of His Own Men: As They Saw General Lee," Everard H. Smith, ed., in *Civil War Times Illustrated* 25 (October 1986), p. 22.

[11]Douglas Southall Freeman, *Lee's Lieutenants: A Study in Command, Volume Two, Cedar Mountain to Chancellorsville* (New York, 1943), pp. 510–514.

Corporal in a cavalry company." James Longstreet, another son of yeoman farmers, also lost his father at an early age and labored under the added disadvantage (in this army) of having no Virginia connections (born in South Carolina, Longstreet had grown up in Georgia under the tutelage of his slave-owning uncle, Augustus Baldwin Longstreet). Richard Ewell was a pop-eyed eccentric who lisped vulgarities and profanity. Only Ambrose Powell Hill's family came close to conferring any kind of recognizable social status on him, and even then, Powell Hill's father was a townsman and a merchant rather than a landholder. Hill was also known to be as rakish and irreligious as "Stonewall" Jackson was a severe and devout Presbyterian.[12]

Lee, by contrast, came from the elite of Virginia Tidewater society and classical Virginia Episcopalianism (even though much of his land and slaves had come from his wife's family and not through Lee's spendthrift and bankrupt father). And although Lee had repeatedly expressed before the war his personal preference for seeing slavery brought to an end at the right time, like most Virginia slaveholders, he found that the right time was never within the foreseeable future. In every respect, Lee was the embodiment of the ideal Virginia planter—decent, gentlemanly, religious, and immovably convinced that slavery was, for the unending present, the best of all possible worlds for African Americans.[13] And he expected, demanded, and received from his subordinate officers precisely the unarguable deference that his herrenvolk lieutenants were conditioned and expected to give to the slaveholding elite of the white South.

Another key to Lee's successes on the battlefield was his cultivation of good relations with Jefferson Davis. The Confederate president originally intended to use Lee in much the same way that Stanton used Henry Halleck, as a general military advisor and liaison between the army and the government, and from March until June, 1862, Lee worked behind a desk in Richmond as an informal military chief of staff to the Confederate president. Although Joseph E. Johnston's wound in the Peninsula campaign forced Davis to put Lee into field command, the two remained in very close communication throughout the war, and Lee's victories on the peninsula convinced Davis to yield to Lee's strategic judgment throughout the ensuing eighteen months. By 1863, Lee had become indispensable to Davis: As Davis wrote to Lee in 1863, to find "someone in my judgment more fit to command, or who would possess more of the confidence of the army, or of the reflecting men of the country, is to demand an impossibility."[14] Thus, Lee was able to exercise, through Davis, an outsize influence over the shape of Confederate military operations and logistics.

[12]The Civil War Memoirs of Captain William J. Seymour: Reminiscences of a Louisiana Tiger, Terry L. Jones, ed. (Baton Rouge, LA, 1991), p. 49; Mills, History of the 16th North Carolina, p. 18; William Garrett Piston, Lee's Tarnished Lieutenant: James Longstreet and His Place in Southern History (Athens, GA, 1987), pp. 2–5; James I. Robertson, General A. P. Hill: The Story of a Confederate Warrior (New York, 1987), pp. 5–7, 303.

[13]Alan T. Nolan, Lee Considered: General Robert E. Lee and Civil War History (Chapel Hill, NC, 1991), pp. 9–29.

[14]Davis to Lee [August 11, 1863], in Official Records, series 1, vol. 29 (part 2), p. 640.

The most important key to Lee's successes was his almost innate aggressiveness. Beneath the statuesque calm and dignity that his soldiers and enemies so admired, Lee was a volcano of aggressive impulses. In the spring of 1862, when he was still a relatively new and untried article, one man asked Colonel Joseph Ives, who knew Lee, whether Lee possessed sufficient vigor and audacity to defend Richmond. "If there is one man in either army, Confederate or Federal, head and shoulders above every other in *audacity* it is General Lee. His name might be audacity. He will take more desperate chances, and take them quicker than any other general in this country, North or South; and you will live to see it, too."[15] Ives's prediction was amply borne out, for Lee easily turned into a different man on the battlefield from the one he was in the drawing room. Lee leaped to the attack at every opportunity, invading the North twice in 1862 and 1863 and taking the tactical offensive in every major battle he fought in those years (except for Antietam and Fredericksburg). The cost in lives for this aggressiveness was not cheap—Lee's men sustained 42,000 casualties in his first four months in command of the Army of Northern Virginia (almost as many men as Albert Sidney Johnston commanded at Shiloh)—but Lee at least achieved in the process the most extraordinary combat victories of the war, and at Second Bull Run, he came as close as any other Civil War general to the complete annihilation of an opposing army. Lee was prepared to fight the Civil War in Virginia as a great Napoleonic conflict, and even after the terrible pounding his army took at Antietam, Lee was ready four days afterward to "threaten a passage into Maryland, to occupy the enemy on this frontier, and, if my purpose cannot be accomplished, to draw them into the [Shenandoah] Valley, where I can attack them to advantage."[16]

On the other hand, each of these parts of Lee's success as a commander also carried within it the seeds of Lee's destruction. Lee's heavy reliance on the talents of his corps commanders to win battles rendered him much too vulnerable, emotionally and strategically, should any of them fall to wounds or death. At Chancellorsville, this was exactly what happened to "Stonewall" Jackson. Accidentally wounded by his own men while performing a risky nighttime reconnaissance, Jackson lost his left arm, and then eight days later, died of complications from the amputation. Lee never found a suitable replacement for Jackson, and with Jackson's death, Lee lost one of the few men capable of turning his audacious plans for offensive warfare into tactical victories. After Jackson, Lee had to depend on Longstreet, whose preference for defensive warfare occasionally led him into outright contradictions of Lee's plans, and on Ewell and Hill, neither of whom ever generated the raw hitting power of Jackson. Similarly, Lee's influence over Davis tended to operate to the advantage of Virginia, and at the expense of the rest of the Confederacy. By 1863, Davis was under substantial pressure from within his own

---

[15]Douglas Southall Freeman, *R. E. Lee* (New York, 1935), vol. 2, p. 92.

[16]Grady McWhiney and Perry D. Jamieson, *Attack and Die: Civil War Military Tactics and the Southern Heritage* (University, AL, 1982), p. 19; Lee to Davis, September 21, 1863, in *Official Records*, series 1, vol. 19 (part 1), p. 143.

government to shift the weight of the Confederate war effort to the West, and reduce the war in Virginia to a defensive holding action. Lee, however, had sacrificed his first career in the United States army for the sake of Virginia, and he was not about to see his second career in the Confederate army compel him to make a similar choice. Hence, Lee tenaciously fought every suggestion made to Davis that the Army of Northern Virginia be denuded to reenforce the West, and his influence over Davis guaranteed, at least until the fall of 1863, that the defense of Virginia would always be able to outweigh the demands for help from the Confederate forces in the West.[17]

Lastly, Lee's keen tactical judgment was inevitably going to be affected by the increasing deterioration of his health and by the deepening sense of fatalism caused by the losses his incessant urge for the offensive produced. By the spring of 1863, Lee was 56 years old, prematurely white-haired, and already suffering from severe arthritis. During the Maryland campaign, his beloved horse, Traveller, bolted while Lee was seated holding his reins, and the general was dragged over the ground by the frightened horse, spraining both wrists and breaking bones in his hands. Then, on March 30, 1863, Lee suffered the first of a series of heart attacks, a premonition of the heart disease that would, after the war, eventually kill him. All of these ills and accidents took a severe toll on Lee's energies, both in camp and in battle. "Old age & sorrow is wearing me away," Lee wrote to his wife, Mary Custis Lee, in March, 1863, "& constant anxiety & labour, day and night, leaves me but little repose."[18] Along with the physical wear and tear of his command, Lee had to cope with the deaths of irreplaceable subordinates like Jackson, and the deaths of his beloved daughter Annie and daughter-in-law, Charlotte Wickham. "I had always counted, if God should spare me a few days of peace after this cruel war was over, that I should have her with me," he wrote after Annie Lee died in 1862, "But year after year my hopes go out, and I must be resigned." And since his Virginia Episcopalianism was one of the principal strongholds of Calvinist Evangelicalism within the Episcopal Church, Lee's sense of resignation increasingly found shape in a mystical submission to the mysterious workings of an all-controlling Providence. "The ties to earth are taken, one by one, by our Merciful God to turn our hearts to Him and to show us that the object of this life is to prepare for a better and brighter world." And yet, as in so many similar cases, Lee's afflictions only made him more willing than ever to throw himself and his army into the balances of battle. "Our country demands all our strength, all our energies," Lee wrote, "If victorious, we have everything to hope for in the future. If defeated, nothing will be left for us to live for. . . . My whole trust is in God, and I am ready for whatever He may ordain."[19]

[17]Thomas L. Connelly, The Marble Man: Robert E. Lee and His Image in American Society (New York, 1977), pp. 202–203.

[18]Lee to Mary Custis Lee [March 9, 1863], in The Wartime Papers of R. E. Lee, Clifford Dowdey and Louis H. Minarin, eds. (Boston, 1961), p. 413.

[19]J. William Jones, Life and Letters of Robert Edward Lee (1906; rept. Harrisonburg, VA, 1978), pp. 200, 207; Freeman, R. E. Lee, vol. 3, p. 268.

Affliction was now, in the summer of 1863, about to be visited on Lee in unprecedented amounts. Lee's victories on the peninsula reinforced all of his inclinations to take the offensive against the federal armies; that, combined with his preoccupation with the protection of Virginia, persuaded Lee that the best way to spare his beloved state from the horrors of war and dishearten northern public opinion was to carry the war north, onto northern territory. A year before, in the fall of 1862, one of his prime motivations for moving into Maryland had been precisely the hope that a Confederate movement north of the Potomac would force a decisive engagement with McClellan, an engagement that would finish what the peninsula had begun either by destroying the federal army or by convincing northern voters before the November 1862 elections that the Confederacy could not be defeated. It would also have helped the logisticial problems of the Army of Northern Virginia in 1862 to recruit and resupply north of the Potomac on the presumably friendly soil of Maryland; and it went without saying that the further upriver along the Potomac Lee could make such an incursion, the closer his army would be to striking at the vital northern rail terminals at Harrisburg, Pennsylvania. But Lee's overall plan for the 1862 Maryland invasion was thwarted by McClellan's discovery of Lee's orders and the battle at Antietam, and Lee had been forced to winter in Virginia after all. In the spring of 1863, Lee was determined to make another raid into the North, and although Hooker's surprise move on the Rappahannock delayed that, Lee was again on the march northward by June with a full army of 75,000 men.

By June 22nd, the advanced elements of Lee's army were already in Pennsylvania, leaving the baffled federals to hop belatedly after them. Just like John Pope's federals eleven months before in northern Virginia, Lee's underfed soldiers were a visitation of famine on the Pennsylvania countryside. Amos Stouffer, a Swiss-German farmer from Chambersburg, Pennsylvania, wrote in his diary that "the Rebs . . . are scouring the country in every direction. . . . They take horses, cattle, sheep, hogs, &c.," and even took over a Chambersburg mill and forced the farmers to grind wheat for them. The Confederates also made off with what they regarded as yet another form of movable property: not only Chambersburg's horses and cattle, but also its "Negroes." Out of a free black population of 451 in and around Chambersburg, more than fifty were rounded up by Confederate soldiers and started south to be sold into slavery.[20] On June 27th, an advance column of Confederate infantry was in Carlisle, Pennsylvania, a short distance across the Susquehanna River from Harrisburg; the next day, another Confederate division was in York.

Once again, however, Lee's plans were thwarted, this time by the loss, not of orders, but of his cavalry. Lee's cavalry commander, J. E. B. Stuart, bolted from the

[20]"The Rebs Are Yet Thick Around Us: The Civil War Diary of Amos Stouffer of Chambersburg," in *Civil War History* 38 (September 1992), pp. 214–215; Wilbur Sturtevant Nye, *Here Come the Rebels!* (1965; rept. Dayton, OH, 1984), pp. 184–185.

long leash Lee kept on his trusted subordinates and managed to become hopelessly separated from the main body of Lee's infantry. Instead of providing Lee with scouting and reconnaissance of the Army of the Potomac, Stuart effectively rode right off the map, leaving Lee strategically blind. This quickly became critical for the Confederates because Lee planned to rendezvous all of his infantry corps together at the crossroads town of Gettysburg, just over the Maryland border in south-central Pennsylvania, on July 1st. But without Stuart to provide scouting services, Lee's infantry unknowingly walked into Gettysburg and found it already occupied by federal cavalrymen. The federal cavalry in Gettysburg numbered only about 3,000 men, but Lee no longer had a Jackson who could be trusted to push ahead on his own initiative without Lee's immediate presence or orders, and the Confederate advance on Gettysburg was stalled for four precious hours by indecision and bad field judgments. The dismounted federal cavalry were not nearly enough to stand up to Lee's infantry for long, but they successfully held up the Confederate infantry outside of the town until the federal infantry could come up and occupy the strategic ridge that ran south of the town.

Once having begun an action, even an unintended one, Lee was unwilling to break it off, and so over the next two days, July 2nd and 3rd, Lee launched two major and futile attacks on the Union positions, hoping to force the federals off the high ground outside Gettysburg. This might have been a fairly good plan to follow, given what had happened at Chancellorsville, and provided the Army of the Potomac was still commanded by someone like Hooker. But Hooker was, by this time, no longer at the head of the Army of the Potomac. Angered over slights he had received from the War Department, Hooker had resigned on June 27th, and Lincoln replaced him with an unimaginative but solid old regular, George Gordon Meade. Lee recognized that Meade would be a very different opponent from either Burnside or Hooker: "General Meade will commit no blunder in my front," Lee remarked, "and if I make one he will make haste to take advantage of it."[21] But even knowing this, Lee allowed his own thirst for the offense to overwhelm the caution he should have shown around Meade. On July 2nd, the second day of Gettysburg, Lee launched a major assault on Meade's left flank, anchored on a small rocky hill called Little Round Top. The attack came within an ace of succeeding, but slipups in timing and deployment tripped up the Confederate attack. Little Round Top itself was saved for the Army of the Potomac by the stubborn defense of the flank of the hill against an Alabama brigade by the 20th Maine Volunteers and their colonel, the former Bowdoin college rhetoric professor, Joshua Lawrence Chamberlain. Out of ammunition, and with their line of battle bent back almost on itself by Confederate attacks, Chamberlain ordered his regiment to charge down the hill at the Alabamians with fixed bayonets. This rare and unanticipated decision to close with the bayonet caught the Confederates so completely by surprise that they broke and ran, and the rest of the attack on the Little Round Top thereafter lost momentum and petered out.

---

[21]Freeman, *R. E. Lee*, vol. 3, p. 64.

The next day, however, on July 3rd, Lee made the same kind of headlong frontal assault, this time sending Major General George E. Pickett and three divisions of Virginians and North Carolinians—approximately 10,500 men— against the center of the Union line of battle. The attack turned into a reverse of Fredericksburg: The Confederates were compelled to cross almost a mile of open ground under a murderous fire of artillery and massed infantry, and although a few Confederates managed to reach the Union line and punch a small hole in it, the attack soon collapsed, with the loss of over 1,100 killed and 4,500 wounded. By the end of the day, it was at last evident to Lee that he could not dislodge Meade from his position at Gettysburg. And with his supplies and ammunition badly depleted, and almost 20,000 casualties from the three days of fighting, Lee wearily ordered the Army of Northern Virginia to retreat.

After ten months of almost unrelieved bad news from the battlefield, the news of Gettysburg came as welcome relief to the North. In the Confederacy, it shattered the myth of Lee's invincibility and raised questions for the first time about Lee's capabilities as a field commander. On August 8th, assuming full responsibility for the defeat at Gettysburg, Lee offered Jefferson Davis his resignation. Davis refused, but at the same time, Lee would never again have complete control of Davis's military policy, and in September, Davis would detach Longstreet's corps from the Army of Northern Virginia and send it west to reenforce Braxton Bragg.

For Lincoln, however, Gettysburg offered only limited consolations. Although jubilant at Meade's victory, he waited in vain to hear of Meade pursuing and destroying the defeated Lee. Instead Meade, in a manner tiringly reminiscent of McClellan, rested his men and then cautiously set off in a perfunctory pursuit of the Army of Northern Virginia. And Lincoln would have to keep on looking for the general who would win the kind of war he had in mind.

2. Advance into the Confederate Heartland

Vicksburg fell to Grant the day after Meade's victory at Gettysburg, and the conjunction of the two events gave the North its happiest weekend in two years of war. But the repulse of Lee's invasion of Pennsylvania and the reopening of the Mississippi probably meant a good deal less in strategic terms than they seemed. Although Gettysburg had inflicted severe wounds on the Army of Northern Virginia, Meade's failure to pursue Lee only ensured that the same cycle of invasions, retreats, and counterinvasions would have to begin all over again in the fall of 1863 or the spring of 1864. As for the Mississippi River, the anxiety Lincoln had felt about reopening the entire length of the river to the Gulf was generated by his youthful memories of how dependent western farmers had always been on the Mississippi for transporting their surpluses to market, and by the croaking of western governors like Oliver Perry Morton of Indiana who was convinced that his legislature would vote to secede and join the Confederacy unless the Mississippi was reopened.[22] But Lincoln's memories were a generation old in 1863, and the mature Lincoln's association as a lawyer with the railroads provided telling evidence of a dramatic shift in market transportation away from the north-south axis of the Mississippi River valley and toward the east-west axis of the railroads that now brought goods more swiftly to Chicago and New York than the steamboat could bring them to New Orleans.

Of course, the conquest of the Mississippi did pay the Union a few dividends. The Confederates surrendered an entire army at Vicksburg—nearly 29,000 men— and the loss of the Mississippi cut them off from Texas, Arkansas, and most of Louisiana. But Braxton Bragg's rebel army was still intact and dangerous in middle Tennessee; and, what was more, none of the regions cut off by the capture of the Mississippi had been an indispensable source of supply for the Confederacy anyway. Whatever their loss did to damage the Confederate war effort, it did not prevent the Confederacy from waging war for almost two more years. In fact, the real heart of the Confederacy's power to carry on the war—its factories, granaries, and rail centers—never had lain along Halleck's or Grant's lines of operation on the Tennessee or the Mississippi. They lay, instead, in upper Alabama and Georgia, around the critical rail centers of Chattanooga and Atlanta, where the remaining pieces of the Confederacy's lateral rail lines still intersected, and around the new government-run gun foundries and iron works at Selma and the great powder works in Augusta.

This meant that the real line of successful operations for the Union in 1862 and 1863 would have to be the same eastern Tennessee line that McClellan had vainly urged Buell to follow back in January of 1862. A good deal more might have been made of this had not Buell shown himself no more eager to pursue his chances in 1862 than McClellan. In the spring of 1862, he had pretty much taken McClellan's view of the war by announcing in a general order that "We are in arms, not for the purpose of invading the rights of our fellow-countrymen anywhere, but to maintain the integrity of the Union and protect the Constitution." Like McClellan in Maryland, he had beaten back Bragg's invasion of Kentucky in the fall of 1862, but Buell's triumph at the battle of Perryville owed more to Bragg's bad judgment than Buell's tactical skills. And then, following the McClellan pattern to its final curve, Buell failed to pursue Bragg and his Confederates and instead settled into comfortable winter quarters in Nashville. Lincoln and the War Department had seen all they wanted to see of this kind of behavior from field officers, and on October 24, 1862, Buell was unceremoniously replaced by Major General William Starke Rosecrans. It would now be up to Rosecrans to finish the long-delayed conquest of eastern Tennessee, seize Chattanooga and Atlanta, and drive a stake into the heart of Georgia and Alabama.

Like so many other high-ranking Union officers, Rosecrans was a West Point graduate, class of 1838, who served in the prestigious Corps of Engineers until

---

[22]William B. Hesseltine, *Lincoln and the War Governors* (New York, 1948), p. 312.

1854, when he resigned and opened up his own business as an architect and engineer. Unlike many of the others, however, Rosecrans was a Democrat and a Roman Catholic, which made him an object of suspicion in an overwhelmingly Protestant culture (James A. Garfield, one of Rosecrans's brigadiers and a radical evangelical preacher, sat up into the wee hours of many mornings with Rosecrans, "talking constantly and incessantly for hours on religion").[23] But in 1861, any real Union man with those credentials was a political godsend who could be used to rally northern Democrats and working-class immigrants, and Rosecrans suddenly found himself rewarded with a brigadier general's commission. A serious student of strategy, paternal and well-loved by every brigade and division he commanded, Rosecrans now took over Buell's 47,000 men, gave them the name "Army of the Cumberland," and on December 26th, moved south out of Nashville after Bragg.

Braxton Bragg, meanwhile, had nearly gone the same way as Buell. Although Bragg was a sharp and careful disciplinarian, he was gravely hampered by an assortment of physical ills, ranging from nightmare headaches to abdominal cramps, which made him quarrelsome with subordinates and a fiend to his soldiers. Rather than risk chances with a fresh invasion of Kentucky, Bragg went into winter quarters at Murfreesboro, Tennessee, approximately forty miles south of Nashville along Stone's River. But there, Bragg recovered his composure and reorganized his 36,000 men into what he now called the "Army of Tennessee." And when Davis visited Bragg and the Army of Tennessee at Murfreesboro in early December, 1862, he was delighted to see that Bragg's men were "in good condition and fine spirits"[24]

Bragg was soon given a chance to use the Army of Tennessee to redeem his reputation. The combative Rosecrans and the Army of the Cumberland moved down to within two miles of Bragg's lines around Murfreesboro on December 30th, and the next day, both armies planned to leap at each other's throats in simultaneous attacks. In the event, however, the Confederates moved first, catching Rosecrans's right flank still at breakfast and scattering them backwards for three miles. The battle might well have been lost right there had not Rosecrans personally rode down the lines and rallied his men in the face of Confederate fire. As for Bragg, the Confederate commander kept on feeding his divisions into the fight piece by piece, feeling all along Rosecrans's battered lines for a weakness. Somehow, the federals held on: one federal division under a scrappy little Irishman named Philip Sheridan lost all three of its brigade commanders killed or mortally wounded, and almost one-third of its men, but it slowed Bragg's attack on the center of the Union line to a halt. At other points, the federals managed to repel Confederate attacks with nothing more than odds and ends of cavalry and, in one

[23]Garfield to Lucretia Garfield, February 13, 1863, in *The Wild Life of the Army: Civil War Letters of James A. Garfield*, F. D. Williams, ed. (East Lansing, MI, 1964), p. 233.

[24]Davis to J. A. Seddon, December 18, 1862, in *Jefferson Davis, Constitutionalist Letters, Papers and Speeches*, Dunbar Rowland, ed. (Jackson, MS, 1923), vol. 5, p. 386.

instance, members of Rosecrans's own headquarters escort. By the time darkness fell, each army had lost close to a third of its men as casualties.

Bragg immediatley jumped to the conclusion that he had won a great victory, and telegraphed Richmond that Rosecrans was falling back. Rosecrans's own officers thought the same way and counseled him to retreat. But Rosecrans had no intention of retreating, and when Bragg awoke the next morning, New Year's Day, the Army of the Cumberland was still there. On January 2nd, Bragg launched a second series of attacks, hoping to prod Rosecrans into the withdrawal that Bragg presumed he ought to be making. Instead, by the end of the day, it was Bragg who became convinced that he had lost the fight and ought to retreat, and during the night of January 3, 1863, Bragg began pulling out of Murfreesboro for another camp twenty miles southward.

Murfreesboro was, like Shiloh, more like a simple slugfest than a model of tactical brilliance, but it temporarily made Rosecrans a national hero all the same. Bragg, meanwhile, was assailed by a mounting tide of criticism from his own officers for uselessly throwing away a victory. Just as at Perryville, Bragg demonstrated a fatal incapacity at Murfreesboro to perform under the stress of combat, and his abrupt decision to retreat was due at least in part to a simple loss of nerve. As one of Bragg's disgusted subordinates remarked, Bragg could easily fight his way straight up to the gates of Heaven, but once there, would doubtless order a withdrawal. One division commander in the Army of Tennessee, Benjamin F. Cheatham, vowed never to serve under Bragg again. Another, Irish-born Patrick Cleburne, politely informed Bragg that no one really trusted his military judgment anymore: "I have consulted all my Brigade commanders . . . and they write with me in personal regard for yourself, in a high appreciation of your patriotism and gallantry . . . but at the same time they see, with regret, and it has also met my observation, that you do not possess the confidence of the Army, in other repects, in that degree necessary to secure success." At this point, even President Davis was ready to relieve him of command, and in March, 1863, Davis tried to persuade Joseph E. Johnston to take over Bragg's command. But Johnston declined Davis's suggestion, and Davis took that as a sign that Bragg had been serverely misjudged by his subordinates. Accordingly, Davis decided to grant Bragg one more reprieve, and in March, he even allowed Bragg to court-martial one of critics, Major General John Porter McCown, who had loudly threatened to leave the Army of Tennessee and go back to farming potatoes until Bragg was relieved.[25]

The situation for the western Confederacy might have looked even bleaker had not Bragg's failures been more than compensated for by the spectacular achievements of one of Bragg's cavalry brigadiers, Nathan Bedford Forrest. By the end of 1862, Forrest had emerged as the single most daring and successful cavalry officer of

[25]Cleburne to Bragg [January 13, 1863], in *Official Records*, series 1, vol. 20 (part one), p. 684; Grady McWhiney, *Braxton Bragg and Confederate Defeat, Volume One: Field Command* (New York, 1969), pp. 374, 378.

the Civil War: In July of 1862, leading only 1,400 cavalry troopers, Forrest had raided Buell's supply lines of over $1 million in weapons and other war material, pulled down bridges and telegraph wires, pulled up railroad lines, and captured over a thousand federal prisoners. In December of 1862, he led a new brigade of 2,100 cavalrymen on a destructive joyride through middle Tennessee that, in two weeks, destroyed fifty bridges and trestles along the Mobile & Ohio Railroad, killed or captured 2,500 federal pursuers, captured ten pieces of artillery and enough Enfield rifles to reequip his own men (and with 500 left over to spare), and generally made a shambles of the federal occupation of middle Tennessee.

Nevertheless, Forrest was an embarrassment to Braxton Bragg. A self-made man, Forrest smacked of the slave market (where he had made a prewar fortune in slave dealing) and his grammar invariably left something to chance. He had no formal military schooling (or any other schooling for that matter), and made up his own earthy maxims of war as he went: *always strike first,* he counseled his artillery commander, the 22-year old John Watson Morton, "In any fight, it's the first blow that counts; and if you keep it up hot enough, you can whip 'em as fast as they can come up"; then, *never let your enemies regain their balance,* or, as Forrest put it, "Get 'em skeered and then keep the skeer on 'em"; finally, *never be intimidated by professional soldiers,* since, as Forrest had discovered, "Whenever I met one of them fellers that fit by note, I generally whipped hell out of him before he got his tune pitched." It was precisely because he had no professional lessons to unlearn about the use of cavalry that Forrest was utterly indifferent to drill and urged his men to attack the enemy directly and without regard for the niceties of the tactics books. "General Forrest, as a commander, was, in many respects, the negative of a West Pointer," wrote his chief of artillery, John Watson Morton. "He regarded evolution, maneuvers, and exhaustive cavalry drill an unnecessary tax upon men and horses." But Forrest's untutored lust for combat might have merely resulted in more casualty-laden melees, had it not been for his natural, baffling gift—a gift possessed by only a few generals in the Civil War, including Ulysses Grant—for sizing up a given tactical situation and instinctively knowing what to do with it.

> [Forrest] had absolutely no knowledge or experience of war gleaned from the study of what others had wrought. General Forrest grasped intuitively and instantaneously the strategic possibilities of every situation which confronted him. . . . His knowledge of men was in most cases unerring; and his ability to inspire and bring out the greatest power and endurance of his men was unsurpassed. . . . His eye for position was almost infallible, and his knowledge of the effect of a given movement on the enemy was intuitive and seemed to come rather from an inner than an outer source of information.[26]

Forrest was a fairly good inkling of what could be done by pressing relentlessly for decisive combat conclusions on the battlefield. Unfortunately, he was also every-

[26]Morton, *The Artillery of Nathan Bedford Forrest's Cavalry* (1909; rept. Paris, TN, 1988), pp. 12, 16–17.

thing that a tightly buttoned regular (like Bragg) ought not to be, and Forrest never ceased to suspect that Bragg had authorized his famous raids chiefly as a means of getting him out of the way.

If so, Forrest's raids were almost the only activity Bragg, or anyone else, would indulge after Murfreesboro. For six months, the Confederate and Union armies, exhausted and bloodied by the battle of Stone's River, were content to rest and refit. Rosecrans's self-confidence had been badly shaken by the carnage at Murfreesboro (his closest friend and adjutant, Colonel Julius Garesché, had been decapitated by a solid shot while riding beside Rosecrans, spattering the general with a mess of blood and brains), and instead of pushing on toward Chattanooga, he carefully fortified himself in Murfreesboro and began demanding reenforcements and supplies. When Stanton refused to send them, and instead began prodding Rosecrans to get the Army of the Cumberland moving southward, Rosecrans went over Stanton's head and began whining to Lincoln in March, 1863, about enemies in the War Department who were denying him the promotion he deserved, the staff members he wanted, and so forth.

And then, on June 23, 1863, Rosecrans's old aggressiveness resurfaced, and the Army of the Cumberland suddenly lurched into action. Bragg's Army of Tennessee was entrenched around Tullahoma, Tennessee, almost halfway between Rosecrans and Chattanooga, inviting an attack as a sure way of revenging itself for Murfreesboro. But Rosecrans deftly feinted to Bragg's left, smartly zigzagged to Bragg's right, and then slipped around behind Bragg in a skillfully executed turning movement that forced Bragg to retreat in confusion to Chattanooga. Rosecrans then paused and waited, until more telegrams from Washington caught up with him, demanding more advances. On August 16th, Rosecrans set off again, this time to turn Bragg's position in Chattanooga, too. Finding an unguarded ferry on the Tennessee River about thirty miles below Chattanooga, Rosecrans threw his army across the Tennessee on the back of a single pontoon bridge, a jerry-rigged trestle, and an assortment of rafts and boats. He then swept around behind Chattanooga, and compelled Bragg to abandon the city on September 8th without firing a shot in its defense. In only ten weeks, Rosecrans had moved the Army of the Cumberland almost a hundred miles southward, had outmaneuvered Bragg into abandoning all of eastern Tennessee and Chattanooga, and had done it all at the price of less than a thousand casualties.

What Rosecrans did not know, however, was that in Richmond, an anxious Jefferson Davis had finally decided that the threat to Chattanooga was dangerous enough to justify desperate measures. At the very same moment that Rosecrans was crossing the Tennessee, Davis overrode Robert E. Lee's objections and sent James Longstreet's corps of the Army of Northern Virginia to reenforce Bragg at LaFayette, Georgia, about twenty-five miles south of Chattanooga. The southern railroads were in such poor condition that it took the first of Longstreet's men ten days to make the 952-mile trip from Richmond to northern Georgia. But by the middle of September, Longstreet and five out of his nine brigades were with Bragg, and

Bragg now determined to use his newly reinforced strength of 47,000 men (not counting Forrest's dismounted cavalry) to strike back at Rosecrans. All unsuspecting, Rosecrans kept on rolling along merrily after Bragg into northern Georgia under the delusion that Bragg was still retreating. Not until September 10th did he realize that Bragg had actually turned and was moving in for the kill. Rosecrans hastily concentrated his four corps—approximately 56,000 men—in the valley of Chickamauga Creek, a dozen miles south of Chattanooga. But before he could devise a plan of action, Bragg struck first.

Chickamauga is a Cherokee word for *river of death,* and for two days, the 19th and 20th of September, Chickamauga Creek fully lived up to its name. The fighting on the 19th was a cautious draw, with Bragg hesitantly testing Rosecrans's defensive lines behind Chickamauga Creek. The next morning, Bragg threw caution to the winds and launched a furious series of frontal assaults on the federal lines that lasted for two hours without gaining much ground. But at 11:00 A.M., Rosecrans mistakenly pulled one of his divisions out of line and sent it in the wrong direction just as Longstreet's Virginians came avalanching down upon the gap so conveniently left for them. The federal right flank simply turned and fled in panic, sweeping Rosecrans and two of his corps commanders with it. "I saw our lines break and melt away like leaves before the wind," wrote Charles Dana, Stanton's second assistant secretary of war who was traveling with Rosecrans as an observer. "Then the headquarters around me disappeared. . . . The whole road was filled with flying soldiers. . . . Everything was in the greatest disorder."[27] By 1:00 P.M., all that was left of Rosecrans's army at Chickamauga was Major General George H. Thomas's corps, which stood its ground against Longstreet on a small hill beside the road to Chattanooga and gave the rest of the beaten Army of the Cumberland time to retreat. Thomas's valiant rearguard action earned him the nickname, "The Rock of Chickamauga," but Thomas was almost the only senior federal officer to emerge from the defeat at Chickamauga with any semblance of reputation intact. The federals lost 16,000 men that afternoon (fully half of them as prisoners) plus 51 cannon and 15,000 rifles, not to mention innumerable horses, wagons, and supplies.

Rosecrans never recovered from the shock of Chickamauga. A disgusted Lincoln imagined Rosecrans waddling in circles, "confused and stunned like a duck hit on the head." Curling up in the defenses of Chattanooga, Rosecrans allowed Bragg to close off the Tennessee River and move the Confederates onto Missionary Ridge and Lookout Mountain, the heights that loomed over Chattanooga. Without full control of the Tennessee, Rosecrans was in a very bad supply position, and within a month, the despondent Army of the Cumberland was facing either starvation or surrender. Here was Vicksburg in reverse, and at last Lincoln decided that it was time to bring Grant onto the scene.

Grant believed that Vicksburg had more than made up the damage done to his

[27]Charles A. Dana, *Recollections of the Civil War with the Leaders at Washington and in the Field in the Sixties* (New York, 1898), pp. 115, 117.

military reputation at Shiloh, and he fully expected that he ought to be given a free hand in mounting a new campaign into the vital interior of Alabama. But Halleck had other plans, none of which included independent action for Grant. "The possession of the trans-Mississippi by the Union forces seemed to possess more importance in his mind than almost any campaign east of the Mississippi," Grant wrote, and he found himself reduced to policing the Vicksburg area "against guerilla bands and small detachments of cavalry which infested the interior."[28] This, however, was not what Lincoln and Stanton had in mind for Grant. Both the president and the secretary of war had been keeping a close and inquisitive eye on Grant ever since the capture of Forts Henry and Donelson in February of 1862, and Lincoln defended Grant after the Shiloh debacle. When Alexander McClure accused Grant of drunkenness and incompetence at Shiloh and urged Lincoln to cashier him, Lincoln "gathered himself up in his chair and said in a tone of earnestness that I shall never forget, '*I can't spare this man; he fights.*' " Francis Carpenter remembered one "self-constituted committee" that visited Lincoln in 1863 to warn the president against Grant's reputed alcoholism. "By the way, gentlemen," Lincoln remarked after hearing them out, "can either of you tell me where General Grant procures his whiskey? Because, if I can find out, I will send every general in the field a barrel of it!"[29]

But behind the jokes, Lincoln remained unsure about Grant, and in 1863, Stanton sent Charles A. Dana to keep an eye on Grant during the Vicksburg campaign and report anything untoward. As it turned out, Dana gave Grant the highest possible praise: "the most modest, the most disinterested, and the most honest man I ever knew, with a temper that nothing could disturb, and a judgment that was judicial in its comprehensiveness and wisdom . . . whom no ill omens could deject and no triumph unduly exalt."[30] That clinched the matter for Lincoln and Stanton. In October, unwilling to face the prospect of the destruction of an entire federal army at Chattanooga, Stanton wired Grant to come up the Mississippi to Cairo, and thence to Louisville, and meet with him personally. Their trains crossed instead in Indianapolis on October 17th, with Stanton boarding Grant's car and mistaking Grant's medical attache for Grant and confidently informing the aide that he recognized him from his photographs.[31] Once the proper identities had been sorted out, Stanton informed Grant that Lincoln had decided to consolidate all federal military operations in the West (except for the occupation of Louisiana) and put Grant in command of them all. Next, Grant was to take himself and whatever troops he had at hand over to Chattanooga to rescue the Army of the Cumberland. Grant never hesitated. The next day, he relieved Rosecrans of command of the Army of the Cumberland and

---

[28]Grant, "Personal Memoirs," in *Memoirs and Selected Letters*, M. D. McFeely and W. S. McFeely, eds. (New York, 1990), pp. 388–389.

[29]Alexander K. McClure, *Lincoln and Men of War-Times* (Philadelphia, 1892), p. 196; Francis B. Carpenter, *Six Months at the White House with Abraham Lincoln* (New York, 1867), p. 247.

[30]Dana, *Recollections of the Civil War*, p. 61.

[31]Bruce Catton, *Grant Takes Command* (Boston, 1968), pp. 34–35.

turned it over to the hero of Chickamauga, George Thomas. Five days after that, Grant himself was in Chattanooga.

What Grant did to lift the siege of Chattanooga looks almost ludicrously simple from a distance, but that only underscores the real genius of his accomplishment. First, Grant reopened the Tennessee River supply line to Chattanooga on October 27th. Then he brought up substantial reenforcements, including two army corps shipped by railroad from the Army of the Potomac under "Fighting Joe" Hooker in October, and two more from the Mississippi under William Tecumseh Sherman by mid-November. With these forces in hand, and with Thomas's Army of the Cumberland, Grant now turned on the complacent Bragg and prepared to drive him off his positions atop Lookout Mountain and Missionary Ridge. The inevitable confrontation came on November 24th and 25th. After a preliminary skirmish, Grant sent Hooker's men up the steep sides of Lookout Mountain (on Bragg's left flank), and threw in Sherman's men at a railroad grade and tunnel on Bragg's right flank. Thomas's Army of the Cumberland, angered and humiliated, were held in reserve in the center to await the results.

As it turned out, Hooker's men easily cleared the Confederates off Lookout Mountain, but Sherman's attack on the tunnel stalled. To relieve pressure on Sherman, Grant ordered Thomas's men to seize the trenches the Confederates had dug along the base of Missionary Ridge. But when the Army of the Cumberland finally got moving, it scarcely bothered to stop at the trenches but kept right on going, up the 200-foot-high face of Missionary Ridge and over the top. The Confederates up on the ridge were taken completely by surprise. The center of Bragg's line caved in like wet paper, and the rest of the Army of Tennessee stumbled back along the roads down to Georgia, with Bragg berating and blaming his men for the disaster. This time, no amount of shifting and excuse could disguise Bragg's incompetence. Instead of crushing Rosecrans in Chattanooga when he could have, Bragg had settled into a comfortable and indolent siege. He had quarreled with the best of his officers again, including a wrathy Nathan Bedford Forrest, who finally descended on Bragg and shook his fist in his face:

> I have stood your meanness as long as I intend to. You have played the part of a damn scoundrel, and are a coward. . . . You may as well not issue any more orders to me, for I will not obey them, and I will hold you personally responsible for any further indignities you endeavor to inflict upon me. You have threatened to arrest me for not obeying your orders promptly. I dare you to do it, and I say to you that if you ever again try to interfere with me or cross my path it will be at the peril of your life.[32]

And then, as though the presence of Grant in Chattanooga meant nothing, Bragg had sent Longstreet's corps off on a wild goose chase to recapture Knoxville. In short, Bragg had done almost everything necessary to destroy the morale and order of the Army of Tennessee, and Chattanooga just about finished it. Five days after

[32]John Allan Wyeth, *Life of General Nathan Bedford Forrest* (New York, 1899), p. 266.

the battle, Bragg was officially relieved by President Davis and recalled to Richmond, where he would finish out the war behind a desk. After Gettysburg, Vicksburg, and Chattanooga, it was now beginning to be a good question in Confederate minds whether there was much of a war left to win.

3. The Problem of the Confederate Nation

For many Southerners, the secession of the southern states from the Union was the ultimate solution to the political and economic problems that confronted them inside the Union. On the other hand, it was also true that, like the soldiers in their armies, the southern people were not always of one mind about which of those problems was the most important. For the Georgia secession convention, secession was an act of racial revolution, a necessary reconstruction of the republican ideology along racial lines so as to secure the existence of "a white man's Republic" and keep African-American slaves firmly in their place as slaves. Alexander H. Stephens, a Georgian and former Whig colleague of Abraham Lincoln, told an enthusiastic audience in Savannah in 1861 that "Our Confederacy is founded upon . . . the great truth that the negro is not equal to the white man. That slavery—subordination to the superior race, is his natural and normal condition. Thus our new government is the first in the history of the world, based upon this great physical and moral truth." One lonely Georgia Unionist was shocked to find how strongly southern women agreed with Stephens. "I had rather every one of my children should be laid out on the *cooling board*," snorted one, "than to have Yankees get my niggers."[33] But other Southerners pulled shy of justifying secession from the Union solely for the sake of protecting slavery. Even among the elite of the planter class, there remained an acute sense of embarrassment over slavery as a necessary but unpleasant economic necessity. Southerners like Edward A. Pollard spoke instead about the preservation of an agrarian republicanism, a culture of leisured and independent agriculture that was standing deliberately aloof from the hard-handed industrial money grubbing of the North. "No one can read aright the history of America," said Pollard, the editor of the Richmond *Examiner*, "unless in the light of a North and a South: two political aliens in a Union imperfectly defined as a confederation of states." The North, envious of the South's "higher sentimentalism, and its superior refinements of scholarship and manners," chose to divert attention away from its real animosity toward southern culture "in an attack upon slavery," but this was "nothing more than a convenient ground of dispute between two parties, who represented not two moral theories, but hostile sections and opposite civilizations."[34] In that light, it was the North that

[33]Marilyn Mayer Culpeper, *Trials and Triumphs: Women of the American Civil War* (East Lansing, MI, 1991), p. 21.
[34]Pollard, *The Lost Cause: A New Southern History of the War of the Confederates* (New York, 1867), pp. 46, 49.

represented revolution against the past, and secession was the South's cultural anti-dote to it.

And then there were those for whom the basic justification for secession arose from neither slavery nor culture, but from the more practical considerations of profits and politics. Southerners like Alabama Governor John Gill Shorter argued that for too long, northern politicians and bankers had been fattening themselves off the tariffs they charged on the imports Southerners needed and the cotton Southerners consigned to their commission houses. Dissolving the Union would result in "deliverance, full an unrestricted, from all commercial dependence upon, as well as from all social and political complicity with, a people who appreciate neither the value of liberty nor the sanctity of compacts." Once independent, the southern states could solve the tariff problem for themselves, and swing firmly into the great network of transatlantic free trade that was centered on the British textile economy. Henry L. Benning of Georgia was sure that

> the South would gain by a separation from the North, for [by] the mere act of separation all these drains would stop running, and the golden waters be retained within her own borders. And the grand option would be presented to her of adopting free trade, by which her consumers would gain eighty millions a year clear money in the consequent lower price at which they could purchase their goods or a system of protection to her own mechanics and artisans and manufactures by which they would soon come to rival the best in the world.

Northerners "know that the South is the main prop and support of the Federal system" declared the New Orleans Daily Crescent in January, 1861. "They know that it is Southern productions that constitute the surplus wealth of the nation, and enables us to import so largely from other countries." And knowing that, "they know that they can plunder and pillage the South, as long as they are in the same Union with us, by other means, such as fishing bounties, navigation laws, robberies of the public lands, and every other possible mode of injustice and peculation." On those terms, it was high time for the southern states to reclaim their individual sovereignty as states, assert the supremacy of "states' rights," and resume an independent status where they could be sure of putting their own affairs first.[35]

What all these interpretations of secession had in common was the language of republicanism—or rather, the language of Democratic republicanism, the strand of classic republicanism articulated best by Andrew Jackson, and which Henry Clay and the Whigs had fought so tenaciously from the 1830s onward. Unlike Whig republicanism, Democratic republicanism was dominated by a preoccupation with individual independence, white equality, and political diversity—which is to say, that they resented centralized federal government and northern financial dominance, excused

[35]Malcolm C. McMillan, The Disintegration of a Confederate State: Three Governors and Alabama's Wartime Home Front, 1861–1865 (Macon, GA, 1986), p. 33; "Henry L. Bebbing's Secessionist Speech," in Secession Debated: Georgia's Showdown in 1860, W. H. Freehling and Craig Simpson, eds. (New York, 1992), p. 142; Southern Editorials on Secession, Dwight L. Dumond, ed. (New York, 1931), p. 408.

slavery on the grounds that its victims were not the "equals" of whites, and opposed every measure of the Whigs to use the federal government to impose banking, taxes, tariffs, and evangelical moralism. However different the reasons offered by Stephens, Pollard, and the others for secession, they all harmonized within a basic Jeffersonian outlook, and in that sense they were all agreed in seeing the Civil War as a crisis within American republicanism itself. For the South in 1861, the only logical solution to this crisis was the final appeal to Democratic republican principles—simple, peaceful secession of the states from a Union gone awry.

But the southern states were not permitted the luxury of a peaceful and uncontested separation from the Union. The commitment of Lincoln and the Republican party to the old banner of Whiggism necessarily meant that the same federal centralization that had antagonized Southerners to the point of secession would now be used to prevent them from breaking away. And so Southerners found themselves compelled to do two things that, as it turned out, flew straight in the face of the principles they held so dear. First, in the interests of survival, the southern states were forced to cooperate with each other, so that they began their war of state sovereignty by immediately subordinating their highly-prized political and commercial interests to a confederation arrangement and the authority of a central government in Richmond. And second, they were forced to wage a major war of national defense, in which it was going to get harder and harder for the central Confederate government to resist tinkering with the slave system in order for the Confederate nation to survive. This meant that the basic question that Southerners would have to answer between 1861 and 1865 was whether it was more important to Southerners to survive as a Confederate nation, even if it cost them both slavery and states' rights, or whether they preferred to clutch their Democratic republicanism to their bosoms and go down to defeat as a noble but lost cause.

At first, the answers to that question seemed easy and risk-free. The convention that assembled in Montgomery, Alabama, in February of 1861 to form a Confederate government for the first wave of seceding states worked hard to avoid any suggestion of ultra Democratic radicalism, and seemed to give remarkably small place to the states'-rights fire-eaters. The convention, in fact, turned itself into the Confederacy's first provisional congress, and the constitution that it adopted for the Confederacy was close replica of the federal Constitution. Just like the old Constitution, it provided for a president, a bicameral congress, and an independent judiciary. Though the Confederate constitution explicitly recognized the principle of state sovereignty in its preamble, no mention about a right to secession was added. The Confederate president was granted powers that even the federal president lacked, such as a line-item veto over appropriations, a six-year term of office, and the provision for cabinet members to be allowed a voice on the floor of the Confederate congress. Even more to the point, the decision to elect Jefferson Davis as provisional president and Alexander H. Stephens as provisional vice-president neatly skipped over the worst of the slavery and state-sovereignty ideologues.

But much of the short shrift given to slavery and state sovereignty in the public deliberations of the provisional congress was pragmatic rather than principled. The seceding states had to placate the substantial portions of their populations that were either resistant to secession or that wanted secession only if it could be done in the safety of a combined group of seceding states. It also went without saying that foreign governments like Great Britain and France would be reluctant to extend themselves on behalf of the South if it seemed to have no recognizable central government to speak to or else one too explicitly devoted to slavery. It was only when the new Confederate constitution was looked at more closely that an inner radicalism became clear, for behind the facade of continuity with the constitutional past, the Confederate constitution was as thoroughgoing an enactment of the old Democratic republican agenda as Lincoln's Congress was a repudiation of it. The sovereignty of the individual Confederate states was asserted right off in the preamble, which stressed that each state was "acting in its sovereign and independent character" to form a "permanent federal government." Even more revealing was its careful definition of what constituted "citizens of the Confederate States," since it graduallly became plain from the Confederate constitution that a Confederate citizen was a participant in the national Confederate government only through his or her status as a citizen of a Confederate state. The states were given authority to initiate constitutional conventions (with consents from only two-thirds of the states needed to ratify amendments) and to remove Confederate officials operating within their boundaries—so that, for instance, obstreperous Confederate judges could no longer rely on the nettlesome example of John Marshall to stymie the diversity of state interests. In a further reminder of how hotly the Democratic memory retained its resentments over the Marshall Court, the principle of judicial review was restricted only to specific constitutional questions (and not "all cases in Law and Equity," as in the federal Constitution). Above all, the Confederate constitution expressly curtailed the authority of the Confederate government to "appropriate money for any internal improvement intended to facilitate commerce. . . ." And remembering how the Whigs had justified such appropriations in the past by appealing to the federal Constitution's promise to promote the "general welfare," the Confederate constitution simply dropped the offending phrase out of its text.[36]

The difficulty with a constitution so strict and pure in its celebration of states' rights was that it might not stand any realistic chance of surviving under pressure. And after the fall of Fort Sumter and Lincoln's call for volunteers in 1861, outside attack was precisely what the Confederacy was facing. As the Americans of an earlier political generation had learned in the War of 1812, no mere league of political interests had the strength to resist a coordinated and well-funded assault on its survival. The Confederacy had at least one major political advantage in this painful process of discovery, and that was the person of Jefferson Davis, its presi-

[36]Marshall L. DeRosa, *The Confederate Constitution of 1861: An Inquiry into American Constitutionalism* (Columbia, MO, 1991), pp. 23, 40–44, 91–101.

dent. As much as he defended the Democratic principles of states' rights and held large numbers of slaves, Davis had long stood aloof from the ultrasecessionists. In fact, despite Davis's reputation as the ideological heir-apparent of John Calhoun, Davis's political outlook on banking, tariffs, and internal improvements had sometimes been as close to Whiggery as a Democrat could be. From the very beginning (and to the disgust of the states' rights fire-eaters), Davis warned the southern people to stop thinking of themselves as citizens of states and start seeing themselves as the members of a new political nation whose overall survival was of greater importance than the survival of any of the separate parts—slavery, culture, states' rights—which made it up. "To increase the power, develop the resources, and promote the happiness of the Confederacy, it is requisite that there should be so much of homogeneity that the welfare of every portion shall be the aim of the whole," Davis warned. "Our safety—our very existence—depends on the complete blending of the military strength of all the States into one united body, to be used anywhere and everywhere as the exigencies of the contest may require for the good of the *whole*."[37] That led Davis to stretch his war powers as president of the Confederacy in precisely the same ways Lincoln stretched his: Davis acted to extend Confederate control over former federal arsenals and navy yards within the Confederate states, to justify Confederate military control over southern rail lines, and to secure presidential oversight of the officer-selection process of the Confederate army, and all before the end of 1862.

Davis's political flexibilities surprised many observers even within his administration, since he was not, in many ways, a particularly charming or attractive personality. Erect in his bearing, rigid in his conception of his own correctness, thin to the point of emaciation and virtually blind in one eye, Davis was crippled throughout the war by bouts of illness that would have killed most normal people, and by levels of political cat-calling that would have killed most politicians. The raw willpower that kept him at the helm of state through all these storms was his greatest asset, but no portrait of the Confederate president can ignore his politically canniness, his ability to draw all but his most violent critics back into cooperation, and his sterling dedication to the idea of a Confederate nation. Like Lincoln, Davis ruthlessly overworked himself and failed to delegate responsibilities; like Lincoln, he turned most of his attention to managing the war effort rather than domestic politics; like Lincoln, he was notoriously inclined to issue pardons to condemned soldiers; and like Lincoln, he tasted tragedy in his presidency in the death of a young son.

If Davis turned out to be a more calculating politician than his enemies imagined, he also turned out to be a far more lackluster military commander in chief than his friends had expected. Although Davis frequently insisted that the Confederacy was not interested in waging a war of aggressive conquest, he fully shared

[37]Davis, in *Jefferson Davis, Constitutionalist: His Letters, Papers and Speeches*, Dunbar Rowland, ed., vol. 5, pp. 52, 462.

Robert E. Lee's preference for offensive over defensive warfare, "that reviled policy of West-Pointism," and he committed the Confederate armies in 1861 to the well-nigh impossible task of policing (and in the case of Kentucky, seizing) every inch of the slave South's immense Ohio and Potomac River boundary lines with the North. After the fall of Forts Donelson and Henry, Davis acknowledged "the error of my attempt to defend all the frontier," but he resented any suggestion that "I have chosen to carry on the war upon a 'purely defensive' system," and he would later sanction Lee's raids north of the Potomac and lend eastern troops to Bragg so that he could go on the offensive against Rosecrans.[38] Far more serious than his strategic misjudgments, though, were Davis's personnel misjudgments. If Lincoln was overly fond of appointing incompetent politicians to generalships, Davis was overly willing to appoint and defend incompetents—Leonidas Polk, Theophilus Holmes, Braxton Bragg—who were either personal friends or else men he believed had been (as Davis was convinced he himself had been) unfairly condemned by unscrupulous and self-interested rivals. At the same time, though, it has to be conceded that in many cases Davis made these appointments knowing full well that he was dealing from the bottom of the deck, and he stood by them through one blunder after another simply because the supply of real military talent in circulation was so limited. "A *General* in the full acceptation of the word is a rare product, scarcely more than one can be expected in a generation," Davis grimly observed to his brother, "but in this mighty war in which we are engaged there is need for half a dozen."[39]

Still, Davis's military miscues were not nearly as harmful to the Confederacy as the lamentable failures of his cabinet and the Confederate congress. Most of Davis's first choices for the Confederate cabinet were dictated by the need to assure the various states that their interests were being represented in the government. His first secretaries of state and war, Leroy Pope Walker of Alabama and Robert Toombs of Georgia, were both brainless political appointees, and neither of them survived the first year of the war in office. Davis's most talented cabinet member, Judah P. Benjamin, was also, unfortunately, his most unpopular. With a Cheshire-cat smile playing around his lips, Benjamin was described by John S. Wise as over-full of "oleaginous" slickness, with a "keg-like form and over-deferential manner suggestive of a prosperous shopkeeper" and "more brains and less heart than any other civic leader in the South."[40] But Davis could not spare Benjamin, and each time Benjamin's political enemies demanded that he be removed, Davis would simply shift him to another post within the cabinet, moving him from attorney

---

[38]Davis to W. M. Brooks, March 13, 1862, and to Varina Davis, June 11, 1862, in *Jefferson Davis, Constitutionalist: Letters, Papers and Speeches*, volume five, pp. 216–217, 272.

[39]Steven E. Woodworth, *Jefferson Davis and His Generals: The Failure of Confederate Command in the West* (Lawrence, KS, 1990), pp. 305–316; William C. Davis, *Jefferson Davis*, p. 504.

[40]Eli N. Evans, *Judah P. Benjamin: The Jewish Confederate* (New York, 1988), pp. 147–148.

general to secretary of war, and then to secretary of state. The weakest link in Davis's chain of cabinet secretaries was the secretary of the treasury, Christopher Memminger. This South Carolina politician's only real fiscal experience was his chairmanship of the old House Committee on Finance, but he had been an important standard-bearer for secession in South Carolina, and the need to accommodate the South Carolinians in the Confederate government compelled Davis to make room for him in the cabinet. It is hard to know where Memminger would have done the least damage, and it was probably Davis's own naivete in financial matters that led him to park Memminger at the treasury. As it turned out, Memminger's tenure as the Confederate treasury chief was as close as one could come to unrelieved disaster without overworking the word. Overconfident as a result of the Confederacy's initial military successes in 1861, Memminger made no effort to prevent northern merchants from removing hard currency (specie) from their southern banks accounts, failed to float loans on the foreign money markets when he could have obtained large sums at cheap rates, and allowed the specie in the vital New Orleans banks to fall into federal hands without hardly stirring when New Orleans was captured by Farragut's ships in April, 1862.

Curiously, Memminger hesitated to capitalize on the South's most valuable commodity, cotton. With a little forethought, Memminger might have bought up the 1861 cotton harvest with Confederate bonds, notes, and securities (counting on the optimism and good will of southern civilians at that moment), and then shipped the cotton through the still-porous blockade to purchase supplies and float new loans. Instead, Memminger dismissed the need for such drastic intervention in the cotton markets, and not until the war had dragged on into 1862 did he reverse himself and attempt to buy up cotton for government use. By then, however, cotton was commanding much steeper prices, and even when he was able to purchase it, he found himself unable to find enough blockade runners willing to ship the cotton at government prices. Not until 1863, when the Confederate congress acted to regulate the blockade-runners, was Memminger assured of a regular means for exporting cotton. Even though this was much too little, much too late, the export of Confederate cotton helped underwrite the Erlanger loan, and it is anyone's guess how much other financial support a cotton-starved Europe might have lent to Memminger if he had acted as decisively in 1861. This forced Memminger to resort more and more to the printing presses to print the money he needed, and he helplessly flooded the Confederate economy with notes and bonds that had little or no backing in either specie or cotton.[41] If there was any single factor that must stand before all the others in the defeat of the Confederacy, it was the stunning failure of Memminger and the treasury to make the Confederate economy work. As late as the fall of 1863, Josiah Gorgas was confident that "there is breadstuff enough" and "war material" sufficient—

[41]Douglas B. Ball, *Financial Failure and Confederate Defeat* (Urbana, IL, 1991), pp. 85–98, 128–129.

men, guns, powder . . . to carry on the war for an indefinite period. . . . The real pinch is in the Treasury."[42]

Davis's difficulties in assembling a competent cabinet were sometimes overshadowed by the political turbulence of the Confederate congress. The provisional congress that first sat in Montgomery was composed of only fifty members, appointed by the state secession conventions and including some of the South's most distinguished men (including a former president of the United States, John Tyler). But once the new constitution was formally adopted and the capital moved to Richmond, a new Confederate congress had to be elected, and when it assembled in November 1861, it turned out to be a very different assembly. The Confederate armies had sucked up a good deal of the Confederacy's experienced leadership, with the result that only about a third of the 257 men who sat in the Confederate congress during the war possessed any previous service in the federal Congress. The rest were either political amateurs or else men with nothing more than the limited experience of serving in state legislatures, who would be likely to speak only for the most narrow and local state interests. And even those who could boast some experience in the old Congress were men whose long struggle to defend slavery there had turned them temperamentally into political outsiders, more inclined to oppose and criticize than to construct. "You would be amazed to see the differences of opinion that exist among the members," wrote Georgia Congressman Warren Akin, "It seems, sometimes, that no proposition, however plain and simple could be made that would not meet with opposition." Absenteeism, drunkenness, and outright brawling on the floor of the house further crippled the effectiveness of the Confederate congress. Georgia Senator Benjamin Hill hurled an inkstand at the head of William Yancey of Alabama; Henry Foote of Tennessee attacked another member with a bowie knife; an outraged female constituent of Missouri Senator George Vest horsewhipped him in the lobby of the capitol. "Some malign influence seems to preside over your councils," complained James Henry Hammond to Virginia Senator R. M. T. Hunter. "Pardon me, is the majority always drunk?"[43]

Mercifully for Jefferson Davis, few challenges to his calls for greater central authority in Richmond emerged from congress during the first ten months of the war. But the sudden loss of Forts Henry and Donelson, followed by the failure to redeem the Tennessee River at Shiloh and the fall of New Orleans, badly jolted southern complacency. On February 27, 1862, only five days after his formal inauguration as Confederate president under the new constitution, Davis suspended the writ of habeas corpus around Norfolk and Portsmouth, Virginia, and he eventually widened his suspension of the writ to include any southern districts threatened by invasion. And on March 28th, he appealed to the Confederate congress to institute

---

[42]*The Civil War Diary of General Josiah Gorgas*, Frank E. Vandiver, ed. (University, AL, 1947) pp. 68, 172.
[43]Clement Eaton, *A History of the Southern Confederacy* (New York, 1954), p. 63; Peter J. Parish, *The American Civil War* (New York, 1975), pp. 218–219; W. B. Yearns, *The Confederate Congress* (Athens, GA, 1960), pp. 15–16.

a selective military draft for all males between ages eighteen and thirty-five. The congress blinked, and on April 16th, passed Davis's Conscription Act (with some important exemptions) by a margin of two-to-one.

The grasp of the conscription bill over the rights of the individual southern states was greater than anything anyone had seen, even in the old Union. Georgia Governor Joseph E. Brown protested the draft in pure Democratic terms as a "bold and dangerous usurpation by Congress of the reserved rights of the States . . . at war with all the principles for which Georgia entered into the revoluton." To Alexander Stephens, Brown added that "I entered into this revolution to contribute my humble mite to sustain the rights of the states and prevent the consolidation of Government, and I am a rebel till this object is accomplished, no matter who may be in power." To the delight of his constituents, Brown defied the draft in the state courts, and promptly appointed large numbers of eligible Georgia males to fictitious state offices in order to exempt them. In South Carolina, Governor Francis W. Pickens was trying to impose a state draft of his own, and attempted to exempt South Carolina draftees from any liability to the Confederate draft. Even in Virginia, the otherwise cooperative Governor John Letcher ordered the superintendent of the Virginia Military Institute to refuse any movement to draft VMI cadets.[44]

The Conscription Act also alienated a far more dangerous segment of southern society by exempting certain classes of skilled workers, and (in response to planter anxieties over the possibility of slave revolts when so many southern white men were being pulled into the armies) the owners, agents, or overseers of plantations with more than twenty slaves. The intentions behind the exemption were plausible enough, but linking slave-ownership to exemption from war service was a spark to the tinder of the nonslaveholders of the South. In effect, this so-called "twenty-nigger law" protected large-scale slave-owning planters—the very people who had the most at stake in this war—from military service, while drafting the small-scale slaveholders and the nonslaveholders who had the least interest in fighting to defend slavery. That, in turn, caused southern yeomen who had been ambivalent about the planters and their slaves anyway, and who rallied to the defense of the Confederacy only because it promised to keep the demons of abolition and black amalgamation from their doors, to wonder once again whether they had more to lose at the hands of the Yankees or the planters. "Never did a law meet with more universal odium than the exemption of slave-owners," warned Senator James Phelan as he wrote to Jefferson Davis in December, 1862. "Its influence upon the poor is most calamitous." And Phelan prophesied all too accurately that the controversial exemptions had "awakened a spirit and elicited a discussion of which we may safely predicate the most unfortunate results."[45]

But Davis turned out to be both stubborn and resourceful is getting his legislative way with the draft. Since the Confederate congress had declined to organize

[44]Albert Burton Moore, *Conscription and Conflict in the Confederacy* (New York, 1924), pp. 24, 298–299.
[45]Moore, *Conscription and Conflict in the Confederacy*, p. 71.

even the rudimentary supreme court allowed by the Confederate constitution, Davis took his defense of the Conscription Act into the Georgia state courts, and to the amazement of onlookers, won. In Richmond, he kept a working majority behind his bills, and lost only one veto to an override in congress. In time, as Confederate military fortunes ebbed away after Antietam and Perryville, he persuaded congress to hand him even more vital powers. In March, 1863, congress authorized quartermaster and commissary officers to confiscate food and animals for the use of the Confederate army, offering as payment a scale of reimbursement at well below market values. A month later, in an effort to raise more revenue and pull some of Memminger's worthless paper currency out of circulation, congress imposed a broad range of stiff direct taxes on the Confederate people, including an 8% property tax, another 10 percent tax-in-kind on livestock and produce, and a graduated income tax up to 15 percent on all yearly incomes over $10,000.[46]

Once again, the howls of the state sovereignty loyalists rebounded from the walls of the state capitols. R. M. T. Hunter, once a member of Davis's cabinet and now a senator from Virginia, turned on the president, and even the vice-president, Alexander Stephens, became a bitter critic of Davis's national policies. Moreover, the tightening of the blockade and the gradual collapse of the Confederacy's own internal transportation system spelled increasing want and dislocation for southern society, and only further undermined popular support for the war and for Davis's programs of nationalization. With the war cutting off southern access to northern markets, shortages of even the most ordinary goods now began to cramp southern life. Although Davis successfully urged cotton planters to switch to planting grains and cereals for the war, much of it had no way to reach vital Confederate markets. The shortages combined with the unreliability of Memminger's unceasing flood of unbacked bonds and notes drove prices on goods to astronomical levels. In Richmond, John B. Jones, a war department clerk, found that "a dollar in gold sold for $18 Confederate money" on November 21st, 1863, while "a genteel suit of clothes cannot be had for less than $700" and "a pair of boots, $200—if good." Two weeks later, after Bragg had been driven off Missionary Ridge, one gold dollar was fetching twenty-eight Confederate ones. On a combined family income of $7,200 in 1864, Jones was forced to buy "flour at $300 a barrel; meal, $50 per bushel; and even fresh fish at $5 per pound." By the end of the year, Richmond hospital steward Luther Swank found flour going at $400 a barrel, sweet potatoes at $40 a bushel, and butter at $11 a pound. In the treasury department, Jones confided to his diary, "some of the clerks would shoot Mr. Memminger cheerfully."[47]

As the price for creating an independent Confederate nation rose higher and

---

[46]Emory Thomas, *The Confederate Nation, 1861–1865* (New York, 1979), p. 198; Yearns, *The Confederate Congress*, pp. 199–200.

[47]Jones, *A Rebel War Clerk's Diary*, E. S. Miers, ed. (New York, 1958), pp. 309, 316, 345, 349; "Inflation Grips the South: Luther Swank reports from a Field Hospital," Horace Mathews, ed., in *Civil War Times Illustrated* 22 (March 1983), p. 46.

higher, more and more Southerners began to kick against the goads. William W. Holden, the editor of the Raleigh *Standard*, began editorializing for a negotiated peace in 1863, only to have soldiers destroy his press; undaunted, he resumed publication of the *Standard* and in 1864 ran for governor of North Carolina against Zebulon Vance on the unspoken promise to take North Carolina out of the war or out of the Confederacy. In the Carolinas and northern Alabama, secret antiwar movements with names like the Order of the Heroes of America in western North Carolina and southwestern Virginia, the Peace and Constitutional Society in the hill country of Arkansas, and the Peace Society in northern Alabama sprang into existence. The yeomen of the piney woods of Alabama had been reluctant secessionists to start with, and by the spring of 1862, Unionists in Winston County were raising recruits for the *Union* army. Overall, at least 100,000 Southerners ended up enlisting to fight against the Confederacy.[48] Others who weren't actually volunteering to fight the Confederates were concealing Confederate army deserters, and before the end of the war, Winston County had sheltered between 8,000 and 10,000 deserters. Some southern counties simply deserted the Confederacy en masse: in western Virginia, the nonslaveholding mountain counties created their own new state of Kanawha in August of 1861—effectively seceding from secession—and in 1863, they were formally admitted to the Union as the state of West Virginia.

Little wonder, then, that congressional by-elections in the fall of 1863 showed a significant drop in confidence in Davis's policies. The number of antiadministration representatives in the Confederate house rose from twenty-six to forty-one, out of a total of 106, while in the Confederate senate, Davis clung to thin majority of fourteen proadministration members out of twenty-six. None of the new members from North Carolina had voted for secession two years before, and one of the Alabama representatives was so plainly in favor of an immediate peace that the congress voted to expel him. And yet, Davis beat back every attempt to unseat his administration. A bill to limit the tenure of cabinet officers to two years died on Davis's desk, and his congressional backers kept turning the trick for him on crucial votes.[49] In fact, far from being intimidated by his administration's losses at the polls, Davis had still more demands to make of congress in the name of Confederate nationhood. When the last session of the first Confederate congress convened in Richmond on December 7, 1863, Davis immediately urged the further expansion of the draft, and added provisions to the conscription laws that allowed the government to reach into the civilian labor pool to reassign and reallocate workers. Two months later, he also obtained a new and expanded suspension of habeas corpus, a supervisory monopoly over all blockade-running enterprises, and on February 17, 1864, a compulsory funding bill that would compel Confederate citizens to pay their taxes either in specie or in government bonds. Once again, the centralizing authority of the Rich-

---

[48]Richard N. Current, *Lincoln's Loyalists: Union Soldiers from the Confederacy* (Boston, 1992), pp. 195–197.

[49]Paul D. Escott, *After Secession: Jefferson Davis and the Failure of Confederate Nationalism* (Baton Rouge, LA, 1978), p. 155; Yearns, *The Confederate Congress*, pp. 224–225, 234.

mond government had further overridden the localism and individualism that three years before had been a major cause of southern secession.

None of these measures, however, could stanch the ebbing of the Confederacy's territory and armies, and so on November 7, 1864, when the second (and last) session of the second congress met, Davis finally decided to trade in the last symbol of the Democratic South in a bid to save the new Confederacy. He asked congress to allow the Confederate government to purchase 40,000 slaves, enlist them as soldiers in the Confederate army, and emancipate them upon completion of their enlistment as a reward for service.

Actually, the proposal to arm the slaves and offer them the carrot of emancipation to guarantee good service had not originated with Davis. It had first been publicly broached on January 2, 1864, by Patrick Cleburne, the Army of Tennessee's Irish-born corps commander. Significantly, Cleburne was not a slave-owner himself and had little interest in slavery. His principal rationale was the preservation of Confederate independence: "As between the loss of independence and the loss of slavery, we assume that every patriot will freely give up the latter—give up the negro slave rather than be a slave himself."[50] But this was asking much more of Southerners in the name of the Confederacy than Cleburne realized; he was, in fact, asking them to surrender the cornerstone of white racism and *herrenvolk* democracy in order to preserve their nation, and that was more than Davis felt he could safely ask. All copies of Cleburne's written proposal were destroyed. But ten months later, Davis felt he no longer had room for choice, and so in November, 1864, Davis introduced his own proposal for arming the slaves to the Confederate house. This time, even Davis's closest political allies stopped short. Howell Cobb, who thought he was fighting the war to preserve slavery and not some elusive Confederate nationalism, warned Davis that "The day you make soldiers of them is the beginning of the end of the revolution. If slaves will make good soldiers our whole theory of slavery is wrong." North Carolina newspapers bitterly attacked the proposal as "farcical"—"all this was done *for the preservation and perpetuation of slavery*" and if "sober men . . . are ready to enquire if the South is willing to abolish slavery as a condition of carrying on the war, why may it not be done, as a condition of *ending the war?*" Without slavery, Virginia Governor William Smith exclaimed, the South "would no longer have a motive to continue the struggle."[51] But the continuing collapse of the Confederate field armies eventually frightened even the most diehard slaveholders in congress, and when General Lee added his endorsement to Davis's plan in February, 1865, the opposition crumbled. On March 13th, with a margin of only one vote in the senate, the congress voted to authorize the recruitment of black soldiers. Twelve days later, the first black Confederate companies began drilling in Richmond.

[50]Howell and Elizabeth Purdue, *Pat Cleburne: Confederate General* (Hillsboro, TX, 1973), p. 267.
[51]Richard E. Beringer, Herman Hattaway, Archer Jones, William N. Still, *Why the South Lost the Civil War* (Athens, GA, 1986), pp. 384–385.

Would African Americans have fought to save the Confederate nation? They just might have, since southern blacks demonstrated repeatedly throughout the war a healthy skepticism of all white intentions and promises, and were prepared to grasp for liberty without regard to who offered it. A skeptical Georgia slave told Union Major George Ward Nichols that it was all well and good that the Union armies had come to bring him freedom, "But, massa, you'se'll go way to-morrow, and anudder white man'll come." Nichols could only nod in agreement: "He had never known any thing but persecutions and injury from the white man, and had been kept in such ignorance . . . that he did not dare to put faith in any white man."[52] On those terms, blacks would take freedom, even if the offer came from Jefferson Davis, rather than wait passively to receive it only from Abraham Lincoln. But in the event, it was really too late for anyone to find out what might have happened. Less than a month after the Confederate congress authorized black enlistment, the war was over and the prospect of black Confederates was left to drift off into the realm of might-have-been. In the end, Davis could not persuade every white Southerner to allow him to override state interests and slave interests fast enough to save the Confederacy as a nation.

Yet, this is not to say that the idea of creating a Confederate nation and a Confederate nationalism was a foreordained failure. The move to recruit black soldiers was a testimony to the fact that the South entered the war short of the resources that would have guaranteed victory, but it also indicated the degree to which Davis and like-minded Southerners had managed to move the Confederacy toward thinking of itself as a nationality whose collective survival was more impor- tant than the preservation of its individual parts. The Confederate nation did not survive the Civil War, but the 94,000 Southerners who died in its battles, and the four years of fire that it sustained in the teeth of the North's industrial and military might, are a warning not to underestimate how close Davis came to building a Confederate nation out of the materials he had in hand. The irony is, of course, that had Davis and the Confederacy succeeded, they would not have been the political nation they thought they were in 1861. For all its protests, the only possible form in which the Confederate nation could have survived would have been the very centralized nation-state that the seceders had been fleeing in 1861.

What Davis needed was time—time to weld together a nation of Democratic republicans, time to persuade slaveholders and nonslaveholders that each served the other's best interests, time to make the kind of mistakes in finance and domestic policy that any politicians must make when they attempt to re-create a nation on untried blueprints. But time was not on the side of the Confederacy. The idea of Confederate nationalism dawned upon Southerners too slowly and too reluctantly for them to make the cultural sacrifices necessary to save it. And after the war,

[52]George Ward Nichols, *The Story of the Great March from the Diary of a Staff Officer* (1865; rept. Williamstown, MA, 1972), p. 59; Clarence Mohr, *On the Threshold of Freedom: Masters and Slaves in Civil War Georgia* (Athens, GA, 1985), pp. 288–289.

Southern whites re-created a newer brand of the old Jacksonian ideology, along with a kind of legal quasi-slavery that allowed them to remain simply a peculiar people rather than a nation.

Further Reading

The movements of the eastern armies that led to the battles of Fredericksburg and Chancellorsville have always stood in the shadow of the great battle that followed them at Gettysburg in the summer of 1863. The Gettysburg campaign has now generated not only its own free-standing bibliographies of material solely devoted to Gettysburg, but even bibliographies of the bibliographies. For the admittedly limited purposes of these listings, it will suffice to point to Edwin B. Coddington's *The Gettysburg Campaign: A Study in Command* (New York, 1968) as the best overall study of the campaign, with Glenn Tucker's *High Tide at Gettysburg: The Campaign in Pennsylvania* (Indianapolis, IN, 1958) being the best single-volume book on the battle itself. Breaking the campaign down into segments, it is possible to begin a detailed reading of Gettysburg with Wilbur S. Nye's excellent study of the Confederate invasion of Pennsylvania, *Here Come the Rebels!* (1965; rept. Dayton, OH, 1984), followed by Warren W. Hassler's fine book on the first day of the Gettysburg battle, *Crisis at the Crossroads: The First Day at Gettysburg* (University, AL, 1970). Harry W. Pfanz's meticulous studies of the second day, *Gettysburg: The Second Day* (Chapel Hill, NC, 1987), and *Gettysburg: Culp's Hill and Cemetery Hill* (Chapel Hill, NC, 1993) are outstanding pieces of strictly military history. The military action of the third day at Gettysburg is dominated by "Pickett's Charge" (even though, in strict truth, it was not Pickett who was in command of the "charge" but his superior, James Longstreet) and it has found a vivid and precisely detailed "microhistory" in George R. Stewart, *Pickett's Charge: A Microhistory of the Final Attack at Gettysburg, July 3, 1863* (Boston, 1959).

In the west, the finest survey of the Confederacy's desperate campaign in 1863 to hold onto its heartland is the second volume of Thomas Connelly's history of the Army of Tennessee, *Autumn of Glory: The Army of Tennessee, 1862–1865* (Baton Rouge, LA, 1971). The Army of Tennessee has been compared, and not favorably, with the Army of Northern Virginia in Richard M. McMurry's brief but pungent *Two Great Rebel Armies* (Chapel Hill, NC, 1989). The major battles fought in the west from the end of 1862 till the dismissal of Braxton Bragg were for many years the orphans of Civil War military history. But since the 1970s, a series of outstanding battle histories has rejuvenated interest in such desperate but almost-forgotten engagements as Murfreesboro (Stones River), Chickamauga, and Chattanooga. James Lee McDonough has borne the burden of this rejuvenation with his *Stones River—Bloody Winter in Tennessee* (Knoxville, TN, 1980) and *Chattanooga: A Death Grip on the Confederacy* (Knoxville, TN, 1987). But, in addition, Peter Cozzens's *No Better Place to Die: The Battle of Stones River* (Urbana, IL, 1990) is an outstanding Civil War battle history, as is Glenn Tucker's much older *Chickamauga, Bloody Battle in the West* (1961; rept. Dayton, OH, 1976).

The overall struggle of the Confederacy to establish not only its independence, but a sense of itself as a separate nation and culture, has been brilliantly surveyed in Emory Thomas, *The Confederate Nation, 1861–1865* (New York, 1979). Alongside Thomas are a series of excellent older histories of the Confederacy, especially E. Merton Coulter's thick *The Confederate States of America, 1861–1865* (Baton Rouge, LA, 1950), Frank Vandiver's brief and sprightly *Their Tattered Flags: The Epic of the Confederacy* (New York, 1970), and Clement Eaton's detail-studded *A History of the Southern Confederacy* (New York, 1954). The four remarkable essays that comprise Drew G. Faust's *The Creation of Confederate Nationalism: Ideology and Identity in the Civil War South* (Baton Rouge, 1988) explain the various attempts of Southerners to create a distinct Confederate culture and ideology. The best place to begin the story of Confederate politics is with Jefferson Davis himself, who provided his own history (and his own interpretation) of Confederate politics in *The Rise and Fall of the Confederate Government*, James McPherson, ed. (New York, 1991). Davis has also been the subject of several major biographies, the most recent and the most outstanding being William C. Davis, *Jefferson Davis: The Man and His Hour* (New York, 1991) and Clement Eaton, *Jefferson Davis* (New York, 1977). Ludwell H. Johnson's "Jefferson Davis and Abraham Lincoln as War Presidents: Nothing Succeeds like Success" in *Civil War History* 27 (March 1981) is a daring and stimulating comparison of Lincoln and Davis in which Davis clearly comes off the better. The fractious politicians Davis dealt with in Richmond have also been analyzed individually and as a group in W. B. Yearns, *The Confederate Congress* (Athens, GA, 1960) and in Thomas B. Alexander and Richard Beringer, *The Anatomy of the Confederate Congress: A Study of the Influences of Member Characteristics on Voting Behavior, 1861–1865* (Nashville, TN, 1972).

The Confederacy's military leadership has generally gotten much higher grades than its political leadership, and more sympathetic biographies along with them. The literature on Lee, like that on Gettysburg, has now spawned its own subcategory of revisionist interpretation, beginning with Thomas L. Connelly's daring and controversial *The Marble Man: Robert E. Lee and His Image in American Society* (New York, 1977). Connelly has been seconded by Alan T. Nolan's *Lee Considered: General Robert E. Lee and Civil War History* (Chapel Hill, NC, 1991). Close behind Lee as an interesting biographical subject is Thomas Jonathan "Stonewall" Jackson, who was the subject of a biography by his chief of staff, Robert Lewis Dabney, even before the Civil War was over. Byron Farwell's *Stonewall: A Biography of General Thomas J. Jackson* (New York, 1992) is a vivid retelling of Jackson's career as Lee's most peculiar lieutenant, but it should be supplemented by the searching interpretative essays on Jackson's character and campaigns in *Whatever You Resolve to Be: Essays on Stonewall Jackson*, A. Wilson Greene, ed. (Baltimore, MD, 1992). James I. Robertson's *General A. P. Hill: The Story of a Confederate Warrior* (New York, 1987) astounded the Civil War historical community by identifying Ambrose Powell Hill's mysterious and debilitating illnesses as a sexually transmitted disease, contracted while a cadet at West Point. The most frequently studied Confederate officer in the West is Nathan Bedford Forrest, whose colorful and combative career has been described in Brian Wills's *A Battle from the Start: The Life of Nathan Bedford Forrest* (New York, 1992). Braxton Bragg had only a half a biographical life from Grady McWhiney until Judith Lee Hallock's *Braxton Bragg and Confederate Defeat, Volume Two* (Tuscaloosa, AL, 1991) completed the two-volume biography McWhiney began in 1969.

The war was hardly over before its survivors began speculating on why the South lost, and among modern attempts to answer that question, the most far-reaching is Richard E. Beringer, Herman Hattaway, Archer Jones, and William N. Still, *Why the South Lost the Civil War* (Athens, GA, 1986). This book needs to be read beside the more hard-headed reasons for Confederate collapse laid out in Douglas E. Ball's *Financial Failure and Confederate Defeat* (Urbana, IL, 1991) and Richard C. Todd's *Confederate Finance* (Athens, GA, 1954). Some of the depth of states'-rights and unionist resistance in the South can be appreciated through reading Georgia L. Tatum, *Disloyalty in the Confederacy* (Chapel Hill, NC, 1934) and Albert Burton Moore's classic account of Confederate draft policies *Conscription and Conflict in the Confederacy* (New York, 1924). More recently, Paul D. Escott's *After Secession: Jefferson Davis and the Failure of Confederate Nationalism* (Baton Rouge, 1978) has surveyed Jefferson Davis's difficulties in selling the notion of a Confederate nation over the hurdles of popular resistance, wartime suffering, and his political enemies. Davis's last, desperate bid to save the Confederacy by sacrificing the South's most potent symbol of localism and independence has been chronicled in Robert F. Durden, *The Gray and the Black: The Confederate Debate on Emancipation* (Baton Rouge, LA, 1972).

CHAPTER 9

World Turned Upside Down

Willard Glazier was a lithe, sharp-witted 19-year-old when he enlisted in the 2nd New York Cavalry in 1861. Starting out as an ordinary private, he soon climbed the ladder of promotion, and at the end of August in 1863, he was commissioned as a second lieutenant for Company M of the 2nd New York. That was where his promotions ended. In a skirmish at New Baltimore, Virginia, on October 19, 1863, Glazier's horse was shot from under him, and he was captured by Confederate cavalry.

Just as neither North nor South had been prepared to wage war, neither had been prepared to deal with one of the major encumbrances of war, the keeping of enemy prisoners. Both governments quickly constructed elaborate exchange systems to get enemy prisoners off their hands and to retrieve their own soldiers. But the exchange systems were cumbersome, and the personnel needed for running them was really needed somewhere else; more often than not, the improvised prisoner camps degenerated into slow-moving pools of maltreatment, humiliation, hunger, and death. Glazier got a taste of this early on, when the Virginia militia who shoved him along the road from New Baltimore to Warrenton neatly stripped him of his watch and his overcoat, and then dumped him into Libby Prison, a converted warehouse that had become Richmond's principal holding pen for Union officers. There, Glazier languished until May, 1864, when Libby Prison was closed down and the inmates piled onto trains that would take them farther south. Glazier then bounced from one prison camp to another in Georgia and South Carolina, until he was finally delivered to a camp near Columbia, South Carolina, in November. There, he and a friend slipped into a column of paroled prisoners who were leaving the camp and made off into the woods.

And there began the most curious part of Glazier's adventures. Without food, weapons, or even decent clothing, Glazier and his friend somehow had to find their way to Union lines from deep within rebel territory, and they had not the faintest idea of how to do it. But Glazier had some unsuspected allies, fashioned for him by the war and emancipation, and he recognized those allies as soon as they came down the road he was standing on. They were, of course, black slaves, for in spite of the conventional wisdom up until 1863, the slaves had known all along that the war and the Yankees meant freedom, and now Willard Glazier was about to have a similar epiphany on that Carolina road. The slaves walked by him, eyeing Glazier and his friend suspiciously. "I reckon deys Yankees," remarked one. "Golly, I hope to God dey is," replied another. Glazier took his chance. "We are Yankees and have just escaped from Columbia," Glazier pleaded. "Can't you do something for us?" The slaves stopped and laughed. "Ob course," they replied eagerly, and one added "I'll do all I can for you, marster. I no nigga if I didn't 'sist de Yankees."

And so Willard Glazier, federal officer and prisoner of the Confederacy, became the ward of the most powerless class of people in the American republic. With black slaves as his providers and guides, Glazier and his friend were passed surreptitiously from one plantation to another. "It was always a pleasant interruption of their lonely tramp to meet any negroes," Glazier's biographer wrote twenty years later. "These people, so patient under oppression . . . were ever faithful and devoted to those whom they believed to be the friends of their race . . . and the cruelties practised upon them seem rather to have opened their hearts to sympathy than to have hardened them into vindictiveness." Eventually, Glazier and his friend met up with two other bands of fugitive Yankee prisoners, and all of them were moved by night with slave guides and sheltered by day in huts and barns and "a corn-fodder house." One slave family found and repaired a boat to get them across the Savannah River; another slave resoled Glazier's worn-out shoes. Twenty miles north of Savannah, on December 15th, Glazier blundered into Confederate pickets and was recaptured. But four days later he slipped away again and found his way once more to "the hut of a negro." Occasionally, he was even able to beg a meal from a hard-eyed white farmer's wife who held no love for Confederate conscription agents and tax gatherers. A free black family near Cherokee Hill, Georgia, found him a guide named March Dasher, another free black who at last guided Glazier to federal lines in northern Georgia on December 23, 1864.

As a white male and an officer, Glazier was the embodiment of a social order in which white men held power and ruled over submissive white women and submissive black slaves. But the chance of war had inverted those relationships: Willard Glazier found himself powerless and completely dependent on the leadership and goodwill of black slaves and farm women. That same inversion would see Willard Glazier's story repeated over and over again throughout the war years, for the Civil War would impose on American society as much social disruption as it did physical destruction. And within that disruption, for one brief and bloody historical moment, an entirely new way of ordering race and gender within a republican society would become possible.

1. By Their Own Strong Arms

After more than a century, nothing blurs the image of the Civil War more than the realization that white Northerners were less than enthusiastic about the Emancipation Proclamation—even though emancipation helped fend off the possibility of outside intervention in the war and provided nearly 200,000 extra soldiers and sailors to help win it. Even among Northerners who genuinely believed that slavery was an evil, emancipation was celebrated largely for the way it secured the triumph of free capitalist labor in the republic, and few whites saw any connection between emancipation and extending republican equality to blacks.

It was clear that many Northerners (Lincoln included) believed that the next step after emancipation was the colonization of African Americans to Central America or the American Southwest, or repatriation to Africa. "The African race here is a foreign and feeble element," explained Lincoln's secretary of state, William Henry Seward, a view echoed by the secretary of the treasury, Salmon Chase, who reluctantly agreed that "the separation of the races" was unavoidable, and that African Americans should seek "happier homes in other lands." Even while he was discussing emancipation with his Cabinet in the summer of 1862, Lincoln was advising a delegation of black leaders that "it is better for us both . . . to be separated." Even though "your race are suffering, in my judgment, the greatest wrong inflicted on any people," it was still a fact—regrettable, perhaps, but a fact all the same—that "even when you cease to be slaves, you are yet far removed from being on an equality with the white race. . . . There is an unwillingness on the part of our people, harsh as it may be, for you free colored people to remain with us."[1]

This was decidedly not a view shared by African Americans. But if numbers and influence meant anything, there did not seem to be much they could do about it. Out of a total population in the United States of 31,443,000 in 1860, African Americans numbered only about 4,441,000, some 14 percent of the population, and of that number, less than 500,000 were free. And even for those who were free, only a small number enjoyed anything like full participation in the political life of their communities or the republic as a whole. Still, from the very beginning, African Americans never saw the war as anything but a war against slavery, and never saw the war against slavery as anything less than a struggle for full equality in the life of the American republic. Hardly had Fort Sumter fallen than Frederick Douglass began agitating, for a no-holds-barred assault on slavery as the central thrust of the war. "The slaveholders themselves have saved our cause from ruin!" Douglass exulted in the summer of 1861, and he exhorted the readers of *Douglass' Monthly* to press "the keen knife of liberty" to southern throats. Instead of a restrained war aimed at the reconciliation of the southern states, Douglass wanted a war of destruction, and especially the destruction of slavery, waged in the South. Appealing to the rhetoric of the "Slave Power" conspiracy, Douglass called on northern whites to see the war not as a political misadjustment over constitutional niceties, but a monstrous conspiracy of slaveholders, hatched for the sake of slavery against the well-being of every American. In such a war, there could be no peace

---

[1]Eric Foner, *Free Soil, Free Labor, Free Men: The Ideology of the Republican Party before the Civil War* (Oxford, 1970), pp. 261–269; Frederick J. Blue, *Salmon P. Chase: A Life in Politics* (Kent, OH, 1987), pp. 83–84; Lincoln, "Address on Colonization to a Deputation of Negroes," in *Collected Works*, vol. 5, pp. 371–372.

without the destruction of slavery. "There is but one . . . effectual way to suppress and put down the desolating war which the slaveholders and their rebel minions are now waging against the American government and its loyal citizens. . . . *The simple way . . . to put an end to the savage and desolating war now waged by the slaveholders, is to strike down slavery itself,* the primal cause of that war."[2]

For Douglass and other northern blacks, the most obvious way to nudge the war for reunion toward a war for abolition was to put black soldiers on the Union firing lines, and in 1861, thousands of northern blacks stepped forward to volunteer. "No nation ever has or ever will be emancipated from slavery . . . but by the sword, wielded too by their own strong arms," wrote a black schoolteacher in the pages of the newspaper *Anglo-African* in 1861. "The prejudiced white men North or South never will respect us until they are forced to do it by deeds of our own."[3] In Pittsburgh, an all-black militia company known as the "Hannibal Guards" offered its services to the governor of Pennsylvania; in Cleveland, Ohio, another company of free blacks published their resolution "That today, as in the times of '76, and the days of 1812, we are ready to go forth and do battle in the common cause of the country." But there was a higher purpose to be served by black volunteers than merely the satisfaction of focusing white attention on a war about black slavery. By volunteering for military service alongside whites, African Americans were laying claim to a tacit equality with whites—to "a common cause" that whites and blacks shared equally—since it only stood to reason that if blacks could fight and die alongside whites, they were certainly fit to vote and work alongside them, too.

And perhaps because the logic of that position was as clear as it was, black volunteers in 1861 were abruptly shown the door by the War Department. There were, in the first place, a series of legal roadblocks to black enlistment, beginning with the militia act Lincoln used to call out the first volunteers, which limited volunteer service to white males (oddly, the U.S. Navy drew no such color line). But far more menacing were the attitudes of white Northerners, who angrily fended off black volunteers with the warning, "We want you d——d niggers to keep out of this; this is a white man's war." Northern whites could read the political logic of black enlistment as easily as any black volunteer, and they wanted no part of it. "The negro is not equal to a white man," insisted Arthur Carpenter, a white Union volunteer, and he was fearful that "being called a united states soldier" would put the African American "upon an equality with us in being allowed to fight with us." Felix Brannigan, a white New York sergeant, wrote in an open letter to a New York City newspaper that "we don't want to fight side and side by the nigger. We think we are too superior a race for that."[4]

[2]David W. Blight, *Frederick Douglass' Civil War: Keeping Faith in Jubilee* (Baton Rouge, 1989), pp. 82–83; McPherson, *The Negro's Civil War*, pp. 37–38.

[3]Alfred M. Green, in *The Negro's Civil War: How American Negroes Felt and Acted during the War for the Union*, James M. McPherson, ed. (New York, 1965), pp. 32–33.

[4]Randall Jimerson, *The Private Civil War: Popular Thought during the Sectional Conflict* (Baton Rouge, LA, 1988), p. 93; McPherson, *The Negro's Civil War*, p. 193.

Many northern blacks recoiled in disappointment and disgust from these re-buffs. But, as Lincoln himself explained, any move to recruit black soldiers in 1861 would have turned white Unionists in the border states against him, a loss that all the black soldiers in the North could not have made up for. "To arm the Negroes would turn 50,000 bayonets from the Loyal Border States against us that were for us," Lincoln told an Indiana delegation that wanted to offer him two regiments of black volunteers in 1862. "It is the determination of the Government not to arm Negroes unless some new and more pressing emergency arises." But by the fall of 1862, with Lee and Bragg rampaging into Kentucky and Maryland, that "new and pressing emergency" seemed to be upon Lincoln. And taking his cue from that "emergency," Frederick Douglass swerved around to a new line of argument: Blacks should be recruited for war service, not because their enlistment would turn the war toward abolition and equality, but because in practical terms black soldiers were a military necessity just to prevent defeat. "Our Presidents, Governors, Generals and Secretaries are calling, with almost frantic vehemence, for men," Douglass ob-served, "and yet these very officers, representing the people and the Government, steadily and persistently refuse to receive the very class of men which have a deeper interest in the defeat and humiliation of the rebels than all others. . . . Men in earnest don't fight with one hand, when they might fight with two, and a man drowning would not refuse to be saved even by a colored hand."[5]

African Americans, however, did not sit idly by awaiting Lincoln's permission to enter the war. Denied the privilege of volunteering in 1861, they found other ways to make the struggle theirs. Over the course of the war, as many as 500,000 slaves escaped from bondage in the South to the Union lines, and the decision of Benjamin Butler to treat them as "contraband of war" set a precedent for allowing runaway slaves to deprive the Confederacy of a critical supply of civilian and military labor. Once under Union flags, over 200,000 blacks found employment in various noncombat roles as teamsters, laborers, and cooks for the Union forces, until by the end of the war, much of the supply structure that kept the Union armies fed, clothed, and armed relied on African Americans who worked as underpaid but free men and women. The very presence of blacks among the federal armies soon forced the commanders of those armies to ask why blacks could not serve equally as well in the armies as soldiers. When the abolitionist General David Hunter took command of the new military district made up of the federally-occupied Carolina Sea Islands around Port Royal, he began organizing black military units on his own hook. In Kansas, the militant free-soil Senator Jim Lane recruited the 1st Kansas Colored Infantry, and when he was notified his new regiment could not be mustered into federal service because no authorization existed for black troops, Lane simply mustered them into his own service and went to war with them. And when

[5]Lincoln, "Remarks to Deputation of Western Gentlemen," in *Collected Works*, vol. 5, p. 357; James M. McPherson, *The Struggle for Equality: Abolitionists and the Negro in the Civil War and Reconstruction* (Princeton, NJ, 1964), p. 47; McPherson, *The Negro's Civil War*, p. 162.

Benjamin Butler took over military command of occupied New Orleans in 1862, he was surprised to find that free Louisiana blacks had already organized three regiments of black militia, complete with French-speaking black officers.

Pressed from behind by the need to fill the Union ranks, and from in front by the eagerness of blacks to fill those ranks, white opposition to black enlistment gradually crumbled. In July of 1862, Major General Philip Kearny, one of the most combative division commanders in the Army of the Potomac, defied George Mc-Clellan's reluctance to talk about emancipation as a war aim and began calling for the recruitment of "black adjuncts to the military" and "a Black Regiment" with "Jamaican Sergants" and white officers that could be given a "trial" on "the frontier garrisons."[6] That same month, Congress enacted its Second Confiscation Act, which included a provision repealing the 1792 ban on black volunteers, and in August, the War Department gave the official go-ahead to the new commander of the Port Royal district, Brigadier General Rufus Saxton, to enlist up to 5,000 black volunteers from the former slaves of the Port Royal plantations. In May, 1863, the War Department established a Bureau of Colored Troops and began recruiting black soldiers directly into federal service. Three states—Massachusetts, Connecticut, and occupied Louisiana—opened up enlistments for several regiments of black state volunteers.

The actual conditions in which these black volunteers found themselves turned out to be something less than ideal. Both the state-recruited "colored infantry" of New England and Louisiana and the new federal units known as United States Colored Troops (USCT) were to be segregated, all-black regiments—all-black, that is, except for the officer grades, which were reserved for whites. When Massachusetts Governor John Andrew tried to issue a state commission as a second lieutenant to Sergeant Stephen Swails of the 54th Massachusetts (one of the two "colored" infantry regiments raised by the Bay State), the Bureau of Colored Troops obstinately refused to issue Swails a discharge from his sergeant's rank, and Swails's promotion was held up until after the end of the war. The black officers of the Louisiana militia were quickly discharged after the black Louisianians were mustered into federal service as the 73rd, 74th, 75th, and 76th USCT. Only in the last months of the war did the War Department reluctantly yield to the demands of the USCT's white officers to commission talented black soldiers, and in the end, only one black officer, Martin R. Delany, rose as high as the rank of major.

Black soldiers also had their patience tried to the point of mutiny by the War Department's decision to pay them only $10 a month (the same pay as teamsters and cooks) instead of the $13 paid to white volunteers, and to issue some black regiments inferior equipment and weapons. Medical services for black soldiers were also thinner on the ground than for white volunteers, and black soldiers died from camp diseases at three times the rate of their white counterparts. Patience also suffered taunts and

---

[6]*Letters from the Peninsula: The Civil War Letters of General Philip Kearny*, W. H. B. Styple, ed. (Kearny, NJ, 1988), pp. 144–145.

humiliation from the white civilians whose nation they were enlisting to save, and from white soldiers whom they were supposed to fight beside. In August, 1862, a mob of immigrant workers, fearful of job competition from free blacks, burned down a black-owned tobacco warehouse in Brooklyn; the following March, an angry mob of whites burned down homes in a black neighborhood in Detroit; in July, 1863, savage riots in New York City resulted in the murder and beatings of dozens of African Americans. In November, the 2nd USCT was mobbed in the streets of Philadelphia as it prepared to board a troop train for New York. And all this had to be added to the threats of the Confederate congress, who interpreted the recruitment of black soldiers as an incitement to "servile insurrection" and threatened to re-enslave captured black soldiers and shoot their captured white officers.

But the chance to lend their own hands to the process of freedom more than made up in most cases for the inequities and harassment visited on African-American volunteers. "It really makes one's heart pulsate with pride as he looks upon those stout and brawny men, fully equipped with Uncle Sam's accoutrements upon them," wrote James Henry Gooding, a black corporal in the 54th Massachusetts, "to feel that these noble men are practically refuting the base assertions reiterated by copperheads and traitors that the black race are incapable of patriotism, valor, or ambition."[7] It also helped that the white officers of the USCT regiments were, on the whole, better-trained and better-motivated than their counterparts among the white volunteers. Since the USCT were mustered directly into federal rather than state service, officer's commissions came through the War Department rather than through politicians in the state capitals, and the Bureau of Colored Troops quickly instituted a rigorous application and examination process to screen whites who wanted to become USCT officers. As a result, most of the officer's commissions in the USCT went to experienced former sergeants and officers from white volunteer regiments, many of whom were ardent abolitionists who saw the USCT as the troops themselves saw it, as a lever for freedom and equality.[8]

Some of the officers, whatever their level of sympathy for these goals, entered the USCT with their perceptions of blacks clouded by the hard growths of racial prejudice and doubts about the capacity of African Americans to stand up to the shock of combat. But once the black troops had their first opportunities in combat, the prejudices and doubts rapidly disappeared. In May, 1863, the black Louisiana militia led six furious assaults on Confederate fortifications at Port Hudson, Louisiana; they were followed the next month by the hand-to-hand defense of Milliken's Bend, Louisiana, by four black and one white Union regiments. Even the commander of the Confederates, Henry E. McCullough, was forced to concede that "This charge was resisted by the negro portion of the enemy's force with considerable

[7]Gooding, On the Altar of Freedom: A Black Soldier's Civil War Letters from the Front, Virginia M. Adams, ed. (Amherst, MA, 1991), p. 9.

[8]Joseph T. Glathaar, Forged in Battle: The Civil War Alliance of Black Soldiers and White Officers (New York, 1990), pp. 107–108.

obstinacy, while the white or true Yankee portion ran like whipped curs almost as soon as the charge was ordered." But the bloodiest laurels for black soldiers were won by the cream of the black volunteers, the 54th Massachusetts, with a blue-stocking white colonel, Robert Gould Shaw, and two sons of Frederick Douglass in its ranks. On July 18, 1863, Shaw and the 54th Massachusetts spearheaded an infantry attack on Battery Wagner, one of the outlying fortifications covering the land approaches to the harbor of Charleston, South Carolina. A full day's worth of bombardment by federal gunboats offshore had failed to silence the Confederate artillery in the fort, and when the 54th raced forward to the fort's walls, their ranks were shredded by Confederate fire. Nevertheless, the 54th swept up over the walls and into the fort, with Shaw and one of his black color-sergeants dying side-by-side on the parapet. The 54th gamely hung on to one corner of Battery Wagner but they were finally pushed off after a stubborn resistance. Sergeant William H. Carney staggered back from the fort with wounds in his chest and right arm, but with the regiment's Stars and Stripes securely in his grasp. "The old flag never touched the ground, boys," Carney gasped, as he collapsed at the first field hospital he could find.

The extraordinary valor of the black troops at Port Hudson, Milliken's Bend, and Battery Wagner sent waves of amazement over the North. Abraham Lincoln, who had been as dubious about the fighting qualities of the black soldiers as other whites, now agreed that "the use of colored troops constitute the heaviest blow yet dealt to the rebellion." Ulysses Grant concurred: In a letter to Lincoln one month after the assault on Battery Wagner, Grant agreed that "By arming the negro we have added a powerful ally. They will make good soldiers and taking them from the enemy weaken him in the same proportion as they strengthen us. . . . This, with the emancipation of the negro, is the heavyest blow yet given the Confederacy."[9] And so did the ordinary Union soldier: "The colored troops are very highly valued here & there is no apparent difference in the way they are treated," wrote one USCT officer in Virginia, "White troops and blacks mingle constantly together & I have seen no single Evidence of dislike on the part of the soldiers. The truth is they have fought their way into the respect of all the army." It was time, now that black soldiers had proven themselves under fire, for white Northerners to begin thinking about what was owed to African Americans at home. "The American people, as a nation, knew not what they were fighting for till recently," wrote Corporal Gooding, but now it was clear that "there is but two results possible, one is slavery and poverty and the other is liberty and prosperity."[10]

---

[9]Grant to Lincoln [August 23, 1863], in The Collected Papers of Ulysses S. Grant, John Y. Simon, ed. (Carbondale, IL, 1982), vol. 9, pp. 196–197; part of Grant's motive in this letter, which suspiciously echoes Lincoln's own words back to him, was certainly Grant's desire to ingratiate himself with Lincoln; still Grant's cooperation and support for black soldiers was critical to the enlistment of 20,000 African Americans in the Mississippi valley in 1863. Howard C. Westwood, "Grant's Role in Beginning Black Soldiery," in Journal of the Illinois Historical Society 79 (1986), pp. 197–212.

[10]Lincoln, "To James C. Conkling" [August 26, 1863], in Collected Works, vol. 6, p. 409; Glathaar, Forged in Battle, p. 168; Gooding, On the Altar of Freedom, p. 19.

But it proved harder to turn the tide of northern white opinion at home than it had been among northern soldiers in the army, and black soldiers were the first to discover this, almost literally in the streets of northern cities. In the great northern urban centers of Boston, New York, and Philadelphia, segregated streetcar systems immediately became a flashpoint for conflict, and especially when, as in New York City, streetcar operators began throwing black soldiers off the cars and into the streets. When the widow of a black sergeant was pushed off a New York City streetcar by a policeman, a public scandal followed, with Horace Greeley's New York *Tribune* growling that "It is quite time to settle the question whether the wives and children of the men who are laying down their lives for their country . . . are to be treated like dogs." In Philadelphia, where white and black abolitionists had been demanding an end to segregation on the city rail lines since 1859, a coalition of Republican and black civic organizations appealed to the city's Democratic mayor, and then finally to the state legislature, to end racial discrimination in public accommodations throughout Pennsylvania. In Washington, D.C., the veteran black abolitionist Sojourner Truth deliberately challenged a whites-only rule on the city streetcars by standing at streetcar stops and screeching "I want to ride!" at the top of her lungs. When a conductor on another streetcar tried to throw Sojourner off the car, he dislocated her shoulder; she promptly hired a lawyer, sued the streetcar company, and forced the company to abandon its racial discrimination policies. "Before the trial was ended," Sojourner announced sardonically, "the inside of the cars looked like pepper and salt."[11]

Not every battle for equality ended so happily. Free northern blacks operated in a largely urban context, where many of them had visible places in northern society and where white allies were fairly close at hand. Among the newly emancipated "freedmen" of the South, the story was significantly different. Lacking education, property, or even a clear sense of what emancipation might mean, slaves slipped away to the Union armies or celebrated their liberation as the Union forces marched southward past them without any certainty of what the next step might be. A federal officer marching down toward Murfreesboro wrote that "at every plantation negroes came flocking to the roadside to see us. . . . They have heard of the abolition army, the music, the banners, the glittering arms . . . [and they] welcome us with extravagant manifestations of joy. They keep time to the music with feet and hands and hurrah 'fur de ole flag and de Union,' sometimes following us for miles." An estimated 10,000 liberated slaves packed up and trailed after William Tecumseh Sherman and his army in 1864, shouting "Yesterday I was a slave, to day I am free. We are all white now."[12] In addition to the half-million slaves who ran away to the Union army, as many as 400,000 more were freed by the advance of the Union armies and subtracted

---

[11]McPherson, *Struggle for Equality*, p. 232; Philip Shaw Paludan, *A People's Contest: The Union and the Civil War, 1861–1865* (New York, 1988), pp. 220–221.

[12]Glathaar, *March to the Sea*, p. 60.

themselves both from their masters and from the Confederate war effort. But they quickly learned that emancipation was only the beginning of a new and uncharted future, and they did not receive much in the way of direction from either northern or southern whites. The federal armies frequently seized newly freed slaves and forced them into service as manual laborers, while embittered southern whites evicted their former slaves from white-owned property and refused to hire "freedmen" to work for them.

In a few places in the South, conscientious whites attempted to intervene and help the freed people toward literacy and economic independence. The northern "Gideonites" who descended on Port Royal in 1862 set up schools and churches, and pressed the Lincoln administration (through their own influential political networks at home) to have the plantations that had been abandoned by Port Royal's white masters before the Union seizure of the Carolina coast divided among the former slaves who had once worked those lands. In 1865, Congress took its own steps for setting the freed slaves up on their feet by organizing the Freedmen's Bureau, which was designed to establish schools, educate blacks in the intricacies of labor contracts, oversee wage and labor relations, and open up public lands to black settlers. But the experiment in land redistribution at Port Royal foundered on the greed of northern white land speculators (who had the money to outbid the former slaves at the open auctions of seized Confederate property) and on postwar legal challenges lodged by former plantation owners who successfully disputed the federal government's wartime authority to seize their property.

In the end, the most important agents for change would be the former slaves themselves. Many simply hit the road, sometimes in a nameless determination to put the scenes of slavery behind them, sometimes in a pathetic search for family members who had been sold away to other parts of the South years before. "They had a passion, not for wandering, as for getting together," wrote one white observer in South Carolina, "and every mother's son among them seemed to be in search of his mother; every mother in search of her children. In their eyes the work of emancipation was incomplete until the families which had been dispersed by slavery were reunited." Others sought to strike down roots in the soil they knew the best. In central Tennessee, the number of farms shot up from 19,000 in 1860 to nearly 30,000 in 1870, with more than three-quarters of that increase representing black farmers who now owned or rented their own land. That did not mean, however, that they were eager to assimilate themselves to white society. Blacks withdrew from the white churches where their masters had ruled over faith and practice, and formed their own congregations. And in defiance of the most vicious symbol of white dominance under slavery, the freed slaves rushed to county courthouses to legalize slave marriages and adopt surnames of their own choosing. In July, 1865, Tennessee's Bedford County courthouse issued marriage licenses to 422 couples—406 of them were black; in nearby Rutherford County that September, 431 black couples had their marriages legalized in a single week. Never again would a white man with an auctioneer's bill in his hand come between black husband and black wife, and never again would an African American be known simply as so-and-so's Tom or Dick or Cuffee or Caesar.[13] Mr. Carver's George would become George Washington Carver; James Burrough's child slave Booker would borrow his stepfather's first name to create a last name for himself and become Booker Taliaferro Washington.

So many of these steps seem so basic, and others so halting, that it is easy to lose sight of how much ground was really gained by African Americans in their stride toward civil equality. On the one hand, it was disappointingly true that outside of New England, where free black males already had some measure of voting rights, not a single northern state initiative to extend voting rights to blacks succeeded during the war, and publicly funded schooling remained closed to blacks in most northern states. But on the other hand, the thick carapace of prejudice and legalized discrimination was also showing clear and open cracks under the hammer blows of the black soldier and the black orator. Five New England cities voted to abolish segregated schools; California and Illinois repealed all of their invidious "black laws" (except, in Illinois, the ban on black voting). On the federal level, Congress repealed exclusionary laws on racial hiring and abolished its restraints on black participation in the federal court system, and on February 1, 1865, John S. Rock was presented by Charles Sumner to plead before the bar of the Supreme Court, the first African American to be admitted as counsel before a court that a decade before had declared that he was not even a citizen. "The Dred Scott Decision Buried in the Supreme Court," ran the New York *Tribune*'s headline, "Senator Charles Sumner and the Negro lawyer John S. Rock [were] the pall-bearers—the room of the Supreme Court of the United States the Potter's Field—the corpse the Dred Scott decision!" For African Americans, the future seemed without limits: Three centuries of bondage had passed away, and even if African Americans had not yet achieved the levels of equality they yearned for, they had still reached levels none had ever dreamed possible before the war. In November, 1864, two weeks after Maryland officially abolished slavery, Frederick Douglass returned to Baltimore for the first time since his flight from slavery twenty-six years before. He was "awed into silence" by the changes the war had wrought, and as he spoke to a racially mixed meeting at an African-American church, he declared that "the revolution is genuine, full and complete."[14]

Douglass was, for once, being an optimist. It was not an optimism widely shared by other racial minorities who found themselves with less at stake and less to gain by the war. By 1861, many of the most familiar Native American tribes had been driven out of their ancient lands east of the Mississippi, and either penned

[13]Leon Litwack, *Been in the Storm So Long: The Aftermath of Slavery* (New York, 1977, 1980), pp. 230, 240–251; Thomas V. Ash, *Middle Tennessee Society Transformed, 1860–1870: War and Peace in the Upper South* (Baton Rouge, LA, 1988), pp. 187, 210.

[14]George A. Levesque, "Boston's Black Brahmin: Dr. John S. Rock," in *Civil War History* 26 (December 1980), pp. 335–336; Blight, *Frederick Douglass' Civil War*, p. 186.

into reservations and "civilized" with white agriculture, education, and churches, or else forcibly relocated west of Mississippi with the tribes of the unsettled western plains. Few of these uprooted eastern tribes had much connection with the larger issue of slavery and disunion, except for the "civilized" Cherokees of the federally designated "Indian Territory" south of Kansas, who had been removed from their Alabama and Georgia homelands in the 1830s and who retained black slavery and a rudimentary plantation system. But like African Americans, Native Americans seized on the war as an opportunity for advancing or protecting political agendas of their own, although in the case of Native Americans, those agendas varied from place to place and tribe to tribe. The Iroquois of western New York had been resisting federal pressure to surrender their reservation lands and move west ever since the 1830s, and during the Civil War many of them stepped forward to volunteer for the Union army on the premise that Iroquois cooperation in winning the war would induce an appreciative federal government to leave them alone on their lands.[15] In southern Minnesota, the failure of the federal government to meet its treaty obligations with the Dakota Sioux of the Minnesota River reservation provoked a bloody uprising in August of 1862 that led to the deaths of over 350 white settlers. In the Indian Territory, intratribal political factions among Cherokee, Creeks, and Seminoles led to a miniature civil war among the tribes, with various factions soliciting Confederate or Union intervention in the territory to promote their own control. On the plains of the unorganized western territories, the seminomadic plains tribes took advantage of the withdrawal of federal regular units to overrun white settlements and communications routes to the Pacific.

But the more Native Americans involved themselves in the Civil War, the more they seemed to lose. As many as 2,000 Iroquois may have volunteered for Union service, including the nearly all-Iroquois 132nd New York, but their willingness to fight for the Union was interpreted by the federal government as a willingness to further assimilate themselves into white culture, and it only fed postwar government pressures to dissolve the New York reservations and absorb the Iroquois "into the great mass of the American people." The Dakota Sioux uprising in Minnesota was brutally suppressed by hastily recalled Union troops, and thirty-eight Sioux and half-Sioux were hanged for their role in the uprising on December 26, 1862. The tribes of the Indian Territory were devastated by fighting between pro-Confederate and pro-Union bands all through the war. And the plains tribes suffered much more in the long run by the withdrawal of the regulars than they could have imagined. In the absence of the regulars, untrained and vengeful white western volunteer regiments took up responsibility for dealing with unruly bands of Cheyenne, Mescalero, Navajo, Commanche, and Kiowa, and the volunteers showed little of the discipline and none of the restraint that the regulars had exercised on western outpost duty. On November 29, 1864, 600 peaceful Cheyenne

[15]Laurence M. Hauptman, *The Iroquois in the Civil War: From Battlefield to Reservation* (Syracuse, NY, 1993), pp. 11–16, 148.

and Arapaho who had camped at Sand Creek, Colorado, under promises of protection by federal troops at nearby Fort Lyon were surprised by a force of Colorado volunteers, determined to avenge Cheyenne raids on white settlements on the Platte River. The Cheyenne chief Black Kettle vainly waved a large Stars and Stripes to prove the peaceful intentions of his village, but the Colorado volunteers cut down 150 Cheyennes and Arapaho, most of them women and children who were then mutilated.[16]

Other, less visible, ethnic and racial groups saw their fortunes fluctuate during the war as well. Stereotyped images among Anglo-Americans defined Jews as cunning moneylenders and "Shylocks." "What else could be expected from a Jew but money-getting?" asked the *Southern Illustrated News* in an 1863 article on "Extortioners." Those prejudices guaranteed that American Jews would be regularly targeted in both North and South as aliens and swindlers who fattened themselves through war contracts and shady dealing and on the sufferings of their presumably Christian neighbors. In December, 1862, Ulysses Grant grew so convinced that "the Jews, as a class" were guilty of "violating every regulation of trade established by . . . Department orders," that he ordered the expulsion of "this class of people" from his Mississippi military district—not thinking that this order included sutlers, civilians, as well as more than a few Jewish soldiers. The protests that erupted over Grant's order went all the way up to Lincoln, who promptly had the order rescinded. Grant's prejudices notwithstanding, 7,000 Jews (out of an American Jewish population of about 150,000) enlisted to fight for the Union and six of them won the Congressional Medal of Honor for bravery in action, while another 1,500 Jewish Americans joined the Confederate forces. Hispanic Americans constituted an even smaller piece of the American ethnic pie, especially since the Anglo-Texans who turned Texas into an American republic and then an American state in the 1840s successfully drove most of Texas's small Hispanic population south into Mexico. However, when Confederate Texans mounted a small-scale invasion of the New Mexico territory in early 1862, a combined force of federal regulars, Colorado militia, and a company of the mostly Hispanic 4th New Mexico Volunteers faced the Texans at Glorieta Pass, on the Santa Fe Trail. Together, on March 28, 1862, the Anglo-Hispanic Union troops administered a thorough drubbing to the Texans, sinking Confederate hopes of western conquest beneath the sands of the New Mexico desert.

Much to the surprise of those who thought that the Civil War would be "a white man's war," the conflict quickly broadened, by policy and by accident, to include a kaleidoscope of races and ethnic minorities, from Battery Wagner to Glorieta Pass. Each of these groups saw the confusion of civil war as a moment of opportunity, whether they had rights and respect to win or political agendas to build or merely scores to settle. None of them saw their hopes fully realized. What is remarkable, though, is how the issues and battles of the Civil War made those

[16]Alvin M. Josephy, *The Civil War in the American West* (New York, 1991), pp. 269–292, 305–316.

hopes soar. "This is essentially a people's contest," Lincoln had told Congress in 1861, a war that would justify the republican ideology's confidence in what Lincoln's Whig forerunner, Daniel Webster, had called "a popular government, erected by the people . . . responsible to the people" and "just as truly emanating from the people, as from the State governments." In 1861, neither Lincoln nor his Congress could have dreamt of the ways in which many different kinds of American people were eager to make that contest a proving ground for a new kind of republican future.

2. The Lives Which Women Have Led Since Troy

For Virginia Governor Henry Wise, the Union was like a marriage of man and woman. "It is with the Union of the States as it is with the union of matrimony," Wise explained in 1860—in it, the husband must be "a good man, a good citizen, a good moralist," and so long as his honor is not questioned by his wife, all within that marriage would be peace. But the moment the wife challenged that authority, then "he will burst the bonds of union, as the burning Wythes were bursted by the vigorous limbs of the yet unshorn Nazarite."[17] This was an eccentric way of understanding the politics of secession and understandable for coming from an eccentric politician. What was more mysterious was the larger implication of Wise's analogy. If secession was equivalent to the disruption of a marriage, then civil war could hardly be less than the overthrow of gender itself, and on Wise's logic, divided Americans could not avoid some uncomfortable reflection on gender roles in American society, not just as symbol but as reality. A house divided was literally a household whose meanings and roles were now being contested, and each individual within this divided American household would feel the impact of that challenge in a different way. For southern slaveholders like Wise, authority and fatherhood were the prerogatives of white men, and the threat posed first by John Brown, and then by Lincoln, and then by the invading Yankee armies was really a threat to strip slaveholders of their "fatherhood" over their slaves and their families. For the African American males whom Wise enslaved, it offered the opportunity to assert a manhood and fatherhood that slavery had stripped away. And as American men struggled to define themselves in the midst of civil war, American women likewise found a fresh series of opportunities to question what gender roles meant in the ambiguous context of a republic.[18]

From time out of mind in European societies, adult males had been assigned the primary role of providers and leaders. The combined risks and necessities of biological

[17]Craig M. Simpson, A Good Southerner: The Life of Henry A. Wise of Virginia (Chapel Hill, NC, 1985), pp. 224–225.

[18]LeAnn Whites, "The Civil War as a Crisis in Gender," in Divided Houses: Gender and the Civil War (New York, 1992), pp. 7, 11.

reproduction limited the mobility of women and restricted them, with but few exceptions, to the subordinate role of giving supporting care to children, performing gender-based "women's work" in agriculture—spinning, carding, butter-making, sewing, making and mending clothes, storing and preparing food, making soap and candles, household cleaning—and yielding to the direction and authority of men. In America, however, recreating these ancient patterns of subordination, like the re-creation of other patterns of European social organization, had been neither easy nor straightforward. The disorientation and disorganization that migration involved, coupled with the example of the Revolution and the heady influence of the republican ideology, made male control over women much less predictable in America. On the other hand, American law continued to be guided by English common law well into the 19th century; and under English common law, marriage very nearly meant the legal annihilation of woman. Up until the point that an adult woman married, she suffered no special restrictions and could own property in the same way as men; but once married, a woman's property and property rights were automatically trans-ferred to her husband, and she was permitted to own nothing in her own name. Married women could not make contracts, could not sue, could not write a will, and could not buy or sell, except over their husbands' signature. The United States might be a republic, but it would be a republic of patriarchs, where adult males controlled public institutions and the organization of their families, and spoke as their families' voices in their communities.[19]

Americans also developed a peculiar twist on the republican ideology that further heightened the walls around gender. The Revolution had transformed the relations of men and women, not into equality, but into new, separate spheres. Republican manhood came to mean virtuous leadership, duty to family and town, and a sense of disinterested responsibility to one's neighbors. The sphere assigned to women was the bearing and rearing of a new republican generation that would have no attachment to monarchy and that would be educated by republican mothers to love liberty, virtue, and commerce rather than interest and privilege. "Republican motherhood," as a subset of the republican ideology, carried within it the assertion that women were the moral superiors of men and were the best fitted to produce "liberty-loving sons," and it glorified motherhood and marriage as a source of emotional fulfillment as well as a substitute for political authority. Republicanism, for women, came to mean trading in claims to a public role as citizens in a republic for a republicanized definition of their private roles as women in families, as wives, and as mothers.

Allied to republican motherhood in the exchange of public for private roles was a redefinition of the relation of husbands and wives within marriage and the rise of what can be called *companionate* or *affective* marriage. Marriage in the 18th century was, like politics in the colonial era, a hierarchy in which men ruled as sovereigns

[19]Toby Ditz, *Property and Kinship: Inheritance in Early Connecticut, 1750–1820* (Princeton, NJ, 1986), p. 119.

and in which marriages were made on the basis of self-interest, economic advancement, or the preservation of family property. In the republican air of the new American Union, such an aristocratic and self-serving concept of marriage was intolerable, especially when stood beside the cult of republican motherhood. So, just as women were now understood to occupy a separate sphere devoted to the vital political function of republican motherhood, husbands were warned that they were to respect a woman's sphere as a complement to their own responsibilities as disinterested republican fathers and citizens. Marriage was now a union of companions, each complementing the other in the private world of the family, and the cement of these unions was to be affection, love, and intimacy, rather than mere interest.[20]

These new definitions of "woman's sphere" also carried with them new stresses. Companionate marriage opened up new opportunities for tension by allowing women a legitimate basis for voicing their own opinions, without at the same time guaranteeing that those opinions would be heeded; and it raised expectations about love and affection for men and women alike that could easily be disappointed. By the same token, republican motherhood only added to, rather than replaced, the age-old responsibilities women had for the gender-based work they had always performed beside their men in American agriculture. And whatever advantages there were in both companionate marriage and republican motherhood pertained only to white women in the American republic. The vast majority of black women in the republic were chattel slaves, and the small number of free black women occupied only the poorest rungs of the economic ladder. There, many deliberately stayed unmarried in order to retain what few property rights they were entitled to.[21]

And yet the dynamic of American republicanism had always been to press for more and greater liberty, independence, and property. Especially with the penetration of the market into more and more of American life, men came to define their duties more in relationship to the market than the community, and more in terms of personal ambition and competitiveness than community responsibility.[22] Women responded in the same way, either by demanding more personal rights themselves, or by retreating more deeply into domestic life. American women gave vent to their frustrations over this changing scenario by writing and by organizing, for they saw in the market mentality only an invitation to economic marginalization, and the prescribed republican response to that was political action. In July, 1848, a group of two hundred women led by Elizabeth Cady Stanton and Lucretia Mott organized a women's rights convention at Seneca Falls, New York. The Declaration of Sentiments adopted by the Seneca Falls convention announced that "the history of

[20]Catharine Clinton, *The Other Civil War: American Women in the Nineteenth Century* (New York, 1984), pp. 12–19.

[21]Suzanne Lebsock, *The Free Women of Petersburg: Status and Culture in a Southern Town, 1784–1800* (New York, 1984), pp. 100–104.

[22]E. Anthony Rotundo, *American Manhood: Transformations in Masculinity from the Revolution to the Modern Era* (New York, 1993), pp. 28–30, 183–186.

mankind is a history of repeated injuries and usurpations on the part of man toward woman, having in direct object the establishment of an absolute tyranny over her," and they concluded by demanding what women in America had possessed in only one place since the Revolution (in New Jersey) and which they had not had at all since 1807—the right to vote. Two years later, they organized a National Women's Rights Convention that denied "the right of any portion of the species to decide for another portion . . . what is and what is not their 'proper sphere': that the proper sphere for all human beings is the largest and highest to which they are able to attain."

The most obvious test of this claim to full participation in the political life of the republic would be war, since the most ancient and durable "proper sphere" was the one that shielded women from involvement in war and assigned to men the role of combatants in wartime. And for that reason, the Civil War opened the most risky of questions concerning what women could or would do within the political structure of a republic. At the most basic level, the outbreak of the Civil War rallied the sectional patriotism of women fully as much as men. Sarah Morgan of Baton Rouge, who kept one of the war's most interesting diaries, did not believe in secession, "but I do in Liberty. . . . The North cannot subdue us. We are too determined to be free." Some of the patriotism was mixed with curiosity and the half-formed expectation that crossing over into the state of war meant entrance to a new social territory. "I've often longed to see a war," wrote Louisa May Alcott in April, 1861, "and now I have my wish." For Alcott, war made her "long to be a man," and thus upset the entire hierarchy of gender values. "Felt very martial and Joan-of-Arc-y," Alcott wrote after a visit to Fort Warren in Boston harbor, "as I stood on the walls with the flag flying over me and cannon all about." The 19-year-old Morgan loathed "women who lounge through life, between the sofa and rocking chair with dear little dimpled hands that are never raised except to brush away a fly." The war excited Morgan to the point of anger at her confinement, and she wrote angrily, "If I was only a man! I don't know a woman here who does not groan over her misfortune in being clothed in petticoats; why can't we fight as well as the men?" Julia LeGrand, another prolific Confederate diary-keeper, also chafed at the bonds of republican womanhood, and complained against leading "the lives which women have led since Troy fell . . . while men, more privileged, are abroad and astir, making name and fortune and helping make a nation."[23]

Almost as an answer to that complaint, a number of American women managed to slip into direct roles in combat by donning men's clothing and volunteering for the armies as men (and given the lax medical examination processes, this turned out to be easier than it might seem). Some of these women, like Lucy Matilda Thompson, were simply following lovers, husbands, or brothers who cooperated in

[23]Alcott, *The Journals of Louisa May Alcott,* Joel Myerson and Daniel Shealy, eds. (Boston, 1989), p. 105; *The Civil War Diary of Sarah Morgan,* Charles East, ed. (Athens, GA, 1991), pp. 74, 77, 85; Marilyn Mayer Culpepper, *Trials and Triumphs: Women of the American Civil War* (Lansing, MI, 1991), p. 39.

the disguise: Thompson saw her husband enlist in the 18th North Carolina in 1861, and then "cut her hair very close . . . oiled her squirrel musket, and went off to enlist" in the same regiment. Not until her husband was killed and she herself wounded in 1862 was Thompson discovered to be a woman and summarily discharged. For other women, the war offered an opportunity, not to follow men but to evade them, and to escape the restraints of custom imposed by a "woman's sphere." Sara Emma Edmonds "was born into this world with some dormant antagonism toward man" and "longed to go forth and do" by killing "one rebel after another." Edmonds managed to serve, with or without male connivance, as a Union nurse, spy, and soldier, and the frontispiece illustration to her 1865 memoirs shows her booted and spurred (and skirted), with a hard-set jaw, stern and straight beside her horse, ready to ride down any opposition—even from her readers.[24]

All told, approximately 400 women, disguised as men, found their way into either the federal or Confederate armies, and some of them managed to elude detection and dismissal until the close of the war. Elizabeth Compton, a Canadian, enlisted seven different times under different names and with different male disguises, serving in the 125th Michigan for eighteen months in one instance before being detected. Jennie Hodgers was mustered into the 95th Illinois in 1862 as "Albert Cashier," survived forty battles and skirmishes, and continued to live as a honored male Civil War veteran until 1911, when an automobile accident disclosed his/her identity. Some women kept their secrets far longer than anyone expected. In 1934, a farmer near the old Shiloh battlefield unearthed nine human skeletons with bits of uniforms and buttons that identified them as soldiers; one of the skeletons was that of a woman.[25]

Other women managed to find near-military roles that gave them a place in uniform without necessarily putting a rifle in their hands. Zouave regiments, for instance, followed the French model by enlisting *vivandieres*, uniformed women auxiliaries like Mary Tebe of the 114th Pennsylvania ("Collis's Zouaves") who followed her husband into the regiment and kept store, collected the regimental wash, and ventured out under fire to bring water to the wounded. Women who could not manage a way into uniform could still find a direct military role as a spy. Precisely because social convention disconnected white women from the waging of war, it was easier for women to obtain and pass along military information without being suspected. Pauline Cushman parlayed her acting talents into an series of elaborate ruses that allowed her to pry information out of admiring and complaisant Confederate officers; Belle Boyd used an equal measure of talent as a northern Virginia coquette to elicit the same kinds of information out of the same kinds of federal officers. At the other social extreme, African-American women were also

[24]Edmonds, *Nurse and Spy in the Union Army: The Adventures and Experiences of a Woman in Hospitals, Camps, and Battle-fields* (Philadelphia, 1865), p. 101.

[25]Richard Hall, *Patriots in Disguise: Women Warriors of the Civil War* (New York, 1993), pp. 20–26, 100–101, 158, 161.

generally dismissed as militarily harmless, a miscalculation that Harriet Tubman and Sara Edmonds used to immense advantage. Tubman, who had escaped from slavery in Maryland twenty years before the war and who had amassed considerable experience venturing south to guide runaways to the North, undertook spying expeditions for the federal troops on the Carolina Sea Islands. Edmonds colored her white skin with silver nitrate to penetrate the Confederate lines on the peninsula in 1862. Whether in uniform or not, the war permitted these women to experiment with a series of dramatic and subversive role-reversals in gender—and in Edmonds's case, a reversal of both gender and race.[26]

And yet none of these reversals was permanent, and most of them involved only the occasional acting-out of a forbidden role within accepted male definitions of those roles. The number of women involved in these escapades was also exceedingly small. By and large, Union and Confederate women stayed within the traditional circle of "women's sphere," and turned their energies to the performance of appropriately defined "war work." "As I can't fight," resolved Louisa May Alcott, "I will content myself with working for those who can."[27] Doing war work, in the most general sense, meant extending the model of republican motherhood to the soldier by continuously attempting to shape the moral life of the sons or brothers a woman might send off to the war. That meant, in the first place, that women were expected to act as recruiters, pushing and shaming men into volunteering. Kate Cumming, a Confederate nurse frankly told a lietuenant from the 24th Alabama that "a man did not deserve the name of a man, if he did not fight for his country; nor a woman, the name of woman, if she did not do all in her power to aid the men. . . . He had the candor to acquiesce in all I said." Sara Edmonds agreed that "the women down South are the best recruiting officers—for they absolutely refuse to tolerate, or admit to their society, any young man who refuses to enlist; and very often send their lovers, who have not enlisted, skirts and crinoline, with a note attached, suggesting the appropriateness of such a costume unless they donned the Confederate uniform at once."[28] Sometimes, the encouragements to enlistment overlapped the boundaries of sexual innuendo: "None but the brave deserve the fair," a Charleston newspaper warned in 1861, and even Jefferson Davis urged Confederate women to prefer the "empty sleeve" of the wounded soldier to the "muscular arm" of the stay-at-home coward.[29]

Having converted the "moral influence" of women to war, "war work" also converted women's domestic skills to war, particularly for making clothes. In 1861,

---

[26]L. C. Sizer, "Acting Her Part: Narratives of Union Women Spies," in *Divided Houses: Gender and the Civil War*, Catharine Clinton and Nina Silber, eds. (New York, 1992), pp. 127–130.

[27]Alcott, *Journals*, p. 105.

[28]Cumming, *Kate: The Journal of a Confederate Nurse*, R. B. Harwell, ed. (Baton Rouge, LA, 1959), pp. 191–192; Edmonds, *Nurse and Spy*, p. 332.

[29]Drew G. Faust, "Altars of Sacrifice: Confederate Women and the Narratives of War," in *Divided Houses: Gender and Civil War*, Clinton and Silber, eds., pp. 175–179.

neither the North nor the South possessed the kind of large-scale clothing manufacturing that the immense numbers of enlistees required for uniforms, and the slack in uniform production had to be taken up by women at home. The Springfield Ladies Aid Society proudly reported in 1862 that it had sewn cotton shirts, drawers, socks, slippers, handkerchiefs, towels, pillow cases, and bandages, and still found time to pack off "large quantities of cornstarch, barley, tea, crackers, soap, jars, jellies, pickles, fruits. . . ." The Ladies Gunboat Fair in Charleston in 1862 was specifically designed to raise money to fund a building program for Confederate ironclads. Other aid organizations began demanding new and unprecedented levels of organizational skill from women. In 1861, 3,000 New Yorkers organized the Women's Central Relief Association, and in a rare but grudging concession by the male directors of the association, twelve women were elected to serve on the governing board. Overall, as many as 20,000 aid societies, great and small, were set up and operating by the end of 1861; South Carolina and Alabama had one hundred each.[30]

Over time, the "war work" of recruitment and support required more and more sacrifice, especially in the South, where the sheer lack of resources drove most of the southern aid societies out of business before the end of 1862. The problem with sacrifice was that, as the war and the casualty lists lengthened, women received so little in the way of reward for these sacrifices. It made increasingly little sense to speak of the reciprocal joys of companionate marriage when the war continued to drain the pool of available males. It also made little sense to praise the moral influence of women when it became increasingly clear that the immense distances covered by Civil War armies unstrung any effective notion of moral control over the men in uniform. Much as Union and Confederate women might try to transport the moral values of home to camp through letters (and the volume of letters to and from the Union army reached the astonishing level of 180,000 a day in 1862) or even to keep their influence more direct by visiting husbands in camp, it was soon apparent that they had little real power to deal with the camp visits of other kinds of women (around the Army of the Potomac's camps near Washington, the number of prostitutes and camp followers mushroomed from 500 to 5,000 in 450 known brothels by 1862). It was hard to mind the bounds of a "woman's sphere" when men were not minding their own.

It was worse when the simple absence of men from farms and shops forced the wives they had left behind to shift for themselves. Although local and state governments made generous promises of support for soldier families, little of that support was ever forthcoming in meaningful quantities. Bereft of the men who formed the traditional center of patriarchal authority, women had to improvise new ways of organizing their lives. Women who had defined their lives by "inside" domestic work now found themselves behind the plow in the fields. "Most of the women

[30]Mary Elizabeth Massey, Bonnet Brigades: American Women and the Civil War (New York, 1966), pp. 34–35; Culpepper, Trials and Triumphs, pp. 256, 258, 261; George Rable, Civil Wars: Women and the Crisis of Southern Nationalism (Urbana, IL, 1991), p. 139.

around here who live on farms have to do all their work alone, their husbands being in the army," wrote a curious soldier in Tennessee. "I got some butter the other day of a woman who has six little children and a place of fifty acres which she has cultivated alone and supported herself and children besides. Don't you think this is doing pretty well for one woman?" But the satisfaction these women derived from "doing pretty well" was more than balanced by the incessant grind of dread and anxiety over the fate of their husbands, brothers, and sons. And when those fears culminated at last in the news of death in battle, the results could range from raw stoicism to outright derangement. Mary Chesnut's friend, Colonel John Hugh Means, was killed at Antietam; Means's wife lay down, covered her face, and a little while after, when "she remained quiet so long, someone removed the light shawl which she had drawn over her head. She was dead." Is it any wonder, Chesnut asked, that "so many women die? Grief and constant anxiety kill nearly as many women as men die on the battlefield."[31]

The toll that privation, dislocation, and death took on the loyalty of women, both to their sections and to their "sphere," was especially severe in the South. Unlike Northerners, women in the Confederacy had to deal with invasion and occupation, which involved everything from vandalism by unruly federal soldiers to conflicts with restless slaves. In some instances, Confederate women put up spirited resistance to the Union occupation forces. After Baton Rouge fell to federal forces in 1862, Sarah Morgan and her sister Antoinette made small Confederate flags for themselves; Morgan "put the stem in my belt, pinned the flag to my shoulder, and walked down town, creating great excitement among women & children" and among the federal occupation troops.[32] In New Orleans, Confederate women grew so hostile and malevolent in their behavior that the occupation commander, Benjamin Butler, issued a general order threatening that "when any female shall by word, gesture, or movement, insult or show contempt for any officer or soldier of the United States, she shall be regarded and held liable to be treated as a woman of the town plying her avocation"—in other words, a prostitute. Butler's "Woman Order" was ill-timed and even more ill-worded—it even aroused unfavorable comment in the British Parliament—but it did underscore Butler's frustration with women who refused to behave passively in the face of male conquest. What Butler failed to see behind the contempt the New Orleans women had for Yankee soldiers was the corresponding contempt they nurtured for the Confederate men who had abandoned them to Butler's unkind embrace; and what Butler's proclamation unwittingly underscored for Confederate women was how exposed and undefended the Confederacy had left them in their hour of peril.[33]

[31]Culpepper, *Trials and Triumphs*, pp. 126, 264; *Mary Chesnut's Civil War*, C. Vann Woodward, ed. (New Haven, CT, 1981), pp. 371, 426.

[32]Morgan, *The Civil War Diary of Sarah Morgan*, p. 67.

[33]George Rable, "Missing in Action: Women of the Confederacy," in *Divided Houses: Gender and the Civil War*, Clinton and Silber, eds. pp. 137–141.

For that reason, by 1862, fewer Confederate women were sending their men off willingly. Some were refusing to keep up farms and others were demanding that the Confederate government return their men. In many cases, southern farm women and planters' wives were forced to rely on male slaves to run their farms and plantations for them, which in most cases dangerously loosened the bonds of slave discipline. The Confederate congress responded sluggishly with a series of conscription exemptions designed to keep the most critically needed men at the most critical jobs. But many of the exemptions, especially the infamous "twenty-nigger law," only fanned the resentment of the yeoman classes without doing much to improve the South's chances.[34] As the blockade further pinched southern resources, even the wealthiest southern women were besieged with the need to economize, while the yeoman farmers slipped into outright poverty. "We are all in a sadly molting condition," wrote Mary Chesnut in the fall of 1863. "We had come to the end of our good clothes in three years, and now our only resource was to turn them upside down or inside out— mending, darning, patching." George Washington Whitman was amazed at the wretched conditions he found among the once-prosperous farms of northern Virginia in 1862: "The villages we have passed through are the most God forsaken places I ever saw, the people seem to have next to nothing to eat as the men have all gone in the Secesh army, and how they are going to get through the winter I dont know."[35] Southern women were being forced to assume roles of independence that neither companionate marriage nor republican motherhood had ever envisioned, and the independence that events foisted on them was not always the kind of independence they might have welcomed. At the same time, however, southern men were becoming ever more critically dependent on women for supplies of food from the fields and clothing from the home. The bargain of separate spheres was turning upside down as the Confederacy weakened, and southern women, far from rallying 'round the flag, now turned on Confederate men in rage. When Confederate cavalry stampeded in panic through Winchester, Virginia, in 1864, "a large number of the most respected ladies joined hands & formed a line across the principal street, telling the cowardly Cavalrymen that they shoud not go any further unless they ran their horses over their bodies." Poorer women who were not quite on the same social level as the "respected ladies" of Winchster stated their disgust more frankly. "The men of Atlanta have brought an everlasting stain on their name," wrote Julia Davison, a disgusted Georgia farmwife. "Instead of remaining to defend their homes, they have run off and left Atlanta to be defended by an army of women and children. . . . God help us for there is no help in man."[36]

---

[34]Paul D. Escott, *After Secession: Jefferson Davis and the Failure of Confederate Nationalism* (Baton Rouge, LA, 1978), pp. 120–121.

[35]*Mary Chesnut's Civil War*, Woodward, ed., p. 459; *Civil War Letters of George Washington Whitman*, Jerome M. Loving, ed. (Durham, NC, 1975), p. 73.

[36]*The Civil War Memoirs of Captain William J. Seymour: Reminiscences of a Louisiana Tiger*, Terry L. Jones, ed. (Baton Rouge, LA, 1991), p. 142; Rable, *Civil Wars*, pp. 74, 80, 84, 101, 140, 171.

These mutterings of disloyalty came mostly from Confederate women who stayed put; a far darker kind of misery awaited those who tried to turn refugee. As early as 1862, federal invasions of northern Virginia and Tennessee were dislodging large numbers of Southerners, mostly women whose men had left for the army and who feared the unlovely rule of Yankee occupiers, and mostly those with slaves who feared that their slaves could not be relied upon anywhere near the northern armies. Over the course of the war, nearly 250,000 Southerners fled from the battle zones to areas deeper within the Confederacy. Taken together with the hundreds of thousands of blacks who were fleeing in the other direction and with the 3 million men sucked up into the whirlwind of the armies as they crossed state after state and river after river, the Civil War was turning into a demographic movement across the eastern half of North America that had no equal in the American memory. Nor did the problems stop once Southerners had gotten away to a reasonable breathing distance from the Yankee invaders. Once removed, refugee planters who had dragged their slaves along with them had no work for the slaves to do and no income from cotton planting to feed them. So, to keep their slaves somehow within the slave system and earning money, refugee planters hired out their slaves in record numbers to public and private war industries, as teamsters, iron workers, and even niter diggers. But this, in turn, only further destabilized the slave work regimen. As slaves moved out of the plantation environment and into the wider boundaries of urban employment for cash, the old systems of supervision broke down, while wartime conditions made it impossible to develop a new work system to absorb the sudden influx of industrial slaves. But even without the excess baggage of slaves, southern women refugees found the incessant string of moves from one unfamiliar place to another, or from one increasingly reluctant brace of relatives to another, to be a counsel of despair. The longer the war rolled on, the more all trace of southern civic life disappeared, as individual survival became the paramount concern.[37] Sarah Morgan and her family fled Baton Rouge under a barrage of Union shells to seek refuge on a plantation near Port Hudson; and then, when the war came up to Port Hudson, they fled again to Lake Pontchartrain, and then finally into occupied New Orleans, where Sarah was sheltered under the roof of her Unionist half-brother. "Give me my home, my old home once more," she lamented, in what could have been the words of every Confederate woman tossed in the tornado of destruction and disappointed expectations for their own womanhood, "O my home, my home! I could learn to be a woman there, and a true one, too. Who will teach me now?"[38]

As the war forced women into new and unaccustomed roles, it simultaneously undermined women's notions of their reliance on men, and introduced them to new views of their own capacities. This was particularly true for women who

[37]Clarence Mohr, *On the Threshold of Freedom: Masters and Slaves in Civil War Georgia* (Athens, GA, 1985), pp. 113, 118, 153–157; Rable, *Civil Wars*, p. 221.

[38]Morgan, *The Civil War Diary of Sarah Morgan*, p. 435.

stepped into the void created by the army medical services' miserable unpreparedness for handling the frightful casualties of Civil War battlefields. Republic womanhood had assigned to women so many domestic roles related to caregiving that it required only the shortfall in male medical personnel before women began to volunteer themselves as nurses, and in a few cases like Mary Walker, as doctors. Before the 1850s, army medicine, like the army itself, had been the preserve of male doctors and male nurses, and women could scarcely find opportunity for medical education in the United States, much less an opening for medical practice. But the work of Florence Nightingale during the Crimean War had cracked that particular wall of gender separation down to its foundations, and Nightingale became the stepping stone for a small number of American women to open up military nursing to women volunteers. Not surprisingly, female nurses were not, at first, welcomed by the doddering army medical establishments. "There is scarcely a day passes that I do not hear some derogatory remarks about the ladies who are in hospitals, until I think, if there is any credit due them at all, it is for the moral courage they have in braving public opinion," wrote Kate Cumming in 1863.[39] But the administrative record soon carved out by Dorothea Dix as the Superintendent of Army Nurses in the North, by Captain Sally Tomkins and her Richmond hospital, and by civilian volunteer nurses on the federal hospital ships on the western rivers soon dampened the carping.

What was far more discouraging to women nurses was the sheer appalling slaughter churned up by battle, and by the dirt and incompetence that pervaded the army medical services. When Cornelia Hancock and a group of army nurses caught up with the Army of the Potomac at Fredericksburg in 1864, they walked into an abandoned church that the army had converted into a hospital. There, "the scene beggared all description." The two male surgeons with them "were paralyzed by what they saw," Hancock wrote home, for "rain had poured in through the bullet-riddled roofs of the churches until our wounded lay in pools of water made bloody by their seriously wounded condition." Louisa May Alcott, who nursed briefly in a military hospital in Georgetown before falling dangerously ill, described her hospital as a "perfect pestilence-box . . . cold, damp, dirty, full of vile odors from wounds, kitchens, wash rooms, & stables."[40] Partly because of these conditions, by the end of the war only 3,200 women had actually served as nurses in the armies, not more than a fifth of the overall number of military nurses. Rather than take the risks posed by nursing, far more women found their ways to new jobs in northern and southern textile mills, hurriedly manufacturing cartridges, clothing, and military equipment under the wide umbrella of government war contracts. The absence of men also created a gap in teaching, another previously all-male profession that now began to admit women, and the explosive

[39]Cumming, Kate: The Journal of a Confederate Nurse, p. 178.
[40]Hancock, South After Gettysburg: Letters of Cornelia Hancock, 1863–1868, H. S. Jaquette, ed. (New York, 1956), p. 92; Alcott, Journals, p. 114.

growth in government paperwork opened up employment for women in govern-ment and treasury offices.

What is not clear is whether these new opportunities, however much satisfac-tion they gave, opened any new windows in the republican ideology for redefining political or social power for women. Many of the wartime positions opened to women were replacement positions for men, and those positions often disappeared as soon as the war was over and the men returned. It was only at incidental moments that a real departure from "separate spheres" for women and genuine movement toward gender equality took shape. In 1863, a core group of women veterans of the Seneca Falls convention organized a Women's National Loyal League, which undertook a massive petition drive in support of an abolition amend-ment to the Constitution. That, in turn, became the organizational platform from which Elizabeth Cady Stanton and Susan B. Anthony launched a parallel move-ment in 1866, the American Equal Rights Association, to ensure a similar constitu-tional amendment that would grant voting rights to women. But the only real weapons Stanton and Anthony had at their disposal were petitions and persuasion, and they gained little ground against the entrenched legal restraints that deprived women in many states, not only of the vote, but of the most basic republican privilege, property ownership. Mary Ashton Livermore, who had already carved out a prominent career as a reformer and religious magazine editor in the 1850s, turned her organizing talents to private fund-raising for the United States Sanitary Commission during the war. But when she attempted to sign a contract for con-structing the fairgrounds for the 1863 USSC Northwestern Sanitary Fair in Chi-cago, she was politely informed that no contract with her signature on it had any legal standing, even if she paid the contractors in cash. Only her husband's signa-ture carried any standing in Illinois law. "By the laws of the state in which we lived, our individual names were not worth the paper on which they were written." In the face of these legal stonewalls, Stanton and Anthony were unable to hold their equal-rights movement together, and the equal-rights drive fractured into a radical wing led by Stanton and Anthony (which continued to press for a national constitu-tional amendment) and a moderate wing, led by Mary Livermore and Henry Ward Beecher, that wanted to limit the campaign to what could be accomplished in state legislatures. None of them lived to see American women gain the right to vote in 1920.[41]

The war brought changes to American women, but only some changes and only to some women. In the confusion caused by the war, both the number of women who left the domestic sphere to find work in the field or the government office or the hospital, and the number of jobs that it was admitted women could do

[41]Massey, Bonnet Brigade, pp. 135–137, 143–149; Livermore, My Story of the War: A Woman's Narrative of Four Years Personal Experience (1889; rept. New York, 1972), pp. 435–436; Wendy Hamand Venet, Neither Ballots nor Bullets: Women Abolitionists and the Civil War (Charlottesville, VA, 1991), pp. 154–155.

increased. But the war that made this movement possible also doomed its further growth, since so much "war work" was the creature of the war itself. Once the war was over, and the legal structure of restraints on women remained unchanged, the tide of women's advances shrank back to its prewar boundaries. This retreat was reinforced by a certain measure of class, as well as gender, expectations. Lower-class and black women had never been part of the "separate spheres" expectation, and both had always worked outside the domestic boundary, and only the national emergency of the war sanctioned the movement of upper-class and middle-class white women in the same outward direction. Once that emergency was over, the class bias of women's work reasserted itself, and women's work outside the family circle reclaimed its stigma of being "poor folks' work."

The Civil War represented both advance and retreat for American women, in a moment of unspeakable turbulence when all the customary handholds disappeared and men and women were forced to find new aways through the storm of conflict. For Clara Barton, who made her Civil War nursing career the foundation for organizing the International Red Cross, the war meant a gain of "fifty years in advance of the normal position which continued peace . . . would have assigned her"; for Susan B. Anthony, the postwar crusader for women's rights, the distractions of the war actually stifled most of the progress women had made toward winning the right to vote.[42] The Civil War thus managed to be a deeply radical event, in the shock waves it sent through American gender relations; but it was also a conservative event, in which American women frequently traded back the radicalism of their words and deeds for the stability and peace that the war took from them.

3. Union Always Swarming with Blatherers

By the end of 1863, the Civil War had taken on new and unexpected shapes for Americans. The political goals of the war had shifted for both Northerners and Southerners, from simple reunion to emancipation in the northern case, and from simple secession to the forging of a new Confederate nationalism in the South. The added turmoil of moving millions of people out of their homes and out of the accustomed tracks of their life-cycles, and the relentlessly lengthening casualty lists from one indecisive battle after another threatened to break up and disorganize an entire generation of American lives. After two years of dislocation, shock, and carnage, Americans were groping in exhaustion for a new way of understanding the meaning and purpose of the war that would give them some idea of why it was being fought. And for those answers they turned to the philosophers, moralists, and clergymen who constituted the intellectual elite of the American republic and made it what Walt Whitman cheerfully described as a "Union always swarming with blatherers."

[42]Massey, *Bonnet Brigade*, pp. 339, 357.

The most famous names that have come down to us from the 1860s as America's "blatherers" are the names of its secular public intellectuals—thinkers, in other words, who had little or no formal connections with religion or with America's small string of colleges. Few of them were exactly irreligious, but their religion assumed ever smaller or ever more eccentric outlines. Chief among these in the North was the noted essayist Ralph Waldo Emerson, a former Unitarian clergyman who had abandoned the ministry to take up a life of writing and lecturing across the country. But the list also included the novelists Herman Melville and Nathaniel Hawthorne, the Whig philosophers Richard Hildreth and Henry Philip Tappan, the historian Francis Parkman, and the future Harvard College president, Charles Eliot Norton. In the South, where intellectuals had even fewer resources to support them and fewer magazines and quarterlies for platforms, an intellectual network based on James Henry Hammond and William Gilmore Simms of South Carolina, Henry Hughes of Mississippi, Josiah Nott (an Alabama physician), and the Virginians Nathaniel Beverley Tucker, Thomas Roderick Dew, Edmund Ruffin, and George Frederick Holmes provided the backbone of southern intellectual life.[43]

But famous as the names of the secular intellectuals appear to modern eyes, they turned out to be extraordinarily unprepared for the immense task of providing explanations and solutions to the complex problems of the war. Part of this was because few of them had ever felt that the American republic was particularly interested in listening to the prescriptions they had given for the moral or ethical dilemmas of American life. They found the "buzz and din" of republican politics distasteful, and since many of both the New England and southern thinkers lived off inherited land and wealth, they lacked much sympathy for the strivings of poor-born men and women like Lincoln. That, in turn, gave them little to admire in republicanism and still less to understand about a civil war in a republic. Led by Emerson, many of the New Englanders withdrew from intellectual engagement with republican political culture and celebrated a radical individualism built upon "self-reliance" and "self-culture." Emerson wanted "to insulate the individual—to surround him with barriers of natural respect, so that each man shall feel the world as his, and man shall treat with man as a sovereign state with a sovereign state," and he held himself aloof from even the most pressing reform movements.

But Emerson was actually less detached from the republican environment than he realized. Much as he admired Immanuel Kant and G. W. F. Hegel, and even dabbled in Oriental mysticism, Emerson's individualism owed a great deal to the empiricism of John Locke, the father-figure of republican political thought, whose influential *Essay Concerning Human Understanding* had interpreted the human knowing process as the discovery of individual artifacts of knowledge by individual minds. Other secular intellectuals, North and South, moved in the opposite direction. The great attraction of Kant and Hegel among secular intellectuals in prewar

[43]Drew G. Faust, *A Sacred Circle: The Dilemma of the Intellectual in the Old South, 1840–1860* (Baltimore, MD, 1977), pp. 83–84.

America was based precisely on their movement away from Locke's hard-headed empiricism. Kant, for instance, aggressively defended the role of intuition in knowledge, and that yielded in the hands of Kant's English and American admirers to a glorification of romantic feelings as the test of truth. Hegel, in a similar fashion, disputed the notion that human society was simply the sum of individual wants and choices, and he endowed the movement of races and peoples with mysterious (and sometimes irrational) collective purposes. "Human progress has arisen mainly from the war of races," wrote Josiah Nott. "All the great impulses which have been given to it from time to time have been the results of conquests and colonizations . . . of new blood and novel influences."[44]

This left neither Emerson nor Nott in a very good position to give advice about the meaning of a republican civil war. Although Emerson was surprised almost in spite of himself with how "a sentiment mightier than logic" was sweeping up even the most detached and self-reliant minds in a "whirlwind of patriotism," few New England intellectuals stayed for long within that whirlwind. Rather than seeing the war as a crusade in defense of republicanism, Parkman and Norton supported the war more for the opportunities it gave young New England bluebloods to demonstrate the individual virtues of heroism, fortitude, and manliness. The death of Robert Gould Shaw at Battery Wagner, for instance, was seen less as a blow for racial justice and more as proof that the republic's wealthy mercantile elite had not grown stagnant and effeminate. Some of the secular intellectuals even hoped that the Civil War would burst Americans' overweening confidence in republicanism and lead to the replacement of republicanism's democratic turbulence by a more orderly and organic notion of society, with themselves as the acknowledged elite.[45] George Templeton Strong, a New York lawyer whose diary is yet another monument in an era of monumental diary-keepers, condemned republicanism's preoccupation with "democracy and equality and various other phantasms." Strong believed that "Universal suffrage has been . . . at the root of our troubles," and he hoped that they "will be dispersed and dissipated and will disappear forever" in the face of civil war. America required the discipline of "a strong government," and Charles Stille, a lawyer and later provost of the University of Pennsylvania, blamed much of the North's inability to bring the war to a swift conclusion on the "hideous moral leprosy" of disloyalty and antiwar dissent "which seems to be the sad but invariable attendant upon all political discussions in a free government, corrupting the very sources of public life. . . ."[46]

---

[44]Nott, *Types of Mankind, Or Ethnological Research . . . Upon their Natural, Geographical, Philological, and Biblical History* (Philadelphia, 1854), pp. 53–54.

[45]George M. Frederickson, *The Inner Civil War: Northern Intellectuals and the Crisis of the Union* (New York, 1965), pp. 55–56, 65–66, 141–144.

[46]Strong, *The Diary of George Templeton Strong,* Allan Nevins and M. H. Thomas, eds. (New York, 1952), vol. 3, p. 66; Charles J. Stille, "How a Free People Conduct a Long War: A Chapter from English History" [1862], in *Union Pamphlets of the Civil War,* Frank Friedel, ed. (Cambridge, MA, 1967), vol. 1, p. 389.

The most stubbornly republican interpretation of the war, from a secular point of view, came from no one less than Abraham Lincoln, who does not figure in most cases as a public intellectual, but who nevertheless happily engaged his bright young secretary, John Hay, in discussions of linguistics and philology "for which the T. [the "Tycoon," Hay's shorthand reference for Lincoln] has a little indulged inclination."[47] Although Lincoln's changing conceptions of the war were mostly embedded in various state papers and qualified by the highly charged atmosphere of political interviews, the fall of 1863 gave Lincoln a clear and unalloyed opportunity to articulate his understanding of the war. The commonwealth of Pennsylvania, following the battle at Gettysburg, had arranged for the reburial of the Gettysburg dead in a new cemetery beside the battlefield, and Lincoln was invited by the organizers to deliver "a few appropriate remarks" at the ceremonies in Gettysburg on November 19, 1863. Lincoln was not the featured speaker at the dedication—that honor went to a New England intellectual, Edward Everett—and he was asked only to make the brief "remarks" that would make the dedication of the cemetery a rhetorical fact. But within the short compass of the 272 words that Lincoln used, he eloquently reaffirmed a republican middle way between the Emersonian individualists and the organic antirepublicans.

Lincoln's Whiggism was never more evident than at the opening of his "remarks": *Fourscore and seven years ago, our fathers brought forth on this continent a new nation, conceived in Liberty, and dedicated to the proposition that all men are created equal.* Unlike the states'-rights Democrats, with their preoccupation with diversity over nationality, Lincoln soared in his first sentence to the Declaration of Independence for authority (the "fourscore and seven" went back to 1776, not the 1789 of the Constitution) and appealed to the existence of a single *nation* rather than a subdividable Union. Within that nation "all men were created equal"—an equality that Lincoln had persistently equated with economic opportunism rather than *herrenvolk* democracy and the balancing of group or sectional interests. The real question of the war was, therefore, whether *this nation or any nation so conceived and so dedicated can long endure*—whether republican government could actually survive in a world where little local oligarchies and special interests within, and hostile monarchies outside, were waiting to tear it to pieces. It was clear in Lincoln's mind that, if things were arranged according to the Democratic model of Calhoun, Jackson, and Jefferson, it would not survive, and the War of 1812 had been the near-evidence of that. In a republic where equality was defined as the protection of some (namely, the planters) and the subsidization of others (namely, the yeomen), all progress would stagnate. A Jacksonian republic would then be a prey to every ambitious empire around it; and every poor-boy Lincoln would be denied what Lincoln wanted most, the precious chance to rise higher. It was vital, for Lincoln, that out of the sacrifices of Gettysburg, Shiloh, Murfreesboro, Chancellorsville,

---

[47]*Lincoln and the Civil War in the Diaries and Letters of John Hay,* Tyler Dennett, ed. (1939; rept. Westport, CT, 1972), p. 72.

and a hundred other places should come *a new birth of freedom*, a turning back of sixty years of almost uninterrupted Jefferson-Jackson-Calhoun rule, which would enshrine the unfettered national idealism of Lincoln's "beau ideal" of a statesman, Henry Clay. And he drove his point home by closing his "remarks" with a deliberate evocation of the great Whig orator, Daniel Webster, and Webster's reply to Robert Hayne, *that government of the people, by the people, and for the people shall not perish from the earth.* For Lincoln, the war was being fought to bring a Whig republic to life at last, a republic of small-scale producers, of free homesteads, and free labor that was not beholden to privileged political or economic powers. The Republican newspapers heartily applauded it: The address was a "brief but immortal speech," editorialized John W. Forney's Philadelphia *Press*. The Democratic papers, predictably, spurned it as "mere trash" and "unworthy of comment."[48]

It was highly significant, too, that Lincoln chose to clothe his appeal at Gettysburg in language that also had little rhetorical connection with the North's secular intellectuals. Even though Lincoln himself professed only the sparest form of religious belief, he had learned early on in his political career to make public peace with American Protestant evangelicalism, and the opening paragraph of his Gettysburg Address was thick with the vocabulary of evangelical Christianity, culminating in the promise of a *new birth of freedom*. Whatever Lincoln's personal religious inclinations, he knew enough about the inclinations of his audience in composing his address to invoke the rhetoric of Evangelical revivalism. Although the story of American religion has often been told in terms of declension and shrinking public influence, the 19th century had seen almost the exact opposite. The overall number of Christian congregations rose from 2,500 in 1780 to 52,000 in 1860, and along with the new congregations came new publication agencies, like the American Bible Society and American Tract Society that spun off a million Bibles and 6 million religious books and pamphlets each year, and a constellation of interlocked social reform and missionary agencies.[49] From a low point immediately after the Revolution, American Protestantism had risen on the wings of evangelical revivalism to unprecedented levels of power and public influence. And just as American religion sought to make sense of Americans' universe for them, American religious leaders now turned their energies to making sense of America's civil war, as well.

At the outbreak of the war, there was little to distinguish the response of the Protestant churches and clergy from their secular counterparts in their burst of sectional patriotism. For the first time in the history of the American military, regimental chaplains became a major presence in every army.[50] But as the war

[48]Joseph George, "The World Will Little Note? The Philadelphia Press and the Gettysburg Address," in *Pennsylvania Magazine of History and Biography* 114 (July 1990), pp. 394–396.

[49]Jon Butler, *Awash in a Sea of Faith: Christianizing the American People* (Cambridge, MA, 1990), pp. 270, 278.

[50]Gardiner H. Shattuck, Jr., *A Shield and a Hiding Place: The Religious Life of the Civil War Armies* (Macon, GA, 1987), pp. 51–52.

lengthened, the meanings American religion attached to the war separated along three distinct lines. The first of these meanings were issued by the religious liberals of mid-century, whose understanding of Christian dogma had been amended and altered by some of the same Kantian and Hegelian sources that influenced the secular intellectuals. The most prominent example of this influence in the North was Horace Bushnell, a Congregationalist minister in Hartford, Connecticut, who had carved out a reputation by horrifying more orthodox Congregationalists with his admiration for a Kantian religion of intuition and feelings. Bushnell, like George Templeton Strong, was convinced that the war had only shown how little popular government was to be trusted, and in 1864, he interpreted "the true meaning of the present awful chapter of our history" as proof that "popular governments, or such as draw their magistracies by election from among the people themselves" were only "feeble pretences of philosophy." Bushnell, who also vigorously opposed extending voting rights to women as a measure that would only further splinter and individualize American politics, wanted a much stronger centralized form of government that would derive its justification, not by popular consent, but by "the ordinance of God." Just what that form would look like, Bushnell hesitated to say. The people should "choose their magistrates," Bushnell allowed, but it would be far better if "not governing the magistrates, the magistrates govern them . . . the sanction of God's Head Magistracy going with it."[51] In like manner, the American Methodist and sometime Confederate government official, Albert Taylor Bledsoe, agreed that civil society "is not a thing of compacts, bound together by promises and paper. . . . It is a decree of God; the spontaneous and irresistable working of that nature, which, in all climates, through all ages, and under all circumstances, manifests itself in social organizations."

Slavery and not republicanism was a more appropriate model for government, argued southern Presbyterian William A. Smyth: "Government involves the idea of slavery. It restricts the wills of men in greater or less degrees, and is to that extent slavery."[52] What a war for Union or independence should produce is more than mere Union or mere independence, but rather an admission that the whole premise of republican ideology, in both its Democratic and Whig versions, had been flawed from the start.

Another more ambiguous way of attaching religious meanings to the war arose from the confessional Protestants—those who drew their religious identities from a conservative theological or dogmatic statement, such as the Presbyterian Church's Westminster Confession, which clearly separated them from the religious liberals. The confessionalists split from the liberals both in terms of theology and in philosophy, since the confessionalists had little use for intuition and "senti-

---

[51]Bushnell, "Popular Government by Divine Right," in God Ordained This War: Sermons on the Sectional Crisis, 1830–1865, D. B. Cheseborough, ed. (Columbia, SC, 1991), pp. 104, 117.

[52]Bledsoe, An Essay on Liberty and Slavery (Philadelphia, 1856), p. 34; Mitchell Snay, Gospel of Disunion: Religion and Separatism in the Antebellum South (Cambridge, 1993), pp. 71–72.

ments mightier than logic," and stuck devotedly to the rigorous empiricism of what became known as Scottish "common sense," or realist philosophy. And yet, for all these differences, the confessionalists often turned out to be as suspicious of republicanism, or at least Whig republicanism, as the liberals. Robert Lewis Dabney, who was nearly as close to being a perfect Presbyterian confessionalist as Southern Presbyterianism offered, did not bother trying to justify slavery as a republican institution: "Our best hope is in the fact that the cause of our defence is the cause of God's Word. . . . It will in the end become apparent to the world, not only that the conviction of the wickedness of slaveholding was drawn wholly from sources foreign to the Bible, but that it is a legitimate corollary from that fantastic, atheistic, and radical theory of human rights, which made the Reign of Terror in France." Dabney was not, like Bushnell or Strong, a critic of republics, but as a Democrat, he believed that the "great *dilemma* of republicks" was how to create a docile labor force, and slavery of course solved this better "than any expedient of free countries."[53]

It was among the Evangelicals, the children of Jonathan Edwards and the great pietist Awakenings of the late 18th and early 19th centuries that the meaning of the Civil War took on its most dramatic and apocalyptic colorings. As Richard Carwardine has shown, American evangelical Protestants had largely adopted the Whigs as their party of choice, and when the Whigs failed to adopt wholeheartedly the moral crusades of the Evangelicals, the withdrawal of northern Evangelicals helped destroy the Whig party and lay the basis for the rise of the Republicans. Southern Evangelicals, by contrast, withdrew from public discourse into private devotionalism, and allowed southern confessionalists to take the the lead in shaping Confederate religion.[54] But the northern Evangelicals swung enthusiastically behind the cause of the Union and of antislavery, and they interpreted the war as a vindication of righteous republicanism. The great Presbyterian preacher and commentator, Albert Barnes (who had opened the 1856 Republican convention with prayer), declared two weeks after Fort Sumter, "Of all the civil and political trusts ever committed to any generation of men, that Constitution is the most precious, for it guards higher interests and secures richer blessings to the world than any other." The result would be, as with Lincoln, the establishment of a Whig republic that would "render the world the abode of industrious freedom, peace, domestic joy, and virtuous intelligence." The American Tract Society's agent, Hollis Read, went a step further when he prophesied in *The Coming Crisis of the World, or the Great Battle and the Golden Age* in 1861 that the Civil War would actually be the prelude to the return of Jesus and the onset of the millennium; it would be "one of the last mighty strides of Providence towards the goal of humanity's final and high destiny."

[53]Dabney, *A Defense of Virginia, and through her, of the South* (1867; rept. Harrisonburg, VA, 1977), pp. 21, 300, 305–306.

[54]Richard Carwardine, *Evangelicals and Politics in Antebellum America* (New Haven, CT, 1993), pp. 99–103, 286–290, 307.

And Methodist bishop Gilbert Haven, who served as chaplain to the 8th Massachusetts, added that a Union victory would make "wars cease to the end of the earth, the millennial glory rest upon the world-Republic and universal liberty, equality, and brotherhood bring universal peace."[55]

No matter what their interpretations of the war, Protestant and secular intellectuals of every stripe set out to institutionalize these meanings. Secular intellectuals, so far as they could be teased out of their studies, and liberal Protestants banded together to create the United States Sanitary Commission in 1861, with the mission of raising and channeling private donations and large-scale giving to the support of the Union army. The USSC was, from the start, an exercise in benevolent elitism. Just as its leaders had no faith in the abstract theories of republican virtue, they had no practical use for unorganized charity, and they struggled throughout the war to redirect homemade clothing, blankets, camp goods, food, and even pen and ink through their own hands. "Neither the blind masses, the swinish multitudes, that rule us under our accursed system of universal suffrage, nor the case of typhoid can be expected to exercise self-control," growled George Templeton Strong, the USSC's treasurer; if good was to be done for the soldier, better that it be done by the elite who really knew how to organize it.[56] Thus, Strong and the USSC's upper-class New York and Boston officers struggled to turn it into the model of what a properly administered nation ought to look like. Beside the USSC, and often in conflict with it, northern Evangelicals organized the United States Christian Commission, which sent 5,000 volunteers into the Union armies to distribute tracts, hold religious meetings, and in general do for the northern soldier's soul what the USSC aimed to do for his body. Evangelical chaplains, in both the Northern and Southern armies, sponsored revival meetings, and especially in the southern armies, the chaplains eased the transition of the southern white male from the structures of rural society to the harsh discipline and jumbled class identities of the army.[57] As early as 1862, large scale "conversion seasons" swept through both Union and Confederate troops: The federal Army of the Cumberland and the Army of Northern Virginia both experienced large-scale revivals of religion during the winter and spring of 1864. And not content with converting soldiers, northern Evangelicals organized the National Reform Association in 1863 to press for the passage of a "Bible Amendment" that would explicitly unite Evangelical Protestantism and republicanism by rewriting the preamble to the Constitution to read: "Recognizing Almighty God as the source of all authority and power in civil government, and acknowledging the Lord Jesus Christ as

[55]James H. Moorhead, American Apocalypse: Yankee Protestants and the Civil War, 1860–1869 (New Haven, CT, 1978), pp. 41, 50, 62, 76.

[56]Strong, Diary, vol. 3, p. 272.

[57]Drew G. Faust, "Christian Soldiers: The Meaning of Revivalism in the Confederate Army," in Journal of Southern History 53 (February 1987), pp. 73–75.

the Governor among the nations, His revealed will as the supreme law of the land, in order to constitute a Christian government. . . ."[58]

But none of America's religious leaders were prepared for the depth or the severity of the wounds that Civil War combat and the disruption of civil society inflicted on these attempts to give meaning to the war. Southern confessionalists like James Henley Thornwell were among slavery's most ardent defenders right up to the point of secession, but then many of them suffered sharp doubts about committing their country to civil war just for slavery's sake, a doubt that tore at the very legitimacy they were trying to drape over it. Thornwell died in 1862, an event that relieved him of the burden that eventually confronted other southern clergymen, of explaining to their people why a cause they had called righteous was slowly collapsing.[59] Northern Evangelicals who had so confidently expected the war to light up the path to the millennium were cruelly disappointed by the profiteering and the corruption, and the uncertain notes on which the war ended looked like anything but a preparation for the return of Jesus Christ to earth. Charles Grandison Finney, who had been smiting slavery with great revivalistic blows for thirty years, warned his Oberlin College students in 1863 that although "The south *must be reformed* or *annihilated,*" still "the *north* are not *yet just.* . . . The *colored man* is still *denied* his *equal rights*" and "is *most intensely hated & persecuted* by a *majority.*" It saddened and angered Finney that after two years of war, "in no *publick proclamation either* north or *south* is *our great national sin recognized.*" No one, however, lost more confidence in religious interpretations of the war than the ordinary soldier. The general disappearance of moral restraint among Civil soldiers mocked the efforts of chaplains and USCC volunteers, at all but the most exceptional moments, to force the war into Christian shape. "It is hard, very hard for one to retain his religious sentiments and feelings in this Soldier life," admitted one New Jersey surgeon. "Every thing seems to tend in a different direction. There seems to be no thought of God of their souls, etc. among the soldiers." But even more than ordinary camp immorality, it was the shock of Civil War combat and the apparent randomness of death on the battle-field that wrecked peacetime faith in an all-knowing, all-loving God. An Illinois surgeon named John Hostetter remarked, "There is no God in war. It is merciless, cruel, vindictive, unchristian, savage, relentless. It is all that devils could wish for." The chaplains talked in vain to Edward King Wightman about divine pur-pose and meaning in the war: "A minister and a soldier are antipodes in senti-ment. The one preaches 'election' and the other fatalism." Even the lay preacher and future president, James A. Garfield, told William Dean Howells after the war that at the sight of "dead men whom other men had killed, something went out of

[58]Morton Borden, "The Christian Amendment," in *Civil War History* 25 (June 1979), p. 160.
[59]William W. Freehling, "James Henley Thornwell's Mysterious Antislavery Moment," in *Journal of Southern History* 57 (August 1991), pp. 383–406.

him, the habit of his lifetime, that never came back again: the sense of the sacredness of life and the impossibility of destroying it."[60]

Although American Protestants had been confident at the beginning of the war that they would be able to interpret the war in ways that their secular counterparts could not, the war itself proved otherwise, and American religion instead became one of the Civil War's major cultural casualties. Never again would evangelical Christianity so dominate the public life of the nation, or come so close to wedding its religious ethos to American republicanism. From the 1860s onward, as Anne Rose has shown, American Protestantism would be increasingly marked by the quiet erosion of faith, and religious experience would become plagued more and more by incessant questioning, by decaying faith, and an increasing appeal to feeling and imagination over and against confessional reason or evangelical conversion.[61] "Perhaps people always think so in their own day, but it seems to me there never was a time when all things have shaken loose from their foundations," wrote one of Finney's correspondents in 1864. "So many are sceptical, doubtful, so many good people are cutting loose from creeds & forms. . . . I am sometimes tempted to ask whether prayer can make any difference." Evangelicals themselves would unwittingly aid this process by withdrawing in confusion from their public roles to concentrate on ever more personalized forms of religious conversion and ever more exotic attempts to hook current events onto the promise of the coming millenium. The public discourse of American intellectuals would, by the 1890s, be taken over by the secular intellectuals who had risked so little in the war, and who had therefore lost so little in it. The secular intellectuals would, of course, be immeasurably aided in this process by the postwar impact of Charles Darwin and Darwin's shocking theory of evolution. But the Civil War proved nearly as deadly to the credibility of American Protestant intellectuals as any of Darwin's apes. Taken together, the Civil War baffled and horrified both secular and Protestant intellectuals, and only in later years, when suffering could be transmuted by memory into moral triumph, and racism effaced by memories of battlefield heroism, could they even begin again to mention the subject. For men of the mind, as well as for men of color and women of all descriptions, the Civil War was a world turned upside down.

Further Reading

The opening vignette of Willard Glazier's descent into powerlessness is drawn from Glazier's own postwar descriptions (which were based on a wartime diary he kept) and on John

[60]From Antietam to Fort Fisher: The Civil War Letters of Edward King Wightman, 1862–1865, E. G. Longacre, ed. (Madison, NJ, 1985), p. 56; James I. Robertson, Soldiers Blue and Gray (Columbia, SC, 1988), p. 227; Gerald Linderman, Embattled Courage: The Experience of Combat in the American Civil War (New York, 1987), p. 128.

[61]Anne Rose, Victorian America and the Civil War (Cambridge, 1992), pp. 17–66.

Algernon Owen's sensationalized biography of Glazier, *Sword and Pen: or, Ventures and Adventures of Willard Glazier* (Philadelphia, 1880). The agitation that African Americans raised for civil rights and military enlistment has been ably discussed in George M. Frederickson, *The Black Image in the White Mind: The Debate on Afro-American Character and Destiny, 1817–1914* (New York, 1971), and James M. McPherson, *The Struggle for Equality: Abolitionists and the Negro in the Civil War and Reconstruction* (Princeton, NJ, 1964). These books are largely concerned with the record of northern blacks, and Leon Litwack's *Been in the Storm So Long: The Aftermath of Slavery* (New York, 1979) should be read for the attention it lavishes on the experience of freedom for former slaves. The record of the African-American soldier, once he was permitted to volunteer, has been chronicled in Dudley Taylor Cornish's *The Sable Arm: Negro Troops in the Union Army, 1861–1865* (New York, 1956), but Cornish's work has been dramatically updated by Joseph Glathaar's *Forged in Battle: The Civil War Alliance of Black Soldiers and White Officers* (New York, 1990). The Civil War in the western territories has usually been told from the viewpoint of military action, without much consideration to the racial and ethnic significance of these small-scale conflicts in the context of a war that was preoccupied with the question of race. Alvin M. Josephy's *The Civil War in the American West* (New York, 1991) offers a highly readable survey of the various actions west of the Mississippi.

Women's history has become its own separate department within American studies, and it has now begun to generate its own subdepartment in Civil War studies as well. One mark of the increasing sophistication of gender and family studies of the Civil War era is *Divided Houses: Gender and the Civil War* (New York, 1992), a collection of essays edited by Catharine Clinton and Nina Silber that offers explorations of childhood, spies, nurses, divorce, and even illicit sex. Catharine Clinton's *The Other Civil War: American Women in the Nineteenth Century* (New York, 1984) offers a useful overview of women's history in the 19th century, but it should be read alongside Nancy F. Cott, *The Bonds of Womanhood: "Woman's Sphere" in New England, 1780–1835* (New Haven, CT, 1977), Mary P. Ryan's *Cradle of the Middle Class: The Family in Oneida County, New York, 1790–1865* (Cambridge, 1981), George C. Rable's *Civil Wars: Women and the Crisis of Southern Nationalism* (Urbana, IL, 1991), and Clinton's own *The Plantation Mistress: Women's World in the Old South* (New York, 1982). The overall disruption of southern communities has been the focus of some of the best social histories of the Civil War, beginning with Gerald M. Capers, *Occupied City: New Orleans Under the Federals, 1862–1865* (Lexington, KY, 1965) and continuing through Peter Maslowski, *Treason Must Be Made Odious: Military Occupation and Wartime Reconstruction in Nashville, Tennessee, 1862–65* (Millwood, NY, 1978), James T. Currie, *Enclave: Vicksburg and Her Plantations, 1863–70* (Jackson, MI, 1980), Thomas V. Ash, *Middle Tennessee Society Transformed, 1860–1870: War and Peace in the Upper South* (Baton Rouge, LA, 1988) and Michael Fellman, *Inside War: The Guerilla Conflict in Missouri during the American Civil War* (New York, 1989).

American culture in the Civil War era and afterward has been surveyed in Anne C. Rose, *Victorian America and the Civil War* (Cambridge, 1992) and Louise A. Stevenson, *The Victorian Homefront: American Thought and Culture, 1860–1880* (New York, 1991), although Stevenson devotes most of her book to the post–Civil War decades. The intellectual life of mid-19th-century America can be best understood through Bruce Kuklick's *Churchmen and Philosophers: From Jonathan Edwards to John Dewey* (New Haven, CT, 1985), which is the finest one-volume survey of the main currents of American intellectual life from the late

18th till the early 20th centuries. George M. Frederickson's *The Inner Civil War: Northern Intellectuals and the Crisis of the Union* (New York, 1965) is still the prevailing interpretation of the involvement of northern intellectuals in interpreting the Civil War, but because he focusses exclusively on the secular intellectuals and the liberal religionists, the record that emerges from his book is quite a dismal one, with northern intellectuals being long on fears for social control and remarkably short on intellectual substance. James Moorhead's *American Apocalypse: Yankee Protestants and the Civil War, 1860–1869* helps to correct the sense of imbalance induced by Frederickson's book, but even so, Moorhead is more concerned with millennialism than with the larger picture of Evangelical Protestants in the Civil War. Another important reminder of the social and interpretive power of Protestantism at mid-century in America is Jon Butler's *Awash in a Sea of Faith: Christianizing the American People* (Cambridge, MA, 1990), while Gardiner H. Shattuck's *A Shield and a Hiding Place: The Religious Life of the Civil War Armies* (Macon, GA, 1987) provides a modern overview of the role played by religion and the religious in the life of the armies. The intellectual background that Protestantism created for interpreting the war can be constructed from the materials in E. Brooks Holifield's elegant little survey, *The Gentleman Theologians: American Theology in Southern Culture, 1795–1800* (Durham, NC, 1978), and for northern Unitarians, Daniel Walker Howe's *The Unitarian Conscience: Harvard Moral Philosophy, 1805–1861* (Cambridge, MA, 1970) presents a scrupulously exact but enormously readable account of the conservative Unitarians up to the outbreak of the war. The significance of the clergy in forming and sustaining homefront morale has been documented in great detail by James W. Silver in *Confederate Morale and Church Propaganda* (New York, 1967). Garry Wills's highly popular *Lincoln at Gettysburg: The Words That Remade America* (New York, 1992) explores the meaning Lincoln attempted to fasten on the war through the Gettysburg Address. Wills's detailed analysis of the structure and rhetorical context of the address is outstanding, but he is less than reliable when he turns to its political meanings. Louis A. Warren's *Lincoln's Gettysburg Declaration: "A New Birth of Freedom"* (Ft. Wayne, IN, 1964) and Frank Klement, *The Gettysburg Soldiers' Cemetery and Lincoln's Address* (Shippensburg, PA, 1993) offer conventional but detailed histories of the writing of the address and its subsequent reputation.

CHAPTER 10

Stalemate and Triumph

David Howe was an officer, but evidently no gentleman.

Around noon on July 14, 1863, Howe turned the corner at the foot of Prince Street, in the mostly Irish North End of Boston. His job was to deliver notice to an unstated number of Prince Street men that their names had been pulled from a drum by draft-enrollment officers, and under the new Federal Enrollment Act, they had ten days to claim exemption, hire a substitute, pay a fee, or face drafting. Serving these notices was not a popular job, and on an upstairs floor in one Prince Street building Howe was confronted by an Irish woman who refused to accept what was probably a notice for one of the men in her family. She must not have found either Howe's manners or his news all that welcome, because after some time spent arguing, the woman hauled off and slapped Howe across the face.

That was when the trouble began.

Enraged at the woman's boldness, Howe announced that as an agent of the United States government, he intended to have the woman arrested, which he may have supposed would shut her up fast. It didn't. She shrieked and howled more loudly, and in short order a curious and not altogether friendly looking crowd began to drift together around Howe. The nervous officer hurriedly descended to the street with the crowd milling after him, and there a quick-witted policeman bundled him into a store at the corner of Prince and Causeway streets and persuaded the crowd to disperse. After a while, the coast seemed clear, and Howe quietly slipped back out into Prince Street with as much of his dignity as he had left. His timing could not have been worse. The crowd from the Irish woman's building had only dispersed long enough to gather up sticks, stones, and reinforcements, and they came boiling down Prince Street just in time to catch Howe out in the open, where they proceeded to beat the draft officer to within an inch of his life.

Howe's erstwhile police protector now sent off for more policemen. But by the time they arrived, the crowd had swollen to over 300 people, and they nearly stomped the hapless coppers to death. Now that it had its blood up, the crowd needed direction, and according to the Boston *Journal*, it got it from "an Irishwoman" who held up "a photograph of her boy who she said was killed in battle," and led them all to Haymarket Street, four blocks away. It was now 2 P.M., and the crowd was numbering near 500.

330

Massachusetts Governor John Andrew was at that moment across the Charles River, listening to the salutarian at the Harvard College commencement drone out a scrupulously esoteric oration in Latin. Andrew was on the point of nodding off when an aide jabbed him awake with an urgent message about a disturbance in the North End. Andrew had been anticipating trouble in Boston, but not over the draft: The all-black 55th Massachusetts had been due to parade through Boston, and Andrew had prudently put the militia and federal artillerymen from the harbor forts on notice in case race-baiting toughs tried to stir up a little trouble. Andrew's face paled at the whispered news, causing the Harvard salutarian to forget his Latinate lines, and the governor abruptly walked off the platform and left the commencement audience stewing in whisper and rumor.[1] By 6 P.M., Andrew had mobilized four companies of militia and a battery of artillery and ordered them to rendezvous at the Cooper Street arsenal, only two blocks from Haymarket Square; in another hour, two companies of federal heavy artillerymen were on their way to the arsenal as well.

The heavy artillerymen were the last to arrive at the Cooper Street arsenal, and they were only just in time. Around 7:30, a mob nearly 1,000 strong roared around the corner of Cooper Street, throwing bricks and bottles and shattering the glass in the arsenal windows. The officers in charge of the troops in the arsenal—federal artillery Major Stephen Cabot and Massachusetts militia Captain E. J. Jones—stepped outside and ordered the crowd to disperse. Instead, the rocks and bottles now came showering down on the two officers, and some of the militia fired a volley over the heads of the crowd to scare them into flight. The volley only maddened the mob, and now the enraged men and women in the street began an attack on the arsenal in earnest, hurling paving stones, bricks, and anything else they could lay hands on. Like the Richmond bread riot three months before, women angrily took charge of the assault, and "one Amazonian woman . . . with hair streaming, arms swinging, and her face the picture of phrenzy . . . rushed again and again to the assault." One neighborhood girl remembered women holding up their infants to the windows of the arsenal and daring the soldiers inside to shoot.

Cabot refused to allow his men to fire. But after forty-five minutes, the crowd began slamming its collected weight against the arsenal doors, and Cabot had no choice but to order one of the six-pounder howitzers his artillerymen had brought with them loaded with a double charge of canister. At 8:15, the door gave way before the mob, and Cabot gave the order to fire. The gun blast blew the mob back into the street, and within a few minutes they had scattered out of sight. Eight people were dead, four of them small children.

The mob was not done, however. Bloodied and desperate, the crowd regrouped around the corner and broke into whatever gun shops they could find for weapons. But as they worked their way down the line of shops that led toward old Faneuil

[1] William B. Hesseltine, *Lincoln and the War Governors* (New York, 1948), pp. 304–306.

Hall, they were headed off by a squad of policemen, two companies of militia, a company of mounted dragoons with drawn sabers, and the mayor of Boston with the Riot Act in his hand. The shiver of sabers in the red summer sunset cowed them, and the mob gradually broke up and faded into the oncoming dusk. By 11 P.M., Boston was quiet again.[2]

And with that, it became apparent even to the most blue-dyed Yankee and the most Radical Republican that Richmond was not the only city in 1863 that was beginning to stagger under the weight of the war's burdens. No city in America was more identified with abolitionism than Boston, no governor had pressed more quickly or more tirelessly to move emancipation and abolition to the front of the war agenda than John Andrew. But the people in the streets of Boston had not been prepared for the costs that a war to emancipate African-American slaves would impose on them, and they had certainly not bargained for the war to turn into a nightmare that requisitioned their sons and brothers and fathers by force, and then sent them off under the Burnsides and Hookers and Buells to be slaughtered to no purpose, or to a purpose linked with black freedom. The temper of the war was failing in the North in 1863. There must be victory, now, and by generals who would stop at nothing less than victory. And there must be political results equal to the sacrifices being made, if not by this administration and this president, then by another. And if the war could not be won on those terms, and won soon, perhaps it might be better to admit that it could never be won at all.

1. If It Takes All Summer

Grant's victory at Chattanooga in November, 1863, brought the federal armies only one-third of the way between their old base in Kentucky and the Confederacy's Atlantic and Gulf coastlines. Now that Grant had complete control over all the western armies, he might choose to push southward directly to Atlanta, and complete the disruption of the Confederacy's western rail links, or shift his line of operations to aim at Mobile, Alabama, which would close one of the Confederacy's last remaining ports and, in the process, roll over the Confederacy's vital foundries and arsenals in northern Alabama.

His first inclination was to strike for Mobile. In August, Grant wrote to Charles Dana, "I am very anxious to take Mobile while I think it can be done," and four months later, he told General-in-Chief Halleck that he wanted "to move by way of New Orleans and Pascagoula on Mobile. . . . A move on Atlanta was a logistical impossibility right now, Grant explained, and instead he proposed to leave only a garrison strong enough to secure Chattanooga, and then move the old Army of the Cumberland via steamboat down to New Orleans. From there, Grant would launch a movement on Mobile that would pinch off the town, capture

[2]William F. Hanna, "The Boston Draft Riot," in *Civil War History* 36 (September 1990), pp. 262–273.

Montgomery and Selma, and maybe even force Lee to abandon the Virginia theater to protect Georgia. In a later letter to Halleck, Grant expanded his views even more dramatically: Washington should give up looking to win the war in Virginia and concentrate its attention on the West instead. Grant was now convinced that the campaigns in Virginia and along the Mississippi were really only so much tactical boxing, and that the only way to strike a really decisive blow at the Confederacy was to slash away at its strategic intestines in Alabama, Georgia, and the Carolinas.[3]

On December 17th, Halleck replied to Grant's Mobile proposal, cautiously authorizing him to proceed, but with the crippling requirement that all of Tennessee first be securely in Union hands. Then, in January, Lincoln authorized General Nathaniel P. Banks to take a joint army-navy expedition up the Red River into the upcountry of Louisiana. Banks's expedition was a political rather than a military move—Lincoln wanted to consolidate the hold of the newly reconstructed government in occupied Louisiana over the rest of the state and perhaps send a useful message to the French in Mexico about federal intentions for Texas. But all the same, it drained away men and supplies Grant had been counting on for his Mobile campaign. Just as he had done after Corinth and after Vicksburg, Grant was forced to sit on his triumphs.

But Grant did not sit still for long in Tennessee anymore than he had in Mississippi the year before. In December, 1863, Congress proposed to reward Grant for the Chattanooga victory by reviving the rank of Lieutenant General, a grade filled only once before in the history of the American Republic, by George Washington. The bill passed the Senate on February 24, 1864, and on March 3rd, Halleck wired Grant to come to Washington to receive the commission. The promotion to lieutenant general did two things for Grant. First, it immediately made him senior in rank to Halleck, who remained only a major general, and effectively booted Grant up to general-in-chief of the federal armies. Halleck, with uncommon graciousness, stepped aside as general-in-chief to make way for Grant and assumed the new post of chief-of-staff to Secretary of War Stanton (which is really the function he had been exercising all along since July of 1862). Second, it brought Grant east to meet with Lincoln and Stanton on March 8th. Two days later, the new lieutenant general rode out to the headquarters of the Army of the Potomac to meet George Gordon Meade and take the measure of the eastern army.

Grant had heard rumors ever since the preceding summer that Lincoln wanted to drop Meade from command of the Army of the Potomac, chiefly because of his failure to follow and destroy Lee after Gettysburg, and the substance of these rumors was that Lincoln meant to bring Grant east as Meade's replacement. Knowing what a political cockpit the Army of the Potomac was, Grant had no desire whatever to

---

[3]Grant to Dana [August 5, 1863], in *The Papers of Ulysses S. Grant*, John Y. Simon, ed. (Carbondale, IL, 1982, vol. 9, pp. 146–147; Grant to Halleck, *Official Records*, series 1, vol. 31, p. 349; Bruce Catton, *Grant Takes Command* (Boston, 1968), pp. 101–102.

offer himself as the next target for eastern military intrigue. In the same letter in August, 1863, that had broached the Mobile plan to Charles Dana, Grant laboriously thanked Dana "for your timely intercession is saving me from going to the Army of the Potomac. Whilst I would disobey no order I should beg very hard to be excused before accepting that command." Even after his appointment as general-in-chief, Grant seems to have been determined to keep his headquarters in the West, and proceed with his plans to give the Army of the Potomac the shorter end of the strategic stick. But Grant was impressed in spite of himself with Meade and the army, and the War Department and various Republican congressional nabobs pressed on Grant the fact that Congress had bestowed the grade of lieutenant general on him principally in the hopes that he would lead the Army of the Potomac into battle against Lee in a super-showdown of tactical wits. "Unless this army of foes [i.e., the Army of Northern Virginia] is defeated and broken, and our Capitol relieved of its fierce frowns," argued Grant's own chief-of-staff, John A. Rawlins, "we cannot hope that the recognition of the rebel government will be much longer postponed by European governments."[4] By the time Grant returned to Nashville, he had decided to move his headquarters to the east and take up general tactical command of the eastern theater. He also revised his plans for operations in Virginia to include yet another overland campaign across the Rappahannock for the Army of the Potomac in order to confront Lee and bring the Army of Northern Virginia to battle.

Grant knew that he was taking considerable risks in coming east. For one thing, he was a Westerner and a stranger with surprisingly little personal grandeur or charisma about him, and it took the Easterners some getting used to a commander who had no interest in fine reviews and hip-hip-hoorah. "Grant . . . paid us a visit yesterday," George Washington Whitman wrote to his mother on April 14, 1864. "There was no grand Review as is generally the case, but the Regiments just fell in line and Grant rode along and looked at them and then went on about his business." A civilian friend of one of Grant's staff officers was amazed that "there is no glitter or parade about him. To me he seems but an earnest business man." Grant was also aware that as a Westerner, he was likely to be resented as an interloper by the Army of the Potomac. "The enlisted men thoroughly discussed Grant's military capacity," Frank Wilkeson remembered. "Magazines, illustrated papers, and newspapers, which contained accounts of his military achievements, were sent for, and eagerly and attentively read." Most of the veterans were skeptical. "Old soldiers, who had seen many military reputations—reputations which had been made in subordinate commands or in distant regions occupied by inferior Confederate troops—melt before the battle-fire of the Army of Northern Virginia, and expose the incapacity of our generals, shrugged their shoulders carelessly." Wilkeson, who would be going into his first campaign under Grant,

[4]Herman Hattaway and Archer Jones, *How the North Won the Civil War: A Military History of the Civil War* (Urbana, IL, 1983), p. 517.

discovered that "Grant's name aroused no enthusiasm. The Army of the Potomac had passed the enthusiastic stage."[5]

Grant anticipated that skepticism, and he even toyed with the idea of bringing McClellan back into the Army of the Potomac at some level to rally its faded enthusiasm. He also wisely retained Meade as official commander of the Army of the Potomac (even though Grant himself would travel with the army and give all the orders that mattered). In some cases, though, Grant was facing problems that political savvy had no way of addressing. This particular army was largely composed of three-year volunteers, and in the spring and summer of 1864, many of those enlistments were due to expire. The constant defeats the army had suffered had badly undermined its morale, and only about half of the Army of the Potomac's veterans would be persuaded to reenlist. Unless he could win some kind of smashing victory and win it soon, this meant that Grant was liable to see a large part of the Army of the Potomac legally desert him.

Staggering as these problems were, Grant managed to stay on his guard about letting the Army of the Potomac eat up all his attention and resources. He still believed that the really decisive blows that would win the war were going to have to land somewhere outside the old battlefields north of Richmond. To that end, Grant also provided for three other simultaneous offensives to begin in the West and below Richmond that would help to realize much of the original plan he had proposed to Halleck. Those three offensives would depend largely on the men Grant designated to lead them. First and foremost, there was William Tecumseh Sherman. Grant proposed to combine George Thomas and the Army of the Cumberland with Grant's old army from the Vicksburg campaign, and put them both under the command of Sherman. At the same time as Grant's overland campaign would open in Virginia, Sherman would advance south toward Atlanta, with the goal of taking Atlanta by the end of the summer. In addition to Sherman, Grant was also looking to Nathaniel P. Banks, the federal military commander of Louisiana. From his base in Union-occupied Louisiana, Grant originally planned that Banks would launch a combined army-navy operation against Mobile. With Sherman occupying the Army of Tennessee, there would be little at hand to defend Mobile, and when the port fell into his hands, Banks could then move his men north through Alabama without serious opposition, wrecking Selma in his path, and then turn east and meet Sherman at Atlanta. Lastly, Grant was looking for help from Major General Benjamin F. Butler, the Massachusetts politician who had outraged New Orleans and made the "contrabands" the beginning of a new federal policy on slavery in 1861. Butler was to take command of two federal army corps (about 33,000 men) and deposit them on the old James River peninsula, below Richmond. While Grant and the Army of the Potomac would clinch Lee in battle

[5]Civil War Letters of George Washington Whitman, Jerome Loving, ed. (Durham, NC, 1975), p. 114; William S. McFeely, Grant: A Biography (New York, 1981), p. 159; Frank Wilkeson, Recollections of a Private Soldier (New York, 1887), pp. 36–37.

along the Rappahannock line, Butler and his men could slip past the thin Confederate defenses on the James, and capture Richmond or at least cut Richmond's rail communications with the rest of the South.

But almost from the first, things began to go wrong with Grant's big strategic picture. For one thing, Banks's private little expedition up the Red River failed to move until March 12, 1864, and when it did, it turned out to be an unpleasant little fiasco that tied up Banks's forces (along with 10,000 of Sherman's men who had been sent to reinforce him) until the end of May. By that time, Banks was a month late just starting for Mobile, and in fact, he never even got that far, and spent the rest of the war in New Orleans. If Grant wanted Sherman to take Atlanta, Sherman would have to do it himself, and without any helpful distractions at Mobile by Banks. Meanwhile, Butler and his "Army of the James" made a brave landing below Richmond on the James peninsula on May 5, 1864. Butler got within five miles of Richmond on May 11th, only to be turned back by a desperate Confederate defense at Drewry's Bluff on May 16th. Butler withdrew back to the James River and entrenched himself on a little bottleneck formed by a bend in the river called Bermuda Hundred. There the Confederates sealed off his little army, like a "bottle tightly corked," and that was where Butler's men stayed for the next year.

But Grant's biggest problem was presented by Robert E. Lee and the Army of Northern Virginia. He was, for one thing, clear that it was Lee's army, and not Richmond, that was the real objective of his campaign. In his orders to Meade, Grant stated with biblical bluntness, "Lee's army will be your objective point. Wherever Lee goes, there you will go also." There would be no more war by the engineers' numbers. On the other hand, Grant did not simply propose to throw himself at Lee, and like Hooker a year before, he chose not to try to force a crossing of the Rappahannock at Fredericksburg. Instead, the Army of the Potomac, with Meade and Grant, 3,500 wagons, 29,000 horses, 20,000 mules, and 120,000 men, splashed across the Rapidan River on May 3rd, and plunged at once into the eerie gloom of the Wilderness.[6] Grant expected that he could move through the Wilderness fast enough to force Lee to fall back upon Richmond, but his immense wagon train bogged down in the narrow rutted roads of the Wilderness, and on May 4th, the army was forced to stop and wait for the line to close up.

This presented precisely the sort of opportunity Lee prayed for, since the tangled and unfamiliar terrain of the Wilderness would eliminate the federal advantages in numbers and artillery and allow the Army of Northern Virginia an even chance in a fight. And this spring, Lee would need all the help that the Virginia terrain could give. Three weeks before Grant crossed the Rapidan, Lee warned Jefferson Davis that "I cannot see how we can operate with our present supplies. . . . There is nothing to be had in this section for man or animals." Lee's

[6]Edward Hagerman, The American Civil War and the Origins of Modern Warfare: Ideas, Organization, and Field Command (Bloomington, IN, 1988), p. 248.

health was so poor that he admitted to his son Custis in April that "I feel a marked change in my strength . . . and am less competent for duty than ever." Lee's three corps commanders—James Longstreet (who had rejoined the Army of Northern Virginia with his corps after Bragg's debacle at Missionary Ridge), A. P. Hill, and Richard Ewell—were all veteran officers with at least a full year of experience at corps command behind them. But each had failed Lee at Gettysburg, and there would remain some question about how reliable their performance would be in the upcoming battles.[7]

The most immediate problem that Lee had to face, however, was concentrating his forces to meet Grant. In the interest of casting his net for supplies as far as he dared, Lee's three army corps, numbering only about 70,000 men, were widely scattered along the south side of the Rapidan. When Lee ordered them to rendezvous to face Grant, one of those corps, moving eastward on the main turnpike through the Wilderness, collided with the vanguard of the Army of the Potomac, heading south on the one usable north-south road through the Wilderness, and a firefight erupted. Meade, anxious to get out of the Wilderness before the main body of Lee's army arrived, tried to shoulder the Confederates aside, only to find too many of them in front. Reserves were called up, and they proceeded to blunder into another Confederate corps coming up to the support of the first one. And so it went on for the next two days, until both armies had thrown everything they had at each other in a confused melee of attacks and counterattacks through the dense underbrush and burning woods, little of it with any sense, but with a total of 18,000 casualties for the Army of the Potomac and another 7,500 or so for the Army of Northern Virginia. By midnight on the evening of May 6th, both armies had lapsed into an uncomfortable quiet, too exhausted and confused to carry the fight on further.

Almost exactly one year before, "Fighting Joe" Hooker had found himself in the same situation and at the same location near the old Chancellorsville House, and he had elected to retreat. Much of the Army of the Potomac must have expected that Grant would follow the same old pattern, a dingy and depressing pattern they had known for three years—attack, stall, withdraw across the Rappahannock. But Grant was not "Fighting Joe," and he was not like anything else the Army of the Potomac had ever seen. In the early morning hours of May 7th, Grant arose, wrote out his orders, ate breakfast, and then moved out onto the road in the predawn darkness with his headquarters staff, past the burning wreck of the Wilderness and the long lines of Winfield S. Hancock's 2nd Corps standing by the roadside—and headed *south*. For the first time since he arrived in the East, the Army of the Potomac began to cheer Grant. "No doubt it was inspired by the fact that the movement was south," wrote Grant with characteristic detachment. "It indicated to them that they had passed through the 'beginning of the end' in the

---

[7]Gary W. Gallagher, "The Army of Northern Virginia in May 1864: A Crisis of High Command," in *Civil War History* 36 (July 1990), pp. 101–107.

battle just fought. The cheering was so lusty that the enemy must have taken it for a night attack."[8] Frank Wilkeson recalled that "Grant's military standing with the enlisted men this day hung on the direction we turned at the Chancellorsville House."

> If to the left, he was to be rated with Meade and Hooker and Burnside and Pope— the generals who preceded him. At the Chancellorsville House we turned to the right. Instantly all of us heard a sigh of relief. Our spirits rose. We marched free. The men began to sing. The enlisted men understood the flanking movement. That night we were happy.[9]

Sixty miles away, in Washington, Lincoln and Stanton had heard nothing from Grant after the last of the Army of the Potomac had disappeared into the maw of the Wilderness, and an aide noticed that the tension was so great for Stanton that he could not even reach for a piece of paper without twitching. But on May 8th, Grant finally had an official dispatch to send to Lincoln, and despite the punishing losses, John Hay noticed for the first time Lincoln was happy with what one of his generals was doing in Virginia. Lincoln remarked to Hay, "How near we have been to this thing before and failed. I believe if any other general had been at the head of that army it would not have been on this side of the Rapidan. It is the dogged pertinacity of Grant that wins." Two days later, Grant sent Halleck a letter that had an even larger measure of "dogged pertinacity" to it: "I am now sending back . . . all my wagons for a fresh supply of provisions and ammunition, and purpose to fight it out on this line if it takes all summer."[10]

Grant rightly suspected that, as badly hurt as his own army was, Lee's was probably even more badly hurt. So, shaking off the blow he had received in the Wilderness, Grant began feeling to his left, seeking to move around the battered flank of Lee's army and out onto the open ground between the Rappahannock and Richmond. His first objective was Spotsylvania Courthouse, a little country cross-roads eleven miles southeast of the Wilderness. If he could get there before Lee, the Army of the Potomac would lie at right angles to Richmond and the Army of Northern Virginia, and Lee would have no choice but to attack him there or abandon Richmond. But once again, the roads were poor, the maps unreliable, and the wagon train took too long, and as a result, Lee managed to beat Grant to Spotsylvania Court House by the afternoon of May 8th.

The Confederates had only a little time to build up their defenses before Grant's army arrived, but by this point in the war, all but the greenest volunteers

---

[8]Grant, "Personal Memoirs," in *Ulysses S. Grant: Memoirs and Selected Letters*, W. S. and M. D. McFeely, eds. (New York, 1990), p. 539; Catton, *Grant Takes Command*, p. 208.

[9]Wilkeson, *Recollections*, p. 80.

[10]Benjamin P. Thomas and Harold M. Hyman, *Stanton: The Life and Times of Lincoln's Secretary of War* (New York, 1962), p. 300; Hay, in *Lincoln and the Civil War in the Diaries and Letters of John Hay*, Tyler Dennett, ed. (1939; rept. Westport, CT, 1972), p. 180; Grant, "Personal Memoirs," in *Memoirs and Selected Letters*, pp. 550–551.

knew how to scratch up effective entrenchments by the rule of the minute. By the time Grant was ready to attack on May 10th, the Army of Northern Virginia was dug into a five-mile long horseshoe-shaped line that no power on earth known to the 19th century could have dislodged. What happened instead was a pointless, bloody, headlong attempt to punch a hole in the west side of the horseshoe. For one moment that evening, a carefully selected division of twelve regiments under Colonel Emory Upton fought its way into the Confederate position, but Upton's men were left dangling without supports and were forced to withdraw. Two days later, on May 12th, Grant tried again, and this time the results were an exercise in military horror. At one point on the Confederate line, in a trench known as "The Bloody Angle," attackers and defenders grappled in vicious hand-to-hand, rifle-to-rifle combat, like two crowds of enraged beasts. The commander of the Vermont Brigade remembered that "it was not only a desperate struggle but it was emphatically a hand-to-hand fight."

> Scores were shot down within a few feet of the death-dealing muskets. A breastwork of logs and earth separated the combatants. Our men would reach over the breastworks and discharge their muskets in the very face of the enemy. Some men clubbed their muskets, and in some instances used clubs and rails. . . . The slaughter of the enemy was terrible. The sight next day was repulsive and sickening, indeed. Behind their traverses, and in the pits and holes they had dug for protection, the rebel dead were found piled upon each other. Some of the wounded were almost entirely buried by the dead bodies of their companions that had fallen upon them. Many of the dead men were horribly mangled, and the logs, trees, and brush exhibited unmistakeable signs of a fearful conflict. [11]

By the close of day, with another 6,800 casualties to add to those in the Wilderness, the Army of the Potomac was still unable to dislodge Lee from his position around Spotsylvania Court House. But Grant had lost nothing of his determination. On May 14th, true to his promise to fight matters out "if it takes all summer," Grant again decided to move around Lee's right.

From that point on, Grant's campaign became a lethal ballet with Lee, with Grant and the Army of the Potomac always looking to slide quickly and deftly around Lee's right, and Lee always moving just fast enough to get his army in front of them again. In a deadly arc of turning movements, over poor roads and through bottomless mud, always dropping closer and closer to Richmond, Grant pushed his army one step ahead of Lee, until finally by the end of May, Grant had fought his way down to another desolate little crossroads called Cold Harbor, only ten miles northeast of Richmond. At that point he ran out of maneuvering room. In front of Grant was Lee, his men arriving just in the nick of time to throw up instant entrenchments; on Grant's left was a familiar and fatal stream, the Chickahominy River, trickling into the James; on the right was the road back north that he had

---

[11]L. A. Grant, in *Official Records*, series 1, vol. 36 (part 1), p. 704.

promised not to take. His options gone, Grant ordered another frontal assault, and the results were even worse than Spotsylvania. In less than a single hour, 7,000 federal soldiers had been shot down.

Now was the moment of decision for Grant: He had sustained 30,000 casualties since crossing the Rapidan a month before, and he was losing still more as regimental enlistments expired. It is on this point, incidentally, that the old story that Grant was a military butcher who simply kept feeding an unlimited supply of Union reinforcements at the Confederates until the Southerners were finally overwhelmed by sheer numbers falls apart. All through the war, Robert E. Lee consistently lost more men in one offensive gambit after another than any federal commander, including Grant; even when facing Grant directly, Lee still lost a higher percentage of his forces in battle than Grant, despite the fact that Grant took the offensive at every point from the Wilderness to Cold Harbor. Nor did Grant always have a bottomless barrel of fresh troops to draw upon. General Andrew Humphreys, Meade's chief of staff, recorded after the war that the Army of the Potomac received only about 12,000 effective reinforcements during the first six weeks of the overland campaign, while it lost not only the names on the bloody casualty lists but also thirty-six infantry regiments who simply chose to go home rather than re-enlist. Over the long haul, Grant husbanded the lives of his men far more effectively than Lee; it was Lee, and not Grant, who bled armies dry.[12]

One other thing that was evident, however, was that Grant was far from overwhelming Lee or anyone else at Cold Harbor, and all Grant had to show for a month's grinding campaigning was the lesson that the Confederates simply could not be beaten by an army marching overland at them. McClellan, of course, had grasped that back in 1862. That was one reason why he had refused to go hunting for the Confederate army south of the Rappahannock, and preferred instead to pin them into a siege of Richmond by way of the James River. Unhappily for McClellan, he was too timid to make his plans work, and his political obstructionism had made anyone else's proposals for sieges and operations along the James guilty by mere association. But Grant had now played all the cards there were to play on the overland route, and the Army of the Potomac was no closer to victory now than when he started. So, he imperturbably sat down and informed Halleck that he intended to change his line of operations from the Fredericksburg-Richmond line to the James River, transfer the Army of the Potomac to the south side of the James, and either barge into Richmond from below or shut Lee up into a siege.

This, of course, was what Halleck and Lincoln had always been sure they must prevent their generals from doing. Lincoln's methodology, ever since McClellan, had been to push his generals after Lee, not Richmond. But Grant merely observed that Lee's men had acquired a considerable knack for entrenching themselves and making head-on attacks a very costly proposition. And besides, Grant was propos-

[12]Catton, *Grant Takes Command*, pp. 240–241.

ing not to attack Richmond but to maneuver Lee out of Richmond and away from the Army of Northern Virginia's vital depots and rail links, thereby forcing the Confederates out into open country where they would be compelled to fight or starve or both. This was essentially the same thing he had done at Vicksburg. And with the memory of Vicksburg in mind, Grant aimed to pull back secretly from the Cold Harbor lines, steal a march down to the James and cross it over a 2,100-foot-long pontoon bridge that remains one of the greatest wonders of military engineering, and wind up on the south side of the river below Richmond while Lee was still in his lines above the city. He would then seize the vital rail junction at Petersburg, twelve miles below Richmond, where all the major rail lines from the rest of the South—Norfolk & Petersburg, Weldon, Southside, Richmond & Danville—came together to form the logistical lifeline of the Army of Northern Virginia. Cut those lines at Petersburg, and both Richmond and the Army of Northern Virginia were doomed to die on the vine. Grant would then link up with Butler's little Army of the James on Bermuda Hundred, march straight in through Richmond's poorly defended back door, and prepare for the final grapple of the armies somewhere in the open country outside Richmond.

Coming from any other general, not a syllable of this plan would have been even remotely acceptable to Lincoln or Halleck—it looked too much like the same dreary plan McClellan had invented for avoiding Lee and spending time and resources grasping at a dot on the map. But Grant had Lincoln's confidence to a degree that no other general had, and the president was inclined to give the general his leash. Lincoln remarked in the spring of 1864 to one of his White House secretaries, William O. Stoddard, that "Grant is the first general I've had" who "hasn't told me what his plans are. I don't know, and I don't want to know. I'm glad to find a man who can go ahead without me." That, of course, was not literally true: Grant had telegraphed all the details to Halleck, Halleck had passed them on to Lincoln, and Lincoln had taken the whole plan in at once. "Have just read your despatch," Lincoln wired Grant while Grant was already on the road. "I begin to see it. You will succeed. God bless you."[13]

On June 12th, Grant quietly evacuated his Cold Harbor lines, moving so swiftly and unobtrusively that Lee knew nothing of the withdrawal until the next morning. Grant then proceeded to execute the biggest turning movement of the war, quick-marching his men, corps by corps, down to the James and across the marvelous pontoon bridge while Lee was still trying to decide where they had gone. By the afternoon of the 15th, two federal army corps were poised at the gates of Petersburg with no more than 2,400 Virginia state militia to bar the way. "The city is ours. There is not a brigade of the Army of Northern Virginia ahead of us," shouted the jubilant men of Frank Wilkeson's battery. "On all sides I heard men assert that Petersburg and Richmond were ours; that

---

[13]T. Harry Williams, *Lincoln and His Generals* (New York, 1952), p. 307; Catton, *Grant Takes Command*, pp. 176–177; Lincoln, "To Ulysses S. Grant" [June 15, 1864], in *Collected Works*, vol. 7, p. 393.

the war would virtually be ended in less than twenty-four hours."[14] But at that moment, both federal corps commanders lost their nerve and failed to press home their attacks. The next afternoon, Grant, Meade, and the rest of the Army of the Potomac arrived, but so had advance elements of the Army of Northern Virginia, and when Grant tried to launch his own attacks on June 16th and 17th, the resistance was already too stiff. Both armies began frantically digging in, and Grant reluctantly conceded that there was nothing left to do but begin a siege at Petersburg and hope for the best.

Grant continued to experiment with ways of breaking the impasse at Petersburg, but none really worked. On July 30th, with Grant's blessing, a regiment of Pennsylvania coal miners exploded an immense mine under the center of the Confederate entrenchments. The mine blew "an enormous hole in the ground about 30 feet deep, 60 feet wide and 1709 feet long, filled with dust, great blocks of clay, guns, broken carriages, projecting timbers, and men buried in various ways—some to their necks, others to their waists, and some with only their feet and legs protruding from the earth."[15] The plan had been for a division of black federal soldiers to rush into the hole created by the mine, peel back the twisted ends of the Confederate line, and allow the rest of the Army of the Potomac to pour through the gap toward Petersburg. But at the last minute, the black division was replaced with a white division that had no training or preparation for the assault, and when the new division rushed into the crater, no one had any clear idea what to do next. The stunned Confederates rallied, sealed off the crater, and after stubborn but disorganized federal resistance, managed to recapture the crater and most of the federal soldiers in it. The Battle of the Crater became simply one more in the long string of the Army of the Potomac's missed chances, and Grant admitted to Halleck, "It was the saddest affair I have witnessed in the war. . . . I am constrained to believe that had instructions been promptly obeyed that Petersburg would have been carried with all the artillery and a large number of prisoners without a loss of 300 men."[16] The lack of a dramatic victory, and the prospect of a long and empty siege, fell dramatically short of what the country had expected from Grant, and the price for that disappointment was liable to be severe: 1864 was an election year, and if Lincoln had nothing to show for three years of war but Grant besieging Petersburg and Richmond for who-knew-how-long, then it was entirely possible that the North would turn to another president and another solution. But there was still one other voice to be heard from before a decision would be made, and that would come from a man who was at that moment almost a thousand miles away, and his name was Sherman.

[14]Wilkeson, Recollections, pp. 157–158.

[15]William H. Powell, "The Battle of the Petersburg Crater," in Battles and Leaders of the Civil War, C. C. Buel and R. U. Johnson, eds. (New York, 1956), vol. 4, p. 551.

[16]Grant to Halleck, Official Records, series 1, vol. 40 (part 1), pp. 17–18.

2. To Atlanta and the Sea

The only piece of Grant's overall strategic plan in 1864 that actually worked was the move he had outlined from Chattanooga to Atlanta, and the principal reason why this part succeeded when so many other parts miscarried was the simple fact that he had entrusted it to William Tecumseh Sherman. What had been little more than a nodding acquaintance between the two men before the war had matured into one of the most formidable friendships in American history, fueled by the company misery is supposed to enjoy: The careers of both men before the Civil War had followed much the same dismal course, for in both cases, the army proved a poor employer, and a West Point education was a poor preparation for anything but army employment. Sherman had veered erratically from the army into banking, then into near-destitution when his San Francisco bank failed, and then into real-estate speculation. He arrived at the year 1857, thirty-seven years old but looking more like a man of sixty, a nervous, fidgety chain smoker with a thin coating of reddish hair and a perpetually scraggly shadow of beard. "I am doomed to be a vagabond," he wrote, "I look upon myself as a dead cock in the pit, not worthy of future notice."[17]

However, in 1859, Sherman successfully applied for the superintendency of the new Louisiana State Military College. There, the transplanted Ohioan spent two of the happiest years of his life, until he gradually came to think of himself as being as much a Louisianan as anything else. He did not particularly like slavery, but he also believed that it was the only condition fit for blacks, and he was perfectly willing to defend Louisiana slavery, if necessary, provided that Louisiana did not put itself beyond the pale by attempting to secede from the Union. "I am willing to aid Louisiana in defending herself against her enemies so long as she remains a state in the general confederacy; but should she or any other state act disunion, I am out." But secession was exactly what Louisiana proposed in 1861, and one week before the state adopted its secession ordinance, Sherman resigned from the Military College and headed north. After a wait of four months, he was summoned to Washington and commissioned as colonel of the 13th U.S. Infantry.

Sherman's first round of Civil War service nearly finished him. He commanded a brigade of infantry at First Bull Run, and then was promoted to brigadier general and transferred to the Department of the Ohio. Unfortunately for Sherman, the department commander resigned, and until the new commander could be appointed and arrive on the scene, Sherman had to assume responsibility for organizing and administering the entire department. The nervous excitement was too great for a man of Sherman's high-strung temperament—he quarreled with the press, began screaming to Washington for 200,000 reinforcements, and insisted on returning runaway slaves to their owners. Finally, on November 15th, Don Carlos Buell showed up to take charge, and Sherman was moved over to Henry Wager Halleck's

---

[17]John F. Marszalek, *Sherman: A Soldier's Passion for Order* (New York, 1993), p. 119.

department in St. Louis. Vengeful newspaper reporters circulated stories that Sherman had actually gone insane, and it looked as though his second military career had gone broke even faster than his bank.

But Halleck discounted the newspaper stories, and when he began moving up the Tennessee River in March of 1862, he gave Sherman command of a division and sent him upriver to Pittsburg Landing to reinforce Grant. There, on April 6th, Sherman's division, posted around the little Shiloh Baptist Church, was the first in the way of the Confederate wave that rolled over Grant's army. To the surprise of his former critics back in Ohio, Sherman displayed an unexpected cool-headedness in the midst of the Confederate onslaught. The peculiar geography of battle transformed Sherman: He personally rallied shattered regiments, plugged up holes in the federal lines, and had four horses shot from under him. Under his direction, the right flank of Grant's army managed to perform the most difficult maneuver in the military textbooks, an orderly retreat under fire. "All around him were excited orderlies and officers," wrote one observer after Shiloh, "but though his face was besmeared with powder and blood, battle seemed to have cooled his usually hot nerves." Halleck obtained Sherman's promotion to major general, and when Grant finally began his great move on Vicksburg at the end of 1862, it was Sherman whom Grant asked Halleck for as a division commander.

Sherman eventually became as indispensable to Grant as "Stonewall" Jackson had been to Robert E. Lee, and like Grant, he made a deep and favorable impression on Charles Dana. "On the whole, General Sherman has a very small and very efficient staff; but the efficiency comes mainly from him," Dana wrote to his chief, Secretary of War Stanton, in July, 1863. "What a splendid soldier he is!"[18] When Grant went east at the end of 1863 to supervise operations in the Virginia theater, there was no question but that Sherman would take command in the West and conduct the operations Grant had planned against Atlanta. Gone forever was the paranoid behavior Sherman had manifested in Kentucky; under Grant's tutelage, he had developed into an energetic field commander, capable of quick decisions and even quicker movement. Instead of waging war by the defensive book, carefully preserving southern property as the armies tiptoed past it, Sherman now began to talk about bringing it all crashing to the earth, about putting the thumbscrews to the South. In September of 1863, he urged Lincoln to turn the war into a campaign of desolation, since desolation was the only language the Confederates would understand.

> I would banish all minor questions, assert the broad doctrine that a nation has the right, and also the physical power to penetrate to every part of our national domain, and that we will do it—that we will do it in our time and in our own way; that it makes no difference whether it be one year or two, or ten or twenty; that we will remove and destroy every obstacle, if need be, take every life, every acre of

---

[18]Dana, *Recollections of the Civil War with the Leaders at Washington and in the Field in the Sixties* (New York, 1898), p. 76.

land . . . that we will not cease till the end is attained. . . . I would not coax them or even meet them half way but make them so sick of war that generations would pass away before they would again appeal to it. . . . The people of this country have forfeited all right to a voice in the councils of the nation. They know it and feel it and in after-years they will be better citizens from the dear-bought experience.

And to a Tennessee lady who objected to manners so cruel, Sherman replied with a shrug: "War is cruelty. There is no use trying to reform it, the crueler it is, the sooner it will be over."[19]

But there was one point on which Sherman had not changed his opinions, and that was the future of the black slaves his soldiers encountered in Tennessee and Mississippi. He bowed to the Emancipation Proclamation as a military necessity, but he consistently declined to use black Union soldiers in combat (though he later on conceded to assigning them garrison duties), and publicly doubted whether freed slaves could be "manufactured into voters, equal to all others, politically and socially." Notions like that had destroyed the career of many an officer in the Army of the Potomac. But the eastern army was Lincoln's and Stanton's army, an army so close to the politicians that it could hardly help but endure close political scrutiny. The western armies were something else: Their uniforms were sloppier, their drill was slouchier, and their overall opinion of themselves was boundlessly higher. Away over the Appalachians, Sherman's politics were less easily noticed, and less of a liability so long as Grant continued to sponsor him and so long as Sherman kept on winning battles. The time would come when politics would catch up with Sherman, and then, it would nearly destroy him.

For now, it was the soldiers in Chattanooga who were Sherman's chief concern. The army Grant left Sherman was something of a hodgepodge. The heart of it was George H. Thomas's 61,000-man Army of the Cumberland. But beside them were several smaller departmental commands Grant had amalgamated for Sherman, including the 24,000-man Army of the Tennessee under a marvelous young engineer named James B. McPherson, and the 13,500 men of the Army of the Ohio under John M. Schofield. Together with his cavalry, Sherman had over 100,000 men at his disposal, along with 254 guns in his artillery train. On the 4th of May (just as Grant was crossing his wagons into the Wilderness), he moved out of Chattanooga, pointed like a dagger at Atlanta.

Opposing him was what was left of the beaten and demoralized Confederate Army of Tennessee. The disaster at Missionary Ridge ought to have spelled the end for this luckless army, had not the individual corps commanders taken over and managed to patch it back together in northern Georgia. At least Braxton Bragg was gone now, and in his place, Jefferson Davis appointed the one-time victor of First Bull Run, General Joseph E. Johnston. Douglas Cater of the 19th Louisiana glowingly described Johnson as "possessed of a magnetism which held such sway over his

[19]Lloyd Lewis, *Sherman: Fighting Prophet* (New York, 1932), pp. 307–308, 330.

army that there was a feeling of security pervading every part of it." Cater found that "the faith our soldiers had in their commander" was so great that "they feared no surprise nor wrong movement."[20] Unfortunately for Johnston, that admiration was not shared by Jefferson Davis, who appointed Johnston to general command in the West in 1863 and watched him allow Vicksburg to fall into Grant's hands with but little interference. That was not the kind of security the Confederacy could afford, and not until Braxton Bragg had nearly destroyed the Army of Tennessee would Davis relent and put it directly into Johnston's hands.

Johnston arrived at the army's winter encampments around Dalton, Georgia, on December 27, 1863, and what he found there was not encouraging. The Army of Tennessee had 70,000 men on its rolls but only 36,000 actually present for duty, and a critical shortage of horses hobbled the cavalry, artillery, and wagons. By the end of April, however, Johnston had successfully reorganized the army, called in furloughs, distributed amnesties to deserters, and scraped together enough reinforcements to swell the Army of Tennessee back up to 53,000 men, with calls out for another 14,000 from Georgia's coastal garrisons and local militia. But this still gave Sherman a three-to-two edge over Johnston, and so Johnston decided that the best campaign would be a defensive one, using the mountains, ridges, streams, and gaps of northern Georgia to stymie Sherman's advance at every step and forcing him to waste time and thin out his supply line. It escaped Johnston's notice that this was a formula largely designed to lose, even if the loss was a slow one. But defensive warfare was Joseph Johnston's long suit, and from the moment Sherman's army clanked out of Chattanooga on the roads toward Atlanta until the middle of July, Johnston and the Army of Tennessee tick-tacked across northern Georgia, holding defensive positions Sherman dared not attack, waiting for Sherman to waste time maneuvering around them, and then slipping back to a new position just as Sherman was about to spring the trap. On June 27th, seething with frustration, Sherman risked an all-out frontal attack on Johnston's positions on Kennesaw Mountain. But in two hours, Johnston's men mowed down 2,000 federals, and Sherman went back to the chessboard war. It took Sherman until the middle of July to cover the 120 miles that separated Chattanooga from Atlanta, and when at last the federal army arrived there, it found Johnston securely entrenched around the city, waiting for Sherman to commence a lengthy and futile siege.

Sherman, with a vulnerable 300-mile long supply line stretching back through Chattanooga to the Ohio River, could not easily afford such a siege. He "did not fear Johnston with re-inforcements of 20,000 if he will take the offensive," but so long as Johnston was safely cooped up inside Atlanta, Nathan Bedford Forrest's cavalry, now based as an independent command in northern Mississippi, could easily slip northward into Tennessee and slice Sherman's supply jugular in half-a-dozen places. Sherman had tried to forestall the threat of such a raid by dispatching

---

[20]Cater, *As It Was: Reminiscences of a Soldier of the Third Texas Cavalry and the Nineteenth Louisiana Infantry*, T. Michael Parrish, ed. (Austin, TX, 1991), pp. 169, 178–179.

Brigadier General Samuel Sturgis and 8,100 cavalry and infantry to find and destroy Forrest. But Forrest, with no more than 3,500 men, found Sturgis first at Brice's Crossroads, and on June 10, 1864, routed Sturgis's men and captured most of their artillery, 176 wagons full of supplies, and 1,500 prisoners. If Forrest could now get loose on Sherman's supply lines while Sherman was bogged down in front of Atlanta, Sherman would have no alternative but to withdraw back into Tennessee, and the last leg of Grant's great offensive would collapse.

At this moment, however, Jefferson Davis stepped in to present Sherman with an unlooked-for gift. However successful Johnston's campaign might have seemed as a defensive operation, it looked to Davis, who had no incentive to think well of Johnston in the first place, as though the general was performing nothing more than a half-hearted retreat when the object of the war in the West was to push the federals back into Tennessee. So, on July 17th, Davis abruptly relieved Johnston and turned the Army of Tennessee over to John Bell Hood. No one could have been more the opposite of Johnston, both temperamentally as well as professionally. Hood had spent most of the war in the Army of Northern Virginia, commanding a brigade of Texans whom he happily and recklessly threw at whatever Union position lay before him. Personally brave to a fault, Hood knew nothing of caution; one old army acquaintance recalled seeing Hood bet $2,500 in a poker game "with nary a pair in his hand." In 1863, he had lost his left arm leading his men at Gettysburg, and three months later, as part of Longstreet's corps at Chickamauga, lost his right leg to a minié ball while personally leading his men into the teeth of federal fire. Aggressiveness like that was just what Davis wanted for the Army of Tennessee, and since Hood was still on the spot in Georgia, it seemed only natural to give the army to Hood to be sure something would be done with it. "Here is Gen. Joseph E. Johnston's reward for shielding his soldiers and inflicting losses on Gen. Sherman's army until his own little army could successfully offer battle and turn back the advancing hosts of Sherman's invaders," Douglas Cater complained. "This change of commander . . . had an effect on the army that was hard to overcome," and from that point on Cater was convinced that Hood would simply drown the Army of Tennessee in blood. "This order sounded the death knell of the Confederate States of America," he added. "The mistake that our soldiers then made was in not laying down their arms and stopping further bloodshed."[21]

For Sherman, Hood's appointment was good news: It meant that the Confederates would at last come out and fight in the open, where Sherman was sure he could beat them. And sure enough, only three days after assuming command, Hood took the Army of Tennessee out of its Atlanta defenses and flung them at the heads of Sherman's columns. Over the next eight days, Hood launched three major assaults, at Peachtree Creek (north of the city), on the Atlanta defenses (east of the city), and at Ezra Church (west of the city), each of which failed to stop Sherman, and all of which taken together cost Hood 13,000 casualties and probably another 2,000

[21]Cater, As It Was, pp. 183–184, 185.

deserters and missing. Hood now slumped wearily into the defenses Johnston had prepared, and settled down to the siege he had been appointed to avoid.

For Sherman, a siege was still a risky proposition; but with Hood in command, he counted on less vigilance than he would have expected from Johnston. Sherman spent the first half of August using his cavalry to feel around behind Atlanta, looking to cut Hood's rail line south of the city. But Sherman's cavalry were no match for the rebel horsemen commanded by General Joseph Wheeler, and at the end of August, Sherman finally concluded that he would have to do the job with infantry instead. On August 28th, leaving only one corps in front of the Atlanta lines, Sherman stole around below Atlanta toward Jonesboro, on the Atlanta & Macon Railroad. There, his men tore up the railroad tracks, heated the iron rails over bonfires of cross ties, and twisted the rails around tree trunks in what became known as "Sherman neckties." Looking out over the deserted federal lines around Atlanta, Hood at first thought Sherman had retreated and that he had won a great victory. Too late, he realized where Sherman really was, and by the time Hood got his army down to Jonesboro, Sherman had finished with the railroad and was ready to deal with Hood. After a stiff, two-day fight at Jonesboro on August 31– September 1, Hood decided to abandon Atlanta and withdraw south. "Atlanta is ours," Sherman telegraphed Lincoln, "and fairly won."

With the fall of Atlanta, the first of Grant's strategic objections was at last in hand. Ironically, the second of these also dropped into federal hands at the same time. On August 5th, David Farragut sailed a combined flotilla of wooden warships and ironclad monitors into the entrance to Mobile Bay, and hammered the Confederate forts at the mouth of the bay into silence. Although a minefield of Confederate "torpedoes" sank one of his prize ironclads, Farragut took his own flagship *Hartford* to the head of the line and plunged into the minefield with the memorable order: "Damn the torpedoes! Full speed ahead." Most of the "torpedoes" turned out to be duds and the rest of the fleet passed safely into the Bay, and handily destroyed Mobile's Confederate flotilla. After three weeks of uninterrupted bombardment by Farragut, the last Confederate fort shielding Mobile surrendered and on August 23, 1864, Mobile Bay was effectively sealed off to blockade runners.

The question now was what to do with Sherman. It was the navy and not Banks's infantry that had locked up Mobile, and so Grant's old idea of federal infantry linking up with Sherman from Mobile was rendered moot. There was little point in stopping with Atlanta, and Sherman urged Grant not to waste his time and men garrisoning northern Georgia. Instead, Sherman proposed to launch a gigantic raid down through Georgia to Savannah, where he could link up with the federal forces occupying the Carolina coastline. "The possession of the Savannah River is more than fatal to the possibility of Southern independence," Sherman argued to Grant over the telegraph. "They may stand the fall of Richmond but not all of Georgia." Sherman gave three reasons for his proposal. First, he could fan out across the rich Georgia countryside between Atlanta and Savannah and destroy everything of any possible logistical value to the Confederacy. The capture of Atlanta had effectively cut off the northern Confederacy (and with it, Lee and the Army of Northern Virginia) from its communications with the arsenals and foundries of northern Alabama. Now Sherman would put the torch to the fields and farms that fed the Confederate armies. Second, he could demonstrate to foreign powers and to the Confederate people how weak and powerless the Richmond government had become, when it could not stop a federal army from trampling across its geographical abdomen. "If we can march a well-appointed army right through his territory, it is a demonstration to the world, foreign and domestic, that we have a power which Davis cannot resist," Sherman told Grant on November 6th. "This may not be war but rather statesmanship, nevertheless, it is overwhelming to my mind that there are thousands of people abroad and in the South who reason thus: If the North can march an army right through the South, it is proof positive that the North can prevail."[22] Third, Sherman expected that by putting his army at the mouth of the Savannah River, he would have a secure supply base for a march north "to join Grant at Richmond" and, in passing, once his march to the coast was complete, to swing north and take Charleston, which had resisted federal land and sea attacks for two years, from behind.

This was, obviously, an outrageously risky proposition, and both Grant and Lincoln objected that such a march would string out Sherman's already lengthy supply lines to even more vulnerable lengths. Also, they pointed out, Sherman made no mention of what might happen if Hood and the Army of Tennessee decided to imitate Bragg's maneuver of 1862 and swing an end-run around Sherman back up into Tennessee. Sherman's reply was the essence of military daring: He did not propose to use a supply line. He was going to conduct a large-scale infantry version of one of Forrest's raids. Like Forrest, he would strip his army down to the bare essentials and encourage his men to forage off the Georgia countryside for whatever else they needed until they struck the coast. "I can make this march, and make Georgia howl!" Sherman assured Grant. "We have on hand over eight thousand head of cattle and three million rations of bread. . . . We can find plenty of forage in the interior of the State."[23] As for Hood, Sherman did not particularly care what the Confederate general did. Sherman would detach 60,000 men under George Thomas to return and hold Tennessee, but he would keep the rest of his army (nearly 62,000 men) on the road to Savannah come what may. "Damn him," Sherman snarled at the mention of Hood. "If he'll go to the Ohio River, I'll give him rations. Let him go north. My business is down south."[24]

Grant mulled the proposition over, and on October 13th, persuaded Stanton to approve it. A month later, Sherman marched out of Atlanta, his bands playing "Glory, glory hallelujah," and one-third of the city of Atlanta going up in flames behind him. Moving in four immense columns, Sherman swept aside the feeble resistance of the Georgia militia and burned a swath fifty miles wide across the state.

[22]Marszalek, *Sherman*, p. 295; Lewis, *Sherman*, p. 431.

[23]Sherman, *Memoirs of General W. T. Sherman*, Charles Royster, ed. (New York, 1990), p. 627.

[24]Sherman, *Memoirs of General W. T. Sherman*, p. 627; Lewis, *Sherman*, p. 430.

He instructed his men to "forage liberally on the country during the march," and it was an order they obeyed with gusto. "This is probably the most gigantic pleasure expedition ever planned," exclaimed one Illinois captain; "We had a gay old campaign," wrote another soldier, "Destroyed all we could not eat . . . burned their cotton & gins spilled their sorghum, burned & twisted their R[ail] roads and raised Hell generally." On December 10th, Sherman turned up outside Savannah and on the 20th, the Confederate defenders evacuated the city before the federals could trap them inside. "I beg to present to you, as a Christmas gift, the city of Savannah," Sherman telegraphed Lincoln, "with 150 heavy guns and plenty of ammunition, and also about 25,000 bales of cotton." Along the way, Sherman's men had confiscated nearly 7,000 mules and horses, 13,000 cattle, 10.4 million pounds of grain, and 10.7 million pounds of animal fodder. All told, Sherman estimated that his march to the sea had cost the Confederacy $100 million in damages, of which four-fifths "is simple waste and destruction."[25]

Meanwhile, just as Sherman had expected, Hood had taken the Army of Tennessee off on a diversionary raid into Tennessee, hoping to compel Sherman to break off his march and follow him back out of Georgia. Contrary to Sherman's expectations, Hood's opportunities for causing serious damage in Tennessee were far greater than had been expected. For one thing, Hood had Forrest's cavalry with him, and that was danger enough on its own terms; for another, George Thomas, who was supposed to be covering Tennessee on Sherman's behalf, was slow to get the infantry Sherman had left him concentrated in one place. If Hood moved fast enough, it was entirely possible that he could isolate parts of Thomas's command while they were still on the roads back to Nashville and annihilate them by pieces.

However, Hood's 39,000 men were pitifully equipped for a November campaign. Hood himself was too much of a physical wreck from his wounds and from the opium and alcohol he took as a cure for pain to seize the opportunities thrown in his path. On November 30th, at Franklin, Tennessee, Hood caught up with part of the force Thomas was supposed to be using to watch him and attempted to destroy it by throwing his men at the federals and their entrenchments in a day-long frontal assault. But those tactics only left Hood with 6,300 casualties, including twelve of his general officers and fifty-five regimental commanders, while the federals slipped away north to join Thomas at Nashville. Unwilling to admit defeat, Hood advanced on Nashville, where Thomas had concentrated his 60,000 men, and tried to besiege it. But on December 15, 1864, Thomas moved out from Nashville and smashed Hood's army in a running, two-day battle. Hood fell back into Mississippi, where he found that he could rally only 15,000 men.[26] The ill-

---

[25]Burke Davis, *Sherman's March* (New York, 1980), pp. 12, 24, 31, 118; Joseph T. Glatthaar, *The March to the Sea and Beyond: Sherman's Troops in the Savannah and Carolinas Campaigns* (New York, 1985), p. 130; Bruce Catton, *Never Call Retreat* (New York, 1965), p. 415–416; Hattaway and Jones, *How the North Won*, p. 654.

[26]Thomas Connelly, *Autumn of Glory: The Army of Tennessee, 1862–1865* (Baton Rouge, LA, 1971), p. 513.

starred Army of Tennessee was finished, and so was Hood, who resigned on January 13, 1865. And so, for that matter, was the Confederacy. Just as Grant had predicted a year earlier, and Sherman had predicted in October, the real heart of the Confederate war effort lay along the terrible line that had stretched from Chattanooga to Savannah, and once that line was in federal hands, the Virginia theater, along with Lee and his fabled army, would perish on the vine.

3. Victory by Ballot

The summer of 1864 was one of the gloomiest seasons of the war for Lincoln and his administration. Grant had bogged down below Petersburg after a campaign that had cost the Union staggering casualties; Sherman was still struggling slowly toward Atlanta; and the *Alabama* was still burning northern merchantships on the high seas. And, to add insult to injury, Lee detached from the Army of Northern Virginia four infantry divisions and four cavalry brigades under General Jubal Early (about 14,000 men) and sent them on a raid into the Shenandoah Valley of Virginia. Lee hoped that Early's raid, like "Stonewall" Jackson's in 1862, would draw off federal troops from the Petersburg siege. In the event, Early not only chased the federals out of the Shenandoah, but on July 11th, even dared to cross the Potomac and make a lunge at Washington. Grant was forced to pull an entire infantry corps out of the Petersburg lines and send it to Washington, where the troops arrived just in time to fend off an attack on the outer ring of Washington's fortifications. Early merely drew off into Maryland, where he had already extorted ransoms from the citizens of Hagerstown and Frederick. When the citizens of Chambersburg, Pennsylvania, refused to pay a ransom of $500,000 to Early for their town, Early unhesitatingly burned it to the ground.

Lincoln faced opposition from other quarters than just Jubal Early in the summer of 1864. Supreme Court interference in his war powers and proclamations remained a vivid possibility until Roger Taney's death in October, and he continued to endure criticism and harassment from the Democrats, and especially from the Peace Democrats who seized on Grant's overland campaign as an example of Republican butchery and incompetence. But with the fall of 1864 meaning another presidential election, Lincoln also now had to deal with a rising tide of disgruntlement from within his own Republican party. Salmon P. Chase, Lincoln's secretary of the treasury, had always considered himself better presidential material than Lincoln, and had been sorely disappointed in 1860 when he was passed over for the Republican nomination. "He never forgave Lincoln for the crime of having been preferred for President over him," wrote Alexander McClure, the prominent Pennsylvania Republican, "and while he was a pure and conscientious man, his prejudices and disappointments were vastly stronger than himself, and there never was a day during his continuance in the Cabinet when he was able to approach justice to

Lincoln."[27] The disappointment had not abated after three years of sitting in Lincoln's Cabinet, and he was particularly incensed at Lincoln's habit of parceling out tasks to the Cabinet secretaries as though they were so many errand boys, rather than sitting and paying earnest heed to the presumably wiser counsel that Chase longed to unburden himself of. "We . . . are called members of the Cabinet," Chase complained, "but are in reality only separate heads of departments, meeting now and then for talk on whatever happens to come uppermost, not for grave consultation on matters concerning the salvation of the country."[28] Now, with the 1864 election looming large and the armies conquering little, Lincoln was looking more and more like a liability to the Republican party, and Chase's moment seemed to have come at last.

In December of 1863, Chase's supporters began building a boom for him as a dump-Lincoln candidate. The marriage of his daughter, Kate Chase, to Rhode Island Governor William Sprague gave Chase a foothold in New England politics, as well as unlocking the Sprague fortune and the Sprague mansion in Washington for the secretary's political uses. In February, 1864, Chase's political manager, Kansas Senator Samuel C. Pomeroy, arranged for the publication of a pro-Chase pamphlet, *The Next Presidential Election*, which declared that a second term for Lincoln would be a national calamity; that the next president needed to be a statesman with a record of advanced economic thinking; and that Lincoln was manifestly inferior to Jefferson Davis as an executive. Though the pamphlet did not expressly advocate a Chase presidency as the alternative, it was clear that no more likely person to fill such a need was then living in the republic than Salmon P. Chase. The pamphlet itself was a cheap, discreditable essay in political character assassination, and it looked all the more cheap for having been distributed to Senator John Sherman's Ohio constituents by means of Sherman's postage-free frank. But the impact might not have been nearly so embarrassing for Chase had not Pomeroy also boiled down its essential points into a "strictly private" circular letter to Republican party backers two weeks later, and named Chase—"a statesman of rare ability and an administrator of the highest order" whose "private character furnishes the surest guarantee of economy and purity in the management of public affairs"—as the proper successor to Lincoln.[29] The idea that Chase would sit in Lincoln's Cabinet and encourage his political foot soldiers to stab Lincoln in the back made party regulars blanch. Chase wrote to Lincoln to swear that he had known nothing about the Pomeroy circular, and even offered to resign from the Cabinet. Lincoln rather pointedly gave Chase's protests a chilly reception, and knowing that it would be easier to keep a leash on Chase's ambition inside the

[27]McClure, *Lincoln and the Men of War-Times* (Philadelphia, 1892), p. 132.

[28]Chase, in *Inside Lincoln's Cabinet: The Civil War Diaries of Salmon P. Chase*, David Donald, ed. (New York, 1954), p. 17.

[29]Burton J. Hendrick, *Lincoln's War Cabinet* (1946; rept. New York 1961), pp. 486–487; Frederick J. Blue, *Salmon P. Chase: A Life in Politics* (Kent, OH, 1987), pp. 223–225.

Cabinet rather than outside, Lincoln refused the resignation. The Chase boomlet had worried Lincoln a good deal, and McClure remembered that it was the only occasion when he had seen Lincoln "unbalanced . . . like one who had got into water far beyond his depth."[30] But Lincoln now had Chase where he wanted him: Chase's chances for the nomination vanished into thin air, and even the Republicans in his native Ohio rejected any notion of his candidacy. At the end of June, Chase offered again to resign, and this time, Lincoln accepted his offer, replacing him with William Pitt Fessenden, the chair of the Senate Finance Committee. That December, Lincoln got rid of Chase once and for all by kicking him upstairs to the Supreme Court, which no one had any hope of using as a springboard for the presidency.

The kind of clash Lincoln had with Chase was really little more than a cloak-room dispute, and it paled by comparison with the struggle Lincoln faced when his fellow Republicans openly declared their disagreements with him on substantial questions of war policy. The Thirty-eighth Congress, which had been elected in the painful 1862 by-elections, counted 102 Republican representatives in the House and thirty-one Republicans in the Senate, which gave them a clear majority over against the seventy-five Democrats in the House and nineteen in the Senate. Of the thirty-one Republican senators, seventeen formed an especially critical core of radical Republican determination that expressed itself time and again in pressing for the swiftest and most extreme solutions to the problems of war policy, including emancipation and black civil rights. The figurehead of the Senate Radicals was Charles Sumner of Massachusetts, and no one could match Sumner's eloquence in pleading for an aggressive prosecution of the war, emancipation, and racial equality. But while Sumner was a great talker, he was less skilled as a practical politician. Far more talented among the Radicals in wielding the political knife was Benjamin Franklin Wade, crude and competent. (Wade was the author of the greatest antislavery one-liner in the history of the Congress: In the debates in the 1850s over the extension of the slavery into the territories, one southern senator shed eloquent tears over the Republicans' refusal to allow him to take his old black "mammy" to Kansas with him; Wade replied that he had no objection to the senator's taking her with him, only to selling her once he got there). Sumner and Wade were joined in radicalism by Zachariah Chandler of Michigan, Henry Wilson of Massachusetts, Lyman Trumbull of Illinois, and the unfortunate Pomeroy of Kansas. Wilson, Wade, Sumner, Trumbull, and Chandler all sat together as one radical phalanx on the right side of the aisle on the floor of the Senate.[31]

Most of the Radicals were party veterans, and many had even longer ties to the old Whig party, and as a result they were inclined to regard Lincoln as a political novice. While Lincoln hesitated over colonization, compensated emancipation,

---

[30]McClure, *Lincoln and Men of War-Times*, p. 134.
[31]Allan G. Bogue, *The Earnest Men: Republicans of the Civil War Senate* (Ithaca, NY, 1981), pp. 97–98, 109–110, 130.

and the recruitment of black soldiers, the Radical Republicans used the majority they achieved in the Senate after the withdrawal of the southern senators to lead the way in expelling Democratic senators of dubious loyalty, in abolishing slavery in the District of Columbia, and in amending the Militia Act to open up recruitment to black soldiers. They also repealed the Fugitive Slave Law, barred the issue of charters to District of Columbia streetcar companies that practiced racial discrimination, and equalized pay for the USCT regiments. The conventional wisdom about these Radical Republicans sees them as vengeful, ambitious men, eager to use emancipation as a means of subduing the South once and for all to northern free-labor capitalism. There may be some debate about their lusts for vengeance or self-aggrandizement, but it is certainly true enough that the Whig-Republican ideology had already persuaded most of them of the virtues of protecting northern industry through high tariffs, of opening western public lands to homesteaders as a means of avoiding the formation of a propertyless urban proletariat, and the replacement of slavery in the South with free labor. It only took the war to convince the Radicals that the South was an obstacle to the triumph of Whig republicanism that the war should remove, and it was they who crafted the confiscation bills in 1861 and 1862 and called for the treatment of rebels as traitors whose penalty, "as established by our fathers, was death by the halter." It was this no-compromise, root-and-branch Whiggism and their determination to make the Republican party the virtual national government that frequently made the Radicals impatient with Lincoln's administration; in 1862, they tried to unseat Seward as secretary of state, and a few obliquely suggested that even Lincoln should resign.

Lincoln, by contrast, has been portrayed as a moderate and far-seeing statesman, desiring only to end the war without bitterness. Lincoln, after all, had won the Republican nomination in 1860 precisely on the grounds that he was more of a moderate than Seward or Chase and could win more votes, while his slowness in moving toward emancipation has been interpreted as proof of his distaste for Radicals. But Lincoln shared more ground with Radical thinking on the key issues of abolition and black civil equality than he often publicized, and it is significant that the Radicals also sought (and got) policy statements from Lincoln for use in directing their legislative campaigns, while he never gave any such support to Republican moderates.[32] Sumner remained a close family friend of the Lincolns all through the war; Lincoln's closest political ally in the House of Representatives was Owen Lovejoy, brother of the abolitionist martyr Elijah Lovejoy and one of the most Radical Republicans in Congress.

If Lincoln resisted the Radicals, it was not so much because of outright disagreements over policy or ideology, but because he was determined to keep the hands of Congress off his presidential prerogatives (especially as commander in chief) and to ward off interparty challenges to his authority as the head of the Republican party. And if the Radicals were impatient with Lincoln, it was not so much because of a

[32]Allan G. Bogue, *The Congressman's Civil War* (New York, 1989), p. 43.

difference of principles, but on differences of timing and political tactics, especially when they concerned the military conduct of the war, abolition, and Lincoln's proposals for reconstructing the Union. As early as December, 1861, the Radicals tried to deal themselves a piece of Lincoln's war powers by creating a seven-member House-Senate committee, known as the Joint Committee on the Conduct of the War, with Wade and Chandler as the unofficial handlers. Although it was never actually stated in so many words, the joint committee was understood as the Radicals' lever for pressuring Lincoln and the Union military into waging a more and more Radical version of the war. In February, 1862, the committee moved first against Brigadier General Charles P. Stone, a McClellanite general who had botched a small-scale military operation at Ball's Bluff on the Potomac. It was clear that Stone was a surrogate for McClellan, whom the Radicals had already come to hate as a Democrat and a half-heart, and as an object lesson, the committee had Stone arrested and imprisoned for six months without so much as a chance to hear the charges—whatever they were—against him. Nothing bound the committee to observe the customary legal safeguards for those it examined, and the hapless generals and politicians who were hauled before it were unable to respond to their accusers, or even (like Stone) to see a copy of the charges that had led to their investigation in the first place. Over the course of the war, the joint committee held 272 meetings and issued eight fat volumes of proceedings, including condemnations of the massacre at Sand Creek and the slaughter of the black soldiers at Fort Pillow in 1864.

Lincoln did not entirely welcome the meddling of the joint committee, and even though Ben Wade offered the president the use of the committee's services to call the House or the Senate into closed-door sessions on war policy, Lincoln ignored what he rightly saw as an attempt to manipulate his prerogatives as president. But much as Lincoln was careful to guard his own constitutional powers from over-eager interference by the joint committee, it is significant that he never tried to suppress the committee, and he occasionally used the threat of the committee's existence to prod reluctant generals into action. By the same token, the committee groused to themselves about Lincoln and occasionally used their hearings to air ill-disguised hints about the direction of war policy, but they never actually challenged the president the way they would challenge and then impeach his successor in future years. The committee, and the Radicals for whom it spoke, recognized in Lincoln an ideological equal but not a practical political one, and their constant agitation for more drastic prosecution of the war amounted to an ongoing criticism, not of Lincoln's principles, but of what they saw as Lincoln's imperfect application of them.[33]

It was not the war, but the shape of the Reconstruction that must follow it that became the most serious issue between Lincoln and the Radical Republicans. Acting on the premise that secession was a legal impossibility, Lincoln urged Congress

[33]Phillip S. Paludan, *The Presidency of Abraham Lincoln* (Lawrence, KS, 1994), pp. 104–105.

to accept new governments for the southern states as soon as a Unionist majority among the citizens could make it ready. On December 8, 1863, Lincoln published a "A Proclamation of Amnesty and Reconstruction," which offered occupied Louisiana a Reconstruction scheme allowing the formation of a new state government under three key terms. First, any inhabitants of Louisiana could obtain a pardon for participating in the rebellion by taking a loyalty oath to the federal Constitution and "all acts of Congress passed during the existing rebellion with reference to slaves" and "all proclamations of the President made during the existing rebellion having reference to slaves, so long and so far as not modified or declared void by decision of the Supreme Court." In other words, with one eye kept firmly on the chance that his actions might be challenged in the federal courts, Lincoln was offering to trade presidential pardons for submission to the Emancipation Proclamation before the Taney court got a chance to void it. The only exclusions Lincoln kept in place would be for high-ranking Confederate military officers, politicians who had resigned federal offices (and who had therefore violated their oath to support the Constitution), and anyone guilty of abusing federal prisoners, "colored persons or white persons." Then, when 10 percent of the 1860 voting population had taken the loyalty oath, occupied Louisiana could reestablish its state government, and any provisions in reestablished state governments that would make black freedom permanent and provide for education of freed slaves "will not be objected to by the national Executive."

Lincoln, not knowing how the war might turn out, hoped to use this proclamation as a means of wedging emancipation into the constitutions of as many occupied states as possible. The Radicals, however, criticized this plan as too flimsy and too unrealistic a foundation for genuine Reconstruction, in Louisiana or anywhere else. A number of the Radicals, headed by Wade and Sumner, argued that the seceding states had committed "state suicide" and should now be treated as conquered provinces and made to pass again through the entire process of territorialization before being readmitted to the Union. And when Louisianans attempted to follow Lincoln's directives and re-create a Louisiana constitution, they unwittingly lent the Radicals a stick to beat them with by endorsing only emancipation and not black voting rights, even for black Louisiana soldiers. Lincoln delicately pointed out this oversight to Michael Hahn, the new Louisiana governor, and pressed Hahn privately to have black voting rights included in the new state constitution. But the damage had been done, and when representatives from the newly reconstructed Louisiana government showed up in Congress in 1864, the Radicals rounded up enough votes to exclude them from sitting.

Then in July, 1864, the Radicals moved take the initiative on Reconstruction out of Lincoln's hands altogether. Henry Winter Davis in the House, and Ben Wade in the Senate, sponsored a bill which, although it stopped short of "territorializing" the seceder states, still upped the ante of Reconstruction far above Lincoln's levels. Instead of the 10 percent of the 1860 voting population specified in the Lincoln proclamation as the requisite for Reconstruction, the Wade-Davis bill demanded the "enrollment" of all the white male citizens of states where "military resistance . . . shall have been suppressed" and the extraction of a loyalty oath from "a majority of the persons enrolled in the State." Once the loyalty of a white majority had been established (and this time no inclusion of black citizens would be permitted, since that would make the readmission process of the Confederate states too quick and painless), the "loyal people" of a state could elect a convention and reestablish their state government. However, no one who had served in the Confederate army or held political office under the Confederacy was eligible to vote for a delegate to this convention or be elected as a delegate. Likewise, no matter what the form of state government eventually drawn up by the convention, no one who had ever served in the Confederate military or civil service could vote for, or be elected to, any office. Moreover, all public debts under the Confederate regime were to be repudiated (which meant that anyone holding Confederate bonds, notes, or currency lost everything they had invested) and "involuntary servitude" was to be "forever prohibited."

What this did, in effect, was to postpone Reconstruction almost indefinitely, since it was difficult to see how half of the present population of any Confederate state could be persuaded to take a loyalty oath to the United States before a long time had passed. Lincoln, who understood perfectly what a shambles the Wade-Davis bill would make of Reconstruction, simply killed it by means of a pocket-veto. He was not unsympathetic to the Radicals' determination that reconstructed governments be genuinely loyal to the Constitution, but he was also convinced that they had forgotten that his administration did not have all the time in the world. Emancipation—the goal both he and the Radicals shared—was as yet only a military action, justified only by military necessity and dignified only by what Lincoln could claim as his war powers. While the war was still on and Union occupation forces clearly held the whip hand, emancipation could be forced down southern throats relatively easily. But let the war end suddenly, or let his administration lose the upcoming election in November to a Democratic peace candidate, and the military justification for emancipation would evaporate at the same moment that the shooting stopped. Civil court challenges to the permanent legality of emancipation would immediately flood into the federal courts, at whose apex sat Roger Taney. Better to take an imperfect Reconstruction that got emancipation onto the books now than delay it so long that a changed political or military climate might make emancipation impossible. Lincoln, in a document issued after Congress adjourned, insisted that he was not "inflexibly committed to any single plan of restoration," and that he was not going to undo the "free State constitutions and government already adopted" in places like Louisiana. But this did little to convince either Davis or Wade. On August 5th, the two Radicals published a defiant manifesto, reminding Lincoln, in terms that Lincoln himself ironically had to acknowledge, that "if he wishes our support, he must confine himself to his Executive duties—to obey and execute, not to make the laws—to suppress by arms armed rebellion, and leave political re-organization to Congress."

But the people whose support Lincoln most dreaded losing, and seemed closest to losing by 1864, were the 21 million citizens of the North and border states; and to Lincoln, it seemed that they, too, had lost faith in him. Emancipation, even delayed as long as it had been by Lincoln, was still far in advance of the racial consciousness of most Americans, and the Democratic press in particular dwelt heavily upon the economic penalties white workers would have to pay if emancipation unleashed a flood of free blacks to come north and compete for jobs. Worse than emancipation, however, was the backlash stimulated by Congress's decision to institute military conscription in 1862 and then adopt a federal conscription law in March of 1863.

No one in Washington in 1861 had really planned to resort to mass conscription to fill the armies, simply because no one had thought it would be necessary. The flood tide of volunteers who enlisted in 1861 seemed to provide all the manpower anyone could possibly want for the war. But the enlistments of the forty two-year regiments that Congress had authorized in 1861 ran out in mid-1863, and as they did, few of the two-year veterans showed much enthusiasm for reenlistment. At the same time, the tide of volunteers who had enlisted in the three-year regiments in 1861 and 1862 had noticeably flattened. In July, 1862, the Radical Republican Senator Henry Wilson of Massachusetts drew up a new Militia Act to replace the outdated 1792 federal militia ordinance, and in addition to setting aside the racial color line and permitting black enlistment, the new act mandated the enrollment by each state of all male citizens between the ages of eighteen and forty-five, and authorized the president to set quotas for each state to meet in the event that a draft would be necessary. In order to avoid resorting to an outright draft of unwilling men, the states tried to stimulate volunteering by offering bounties to recruits. "Most of us were surprised," wrote one Pennsylvania volunteer in 1862, "when, a few days after our arrival in [Camp Curtin], we were told that the County Commissioners had come down for the purpose of paying us each the magnificent sum of fifty dollars. At the same time, also, we learned that the United States Government would pay us each one hundred dollars additional."[34] By 1863, these bounties were no longer a surprise. Considering that the average workingman's annual wages ranged between $300 and $500 in the 1860s, these bounties were not inconsiderable sums of money, and reluctant volunteers could frequently be enticed into service by the prospect of a bounty that could buy enough land for a farm or a homestead. The prime difficulty with the bounty system—apart from the appearance it gave of bribing northern males to do their civic duty—was how liable it was to abuses of various sorts. Communities and states eager to fill up state volunteer quotas found themselves competing with other communities and states for volunteers, and presently the politicians began a bidding war for recruits, offering multiple bounties that could run over $1,000 when finally added up. That, in turn,

[34]William J. Miller, *The Training of an Army: Camp Curtin and the North's Civil War* (Shippensburg, PA, 1990), p. 106.

invited the appearance of "bounty jumpers," who enlisted in one state or community to receive a bounty, then deserted and reenlisted under another name in another state to pick up another bounty. One bounty jumper, John O'Connor, who was caught in Albany, New York, in March of 1865 confessed to having bounty jumped thirty-two times before being caught.[35]

If the bounties were the carrot for enlistment, then the draft was clearly the stick. And it did not take long for a draft to become necessary: Little more than two weeks after the passage of the new Militia Act, Lincoln authorized Stanton to initiate a draft that would yield 300,000 men. On August 9th, Stanton issued orders describing how the governors of the states who could not voluntarily meet state quotas were to implement the enrolling and drafting of soldiers. Unhappily, the formula for establishing state quotas was complex and unclear, various categories of exemptions from the draft were fuzzy, and above all, draftees were permitted to hire substitutes in what amounted to a personalized bounty system. In Chester County, Pennsylvania, where the county quota for enlistments was set at 1,800 men, local notables passed the hat to raise a bounty fund they hoped would entice volunteers to fill up the county quota; another 300 draftees, like Samuel Pennypacker, hired a substitute. "My grandfather . . . paid $300 for a substitute in Norristown who was only too willing to go to the front in my stead. I do not know of his name or his fate."[36]

But the need for men in this war was insatiable, and so, in March, 1863, Congress passed an Enrollment Act that bypassed the state governments entirely and created a series of federal enrollment boards to take responsibility for satisfying the federally assigned state quotas. Each congressional district was expected to establish a three-member board headed by a provost marshal that would draw up a roll of all eligible males within its district. Despite the anger and anxieties it touched off, enrollment did not necessarily mean conscription. Although each congressional district was issued a quota of volunteers to recruit for each draft call, men would be drafted only from those districts that otherwise failed to meet that quota through volunteering. Districts that provided sufficient volunteers, or bounties high enough to lure volunteers, would not need to draft anyone. In the end only seven northern states were liable to all four draft calls issued under the Enrollment Act. Even conscription itself did not necessarily translate into war service. Of the 292,000 names drawn from the enrollment lists for the first draft call in 1863, less than 10,000 actually wound up in uniform. Most of the rest were released for disability or on claims to exemption, while another 26,000 hired substitutes (among the hirers being a future president of the United States, Grover Cleveland). Over 50,000 Northerners escaped service by another provision in the Enrollment Act known as "commutation," which allowed draftees to pay $300 as an exemption

[35]James W. Geary, *We Need Men: The Union Draft in the Civil War* (DeKalb, IL, 1991), pp. 32–48.
[36]Douglas R. Harper, *If Thee Must Fight: A Civil War History of Chester County, Pennsylvania* (West Chester, PA, 1990), p. 204.

fee to escape the draft. Even when the three subsequent draft calls in 1864 and 1865 are added to these figures, no more than 47,000 men were actually conscripted into the Union armies.[37]

And yet, despite the loopholes and commutation provisions, the idea of a compulsory military draft was still a strong dose for Americans to swallow, especially since after 1863 conscription meant fighting in a war to free black slaves. Moreover, the commutation fee cast the ugly specter of class conflict over the draft: A wealthy man might have no difficulty coming up with the $300 or with finding and hiring a substitute, but a workingman faced an economic wall that might be too high to scale, while the availability of substitutes grew scarcer with each passing month of the war. That, together with the inherently repulsive notion that in a democracy someone could hire a substitute to get shot in his place, provoked the bloodiest sort of response among the poor and immigrants, and antidraft disturbances erupted within days of the implementation of the Enrollment Act and a new draft call. The worst incident of antidraft violence erupted in New York City on July 13, 1863, two days after the first draft of names was drawn by the chief clerk of the 9th Congressional District. From the beginning of the war until the summer of 1863, New York City had been a hotbed of labor unrest: As men marched off to war and as war contracts sent manufacturing production soaring, New York workingmen found that labor was suddenly at a premium, and they moved to use the situation to bargain and strike for higher wages. Rumors that the government would use prisoners-of-war and even South Carolina blacks to break strikes against war-related business had already inflamed working-class tempers when the Enrollment Act became public in the spring of 1863. The terms of the act looked like nothing so much as an attempt to draw workingmen out of a highly attractive labor market and send them into battle so that more blacks could be free to compete for wages and break up strikes—all the while offering a $300 commutation fee for the factory owners and their sons.[38] And when, on July 13th, the provost marshal for 9th Congressional District began to pull names from a large drum, the angry crowds of workingmen erupted. For four days, mobs of white workingmen attacked and burned the homes of Republican politicians, tried to demolish Horace Greeley's New York *Tribune,* burned the Colored Orphan Asylum to the ground, and lynched any African Americans they happened to lay their hands on.

Eventually, federal troops were brought into New York City; they calmly shot the rioters down, and the riots collapsed. But riots popped up elsewhere—in Boston, in Milwaukee, in the marble quarries of Vermont, and across the upper Midwest—and they were often linked, like the New York City riots, to labor disputes. In the Pennsylvania coalfields, bitter labor disputes between miners and

---

[37]James W. Geary, We Need Men, pp. 54–63, 67–70, 83–84.

[38]Earnest A. McKay, The Civil War and New York City (Syracuse, NY, 1990), pp. 197–212; Iver Bernstein, The New York City Draft Riots: Their Significance for American Society and Politics in the Age of the Civil War (New York, 1990), pp. 7–14.

mine-owners were dragged into the operation of the draft when appointments as provost marshals and enrollment officers went to mine officials and the families of mine owners, thus ensuring that the draft would be used, and perceived, as a weapon in labor disputes. "Now is the time for the operators . . . to get rid of the ringleaders engaged in threatenings, beatings, and shooting bosses at the collieries and put better men in their places," argued one Pennsylvania coal mine owner. "It is far better to send them into the army and put them in the front ranks, even if they are killed by the enemy, than they should live to perpetuate such a cowardly race." Miners took their cues from such lines, evading the draft and waylaying enrollment officers as just one more aspect of their struggle against the mine bosses. Unfortunately for the miners, the mine owners had the authority of the federal government behind them: In Luzerne County, 100 miners were arrested and 70 were imprisoned in the dungeons at old Fort Mifflin in Philadelphia.[39]

Aggravating all of these problems for Lincoln behind the lines was the depressing fact of the uniformly bad news *from* the lines in the summer of 1864. In May, a Radical Republican splinter group called a convention in St. Louis to dump Lincoln and nominate John Charles Frémont for the presidency instead. In late August, the Democratic national convention adopted a "peace and union" platform for the 1864 presidential campaign, and it was obvious that they would nominate as their candidate Lincoln's former general, George Brinton McClellan. The little general had become the darling of Lincoln's Democratic critics, and he had allowed himself to be advertised for the nomination for over a year. "I think that the original object of the war . . . the preservation of the Union, its Constitution & its laws, has been lost sight of, or very widely departed from," McClellan wrote in July of 1864 when the Republican Francis Blair attempted to elicit from him a statement for the newspapers that he would *not* be interested in the Democratic presidential nomination. "I think the war has been permitted to take a course which unnecessarily embitters the inimical feeling between the two sections, & . . . I deprecate a policy which far from tending to that end tends in the contrary direction." This was as much as begging for the Democratic nomination, and when the Democratic convention met in Chicago a month later, McClellan was the easy winner. He was also confident that, at least this time, he would be the easy winner of a national campaign. In his acceptance letter on September 4, 1864, McClellan confidently declared that "I believe that a vast majority of our people, whether in the Army & Navy or at home, would, with me hail with unbounded joy the permanent restoration of peace on the basis of the Federal Union of the States without the effusion of another drop of blood."[40]

Abraham Lincoln was not sure that McClellan was wrong. On August 23rd, a

[39]Grace Palladino, *Another Civil War: Labor, Capital, and the State in the Anthracite Regions of Pennsylvania, 1840–1868* (Urbana, IL, 1990), pp. 124–135.

[40]*The Civil War Papers of George B. McClellan: Selected Correspondence, 1860–1865*, Stephen W. Sears, ed. (New York, 1989), pp. 584, 590–591.

morose Lincoln wrote out a memorandum that he folded and had all the members of his Cabinet endorse without reading. Inside its folds, it pledged the Cabinet to back any last-ditch effort of Lincoln's to win the war in the event that the November election went against them:

> This morning, as for some days past, it seems exceedingly probable that this Administration will not be re-elected. Then it will be my duty to so co-operate with the President elect, as to save the Union between the election and the inauguration; as he will have secured his election on such ground that he can not possibly save it afterwards.

Lincoln was not even sure he could rely on Grant, and he told Alexander McClure that, as far as he knew, "I have no reason to believe that Grant prefers my election to that of McClellan." Looking back, McClure had been certain that "there was no period from January, 1864, until the 3rd of September of the same year when McClellan would not have defeated Lincoln."[41]

But in fact it was not going to turn out that way. On the day Lincoln drafted his letter, Farragut battered the last Confederate resistance on Mobile Bay into submission; a week and a half later, Atlanta fell to Sherman; the *Alabama* went to the bottom of Cherbourg harbor in June, and in October, one of Grant's protegés, an aggressive knockdown brawler named Philip Sheridan, cleared Virginia's Shenandoah Valley of Jubal Early's Confederates in a spectacular miniature campaign. These triumphs buoyed northern morale higher than it had been since Vicksburg and made talk of peace seem like a giveback of victory. And to make matters worse for the Democrats, McClellan alienated the peace faction of the party (including his vice-presidential nominee, George Pendleton, "an avowed peacemonger" according to George Templeton Strong) by insisting that reunion rather than peace be made the first priority of the platform. McClellan had no intention of espousing any peace platform that simply allowed the Confederacy to go its own way as an independent nation; he would make whatever concessions the Confederates asked so long as those concessions led the Confederacy back into the Union, but if the Confederate government was not interested in reunion, then "we must continue the resort to the dread arbitrament of war." McClellan was aware that this would cost him the support of the hard-core peace Democrats, but he could not reconcile the battles he had fought and the lives that had been lost with a settlement that permitted the North and South simply to walk away from each other like strangers. "I intend to destroy any and all pretense for any possible association of my name to the Peace Party," McClellan wrote two weeks before the election. "I, for one, could not look in the face of my gallant comrades of the Army & Navy who have survived so many bloody battles, & tell them that their labors and the sacrifices of such

[41]Lincoln, "Memorandum Concerning His Probable Failure of Re-election," in *Collected Works*, vol. 7, p. 514; McClure, *Abraham Lincoln and Men of War-Times*, pp. 124, 203.

numbers of their slain & crippled brethren had been in vain."[42] As a result, Democratic loyalties were divided at just the moment when only united effort could hope to upset the incumbent Republicans.

And so, almost when it was past expectation, Lincoln was handed hope again for the war—or rather, for both of his wars. On September 17, 1864, Frémont, the Radical splinter candidate, withdrew his competing nomination and Lincoln was allowed to go on, bearing the party banner, alone. And not only the banner of the Republicans—in a last appeal to the war Democrats, he had chosen as his vice-presidential candidate a Tennessee Union Democrat named Andrew Johnson, and announced he would not run under the banner of the Republican party only, but on the "National Union Ticket." On election day, November 8, 1864, Lincoln and Johnson carried 55 percent of the popular vote, and 212 out of 233 electoral votes, while the Republicans in Congress won 145 out of 185 seats in the House and 42 out of 52 in the Senate. But most surprising of all, Lincoln garnered 78 percent of the votes of the soldiers, including the Army of the Potomac, thus destroying forever the mystique of McClellan as the hero of the armies. At last, Lincoln had the political mandate that had eluded him for the four years of his first term. It now remained to be seen how he would win the war that still waited for him down below Petersburg.

Further Reading

The long and bloody "Overland Campaign" that Grant waged against Lee has been ably chronicled in Clifford Dowdey's venerable *Lee's Last Campaign: The Story of Lee and His Men Against Grant—1864* (New York, 1960), Noah A. Trudeau's *Bloody Roads South: The Wilderness to Cold Harbor, May–June 1864* (Boston, 1989), Robert Garth Scott's *Into the Wilderness with the Army of the Potomac* (Bloomington, IN, 1985), and William Matter's *If It Takes All Summer: The Battle of Spotsylvania* (Chapel Hill, NC, 1988). The siege Grant was forced to begin at Petersburg has picked up a number of new admirers, beginning with Noah Trudeau's *The Last Citadel: Petersburg, Virginia, June 1864–April 1865* (Baton Rouge, LA, 1991) and including several books on particular parts of the Petersburg siege, such as Richard Sommers's weighty book on the early siege operations in the fall of 1864, *Richmond Redeemed: The Siege of Petersburg* (New York, 1981) and Michael Cavanaugh and William Marvel, *The Horrid Pit: The Battle of the Crater* (Lynchburg, VA, 1989). A valuable adjunct to these books is William Frassanito's photographic history of the overland campaign, *Grant and Lee: The Virginia Campaigns, 1864–1865* (New York, 1983), which complements his earlier two photographic "then-and-now" books on Gettysburg and Antietam.

Grant's operations in Virginia were only one part of his overall strategic plan for 1864, and he depended heavily on the successes won in Georgia by William Tecumseh Sherman.

---

[42]McClellan to Allan Pinkerton, October 20, 1864, in *Civil War Papers of George B. McClellan*, pp. 591, 615; George Templeton Strong, *The Diary of George Templeton Strong*, Allan Nevins and M. H. Thomas, eds. (New York, 1952), vol. 3, p. 483.

Lloyd Lewis's *Sherman: Fighting Prophet* (New York, 1932) is a rare masterpiece of literary craft and remains the most outstanding Sherman biography, although it is marred in discussing Sherman's racial prejudices by Lewis's disparaging comments on black soldiers. Opposite Sherman in northern Georgia was Joseph Johnston, who has been studied most recently by Craig Symonds in *Joseph E. Johnston: A Civil War Biography* (New York, 1992). Johnston's decision to settle into a siege around Atlanta was his undoing, and the siege itself has been marvelously spoken for in Albert Castel's *Decision in the West: The Atlanta Campaign of 1864* (Lawrence, KS, 1992). Johnston's replacement has also won a biography, Richard M. McMurry, *John Bell Hood and the War for Southern Independence* (Lexington, KY, 1982). Hood's battle at Franklin was a particular exercise in tactical folly, and has attracted the notice of Wiley Sword in *Embrace an Angry Wind: The Confederacy's Last Hurrah, Spring Hill, Franklin and Nashville* (New York, 1992) and James McDonough and Thomas Connelly in *Five Tragic Hours: The Battle of Franklin* (Knoxville, TN, 1983).

Lincoln's difficulties with the Radicals of his own party have been the subject of ongoing debate since Lincoln's death. On the one hand, Hans L. Trefousse's *The Radical Republicans: Lincoln's Vanguard for Racial Justice* (New York, 1968) makes a passionate plea for interpreting the Radicals as Lincoln's secret agents for promoting policies Lincoln could not afford to openly endorse. On the other hand, T. Harry Williams's *Lincoln and The Radicals* (Madison, WI, 1941) just as passionately argues that Lincoln was a moderate who struggled in vain to keep the Radicals from turning the war into a political vendetta against the South. The actual development of Reconstruction policy has been explained by Herman Belz in *Reconstructing the Union: Theory and Policy During the Civil War* (Ithaca, NY, 1969) and Michael Les Benedict, *A Compromise of Principle: Congressional Republicans and Reconstruction, 1863–1869* (New York, 1974). Individual biographies of the Radicals are surprisingly harder to come by, although Hans L. Trefousse's *Benjamin Franklin Wade: Radical Republican from Ohio* (New York, 1963), David Donald's *Charles Sumner and the Rights of Man* (New York, 1970), Ernest McKay's *Henry Wilson: Practical Radical* (Port Washington, NY, 1971), and Richard Sewall's *John P. Hale and the Politics of Abolition* (Cambridge, MA, 1965) are outstanding exceptions to this rule. A clearer view of just who the Radicals were as a group emerges from Allan G. Bogue's *The Earnest Men: Republicans of the Civil War Senate* (Ithaca, NY, 1981), which used mathematical analyses of roll-call votes to identify the core of Radical leadership in the Senate.

Some of the most controversial legislation written by the congressional Radicals concerned conscription. James Geary's *We Need Men: The Union Draft in the Civil War* (DeKalb, IL, 1991) is a clear, precise, and highly illuminating analysis of conscription in the North, and carefully distinguishes the various drafts and draft calls, who was most likely to be conscripted, and how many draftees actually wound up in the federal armies. In addition to Geary, Eugene C. Murdock's *One Million Men: The Civil War Draft in the North* (Madison, WI, 1971) remains an important contribution to the draft literature because of his careful analysis of the peculiarities of the bounty system. The most notorious response to the draft in the North was the New York City draft riot. Iver C. Bernstein's *The New York City Draft Riots: Their Significance for American Society and Politics in the Age of the Civil War* (New York, 1990) skillfully sets the riots against the background of New York labor and racial unrest during the war, while Adrian Cook's *The Armies of the Streets: The New York City Draft Riots of 1863* (Lexington, KY, 1974) provides the best overall narrative of the New York rioting. New York, however, can only lay claim to the most terrible outbreak of antidraft violence:

Grace Palladino's *Another Civil War: Labor, Capitol, and the State in the Anthracite Regions of Pennsylvania, 1840–1868* (Urbana, IL, 1990) traces the major outbreaks of antidraft resistance in Pennsylvania, while J. Matthew Gallman's *Mastering Wartime: A Social History of Philadelphia during the Civil War* (Cambridge, MA, 1990) devotes substantial attention to the question of why the North's other great metropolitan center did not go up in similar flames.

CHAPTER 11

A Dim Shore Ahead

 For a man who believed in the "cold, calculating, unimpassioned" power of "reason" to order his life, Abraham Lincoln retained a peculiar interest in the folk religion of dreams, portents, and signs. Herndon thought Lincoln was "superstitious," and claimed that Lincoln had consulted an African-American fortuneteller "to give him his history, his end, and his fate," and once tried to cure his son Robert of a dog's bite with "a supposed mad stone." Lincoln described to John Hay and Francis Carpenter a portent he had seen just after his nomination for the presidency in 1860. Exhausted from the celebrations, Lincoln was resting "on a lounge in my chamber" when he saw a reflection of himself in the "swinging glass" that sat on top of a bureau opposite the couch. "My face, I noticed, had two separate and distinct images. . . . I was a little bothered, perhaps startled, and got up and looked in the glass, but the illusion vanished." He lay down, the "illusion" returned, "and then I noticed that one of the faces was a little paler—say, five shades—than the other." He went home troubled by the strange double image, and a few days later, he tried to conjure it up before a mirror at his home. He did, and it worried Mary, who was sure he was playing with something dangerously occult. "She thought it was a sign that I was to be elected to a second term of office and that the paleness of one of the faces was an omen that I should not see life throughout the last term."[1]

More than omens in mirrors, it was dreams that haunted Lincoln. In June, 1863, when Mary and Tad Lincoln were visiting in Philadelphia, Lincoln wired her to put the boy's small gift pistol away: "I had an ugly dream about him." But it was the recurring dreams about assassination that particularly preyed on Lincoln's mind. He alarmed both Mary and his self-appointed bodyguard Ward Hill Lamon by describing a dream in which he was awakened in the White House by the sound of weeping and sobbing. Seeing himself rise in the dream, his dream-self moved from room to room in search of the sound until he came to the East Room of the White

[1]Herndon, "Lincoln's Superstitions," in *The Hidden Lincoln, From the Letters and Papers of William H. Herndon,* Emanuel Hertz, ed. (New York, 1938), pp. 409–410; Lloyd Lewis, *Myths after Lincoln* (New York, 1929, 1941), pp. 289–298; Francis Carpenter, *Six Months at the White House with Abraham Lincoln* (New York, 1867), pp. 163–165.

House, where he found a "throng of mourners," a guard of soldiers, and a catafalque, where a body was lying in state. Lincoln's dream-self asked one of the soldiers, "Who is dead in the White House?" The answer was chilling: "The President. He was killed by an assassin."[2] Lamon, whom Lincoln had appointed United States marshal for the District of Columbia, was already uneasy for Lincoln's safety in Washington, and on election night in 1864, he went to the extreme of curling up like a guard dog outside Lincoln's door in a blanket, armed with a collection of knives and revolvers. Lincoln thought Lamon "insane upon the subject of his safety," but it was a derangement that also possessed Secretary of War Edwin Stanton, who made sure that Lincoln's carriage had a secure cavalry escort, that a company of infantry guarded the White House grounds, and that a District of Columbia policeman accompanied the president whenever Lincoln went to the theater.[3]

Sometimes, though, the dreams pointed to happier conclusions. His dreams about the dead Willie gave Lincoln a comfort that eluded Mary. And there was a particular dream that came back to him again and again, and always just before the arrival of good tidings. In this dream, his dream-self stood on the deck of "some singular, indescribable vessel" pointed toward a dim shore ahead. He had dreamt this dream just before some of the most important victories of the war, and he had it again in April, 1865. As he told his Cabinet at a meeting the next morning, he knew that it meant that good news was once again on the way. "I think it must be from Sherman," Lincoln explained. "My thoughts are in that direction, as are most of yours."[4] But perhaps the dream had a meaning wider than Sherman. There was a dim shore ahead for the whole nation in the spring of 1865, an unmapped future that would involve reintegrating the Confederate states back into the political Union, bringing African Americans into the full citizenship that their centuries of unrewarded labor had earned them, and manhandling the old Democratic South into the new Republican future of railroads, markets, and free labor. But, as Lincoln told his Cabinet that day, he was confident that his dream was proof that the dimness would yield to certainty, and that the everything that was now confused, bloodied, and embittered would all be sorted out at last. Good news, soon.

General Grant had been sitting in on the Cabinet meeting that morning. The president had earlier asked if the general and his wife would be interested in attending Ford's Theatre that night, where the Lincolns had promised to go to see actress Laura Keene's benefit performance of *Our American Cousin*. The general, pleading conflict of schedule, declined. The Lincolns would have to find someone else to join them in the box at the theater that night. Perhaps by that time, Lincoln would hear of the good news his dream had promised.

[2]Lamon, *Recollections of Abraham Lincoln, 1847–1865* (Chicago, 1865), pp. 115–116, 266.

[3]Benjamin P. Thomas and Harold Hyman, *Stanton: The Life and Times of Lincoln's Secretary of War* (New York, 1962), pp. 319, 393–401.

[4]Welles, *Diary of Gideon Welles* (New York, 1911), vol. 2, pp. 282–283.

1. The Passing of the Dead

Sherman's march to the sea delivered a fatal body blow to the Confederacy. The fragile network of southern railroad lines had already been badly cut up by Rosecrans's capture of Chattanooga in 1863, while the fall of Atlanta to Sherman a year later wrecked the single most important rail junction between the lower Confederacy and Virginia. The march to the sea finished off what was left of the shorter regional rail lines in Georgia and made it almost impossible to keep Lee's army in Virginia supplied with food and ammunition from the granaries and factories of the lower South.

The situation for Lee was made even gloomier by the siege of Petersburg. Pinned through the winter of 1864–65 into a maze of trenches south of the city, Lee's Army of Northern Virginia was unable to disperse and supply itself from the Virginia countryside, as it had done in years past. Only by clinging to the Weldon & Petersburg Railroad (which ran south from Petersburg to North Carolina) and the Southside Railroad (which ran west to Lynchburg and the Shenandoah Valley) did Lee manage to keep supplies filtering into the hands of his army. "There is nothing within reach of this army to be impressed," Lee despondently informed the Confederate secretary of war. "The country is swept clear; our only reliance is upon the railroads."[5] But even those lines were unsure and vulnerable to Grant's unceasing pressure. In August, Grant suddenly reached westward from his own lines and cut the Weldon and Petersburg railroad. Later in October, Philip Sheridan, Grant's fiery and versatile lieutenant, tracked down and defeated Jubal Early's small Confederate force in the Shenandoah and proceeded to lay waste to the entire valley.

For the first time in the war, the Army of Northern Virginia began to suffer a crisis in morale. "The common soldier perceived that the cause was lost," wrote Sara Agnes Pryor, the wife of a Confederate officer. She could read collapse in the streets of Petersburg, since (as Pryor acidly remarked) the town had never been "so healthy":

> No garbage was decaying in the streets. Every particle of animal or vegetable food was consumed, and the streets were clean. Flocks of pigeons would follow the children who were eating bread or crackers. Finally the pigeons vanished having been themselves eaten. Rats and mice disappeared. The poor cats staggered about the streets, and began to die of hunger. . . . An ounce of meat daily was considered an abundant ration for each member of the family.[6]

Lee's men could read collapse even more clearly in the letters that filtered through into the hands of the Confederate soldiers below Petersburg. Those letters now

[5]Lee to Seddon, *The Wartime Papers of Robert E. Lee*, Clifford Dowdey and Louis Manarin (Boston, 1961), p. 881.
[6]Mrs. Roger A. Pryor, *Reminiscences of Peace and War* (New York, 1904), p. 267.

began to tell the terrible tale of civilian starvation, the devastation of Yankee raiders, and the relentless impressment of the pitiful fruits of southern agriculture by the Confederate war department. "We have been impressing food and all the necessaries of life from women and children, and have been the means of driving thousands from their homes in destitute condition," Lee admitted sadly to James Longstreet in February, 1865. The suffering of Confederate women now reached the breaking point, and their letters, in effect, announced their withdrawal of support for the war by encouraging their men to withdraw themselves from the Army of Northern Virginia. "The Condition of the country at large was one of almost as great deprivation & suffering as the army itself," wrote Edward Porter Alexander, the chief of artillery in Longstreet's corps. "Naturally, the wives & mothers left at home wrote longingly for the return of the husbands & sons who were in the ranks in Virginia. And naturally, many of them could not resist these appeals, & deserted in order to return & care for their families."[7] Beginning in early January, 1865, men began to desert by the hundreds, and then the thousands: Over a period of ten days in February, the army lost 1,094 men to desertion; between February 15 and March 18, 1865, almost 8 percent of Lee's army disappeared either into the Union lines or into North Carolina. Lee himself turned harsh and punitive in an attempt to stop the flow of desertions. On February 25th, he rejected a captured deserter's appeal for mercy without even reading the appeal and ordered the man shot. "Hundreds are deserting nightly," Lee explained to the Confederate adjutant general, Samuel Cooper, "and I cannot keep the army together unless examples are made of such cases." It did little good. "If we stay here," wrote one Union officer who had passed forty deserters through his lines in forty-eight hours, "the Johnnies will all come over before the 4th of July."[8]

For Grant, the issue was now to keep pushing. On the other side of the siege lines at Petersburg, the resolve of the Confederates, which had seemed so formidable when the siege began the summer before, was visibly weakening, and the real question increasingly seemed to be whether Grant would be able to keep Lee from slipping out of Petersburg before he could deliver a knockout blow. As for Sherman, he was opposed by little more than 20,000 Confederates. The old Army of Tennessee had been broken up after Hood's resignation, and its last effective pieces had been shipped over to the Carolinas to join what was left of the forlorn and homeless garrison of Wilmington, North Carolina, to threaten Sherman. At the urging of the Confederate congress, command of this patchwork army was at last given back to Joseph E. Johnston by a grudging and suspicious Jefferson Davis on February 22, 1865. Sherman was mildly apprehensive at the return of Johnston, but Johnston

[7]Alexander, *Fighting for the Confederacy: The Personal Recollections of General Edward Porter Alexander*, Gary Gallagher, ed. (Chapel Hill, NC, 1985), pp. 508–509.

[8]Lee to Longstreet, and Lee to Cooper [February 25, 1865], in *Official Records*, series 1, vol. 46, p. 1258; Douglas S. Freeman, *Lee's Lieutenants: A Study in Command* (New York, 1944), vol. 3, pp. 623–624; Bruce Catton, *A Stillness at Appomattox* (New York, 1953), p. 330.

knew that it was too late to do any serious damage to Sherman. "In my opinion these troops form an army too weak to cope with Sherman," Johnston sighed. All that Lee could advise him was to "hope for the best."[9]

With such small Confederate forces left in the Carolinas, Grant's first inclination in December had been to pull Sherman and his army out of Georgia entirely, and use the navy to transport them up to the James River, where they could reinforce Grant for a fresh assault on Lee in the spring. But Sherman demurred, insisting that he could accomplish much more by setting off on yet another raid, this time up into the Carolinas, where he could help close down Wilmington and Charleston, the last remaining blockade-running ports, and wreck the Army of Northern Virginia's rail lines and supply centers in the Carolinas. Sherman enlisted Halleck as an ally in his cause, and on December 18th, Grant once more gave way to Sherman and authorized this new raid. In one month, after pausing to rest and refit in Savannah, Sherman and his army were once again on the march. In their path was South Carolina, the state whose secession lay at the beginning of the war, and Sherman's men were determined to make South Carolina suffer in retribution. "South Carolina cried out first for war," one of Sherman's Iowans swore, "and she shall have it to her heart's content. She sowed the Wind. She will soon reap the whirlwind." Now Sherman's men pillaged and burned without any regard for the needs of forage or food, leaving "a howling wilderness, an utter desolation" behind them. On February 17th, the state capital, Columbia, fell, and that evening an immense fire blackened the central part of the city. Sherman was accused of having deliberately set the fire as a gesture of revenge, and though he denied the charge, he felt little sorrow over it. "Though I never ordered it and never wished it, I have never shed many tears over the event, because I believe it hastened what we all fought for, the end of the war."[10]

Lincoln, too, had plans for the spring. One of them concerned emancipation. All of Lincoln's actions to end slavery, including the Emancipation Proclamation itself, had been taken on the basis of his presidential war powers. But the Dred Scott decision, banning the federal government from interfering with slavery as legal property, still stood as the last word of the federal courts on the subject, and Lincoln had been acutely aware all through the war how easily a postwar legal challenge could cripple or wipe out everything his wartime proclamations had created. Even then, his war powers had given him no authority to deal with slavery in the border states that had not joined the rebellion, so that slavery in Kentucky, Missouri, and Delaware might easily emerge on the other side of the war fully and legally intact (Kentucky and Delaware had both gone for McClellan in 1864). Only a constitutional amendment forever outlawing slavery across the entire country

[9]Craig L. Symonds, *Joseph E. Johnston: A Civil War Biography* (New York, 1992), p. 344.

[10]Joseph T. Glatthaar, *The March to the Sea and Beyond: Sherman's Troops in the Savannah and Carolinas Campaigns* (New York, 1985), pp. 79, 142; James M. Merrill, *William Tecumseh Sherman* (New York, 1971), p. 283.

could secure the wartime gains made for emancipation. However, the Constitution had only been amended twelve times, and ten of those had been tacked on virtually at the time of its ratification. No other amendment had been offered for passage by Congress and the states since 1804, and Lincoln seems to have been reluctant to risk the appearance of tampering with the Constitution. Moreover, the Radical Republicans in the Senate had adopted an abolition amendment in April of 1864, only to see it fail, by a vote of 93 to 65, to obtain the necessary two-thirds majority needed in the House.

But eventually Lincoln could see no other way forward for black freedom, and he insisted on making a thirteenth amendment part of the platform he had run on in the 1864 election. On December 6, 1864, in his annual message to Congress, Lincoln urged Congress to make the mandate of his reelection as grounds for reconsidering the emancipation amendment. By the time renewed debate on the amendment began in the House on January 6th, Lincoln was ready to step out of his usually passive role with Congress and buttonhole former Whigs and Democrats to bring them into line (among the political horsetrading he performed was the promise to a New York Democrat of a plum patronage position in exchange for his vote). When the House roll was called on January 31, 1865, the proposed amendment squeaked through with just three votes to spare, 119 to 56. "I wish you could have been here the day that the constitutional amendment was passed forever abolishing slavery in the United States," wrote Charles Douglass from Washington to his father, Frederick Douglass. "Such rejoicing I never before witnessed, cannons firing, people hugging and shaking hands, white people, I mean, flags flying. . . . I tell you things are progressing finely." Lincoln's own Illinois, appropriately, was the first state to ratify the new amendment, followed by Pennsylvania and Massachusetts.[11]

It was less clear-cut who was winning on the subject of Reconstruction. Lincoln interpreted his reelection as yet another mandate to press for renewed approval of his Louisiana reconstruction plan, but the Radicals remained reluctant to endorse a plan that fell so far short of clearly overturning the old racial and economic order of the South. Lincoln was far from blind to faults of the Louisiana plan. But he seems to have been eager to bring as many of the former rebel states into Reconstruction as fast as they could be gotten there *first*, and then worry about opening the ears of Southerners to his none-too-delicate hints to include emancipation and black civil rights as part of their new constitutions. Lincoln's admirers, then and now, have been inclined to lay this up to his generosity and desire to end the war on a note of forgiveness. That certainly seemed to be the message Lincoln had for the country when he stood on the Capitol steps on a blustery fourth of March to take his second oath of office as president. In the brief address he gave before taking the oath, Lincoln reviewed the fundamental causes of the war—

[11]Hans L. Trefousse, *The Radical Republicans: Lincoln's Vanguard for Racial Justice* (New York, 1969), pp. 298–300; David W. Blight, *Frederick Douglass' Civil War: Keeping Faith in Jubilee* (Baton Rouge, LA, 1989), p. 186.

slavery, the demand for slavery's extension westward into the territories, the idea that the Constitution permitted secession from the Union when those demands were not met. But he also took the opportunity to set these immediate causes of war in the context of a larger moral question. Lincoln urged Northerners and Southerners alike to admit (as John Brown had prophesied before his execution in 1859) that the war was a common judgment on a sin that the whole nation, and not just one section, had been guilty of. Perhaps, Lincoln speculated, the ultimate, metaphysical meaning of the war was not about republicanism but about the mysteries of divine providence and moral judgment. Lincoln the secularized fatalist, and behind him Lincoln the child of Calvinist predestination, combined now to see the war as a strange and inexplicable movement of God. In this life, the Bible had told him, "offences" are unavoidable, but no one guilty of those offences has the right to plead inability and innocence. If the time had now come, at whatever the cost, to rip up slavery by the roots, then human beings could only bow their heads to that cost as the price of a life in which "offences must needs come." Perhaps it will only be justice, Lincoln said, that "all the wealth piled up by the bond-man's two hundred and fifty years of unrequited toil shall be sunk" and "every drop of blood drawn with the lash" shall now "be paid by another drawn with the sword." And if so, "it must still be said, 'the judgments of the Lord are true and righteous altogether.' " Americans must not waste their energies now in judgment—that belonged to the inscrutable God who moved all things in such mysterious ways—but in the one exercise that still was within their grasp, that of mercy.

> With malice toward none; with charity for all; with firmness in the right, as God gives us to see the right, let us strive on to finish the work we are in; to bind up the nation's wounds; to care for him who shall have borne the battle, and for his widow, and his orphan—to do all which may achieve and cherish a just, and a lasting peace, among ourselves, and with all nations.

Eloquent as these words were as religious philosophy, they were also read as a promise of a speedy and painless reconstruction. Certainly, speed was part of Lincoln's Reconstruction agenda, for in pragmatic terms, it was in the best interests of the newly freed slaves that new governments be installed in the rebel states while the federal military still had wartime authority to do so. After four years of war, Congress had still passed the Thirteenth Amendment by only the slimmest of margins; and efforts by the Radicals to promote a Reconstruction bill in Congress guaranteeing the freed slaves the right to vote had died on the floor. The painful truth was that, even with the Thirteenth Amendment in hand, Lincoln could not wait for Congress to secure the rights of the freed slaves once the war was over. But it was another question entirely whether Lincoln thought Reconstruction ought to be painless. Much as Lincoln was happy to have Salmon Chase out of the Cabinet, his decision to appoint Chase as Taney's successor on the Supreme Court was also a signal that he intended to close off any postwar legal appeals from the war's military results. He signed the Freedmen's Bureau bill, which effectively created a national agency that would shield African Americans from the designs of postwar southern state governments, and by April, 1865, Lincoln himself was calling on the Louisianans to open "the elective franchise" to the "very intelligent" among African Americans and "those who serve our cause as soldiers."[12]

It was with speed uppermost in his mind, though, that at the end of March, 1865, Lincoln came down to the James River to confer with Grant and with Sherman, who had come up from the Carolina coast by steamer for the meeting. There, Lincoln talked to his premier generals about the kind of terms he wanted given to the South and its armies, if and when they surrendered. He advised them to give conditions they thought would induce surrender of the Confederate armies as a whole, since it would be better to let them give up their arms as organized groups rather than pressing the Confederates so hard that they broke up into innumerable guerrilla bands. He expressed the hope that Jefferson Davis could be allowed to escape the country, rather than running the risk of a sensational treason trial; and Sherman remembered Lincoln suggesting that the generals might even offer to recognize the existing rebel state governments, especially in North Carolina, as an inducement to surrender "till Congress could provide others."[13] These comments, which Sherman swore by to his dying day, suggest that for Lincoln, the balance between speed in ending the war and the degree of pain involved in Reconstruction was constantly shifting, as Lincoln sought to bring the progress of the war and political acceptability of black civil rights in the South onto something approaching the same timetable. Lincoln had been willing as early as mid-1863 to allow friends and intercessors to open up secret negotiations with Richmond that involved reunion schemes imposing only limited emancipation and promises of federal assumption of Confederate debts. As late as February, 1865, Lincoln himself came down to Hampton Roads to meet with a Confederate peace commission headed by his old friend and now Confederate vice-president, Alexander Stephens, and he offered compensation in the form of $400 million in United States bonds if the Confederate states would rejoin the Union and adopt the Thirteenth Amendment *prospectively* (in other words, to adopt it with the understanding that it would be only gradually phased in over a period of—as Stephens later claimed Lincoln said—five years). But in each case, the clandestine negotiations foundered on Lincoln's insistence that the Confederate states abandon all claim to negotiate with the United States as a separate government, and the Hampton Roads Conference turned up empty after Jefferson Davis rejected its terms outright. By the time Lincoln met with Grant and Sherman at the end of March, he was still struggling to bring his two agendas together: Just as Sherman had believed he would, Lincoln shortly afterward authorized members of the Virginia legislature to begin organizing themselves in order to return to the Union, provided that they understood there would be "No receding by the Executive of the United States on the slavery

[12]"Last Public Address," April 11, 1865, in *Collected Works*, vol. 8, p. 403.
[13]Sherman, *Memoirs of General W. T. Sherman*, Charles Royster, ed. (New York, 1990), pp. 810–813.

question." And then, after reflecting on the inadequacies of this proposal, Lincoln canceled it a week later.[14]

Sherman, and possibly Grant as well, mistook Lincoln's notorious instinct for the fastest solution to a problem as a willingness on his part to negotiate about the actual political outcome of the war, and as a result, both Grant and Sherman came away from their meeting with the president in possession of a certainty about Lincoln's easy-going intentions Lincoln himself did not entirely share. Neither Grant nor Sherman could have realized how quickly they were going to have to deal in hard terms with that uncertainty, since both generals had warned Lincoln that at least one more major battle in Virginia would probably have to be fought. That apprehension was not necessarily misplaced, either, since Lee staged a breakout attempt from the Petersburg lines on March 25th, lunging out at Fort Stedman, on the far right of Grant's lines. But the attack was beaten back, and with it, the last of the Army of Northern Virginia's fabled aggressiveness faded. On March 28th, Grant once again began sliding the Army of the Potomac around to the left, looking to cut Lee's last big supply line into Petersburg, the Southside Railroad. On April 1st, Philip Sheridan's 12,000 cavalrymen, supported by the infantry of the 5th Corps of the Army of the Potomac, overran the last Confederate outpost on the extreme end of Lee's lines at Five Forks, effectively shutting off the Southside Railroad. At 4:00 A.M. the next morning, the entire left of the federal line went over the top against Lee's trenches, and only the stubborn resistance of two small Confederate forts kept the entire Army of Northern Virginia from collapsing into federal hands that night.

That one night, however, was enough for Lee. After informing Jefferson Davis that the Petersburg lines could no longer be held, he skillfully pulled his army out of the Richmond fortifications and crossed what was left in the Petersburg trenches over onto the north side of the Appomattox River. Lee then turned west, designating Amelia Court House as the rendezvous point for the whole army. Once there, he planned to meet the last supply trains out of Richmond and pick up a spur line of the Richmond and Danville Railroad that would take the Army of Northern Virginia south to join Johnston in the Carolinas. Davis, with a small escort, and the official papers and records of the Confederate government, also headed west, staying ahead of Lee and the army and ultimately escaping to the south. Richmond was abandoned, left to its mayor to be surrendered to Grant on April 3, 1865. Fires set by the Confederate provost marshal to destroy the arsenal and magazines roared out of hand, and rioters and looters took to the streets until at last federal soldiers, their bands savagely blaring "Dixie," marched into the humiliated capital and raised the Stars and Stripes over the old capitol building.

Lee, meanwhile, struggled westward to Amelia Court House. He was dogged by two major problems, one of which was the geographical position of his army. Except

[14]"To John A. Campbell," April 5, 1865, and "To Godfrey Weitzel," April 12, 1865, in Collected Works, vol. 8, pp. 386, 406–407.

for the troops Grant detached to occupy Richmond, he and the Army of the Potomac were on the south side of the Appomattox River, and as soon as Lee bolted westward, so did Grant, pacing Lee step for step on his side of the Appomattox, keeping between Lee and the never-never land to the south, never letting the Confederate general get far enough ahead to curl around the head of the federal columns and break for the Carolinas. Lee's other problem surfaced as soon as he concentrated his men at Amelia Court House on April 5th. In the last hours in Richmond, no one in the Confederate war department had thought to give the orders that would send the supply trains to meet Lee, and Lee found absolutely nothing waiting for him there. He was forced to waste an entire day, foraging enough corn and bacon just to keep going, and by the time he was ready to move on, he found that Sheridan's cavalry had cut the rail line eight miles below Amelia Court House. With Grant's infantry now breathing down his neck, Lee had no choice but to strike westward again, this time toward Lynchburg, where there were Confederate reinforcements and more supplies to be had.

By now, Grant was rapidly closing in on the fleeing Confederates. On April 6th, Federal infantry and cavalry caught up with Lee's rear guard as it was crossing a little tributary of the Appomattox River called Sayler's Creek, and sliced off 6,000 prisoners with hardly any effort. In a desperate effort to keep Grant from getting any closer, Lee had the bridges over the Appomattox burned, but on the morning of April 7th, one federal corps discovered a neglected wagon bridge over the river and crossed it in hot pursuit. Lee now had one hope, and only one: If he could reach Appomattox Station before the federal infantry, he could be supplied there from Lynchburg, and perhaps make a stand that would force Grant to back off and give him maneuvering room. But it turned out to be impossible. Sheridan's cavalry and two infantry corps got to Appomattox Station on the evening of April 8th, while Lee was still several miles back up the road. Stopped in front by Sheridan and pressed from behind by Grant, Lee knew by mid-morning that at last the end had come. "In ten minutes more," wrote Union Brigadier General Thomas C. Devin about that morning, "the charge would have been ordered for the whole line and we would have been on and over them like a whirlwind." Grant and Lee had sent several notes to each other under flags of truce on April 7th and 8th concerning a possible meeting, and now Lee sadly asked to see Grant personally. "Our men were terribly vexed at the truce," wrote the bemused Devin. "It was laughable to see the old troopers come up to the edge of the hill [overlooking the Confederate positions], look down at the position of the Rebs and go back growling and damning the flag of truce."[15]

Grant, who had been pounding along at the head of his army, leaving bag and baggage days behind in the dust, was at that moment in the throes of a migraine, "but the instant I saw the contents of the note I was cured." Lee selected as a meeting place the home of Wilmer McLean in the little crossroads village of

[15]Devin, "Didn't We Fight Splendid," in *Civil War Times Illustrated* 17 (December 1978), p. 38.

Appomattox Court House, about four miles above Appomattox Station. Grant arrived with his staff, painfully self-conscious of the contrast between Lee, immaculate in a full general's uniform and dress sword, and himself, clad in the only things he owned in the absence of his baggage, a pair of muddy boots and a standard-issue frock coat with his lieutenant-general's shoulder straps sewn on. The meeting was formal, and after some polite chit-chat between Grant and Lee about old Mexican War times, they got down to business. Grant's terms, bearing in mind his discussions with Lincoln, were surprisingly mild. No more unconditional surrender: All Confederate soldiers would surrender their arms and promptly be paroled (no ghastly death march to a prison camp, no imprisonment of Confederate officers pending treason trials); all officers could retain their swords and other side arms; and paroled soldiers could claim any captured horses and mules they wished to take home with them. The terms were written out; Lee signed them, and then it was all over, and Lee went back to his little army. George Henry Mills of the 16th North Carolina watched Lee ride slowly back up the road toward his regiment: "As he passed the men all ran down to the road and surrounded him, everyone trying to shake hands with him, many of them in tears." Lee took off his hat and spoke briefly. "Boys, I have done the best I could for you. Go home now, and if you make as good citizens as you have soldiers, you will do well, and I shall always be proud of you. Goodbye, and God bless you all." To Mills, Lee "seemed so full that he could say no more, but with tears in his eyes," he rode off toward his headquarters, "and that was the last we ever saw of him."[16]

On April 12th, the Army of Northern Virginia marched out of its pitiful little camp for the last time, and now numbering no more than 25,000 men, the Confederates tramped defiantly down their last road, to where the Army of the Potomac was drawn up, on either side, to watch them stack their still-gleaming weapons and furl their shredded, star-crossed battle flags. Waiting for them by the roadside was the 1st Brigade, 1st Division, 5th Corps, under the command of Major General Joshua Lawrence Chamberlain. Four years before, Chamberlain had been a professor of rhetoric at Bowdoin College; two years before, at Gettysburg, Chamberlain and his 20th Maine Volunteers had held Little Round Top and saved the day for the Army of the Potomac. Now, commanding his own brigade, Chamberlain impulsively brought his men to attention and ordered a salute to the ragged Confederates. At the head of the Confederate column rode General John B. Gordon, who was startled and uncertain at what Chamberlain's men were about to do. But then, as it dawned on Gordon what Chamberlain meant, he slowly and deliberately returned it.

. . . when the head of each division column comes opposite our group, our bugle sounds the signal and instantly our whole line from right to left, regiment by regiment, in succession, gives the soldier's salutation, from the 'order arms' to the

---

[16]Mills, *History of the 16th North Carolina Regiment* (1903; rept. Hamilton, NY, 1992), p. 68.

old 'carry'—the marching salute. Gordon at the head of the column, riding with heavy spirit and downcast face, catches the sound of shifting arms, looks up, and taking the meaning, wheels superbly, making himself and his horse one uplifted figure, with profound salutation as he drops the point of his sword to the boot toe; then facing to his own command, gives word for his successive brigades to pass us with the same position of the manual,—honor answering honor. On our part not a sound of trumpet more, nor roll of drum; not a cheer, nor word nor whisper of vain-glorying, nor motion of man standing again at the order, but an awed stillness rather, and breath-holding, as if it were the passing of the dead![17]

Two days later, far away in Raleigh, North Carolina, William Tecumseh Sherman received a note from Joseph E. Johnston, asking if he was willing to make "a temporary suspension of active operations." Johnston had never really been able to stop Sherman once he had rolled out of Georgia. Charleston, which had defied everything the federal navy could throw at it from the sea, dropped tamely into Sherman's bag as his fire-eyed army marched past on land. On March 6th, Sherman's men splashed across the Pee Dee River into North Carolina, making a union with Grant only a matter of a few weeks. Johnston made just one serious effort to slow Sherman down, at Bentonville, North Carolina, on March 19th, but Sherman merely brushed him aside. On April 12th, Johnston was summoned to Greensboro, North Carolina, by Jefferson Davis, who had escaped from Virginia and who spoke hopefully of raising new armies to carry on the war. Johnston briefly told him that "to attempt to continue the war" was hopeless and would be "the greatest of human crimes." Davis wearily gave him permission to open negotiations with Sherman, and on April 14th, Johnston sent his note through the lines, begging to be given the same terms Grant had given Lee.

Another 200 miles south, in Charleston harbor, an immense crowd of Federal soldiers and New York celebrities had gathered in the ruins of Fort Sumter to watch Major General Robert Anderson once more raise the same flag he had taken down four years before, to the day. Everywhere, the red slashed banners of the Confederacy were coming down, and the old flag was going up again, and the war would be over.

But there was one last act in the drama to be played out, and with cunning appropriateness, it would be played out in a theater, almost on stage. On Good Friday, April 14th, President Lincoln met his Cabinet in a rare mood of relaxation and good humor, and told them of the dream he had dreamt that always promised good tidings. In the evening, he and Mary were joined by the only couple they could persuade to spend Good Friday with them at the theater, Clara Harris (the daughter of New York Senator Ira Harris) and her fiancé, Major Henry R. Rathbone. Together, they set out in the presidential carriage for Ford's Theatre, only a short distance from the White House, to watch Laura Keene in her 1000th

[17]Chamberlain, *The Passing of the Armies: An Account of the Final Campaign of the Army of the Potomac, Based upon Personal Reminiscences of the Fifth Army Corps* (1915; rept. Dayton, OH, 1982), p. 261.

performance in a popular comedy of manners called *Our American Cousin*. Keene's appearance was to be part of a benefit performance for disabled Union soldiers, and the theater's owner, John Ford, had beseeched the Lincolns to attend that night in order to boost gate receipts. Sure enough, when the Lincolns arrived shortly after curtain time, the theater was packed to its 1,700-seat capacity, and the little orchestra in the pit struck up a rousing 'Hail to the Chief' as the Lincolns made their way to a private box overlooking stage left. The cast cheerfully ad-libbed "many pleasant allusions" to the president into their lines, recalled War Department clerk James Knox, who was sitting in the audience, "to which the audience gave deafening responses, while Mr. Lincoln laughed heartily and bowed frequently to the grateful people."[18]

Somewhere, in the confusion of the surrender celebrations and the hectic gaiety of the theater, the security net Lamon and Stanton had drawn around Lincoln fell down: Lamon was in Richmond on government business, and John Parker, the District of Columbia policeman Stanton had detailed to guard the president, sauntered casually away from the door of the box to get a better view of the play. At approximately 10:00 P.M., a 26-year-old actor, John Wilkes Booth, slipped up a back stairway to the outer door of the president's box. He was stopped there by someone, possibly the chicken-brained policeman, Parker, but Booth merely showed him his card and assured him that the president, who was known to be fond of actors, had asked to see him.

Booth was a member of one of the greatest acting families of the day—his brother Edwin was an outstanding Shakespearean whom Lincoln greatly admired—but he was also a rabid Confederate sympathizer. He had gathered around him a weird little coterie of conspirators—a Confederate deserter named Paine, a half-wit named David Herold, and a few others of even lower mental visibility—who were pledged to take personal revenge on Lincoln and his administration. Booth had originally planned, with the help of the Confederate secret service, to kidnap Lincoln and deliver him to Richmond. But the collapse of the Confederate armies convinced Booth that a more dramatic step was needed. Instead of kidnapping Lincoln, he would murder him in public, while his co-conspirators simultaneously assassinated the vice-president, the secretary of state, and General Grant. Booth only learned about the special performance of *Our American Cousin* and Lincoln's agreement to attend on the morning of the 14th, when he stopped at Ford's Theatre to pick up some mail. But the plan formed at once in his mind, and that night, he and his peculiar gaggle of friends were ready to strike. Using his familiarity with the building and staff, Booth was able to walk unnoticed into the theater, ascend to the packed galleries, and quietly open the outer door to the passageway leading to the president's box.

Once inside the narrow anteroom, Booth wedged the outer door shut to ensure

[18]Harold Holzer, "Eyewitnesses Remember the 'Fearful Night,' " in *Civil War Times Illustrated* 32 (March/April 1993), p. 14.

he would not be discovered and waited until the one point in the play when all but one of the actors had left the stage. Then, drawing a small derringer, he opened the inner door of the presidential box, stepped up behind Lincoln, and shot him behind the left ear. For a second, no one in the house moved. Major Rathbone tried to seize Booth, but Booth had a knife in his other hand, which he used to slash Rathbone's arm, cutting an artery. Then Booth vaulted over the rail of the box and onto the stage, ran past the dazed stagehands to the theater's side door, where a horse was tied for him, and galloped off into the dark of the Washington streets. At the same instant, Lincoln slumped forward in the special rocking chair that Ford had provided for him in the box, while Mary, "on her knees uttered shriek after shriek at the feet of the dying president." Soldiers and civilians began smashing on the door of the box, and were finally let in by the bloodied Major Rathbone. An army surgeon, Dr. Charles A. Leale, who had been sitting in the audience only forty feet from Lincoln's box, was beside the president in minutes and helped to lay him out prostrate on the floor of the box; another military surgeon, Charles S. Taft, was sitting down with the orchestra, and was quickly boosted up to the box from the stage. Leale, whose specialty was gunshot wounds, could see at once that Lincoln's wound was mortal. But he managed to keep Lincoln's uneven breathing going, and the unconscious president was moved across the street to a room in a boarding house. There, at 7:22 A.M. the next morning, with members of his Cabinet around his deathbed and his wife sobbing insanely in the front parlor, Abraham Lincoln died. "Now," said Edwin Stanton, as tears streamed freely down his cheeks, "he belongs to the ages."

2. Treason Must Be Made Infamous

Supreme Court Chief Justice Salmon P. Chase remembered the night of Lincoln's assassination as "a night of horrors." This was true for Chase, not only because of the shame and brutality of Lincoln's murder and the possibility that Chase "was one of the destined victims," but also because of what Lincoln's death now meant for a peace process that had only just begun. Chase arose early the next morning—"a heavy rain was falling, and the sky was black"—and met with Attorney General James Speed to discuss the procedures earlier chief justices had used for swearing in vice-presidents as the new president. But the conversation lingered over "the late president," and Speed mournfully shook his head over the impact Lincoln's murder would have on the plans for southern Reconstruction. "He never seemed so near our views," Speed remarked. "At the [Cabinet] meeting he said he thought [he] had made a mistake at Richmond in sanctioning the assembling of the Virginia Legislature and had perhaps been too fast in his desires for early reconstruction."[19]

[19]Inside Lincoln's Cabinet: The Civil War Diaries of Salmon P. Chase, David Donald, ed. (New York, 1954), pp. 267–268.

Lincoln's uncertainty about the speed of Reconstruction is not surprising. Even if the war had accomplished nothing else, the Emancipation Proclamation and the freeing of hundreds of thousands of southern slaves had made a simple restoration of the prewar status quo unthinkable and repeatedly forced Lincoln to confront the fact that emancipation would compel some dramatic and long-term reshuffling of southern white society. Emancipation had already posed troubling questions for northern whites on the streetcars of major northern cities; it could hardly help raising greater questions in the South, where the economic underpinnings of the southern states were bound up with African-American slavery. And it was still not clear what freedom actually meant for African Americans, or even (until the Thirteenth Amendment was formally ratified in December) whether freedom was a fact for all the slaves. As the federal armies rolled over large parts of the South, southern white Unionists sprang up to seize political control of southern state capitals, but their attentions were mostly preoccupied with evening-up political scores with the secessionists who had plunged them into the war rather than with the civil rights of the newly freed slaves. Even in Louisiana, where Lincoln had taken more than a presidential interest in the structure of a new government, he had been unable to persuade the new white Unionist government to make any provision for black civil rights.

This unwillingness to look the most important of the war's consequences in the face inspired deep mistrust of southern whites, loyalist and rebel alike, in the minds of the Radical Republicans in Congress. They had little of Lincoln's persistent confidence that border-state and southern Unionism could be relied on to reconstruct the Confederate state governments, and as early as 1864, their dissatisfaction with Lincoln's reliance on loyalist white regimes in the occupied zones of the South helped spark the unrest within the Republican party that resulted in the Wade-Davis Manifesto. Even after John Wilkes Booth was tracked down and shot by federal cavalrymen in Virginia on April 26th, the Radicals remained convinced that Booth had only been acting as an agent for a larger Confederate conspiracy to frustrate federal victory. The Radicals, led by Sumner, Wade, Chandler, and Wilson in the Senate, and by Thaddeus Stevens in the House, wanted more from the South for all the treasure and blood that had been spilled than a mere agreement to stop the fighting. "In my view, the war has just begun," announced the veteran abolitionist orator, Wendell Phillips. Merely subtracting slavery from the southern social equation was not enough. "You do not annihilate a social system when you decree its death," Phillips explained. "You only annihilate it when you fill its place with another." And what Phillips and the Radicals wanted was the complete evisceration of the southern political, social, and economic system and its replacement with a practical and forward-looking Whig Republicanism based on free labor, small-scale market production, and universal education. "The whole fabric of southern society *must* be changed," insisted Thaddeus Stevens, "and never can be done if this opportunity is lost. How can republican institutions, free schools, free churches, free social intercourse exist in a mingled community of nabobs and serfs? . . . If the South is ever to be made a safe Republic let her lands be cultivated by the toil of the owners, or the free labor of intelligent citizens."[20]

The most important source of support for the Radical agenda came from the freed slaves themselves, who at once began to organize Loyal Leagues, Equal Rights Leagues, and Union Leagues in the South to demand equal rights. African Americans, wrote Frederick Douglass, wanted "no war but an Abolition war," and they now wanted "no peace but an Abolition peace; liberty for all, chains for none; the black man a soldier in war; a laborer in peace; a voter at the South as well as the North; America his permanent home, and all Americans his fellow-countrymen." In November, a special election was held in Louisiana to elect former Union army officer Henry Clay Warmoth as Louisiana's first Reconstruction "delegate" to Congress. Although an election for the Louisiana governorship was also scheduled, the governor's race was not open to black voters; but Warmoth's race was for a national office where no restrictions were placed on the race of the voters, and on November 6th, over 19,000 African Americans came to parish polling places to cast what amounted to their first votes for a national office. For their own part, the Radicals were helping to inch along the progress toward black voting rights by establishing in March 1865 the Bureau of Refugees, Freedmen and Abandoned Lands, which was known simply as the Freedmen's Bureau. The bureau was originally conceived as a relief agency, with a mandate largely concerned with the feeding, clothing, and education of displaced slaves. But it had within it the germ of radicalism, since education was clearly linked in the Radicals' mind with preparation for voting rights.

The bureau might also have an economic role to play in Reconstruction, too, since the bill that created the Bureau authorized it to divide up plantation lands that had been seized from southern whites for nonpayment of taxes or confiscated as retribution for rebel war service, and assign "not more than forty acres" of these lands to black applicants as their own farms. The wording of the legislation was far from clear: The title to the lands the bureau distributed was only "such title thereto as the United States can convey," which meant that it could easily be challenged in the state courts by former landowners. But the former slaves saw at once that education and political rights would never be secure unless they also possessed the economic power that came with property rights, and they caught up the bureau's lands for their own small farms as fast as they were offered. They had no compunction about taking over their former masters' property as their own. "We has a right to the land where we are located," explained an African American named Bayley Wyatt, "For why? I tell you."

> Our wives, our children, our husbands has been sold over and over again to purchase the lands we now locates upon; for that reason we have a divine right to

[20]Phillips, in *The Radical Republicans and Reconstruction, 1861–1870*, Harold Hyman, ed. (Indianapolis, IN, 1967), pp. 480, 483; Kenneth M. Stampp, *The Era of Reconstruction, 1865–1877* (New York, 1965), p. 127; Peyton McCrary, "The Party of Revolution: Republican Ideas About Politics and Social Change, 1862–1867," in *Civil War History* 30 (December 1984), pp. 330–350.

the land. . . . And den didn't we clear the land, and raise de crops ob corn, ob cotton, ob rice, ob sugar, ob everything. And den didn't dem large cities in de North grow up on de cotton and de sugars and de rice dat we made? . . . I say dey has grown rich and my people poor.[21]

This was the voice that Lincoln had begun listening to in the closing weeks of the war, and at the Cabinet meeting on the morning of his assassination, he endorsed a plan drawn up by Secretary of War Stanton that would have put a stop to the organization of civilian governments in the Confederate states and substituted military occupation under military governors who could ensure that black civil rights would be enforced.[22] This represented yet another shift, this time away from what he had suggested to Sherman and Grant less than a month before, and one can only wonder where it would have taken Lincoln had he lived. But the Radicals were sure they knew. When Sherman met with Joseph Johnston to negotiate the surrender of Johnston's broken-down little army of Confederates at Durham Station, North Carolina, on April 17th, Sherman offered Johnston the kind of terms he thought Lincoln had authorized: All remaining Confederate armies were to be disbanded and "deposit their arms and public property" in their respective state arsenals; a general amnesty; reestablishment of the federal courts; and "the recognition by the Executive of the United States, of the several State governments, on their officers and Legislatures taking the oaths prescribed by the Constitution of the United States. . . ." No judgment, trials, or imprisonment, no mention of slavery, and clearly no allusion to black civil rights. These arrangements were far beyond Sherman's powers as an army commander to grant, even in the fairest of seasons; and as Sherman was to learn, they were infinitely beyond what Stanton as secretary of war and the Radicals in Congress were willing to tolerate. One of Sherman's staff members hand carried the surrender terms to Washington, where Stanton read them on the afternoon of April 21st. That evening, Stanton called in Grant and erupted, and the next day, the secretary of war released a public repudiation of Sherman's agreement and sent Grant down to North Carolina to rein him in. Humiliated, Sherman withdrew the surrender terms and accepted Johnson's surrender on April 26th on terms similar to those Grant had written out for Lee at Appomattox. A different tune for Reconstruction had been called for, and Sherman had no choice but to dance to it.

Another man who was going to have to join that dance was the new president, Andrew Johnson. Lincoln's selection of Andrew Johnson as his running mate in the 1864 election was a baffling proposition even to people who knew both of them. In some respects it was a marriage of political convenience rather than principle. Johnson was an old-line Tennessee Democrat who worshiped at the political shrine of the man Lincoln loathed, Andrew Jackson. But like Jack-

[21]Eric Foner, *Nothing But Freedom: Emancipation and Its Legacy* (Baton Rouge, LA, 1983), p. 56.
[22]Thomas and Hyman, *Stanton*, pp. 357–358.

son, Johnson was a fervent Unionist. Appointed military governor of Tennessee in 1862, Johnson had meted out a harsh justice to rebel planters and promised black Tennesseans in 1864 that he would "be your Moses, and lead you through the Red Sea of war and bondage to a fairer future of liberty and peace." It was public commentary of that sort, along with Lincoln's eagerness to demonstrate to the border states that southern yeomen were turning their backs on the Confederacy, that moved Lincoln to replace his first vice-president, Hannibal Hamlin, with Johnson. Lincoln's concern for wooing border votes was not misplaced in that anxious electoral summer of 1864, but his concern caused him to miss the fact that Johnson's Unionism was really an expression of his yeoman's hatred for the white planters, not of sympathy for black slaves. Although their backgrounds in rural poverty and their rise to success through politics made Johnson and Lincoln look superficially similar, Johnson was a simon-pure Jacksonian whose real energies were consumed with destroying the old white social order in the South, not with the thousands of African Americans who required education, protection, and a fresh start in life. "Damn the Negroes," Johnson told one Tennessee correspondent, "I am fighting these traitorous aristocrats, their masters," and even Johnson's private secretary admitted that Johnson "exhibited a morbid distress and feeling against the negroes."[23]

Initially, the Radical Republicans made the same mistake about Johnson. On the afternoon of the day Lincoln died, a delegation of Radicals headed by Ben Wade (as the chair of the Joint Committee on the Conduct of the War) called on Johnson to take his political temperature, and Johnson enthusiastically assured them that they could "judge of my policy by my past. . . . *Treason* is a crime; and *crime* must be punished. . . . Treason must be made infamous and traitors must be impoverished." This sounded, to the Radicals, like an endorsement for the redistribution of the lands and property of slave-owners and Confederate officials, and severe punishments for those who had led the South into secession. "Johnson, we have faith in you," boomed Wade. "By the gods, there will be no trouble now in running the government." And Johnson fortified Wade's confidence two days later by suggesting that a good example might be set to traitors by hanging a good baker's dozen of the Confederate leaders.[24] Not having many Confederate leaders so easily at hand, Johnson instead concentrated on arresting and punishing Booth's co-conspirators. Scores of suspects were arrested by Stanton and eight were put on trial before a hard-jawed military tribunal. Four of them were hanged on July 7, 1865.

And yet, for all the appearances of grim-faced radicalism in Johnson, Wade and his colleagues could not have been more wrong about the new president. Not only

[23]Hans L. Trefousse, *Andrew Johnson: A Biography* (New York, 1989), p. 183; James M. McPherson, *The Struggle for Equality: Abolitionists and the Negro in the Civil War and Reconstruction* (Princeton, NJ, 1964), p. 317.

[24]Hans L. Trefousse, *Benjamin Franklin Wade: Radical Republican from Ohio* (New York, 1963), p. 249–250.

was Johnson's support for Reconstruction limited to what it could do for southern whites rather than southern blacks, but Johnson's Democratic political instincts set him against almost every other part of the Republican domestic agenda, including protective tariffs for American industry, the new national banking system, the use of paper money by the federal government rather than gold, and federal investment in internal improvements. "The aristocracy based on $3,000,000,000 of property in slaves . . . has disappeared," Johnson rejoiced,

> but an aristocracy, based on over $2,500,000 of national securities, has arisen in the Northern states, to assume that political control which the consolidation of great financial and political interest formerly gave to the slave oligarchy. . . . We have all read history, and is it not certain, that of all aristocracies mere wealth is the most odious, rapacious, and tyrannical? It goes for the last dollar the poor helpless have got; and with such a vast machine as this government under its control, that dollar will be fetched. It is an aristocracy that can see in the people only a prey for extortion.[25]

If Johnson had a solution to the problems posed by the former slaves, it was bounded on the one side by his refusal to grant them any kind of political equality with white men, and on the other side by his assertion that the best conclusion to the story of the African American in America would be a fast ship back to Africa.

Just how deeply the Radicals had misjudged Johnson became apparent when the president issued his own preliminary plan for Reconstruction on May 29, 1865. It was, for all intents and purposes, what Sherman had offered Joe Johnston, only in more spacious detail. Acting on the old Democratic assumption that national government needed restraint, and that the sooner the state governments were restored to their normal position, the better, Johnson proposed to reconstruct the Confederate state governments by personally appointing a civilian provisional governor for each state. The governor would organize a convention that would repudiate the state's secession ordinance, disallow any obligation to pay off Confederate war debts, and write new voting laws; then, regular elections for governor, state legislature, and Congress could be held, and the new state legislatures would ratify the Thirteenth Amendment. This at once posed the question of who would be eligible to serve in such conventions, since the South was now flooded with former Confederate soldiers and officers who would be only too happy to take control of the new state conventions and keep African Americans as close to legal peonage as possible. Johnson answered that question in an accompanying proclamation in which he offered sweeping pardons and amnesty to former Confederates, and "restoration of all rights of property, except as to slaves," even in cases where confiscation proceedings "have been instituted."

Both Radical and moderate Republicans were astounded: "My Dear Wade," wrote Charles Sumner to Ben Wade, "The rebels are all springing into their old life,

---

[25]Stampp, *Era of Reconstruction*, p. 57; McPherson, *Struggle for Equality*, p. 346.

& the copperheads also. This the President's work. . . . We must let him know frankly, that we will not follow his fatal lead. . . . We must also let the country know that we will not consent to this sacrifice."[26] The aging evangelist, Charles Grandison Finney, denounced Johnson as a "piece of rottenness under the nose of God." But Johnson was undaunted. He had already signaled his intentions on May 9th by recognizing the legitimacy of a Unionist Virginia legislature, and as he passed out pardons on application, he proceeded to appoint provisional governors for North Carolina, Texas, Georgia, Alabama, Mississippi, Florida, and South Carolina (he also recognized the state governments that had already been erected in Louisiana, Arkansas, and his own Tennessee). The pardons allowed the provisional governors to make patronage appointments, and to shore up their own political futures, many of them appointed unblushing and newly pardoned Confederates to state offices. The state conventions they called dutifully ratified the Thirteenth Amendment, but none of them extended voting rights to African Americans, and South Carolina even balked at repudiating its share of Confederate debt. Instead of being hanged, Confederate leaders were at first surprised by Johnson's generosity, then relieved, and then defiant. Carl Schurz observed that the surrenders of the Confederate armies had made public opinion in the southern states "so despondent that if readmission at some future time under whatever conditions had been promised, it would have been looked upon as a favor." But when "day after day went by without bringing the disasters and inflictions which had been vaguely anticipated," Southerners grew more secure and resistant, "until at last the appearance of the . . . proclamation substituted new hopes for them." Christopher Memminger put it more simply: Johnson "held up before us the hope of a 'white man's government,' and this led us to set aside negro suffrage. . . . It was natural that we should yield to our old prejudices."[27]

This overconfidence, however, was the undoing of what became known as "presidential Reconstruction." Several southern conventions only repealed secession rather than repudiating it; the new state legislature in Mississippi refused to ratify the Thirteenth Amendment, and a few only ratified it with the proviso that the states and not the federal government had the right to determine the political future of African Americans from that point on; in Arkansas, the legislature actually appropriated funds to pay pensions to Confederate veterans. In fact, rather than granting new rights to African Americans, the Johnson governments strove to take as many away as possible. In a series of "black codes," Mississippi and South Carolina passed labor laws that bound blacks to employers almost as tightly as slavery once had to masters. Other southern black codes established patterns of racial segregation that had been impossible under slavery, barred Afri-

---

[26]Sumner to Wade [August 3, 1865], in *The Selected Letters of Charles Sumner*, B. W. Palmer, ed. (Boston, 1990), vol. 2, pp. 320–321.

[27]Memminger to Schurz [April 26, 1871], in Schurz, *Speeches, Correspondence and Political Papers of Carl Schurz*, Frederic Bancroft, ed. (New York, 1912), vol. 2, p. 256.

can Americans from serving on juries or offering testimony in court against whites, and made "vagrancy" and "mischief" offenses punishable by fines or imprisonment. But the most visibly outrageous actions of the presidential Reconstruction governments involved the people who found top-level state employment in the Johnson governments, and the representatives they sent to Washington to sit in Congress. Across the lower South, former Confederates moved right back into the places of state power and office they held before the war; Alexander Stephens, former Confederate vice-president and now pardoned by Johnson, was elected by the Georgia legislature to the Senate.[28] And along with the restoration of white power, came an upsurge of antiblack violence. "You have doubtless heard a great deal of the Reconstructed South, of their acceptance of the results of the war," wrote a Freedmen's Bureau agent in South Carolina. "This may all be true, but if a man . . . had the list of Negroes murdered in a single county in this most loyal and Christian state, he would think it a strange way of demonstrating his kindly feelings toward them."[29]

When the 39th Congress assembled in December, 1865, the mutterings against presidential Reconstruction had become noisy. Johnson himself seems to have been puzzled by the summer's events, first by the speed with which his Reconstruction plans seemed to go awry, and second by the peculiar reluctance of several northern states to endorse state referendums of their own about black voting rights. But there was no such confusion in the Radicals' minds, and they played skillfully on the fears of moderate Republicans by painting stark pictures of a revived Democratic party that would upset the banking system, repudiate the national debt, and pull down the protective tariffs of the war years. When the representatives of the new Johnson governments appeared at the opening of Congress on December 4th to take their seats, the cooperative clerk of the House of Representatives omitted their names from the roll call and refused to recognize them. The House Radicals, with Thaddeus Stevens in the lead, then seized the initiative by referring the entire matter of southern Reconstruction to a joint House-Senate Committee on Reconstruction (which would be, for all practical purposes, a reincarnation of the Joint Committee on the Conduct of the War); in the Senate, Wade and Sumner were ready with a bill for black voting rights in the District of Columbia and resolutions banning the readmittance of any state to the Union that did not also endorse equal voting rights for all adult males, regardless of color.

The stage was now set for a direct confrontation betwen the president and the Radicals of what was supposed to be his own party. It would center largely on two related issues: The first, of course, was black civil rights, and whether the former Confederate states could be compelled by the federal government to grant African Americans full civil equality. Assuming the federal government did, indeed, have

[28]Eric Foner, *Reconstruction: America's Unfinished Revolution, 1863–1877* (New York, 1988), pp. 188–194, 199–209; Stampp, *Era of Reconstruction*, pp. 67–68, 76, 79.
[29]Richard N. Current, *Those Terrible Carpetbaggers: A Reinterpretation* (New York, 1988), p. 45.

the authority to regulate state Reconstruction policy, the question then became whether that authority belonged to the president or to Congress. As they had with Lincoln, the Radicals argued that secession was tantamount to state suicide, and that the former southern states were now in the position of territories—which the Constitution clearly placed under the oversight of Congress. "Congress alone is authorized to deal with the subject of reconstruction," wrote one Radical congressman to Charles Sumner, and that grant of authority included an unprecedented level of intervention in local southern affairs. "Our safety and the peace of the country require us to disenfranchise the rebels and to enfranchise the colored citizens in the revolted states and thereby confide the political power therein to . . . safe hands."[30] Armed with that conviction, Thaddeus Stevens rose to launch the first strike in a two-year-long campaign against Johnson and his Reconstruction plan. The states, Stevens declared on December 18th, had taken themselves completely out of the Union by seceding, and only one way was provided for in the Constitution for admission, that of territorialization. And in the process of readmitting these nonstates, it was imperative that black voting rights and land reform be made a requirement for rejoining the Union. This led, at the beginning of 1866, to the introduction of a national civil rights bill that guaranteed "full and equal benefit of all laws and proceedings for the security of person and property" to "all persons born in the United States . . . of every race and color. . . ." And then, as an adjunct to the civil rights bill, the Radicals pushed to passage a bill that renewed the mandate of the Freedmen's Bureau (since the bureau would be given much of the responsibility as a federal watchdog for violations of the civil rights bill).

Johnson interpreted these actions as an assault on his presidential authority as well as on his old Democratic republicanism and deference to state and local power—which is precisely what they were. But unlike Lincoln, who had defused attacks like these by moving softly around them, Johnson hurled the full force of his anger at the Radicals. On February 7th, Johnson received a delegation of African-American leaders, headed by Frederick Douglass, and proceeded to harrangue them on the impossibility of granting political equality to blacks. When Douglass tried to object, Johnson cut him short, and Douglass took his objections out the door with him and published them in a Washington newspaper. "I know that d——d Douglass," screeched Johnson when he read Douglass's comments, "he's just like any nigger, & he would sooner cut a white man's throat than not."[31] Having turned from playing Moses to playing Pharoah, Johnson struck back next at Congress. On February 19th, he vetoed the Freedmen's Bureau bill, arguing that Congress had no right to legislate on behalf of states it was determined to bar from their due representation

---

[30]Hans L. Trefousse, *The Radical Republicans: Lincoln's Vanguard for Racial Justice* (New York, 1969), p. 316.

[31]William S. McFeely, *Frederick Douglass* (New York, 1991), p. 247; Trefousse, *Andrew Johnson*, pp. 241–242.

in Washington, with the emphasis falling clearly on Johnson's contention that the southern states were still states. Three days later, in a Washington's birthday speech at the White House, Johnson linked himself to Andrew Jackson, fighting off a new set of enemies of the Union, and when a voice in the crowd asked him to name names, Johnson foolishly singled out Stevens, Sumner, and Wendell Phillips. And then, as if to crown all of these gaffes, Johnson vetoed the civil rights bill on March 29th, effectively burning whatever bridges he still had to the Republican party that had nominated him. Even the moderate Republicans were aghast at Johnson's recklessness, especially since the civil rights bill had been crafted by Lyman Trumbull of Illinois specifically as a compromise measure to appease Johnson.

Rather than managing Congress, Johnson had only succeeded in colliding with it, and his heavy-handed invocation of Jacksonian Democratic ideas cost him whatever small political base within the Republican party he might have hoped to hold. On April 9th, Congress successfully overrode Johnson's veto of the civil rights bill (the Senate managed the override by a single vote); a second version of the Freedmen's Bureau bill was passed, and when Johnson vetoed it again, Congress overrode that veto, too. On April 30th, determined to put black civil rights beyond the reach of Johnson's interference and vetoes, William Pitt Fessenden in the Senate and Thaddeus Stevens in the House introduced a proposal for a new constitutional amendment that barred any state from restricting "the privileges or immunities" of "born or naturalized" citizens concerning "life, liberty, or property . . . without due process of law." This effectively removed the definition of both citizenship and voter eligibility from state jurisdiction and handed it to the federal government. But the amendment went on to expel from Congress any member of the House or Senate, or any civil or military officer of the United States, who had been "engaged in insurrection or rebellion against the same, or given aid or comfort to the enemies thereof," and imposed repudiation of the Confederate debt on the former Confederate states. Predictably, Johnson gagged on the amendment. But since amendments to the Constitution do not require a presidential signature, both houses of Congress passed this Fourteenth Amendment by the required two-thirds majority in June, 1866, and sent it on to the state legislatures for ratification without even bothering to send Johnson a notification resolution.

Johnson attempted to fight back with what powers he still had in hand, but by the summer of 1866, even the small standing he had as president was dwindling. In a desperate bid to rally popular support for his collapsing Reconstruction plan, Johnson embarked on a whirlwind speaking tour of the North, dragging a reluctant General Grant with him to provide moral support. A National Union Convention, designed to unite moderate Republicans and northern Democrats behind Johnson, met in Philadelphia in August, but it was upstaged by a Radical-sponsored Southern Loyalists convention that paraded through the streets of Philadelphia in September to hear Frederick Douglass and Quaker activist Anna Dickinson offer impassioned appeals for black equality. Johnson, for his part, could not seem to open his mouth without offending people, and his rough country mannerisms (unsmoothed as Lincoln's had been by a lifetime of trying to elude his origins) dampened support across the North rather than rousing it. When a heckler in Cleveland called out that Johnson couldn't look a man in the face, Johnson lost all self-control and began shouting,

> I wish I could see you; I will bet now, if there could be a light reflected on your face, that cowardice and treachery could be seen in it. Show yourself. Come out here where we can see you. If ever you shoot a man, you will stand in the dark and pull your trigger. . . . Those men—such a one as insulted me here tonight—you may say, has ceased to be a man, and in ceasing to be a man shrunk into the denomination of a reptile, and having so shrunken, as an honest man, I tread on him.[32]

In the congressional by-elections that November, the Republicans crushed Johnson's moderate and Democratic friends, and gave the Radicals a veto-proof majority in both houses of Congress. Johnson had now lost control, not only of his public image, but of his administration. Even Tennessee, to Johnson's embarrassment, gave up on him and ratified the Fourteenth Amendment as part of a deal that would guarantee the readmission of the state's Representatives and Senators to Congress on Congress's terms. "We have fought the battle and won it," crowed "Parson" Brownlow, who was now Tennessee's Republican governor and the deadly political enemy of Andrew Johnson. "Give my respects to the dead dog in the White House."[33]

3. The Government of the United States Abandons You

The results of the congressional by-elections in November, 1866, were an open invitation to the Radicals, with Thaddeus Stevens at the head of the House and Ben Wade the new president pro tem of the Senate, to take up the reins of Reconstruction from Johnson's faltering hands and substitute a congressional plan. They acted first on January 22, 1867, by passing a bill that called the newly elected 40th Congress to order on March 4, 1867, immediately after the close of the 39th Congress rather than in the following December, so as to give Johnson no opportunities for mischief during a congressional recess. With that foundation securely under foot, the Joint Committee on Reconstruction turned to the scaffolding of congressional Reconstruction, and on March 2, 1867, Congress enacted the first of several major Reconstruction acts. Declaring that "no legal State governments or adequate protection for life or property now exists in the rebel states," the First Reconstruction Act turned the Johnson governments into provisional civilian administrations and consolidated most of the old Confederacy into five "military districts": Virginia would constitute the first, the Carolinas the second, Georgia, Alabama, and Flor-

[32]Stampp, Era of Reconstruction, pp. 114–115.
[33]D. M. DeWitt, The Impeachment and Trial of Andrew Johnson (1903; rept. New York, 1967), p. 100.

ida the third, Mississippi and Arkansas the fourth, and Texas the fifth. Each district would be supervised by an army general appointed by the president, and other army officers and Freedmen's Bureau agents would act as adjuncts to the civilian adminis- trations in properly registering voters. This legislation fell considerably short of outright military occupation. What it really created was a parallel administration not unlike the procedures used in organizing the territories: The civil governments would continue to exist, but the army would have overall supervision of the civil process and would fine-tune the process of civil government until the state regimes began to look like what Congress wanted. Only when "the people of any one of said rebel States"—which included all adult males regardless of "whatever race, color, or previous condition" but not former Confederates—were willing to write a new state constitution embracing the Thirteenth and Fourteenth Amendments would Con- gress recognize a southern state again.

President Johnson, of course, vetoed the act. The Radicals anticipated this, and Congress overrode the veto without hesitation. In fact, they anticipated more than just Johnson's veto: On the same day as Congress passed the First Reconstruc- tion Act, a rider was attached to a military appropriations bill limiting Johnson's ability to make military appointments and issue orders to military commanders and forced the president to pass all of his orders through the general-in-chief (which in this case was Grant). This would ensure, as much as it was possible, that the new district commanders would see themselves as more answerable to Grant and to Congress than to the president. And to make sure that Johnson would not try to circumvent the operation of the Reconstruction Act through his use of civilian patronage appointments in the South, Congress added the Tenure of Office Act, which prevented the president from replacing any civil officeholder until the Sen- ate approved a successor for that office (if the Senate was in recess, the president would be allowed only to "suspend" an officeholder until the Senate reconvened). The last stone in the new edifice of Reconstruction was the Second Reconstruction Act, passed on March 23, 1867, which established the procedures for registering eligible white and black voters—and excluding any southern participants "in any rebellion or civil war against the United States." Johnson vetoed them all; Congress just as easily overrode the vetoes.

Johnson's presidency was by this point so impotent that simply getting rid of him seemed worth considering, especially since Ben Wade, as the president pro tem of the Senate, would be his constitutional successor. Discussions among the Radi- cals about impeaching Johnson and removing him from the presidency had flickered as early as his veto of the civil rights bill in 1865, but not until January, 1867, did the Republican congressional caucus begin seriously considering such a move. Once considered, however, action quickly followed: On January 7th, James Ashley, the Radical Ohio Representative who had been the floor manager for the Thirteenth Amendment, moved Johnson's impeachment on the grounds of "corrupt" use of the presidential veto and appointment powers. The effort died in the House Judiciary Committee, which found no specific evidence it could use as the basis for impeachment proceedings beyond Johnson's political truculence. When the 40th Congress officially assembled in March, Ashley tried again, hoping that a new Judiciary Committee would be more favorable. But the new committee had no more desire to challenge the president than its predecessor, and in June, the impeachment proposal was dropped again. Emboldened by these failures, Johnson struggled to regain the initiative through a compliant General Grant by restraining the military commanders from implementing the registration procedures; and when Philip Sheridan, the military commander for Texas and Louisiana, showed himself a little too zealous in carrying out the Radical program, Johnson dismissed him. This set off a new flurry of impeachment demands, this time from Thaddeus Stevens and the Joint Committee on Reconstruction. But once again, no one could produce any hard evidence that Johnson had broken a law, and in July, 1867, the Radicals had to content themselves with passing a Third Reconstruction Act that transferred Johnson's powers of dismissal to Grant and beefed up the civil restrictions on former Confederate soldiers and officials.

However, this was not nearly enough of a victory for Johnson. If Grant was now to inherit most of the military powers that Johnson thought properly belonged to himself, Johnson was determined to control Grant, and to that end he proposed evicting the secretary of war, Edwin M. Stanton, and installing Grant in his place. Grant's reaction was evasive, and with good reason, since Stanton was a friend of the Radicals and such a move would bring Johnson into collision with the Tenure of Office Act. But Johnson had decided that by now he had nothing to lose. A few days after Congress adjourned for the 1867 summer recess, Johnson informed Stanton that "Public considerations of a high character constrain me to say that your resignation as Secretary of War will be accepted." Stanton (who had been secretly warned by Grant of Johnson's plans) refused to offer any such resignation until Congress reassembled in December, and Johnson announced that, under the terms of the Tenure of Office Act, Stanton was now "suspended" and Grant would function as the interim secretary of war. There matters hung until December, while Johnson hoped that the case could be diverted into the courts, where he could rely on the Supreme Court to rule the Tenure of Office Act unconstitutional. But Congress moved first, and on January 13th, the Senate refused to approve Stanton's removal from office and ordered him back to his post. Grant, who prudently declined Johnson's order to defy the Senate, obligingly turned the key of the war office over to Stanton, who then barricaded himself in his old chamber. Johnson frantically began casting around for a more willing replacement for Stanton, considering George McClellan, William Sherman, and even a war office clerk by turns. He finally prevailed on Adjutant General Lorenzo Thomas to take on the job, and on February 21st, Johnson officially dismissed Stanton.

The uproar in Congress over this fresh assault on the Tenure of Office Act was immediate, and two days later, the House voted to impeach Johnson by a landslide vote of 128 to 47. On March 5th, the Senate convened itself as a court to begin hearing the testimony that would lead to Johnson's conviction. The trial itself was a fairly wearisome affair—Johnson refused to appear personally and carried out his defense through his lawyers. Most of the arguments turned on the constitutional niceties of the Tenure of Office Act and other congressional legislation, and nearly every one of the spectators who daily crowded the Senate galleries knew that the decision would be settled by politics rather than evidence. When the Senate at last voted on Johnson's guilt on May 16, 1868, a critical group of moderate Republicans headed by William Pitt Fessenden pulled shy of condemning the president, and Johnson was saved from conviction by a single vote.[34] The victory, however, proved an empty one. Two weeks later, the Republican National Convention met in Chicago and nominated Ulysses S. Grant as the Republican candidate for president. Johnson tried to stimulate some interest among his former Democratic friends about getting the Democratic nomination, but the Democrats wanted no more to do with Johnson than the Republicans. Instead, they nominated Horatio Seymour, the wartime governor of New York. Grant won handily, and the South was made safe for Reconstruction.

The sound and the fury in Washington was only one part of the Reconstruction struggle. An equally critical part was being played out in the South, where the congressional Reconstruction governments were already building a new economic and political order for the old Confederacy. Since the Reconstruction Acts stripped voting rights from former Confederate leaders, much of the new political leadership of Reconstruction had to come from white southern Unionists and from northern activists and soldiers who had settled in the South after the war. For almost a century after Reconstruction, the conventional view of these northern reconstructors portrayed them as political vultures, a pack of opportunists and adventurers who hurriedly packed their belongings into cheap "carpet bags" for the trip South (hence the name "carpetbaggers") and proceeded to pick the bones of the defeated South clean, while southern white Unionists were dismissed as "scalawags" who betrayed the South in return for the corrupt spoils of Reconstruction government. But the so-called "carpetbaggers" were a much more diverse lot than the stereotype allowed: Some, like the "Gideonites" at Port Royal, South Carolina, were idealists and educators who wanted to improve the lives of the freed slaves and turn them into productive models of small-scale republican farmers; some, like Lincoln's secretary John Hay, saw economic opportunities in the South, and for $500 bought a Florida orange grove that was soon producing an annual crop worth over $2,500; others, like Colonel George Eliphaz Spencer of New York, were simply following a pattern already established by prewar northern investors, buying up southern cotton and brokering its sale to a cotton-starved Europe for a whopping annual profit of $40,000; and still others, like Captain John Emory Bryant of the 8th Maine, joined the Freedmen's Bureau and moved from there into Georgia politics as one of the founders of the infant Georgia Republican party. Many of the carpetbaggers, in fact, were actually welcomed by Southerners for the badly needed

[34]Michael Les Benedict, *The Impeachment and Trial of Andrew Johnson* (New York, 1973), pp. 168–180.

investment capital they brought into the war-scorched South, and they came largely from the ranks of the same middle-class businessmen and professionals who filled the ranks of the Republican party.[35]

The carpetbaggers struck up political alliances with the disgruntled southern yeomen "scalawags" who, like Andrew Johnson, blamed the South's destruction on the planters and were happy to engineer a new Republican political order. The carpetbaggers struck up an even more critical alliance with the former slaves and with the tiny cadre of free southern blacks who at first formed the core of black political leadership in the South. Once congressional Reconstruction torpedoed the "black codes" and forced the Fourteenth Amendment upon the southern states, black voters entered into southern political life in substantial numbers. Over 2,000 black men held political offices ranging from Hiram Revels, who took over Jefferson Davis's old Mississippi Senate seat in 1870, and P. B. S. Pinchback, the governor pro tem of Louisiana in 1872, all the way down the scale of office to sheriffs, registrars, and justices of the peace. Although later critics of Reconstruction would ridicule these black officeholders as barefoot illiterates fresh from the cotton fields, almost half of them were born free, and the sprinkling of college graduates, lawyers, and Union army veterans among African Americans who held office holds up at least as well (given the paucity of opportunities for education and advancement in the Confederate South) by comparison with the prewar patterns of white officeholding.[36]

The new civil governments that this three-way alliance created under the eye of the federal military district commanders were far from perfect. True to at least one aspect of the legend of the carpetbaggers, they spent money on an unprecedented scale, and raised southern taxes to extraordinary levels to finance that spending, all of which later led to accusations that the money had been squandered on shady contracts and corrupt deals. In South Carolina, the tax rates doubled even though the war had wiped out property values; and while the state debt jumped from $5.5 million in 1868 to over $15.7 million in 1871, legislators voted themselves a free bar and even a bonus of $1,000 to the speaker of the house to cover his losses at the racetrack. But much of this political vulgarity stemmed from the sheer confusion and dislocation of the postwar years, and much of the vastly increased taxing and spending went into the rebuilding of the southern economy. In the postwar South, where the infrastructure of roads, rail lines, and harbors had been devastated by the war and where public education before the war had been almost nonexistent, there was very little alternative to vastly increased taxation and spending if the economy were to be rejuvenated and the educational system brought up to par with the North. That there was graft and corruption in the Reconstruction governments is certainly true; the question is whether it amounted to any more

[35]Current, *Those Terrible Carpetbaggers*, pp. 29–31; Ruth Currie-McDaniel, *Carpetbagger of Conscience: A Biography of John Emory Bryant* (Athens, GA, 1987), pp. 40–41; Foner, *Reconstruction*, pp. 294–295.
[36]Eric Foner, "Introduction" to *Freedom's Lawmakers: A Directory of Black Officeholders During Reconstruction* (New York, 1993), pp. xiii–xxxi.

than what normally occurs in situations of massive postwar or postdisaster rebuilding. What is also certain is that, whatever the degree of corruption that plagued the
congressional Reconstruction governments, they brought vast numbers of new voters, both newly free blacks and southern yeomen, into a more broadly based republican process than had ever before prevailed in the South.[37] By the end of 1868, this
new alliance of southern blacks and southern and northern whites had completely
reconstructed the constitutions of six of the southern states and incorporated the
Fourteenth Amendment into the political heartland of the old Confederacy.

In despair, some of the most ardent old secessionists counseled accommodation
or even outright capitulation. Robert E. Lee's old lieutenant, James Longstreet,
accepted the lucrative federal post of customs surveyor in Republican New Orleans
and campaigned for Grant in 1868; former Georgia Governor Joseph Brown also
joined the Republicans and counseled cooperation with the Radicals; J. D. B.
DeBow revived the old DeBow's Review and called upon Southerners to encourage
the immigration of northern workers and northern industry. In 1869, when Congress adopted a Fifteenth Amendment that specifically prohibited any abridgment
of voting rights "on account of race, color, or previous condition of servitude," the
new southern governments ratified it in less than a year. By 1870 all of the former
Confederate states had been satisfactorily reconstructed and readmitted to the
Union.[38] The Civil War, at least in the sense that secession had made it, now
seemed complete.

And yet despite the apparent successes of congressional Reconstruction, the
health of the Reconstruction governments remained critically dependent on two
restraints: One was the continued exclusion of the most dangerous ex-Confederates
from political power in the South, and the other was continued support and encouragement from Washington, especially in the form of federal soldiers who would be
available to enforce the civil rights statutes. And over the length of Ulysses S.
Grant's two terms as president, from 1869 until 1877, both of those restraints
gradually melted away. Some of the slow erosion of Washington's support for Reconstruction occurred simply from attrition. Thaddeus Stevens died in August of 1868,
asking to be buried in a segregated cemetery for African-American paupers so that
"I might illustrate in death the principles which I advocated through a long life,
Equality of man before his Creator."[39] The next year, Ben Wade lost his powerful
Senate seat when the Ohio legislature was captured by Democrats; Edwin Stanton
died on Christmas Eve, 1869, only four days after Grant nominated him to sit on
the Supreme Court; James Ashley accepted the territorial governorship of Montana

---

[37]F. B. Simkins and R. H. Woody, South Carolina During Reconstruction (Chapel Hill, NC, 1932), pp.
137–138, 148, 155, 175; Michael Perman, The Road to Redemption: Southern Politics, 1869–1879 (Chapel Hill, NC, 1984), pp. 33–34, 81; James S. Allen, Reconstruction: The Battle for Democracy (New York,
1937), pp. 140–144.

[38]Stampp, Era of Reconstruction, pp. 144–145, 174–182; Foner, Reconstruction, pp. 372, 382, 384–385.

[39]Richard N. Current, Old Thad Stevens: A Story of Ambition (Madison, WI, 1942), p. 320.

from Grant and left Congress; Salmon P. Chase drifted back to his old Democratic friends and died in the spring of 1873; Charles Sumner followed him the next year, pleading with Congress to pass a newer and more stringent civil rights bill (which it did in 1875). Without the cutting edge provided by Stevens, Wade, and Sumner, the other Radicals lost their taste for bold interventions in state affairs.

As it was, they got little enough encouragement from President Grant. Although Grant's presidency has frequently been portrayed as a miasma of corruption, presided over by a military genius who turned out to be a political nincompoop, his administration was probably no more spotted than most prewar governments—James Buchanan, for instance, presided over one of the most corrupt Cabinets in the 19th century—and not much worse, in fact, than the graft and bribery that went on under the table of Lincoln's wartime administration. Grant was also more politically skilled than his critics estimated, as his adroit sidestepping of Andrew Johnson demonstrated. On the other hand, it was also true that Grant was not a political risk taker. His slogan—"Let us have peace"—guaranteed that he would take equal offense at the prodding of both Radicals and Democrats, unless the prodding was skillfully handled, and as the Radicals lost the services of Wade, Ashley, Stevens, and Sumner, that prodding became progressively more flaccid. In disgust, many of the surviving Radicals staged a backdoor rebellion in 1872 in an effort to dump Grant from the party ticket, and they eventually ran Horace Greeley as the joint presidential nominee of both the Liberal Republicans and the Democrats. Greeley was crushed in the election, but the divisions the Liberal Republican movement made in the party ranks only further weakened the resolve of the Republicans to actively enforce the Reconstruction legislation their party had created. In the fall of 1875, when gun-toting whites in Mississippi attacked Republican political rallies in Yazoo City and Jackson, the Republican governor, a former Union army general named Adalbert Ames, appealed to Grant for troops to put down the rioters. Officially, Grant promised Reconstruction governors "every aid for which I can find law or constitutional power"; unofficially, Grant and his attorney general informed Ames that "The whole public are tired out with these annual autumnal outbreaks in the South and the great majority are now ready to condemn any interference on the part of the government." No troops were sent; the federal forces already stationed in Mississippi remained in their barracks, and the following spring Ames resigned.[40]

The failure of Radical Republican nerve after 1870 is linked, as Grant's telegram to Ames indicated, to a larger loss of interest in Reconstruction across the North. As the Civil War and its burning issues receded from memory, as a new generation and a new decade turned its energies westward, as a new flood of immigrant labor (for whom the Civil War was only a topic of incidental interest, and for whom African Americans represented only an unwelcome source of compe-

[40]William S. McFeely, *Grant: A Biography* (New York, 1981), pp. 419–425; Current, *Those Terrible Carpetbaggers*, pp. 321–327.

tition for jobs) poured into the ports of the east coast and California, Reconstruction became simply an expensive holdover from a political era that was rapidly closing. As early as 1867, Illinois Radical Elihu Washburne was warned that, even though "the Republican Party have done a great work for the Negro . . . we should be satisfied *for the present* with what we *have* done, and protect him in the rights we have given him in those States where he was formerly a Slave and had no rights at all, but here we should stop. . . ."[41] It was easy, after five more years of political infighting, to believe that with congressional Reconstruction and the Fifteenth Amendment, everything had been done for the African American that ought to be done. In fact, some of the most important aspects of a complete Reconstruction remained ominously incomplete. The ex-slaves now had political rights, but even the most ultra of the northern Radicals hesitated over the question of land reform and the seizure and redistribution of former rebel-owned plantations. Much as the old republican economy had praised the independent property owner as the foundation of republican liberty, that very same conviction restrained the Radicals from the wholesale appropriation of someone else's property—even rebel property—to make property owners out of the freed slaves. In large measure, the Radicals' willingness to use military force and army generals to ensure black voting rights was simply an effort to substitute armed federal force for the more unappetizing alternative of land redistribution. But political rights divorced from economic rights, and from economic clout, can easily turn weightless, and once the political will to enforce black voting rights began to dissipate, the entire structure of African Americans' hard-won civil equality began to lift apart and dissolve.

And then, by the end of Grant's second administration, it started to disappear entirely. In 1873, a massive economic depression, triggered in the United States by the financial collapse of Jay Cooke, turned northern attention away from the political survival of Reconstruction to the economic survival of the northern economy. At the same time, the Supreme Court, ever the stronghold of Democratic disgruntlement since Dred Scott, handled down a critical civil rights decision on an 1873 appeal by New Orleans butchers against a Louisiana state charter that monopolized meat packing in New Orleans. In the *Slaughterhouse Cases,* the butchers sued under the equal protection provisions of the Fourteenth Amendment; but the Supreme Court replied that the amendment only applied to equal protection under *federal* law, not state law. This removed at one stroke the federal protections that Reconstruction had placed around black civil rights at every level, and in fact, in 1883, the Supreme Court took the added step, in *United States v. Stanley,* of reinterpreting the Fourteenth Amendment as applying only to states as corporate entities and not to individual persons, and on that ground, striking down the 1875 Civil Rights Act as an unwarranted federal interference in local and state affairs. "We have been, as a class, grievously wounded, wounded in the house of our friends," declared the aging Frederick Douglass. "I look upon it as one more shock-

---

[41]Trefousse, *The Radical Republicans,* p. 373.

ing development of that moral weakness in high places which has attended the conflict between the spirit of liberty and the spirit of slavery from the beginning. The whole essence of the thing is a studied purpose to degrade and stamp out the liberties of a race. It is the old spirit of slavery, and nothing else."[42]

As the determination of federal authority weakened, the failure of the Reconstruction governments to put a solid economic footing under black civil rights slowly allowed the free-spending Republican administrations of the old South to sink into political quicksand. Without land, the former slaves were forced into sharecropping arrangements on white-owned land that bound them into new webs of dependency on white landowners. As white economic leverage over African Americans increased, their willingness to challenge southern whites politically shrank. As it was, in none of the reconstructed states did African Americans ever have total control of the Reconstruction government, and only in South Carolina, Mississippi, and Louisiana did blacks ever gain a majority of the registered voters. Now, even those majorities began to falter, and African Americans soon learned that there were few whites left with the endurance or willingness to shore those majorities up. Southern Unionist "scalawags" had only entered into the Reconstruction alliance with misgiving, and over time, the enemies of Reconstruction were able to play on the residual loyalty of herrenvolk democracy at least enough to paralyze southern white support for black civil rights. The northern carpetbaggers were longer in their support of southern blacks, but the depression of 1873, with its catastrophic fall in world agricultural prices, ruined the economic base of the carpetbaggers and forced many of them to sell out. The Northerners who worked for the Freedmen's Bureau were gone after 1869, when Congress unwisely closed the bureau down, and the federal troops who had been stationed in the South to stiffen the resolve of the Reconstruction governments were gradually cut back by a cost-conscious Congress to only 3,000 men in 1876.

But southern whites did not wait for the Reconstruction governments to stagger to their end unaided. It would be interesting to speculate what might have happened if Andrew Johnson had obeyed his original impulse in the spring of 1865 to hang a dozen, or even more, of the Confederate leaders, since a punitive action on that scale would have decapitated the potential leadership of any future southern resistance. Instead, Johnson issued over 13,000 pardons to ex-Confederate officers and officials, and as the political resolve of President Grant and the Congress evaporated, many of the former Confederate leaders stepped forward to reassert their old roles. Sometimes, those roles involved a simple resumption of hostilities, only this time in the form of terrorism against blacks and their white Republican allies. Quasi-guerrilla movements like the Knights of the White Camelia and the Ku Klux Klan became, in effect, the armed struggle of the old southern white leadership and the southern Democrats to restore whites-only rule in the South. In

[42]Douglass, *The Life and Writings of Frederick Douglass*, Philip S. Foner, ed. (New York, 1955), vol. 4, pp. 393, 402.

a few cases, like Arkansas Unionist Governor Powell Clayton, the Reconstruction governments successfully struck back and routed the Klan. More often, it was easier to inundate Washington with demands for federal military protection—demands which, under the Grant administration, were treated with mounting annoyance as tokens that the Reconstruction governments were failures, and that it might be better to let political matters in the South take their course with a minimum of federal intervention. Playing to that concern, other southern Democrats portrayed themselves as "Redeemers," struggling to free themselves, not from blacks, but from corrupt and bribe-ridden regimes. To sweeten their image, many of the Redeemers promoted the policy of a "New Departure" in which the interests of both blacks and whites for better government would converge in the election of virtuous southern Democrats who, in public at least, had made their peace with Reconstruction.[43] Once installed, however, "Redeemer" governments turned their first attention to disenfranchising African Americans through literacy tests and poll taxes, fastening the bondage of sharecropping and indebtedness on black farmers, and eventually, by the end of the century, creating elaborate codes of "Jim Crow" laws that rigorously segregated African Americans into the poorest housing, the worst educational opportunities, and political oblivion. By the mid-1870s, black voters were being systematically intimidated away from polling places, while the uncertain courage of southern Unionists was plainly faltering. As the once-formidable Republican voter base paled and faded, the road to white Democratic Redemption lay fearfully open.

The presidential election of 1876, which pitted Republican Rutherford B. Hayes against New York Democrat Samuel J. Tilden, has generally been singled out as the end of Reconstruction. Actually, southern Redeemers had been picking off isolated Reconstruction governments all through the 1870s, until by 1876, only South Carolina, Florida, and Louisiana were still under some form of Republican rule. In the fall of 1876, the twenty-six-year-old Republican lock on the White House was closely challenged by Tilden and the promise of the Democrats to sweep away the corruptions of the Grant administration. Tilden might have won the election—in fact, should have won it, since he topped Hayes by a quarter of a million popular votes, and ought to have been awarded the 185 electoral votes needed to win—but the southern and northern wings of the Democratic party had fractured over the disposition of lucrative new harbor-clearing projects and a new transcontinental rail line that southern Democrats wanted built from Memphis and New Orleans westward through Texas. In the five politically volatile months between the election and inauguration day, Hayes and the southern Democrats patched together an electoral deal permitting the Republicans to claim favorable recounts in Louisiana, Florida, and South Carolina in exchange for the proposed "internal improvements" and a promise of noninterference by federal troops in future southern elections. On March 1, 1877, Hayes was declared president-elect by a margin of exactly one electoral vote. The next day, President Grant informed

[43]Perman, *Road to Redemption*, pp. 16–17, 58–60, 66.

the Reconstruction governments that he would no longer respond to their requests for federal troops to protect black voters.[44]

Hayes was officially inaugurated three days later, and he immediately appointed an ex-Confederate as his postmaster general, one of the most influential patronage-dispensing posts in the federal government. On April 10th, Hayes refused to intervene in the disputed South Carolina governor's election, and withdrew the federal troops that had been protecting Republican Governor Daniel Chamberlain in the state house in Columbia. Chamberlain, seeing the handwriting on the wall, conceded the election to one of Robert E. Lee's former cavalry chiefs, Wade Hampton. "Today," Chamberlain bitterly informed his disheartened black supporters, "by order of the President whom your votes alone rescued from overwhelming defeat, the Government of the United States abandons you, deliberately withdraws from you its support, with the full knowledge that the lawful government of the State will be speedily overthrown." In Mississippi, Republican ex-Governor Adalbert Ames wrote out what may serve as the epitaph of Reconstruction:

> Yes, a *revolution* has taken place—by force of arms—and a race are disenfranchised—they are to be returned to a condition of serfdom—an era of second slavery. Now it is too late. The nation should have acted but *it* was 'tired of the annual autumnal outbreaks in the South' . . . . The political death of the Negro will forever release the nation from the weariness from such 'political outbreaks.'[45]

Well, not forever. But for then, the Civil War and its era were finally over.

Further Reading

Two recent and highly illuminating studies of America's premier political murder are William Hanchett, *The Lincoln Murder Conspiracies* (Urbana, IL, 1983), which explodes much of the mythology surrounding John Wilkes Booth, and Thomas Reed Turner, *Beware the People Weeping: Public Opinion and the Assassination of Abraham Lincoln* (Baton Rouge, LA, 1982). Reconstruction also enjoys a substantial and surprisingly colorful bibliographical history. The publication of Kenneth Stampp's *The Era of Reconstruction, 1865–1877* (New York, 1965) turned on its head a century of interpretation that had accepted with little question the version of Reconstruction history portraying Reconstruction as a fanatical and utopian coup, launched by the Radical Republicans in violation of Lincoln's intentions and carried out by a hungry swarm of political vultures known as the Carpetbaggers and their incompetent black allies. Stampp sharply revised the reputation of Radicals and Carpetbaggers, and placed the entire Reconstruction effort on the high moral ground of a struggle for equal rights. Thirty years later, Stampp's terse and comparatively short book is still in many ways the best single-volume history of Reconstruction. The revisionist path blazed by Stampp has enjoyed many

[44]C. Vann Woodward, *Reunion and Reaction: The Compromise of 1877 and the End of Reconstruction* (Boston, 1951), pp. 166–169, 191–202, 216.
[45]Current, *Those Terrible Carpetbaggers*, pp. 323, 361.

followers, but none has towered so greatly above the rest as Eric Foner, whose *Reconstruction: America's Unfinished Revolution, 1863–1877* (New York, 1988) expands Stampp's focus to include wartime Reconstruction and other national political and economic developments; he also develops many of Stampp's themes from a wealth of printed and unpublished sources.

Andrew Johnson has attracted little favorable press, but he has enjoyed a number of able biographies. Albert Castel's *The Presidency of Andrew Johnson* (Lawrence, KS, 1979) and Eric L. McKitrick's *Andrew Johnson and Reconstruction* (Chicago, 1960) both offer useful surveys of Johnson's presidential policies, while Hans L. Trefousse's *Andrew Johnson: A Biography* (New York, 1989) sets him clearly in the ideological world of the Democratic party. Michael Les Benedict offers a detailed account of Johnson's impeachment in *The Impeachment and Trial of Andrew Johnson* (New York, 1973). Johnson's ill-starred attempt to impose presidential Reconstruction on the South and on Congress has been treated in Roberta Sue Alexander, *North Carolina Faces the Freedmen: Race Relations During Presidential Reconstruction, 1865–1867* (Durham, NC, 1985), and in Dan T. Carter, *When the War Was Over: The Failure of Self-Reconstruction in the South, 1865–1867* (Baton Rouge, LA, 1985), who portrays the presidential Reconstructors more sympathetically than most accounts do, but also concedes that their views and political power base were inadequate to sustain the weight of a genuine reconstruction. Johnson's successor and quondam subordinate, Ulysses Grant, has received much gentler treatment from Brooks D. Simpson in *Let Us Have Peace: Ulysses S. Grant and the Politics of War and Reconstruction, 1861–1868* (Chapel Hill, NC, 1991).

The subsequent fate of Reconstruction has been dealt with in a series of important books in the 1970s and 1980s that examined the impact of Reconstruction policies on a number of individual states, including Richard Lowe, *Republicans and Reconstruction in Virginia, 1856–1870* (Charlottesville, VA, 1991), Jerrell H. Shofner, *Nor Is It Over Yet: Florida in the Era of Reconstruction, 1863–1877* (Gainesville, FL, 1973), Elizabeth Studley Nathans, *Losing the Peace: Georgia Republicans and Reconstruction, 1865–1871* (Baton Rouge, LA, 1968), and especially William C. Harris, *The Day of the Carpetbagger: Republican Reconstruction in Mississippi* (Baton Rouge, LA, 1979), who in a revision of the revisionists treats the Redeemers' promises of an equitable racial settlement after 1877 more seriously than Stampp or Foner and blames the Republicans for their own downfall for ignoring Mississippi's domestic economic plight. The six essays collected by Otto Olsen in *Reconstruction and Redemption in the South* (Baton Rouge, LA, 1980) are also skeptical of the optimism of Reconstruction's revisionist history, and express suspicions about the genuine Radicalism of the Republicans. Louisiana's Reconstruction was the longest and most controversial, and appropriately, it has garnered a large share of Reconstruction studies, including C. Peter Ripley's *Slaves and Freedmen in Civil War Louisiana* (Baton Rouge, LA, 1976), which suggests that Radical Reconstruction accomplished comparatively little, Joseph G. Dawson's *Army Generals and Reconstruction: Louisiana, 1862–1877* (Baton Rouge, LA, 1982), and Ted Tunnell's *Crucible of Reconstruction: War, Radicalism, and Race in Louisiana, 1862–1877* (Baton Rouge, LA, 1984).

A number of the participants in Reconstruction have earned their own biographies. Richard N. Current offers an elegant and determinedly revisionist collective biography of the major southern Republicans in *Those Terrible Carpetbaggers: A Reinterpretation* (New York, 1988). Other biographies of Reconstructors, black and white, include Loren Schweninger, *James T. Rapier and Reconstruction* (Chicago, 1978), a biography of a black Alabama Republican who turned out to be something less than a Radical, William S. McFeely, *Yankee Stepfather: General O. O. Howard and the Freedmen* (New Haven, CT, 1968), and Ruth Currie-

McDaniel, *Carpetbagger of Conscience: A Biography of John Emory Bryant* (Athens, GA, 1987). The Scalawags have also enjoyed some much-needed attention in Sarah Woolfolk Wiggins's *The Scalawag in Alabama Politics, 1865–1881* (University, AL, 1977), where the Scalawags appear as an important force in the creation of Alabama Reconstruction.

African Americans were supposed to be the principal object of congressional Reconstruction policies, although in many cases, they turned out to be its chief victims. The various roles carved out by the former slaves in the Reconstruction South are examined in Leon Litwack, *Been in the Storm So Long: The Aftermath of Slavery* (New York, 1979), Barbara J. Fields, *Slavery and Freedom on the Middle Ground: Maryland During the Civil War Era* (New Haven, CT, 1985), Eric Foner, *Nothing But Freedom: Emancipation and Its Legacy* (Baton Rouge, LA, 1983), Thomas Holt, *Black Over White: Negro Political Leadership in South Carolina During Reconstruction* (Urbana, IL, 1977), and Joel Williamson, *After Slavery: The Negro in South Carolina During Reconstruction, 1861–1877* (Chapel Hill, NC, 1965).

Epilogue

 It was not until August 20, 1866, that President Andrew Johnson officially declared that the Civil War was "at an end and that peace, order, tranquility, and civil authority now exist in and throughout the whole of the United States of America." Peace certainly enough existed, at least in the sense that the organized shooting was by then long over, but tranquility was quite another matter. The federal War Department put the figures for Union army battle deaths at just over 110,000 men, with another 250,000 dying of disease, accidents, and even sunstroke; the number of wounded, which could mean anything from minor punctures to double amputation and blindness, was pegged at another 275,000. Added to the 7,000 or so navy dead and wounded, the butcher's bill for the preservation of the Union amounted to at least 640,000 dead and wounded. In practical terms, eight out of every 100 men of military age in the North died during the war, and sixteen out of every 100 who actually served perished and one out of every ten was wounded. Attached to each of these figures were widening networks of parents or dependent families that saw their breadwinners and children lost or horribly mutilated emotionally and physically by the war. By 1900, the federal government would be paying pensions to nearly one million Union veterans or their dependents in what amounted to the nation's first social security system. And the cost of the ongoing pension burden only came after the immediate costs of the war itself, which (according to one estimate in 1879) tipped the scales at just over $6 billion (or, to look at it another way, approximately $300 for every man, women, and child in the North, in an era when $300 to $500 was a reasonable workingman's annual wage). The costs to the Union were, in short, staggering beyond anyone's expectations.[1]

But these costs paled in comparison with the toll the war exacted from the Confederacy. Confederate war deaths were, in terms of overall numbers, fewer than

[1]Maris A. Vinovskis, "Have Social Historians Lost the Civil War? Some Preliminary Demographic Speculations," in *Toward a Social History of the American Civil War: Exploratory Essays*, M. A. Vinovskis, ed. (Cambridge, MA 1990), pp. 1–12, 21–28; E. B. Long, "The People of War" and "Economics of War" in *The Civil War Day-by-Day: An Almanac, 1861–1865* (New York, 1971), pp. 700–722; Claudia D. Goldin and Frank D. Lewis, "The Economic Cost of the American Civil War: Estimates and Implications," *Journal of Economic History* 35 (June 1975), pp. 299–326.

the Union's, since the Confederacy lost approximately 94,000 killed in battle while another 164,000 died of various diseases. But the Confederacy had a far smaller pool of military manpower to draw upon: Not only was the military-age population of the South smaller but it was restricted until the very end of the war to whites, so that the war cut a far wider swath through the racial power structure of the South than the numbers may at first suggest. All told, as many as nine out of every 100 available southern white men were killed. Adding to that figure the deaths from disease, this means that one out of every three Confederate soldiers never came back. It is almost impossible to estimate how many southern civilians may have died from war-related causes related to the general disruption. What is certain is that up to four-fifths of the prewar southern economy vanished into the smoke that hung over the devastated Confederacy. Of the $7.2 billion worth of southern property listed in the 1860 census, $2.4 billion existed in the form of slaves, which were the chief capital investment of cotton agriculture. The Emancipation Proclamation and the Thirteenth Amendment simply erased the slave assets of the South, while the money that Southerners had converted into Confederate bonds and notes disappeared the moment it became clear that the United States government had no intention of assuming any part of the Confederate government's debt obligations. Added to the disappearance of these assets was the sheer physical destruction caused by the unorganized plunder and wreckage of Confederate impressment officers and Yankee foragers. As much as 43 percent of the South's nonslave agricultural assets were destroyed by the war: a third of the cattle horses and mules of the South were gone, and southern farm values fell by half. In Alabama, per capita wealth among white farmers fell to one-sixth of what it had been in 1860; in Georgia, one-quarter of the state's rail lines were piles of useless, twisted iron, $272 million in slave assets were gone, and the state controller general helplessly estimated that "almost four-fifths of the entire wealth of Georgia had been destroyed or rendered unproductive."[2] By 1870, the accumulated value of all southern property stood at only $2.05 billion, which means (after wartime inflation is factored in) that the war cost the South betwen five and eight billion dollars.

The northern economy, by contrast, found itself driven forward and upward by the war, although not quite in the ways that later observers described and certainly not in a uniform fashion. In a major northern urban center like Philadelphia, the economic impact of secession and government war contracts was broad rather than deep. Some Philadelphia manufacturers made sizeable personal profits out of war contracting. But the overall structure of the Philadelphia economy, not to mention its politics, underwent little reorganization during the war. In Chicago, however, the city's meat-packing industry tripled in size between 1861 and 1863 as Chicago

[2]Eric Foner, *Reconstruction: America's Unfinished Revolution, 1863–1877* (New York, 1988), pp. 125, 129; Mary A. DeCredico, *Patriotism for Profit: Georgia's Urban Entrepreneurs and the Confederate War Effort* (Chapel Hill, NC, 1990), p. 115; Douglas B. Ball, *Financial Failure and Confederate Defeat* (Urbana, IL, 1991), pp. 300–301.

contractors assumed the burden of shipping immense amounts of pork and beef to the western armies. That growth flushed huge waves of new tax money into the city coffers, and led to the reorganization of the tax and ward system of the city, and ultimately, to Chicago's famous "machine" politics. The war also helped lay the foundations for New York City's "machine" politics and the rise of William Marcy ("Boss") Tweed (the leader of Tammany Hall) by undermining the traditional authority of city Democratic politicians and making way for Tweed's masterfully efficient brand of municipal corruption. Even in Pennsylvania's rural Chester County, the war multiplied land values and boosted the Phoenix Iron Works in Phoenixville to a competitive level with British ironmakers. But it also starved to death the cotton and woolen mills that had been the original foundation of northern rural industry in the first half of the 19th century, and wiped out the small-scale iron mills that once occupied the banks of Chester County's Brandywine Creek.[3] As much as northern industrial might was vital to providing the weight of arms and material that gave the Union armies victory, much of its astounding output was channeled to the production of wartime articles, from siege guns to buttons, which had no peacetime value or market and which disappeared once the war was over.

If there was any segment of northern industry that enjoyed a boost from the war, it was the railroads. No single technological innovation of the 19th century was dearer to the heart of Whig republicanism than the railroad, and no industry meant more to the support of the armies than the private railroad companies that Stanton harnessed to the Union war effort. With the Democratic presence in Congress crippled by the withdrawal of the southern Democrats in 1861, the Republicans sparked a massive series of federally underwritten railroad projects, beginning in 1862 with the chartering of the Union Pacific and Central Pacific corporations to build a transcontinental line. This was followed in 1864 by the chartering of the Northern Pacific, another transcontinental line to run from Lake Superior to the Puget Sound, the Atlantic and Pacific in 1866, and the Texas Pacific in 1871. All told, the federal government handed the rail corporations 158 million acres in public lands and over $64 million in federal bonds to underwrite construction. By the 1870s, one-third of all the iron being manufactured in the United States was going into rails.[4] The same story was repeated on the state level, especially in the South where the southern rail system was forced to rebuild even what little it had started out with in 1861. That, in turn, created a host of large-scale subsidiary industries in machines and tools that helped make the great

---

[3] J. Matthew Gallman, Mastering Wartime: A Social History of Philadelphia During the Civil War (New York, 1990), pp. 299–328; Robin L. Einhorn, "The Civil War and Municipal Government in Chicago," in Toward a Social History of the American Civil War, pp. 132–138; Iver Bernstein, The New York City Draft Riots: Their Significance for American Society and Politics in the Age of the Civil War (New York, 1990), pp. 195–196; Douglas R. Harper, If Thee Must Fight: A Civil War History of Chester County, Pennsylvania (West Chester, PA, 1990), pp. 363–367.

[4] Louis M. Hacker, The Triumph of American Capitalism: The Development of Forces in American History to the End of the Nineteenth Century (New York, 1947), pp. 370–371.

ironworks (like Phoenix) immensely profitable, but that left the small-scale prewar mills dropping ever farther behind.

And yet, even the boost given to the railroads by the war was tangential rather than direct; it was not so much the war as the free hand a Republican Congress was given in 1862 to fund railroad construction, which put new sources of wealth behind the railroad industry, and any other excuse to override Democratic opposition to such "internal improvements" would probably have produced the same result. It was not northern industry or the northern railroads that benefited most from the war so much as it was northern agriculture and northern finance. The outbreak of the war and its demands for foodstuffs neatly coincided with the mass introduction in the late 1840s and 1850s of mechanical seeders, steel plows, and the McCormick reaper, and the potent combination of wartime demand and machine-based productive capacity combined to swell the production of northern wheat and oats by 35 percent, northern wool by 66 percent, and northern potatoes by 28 percent; exports of wheat, even during the war, doubled during the war years over the prewar export levels, as did exports of pork and corn. Moreover, northern wartime price inflation helped northern farmers pay off their land indebtedness with cheap greenbacks and doubled land values in major western states like Illinois and Iowa.[5]

Northern financiers benefited in even more remarkable ways. The seven Democratic administrations that straddled the first six decades of the 19th century, by holding the government's role in the economy strictly to exchanges of hard coin, had given little if any encouragement to the development of American finance, and a good deal of the capitalization of American industry in the 1820s and 1830s had to be imported from abroad. But the war and the Republicans changed that: The threat of civil war drove foreign investors off the American securities market and allowed American investors to step into the vacuum; the Republicans dismissed the Democrats' abiding suspicion of the financial markets and took the nation off the gold standard; and the immense amounts of money needed to carry on the war created a new class of financiers— bankers, insurers, brokers like Jay Cooke—who dealt in unprecedented volumes of cash, goods, and securities. The creation of the national banking system in 1863, and the subsequent disappearance of state bank currencies from northern circulation, helped to further centralize massive financial power in the hands of a few financiers.[6]

Nonetheless, these entries on the profit side of the war's ledger were mottled with failures and ambiguities. Northern finance quickly outstripped the capacity of the federal government to oversee and regulate it, and the financial community soon found itself agitating for a return to the gold standard, not to restrain the

[5]Paul W. Gates, *Agriculture and the Civil War* (New York, 1965), pp. 375–377; Hacker, *American Capitalism*, pp. 398–399.

[6]Richard F. Bensel, *Yankee Leviathan: The Origins of Central State Authority in America, 1859–1877* (New York, 1990), pp. 241, 252, 282.

freewheeling dealings of the financial markets, but to slow down currency inflation and attach the markets to a standard independent of federal control. This meant, in effect, returning the United States to its dependence on the international flow of specie, especially through the hands of British financiers, and when the British financial markets failed in 1873, they carried Jay Cooke and the other American financiers down with them. The general fall in international prices hit agriculture the hardest, and the farmers who had rashly expanded westward on the balloon of increased wartime production and cost-free homesteading now suddenly found themselves tied to distant markets where their goods sold for less and less. Lincoln and the Republicans had feared the threat of a propertyless urban proletariat, but neither he nor the other Republicans could have guessed in the 1860s that the farmers and homesteaders whom they had opened the western territories to would also become the seedbed for successive waves of fear, frustration, and populist agitation. The territories had been kept safe from slavery, but they had not been kept safe from the fluctuations of the market. This does not mean, however, that an urban proletariat failed to materialize. The new large-scale industries that were either created by the war, or created by the new finance capitalists whom the war spun off, drew more inexpensive immigrant labor through America's ports than the territories could absorb. Annual immigration, which in 1860 amounted to approximately 150,000 people, had swelled by 1880 to 450,000 per year, and the urban centers of the industrializing North gradually turned into the dependent, wage-earning metropolitan ant heaps that republican ideology had long feared.

That ideology may well have been one of the principal casualties of the Civil War. "The deepest irony" of the war, writes British historian Peter Parish, lies in the fact that "the Northern victors in the war believed for the most part that they had succeeded in protecting an economic and social system . . . of small units, individual enterprise, and open opportunity," but instead the war actually fostered "a new industrial society of complex technology, huge mills and factories, giant corporations and teeming cities."[7] Although Lincoln had spoken optimistically at Gettysburg about how the war would spark a renewed dedication to republicanism, the sheer scale of bigness that it generated made nonsense of the small-producer ethic upon which Lincoln's Whig Republicanism was based. "The truth is that Lincoln was no prophet of a distant day," commented Helen Nicolay in 1912, drawing on the store of wartime reminiscences gathered up by her father, John Nicolay, Lincoln's personal secretary. "His early life was essentially of the old era. He made his own career by individual effort."[8] The war created a scale of commerce, and then government involvement in support of commerce, and then corruption, that made mockery of careers built on the small-producer republican ethic of "individual effort." Once called into being, the mass organizational structures the Civil War created and apprenticed a generation of Americans to replicated themselves in

[7]Peter Parish, *The American Civil War* (New York, 1975), pp. 631–632.
[8]Helen Nicolay, *Personal Traits of Abraham Lincoln* (New York, 1912), pp. 381–382.

everything from the mass production of meat (which Philip Armour helped develop out of wartime contracts in Chicago) to the giant Corliss steam engine that powered the 1876 Centennial Fair in Philadelphia's Fairmount Park. Even the good Whig intentions embodied in the homesteading and banking acts galloped swiftly out of the control of the bewildered Republican politicians. They produced, in the process, almost all the results that Democratic nay-sayers from Andrew Jackson onward had predicted would be the end result of Whiggism, and the Liberal Republican alliance with the Democrats in 1872 was in large part a confession that the staggering new scales of labor and production the war had erected made prewar slogans about free soil, free labor, and free men sound quaint rather than compelling. After the war, "I found that I had got back to another world," said the title character of William Dean Howells' novel *The Rise of Silas Lapham*. "The day of small things was past, and I don't suppose it will ever come again in this country." As uneasy Republicans like Howells (who had written Abraham Lincoln's 1860 campaign biography) contrasted the immense profits reaped by postwar financiers and industrialists with the rising numbers of wage laborers whose hope for economic independence grew dimmer and dimmer as wage rates fell after 1873, there seemed less and less substance in Lincoln's old axiom about workers working for others one year, then working for themselves on their own farms or in their own shops the next, and then employing other up-and-coming workers the year after. Not free labor and independent ownership, but "industrial feudalism" (in James Garfield's phase) now looked like the future.[9]

The choice facing the Republicans was whether to dig in and resist the new industrial economy of scale they had helped to father, or find in it enough resemblance to the old self-disciplined ethic of Whiggism to permit accommodation. The first alternative would have driven them back into the arms of Andrew Jackson; they chose the latter, and so the successive Republican administrations that (except for the two presidential interregnums of Grover Cleveland) dominated the federal government slowly became inextricably bound up with the expansion and privileges of American industrial capitalism. In the same year that Hayes's Republican administration allowed the Reconstruction governments to fall, that same administration unequivocally committed itself and the troops it could not spare for the South to the suppression of a railway labor uprising. This, in turn, created a pattern of assimilation between the federal government and industrial capitalism that reached its high point in the Pullman Strike of 1894, which saw Cleveland, a Democratic president, commit federal troops to the destruction of an even greater railway strike on the slim pretext that it endangered the U.S. mail system. The rhetoric of the republican ideology, which had guided American political discourse since the founding of the republic, dropped mysteriously from the currency of both Republicans

[9]Foner, *Reconstruction*, pp. 477, 488–493, 497; Morton Keller, *Affairs of State: Public Life in Late Nineteenth-Century America* (New York, 1977), p. 185; Richard Hofstadter, *The American Political Tradition and the Men Who Made It* (New York, 1948, 1973), pp. 105–106.

and Democrats in the "Gilded Age." In place of the old Whig-Democrat juxtaposition of liberty and power, a new political tension arose, more in touch with the new economic realities of the postwar era, which pitted "democracy" (economic egalitarianism) against "free markets" (laissez-faire economic individualism). And when, in 1929, the international network of capitalist finance collapsed in an even more horrifying depression than the catastrophe of 1873, the Republican party went into an ideological shock from which it has never entirely recovered. In this sense, free-labor Republicanism lost the Civil War as surely as slaveholding Democrats. The creation of a national capitalist hegemony, built from urban-based, unregulated industry, was not what Lincoln had in mind when he prophesied the coming of a nation of self-made artisans and professionals.[10]

The confusion of purpose that the palsy of republicanism created led to a larger confusion in the postwar years over the purpose of the war and the way it should be remembered. The veterans of the Union armies quickly melted back into the civilian population with a minimum of tension, separating into the spectrum of class and occupation they had temporarily left behind. But in the 1880s, their anxiety over the new social order and the effacement of the old republican ideology led to the extraordinary rebirth of the Grand Army of the Republic, a fraternal organization originally founded in 1866 but which now became one of the principal refuges for old soldiers who had fought for a very different world than the one they found growing about their ears. In over 7,000 G.A.R. posts across the United States, former soldiers once more forgot their class identities in a bath of sentimental memory, reestablished a ritualized camp geography in the post buildings, and preached the fading glories of manly independence and disinterested republican virtue. Likewise, the northern evangelicals, who had so confidently anticipated a republican millennium at the end of the war, now retreated before the intellectual onslaught of Darwin and the "Social Darwinism" that so conveniently apologized for the social and economic inequities of American capitalism. Some, like Dwight L. Moody and John Wanamaker, struggled to harmonize Christ and capitalism; others, like Walter Rauschenbusch, rejected capitalism but lost the classic evangelical hold on Christ; many more, like Jonathan Blanchard of Wheaton, withdrew behind the private ramparts of religious institutions and coded their religious republicanism in what became known to 20th-century Americans as "fundamentalism." As they did so, work and careers in the massive new industrial order replaced religion as the central definition of American personality, and self-interest and individual satisfaction nudged the Edwardsean passion for disinterested benevolence into the wings.[11]

[10]Eric Foner, *Politics and Ideology in the Age of the Civil War* (New York, 1980), pp. 32–33, 124–125; Nell I. Painter, *Standing at Armageddon: The United States, 1877–1919* (New York, 1987), pp. xvii–xliv.

[11]Stuart McConnell, *Glorious Contentment: The Grand Army of the Republic, 1865–1900* (Chapel Hill, NC, 1992), pp. 85–118; Anne C. Rose, *Victorian American and The Civil War* (New York, 1992), pp. 68–78.

Southerners also struggled with the meanings of the war. The spectacle of President Johnson's public combat with the Radical Republicans awoke defeated white Southerners to the realization that the northern war effort was a coalition, not a monolithic antisouthern movement, and that within the coalition, moderate and Radical Republicans, War Democrats, abolitionists, free blacks, and colonizationists stood together mainly because the South had forced them to an inalterable choice between the Union and slavery. Some parts of this coalition were quite satisfied once the Union had been secured and cared little or nothing about the future of the African American. It was the genius of the Redeemers to realize that the path toward the restoration of white supremacy and Jacksonian democracy in the South lay in splitting that coalition. To that end the Redeemer governments advertised themselves as benign representatives of a "New South" who would relieve the North of the burden of Reconstruction and black civil rights, a burden that the Redeemers rightly suspected that most Northerners never really wanted to shoulder in the first place, and one they had accepted because the only alternative to Reconstruction any of them knew was the slave regime of the old South. The New South mythology, which burst into full flower in the 1880s, worked to allay northern concern that the abandonment of Reconstruction was tantamount to a reversal of Appomattox. Proponents of the New South first asserted that it was southern concern for its unique sectional identity and not slavery that had been the cause of secession, and then assured Northerners that the South had learned its lesson and was willing to embrace the northern economic order and judge itself by northern standards. The first assertion allowed New Southers to suggest that race was not, after all, the main concern of the war; the second allowed them to suggest that the North and the federal government could safely let the South govern its own affairs, political as well as racial.[12] In his famous 1886 speech to the New England Society of New York, Henry Grady, the 36-year-old editor of the Atlanta Constitution, promised that, as the New South "stands upright, full-statured and equal among the people of the earth," it will understand "that her emancipation came because through the inscrutable wisdom of God her honest purpose was crossed, and her brave armies beaten." As Southerners reflected on the war, declared Grady, they were now "glad that the omniscient God held the balance of battle in His Almighty hand and that . . . the American Union was saved from the wreck of war."[13]

There were two serious problems with the New South image, one of which was that many Southerners were unwilling to make even this much of a concession for the sake of Redemption, and the other of which was that much of it simply wasn't true. Far from bravely admitting that the South was wrong and asking to be trusted

[12]Richard M. McMurry, "The War We Never Finished," in Civil War Times Illustrated 28 (November/ December 1989), pp. 62–71.
[13]Grady, "The New South," in J. Chandler Harris, Life of Henry W. Grady, Including His Writings and Speeches (New York, 1890), pp. 82–93.

again for that honesty, many ex-Confederates and unreconstructed Democrats in-sisted that they had been right all along and that they hadn't the faintest interest in asking northern pardon for any of it. "Had we been true to our God and country," wrote Kate Cumming, "with all the blessings of this glorious, sunny land, I believe we could have kept the North, with all her power, at bay for twenty years."[14] This countermythology of the so-called "Lost Cause" (the term was coined by Edward Pollard in 1866) defended the old order, including slavery (on the grounds of white supremacy), and in Pollard's case, even predicted that the superior virtues of the old South would cause it to rise ineluctably from the ashes of its unworthy defeat. "Civil wars, like private quarrels, are likely to repeat themselves, where the unsuccessful party has lost the contest only through accident or inadvertence," Pollard defiantly wrote. "The Confederates have gone out of this war, with the proud, secret, deathless, *dangerous* consciousness that they are THE BETTER MEN, and that there was nothing wanting but a change in a set of circumstances and a firmer resolve to make them the victors."[15] While the New Southers tried to promote sectional reconciliation, and staged carefully orchestrated reunions of "the Blue and the Gray" at Gettysburg in 1888, 1913, and 1938, the devotees of the Lost Cause spurned such gestures, and staged observances of Jefferson Davis's birthday, orga-nized the United Confederate Veterans and the United Daughters of the Confeder-acy, and paraded the slashed red Confederate battle flag down dusty southern streets on one Confederate Memorial Day after another. Jubal Early, who may stand as the single most unreconstructed rebel of them all, refused even to contribute funds to a monument to Robert E. Lee in Richmond when he learned that the pedestal would be carved from Maine granite.[16]

A far greater difficulty in making a case for the New South was the persistent and intractable backwardness of the southern economy. To be sure, not everything about the post-Reconstruction South was necessarily a step backwards: Republicans continued to hold onto some southern counties and districts for decades after the end of Reconstruction, and in a number of places African Americans continued to vote, and (thanks to the patronage appointments of successive Republican presi-dents) to hold federal offices in the South. And in further defense of the New Southers, it was also true that the southern states welcomed with undisguised relief the influx of northern railroaders, miners, and loggers who fanned out across the South in the 1880s and 1890s as the mining and timber reserves of the far West were gradually depleted. Southern women retained a greater number of the social freedoms that the war had put in their path for longer than their northern counter-

---

[14]Kate Cumming, *Kate: The Journal of a Confederate Nurse*, R. B. Harwell, ed. (Baton Rouge, LA, 1959), p. 292.

[15]Pollard, *The Lost Cause: A New Southern History of the War of the Confederates* (New York, 1867), p. 729.

[16]Michael Kammen, *Mystic Chords of Memory: The Transformation of Tradition in American Culture* (New York, 1991), pp. 102–121.

parts, including a greater freedom to work and to run businesses. But all the same, not even the most optimistic New Southers could deny for long that the South remained an economic backwater—that its experiments in developing domestic steel and iron industries were a failure, that its networks of postwar textile mills were built on the exploitation of uprooted white workers, most of whom were women and children, that its lumbering industry mostly fed the commercial appetites of the North and left southern hillsides wasted and denuded, that southern per capita income in 1900 still stood at only half that of the rest of the nation. Above all, they could not deny the ugly fact of racial injustice. From the 1880s onward, the post-Reconstruction white governments grew unwilling to rely just on intimidation and violence to keep African Americans away from the ballot box and themselves in power, and turned instead to systematic legal disenfranchisement. And recognizing the close intersection of economic status and political power, southern state governments gradually imposed rigorous segregations of black and white that ensured that blacks would receive the scantiest education, occupy only the second-class railway cars and the bottom rung of the economic ladder. In the broadest sense, segregation apportioned the towns and the cities to whites, and the fields to blacks, and bound blacks to an agricultural peonage—whether in the form of share-cropping or debt tenancy—that smothered the resourcefulness and economic potential of three-fifths of the southern population. In the name of white supremacy, the South marginalized itself.[17]

Behind the facade of reconciliation and racial paternalism that the New Southers erected, there was far more common ground between the New South and the Lost Cause than either of its proponents was eager to admit. Both, for instance, seized on Robert E. Lee and canonized him after his death in 1870 as a kind of Protestant saint.[18] For the New Southers, Lee's dignified surrender of the Army of Northern Virginia was a model of Christian fortitude in the face of disaster. And then, in the years following Appomattox, his willingness to help rebuild Washington College, a war-shattered Virginia educational institution, as the college's first postwar president set yet another example of patience and hope. And to add charity to the lengthening list of Lee's virtues, the New Southers warmed to Lee's repeated exhortations to young Virginia men to put the war behind them and cultivate the arts of peace. All of these pieces of Lee's character seemed to underscore the determination of the South to face the future as part of the reunited American nation. It also gave white Northerners a Southerner of commanding nobility whom they could admire as a fellow American, thus inviting Yankees to forget the violence of the war in a haze of national and white racial brotherhood. By 1900, national magazines were admiring

[17]Edward Ayer, *The Promise of the New South: Life After Reconstruction* (New York, 1992), pp. 8, 37, 42, 77, 146, 102–104, 110–111, 137–146; Paul Gaston, *The New South Creed: A Study in Southern Mythmaking* (New York, 1970, 1973), pp. 202–203.

[18]Thomas L. Connelly, *The Marble Man: Robert E. Lee and His Image in American Society* (New York, 1977), p. 95.

Lee as "the pride of the whole country," and a writer in *Harper's Weekly* was amazed to find "that the American people at the beginning of the twentieth century would be claiming Robert E. Lee . . . as the pride of the whole country." But Lee also played a vital role in the mythology of the Lost Cause. Neither Cumming nor Pollard had an easy answer to why, if the southern armies had contained "THE BETTER MEN," God had let the South lose to the grasping, mercenary, and infidel Northerners. In Lee, they found a solution, for Lee's courageous and humble bearing showed them that suffering might be a nobler calling than victory, and that the South could claim through Lee that it had surrendered, not to superior political morality, but only to superior numbers.[19] In the face of an aggressive and domineering northern capitalism that the Lost Cause had no intention of capitulating to, Southerners found in Lee a sanction for economic backwardness. In time, not only Lee but even the Confederate battle flag was invested with new, less rigid meanings, and it gradually evolved into a symbol of southern regional pride and rebellious American individualism, rather than the militant defense of slavery and secession.

It is these confusions of meaning and disappointment of intentions that help explain why the Civil War occupies so small a representative space in American high culture. The American Civil War never gave birth to a national epic, an American *War and Peace,* and with the exception of Stephen Crane's psychological novella, *The Red Badge of Courage,* and Ambrose Bierce's frighteningly bitter short stories, America's major writers in the postwar period passed the Civil War by on the other side. Although the published output of Civil War–related novels and stories is fairly considerable, their strength lies in their sheer quantity rather than their quality. Kathleen Diffley's survey of sixteen popular American magazines betwen 1861 and 1876 turned up over 300 short stories connected with the war, but hardly any of them were memorable and almost all of them were devoted to themes of reconciliation, redemption, and compassion rather than the unresolved conflicts or terrors of the war.[20] American poets seemed moved by the war only for the production of banality, like John Greenleaf Whittier's "Barbara Frietchie" in *In War Time* (1864) or Thomas Buchanan Reid's "Sheridan's Ride." Only Walt Whitman, among the American poets of the Civil War era, wrote wartime verse in *Drum-Taps* (1865) and *Sequel to Drum-Taps* (1865–1866) capable of piercing the façade of romance and glory without indulging a cheap pacifism. Not until the 1920s did Stephen Vincent Benét come the closest of any American poet to creating, in *John Brown's Body* (which won the Pulitzer Prize in 1929), an Iliad for the Civil War. Similarly, Civil War–related art rarely rose above the technical level of newspaper illustration, and only a handful of genuinely extraordinary paintings from Winslow Homer, Xanthus R. Smith, Conrad Wise Chap-

[19]Thomas Connelly and Barbara Bellows, *God and General Longstreet: The Lost Cause and the Southern Mind* (Baton Rouge, LA, 1982), pp. 73–75, 82–83.
[20]Kathleen Diffley, *Where My Heart Is Turning Ever: Civil War Stories and Constitutional Reform, 1861–1876* (Athens, GA, 1992), pp. 5, 76.

man, and Gilbert Gaul are available to compete with the far vaster output of American artwork on the urban North and the cowboy West. As Harold Holzer and Mark Neely have recently remarked, "No Civil War painting yet uncovered responded to the opportunity to show the nightmare of war." Civil War art was obsessed with portraying battles and leaders of the war in a glow of outdated Napoleonic glory as some of those same leaders had been conducting the war by Napoleon's rules. And like the soldiers, the artists "failed in any way to suggest the demise of individual courage as a significant battle factor."[21]

The single greatest collection of cultural artifacts tossed up by the war was its popular music, and many of the Civil War's tunes—Daniel Emmett's "Dixie," Julia Ward Howe's "The Battle Hymn of the Republic," George Root's "The Battle Cry of Freedom," Patrick Gilmore's "When Johnny Comes Marching Home," and Henry Clay Work's "Marching Through Georgia" and the rollicking "Kingdom Comin' "— are still so sturdy and recognizable that they instantly conjure up associations with the Civil War. But once the arena of popular music is left behind, there is very little of the war to be heard in American music: Charles Ives toyed with Civil War melodic fragments, and worked "The Battle Cry of Freedom" into a particularly heart-rending moment in his *Three Places in New England,* and Aaron Copland set the words of Lincoln against the heroic background of his *A Lincoln Portrait.* Beyond that, only a handful of occasional pieces, a stray symphony here, a choral arrangement there, even notice the Civil War. Ironically, the most recurrent artistic shape the Civil War took was statuary, some of it—like Augustus St. Gaudens's memorial on Boston Common to Robert Gould Shaw and the 54th Massachusetts—is work of awesome emotion and real genius; but by and large, the Civil War monument has been treated more as a joke than a genre. Along the same lines, the dearth of great Civil War fiction has never been overshadowed by the immense production of Civil War regimental histories, a quirky and revealing species of nonfiction with a virtually unique place in American letters, but one which American literary critics have yet to notice. Even Edmund Wilson's *Patriotic Gore,* the most famous study of American Civil War–related literature, makes no allusion to the regimental histories that blossomed in far greater numbers after the 1880s than the novels and memoirs upon which he lavished so much attention.

Much of this neglect is an extension of American uncertainty about the questions the war was fought over and the answers it was supposed to have given. A war that began for the sake of restoring the American Union turned, and with less unanimity and less orderliness than expected, into a war to broaden the definition of republicanism beyond the barriers of race by destroying a racially based system of bondage and raising the bondspeople to civil equality with the rest of the republic. And then after 1865 it inexplicably turned back again into a contest for national

---

[21]Roger G. Kennedy, "Mourning a National Casualty," in *Civil War Times Illustrated* 27 (March 1988), pp. 34–38, 45–46; Holzer and Neely, *Mine Eyes Have Seen the Glory: The Civil War in Art* (New York, 1993), p. 306.

reunion, with the settlement of racial equality left dangling in the air. The Civil War was not a revolution, unless the word *revolution* is to be used indiscriminately to describe any critical moment of change, because what was at stake was not a rebellion against republicanism but a struggle to expand its meaning. North and South, Democrat and Republican, considered themselves in 1861 to be republicans, and the Confederacy did not imagine that it was imperiling republicanism by breaking up the Union. Democratic republicanism had always glorified localism and private independence as the essence of the republican ideology. But localism alone would not have triggered civil war—at least not in America in the 19th century, where the kind of localism that could really set peoples' teeth on edge had hardly had breathing room to take root—and that was why the goals of the war and the redefinition of republicanism had to become a northern war aim if the North was ever to prevail. It was the exercise of slave labor, sharpened by the hateful whettings of racism, that inspired such ardent defenses of Democratic principles, and which made the shattering of a republican Union thinkable.

The press of war briefly brought that fact into clear focus for a number of Northerners and Southerners alike. But once the war was over, the soft tidal return of racial mythologies robbed the war of its most ambitious meaning. And ignoring the centrality of race consigned subsequent interpretations of the war to futility. Without the canker of race, there would never have been slavery in the South as late as 1861; without race, there would have been no argument over the territories and no need for the fatal game of balances; without race, there would have been no Redeemers, no segregation, none of the monumental injustice of one human being to another that made foolishness of American claims over the next century that it was going to save the world for democracy. That Americans failed to face up to this after the war doomed Reconstruction, just as it doomed almost every attempt by American writers and artists to tell an epic story whose meaning they could not fathom and could only fear. The closest one comes in American literature to a frank appreciation of race as the hidden issue of the Civil War is not in the writings of the northern victors, but in the galaxy of great 20th-century southern novelists, from William Faulkner to Walker Percy. Although none of these writers wrote directly about the Civil War, the war and its aftermath hang thick in the atmosphere of the South they describe. Faulkner's Gavin Stephens, in *Intruder in the Dust*, assures his nephew that

> For every Southern boy fourteen years old, not once but whenever he wants it, there is the instant when it's still not yet two o'clock on that July afternoon in 1863, the brigades are in position behind the rail fence, the guns are laid and ready in the woods and the furled flags are already loosened to break out and Pickett himself with his long oiled ringlets and his hat in one hand probably and his sword in the other looking up the hill waiting for Longstreet to give the word and it's all in the balance, it hasn't happened yet, it hasn't even begun yet, it not only hasn't begun yet but there is still time for it not to begin against that position and those circumstances. . . .[22]

[22]Faulkner, *Intruder in the Dust* (New York, 1948), p. 194.

And all of them acknowledge the poisonous role that race has played in the construction of a southern mentality. Race was the great ulcer of the southern innards, wrote Walker Percy, the South's unending shirt of flame,

> . . . and hasn't it always been that way ever since the first tough God-believing, Christ-haunted, cunning violent rapacious Visigoth-Western-Gentile first set foot here with the first black man, the one willing to risk everything, take all or lose all, the other willing just to wait and outlast because sooner or later the first would wake up and know that he had flunked, been proved a liar where he lived, and no man can live with that. And sooner or later the lordly Visigoth-Western-Gentile-Christian-Americans would have to falter, fall out, turn upon themselves like scorpions in a bottle.[23]

By contrast, northern literature fled from the war and from race: Longfellow, Lowell, and Whittier can all be read without much inkling that they had lived through an immense crisis in American republicanism, or any inkling at all that it had something to do with race. Instead, northern writers consumed themselves in an iconoclastic frenzy that ended in the 1920s with their wholesale exile and alienation—Henry James (whose brother served as an officer in the 54th Massachusetts), Fitzgerald, Hemingway—from American society.[24]

There were other Northerners who, like the bitter-enders of the Lost Cause, managed to cling resolutely to the visions they had seen written in burnished rows of steel. The Grand Army of the Republic angrily rejected all the appeals for reconciliation issued by the New Southers and energetically condemned the defiant hostility of the Lost Cause. They harshly criticized public displays of the Confederate flag, resisting any attempt to transform its meaning into a national symbol, and when the G.A.R. began to suspect in the 1890s that schoolbook publishers were toning down their accounts of the Civil War to accommodate southern views and promote southern sales, it mounted a campaign to bring its gray-haired members into public school classes to tell the story of the war as they had experienced it. In 1937, when the United Confederate Veterans gently extended an invitation to the G.A.R. to join it in what amounted to the last great Blue and Gray reunion at Gettysburg, the ninety-year-old veterans at the G.A.R.'s 71st Encampment in Madison, Wisconsin, were adamant that no displays of the Confederate battle flag be permitted. "No rebel colors," they shouted, "What sort of compromise is that for Union soldiers but hell and damnation."[25] An even more resolute objection came from Frederick Douglass, who fought virtually to his dying day in 1895 to keep the eyes of Americans fixed firmly on his vision of a war that had been fought for freedom and not just Union. "We

---

[23]Percy, *Love in The Ruins: The Adventures of a Bad Catholic at a Time Near the End of the World* (New York, 1971, 1989), p. 49.

[24]Thomas Fleming, "The Civil War and American Destiny," in *National Review* (November 6, 1987), pp. 48–53.

[25]Stan Cohen, *Hands Across the Wall: The 50th and 75th Reunions of the Gettysburg Battle* (Charleston, WV, 1982), p. 40.

are sometimes asked in the name of patriotism to forget the merits of this fearful struggle," Douglass declared in 1871, "and to remember with equal admiration those who struck at the nation's life, and those who struck to save it—those who fought for slavery and those who fought for liberty and justice." He would have nothing of it. "I am no minister of hate," he concluded, "but . . . may my tongue cleave to the roof of my mouth if I forget the difference between the parties to that . . . bloody conflict." It was repentance and not reconciliation that Douglass wanted from the South. "The South has a past not to be contemplated with pleasure, but with a shudder," he wrote in 1870. "She has been selling agony, trading in blood and in the souls of men. If her past has any lesson, it is one of repentance and thorough reformation." More than a decade later, Douglass was still not satisfied: "Whatever else I may forget, I shall never forget the difference between those who fought to save the Republic and those who fought to destroy it."[26]

Douglass might not have forgotten, but others did. The G.A.R., to its shame, bent to northern racism and segregated its posts, and in too many cities in too many Memorial Day parades, black veterans were forced to march in the rear, behind the white veterans.[27] The loss of meaning that Douglass feared is the final tragedy in an era of tragedies, and it took Americans another century and the experience of struggle with tyrannies far more frightening in scale to recapture the opportunities and dimensions of what was won and what was lost in the Civil War era. But because the Americans of those years strayed off the path they might have trod at the end of the war—that path that Lincoln and Douglass, and even Lee and Davis, knew lay toward racial hope and civil justice—does not mean that the Civil War is merely a tragedy. In 1886, the survivors of Battery B of the First New Jersey Artillery gathered together at Gettysburg with the other survivors of the 3rd Corps of the Army of the Potomac to stroll over the battlefield and visit the graves of the battery's dead in the national cemetery that Lincoln had dedicated twenty-three years before. One elderly man in Battery B's group, who had lost his son at Gettysburg, listened as the old battery mates stood by the boy's grave and "praised his boy's pleasant ways, genial, kindly disposition, and brave deeds." The man was unconsoled. "My boy, my boy, O God, why did you take my boy? He was all I had," he sobbed. It was one of the wives of the ex-artillerymen who at last took the old man by the arm and turned him toward the flag on the cemetery flagstaff: "Your boy died for that flag, and while this nation endures his deeds will never be forgotten. When you and I are dead, patriots, standing where we are now, will remember his name and fame."[28] It was a beautiful and quintessentially Victorian moment of nationalistic melodrama, but it under-

[26]David W. Blight, Frederick Douglass' Civil War: Keeping Faith in Jubilee (Baton Rouge, LA, 1989), pp. 222–223, 239.

[27]Joseph T. Glatthaar, Forged in Battle: The Civil War Alliance of Black Soldiers and White Officers (New York, 1990), p. 264.

[28]Michael Hanifen, History of Battery B, First New Jersey Artillery (1905; rept. Highstown, NJ, 1991), pp. 82–83.

scores a point often missed in the terrible toll of the Civil War's might-have-beens, and that is that the republic *survived*. It was not the same republic by 1886, and in the age of industrial empire that followed, the republican ideology that Lincoln had given its last full measure of devotion in the Gettysburg Address would be transformed into a new political language of democracy and markets. But it was still a republic.

And it was a united republic, undivided by sectionalism even if its unity was marred by racism. And it would be that unity that eight decades later would be almost all that stood between civilization and the universal midnight of Nazism, and the same unity that a hundred years later would finally rise up to hear Martin Luther King, Jr., summon a nation back to the unfinished work of justice and equality. The notion that the states had made the Union and could withdraw from it at will was dead and gone forever, and no better evidence of that exists than the disappearance, after 1865, of the word *Union* from the ordinary American's political lexicon, and its replacement by the single term *nation*. And slavery was gone, too, and though other forms of injustice would come and go, at least that most egregious contradiction of a republic of liberty was erased for good. In fact, as postwar industrialization made independence less and less likely for the American working class, liberty came to be identified with equality, and the Civil War became the moment when egalitarianism and not virtue or property became the chief component of American political freedom.

Whatever else the Civil War failed to accomplish, and whatever questions it left unanswered, there was at least this: What kind of America would we live in, and what kind world would we live in, if the American republic had fragmented into two, or maybe three, or even four and five pieces, in 1865? Or if the institution of slavery had survived, either in an independent southern Confederacy or as the foundation of the new western states whose future had been Abraham Lincoln's greatest concern? Each year on September 17th, the anniversary of the battle of Antietam, United States Supreme Court Justice Oliver Wendell Holmes, who had been a lieutenant in the 20th Massachusetts at Antietam, presented a red rose to his fellow justice, Edward Douglass White, a former Confederate soldier from Louisiana whom Holmes joined on the Court after Holmes's appointment by President Theodore Roosevelt in 1902. It was the kind of sentimental gesture that Holmes was occasionally guilty of, and which Frederick Douglass would have deplored. But Justice White took the point, all the same. "My God," the old Confederate would mutter in palpable horror as he reflected on the war he had lost, "My God, if we had succeeded."[29]

[29]Liva Baker, *The Justice From Beacon Hill: The Life and Times of Oliver Wendell Holmes* (New York, 1991), pp. 438–439.

Index